The Realist

CARTOONS

THE REALIST SEAL OF APPROVAL
THE REALIST SEAL OF APPROVAL

Publisher and Executive Editor: GARY GROTH
Senior Editor: J. MICHAEL CATRON
Art Director: JACOB COVEY
Cover Artist : JAY LYNCH
Production: PRESTON WHITE and PAUL BARESH
Associate Publisher: ERIC REYNOLDS

Fantagraphics Books, Inc.
7563 Lake City Way NE
Seattle, WA 98115
(800) 657-1100

Fantagraphics.com. · Twitter: @fantagraphics · facebook.com/fantagraphics.

Special thanks to Michael Dooley, R.C. Harvey, Jim Lippard, Jay Lynch, J. David Spurlock

First edition: December 2016
ISBN 978-1-60699-894-6
Library of Congress Control Number: 2015959061
Printed in Korea

The Realist
CARTOONS

EDITED BY

PAUL KRASSNER

AND

ETHAN PERSOFF

FANTAGRAPHICS BOOKS

SEATTLE

Dedicated to the memory of Wally Wood,
Joel Beck, Spain Rodriguez, and Bhob Stewart

To Pat Thomas,
who gently wheedled me into Fantagraphics.

To Ethan Persoff,
whose production talent is beyond diligence.

To Gary Groth,
my publisher who became a friend I've never met.

The Realist

AN INTRODUCTION BY
PAUL KRASSNER, PUBLISHER

★ ★ ★ ★ ★ ★ ★

"It is the test of a good religion whether you can joke about it." – G.K. CHESTERTON

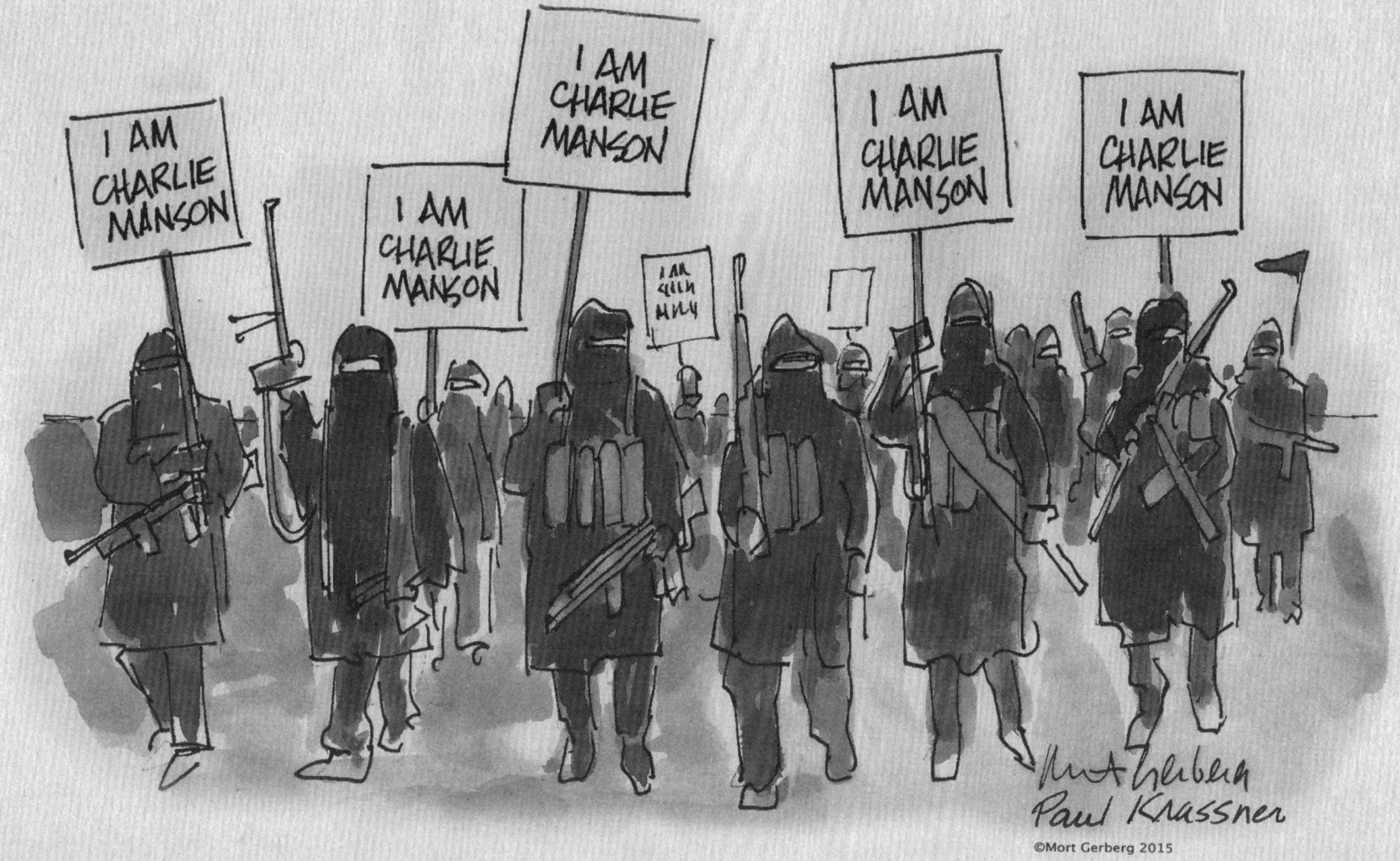
I AM CHARLIE MANSON
I AM CHARLIE MANSON
I AM CHARLIE MANSON
I AM CHARLIE MANSON
I AM CHARLIE MANSON
Mort Gerberg
Paul Krassner
©Mort Gerberg 2015

When the news broke about the assassinations of the *Charlie Hebdo* cartoonists in Paris, Michael Dooley, author of *The Education of a Comics Artist,* sent me an email: "I'm writing the intro to a feature that *Print* magazine will post online about the tragedy, and I'd like to include a comment from you. Any angle you want to approach it from is fine. Possible to email it to me at your soonest convenience, please?"

My hurried reply:

This massacre is an awesome outrage, even to liberals and conservatives alike – HBO left-wing comedian Bill Maher and Fox News right-wing journalist Bernard Goldberg had in common their plea urging newspapers to publish the offensive Charlie *cartoons – although some dinosaur Republicans might try to blame Obama.*

It's a horrendous violation of basic semantic principles, such as 'The menu is not the meal' and 'The map is not the territory.' And what could happen in America? Security guards protect the Onion *offices? Treat* Funny or Die *as Islamic marching orders? Invade the cyberspace of NBC for broadcasting* Saturday Night Live *until it morphs into* Saturday Night Dead *if it's not already deceased?*

As an atheist, I perceive the irony of those assassins shouting "God is great" to justify their insane act in the name of a deity that I believe doesn't exist. Religions continue to rationalize their dogma, from birth to death – and then comes the hereafter for these Muslim murderers where all those virgins supposedly waiting to greet them in Nirvana are busy reading Lysistrata. *OMG has declared war on LOL.*

I forwarded that to some cartoonist friends. Decades-long *New Yorker* contributor Mort Gerberg responded, "Clap, clap! Neatly done – although my own thought might be that LOL has morphed into OMG." I told him my idea for the cartoon above that I would've assigned to an artist if I were still publishing *The Realist*. Gerberg submitted it to the *New Yorker*, and it was rejected. I suddenly got a feeling of *déjà vu*, from back when the *New Yorker* would reject his cartoon, then he – among other artists and other periodicals – would send their cartoons to me, and I would publish 'em in *The Realist*.

My favorite syndicated comic strip in response to the massacre of slain cartoonists was Wiley Miller's *Non Sequitur*. It depicted a sidewalk artist who "finally achieves his goal to be the most feared man in the world," his placard advertising "Caricatures of Muhammad While You Wait!" It seemed safer to target America's leading misleaders.

When George W. Bush and Dick Cheney appeared together before 9/11 commission members – in private and not under oath – they inspired several editorial cartoons around the country showing Cheney as a ventriloquist and Bush as his dummy, so there was no need for such a cartoon in *The Realist*. One caption read, "No wonder Cheney talks out of the side of his mouth." No wonder that, when Bush had a colonoscopy, the doctors discovered the fingerprints of Cheney's right hand on the five polyps they removed. Those polyps turned out to be benign, although the host was malignant.

Now, at the risk of revealing my false humility, allow me to quote from an article, "Why Doesn't America Have Its Own *Charlie Hebdo*? A Brief History of American Satire Since the 1950s," in *Time* magazine: "Perhaps the satire magazine that most closely resembles *Charlie Hebdo* in terms of inflammatory imagery was *The Realist,* created by Paul Krassner. The most notorious items from this publication appeared in 1967, including the 'Disneyland Memorial Orgy,' an illustration of classic animated Disney characters engaged in a variety of obscene acts, and 'The Parts Left Out of the Kennedy Book,' a graphic short story containing a scene in which Lyndon B. Johnson sexually penetrates John F. Kennedy's corpse ..."

I n 1953, while still in college, I started working at an anti-censorship paper, *The Independent,* published by Lyle Stuart. When Stuart subscribed to the comic book *Mad* and included a fan letter, *Mad* publisher Bill Gaines wrote back, revealing that he had been a charter subscriber to *The Independent*. Gaines signed his letter, "In awe." This led to their friendship, which led to a business relationship. Stuart accepted a position as general manager, and the office of *The Independent* moved downtown to what was unofficially known as the *Mad* building.

We were on the seventh floor, right next door to the *Mad* office. The first time I met Gaines, he was chasing his secretary around the room, trying to stamp "FRAGILE" on her forehead. Apparently this was a courtship rite, because they eventually got married. Since I was working for Stuart, I would also be doing things for *Mad*.

My first errand was to deliver a package to the comedians Bob and Ray while they were doing their morning radio show at WINS. They were just sitting there, relaxed and reading newspapers while a commercial was on. They had been preceded the night before by the debut of Alan Freed – who invented the term *rock and roll*, acting it out as he banged the table and shouted along with the records he played. Bob and Ray were speculating about Freed's secret musical taste: "I'll bet he goes home and listens to Andre Kostelanetz."

Ultimately, to avoid government censorship, several publishers formed the Comics Magazine Association of America, which would require a stamp of approval on the cover of every comic book, guaranteeing that the contents were "wholesome, entertaining, and educational." Rather than risk the loss of distribution, publishers toned down their material to meet those subjective standards.

Meanwhile, *Mad* editor Harvey Kurtzman had been lobbying Gaines to change the format from a comic book to a magazine and, when faced with the prospect of losing Kurtzman, Gaines acceded: *Mad* comics became *Mad* magazine. A side benefit of the transformation meant that *Mad* was now outside the reach of the Comics Code. But while Mad survived with its irreverence undiluted, the tension between Gaines and Kurtzman was diluted only slightly.

I flew to Florida with Lyle and his wife Mary Louise for a vacation at her folks' ranch. It was the first time I had ever been on a plane. Once there, I soon experienced another first – riding a horse. I clowned around by sitting in the saddle facing backward – and so I didn't see that tree limb coming. It knocked me off the horse.

At almost the same moment, Mary Louise called to Lyle from the house, and, when Lyle determined that I wasn't injured, he helped me up and the two of us ran back there. There was a long-distance call waiting for him.

When he picked up the phone and said "Hello," a voice asked, "Lyle?" He answered, "Yes." Then the voice on the other end said, "Fuck you," and hung up. Lyle recognized the voice, laughed, and said, "That was Bill."

The phone rang again. This time Gaines said, "I'm in trouble." He told Lyle that Harvey Kurtzman was demanding 51% of *Mad*'s stock or he would quit. Kurtzman was waiting outside Gaines's office that very minute for a decision.

"Bill, listen to me and do exactly what I say," Lyle advised. "Call Kurtzman in, open the window behind you and throw him out."

"I'm serious," Gaines said.

"*I'm* serious," Lyle said. "You have no choice here. Fire him *now*."

"If I do, what'll I do for an editor?"

"Hire Al Feldstein. He did a good job with *Panic*."

And that's exactly what Gaines did, although it seemed strange, since Lyle had previously not been speaking to Feldstein. One afternoon, Lyle passed Gaines and Feldstein together in the corridor. He greeted Gaines but ignored the confused Feldstein.

"Just because Lyle got you the job," Gaines explained, "don't expect him to say hello to you."

I n 1955, I had an idea that *Mad* bought. I wrote the script and Wallace Wood (we called him "Wally" then) did the artwork. My premise was, "What if comic-strip characters answered those little ads in the back of magazines?" Orphan Annie would get Maybelline for her eyes. Dick Tracy would get a nose job. Alley Oop would get rid of his superfluous hair – only to reveal that he had no ears. But Al Feldstein wouldn't include Good Old Charlie Brown responding to the "Do You Want Power?" ad, because he didn't think the *Peanuts* strip was well known enough yet to parody. Nor would Popeye's flat-chested girlfriend, Olive Oyl, be permitted to send away for a pair of falsies. I complained to Bill Gaines.

Gaines said, "My mother would object to that."

"Yeah," I said, "but she's not a typical subscriber."

"No, but she's a typical mother."

His mother would have objected to my final panel, which was also excluded from that spread, depicting a group of comic-strip bachelors – including Air Force pilot Steve Canyon, Dr. Rex Morgan, and detective Kerry Drake – who had sent for *Those Little Comic Books That Men Like* and were now all slobbering over these crude drawings of themselves performing sex acts that they were otherwise never allowed to enjoy.

I sold a few other ideas to *Mad*, but when I suggested a satire on the pros and cons of unions, Feldstein wasn't interested in even seeing it because the subject was "too adult." Since *Mad*'s circulation had already gone over the million-and-a-quarter mark, Gaines intended to keep aiming the magazine at teenagers.

"I guess you don't wanna change horses in midstream," I said.

"Not when the horse has a rocket up its ass," Gaines replied.

That was the exact moment of conception, the impregnation of my notion to publish a satirical magazine for grown-ups. This was before *National Lampoon* or *Spy* or *The Onion*, before *Doonesbury* or *Saturday Night Live, Politically Incorrect, The Daily Show, The Colbert Report,* or *Last Week Tonight With John Oliver*.

I had no role models, and no competition, just an open field mined with taboos waiting to be exploded. I would have to make it up as I went along. My goal was to communicate without compromise. It was a leap of faith. There just *had* to be others out there who were also the only Martians on their block. If I were the only one, there would be no hope. And so, in 1958, *The Realist* was born.

I found a quotation from Groucho Marx: "Satire is *verboten* today. The restrictions – political, religious, and every other kind – have killed satire." Then I began contacting writers and cartoonists, exchanging ideas and giving assignments, trying to help bring satire back to life. I started with John Francis Putnam, the art director at *Mad*. He designed *The Realist* logo and also wrote the first column, "Modest Proposals." Although *Mad* staffers were not allowed to have any outside projects, Putnam was willing to risk his job to write for *The Realist*. Bill Gaines appreciated that and made an exception for him.

And then, late one extremely hot night that spring, alone and literally naked, I was sitting at my desk in Lyle's office, preparing final copy for the first issue, to be dated June. I was supposed to have everything ready for the printer the next morning. I felt exhausted, but there was one final piece to write. My bare buttocks stuck to the leather chair as I borrowed a satirical form from *Mad* and composed "A Child's Primer on Telethons." It had to do with testing atomic bombs.

T*he Realist* became a central clearing house for cartoons that were considered in bad taste or too controversial for mainstream media. In 1961, an unsolicited comic strip arrived from editorial cartoonist Frank Interlandi. It showed a man walking along and eyeing a poster of a mushroom cloud with the question, *If a Bomb Falls, What Would You Do?* He continued walking as his answer appeared in a thought balloon: "I'd shit!"

Interlandi wrote: "Actually, I did the cartoon with the intention of sending it to the syndicate, but when it came to putting the punch line in, I couldn't think of anything but 'I'd shit!' The more lines I tried, the less funny it got, and the surer I was that the original line was the best and only one – it was a genuine reaction; the feeling of being helpless and returning to infantilism. But why do I have to explain a cartoon? Naturally I knew the syndicate would reject it, so they never did see it, but I wanted to see it printed and I thought of you."

At a convention of editorial cartoonists, several artists observed that Interlandi's drawing should have won a Pulitzer Prize, but they knew it couldn't.

In 1962, when abortion was still illegal, I published a cartoon by Mort Gerberg depicting a Mother Goose character – the old lady who lived in a shoe and had so many children she didn't know what to do – speaking on the phone: "Dr. Burnhill? – Uh, you don't know me, but, uh, I've been told that you could, uh, perform a certain, uh, operation..."

It turned out that there was an *actual* Dr. Burnhill, an obstetrician-gynecologist, who called me in distress after patients started bringing that issue of *The Realist* to his office. Although I apologized to the doctor, every succeeding cartoon by Gerberg would include a character named Burnhill.

W**hen** I moved in 1963, John Francis Putnam decided to give me a housewarming gift. He designed the word "FUCK" in red-white-and-blue lettering festooned with stars and stripes. Now he needed a second word, a noun that would serve as an appropriate object for that verb. He suggested "AMERICA," but that didn't seem right to me. It certainly wasn't an accurate representation of my feelings.

I was well aware that I probably couldn't publish *The Realist* in any other country. This was the paradox of America – that I had the freedom to criticize so openly those unspeakable horrors being committed by the government in the name of the people. Besides, a poster saying "FUCK AMERICA" simply lacked a certain sense of irony.

There was at that time a severe anti-Communist hysteria burgeoning throughout the land. The attorney general of Arizona had rejected the Communist Party's request for a place on the ballot because state law "prohibits official representation" for Communists and, in addition, "The subversive nature of your organization is even more clearly designated by the fact that you do not even include your Zip Code."

Alvin Dark, manager of the Giants, had announced, "Any pitcher who throws at a batter and deliberately tries to hit him is a Communist." And singer Pat Boone had declared at the Greater New York Anti-Communism Rally in Madison Square Garden, "I would rather see my four daughters shot before my eyes than have them grow up in a Communist United States. I would rather see those kids blown into Heaven than taught into Hell by the Communists."

So I suggested "COMMUNISM" as the second word, since the usual correlation between conservatism and prudishness would provide the incongruity that was missing. Putnam designed the word "COMMUNISM" in red lettering emblazoned with hammers and sickles. Then he presented me with a patriotic poster that proudly proclaimed "FUCK COMMUNISM!" – suitable for framing. I wanted to share this sentiment with *Realist* readers, but my photo-engraver refused to make a metal plate, explaining, "We got strict orders from Washington not to do stuff like this."

I went to another engraver, who said no because they had been visited by the FBI after making a metal plate of a woman with pubic hair. So in addition to publishing a miniature black-and-white version of the poster in *The Realist*, I offered full-size color copies by mail. And if the post office interfered, I would have to accuse them of being soft on Communism.

The first person to buy a poster was an employee of Radio Free Europe. After a few days, the security people took it off his office wall. His employer explained that it was funny but he didn't want women to see it. The Fuck Communism! poster was purchased by an Episcopalian priest, a mayor, an astronaut, and by college groups for mock political conventions.

Authors Norman Mailer, Terry Southern, and Joseph Heller sent posters out as Christmas gifts. Chicago disc jockey Dan Sorkin kept one in the front window of his home, just waiting for any Commie sympathizer to *dare* criticize him. Somebody gave a Fuck Communism! poster to Gus Hall, head of the Communist Party. And he accepted it.

"People have been saying that to me for years," he laughed.

In London, the head of the U.N. mission to Ethiopia spotted a *Playboy* executive's poster and commandeered it for his office in Addis Ababa. Playwright Arthur Cowan had one framed and shipped it to England with instructions that it be installed in his Rolls-Royce. Country Joe McDonald stuck one on his car bumper and almost got arrested by a confused traffic cop. Journalist Paul Jacobs brought a couple of posters to Washington and gave them to Secretary of Labor Willard Wirtz and Peace Corps Director Sargent Shriver. Shriver kept the poster in a back room and used it to beguile selected Peace Corps recruits.

One subscriber bought 25 posters and asked me to send them to, among others, J. Edgar Hoover, the John Birch Society, and 1964 presidential candidates Barry Goldwater and Lyndon Johnson – all with a personal note from me: "Dear So-and-So: A reader of ours thought you might get a chuckle out of the enclosed patriotic poster."

Senator Goldwater's response to receiving a Fuck Communism! poster crystallized the generic spirit of political campaigns everywhere and forever: "Your comments and suggestions mean a great deal to me," his form letter stated. "You may be sure that I will keep them in mind as the campaign progresses. I want you to know I appreciate your taking the time and trouble to write."

A couple who lived on a former ferry that they had docked at the houseboat community in Sausalito, California, stapled a Fuck Communism! poster to their floating home. One afternoon, a sheriff's captain marched down the gangway, climbed up onto the ferryboat, tore the poster down, and ripped it to shreds. He proceeded to arrest the couple for "outraging public decency." Newspapers reporting the arrest described the poster as a "blunt anti-Communist sign" and "a colorful attack on Communism," substituting asterisks or dashes for "fuck."

A jury was finally selected, but when the bailiff removed three teenage girls from the courtroom to spare their ears, the defense moved for a dismissal. The judge refused to grant the motion, but charges were dismissed before the case came to trial. The district attorney said that he had received assurances that the incident was "an isolated case and repetition is unlikely."

At a Midwestern college, one graduating student held up a Fuck Communism! poster as his class was posing for the yearbook photograph. Campus officials found out and insisted that "FUCK" be airbrushed out. But then the poster would read: COMMUNISM! So that was airbrushed out, too, and the yearbook ended up publishing a class photo showing the student holding up a blank poster.

Writer Robert Scheer was doing research for a booklet, *How the United States Got Involved in Vietnam*, to be published by the Fund for the Republic. He was frustrated because he wanted to witness firsthand what was going on in Southeast Asia, but they wouldn't send him.

Since *The Realist* had already sold a couple of thousand Fuck Communism! posters at a dollar each, I made out a check for $1,900, the

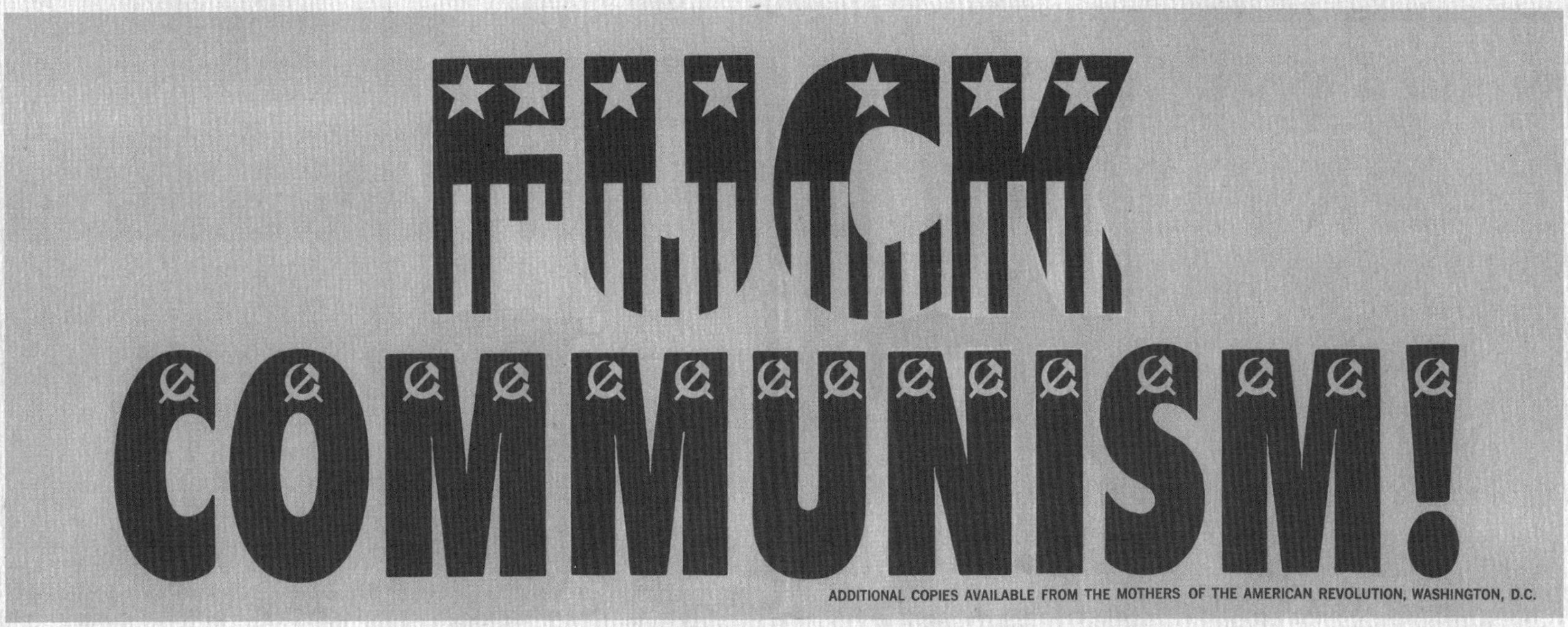
FUCK
COMMUNISM!
ADDITIONAL COPIES AVAILABLE FROM THE MOTHERS OF THE AMERICAN REVOLUTION, WASHINGTON, D.C.

ORIGINAL "FUCK COMMUNISM" TYPOGRAPHY AND DESIGN BY *MAD* MAGAZINE ART DIRECTOR JOHN FRANCIS PUTNAM, WHO ALSO DESIGNED THE *REALIST* LOGO.

price of a round-trip airline ticket for Scheer. He traveled to Vietnam and Cambodia, then wrote his seminal report. He also wrote an article for *The Realist*, titled "Academic Sin," documenting the role of Michigan State University professors in the Diem dictatorship.

Proceeds from another poster – originally a *Realist* cartoon depicting an anthropomorphic deity sodomizing Uncle Sam with the legend *One Nation Under God* – were used to bail the artist Frank Cieciorka out of jail after he was arrested for voter registration work in Mississippi.

More than four decades after I gave Bhob Stewart an illustration assignment, he wrote on his blog *Potrzebie* (a Polish word meaning "need," borrowed from a running gag in *Mad* magazine):

> *In 1965, Paul Krassner and I collaborated on a spoof of Jules Feiffer's weekly comic strip for* The Realist, *Paul's influential magazine of "freethought criticism and satire." I did a line drawing of Feiffer and made four copies to paste down amid copy written by Paul. My contribution to the writing was a reference to Feiffer's black panels similar to the* Little Lulu *pages of Tubby and Little Lulu talking in darkened rooms. Some were fooled by the parody. ...*
>
> *The signature does not say 'Feiffer.' It clearly reads 'PKbhob,' but I tried to trick the eye and create an illusion that would resemble Feiffer's signature. I made an effort to extend such an illusion throughout by duplicating Feiffer's familiar layout, the use of a repetitive image and an attempt to mimic Feiffer's lettering style, complete with a double line on the emphasized words.*
>
> *The cartoon appeared on the front cover of the October 1965 issue of* The Realist *(#63) directly beneath* A Little Play *by Feiffer. This was very much in the previously established prankster nature of* The Realist, *but the juxtaposition did not make Feiffer happy. Especially when he began to get phone calls from friends congratulating him on finally doing a self-satire.*
>
> *Feiffer demanded a clarification, so Paul told him to write a letter....*
>
> *Feiffer's reaction reminded me of something [radio personality] Henry Morgan once said: 'I can dish it out, but I can't take it.' A few years later, Feiffer actually did do a cartoon about himself in an ad to promote one of his books.*

In 1985, I published a full-page comic strip ostensibly "written and directed by Woody Allen" after Mia Farrow accused him of incestuous behavior – written by me, artwork by Kalynn Campbell – titled, "Honey, I Fucked the Kids." Stewart Brand requested permission to reprint it in the *Whole Earth Review*. Brand's printer, however, refused to print it. Brand "published" it anyway – totally blacked out – with an explanation.

When Walt Disney died in December 1966, I remembered two things that he had said. One was, "I love Mickey Mouse more than any woman I've ever known." In 1945, Aldous Huxley was a consultant on the filming of *Alice in Wonderland*, and there were rumors that Huxley had turned him on with magic mushrooms. A year later, Disney said, "If people would think more of fairies, they would forget the atom bomb."

There was an urban myth that Disney's body had been frozen, although it was actually cremated. Somehow I had expected Mickey Mouse and Donald Duck and all the rest of the gang to attend the funeral, with Goofy delivering the eulogy and the Seven Dwarves serving as pallbearers.

After his death, I went to Disneyland with a couple of friends, one a lawyer whose dog jumped into the car as we were leaving his home. Dogs weren't allowed in Disneyland. Neither were male humans who had long hair or beards, except for musicians, so neither the Beatles nor Jesus Christ would have been permitted to enter Disneyland unless they were performing there.

We bluffed our way in with the dog by convincing a ticket-taker that the manager had given us permission earlier on the phone inasmuch as the dog was needed to guide my friend with impaired eyesight. Inside, we continued to fake it by explaining that the dog had already been cleared by the ticket-taker, until a large man with a small walkie-talkie approached us and offered us a choice of putting the dog in the Disneyland kennel or leaving altogether. My lawyer friend complained that this exception to their rule had been arranged two weeks ago, and he asked to speak to the chief of security.

"I *am* the chief of security."

"Just the man I want to see."

Of course, the canine in question was not a seeing-eye dog, not even a German shepherd. It was just a good old bloodshot-eyed basset hound. There was no metal brace for the owner to hold onto, only a rotting, knotted leather leash, and the dog kept stumbling all over the ground, sniffing for a place to pee. Apparently, no dog had ever previously peed in Disneyland, not even Pluto.

We decided to leave. But we were entitled to a refund. So, while the others waited at the gate, I was escorted to a building called City Hall. Inside, a woman was requesting that her lost child be paged over the loudspeaker, but she was refused because it wasn't considered an emergency. I asked an administrator if there had been any special ceremony when Walt Disney had died.

"No, we kept the park open. We felt that Mr. Disney would have wanted it that way."

"Well, wasn't there *any* official recognition of his passing?"

"We did fly the flag at half-mast for the rest of the month."

Walt Disney's death occurred in the same year as *Time* magazine's famous "Is God Dead?" cover, and it occurred to me that Disney had indeed served as the Creator of that whole stable of his imaginary characters who were now mourning in a state of suspended animation. He had been *their* Intelligent Designer, and he had repressed all their baser instincts.

Now that Disney had departed, they could finally shed their cumulative inhibitions and participate together in an unspeakable Roman binge, to signify the crumbling of an empire. In real fake life, Mickey Mouse was a convict in a chain gang when he met Pluto. In World War II, his name was the password for the D-Day invasion. And Snow White warned military personnel about the dangers of venereal disease.

I contacted Wallace Wood and, without mentioning any specific details, I told him my general notion of a parody starring all Disney's characters, who were now reeking with horniness. Wood accepted the assignment, and he presented me with a magnificently degenerate montage. In 1967, I published *The Disneyland Memorial Orgy* as a black-and-white centerspread in *The Realist*.

In Baltimore, the Sherman News Agency distributed that issue with the middle four pages removed. One employee said that the Maryland State Board of Censors had ordered this – that it was the only way *The Realist* could be sold in that state – but while there actually was a Maryland State Board of Censors (now defunct), it was concerned with movies, not magazines. Sherman's had merely taken what they considered to be a precaution. I was able to secure the excised pages and offered them free to any Baltimore reader who had bought a partial magazine.

The centerspread in that issue of *The Realist* was so popular that I published it as a poster. The Disney corporation considered a lawsuit but realized that *The Realist* was published on a proverbial shoestring, and besides, why bother causing themselves further public embarrassment? They took no action against me, and the statute of limitations finally ran out.

Meanwhile, the poster was pirated – painted in black-light day-glo colors, supposedly copyrighted in my name (spelled wrong) and widely distributed. I didn't sue the pirate, but Disney did, and that case was settled out of court for $5,000.

In 2005, artist Joseph Robert Cowles did the restoration process of what he described as "a high-resolution digital image of how the folded, soiled, and shopworn black-and-white poster looked when I began." The result of his digitally coloring the original artwork was a beautiful poster in "authentic Disney colors." It was enlarged and printed on glossy paper. It's available at my website. And, yes, I had it copyrighted. Really.

When the Cuban missile crisis occurred in 1962, Bob Dylan was inspired to write "A Hard Rain's A-Gonna Fall." And Richard Guindon created his most popular cartoon for *The Realist*, which I featured on the cover. It depicted a reclining nude woman, leaning on her elbow with her back to us. Her buttocks fashioned a globe with latitudinal and longitudinal lines, and she faced a couple of faceless men, both naked except that one was wearing boxer shorts with stars and stripes while the other had a hammer-and-sickle tattooed on his chubby arm. The Kennedy-like American was gesturing toward the Khrushchev-like Russian as he said to the Earth-woman: "It's his turn now and then me again."

That cartoon captured a certain feeling of powerlessness that permeated the country. Two Broadway stars – Orson Bean in *Subways Are for Sleeping* and Anthony Newley in *Stop the World, I Want to Get Off* – had it framed on their dressing room walls, even while certain bookstores and newsstands were displaying that issue face down.

And political satirist Mort Sahl chastised me: "I think *The Realist* is probably the most vital publication in America, but I don't think the magazine should dissipate its time on *crudeness*. I don't mind telling you, that kind of thing is offensive to me. I don't think that both the United States and Russia are raping the world."

"Now you used the word *rape*," I said. "How do you know that the female representing the Earth was not being submissive?"

"Or even seductive," Sahl said. "Well, I'll never know. I didn't see her face in that cartoon. You didn't emphasize that part, you know."

Guindon's longest cartoon was a 9-page comic strip about Syria in the May 1968 issue. While compiling this book, I emailed him: "I'm going through all the issues of *The Realist* for a collection, and you were soitanly brilliant and prolific..."

He replied: "Actually you co-authored much of my work in a sense simply by being who you are. We all got spoiled working for you because you set a hell of an example in your own work. No one of us wanted to disappoint. That's different than just wanting to get into *The Realist*. You created a culture and fathered quite a loose-knit staff. Thank you for letting me be a part of it."

What more gratifying feedback could an editor possibly want? So much appreciation goes to Guindon and all the other artists who contributed their cartoons to *The Realist*. Here and now, it's such a pleasure to share them with our invisible audience once again. Enjoy your ass off.

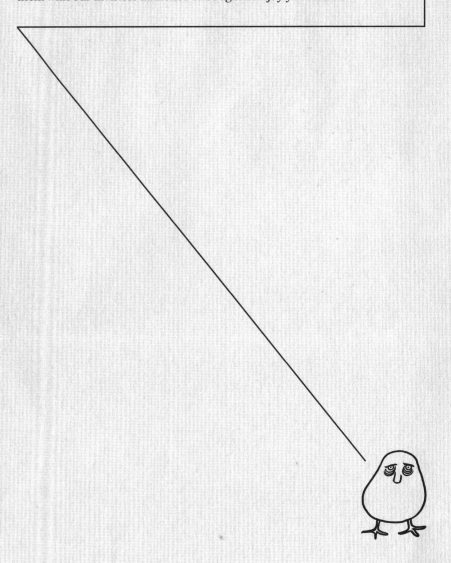

EDITOR'S NOTE

This nicely designed collection is a vital piece of history with many very funny jokes.

The Realist was an uncensored, independent publication, and a significant influence on underground media that followed. It was first published from 1958-1974 as a newsprint magazine (usually 24-32 pages in length) and was sold through subscription and at newsstands. The second run of the paper reemerged in the Xerox DIY-era of the 1980s and ran as a subscriber-based newsletter (typically eight pages each time) from 1985-2001.

It's a joy to view this vast survey of nearly fifty years of comics in one volume.

For academic evaluation, the sequences of images in this book are presented largely in the order they originally appeared in print. This structure provides a useful thematic grouping, based on date and cultural events. Specific sets of political ideas, anxieties, and senses of humor are evident throughout the run of the magazine.

Readers are encouraged to identify their own thematic clusters of topics addressed. For example, early strips in the 1950s focus on global anxiety over nuclear weapons, and an over-reaction to communism. Once the comics hit the early 1960s, racial inequality and civil rights take a pronounced center stage. Religious misconduct is addressed throughout, along with lampoons on the hypocrisies of the war on obscenity. It's also a good humorous guess (if you look for it) when many of the cartoonists herein discover LSD and pot. The magazine develops a definite looseness when it hits the 1970s. And when it returns in the 1980s, it provides a vital final performance as a shrewd political jester, slicing and hammering away at the emerging 24-hour reality news cycle of the 1990s.

Artist attribution, along with date of publication, has been indicated with each cartoon. If no artist is listed, it was not possible to identify the artist credit for that strip, or the signature was unable to be clearly discerned. We regret these attribution omissions. A list of annotations complete this volume at the back of the book, with historical references for certain strips that might require explanation. These annotated strips are indicated with an asterix and annotation ID number.

Have fun,

Ethan Persoff, June 2016

(CO-CONSPIRATOR, *THE REALIST CARTOONS* AND EDITOR/ARCHIVIST OF *THE REALIST* ARCHIVE PROJECT)

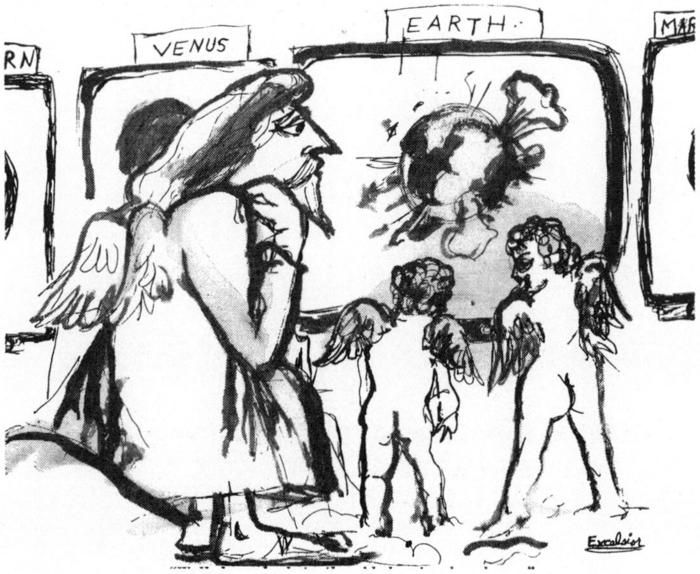
VENUS
EARTH
Excelsior

"Well, boys, back to the old drawing board..."

EXCELSIOR. THE REALIST #1, JUNE-JULY 1958.

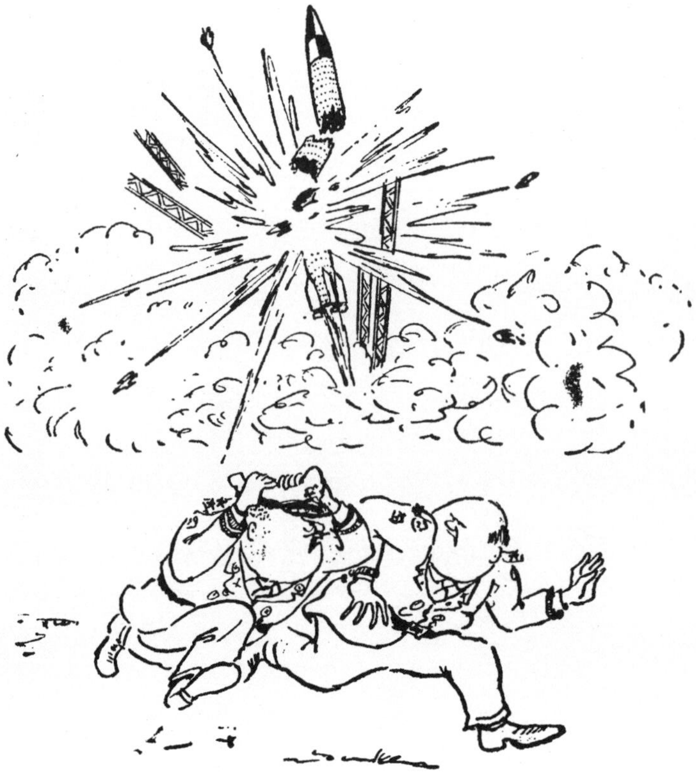

"This experiment has just become top secret..."

DRURY MARSH. THE REALIST #1, JUNE-JULY 1958.

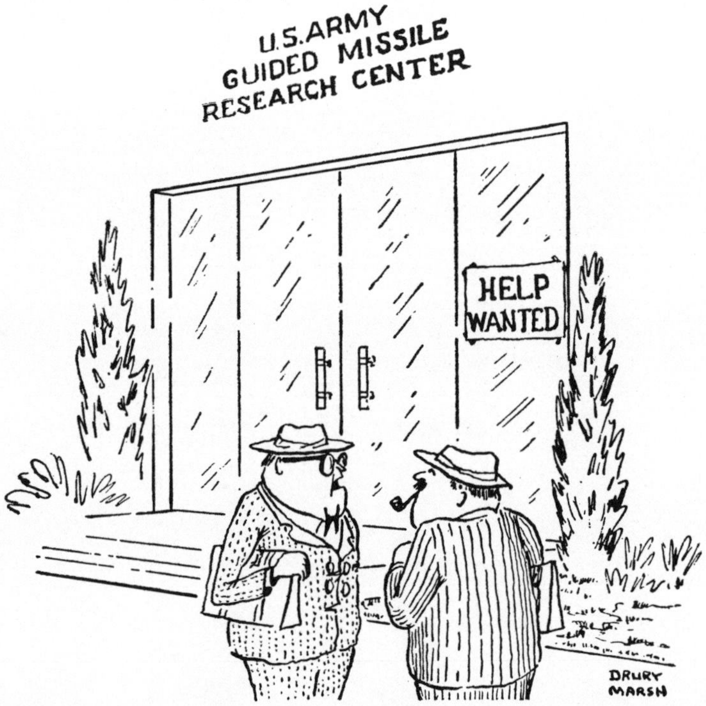
U.S. ARMY
GUIDED MISSILE
RESEARCH CENTER
HELP
WANTED
DRURY
MARSH

"They would have hired me only
I don't speak German..."

DRURY MARSH. THE REALIST #1, JUNE-JULY 1958.

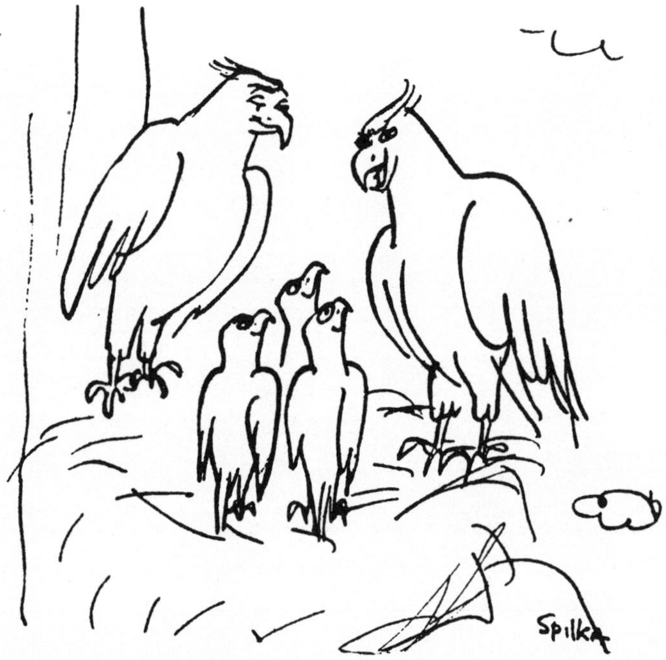
Spilka

"Remember, children, the family that
preys together stays together."

SPILKA. THE REALIST #4, NOVEMBER 1958.

STUDIO
A
STATION
TV
M.N. DAWS, M.D.
DRURY MARSH

"You're going to have to
give up smoking..."

DRURY MARSH. THE REALIST #1, JUNE-JULY 1958..

PAX VOBISCUM
ET CUM SPIRITU
BEATUS VIR

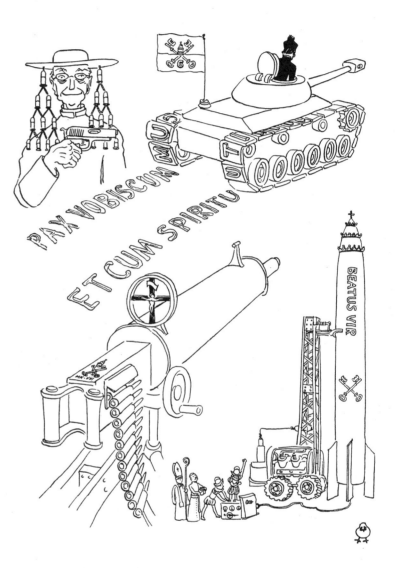

God Is On The Side Of The Heaviest Guns

"The Vatican, as a sovereign state, fulfills many of the normal functions of government in that both censorship and a prison are maintained. (The latter is almost never used.) The above is a pictorial speculation on what might happen if the Vatican set up a military establishment like other states, with a modern armed force of its own to implement the long-established *moral* force."

JOHN FRANCIS PUTNAM. THE REALIST #4, NOVEMBER 1958.

The Filtered Man's Thinker . . .

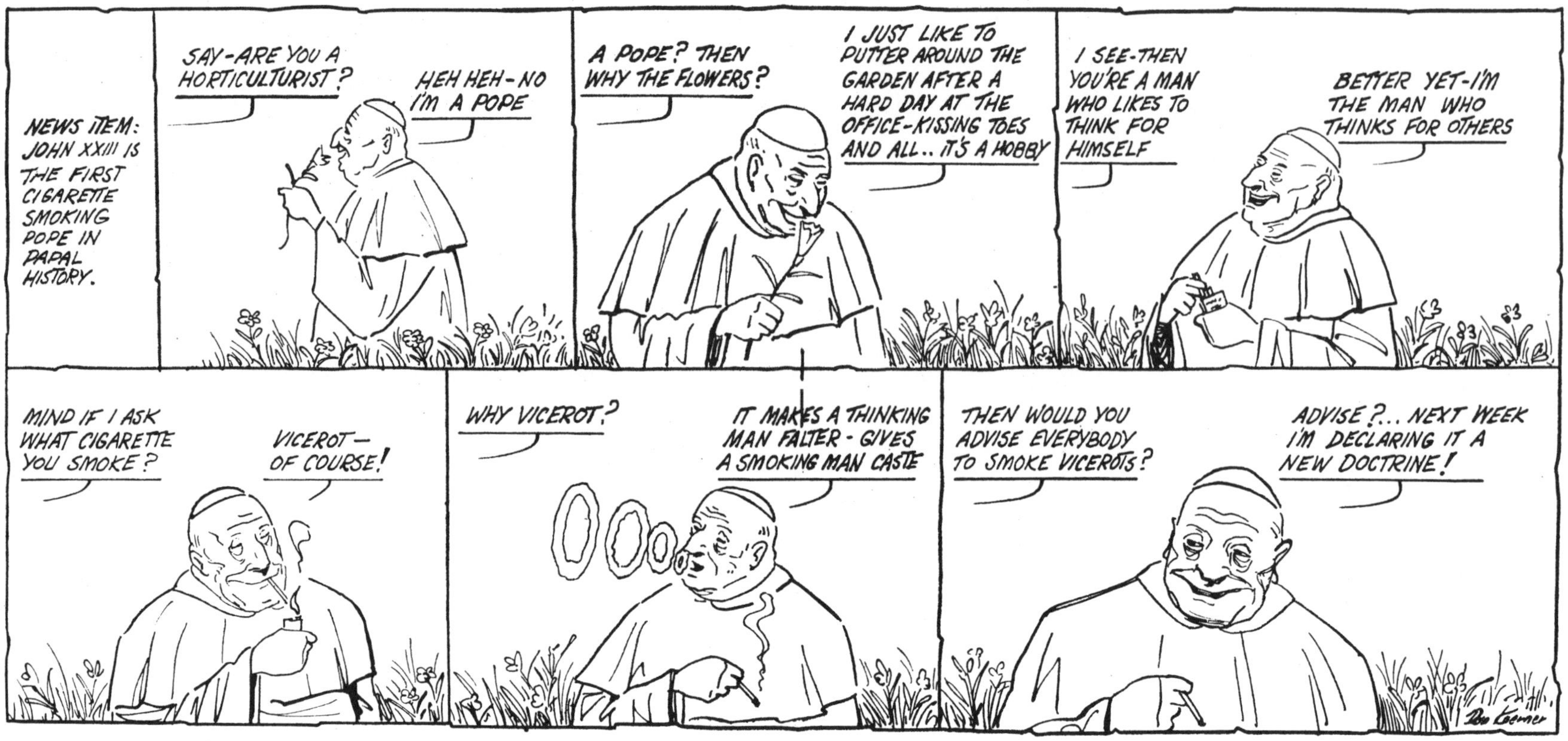
NEWS ITEM: JOHN XXIII IS THE FIRST CIGARETTE SMOKING POPE IN PAPAL HISTORY.
SAY-ARE YOU A HORTICULTURIST?
HEH HEH-NO I'M A POPE
A POPE? THEN WHY THE FLOWERS?
I JUST LIKE TO PUTTER AROUND THE GARDEN AFTER A HARD DAY AT THE OFFICE-KISSING TOES AND ALL.. IT'S A HOBBY
I SEE-THEN YOU'RE A MAN WHO LIKES TO THINK FOR HIMSELF
BETTER YET-I'M THE MAN WHO THINKS FOR OTHERS
MIND IF I ASK WHAT CIGARETTE YOU SMOKE?
VICEROT— OF COURSE!
WHY VICEROT?
IT MAKES A THINKING MAN FALTER - GIVES A SMOKING MAN CASTE
THEN WOULD YOU ADVISE EVERYBODY TO SMOKE VICEROTS?
ADVISE?... NEXT WEEK I'M DECLARING IT A NEW DOCTRINE!

DON KOEMER. THE REALIST #10, AUGUST 1959

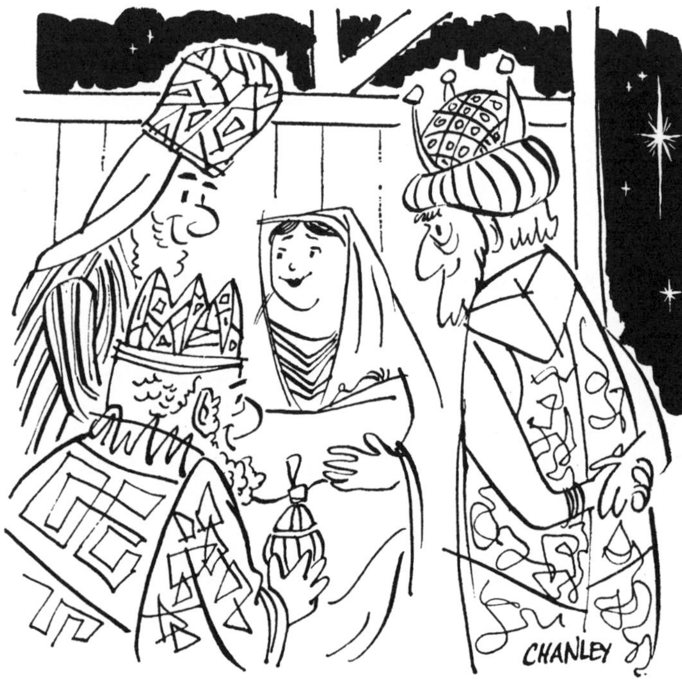
CHANLEY

"Bless his heart, he looks just like his daddy."

CHANLEY. THE REALIST #14, DECEMBER 1959-JANUARY 1960

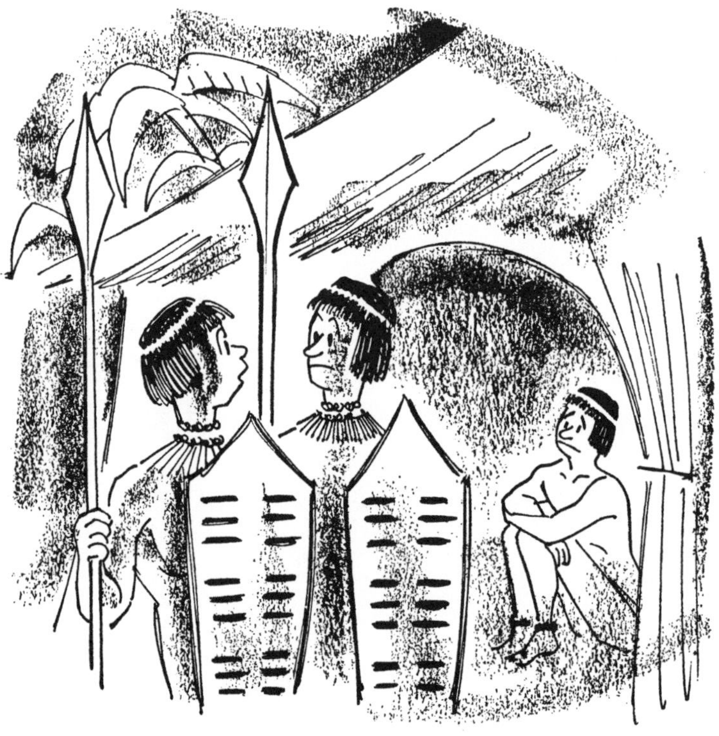

"He's waiting to confess a mortal sin—
he lied to Margaret Mead."

ED FISHER. THE REALIST #9, JUNE-JULY 1959. *1

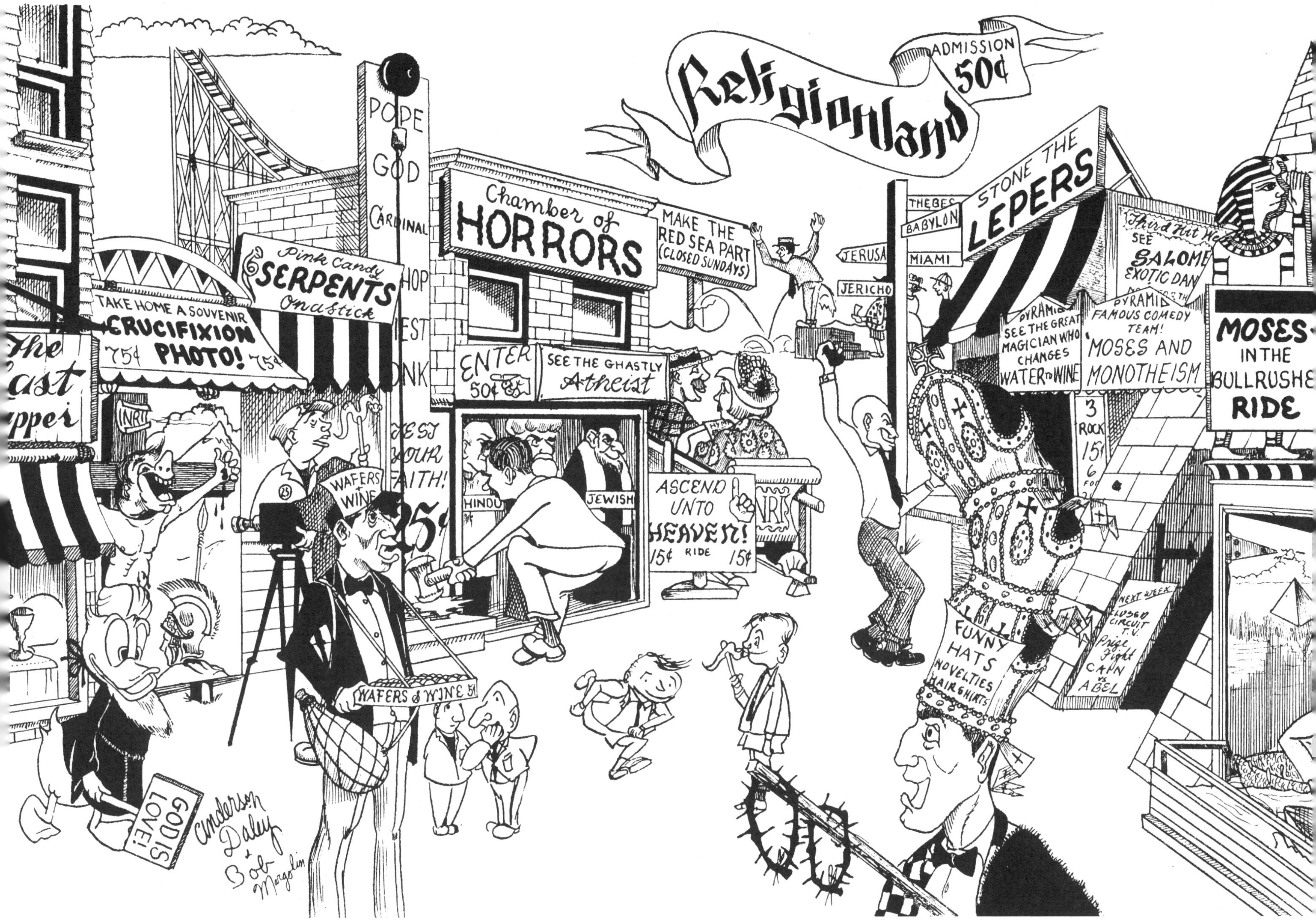
Religionland
ADMISSION 50¢
POPE
GOD
CARDINAL
Chamber of HORRORS
MAKE THE RED SEA PART (CLOSED SUNDAYS)
STONE THE LEPERS
THEBES
BABYLON
MIAMI
JERICHO
Pink Candy SERPENTS On a stick
TAKE HOME A SOUVENIR CRUCIFIXION PHOTO! 75¢ 75¢
INRI
ENTER 50¢
SEE THE GHASTLY Atheist
HINDU
JEWISH
ASCEND UNTO HEAVEN! 15¢ RIDE 15¢
WAFERS + WINE
WAFERS & WINE 5¢
GOD IS LOVE!
SEE THE GREAT MAGICIAN WHO CHANGES WATER TO WINE
PYRAMID FAMOUS COMEDY TEAM! MOSES AND MONOTHEISM
SEE SALOME EXOTIC DAN
MOSES IN THE BULLRUSHE RIDE
FUNNY HATS NOVELTIES HAIR SHIRTS
NEXT WEEK CLOSED CIRCUIT T.V. Prize Fight CAIN vs ABEL
Cinderson Daley + Bob Margolin

CINDERSON DALEY AND BOB MARGOLIN. THE REALIST #20, OCTOBER 1960.

1)
2)
3)
4)
5)
6)
7)
8)
R. WEINER

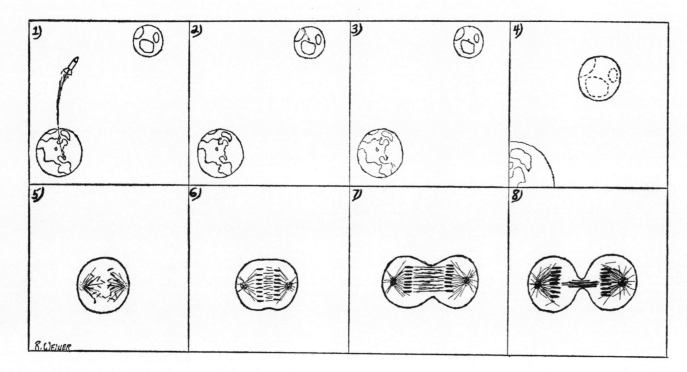

R. WEINER. THE REALIST #20, OCTOBER 1960

STELLA. THE REALIST #21, NOVEMBER 1960.

YE MUST BE
BORN
AGAIN!
ERIC

"Mister, they won't let any kids in without an adult —
would you take me to see Elmer Gantry?"

ERIC. THE REALIST #21, NOVEMBER 1960.*2

The Adventures of Churchman

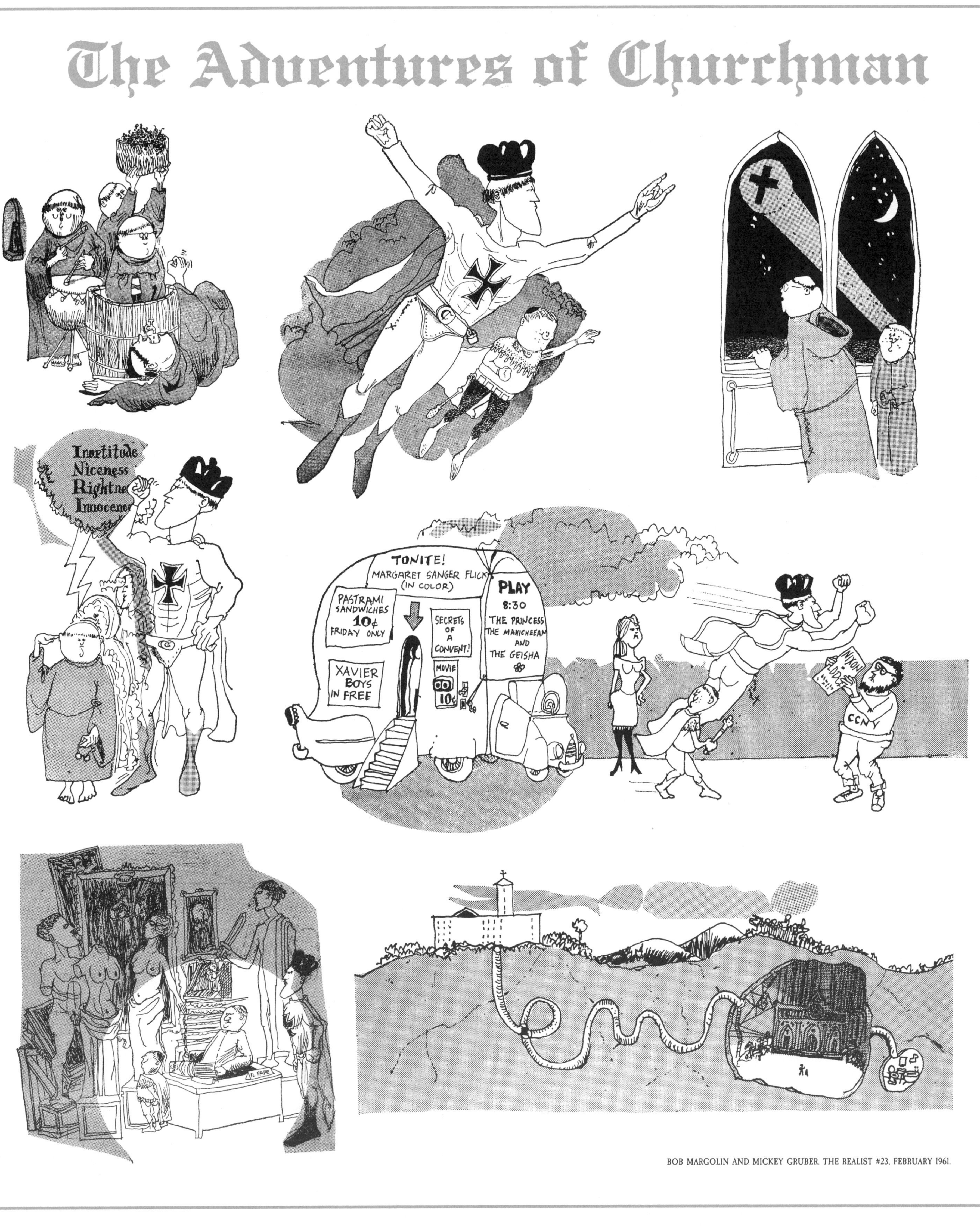
Inertitude
Niceness
Rightne
Innocenc
TONITE!
MARGARET SANGER FLICK
(IN COLOR)
PASTRAMI SANDWICHES 10¢ FRIDAY ONLY
SECRETS OF A CONVENT!
PLAY
8:30
THE PRINCESS
THE MANICHEEAN
AND
THE GEISHA
XAVIER BOYS IN FREE
MOVIE
10¢
NIXON
LODGE
CCNY
IL PAPE

BOB MARGOLIN AND MICKEY GRUBER. THE REALIST #23, FEBRUARY 1961.

Pitin

PITIN. THE REALIST #23, FEBRUARY 1961.

RADIO SWAN
FRESQUITO FRESQUET

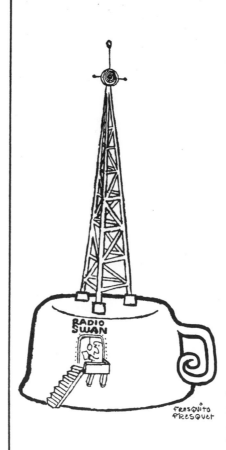

Impropaganda

This chamber-pot of a radio station originally appeared as a full-page, captionless illustration on the back cover of the humor weekly, "El Pitirre" (a small bird indigenous to Cuba which, symbolic of the revolution, attacks vultures). The U.S. State Department pays for the counter-revolutionary broadcasts which emanate from Swan Island, and whose program content ranges from telling Cubans their children will be taken away, to warning them that the Russians are adding a drug to their food and milk which automatically turns people into Communists.

FRESQUITO FRESQUET. THE REALIST #23, FEBRUARY 1961.

I LIKE IKE

THE REALIST #23, FEBRUARY 1961. *3

Have Faith!

THE REALIST #89, MARCH-APRIL 1971.

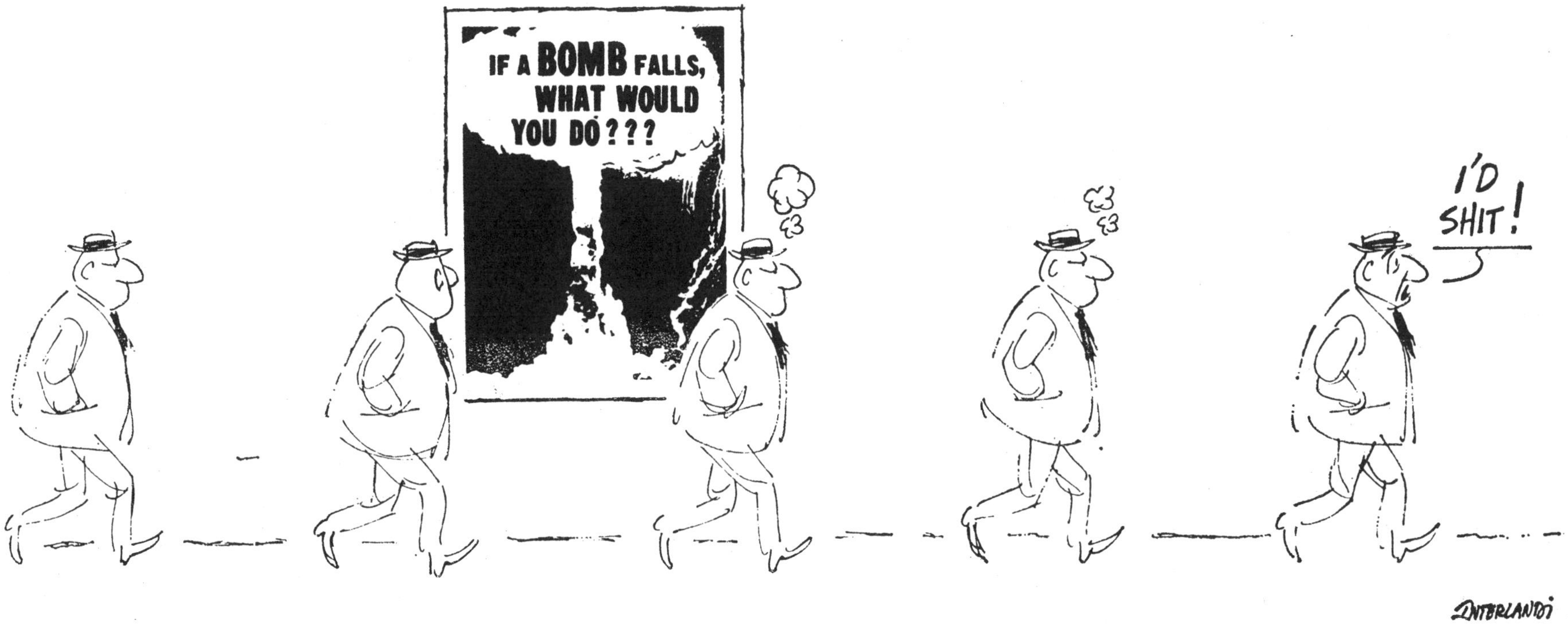
IF A BOMB FALLS, WHAT WOULD YOU DO???
I'D SHIT!
INTERLANDI

FRANK INTERLANDI. THE REALIST #23, FEBRUARY 1961. *4

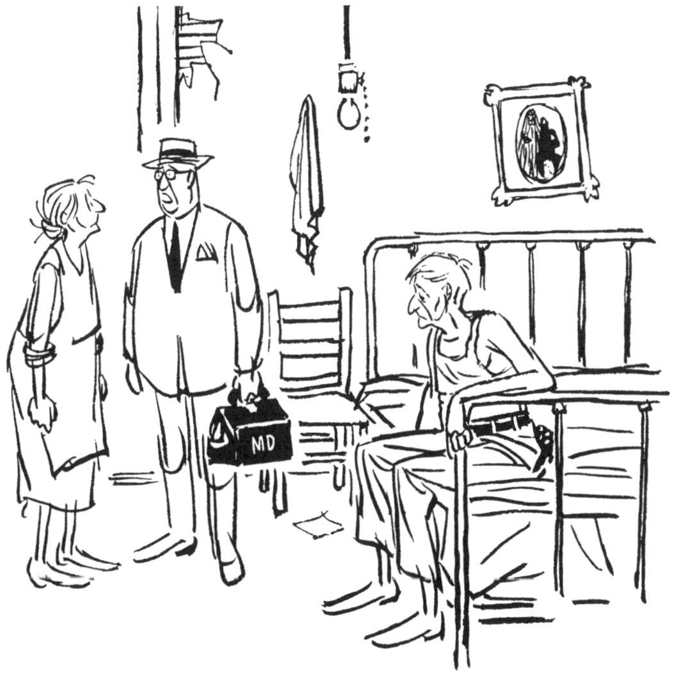
MD

"I hate to charge, but you know what Barry Goldwater says—'People start getting things for nothing, they lose their initiative...."

FRANK INTERLANDI. THE REALIST #24-25, MARCH-APRIL 1961. *5

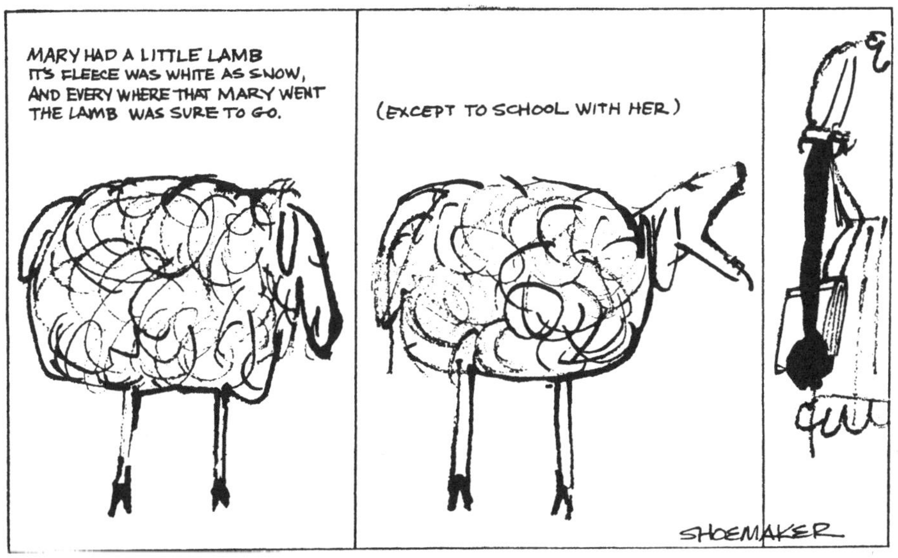
MARY HAD A LITTLE LAMB
ITS FLEECE WAS WHITE AS SNOW,
AND EVERY WHERE THAT MARY WENT
THE LAMB WAS SURE TO GO.
(EXCEPT TO SCHOOL WITH HER.)
SHOEMAKER

HOWARD SHOEMAKER. THE REALIST #24-25, MARCH-APRIL 1961. *6

WORLD CONSCIENCE
"In origin, nature, structure, and general conduct the Franco regime is a fascist regime patterned on, and established largely as a result of aid received from Hitler's Nazi Germany and Mussolini's Fascist Italy."
—from the United Nations indictment of Spain, 1946

THE REALIST #24-25, MARCH-APRIL 1961.

L. HERMAN
אידישע' פאַרשער וואָס האָט דער ערשטער פאַרשפּרייט די

L. HERMAN. THE REALIST #24-25, MARCH-APRIL 1961. *7

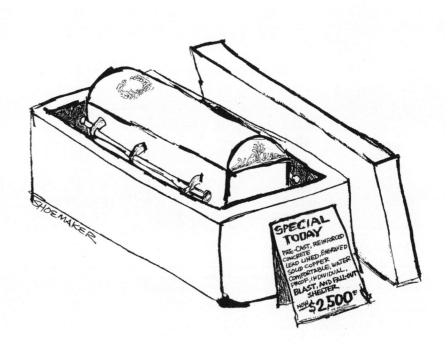

SHOEMAKER
SPECIAL TODAY
PRE-CAST, REINFORCED CONCRETE LEAD LINED, ENGRAVED SOLID COPPER COMFORTABLE, WATER PROOF, INDIVIDUAL, BLAST, AND FALL-OUT SHELTER
NOW $2,500

HOWARD SHOEMAKER. THE REALIST #24-25, MARCH-APRIL 1961.

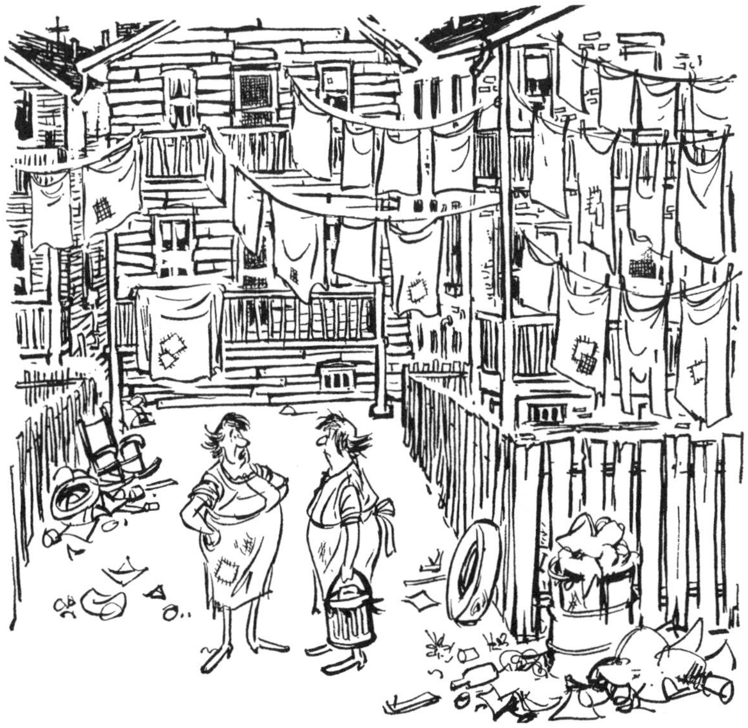

"I'll tell you why the world is in such a turmoil —
everybody wants a standard of living like ours, that's why ..."

FRANK INTERLANDI. THE REALIST #27, JUNE 1961.

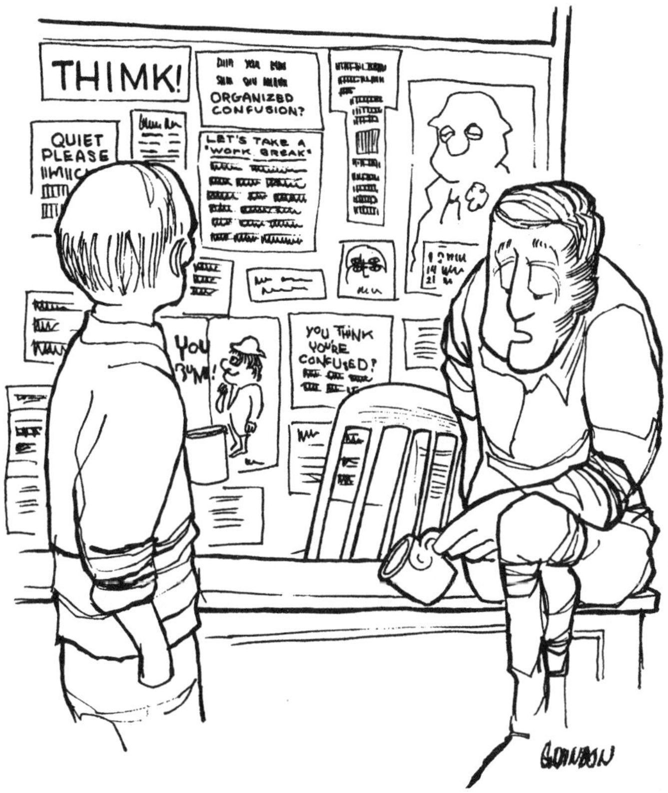
THIMK!
ORGANIZED CONFUSION?
QUIET PLEASE
LET'S TAKE A 'WORK BREAK'
YOU THINK YOU'RE CONFUSED?
GUINDON

"They don't really help — I still hate my job."

RICHARD GUINDON. THE REALIST #27, JUNE 1961.

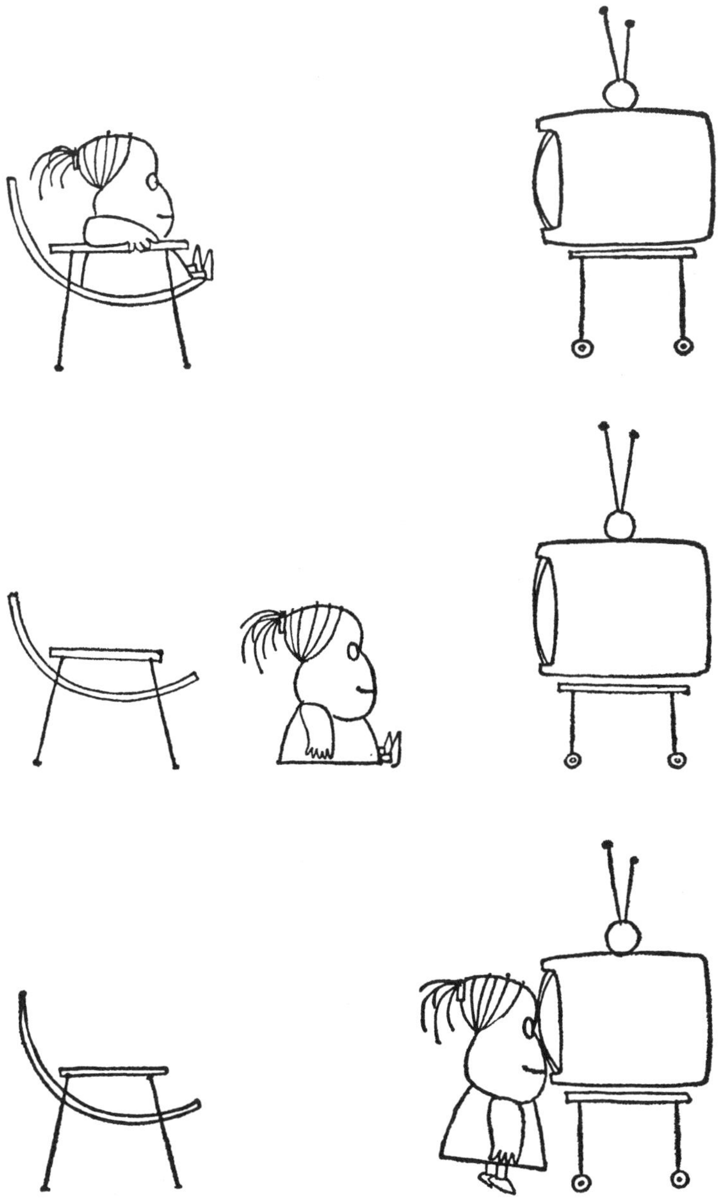

THE REALIST #26, MAY 1961.

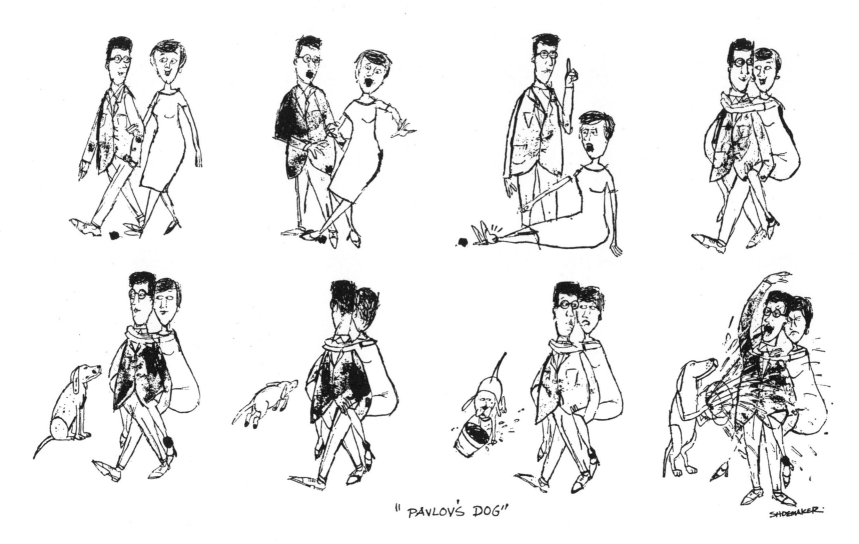

" PAVLOV'S DOG"
SHOEMAKER

HOWARD SHOEMAKER. THE REALIST #26, MAY 1961.

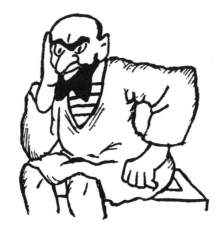

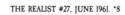

". . . Refresh my bowels
in The Lord."
St. Paul, Philemon 1:20

THE REALIST #27, JUNE 1961. *8

BUY A
PHALLUS
SYMBOL
25¢
donnis

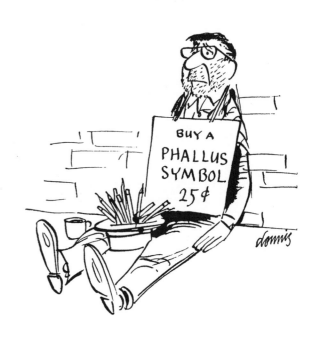

DON ADDIS. THE REALIST #26, MAY 1961.

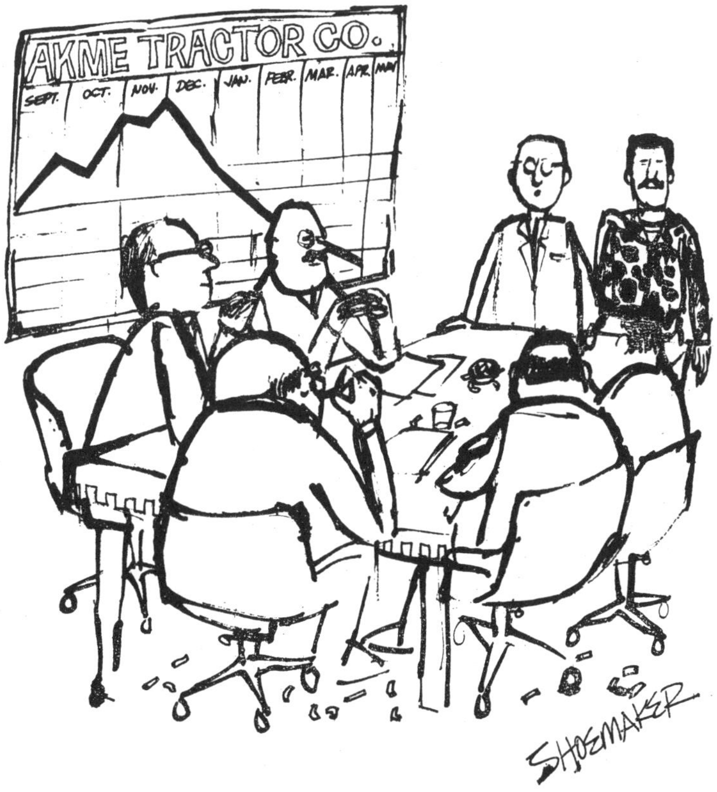
AKME TRACTOR CO.
SEPT. OCT. NOV. DEC. JAN. FEBR. MAR. APR. MAY
SHOEMAKER

"Gentlemen, Gonzales here has a rather unique sales promotion idea."

HOWARD SHOEMAKER. THE REALIST #27, JUNE 1961. *9

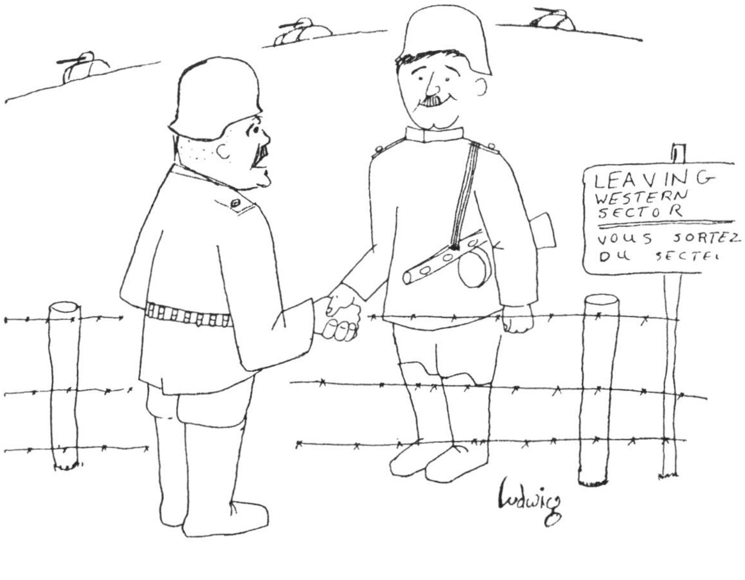
LEAVING WESTERN SECTOR
VOUS SORTEZ
Ludwig

"Afrika Korps, 1943 — no? Ach, maybe Belgium, 1940 ..."

LUDWIG. THE REALIST #28, AUGUST 1961. *10

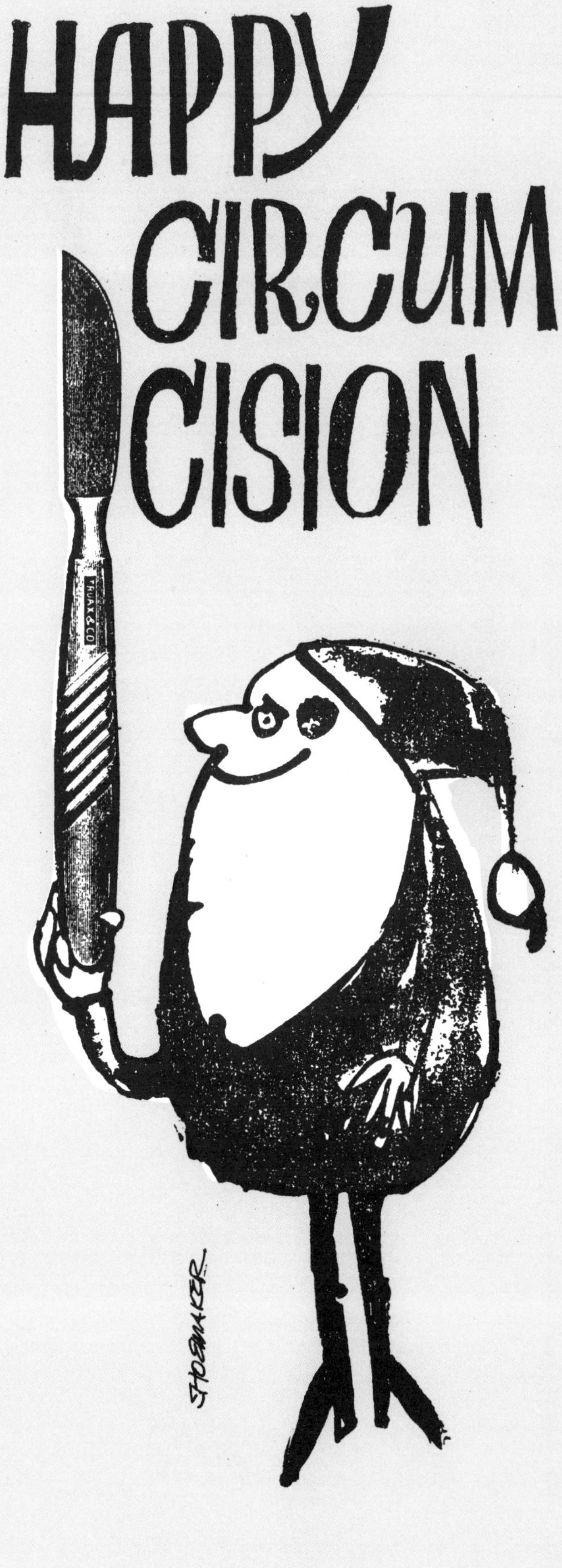
HAPPY
CIRCUM
CISION
SHOEMAKER

HOWARD SHOEMAKER. THE REALIST #27, JUNE 1961.

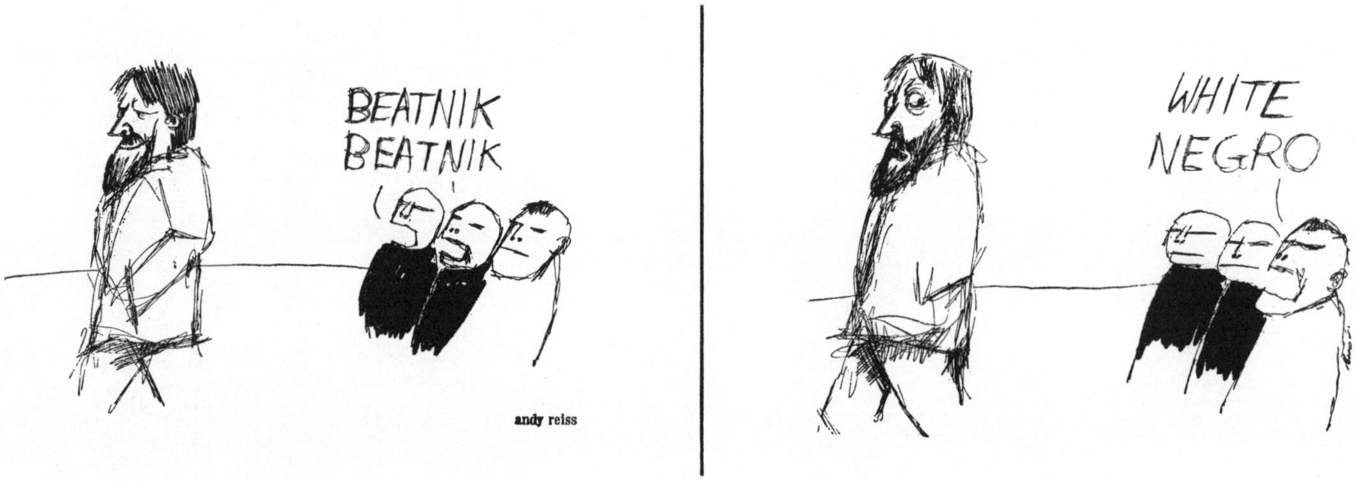
BEATNIK
BEATNIK
andy reiss
WHITE
NEGRO

ANDY REISS. THE REALIST #28, AUGUST 1961. *11

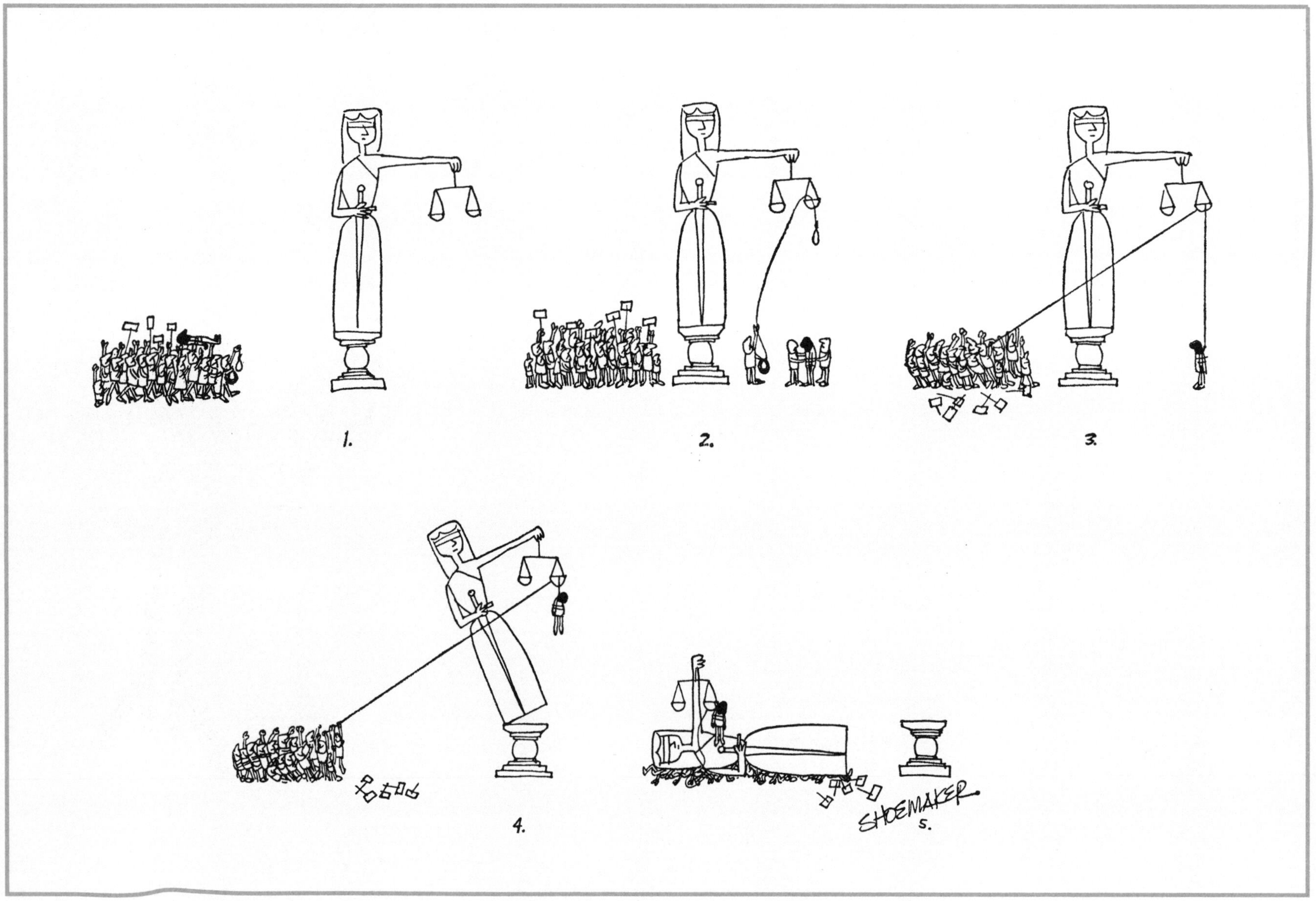
1.
2.
3.
4.
SHOEMAKER
S.

HOWARD SHOEMAKER. THE REALIST #28, AUGUST 1961.

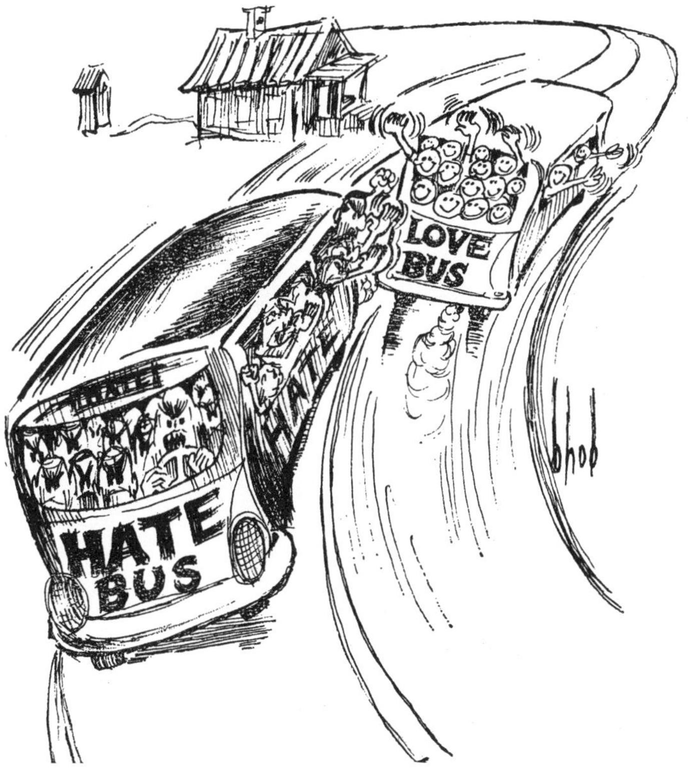
LOVE
BUS
HATE
HATE
BUS
bhob

Segregated Buses

BHOB STEWART. THE REALIST #27, JUNE 1961.

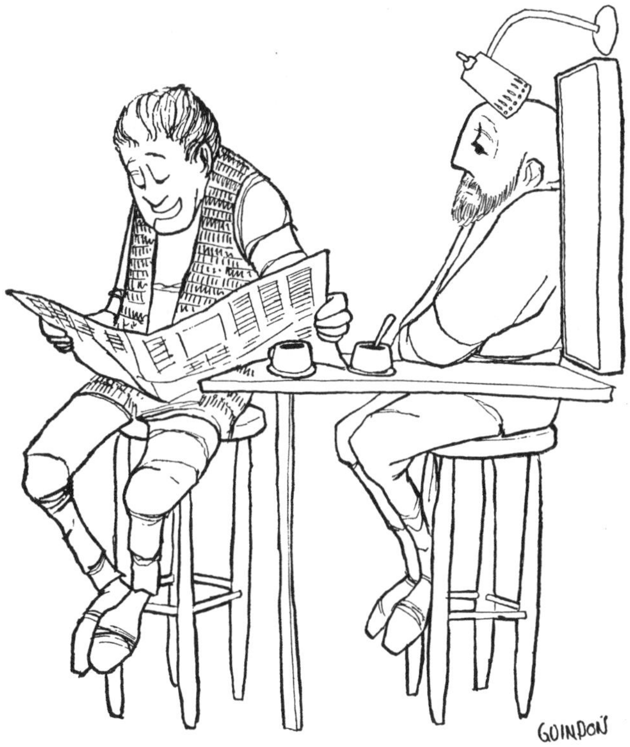
GUINDON

"I see where the nation is facing the greatest challenge of its history."

RICHARD GUINDON. THE REALIST #28, AUGUST 1961.

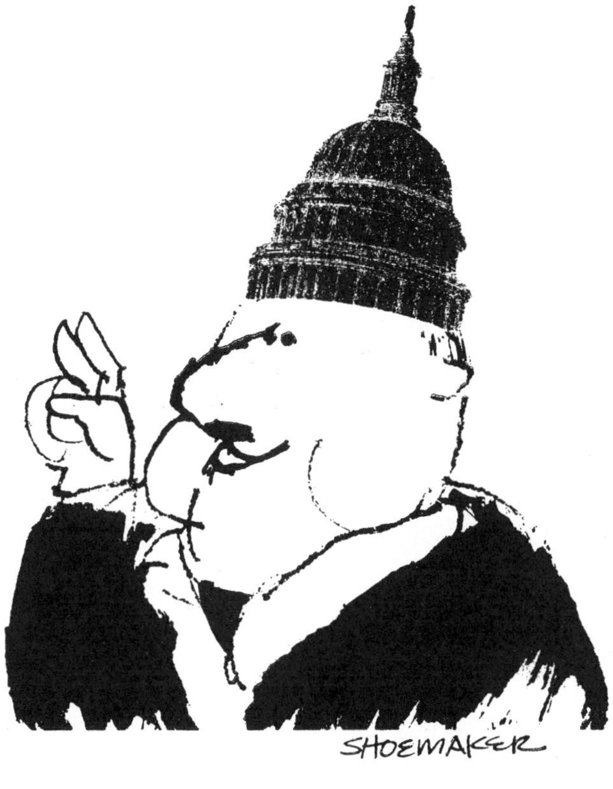
SHOEMAKER

HOWARD SHOEMAKER. THE REALIST #28, AUGUST 1961.

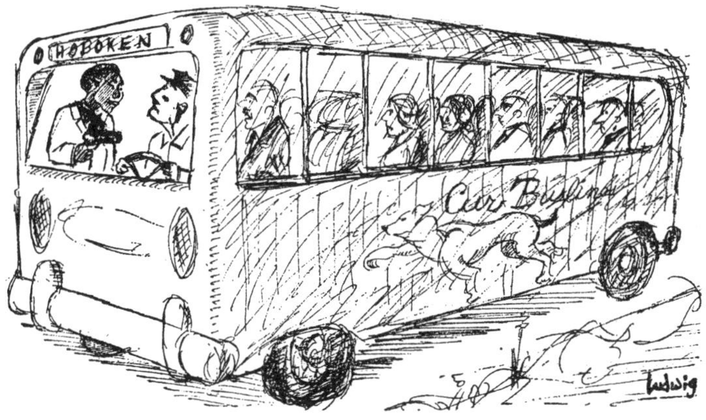
HOBOKEN
ludwig

"Drive to Monroe, North Carolina..."

LUDWIG. THE REALIST #28, AUGUST 1961. *12

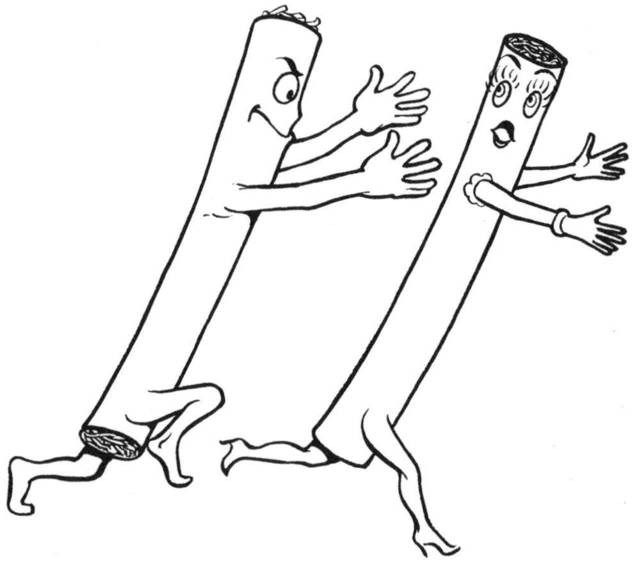

"No, no—not without a filter..."

THE REALIST #29, SEPTEMBER 1961.

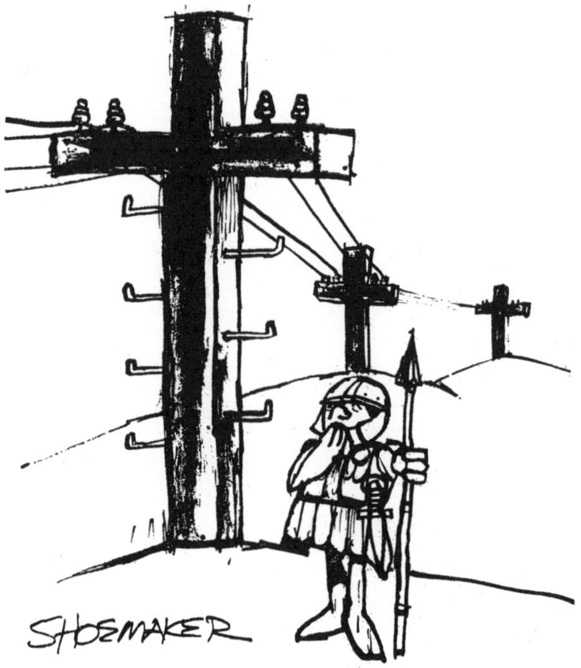
SHOEMAKER

HOWARD SHOEMAKER. THE REALIST #29, SEPTEMBER 1961.

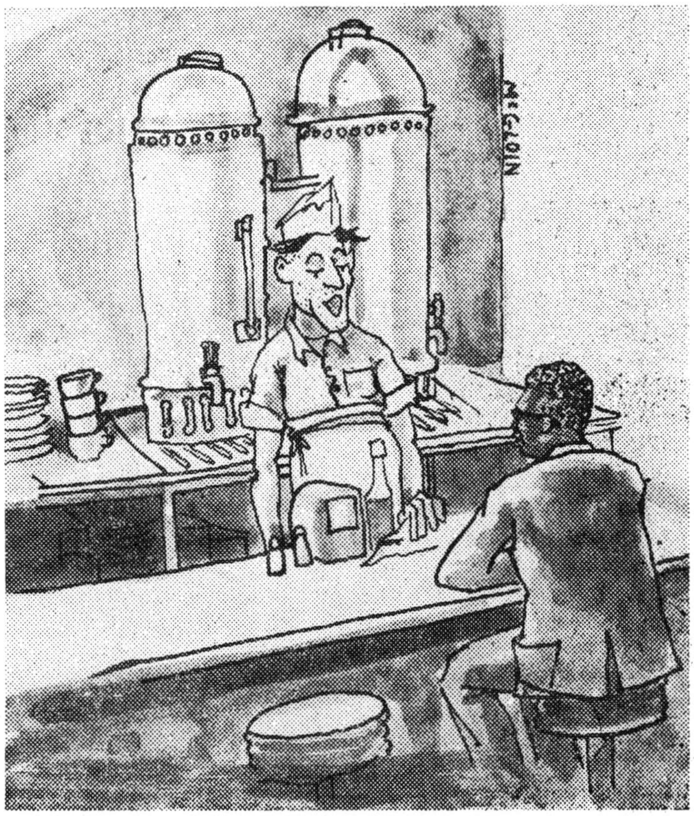
McGLOIN

"Oh, an exchange student from Ghana —
that's different — at first I thought you was a nigger."

MCGLOIN. THE REALIST #29, SEPTEMBER 1961.

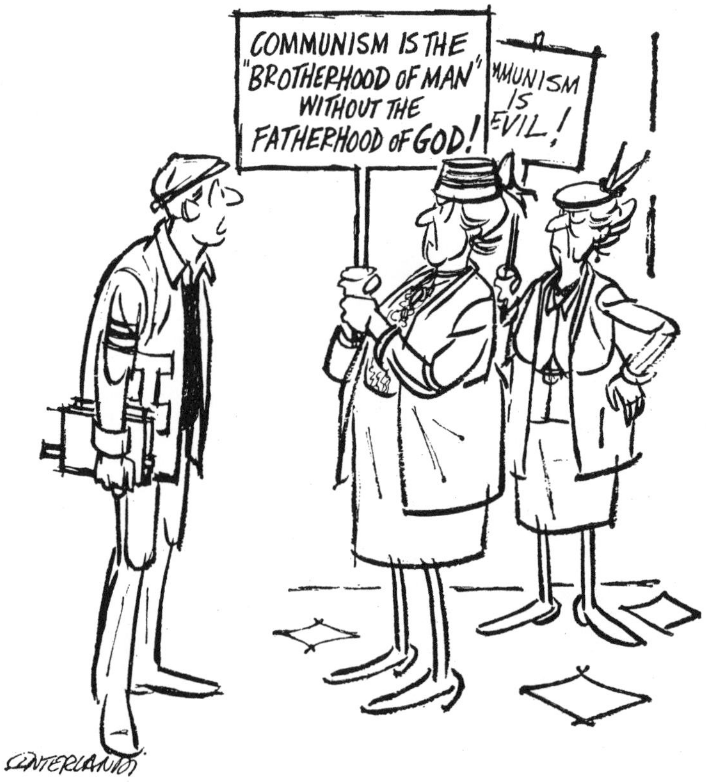
COMMUNISM IS THE "BROTHERHOOD OF MAN" WITHOUT THE FATHERHOOD OF GOD!
MMUNISM IS EVIL!
INTERLANDI

"But ladies — where does that leave the agnostic-misanthrope?"

FRANK INTERLANDI. THE REALIST #29, SEPTEMBER 1961.

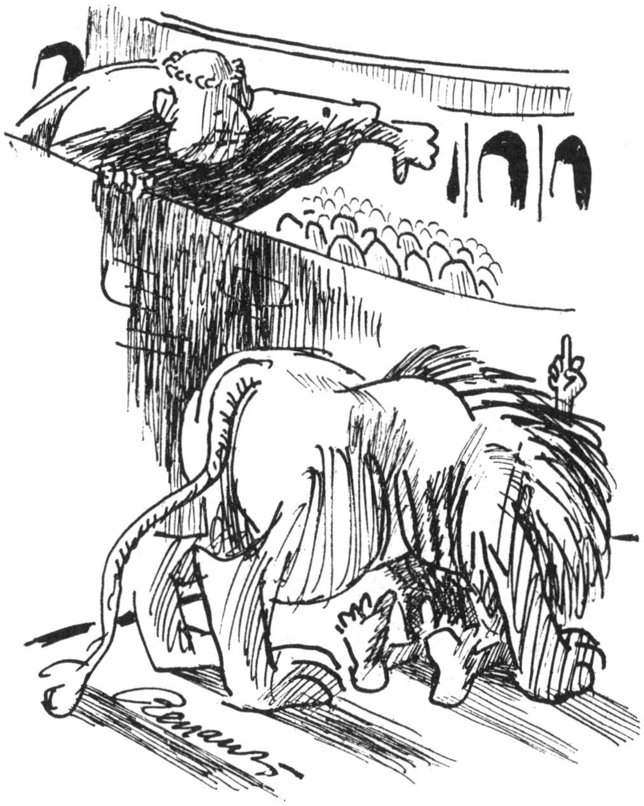

RENAULT. THE REALIST #29, SEPTEMBER 1961. *13

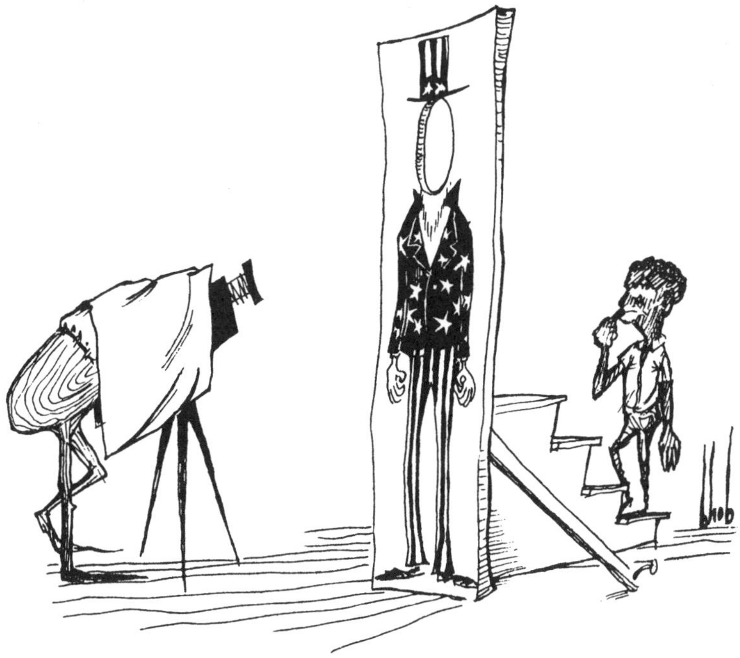

BHOB STEWART. THE REALIST #29, SEPTEMBER 1961.

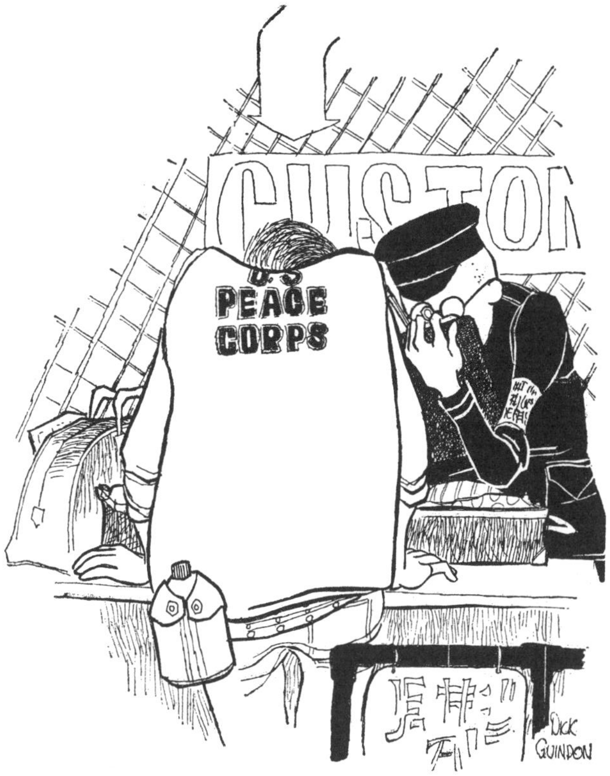
PEACE
CORPS
DICK
GUINDON

"Come on, slant-eyes, hurry up ..."

RICHARD GUINDON. THE REALIST #29, SEPTEMBER 1961. *14

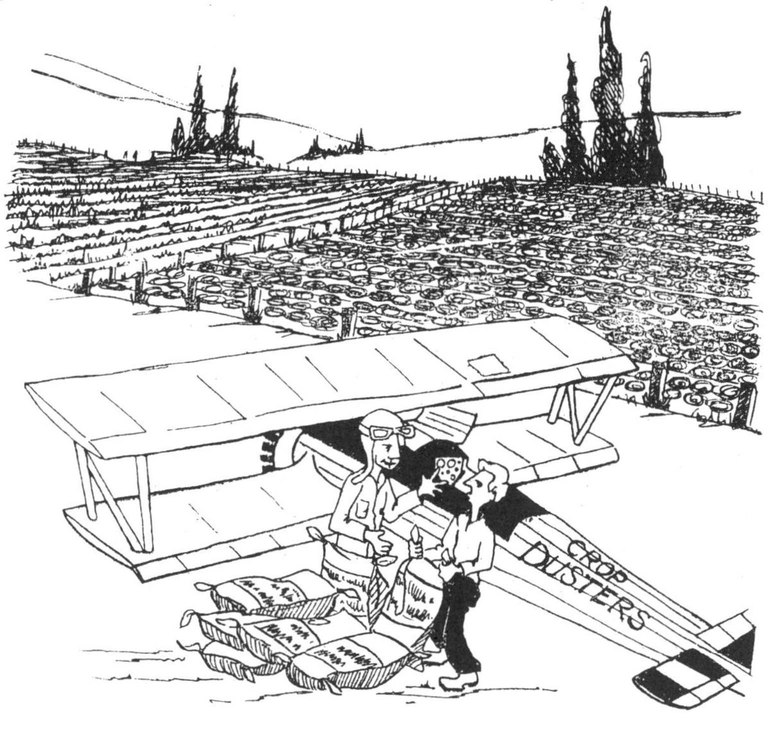
CROP
DUSTERS

THAT'LL BE THE DAY: "Say, do you think this stuff we're spraying on the lettuce might poison the people who eat it?"

THE REALIST #30, DECEMBER 1961.

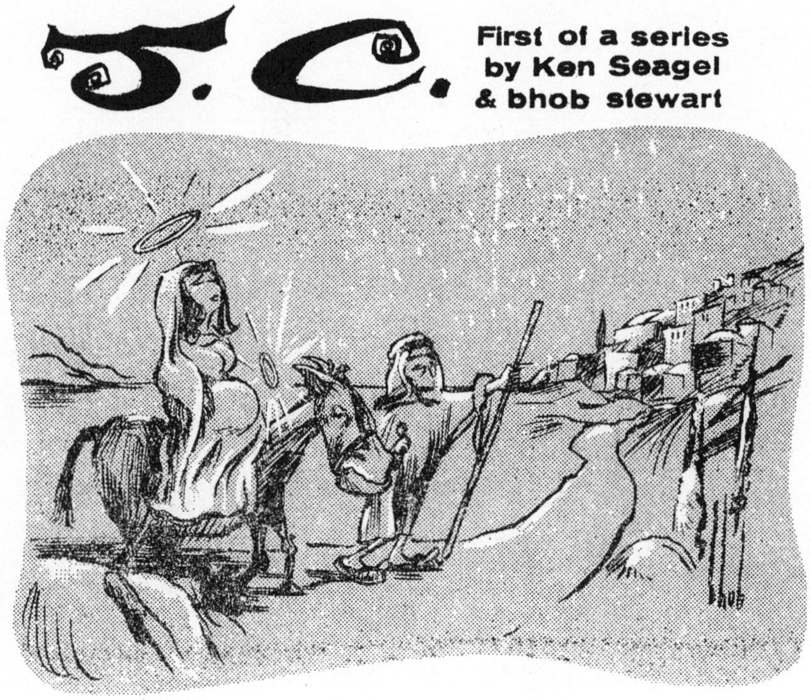
J.C.
First of a series
by Ken Seagel
& bhob stewart

KEN SEAGLE AND BHOB STEWART. THE REALIST #31, FEBRUARY 1962.

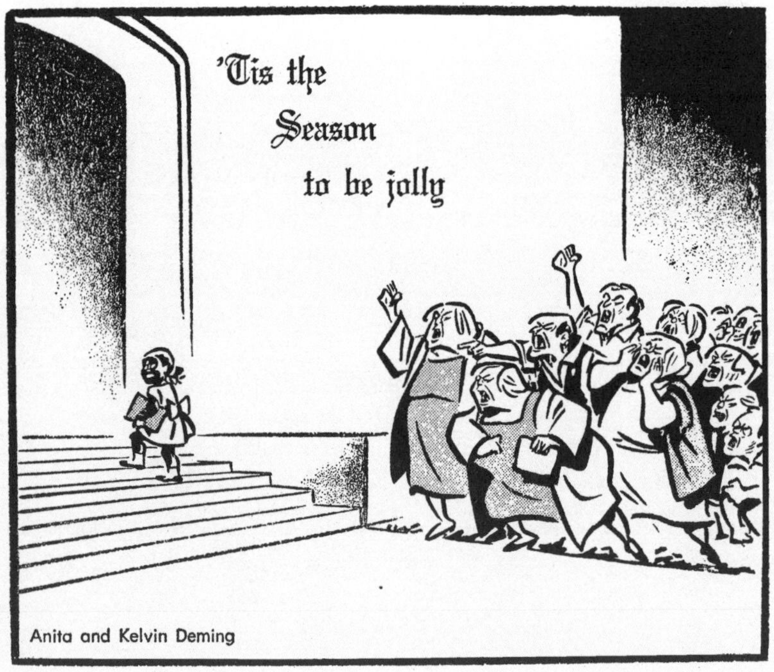
'Tis the Season to be jolly
Anita and Kelvin Deming

ANITA AND KELVIN DEMING. THE REALIST #30, DECEMBER 1961. *15

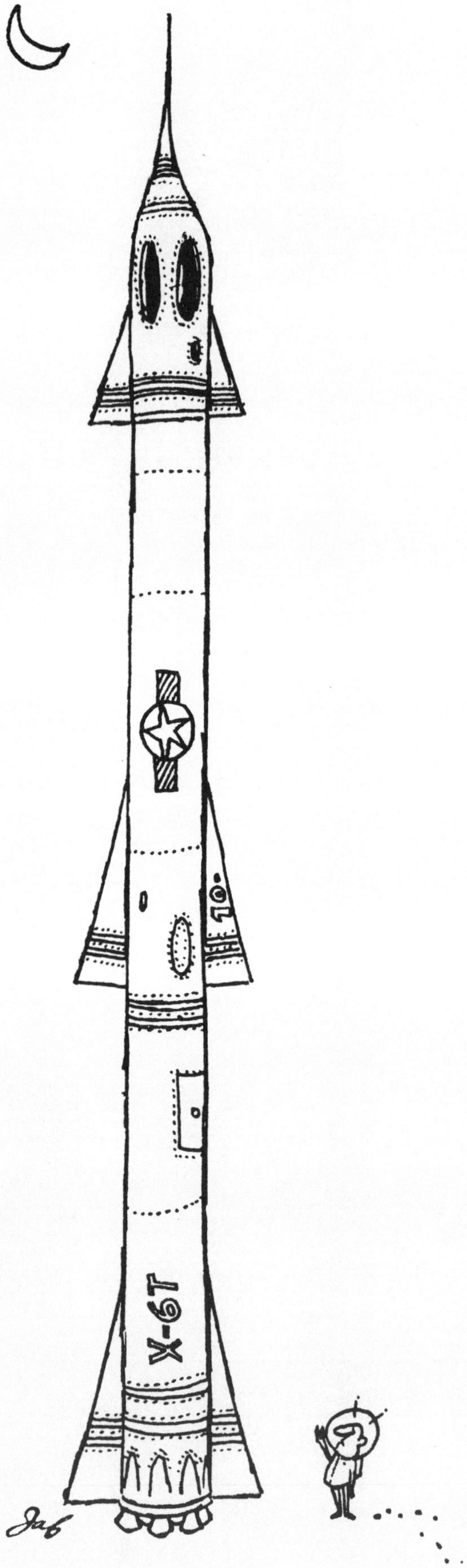
X-6T

"Oh — fuck it ..."

JAMES "JAF" FRANKFORT. THE REALIST #29, SEPTEMBER 1961.

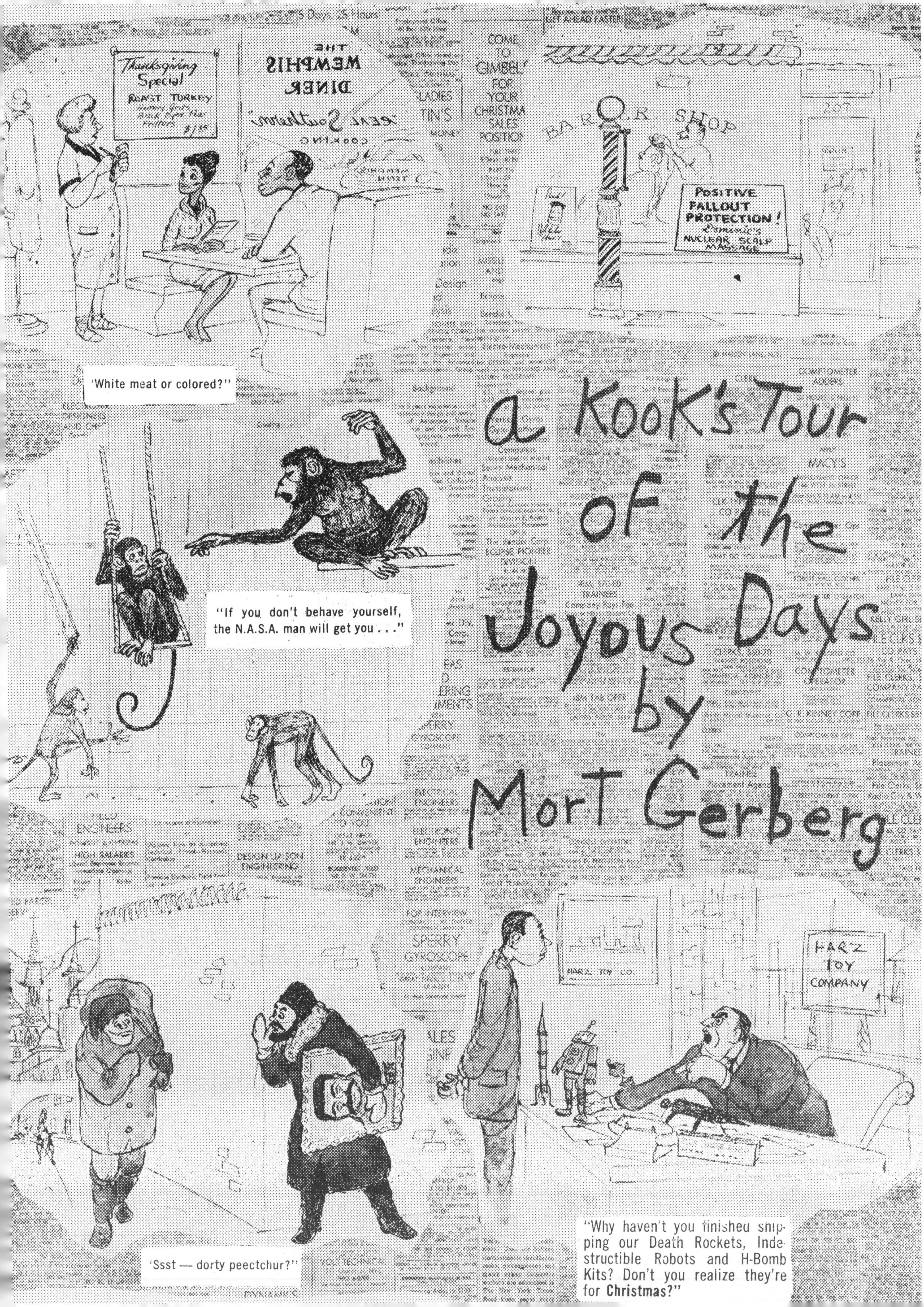
a Kook's Tour of the Joyous Days by Mort Gerberg
Thanksgiving Special Roast Turkey
POSITIVE FALLOUT PROTECTION!
NUCLEAR SCALP MASSAGE
'White meat or colored?"
"If you don't behave yourself, the N.A.S.A. man will get you . . ."
HARZ TOY COMPANY
'Ssst — dorty peectchur?"
"Why haven't you finished shipping our Death Rockets, Indestructible Robots and H-Bomb Kits? Don't you realize they're for **Christmas?**"

MORT GERBERG. THE REALIST #30, DECEMBER 1961.

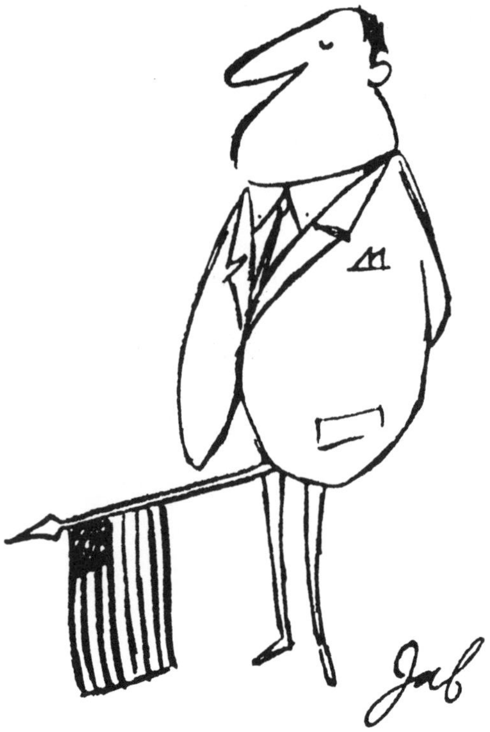
Jaf

"The Power of Kinky Thinking"

JAMES "JAF" FRANKFORT. THE REALIST #30, DECEMBER 1961.

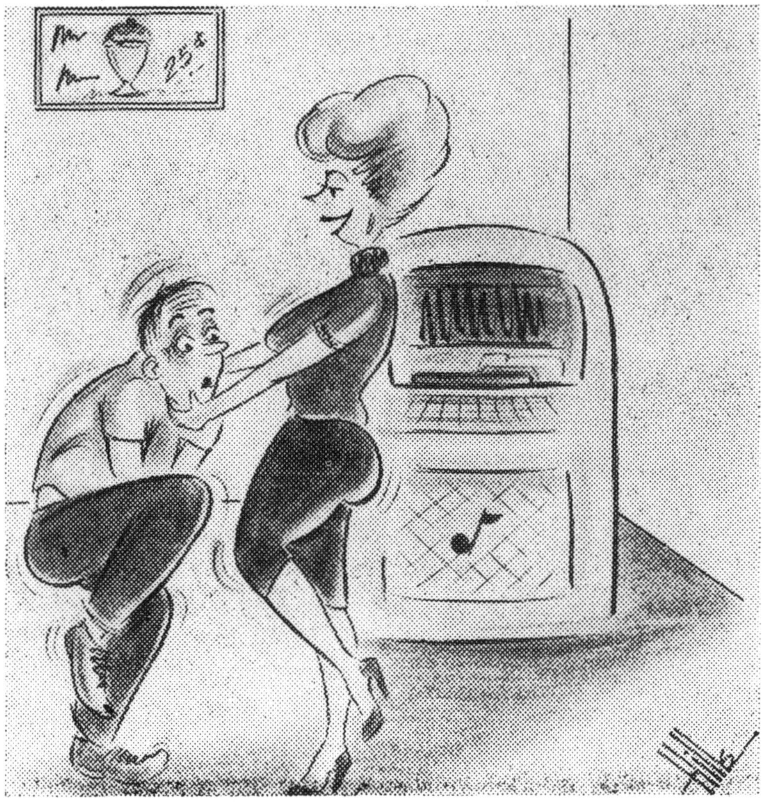

"Unless you straighten up, silly, I can't finish teaching you how to dance the Twist ..."

HILLS. THE REALIST #30, DECEMBER 1961.

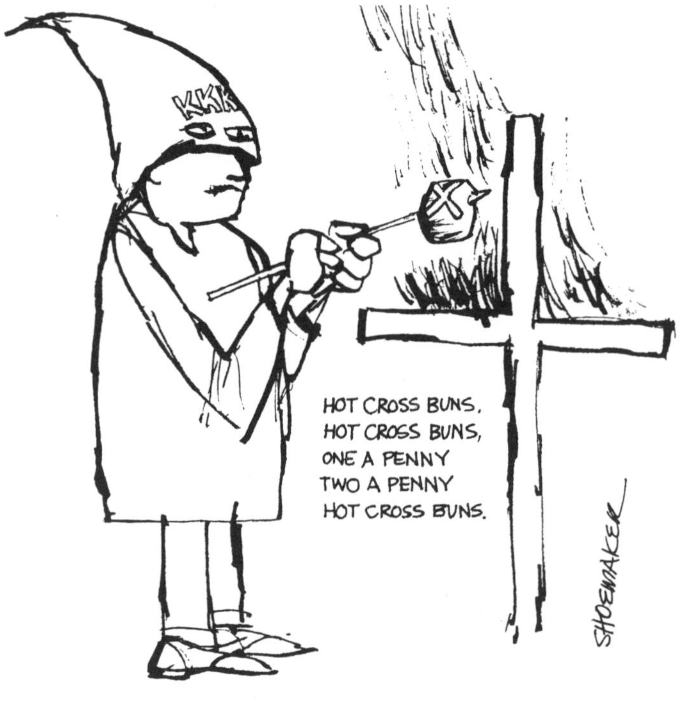
KKK
HOT CROSS BUNS,
HOT CROSS BUNS,
ONE A PENNY
TWO A PENNY
HOT CROSS BUNS.
SHOEMAKER

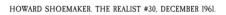

HOWARD SHOEMAKER. THE REALIST #30, DECEMBER 1961.

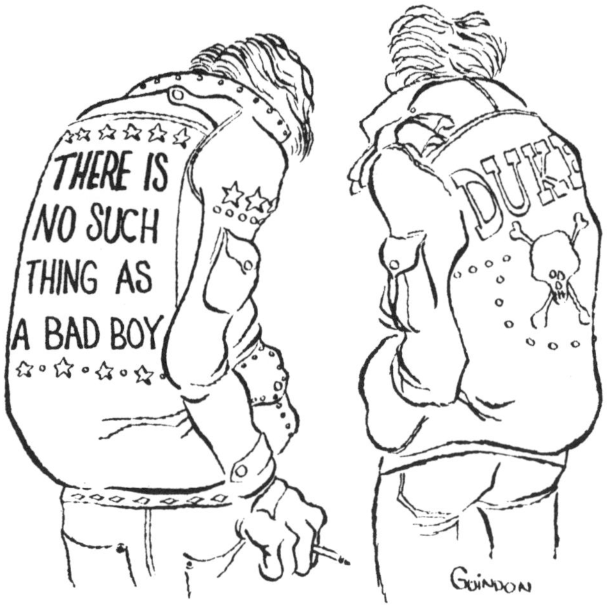
THERE IS
NO SUCH
THING AS
A BAD BOY
GUINDON

RICHARD GUINDON. THE REALIST #31, FEBRUARY 1962.

WALDMAN

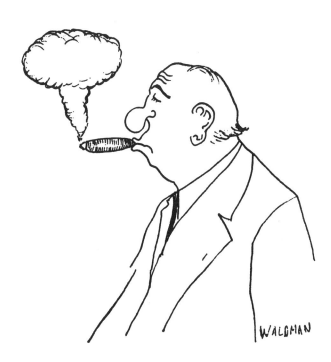

WALDMAN. THE REALIST #31, FEBRUARY 1962.

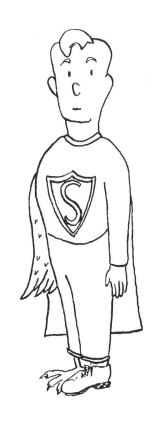

THE REALIST #30, DECEMBER 1961.

WATCH YOUR STEP
WENDE

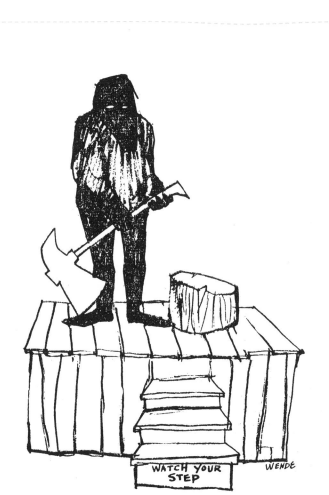

WENDE. THE REALIST #31, FEBRUARY 1962.

NeighboRhood
Pilot
Project
ReMedial Reading Center
FUC U
GUINDON

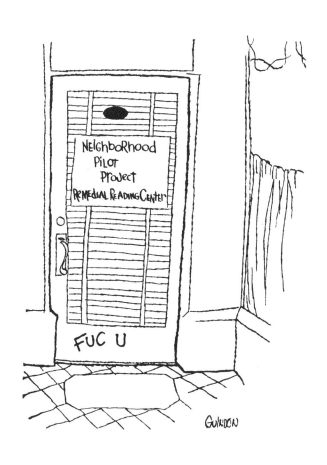

RICHARD GUINDON. THE REALIST #31, FEBRUARY 1962.

SURVIVAL IS IN FASHION

by Edward Koren

This year's theme in men's clothing is styled by the National Academy of Sciences:

"Adequate shielding is the only means of preventing radiation casualties."

Four of the more popular models are illustrated here.

1. The distinctive "diplomat" business suit. Superior protection is combined with "lithe-line" mobility in this steel-and-aluminum classic.

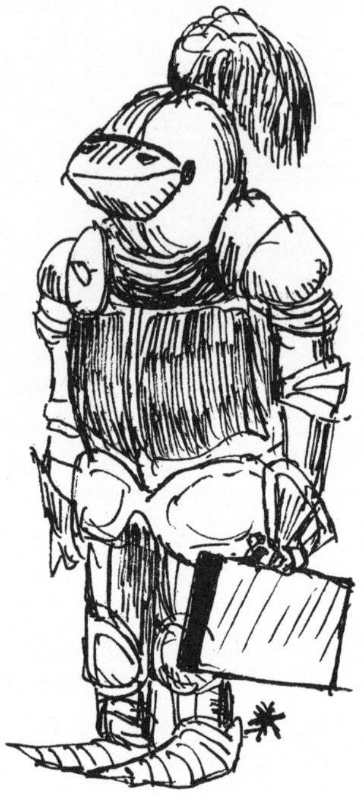

2. Nature's most invulnerable animal has provided this "executive retreat" with maximum self-contained safety, proven capabilities.

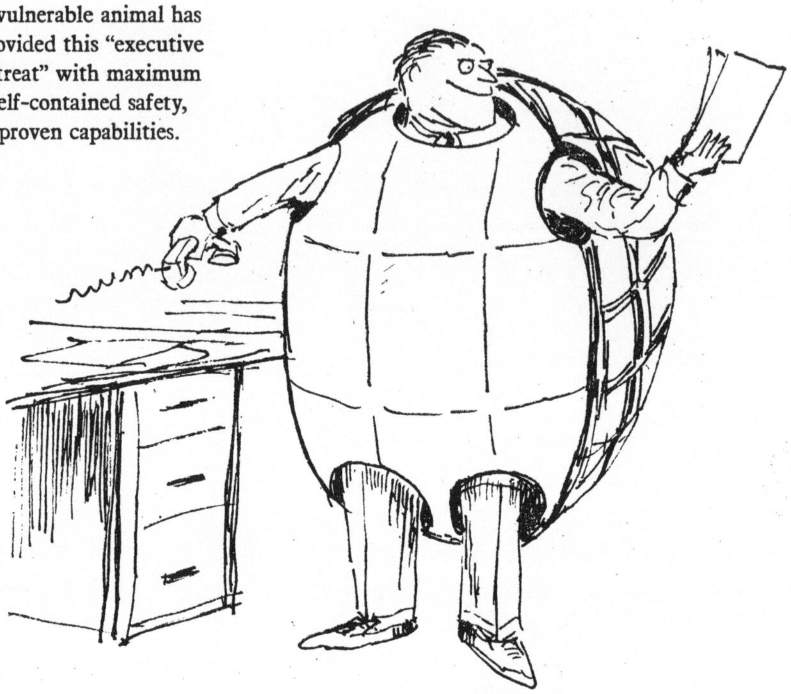

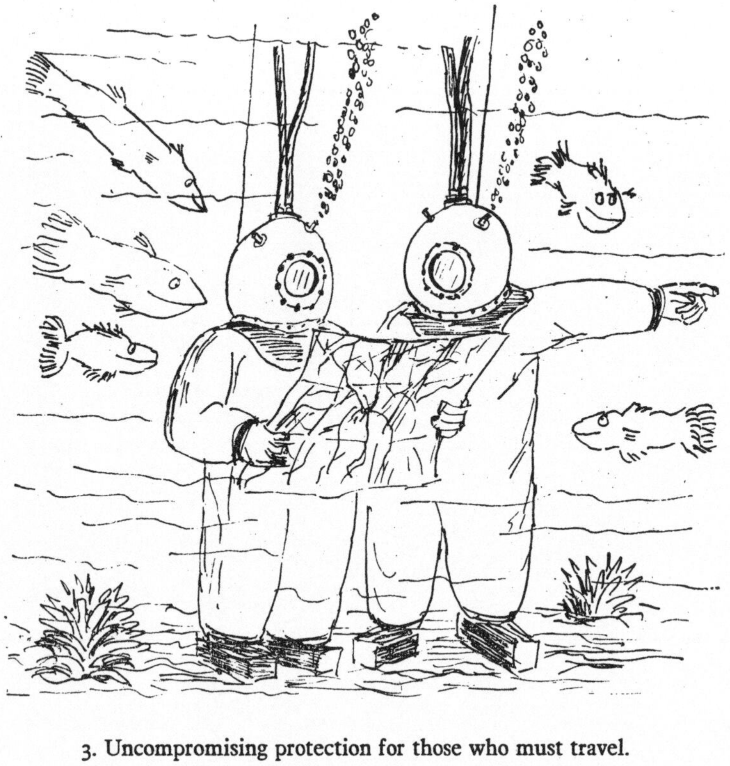

3. Uncompromising protection for those who must travel. Attractive single-piece "down-under" suit available in a wide variety of patterns and colors.

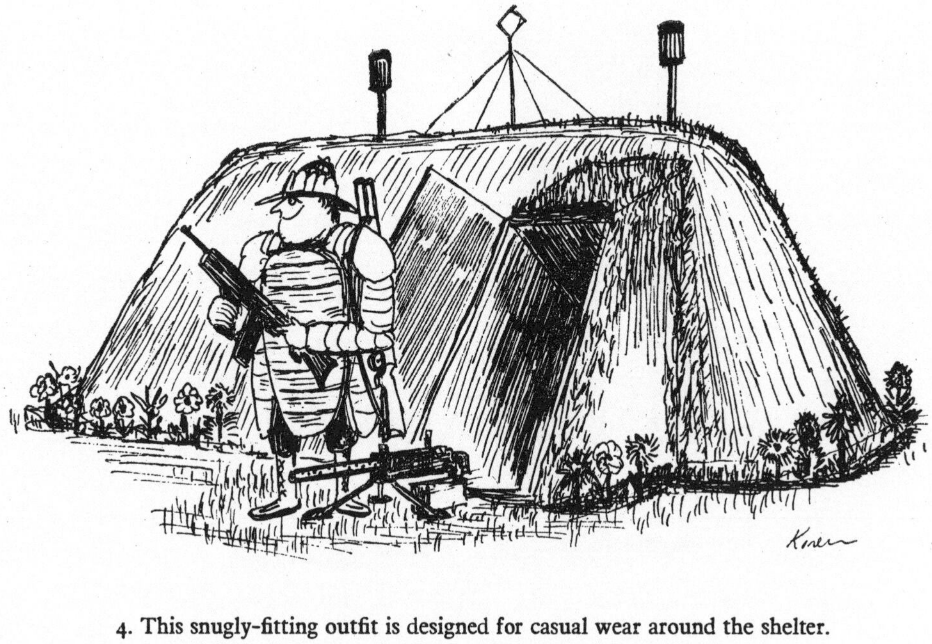
Koren

4. This snugly-fitting outfit is designed for casual wear around the shelter. Entirely bullet-proof, zippered ammunition pockets, padded cap.

EDWARD KOREN. THE REALIST #31, FEBRUARY 1962.

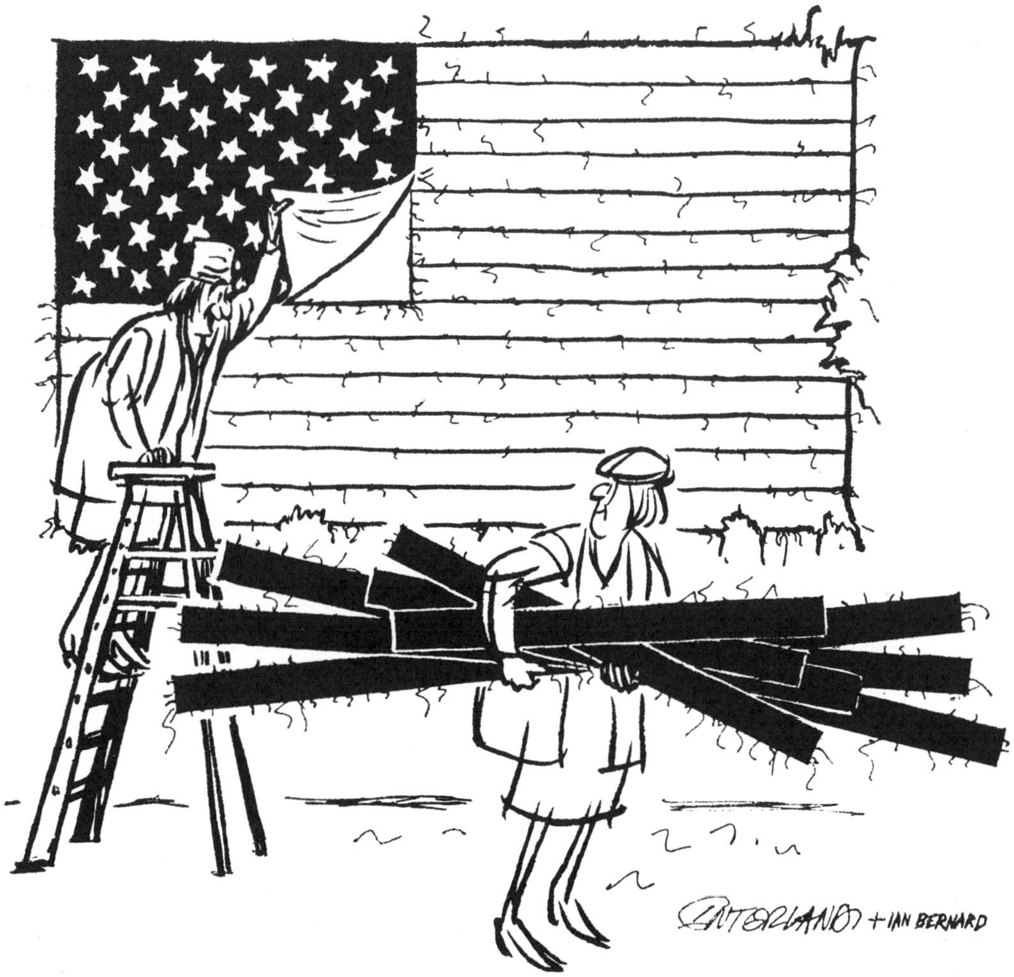
INTERLANDI + IAN BERNARD

"As long as we're taking the Red out of the Red-White-and-Blue, let's get rid of the blue and make our country completely white ..."

FRANK INTERLANDI AND IAN BERNARD. THE REALIST #31, FEBRUARY 1962. *16

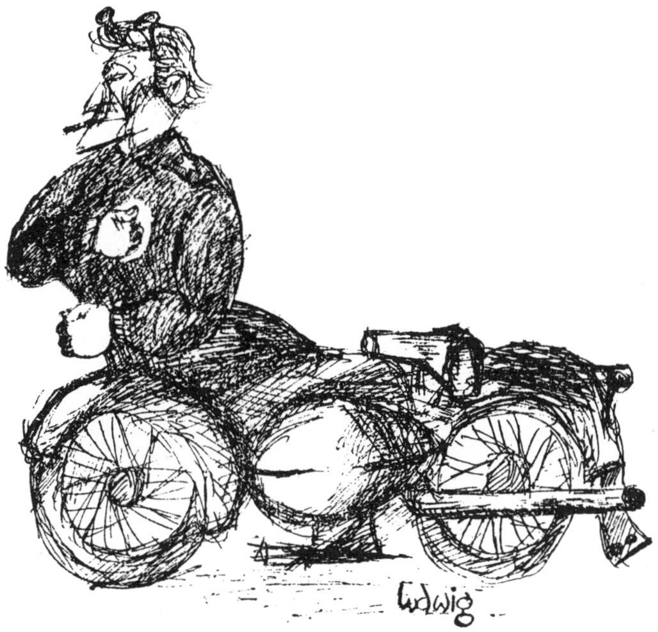
Ludwig

LUDWIG. THE REALIST #31, FEBRUARY 1962.

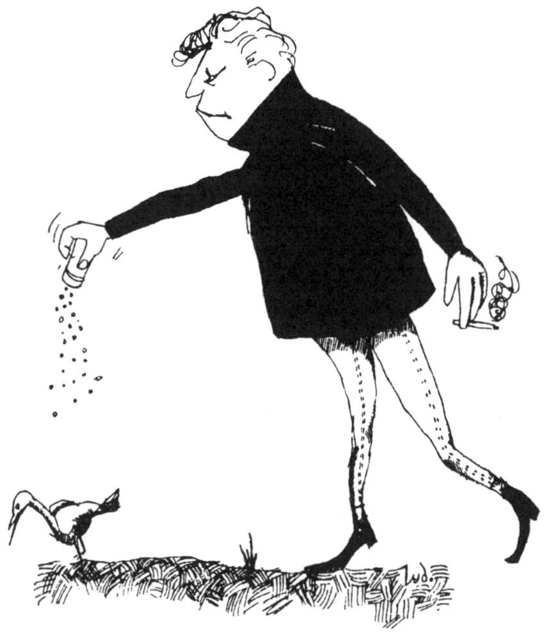

THE REALIST #31, FEBRUARY 1962.

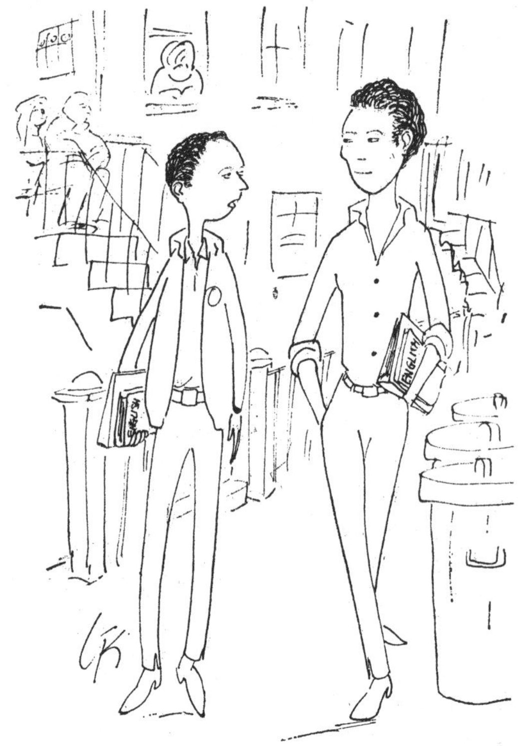
ENGLISH

"Man, Jose, these foreign languages are a real drag ..."

THE REALIST #31, FEBRUARY 1962.

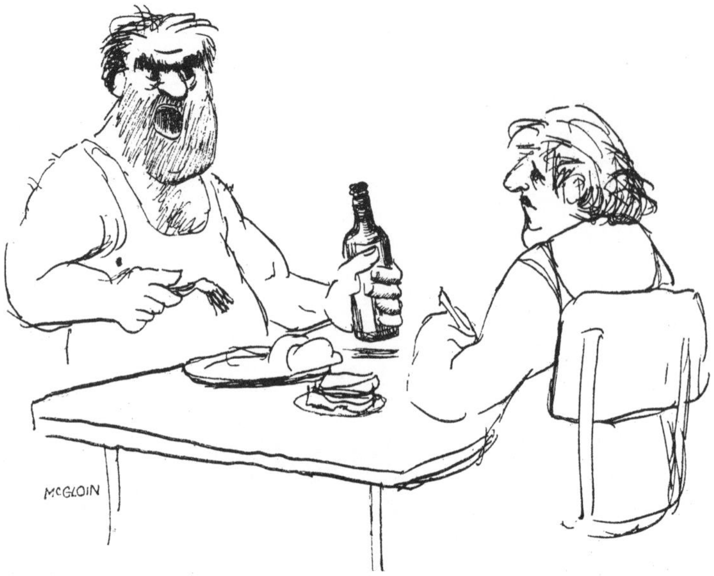
MCGLOIN

"When I wanna know what Kennedy drinks with his meals, I'll ask him ..."

MCGLOIN. THE REALIST #31, FEBRUARY 1962.

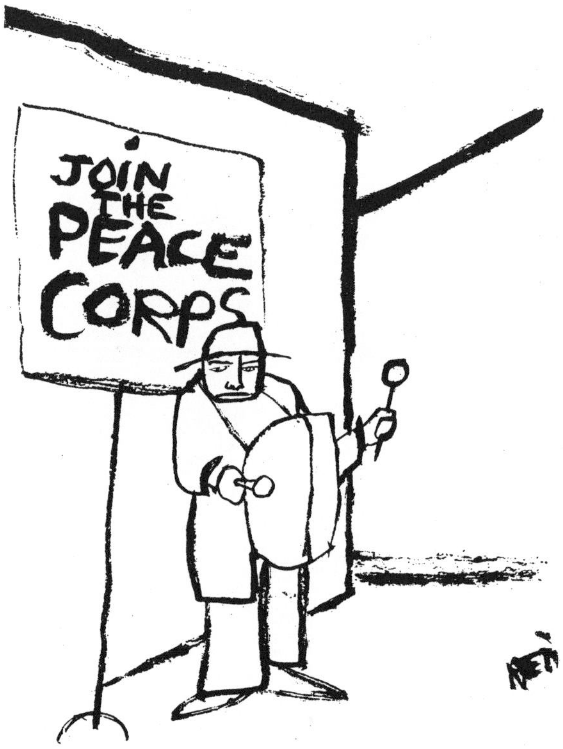
JOIN THE PEACE CORPS

THE REALIST #31, FEBRUARY 1962.

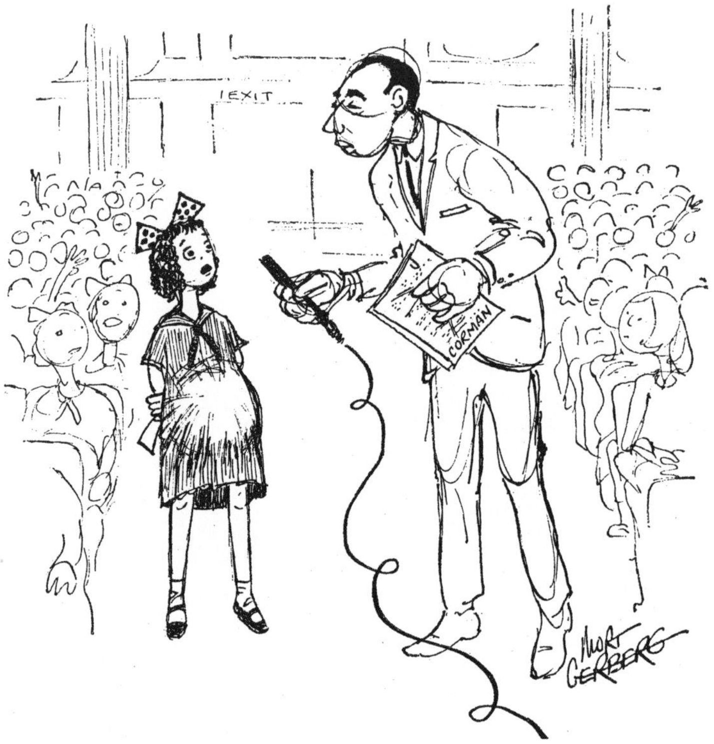
EXIT
CORMAN
MORT GERBERG

"... while *our* half of the class used the *rhythm* method ..."

MORT GERBERG. THE REALIST #31, FEBRUARY 1962. *17

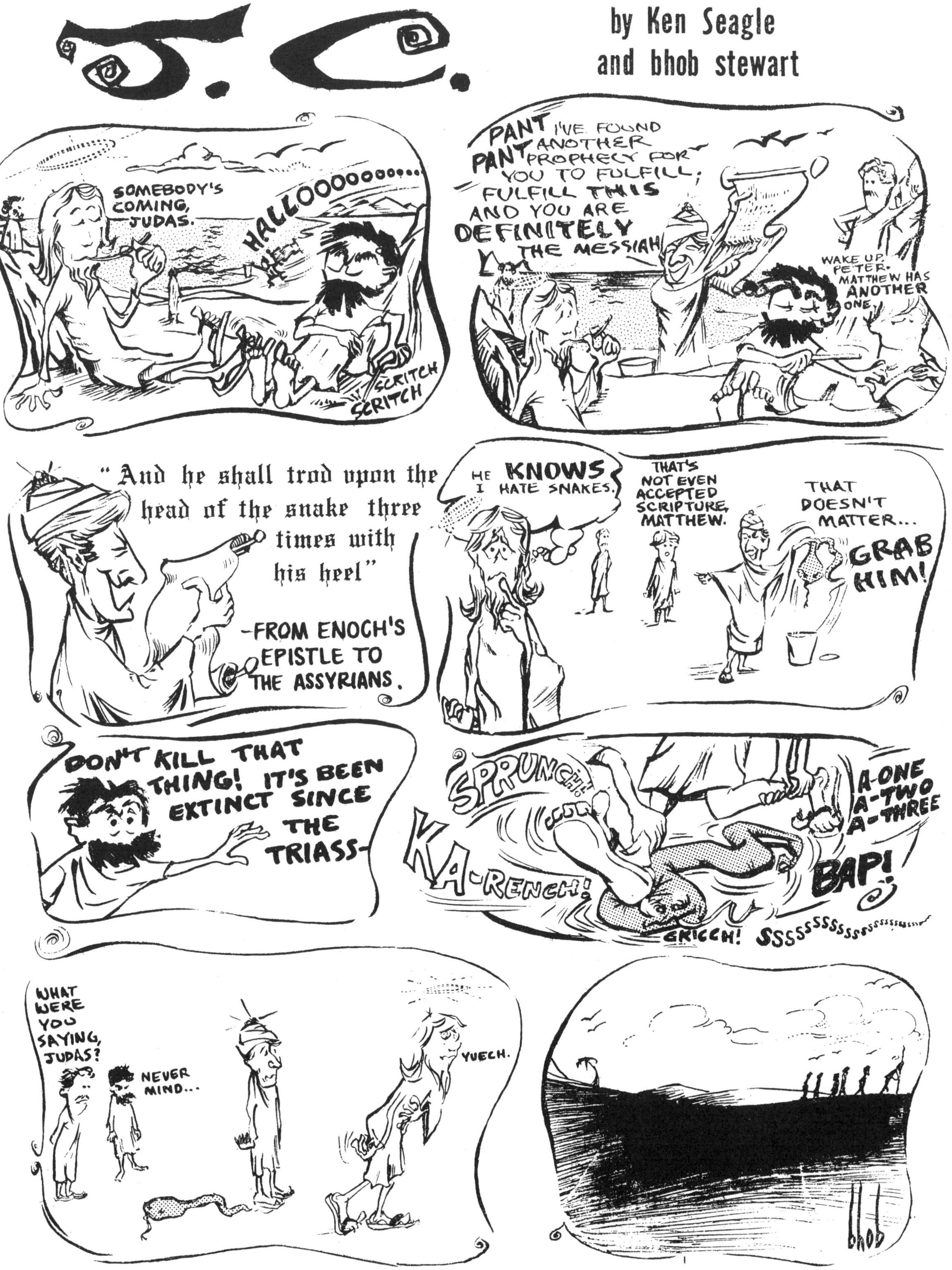
J.C.
by Ken Seagle and bhob stewart
SOMEBODY'S COMING, JUDAS.
HALLOOOOOOoo...
SCRITCH SCRITCH
PANT PANT I'VE FOUND ANOTHER PROPHECY FOR YOU TO FULFILL; FULFILL THIS AND YOU ARE DEFINITELY THE MESSIAH
WAKE UP, PETER. MATTHEW HAS ANOTHER ONE.
"And he shall trod upon the head of the snake three times with his heel"
-FROM ENOCH'S EPISTLE TO THE ASSYRIANS.
HE KNOWS I HATE SNAKES.
THAT'S NOT EVEN ACCEPTED SCRIPTURE, MATTHEW.
THAT DOESN'T MATTER...
GRAB HIM!
DON'T KILL THAT THING! IT'S BEEN EXTINCT SINCE THE TRIASS-
SPRUNCH!
A-ONE A-TWO A-THREE
KA-RENCH!
BAP!
GRICCH!
SSSSSSSSSSSS
WHAT WERE YOU SAYING, JUDAS?
NEVER MIND...
YUECH.
bhob

KEN SEAGLE/BHOB STEWART.
THE REALIST #30, DECEMBER 1961.

GUINDON

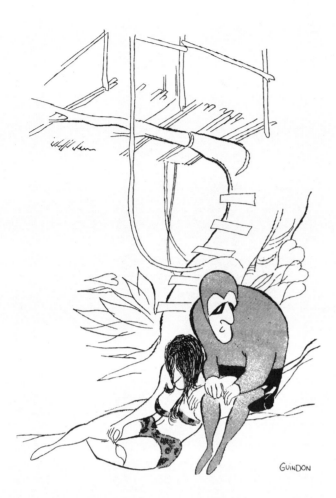

"Jane ... I feel like the lowest ... dirtiest ... most rotten friend a guy ever had."

RICHARD GUINDON. THE REALIST #31, FEBRUARY 1962. *18

BAN
THE
OMB

THE REALIST #32, MARCH 1962.

JAMES "JAF" FRANKFORT. THE REALIST #32, MARCH 1962. *19

NIX TO NELSON
DEFEAT ROCKEFELLER
BEAT ROCKY!
BEAT ROCKEF

"And what's more, my opponent is mentally cruel ..."

MORT GERBERG. THE REALIST #32, MARCH 1962. *20

JIM CROW MUST GO!
MEN'S ROOM WHITES' ONLY

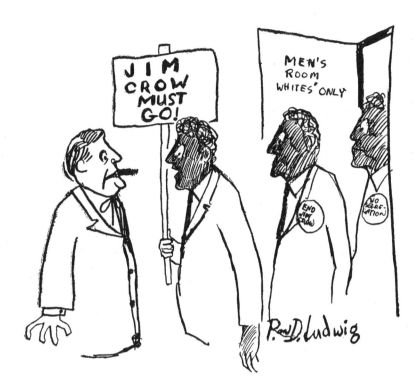

"I'm afraid that we'll have to refuse to leave;
we're staging a shit-in."

LUDWIG. THE REALIST #32, MARCH 1962. *21

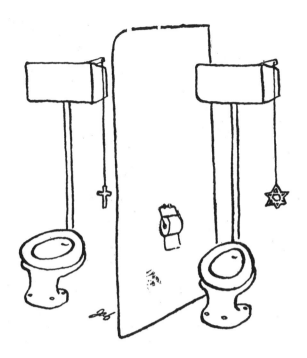

JAMES "JAF" FRANKFORT. THE REALIST #32, MARCH 1962.

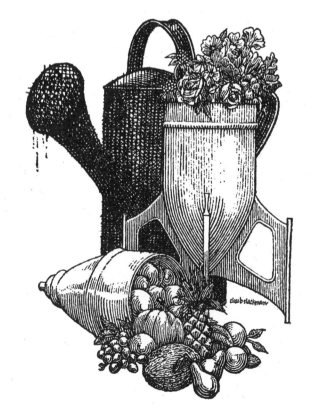

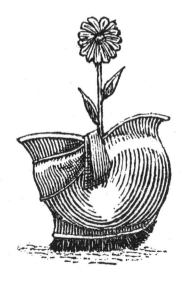

THE REALIST #32, MARCH 1962. *22

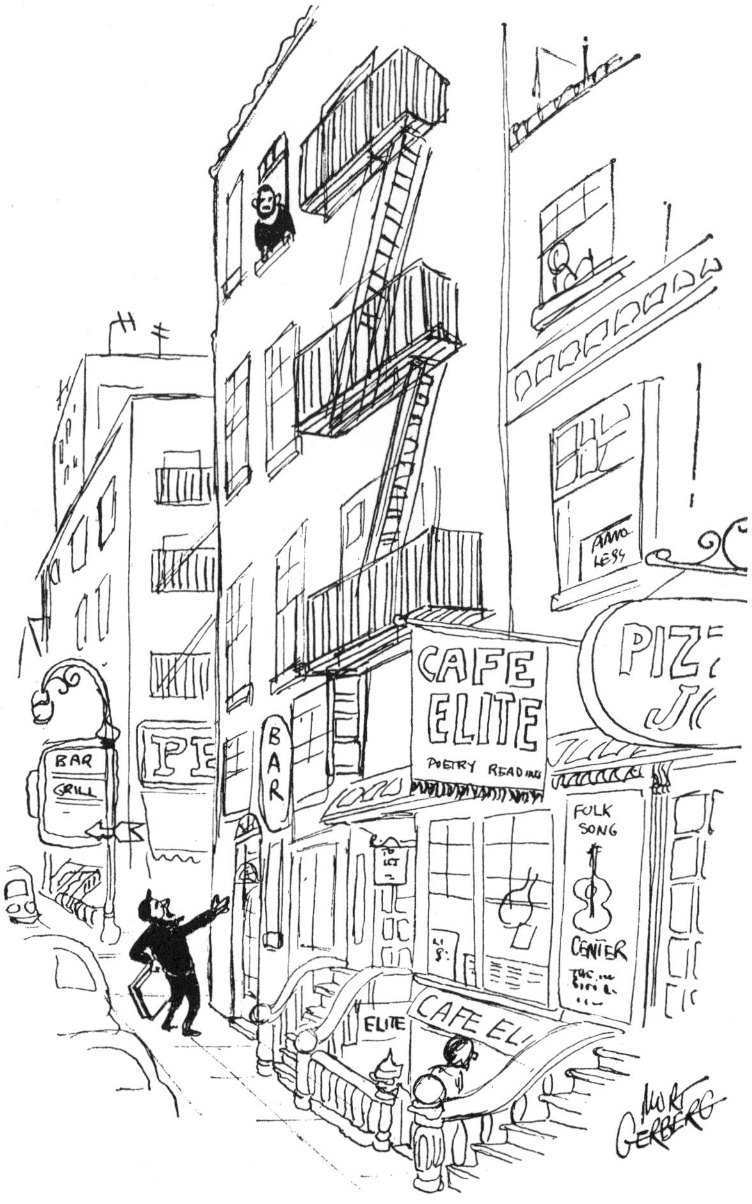
CAFE ELITE
POETRY READING
BAR
BAR GRILL
FOLK SONG
CENTER
ELITE
MORT GERBERG

"Oh, c'mon down for one beer — who d'ya think you are, Salinger?"

MORT GERBERG. THE REALIST #34, MAY 1962. *23

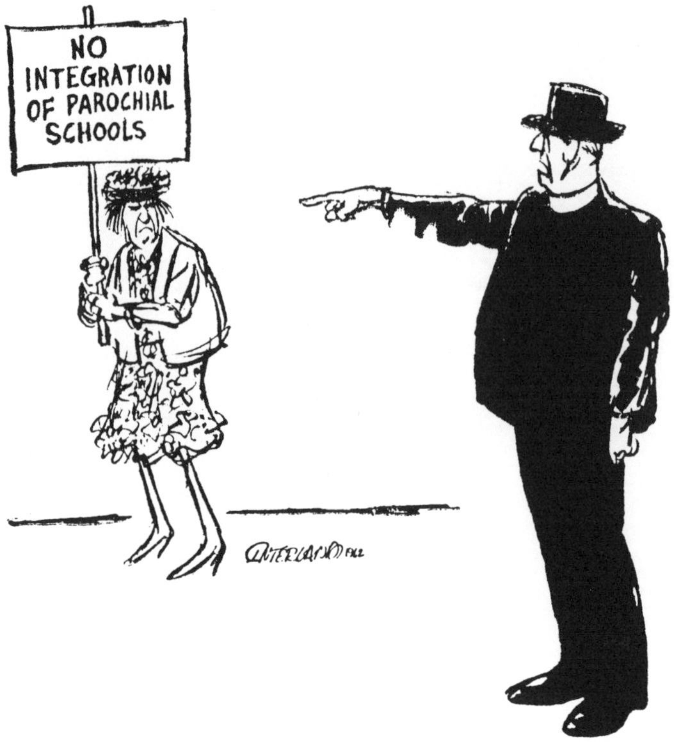
NO INTEGRATION OF PAROCHIAL SCHOOLS

"Madam, y'all can go to Hell!"

FRANK INTERLANDI. THE REALIST #32, MARCH 1962.

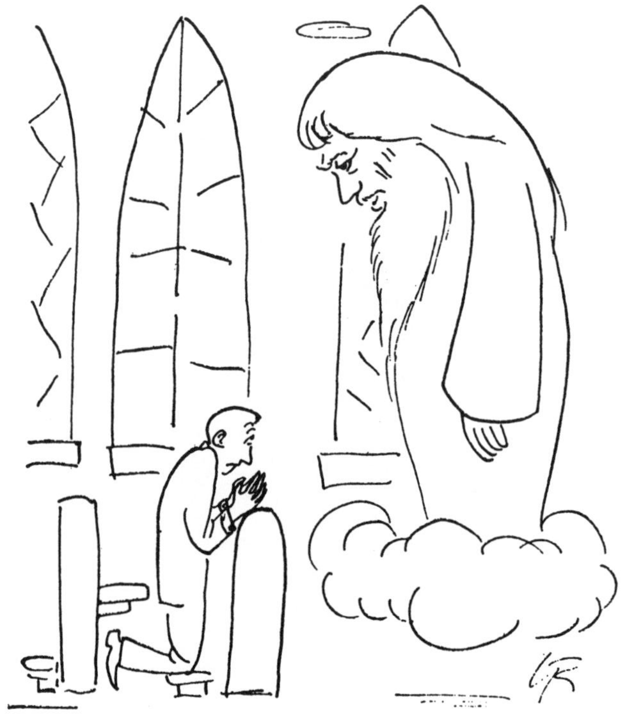

"Yes?"

THE REALIST #33, APRIL 1962. *24

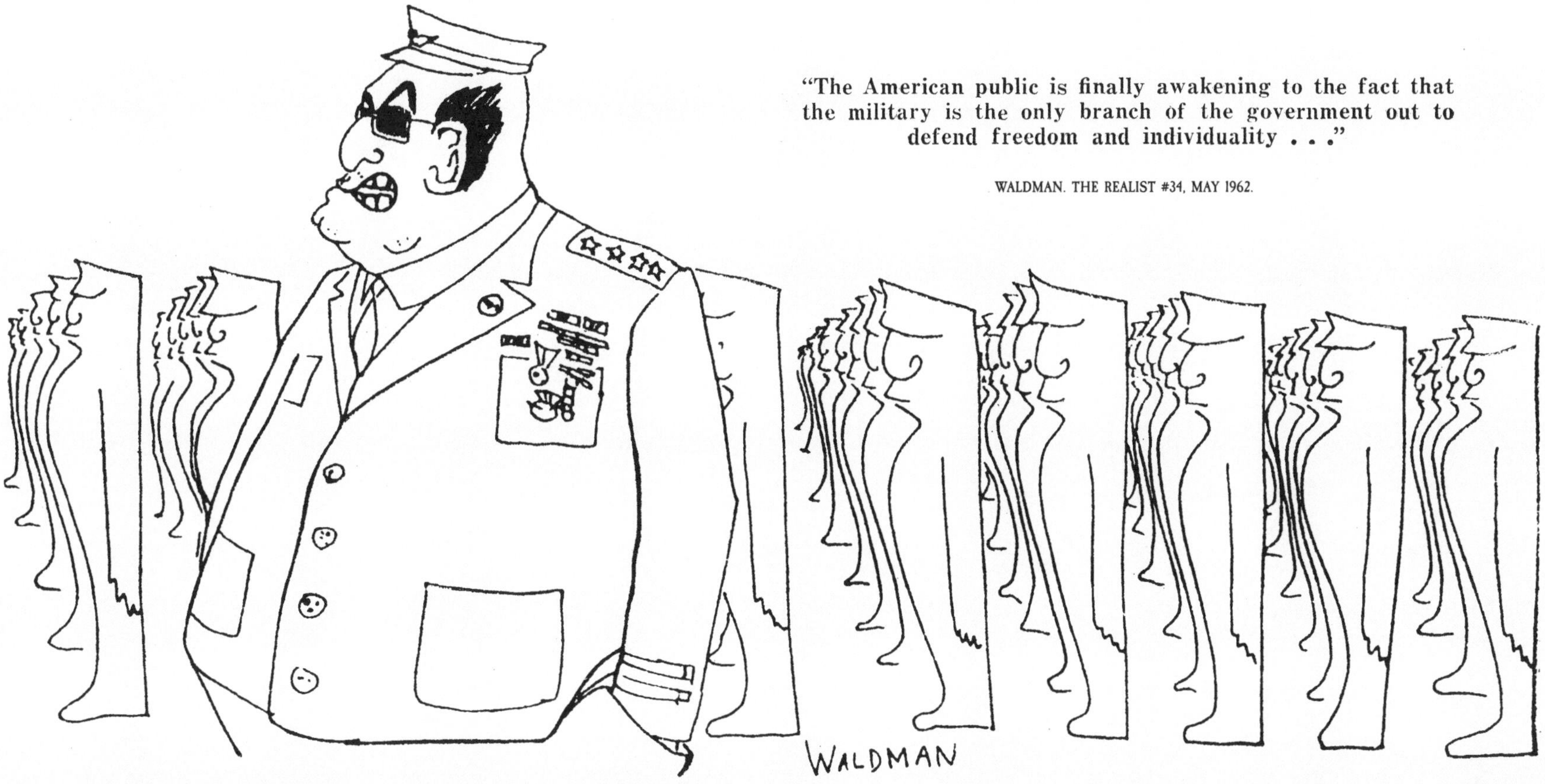
WALDMAN

"The American public is finally awakening to the fact that the military is the only branch of the government out to defend freedom and individuality . . ."

WALDMAN. THE REALIST #34, MAY 1962.

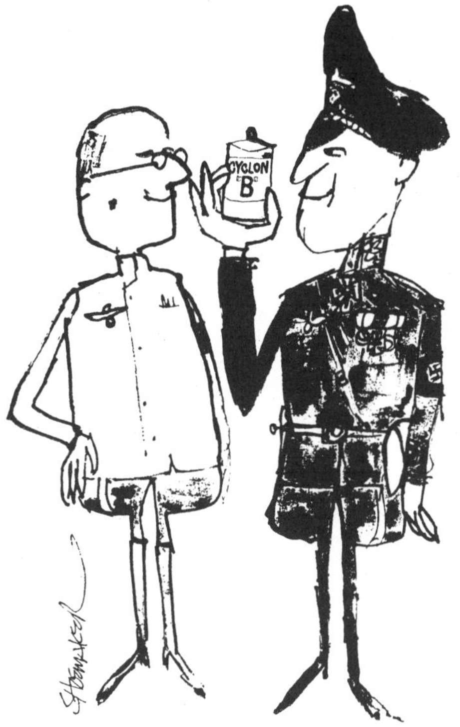
CYCLON
"B"

"Man, that's a gasser."

HOWARD SHOEMAKER. THE REALIST #34, MAY 1962. *25

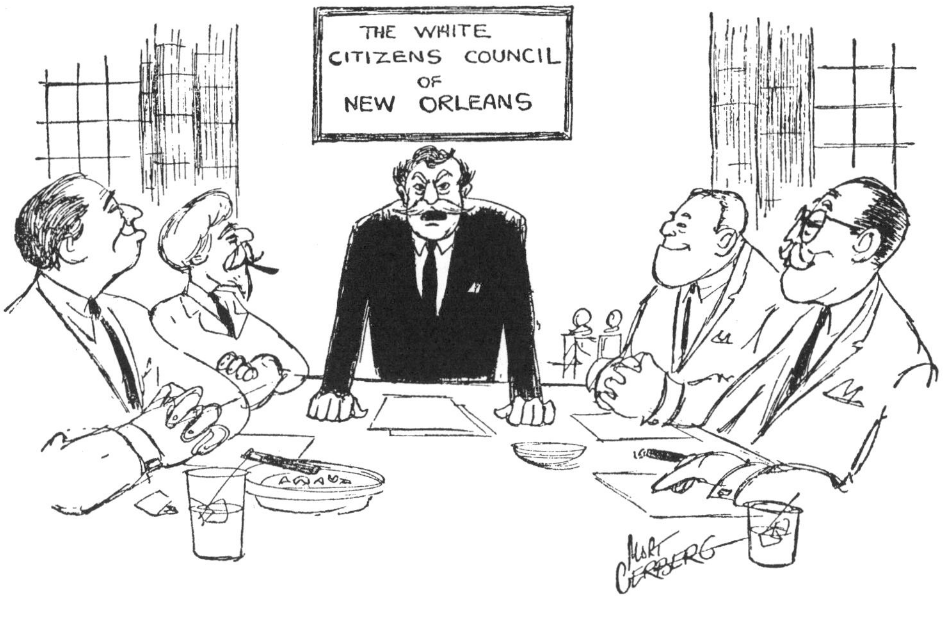
THE WHITE CITIZENS COUNCIL OF NEW ORLEANS
MORT GERBERG

"Gentlemen, it's time for Phase Two — shipping them C.O.D. ..."

MORT GERBERG. THE REALIST #35, JUNE 1962. *26

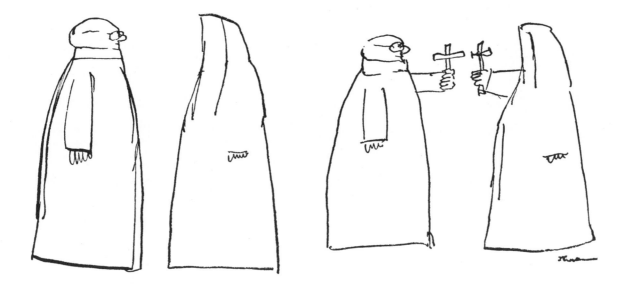

"I'll show you mine, if you show me yours ..."

THE REALIST #35, JUNE 1962.

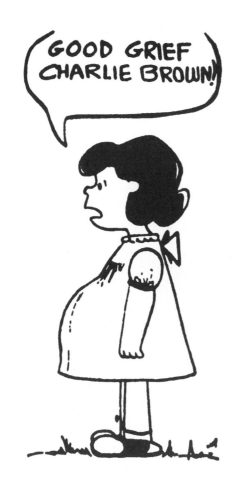

GOOD GRIEF CHARLIE BROWN!

THE REALIST #35, JUNE 1962. *27

freethought criticism and satire

The Realist

the magazine of criminal negligence

No. 35

35 Cents

... beginning our fifth year of publication ... Special Offensive Issue ... featuring "An Impolite Interview with an Abortionist" ... Lenny Bruce on "The Great Hotel Robbery" ... William Worthy on "Mass Media Irresponsibility" ... a report on what happened when this little magazine rattled a possible skeleton in President Kennedy's closet ... a plan for a Humanist Social Work Organization ... a new game—"Who Would You Kick Out of Bed?" ... futile fun with farmers, Adolf Eichmann, God and "The Realmate of the Month"

THE U.S. SAILORS RENDERED IMPOTENT BY A 6 MONTHS CRUISE ON A NUCLEAR SUB COLORING BOOK

... and some Realist Coloring Books for Colorless People Who Have Lost Their Crayons, bla bla bla ...

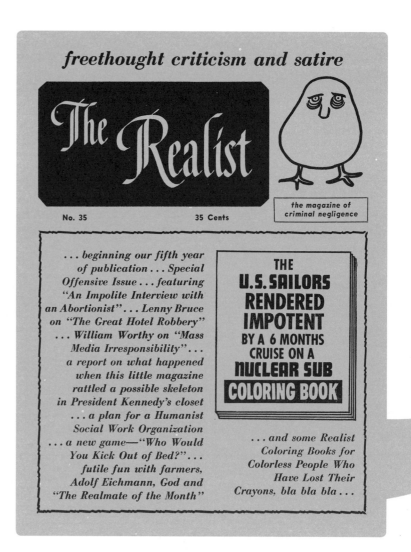

JOHN FRANCIS PUTNAM. THE REALIST #35, JUNE 1962. *28

BLACK MUSLIM KILL ALL THE WHITE MUTHAFUKKAS COLORING BOOK

WOP COLORING BOOK

JAP ATROCITIES AGAINST AMERICAN ARMY NURSES! COLORING BOOK

THE SEXY CATHOLIC NUNS IN black lace underwear COLORING BOOK

The BRAILLE COLORING BOOK FOR USE WITH FINGER PAINT

George Lincoln Rockwell's JEW BASTARD COLORING BOOK

AUSCHWITZ COOKING AND COLORING BOOK

THE SPASTIC COLORING BOOK

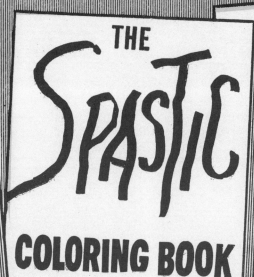

THE POLICE KICKING SHIT OUT OF NON-VIOLENT BAN the BOMB DEMONSTRATORS COLORING BOOK

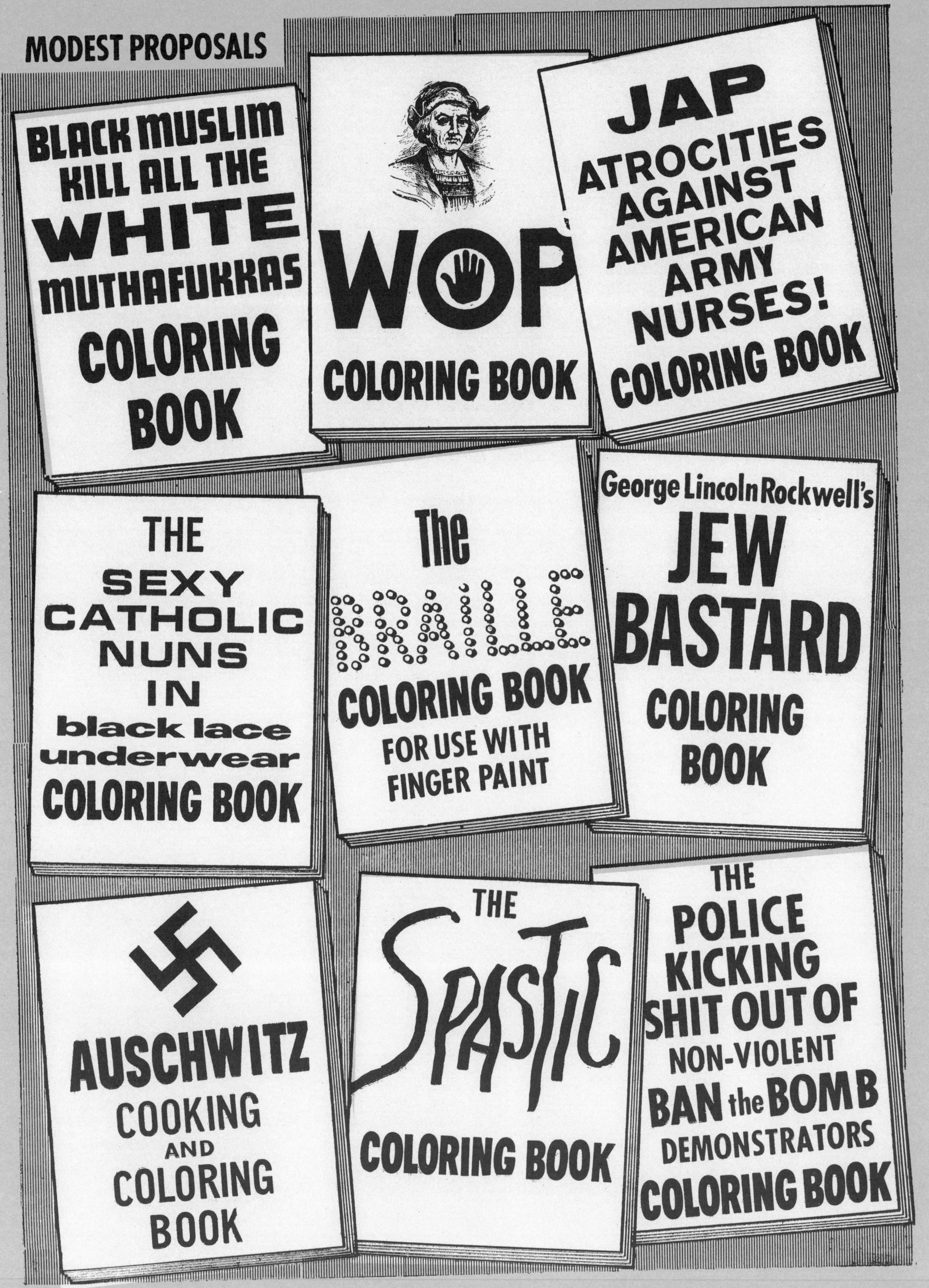

MICHAEL GOLDMAN AND EDWARD KOREN.

THE REALIST #35, JUNE 1962.

U.S. SEEKS CHANGE IN FARMER IMAGE:

Administration in Campaign to Portray Growers As Heroes of Economy
—Headline in N.Y. Times

"Agriculture is the nation's Number One success story."
—Secretary of Agriculture Orville Freeman

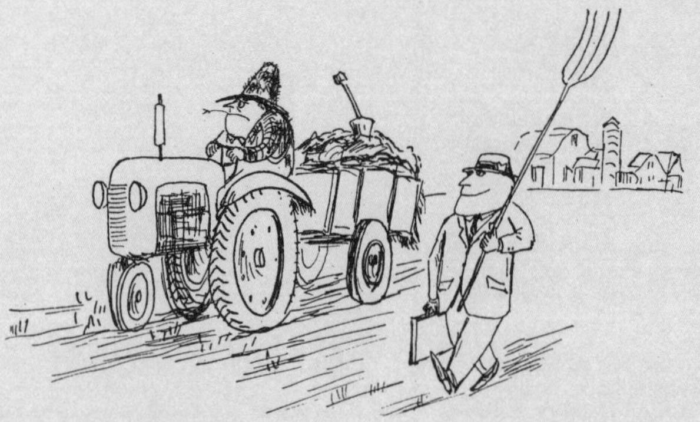

1. We all know what a hero of the American economy looks like, and it is indeed a relief to find an American farmer dressing the part. Here we see Rufus Poore walking to work, a striking contrast to the grubby old-style farmer on the left. Trim in dacron and cotton, quietly efficient in natural shoulders, slim foulard, and calf-skin attaché case, Poore is a decision maker, an influential, a success. The American hero today is a man with an office, and clearly that is where Rufus Poore is going. He glances warily up at the pile of manure on the cart; here is another image that will bear some changing. "We'll make it smell like toothpaste," thinks Poore, "and package it in gay cellophane wrappers. Ain't gonna be no flies on *us*."

2. "Turnip-wise, we've got a market to create," barks dynamic, trend-setting farmer Poore to his distribution team. "For centuries, turnips have been considered food for hogs, but now, boys—and listen closely because I'm playing the theme—turnips are food for thought. The ball's in play. Run with it." The brainstorming begins. Aides hover about with memoes, sketches, charts. "Turnips are fun"—hazards a pipe-smoking idea man, but Poore tops him: "Turnips are a Fun Tuber!" Team techtonics pay off. The pitch is finalized: *Turnips—the food for thinking men.* "Parity, shmarity," cracks Poore. "We'll make a million."

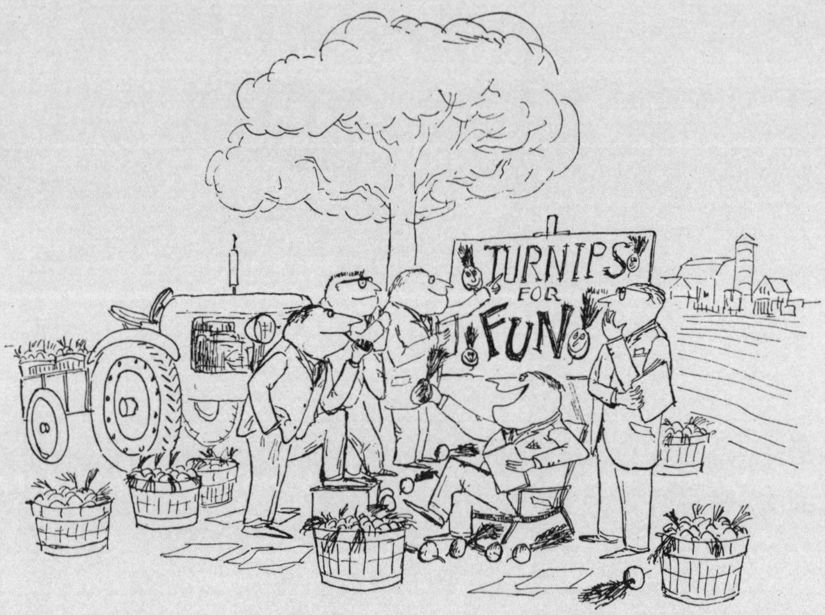
TURNIPS
FOR
FUN

3. Poore strives for good labor-management relations. These animals have a real "say" in the operation, and the hogs, for example, take an active part in the management of their pen. Employee inventions are encouraged. "Bessie" (left foreground), a prime breeder, is one typical example of high-incentive programming for high-efficiency return. She devised a new feeding technique that allows *nearly total snout-immersion* in the trough at peak intake periods, for which she received both a lump-sum bonus of bran mash and a yearly increment of swill. The two grateful chickens in the picture have also made contributions to feeding procedure ("hunt and peck is a thing of the past," cackles one) and have been rewarded with an extra two-week vacation on full feed in the lovely days just before slaughtering time. In return, Poore demands practicality and devotion to duty. As he puts it, in a telling epigram: "A head in the trough is worth two in the clouds."

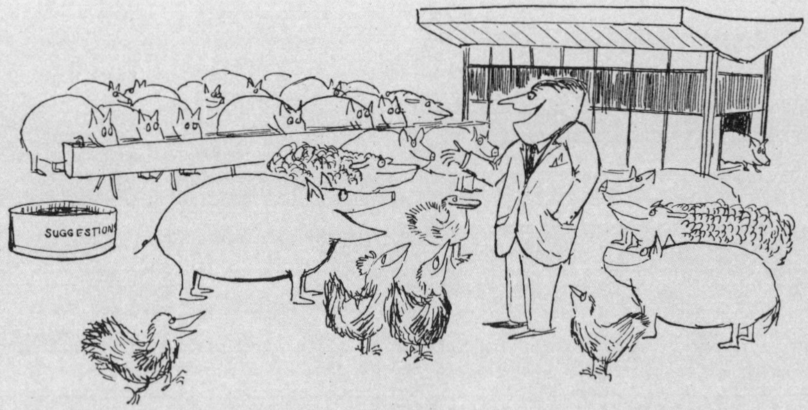
SUGGESTIONS

4. "Think big, work big, play big!" Hard-driving Rufus Poore turns homeward, plowing the back forty in his Fiametta 3.5. The cocktail hour is drawing nigh and farmers' wives begin to rise like mermaids from the old swimming hole, which adjoins the Poore homestead. In the background, a photographer from *Holiday* magazine scrambles to get enticing shots of this rural paradise. A network crew is busy shooting scenes for a documentary report, *The Farmer Lives the Life.* The film is being shot in Washington, Palm Beach, Venice, the Riviera and Rufus Poore's farm.

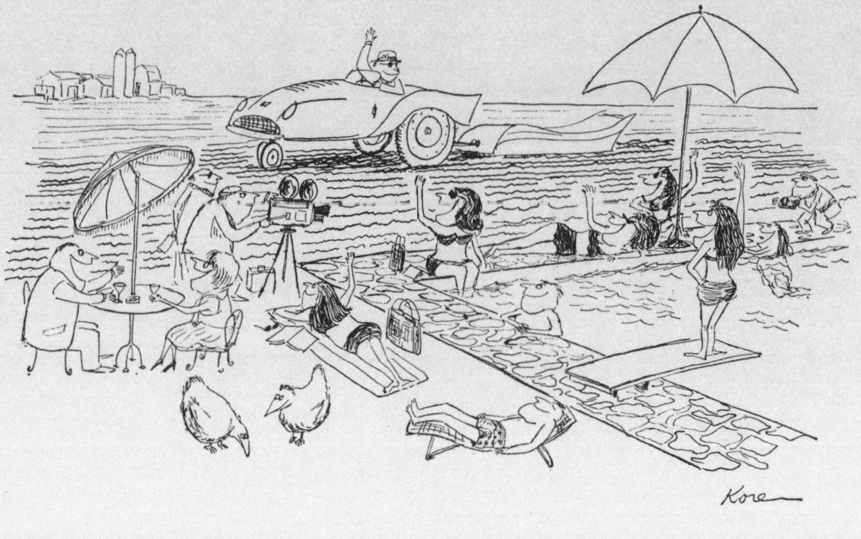

—Michael Goldman and Edward Koren

"... and if I cop the final thrill before I wake ..."

FRANK INTERLANDI. THE REALIST #35, JUNE 1962. *29

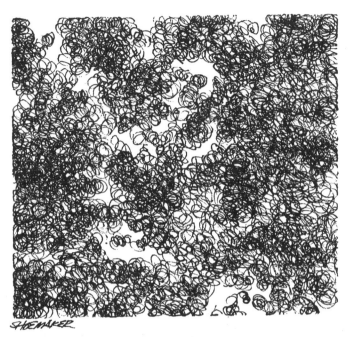

REALMATE OF THE MONTH

Here is a delightful close-up of our Miss August in all her natural beauty. Natalie August is a sprightly fashion model who works part-time as a pert supermarket checkout-counter clerk. Since we didn't have enough trading stamps for a camera, this pin-up picture is actually a composite of castoff material gathered for the Realist by photo re-touchers from Playboy, Escapade, Rogue, Nugget, Gent, Swank, Dude, and Life Magazine.

Natalie, who majored in Bicycle-Riding at Bennington, considers herself to be a philosophical rationalist. "I used to believe in reincarnation," she remarked to us, "but that was in my other life." She is just wild about jazz, sports cars, onanism, skiing, and over-charging customers. She admits, however, to having a morbid fear of men, psychoanalysis, shopping-carts, snow, and air-brushes.

Her rousing ambition: to win circulation and influence fantasies.

HOWARD SHOEMAKER. THE REALIST #35, JUNE 1962. *31

"Dr. Burnhill? — uh — you don't know me, but — uh —
I've been told that you could — uh — perform a certain —
uh — operation —"

MORT GERBERG. THE REALIST #35, JUNE 1962. *30

The Stripper
by Mike Thaler

MIKE THALER. THE REALIST #36, AUGUST 1962.

REPEAT
YE
SINNERS

THE REALIST #38, SEPTEMBER 1962. *32

"He loves me ... He loves me not ... He loves me ..."

THE REALIST #35, JUNE 1962. *33

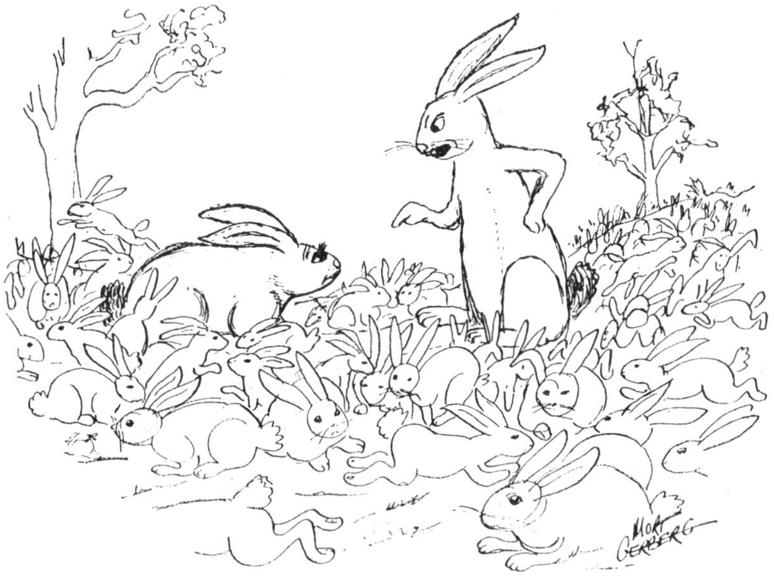
MORT GERBERG

"I don't care what the church says — don't you think this is getting a little ridiculous?"

MORT GERBERG. THE REALIST #37, SEPTEMBER 1962.

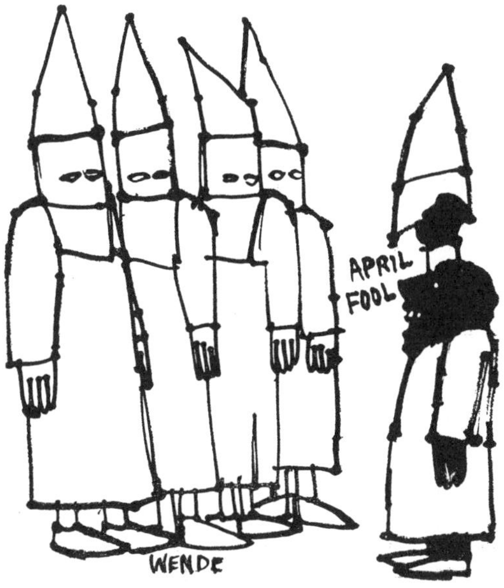
APRIL FOOL
WENDE

WENDE. THE REALIST #37, SEPTEMBER 1962.

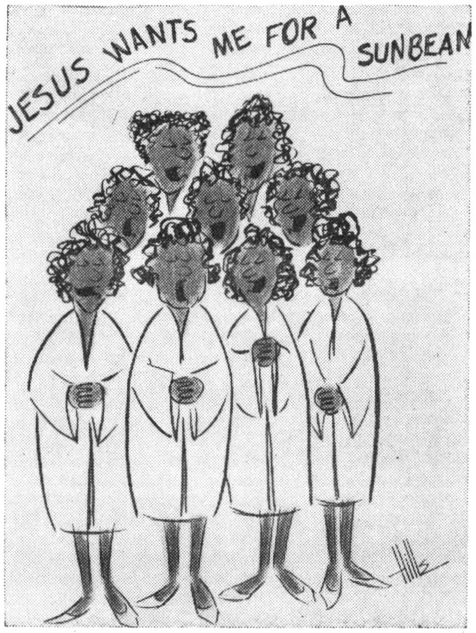
JESUS WANTS ME FOR A SUNBEAM
Hills

HILLS. THE REALIST #37, SEPTEMBER 1962. *34

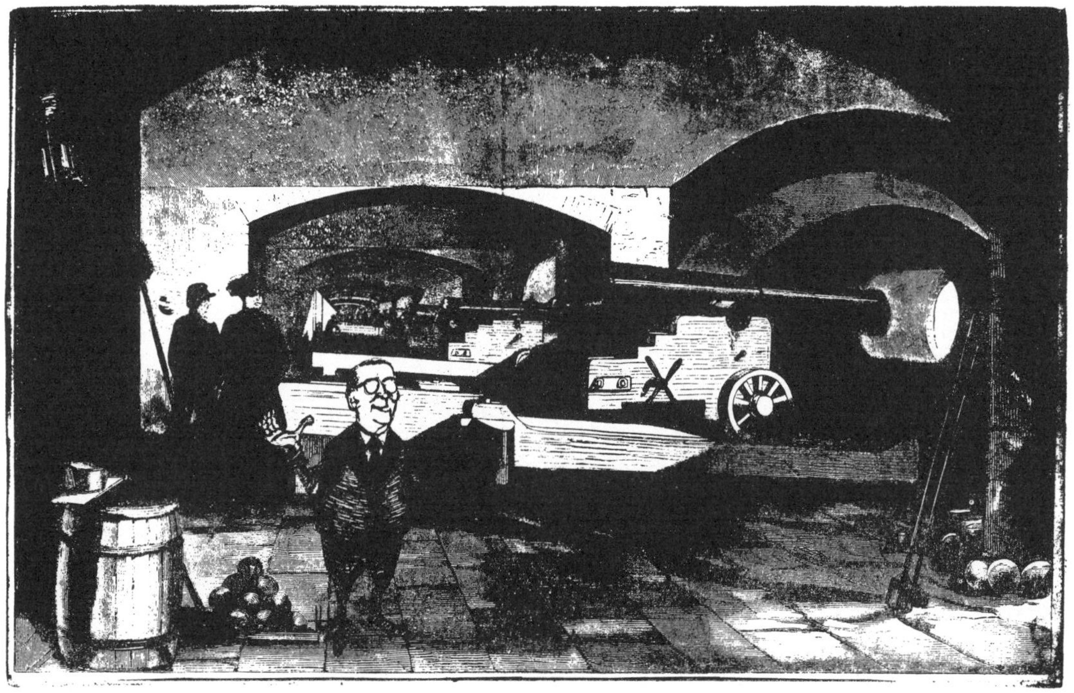

"As Guhvnor, Ah take a puhsonal pride in ouah campus facilities heah at Ole Miss."

THE REALIST #37, SEPTEMBER 1962. *35

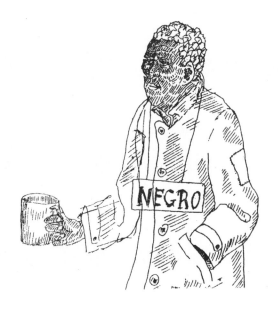

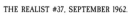

THE REALIST #37, SEPTEMBER 1962.

JAMES "JAF" FRANKFORT. THE REALIST #37, SEPTEMBER 1962.

"It's his turn now and then me again . . ."

RICHARD GUINDON. THE REALIST #39, NOVEMBER 1962.

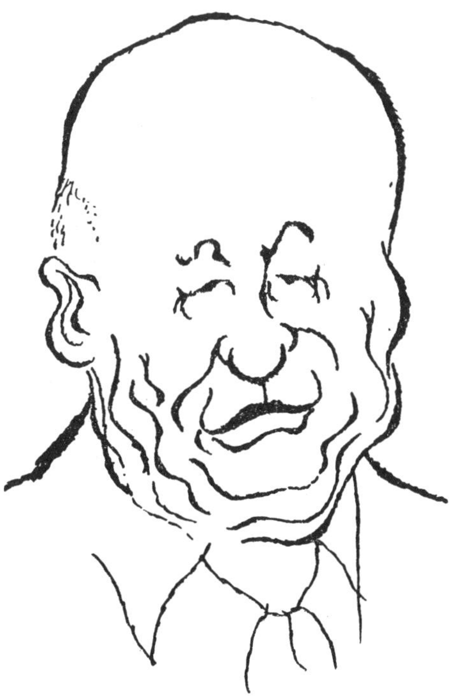

"Last time I let Nixon wag his finger in my face for the photographers, so I figured now I should do something to give the Democrats equal time ..."

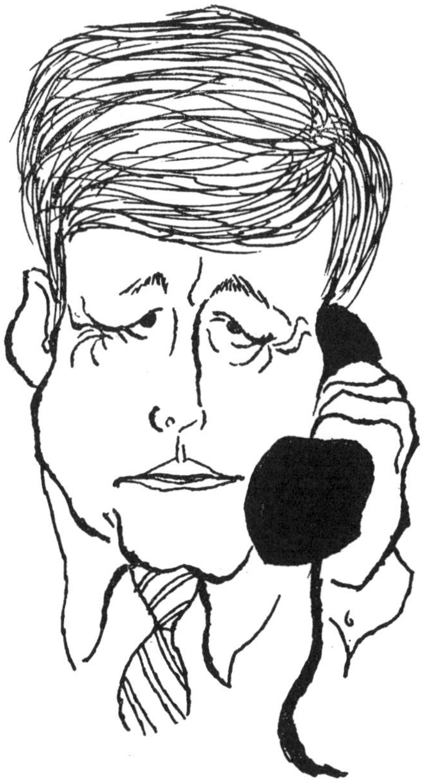

"Yes, Mr. Hearst, I understand — that's a very generous offer — we supply the photos of the missile sites and you supply the war."

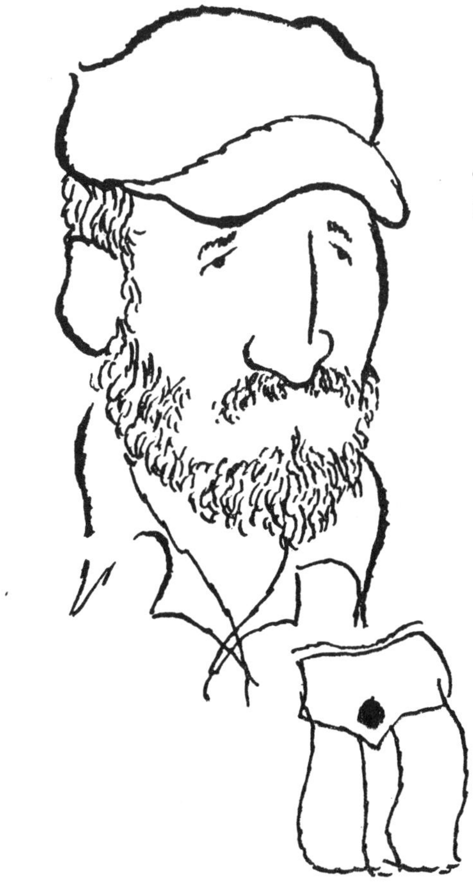

"Inspection? Okay, I'll show you mine if you'll show me yours ..."

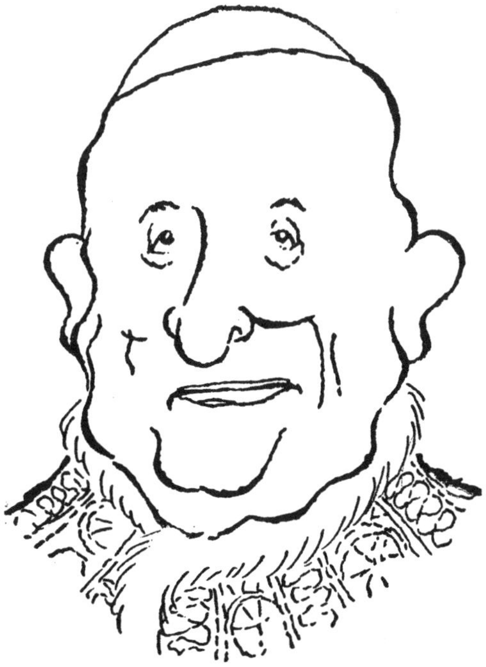

"The Ecumenical Council has approved a birth control pill for married women; it is held firmly between the knees ..."

RICHARD GUINDON. THE REALIST #39, NOVEMBER 1962. *36

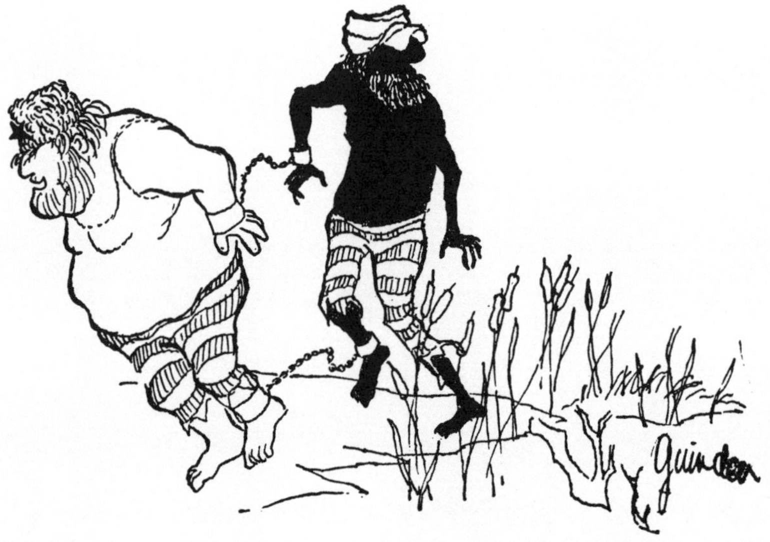
Guindon

"We're almost to my plantation ..."

RICHARD GUINDON. THE REALIST #39, NOVEMBER 1962. *37

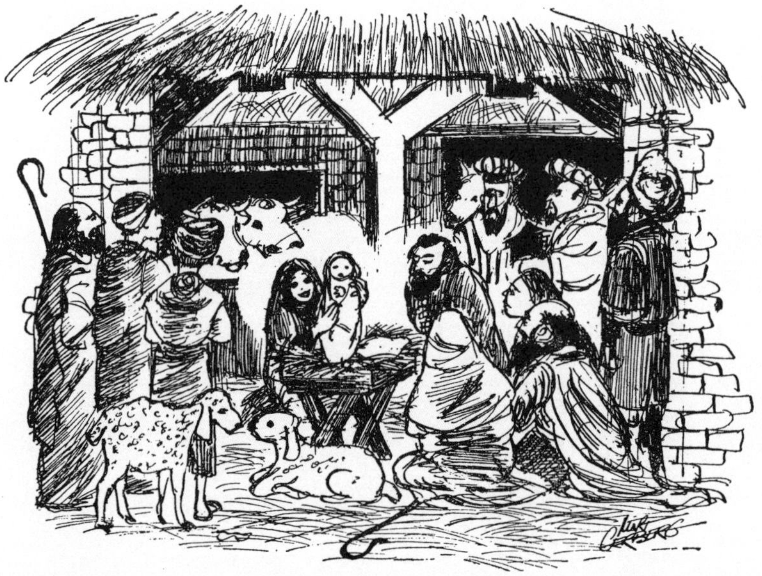

"My son, the saviour ..."

MORT GERBERG. THE REALIST #39, NOVEMBER 1962.

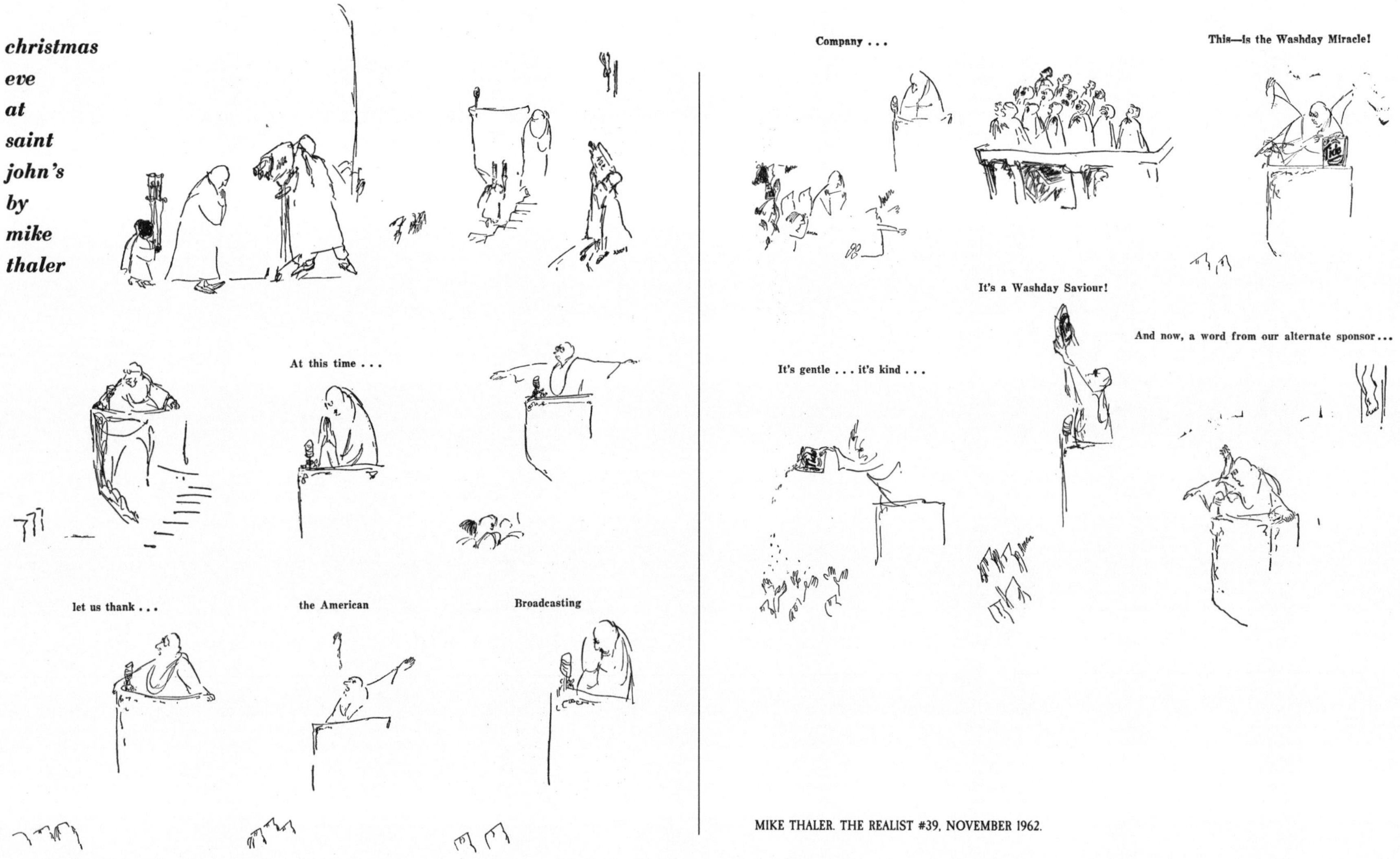
christmas
eve
at
saint
john's
by
mike
thaler
At this time . . .
let us thank . . .
the American
Broadcasting
Company . . .
This—is the Washday Miracle!
It's a Washday Saviour!
It's gentle . . . it's kind . . .
And now, a word from our alternate sponsor . . .

MIKE THALER. THE REALIST #39, NOVEMBER 1962.

WEST
BERLIN
GUINDON

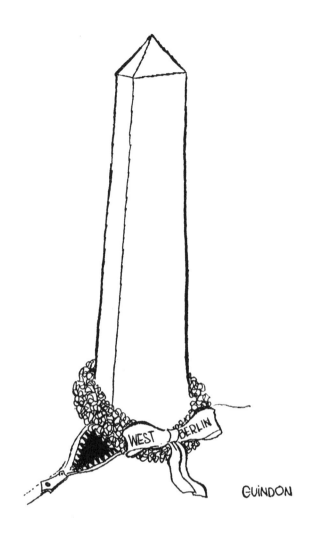

RICHARD GUINDON. THE REALIST #39, NOVEMBER 1962.

oh priest, I Have sinned! I MADE LOVE TO MY FATHER, MY SON, MY UNCLE, MY DAUGHTER AND MY PET TURTLE! WHAT SHALL I DO?
DEFINE YOUR TERMS.

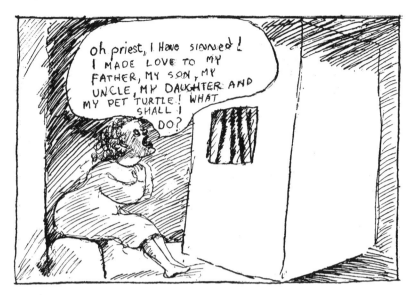

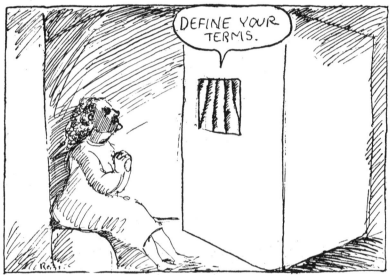

THE REALIST #39, NOVEMBER 1962.

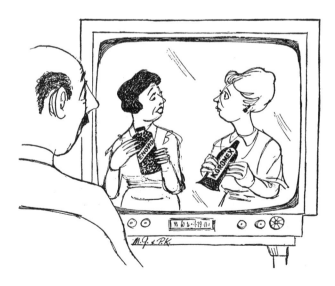

"Hey — are you still using that greasy kid stuff?"

MORT GERBERG. THE REALIST #39, NOVEMBER 1962. *38

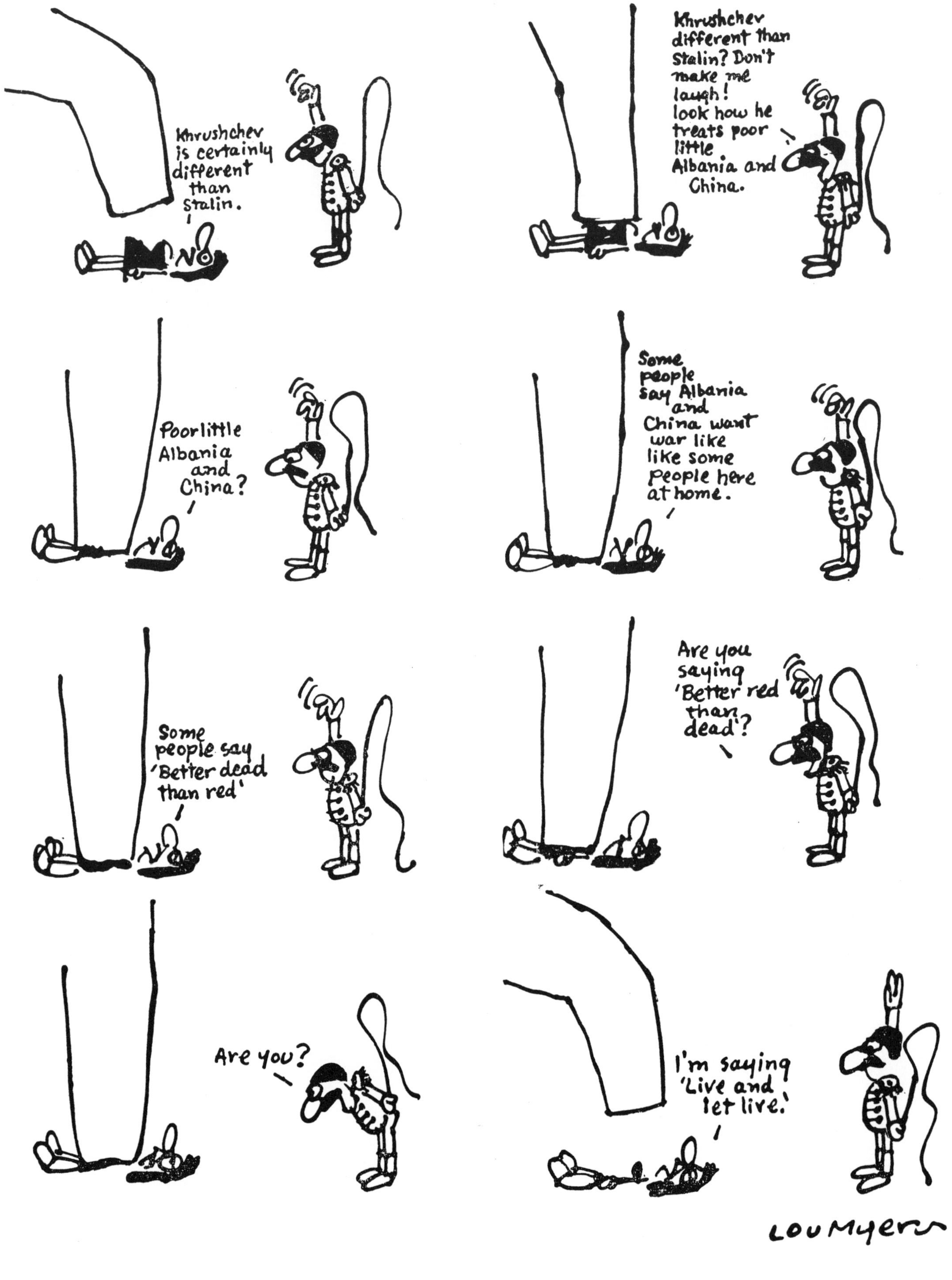
Khrushchev is certainly different than Stalin.
Khrushchev different than Stalin? Don't make me laugh! look how he treats poor little Albania and China.
Poorlittle Albania and China?
Some people say Albania and China want war like like some people here at home.
Some people say 'Better dead than red'
Are you saying 'Better red than dead'?
Are you?
I'm saying 'Live and let live.'
LOU MYERS

LOU MYERS. THE REALIST #39, NOVEMBER 1962.

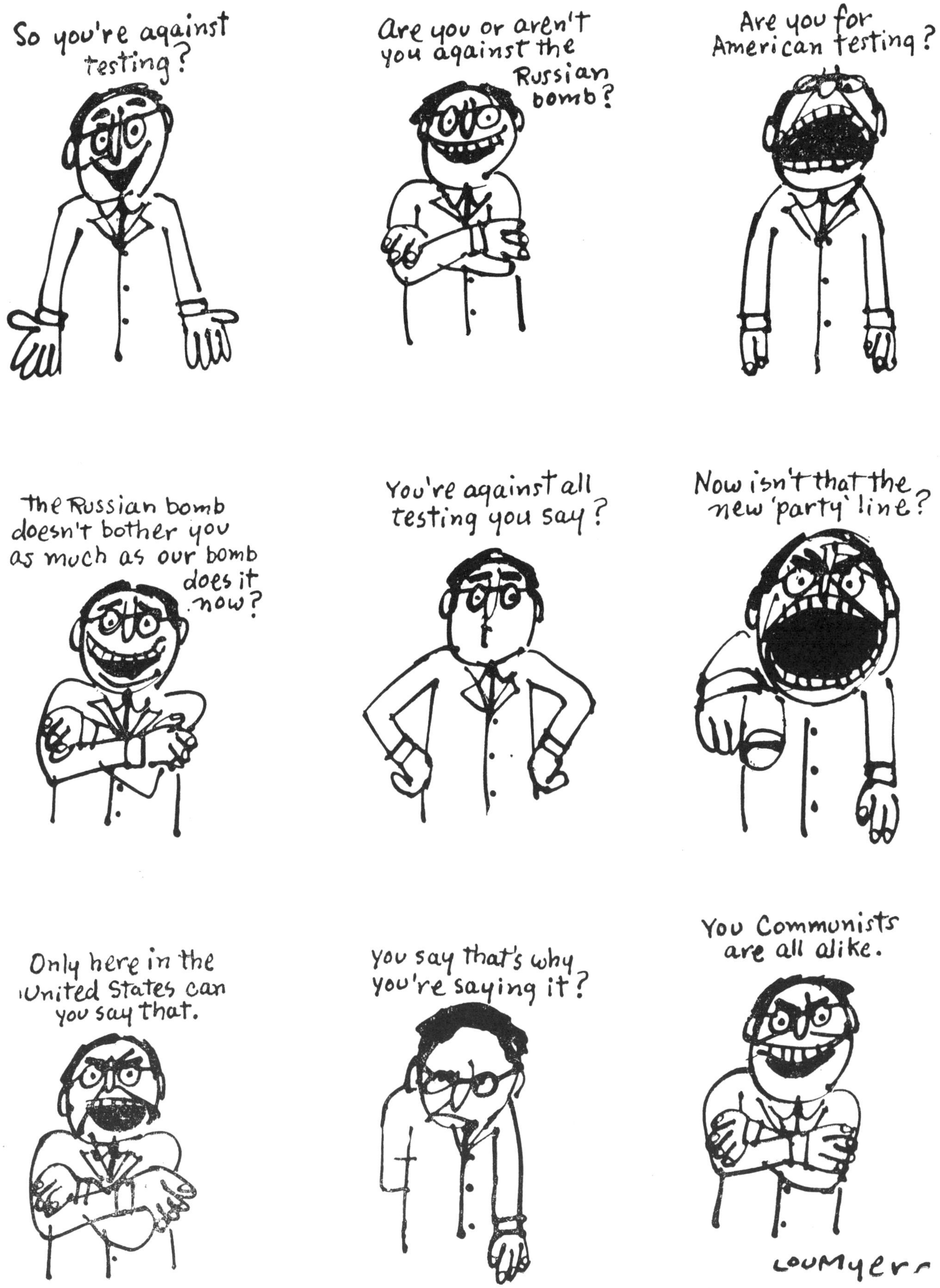
So you're against testing?
Are you or aren't you against the Russian bomb?
Are you for American testing?
the Russian bomb doesn't bother you as much as our bomb does it now?
You're against all testing you say?
Now isn't that the new 'party' line?
Only here in the United States can you say that.
You say that's why you're saying it?
You Communists are all alike.
LouMyers

LOU MYERS. THE REALIST #40, DECEMBER 1962.

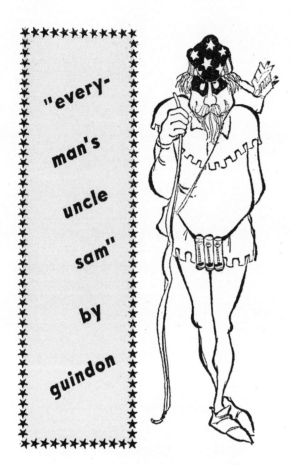

"every-man's uncle sam" by guindon

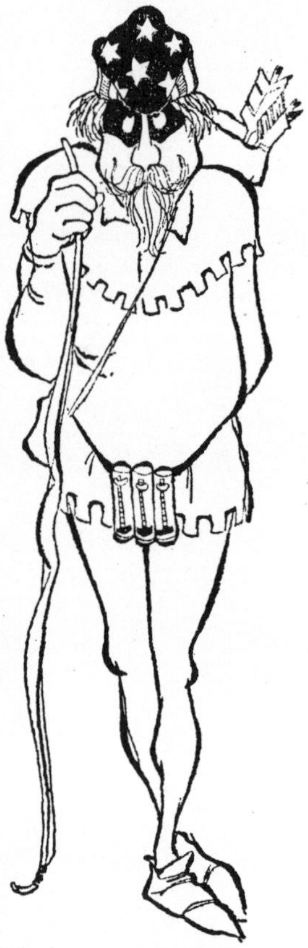

"I wish to contribute $.................. to fight for justice and equal opportunity for American Indians ... Contributions are income tax deductible." — advertisement in *The New Yorker*

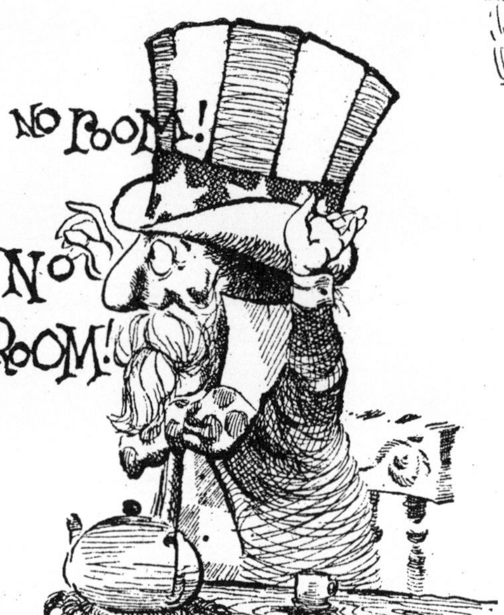
NO ROOM!
NO ROOM!

"The book [*The Liberal Papers*] recommends recognition of Red China and her admission to the United Nations ... " — The Republican Congressional *Newsletter*

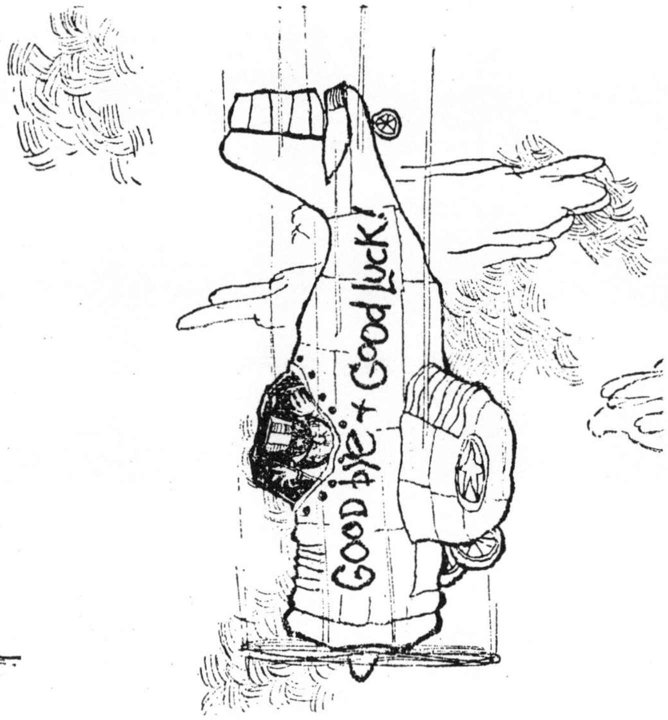
GOOD bye + Good Luck!

"Better to face the *chance* of being dead, than the certainty of being red." — William F. Buckley, *The National Review*

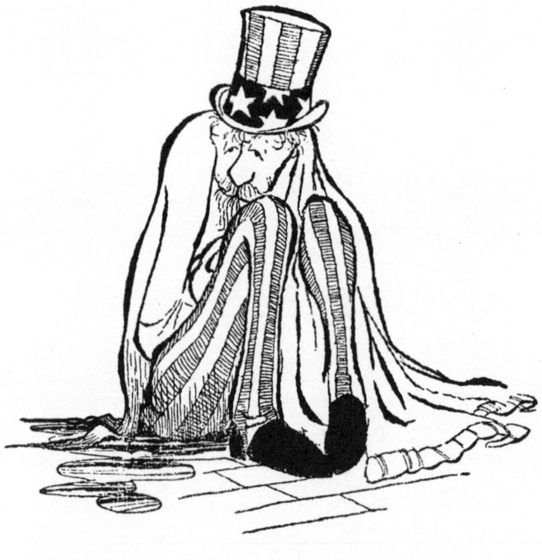

"Dr. Salk ... remarked on the prevailing misuse of drugs and wondered 'How many decisions are being made in Washington, D.C. by persons under the influence of tranquilizers.'" — The *Manchester Guardian*

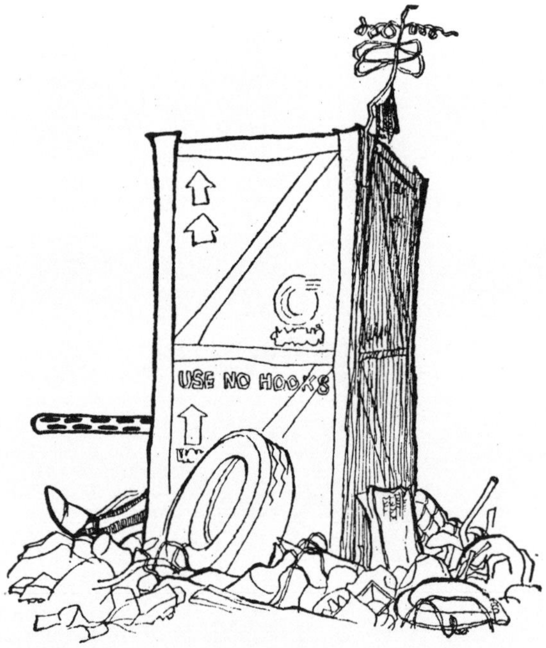
USE NO HOOKS

"How's about joining me in a five year plan for survival: 1. Abolish labor unions. 2. Discontinue social security. 3. Dump the U.N. 4. Quit talking and start shooting. 5. So long Supreme Court ... " — Letter to the *Minneapolis Daily Herald*

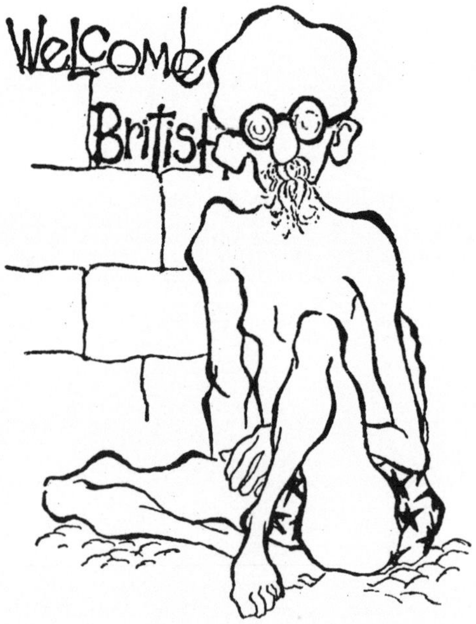
WelCome British

"Psychiatrist Jerome Frank ... urges 'detailed sophisticated, hard-headed analyses of possible methods of non-violent struggle' ... so that disarmed Americans could resist even a nation that attempted military occupation of the United States." — The *New Republic*

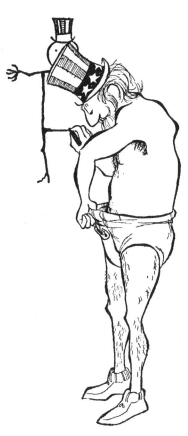

"Sex I say sex is the red open mouth
that has eaten into all American life..."
—Seymour Krim, *Views of a Nearsighted Cannoneer*

QUERY

If the bombs go boom
And the world is creamed—
What happens to all those trading stamps
That have to go unredeemed?
—Avey Corman

Heal!

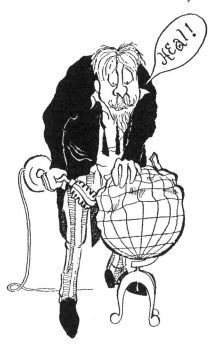

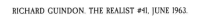

"2:30 PM, WNBC—Catholic Hour:
'Nagasaki: Cradle of Christianity.'"
—*Daily News* radio schedule

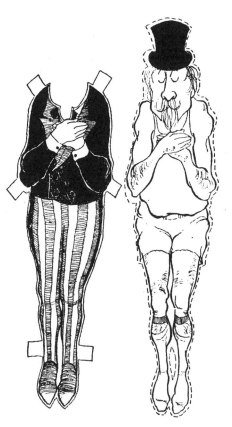

"Patriot and Patriotism: 21W 37N 47N ...
420W 425Q (See Country; Native Land;
Death and War; Dying)"
—Index, *Bartlett's Familiar Quotations*

RICHARD GUINDON. THE REALIST #41, JUNE 1963.

do You
THANK GoD
YoU CAN S

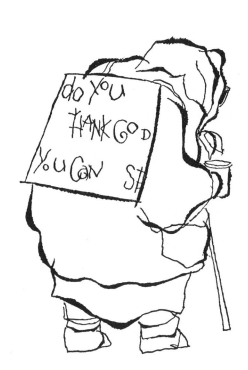

RICHARD GUINDON. THE REALIST #41, JUNE 1963.

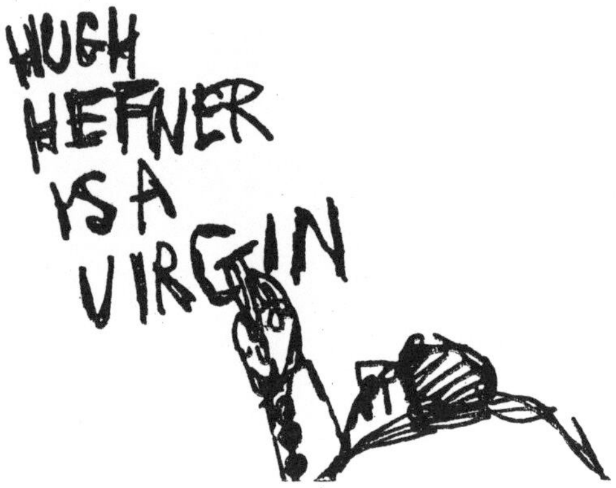
HUGH
HEFNER
IS A
VIRGIN

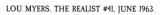

LOU MYERS. THE REALIST #41, JUNE 1963.

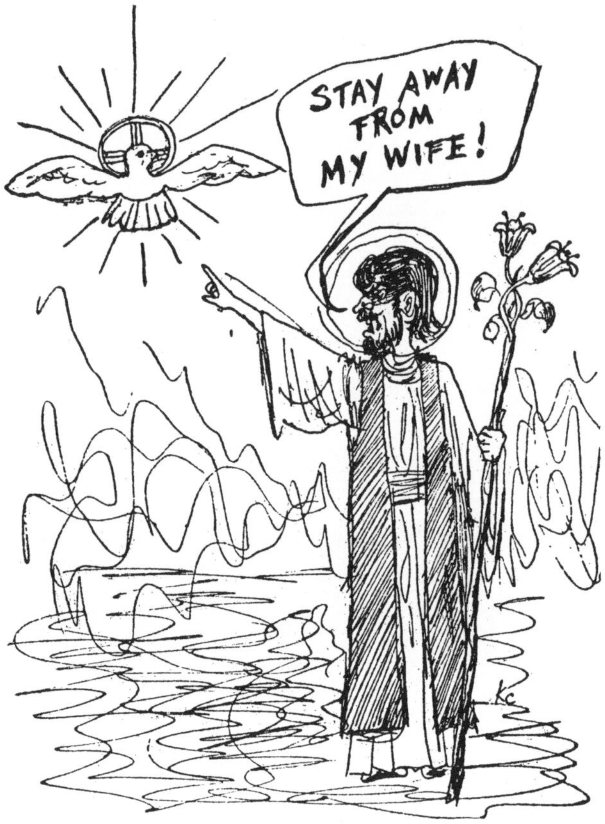
STAY AWAY FROM MY WIFE!

THE REALIST #41, JUNE 1963.

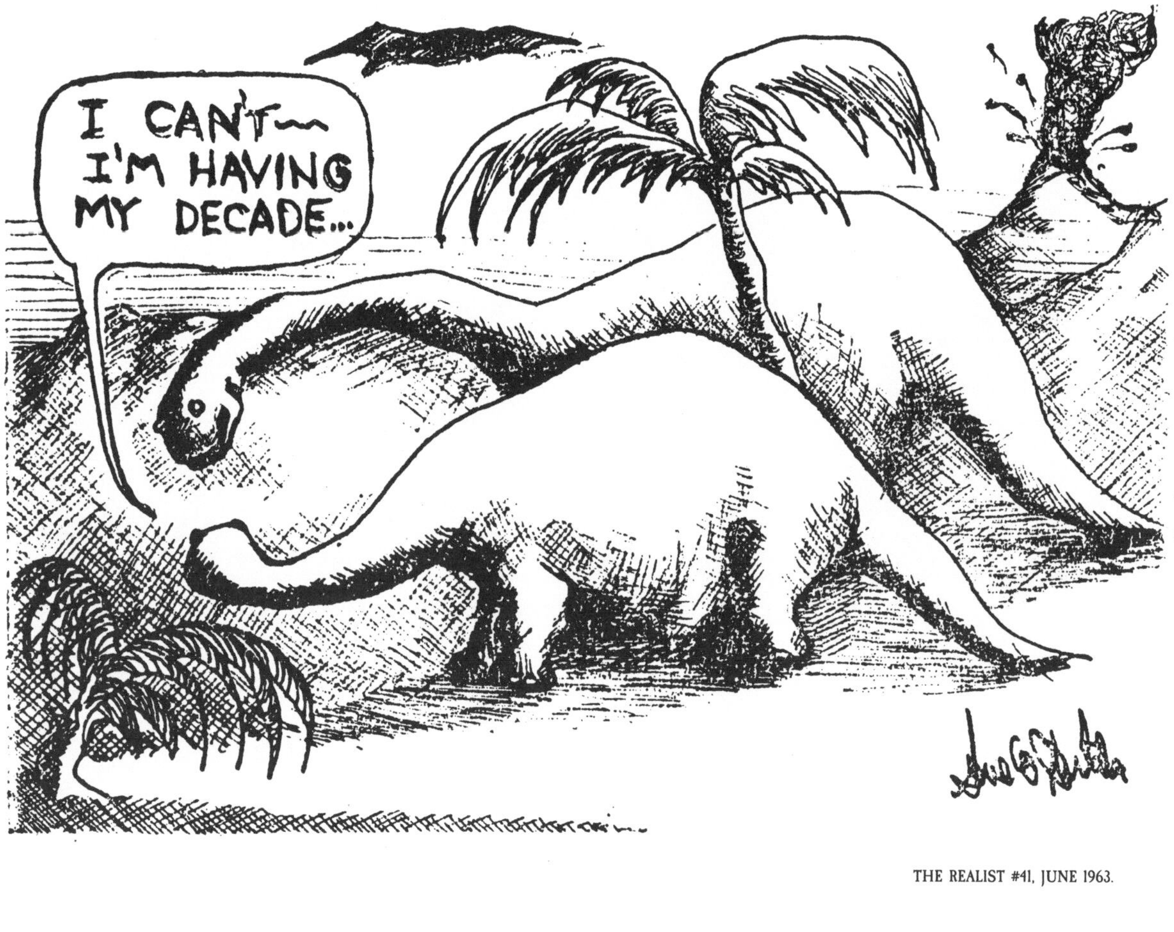
I CAN'T— I'M HAVING MY DECADE...

THE REALIST #41, JUNE 1963.

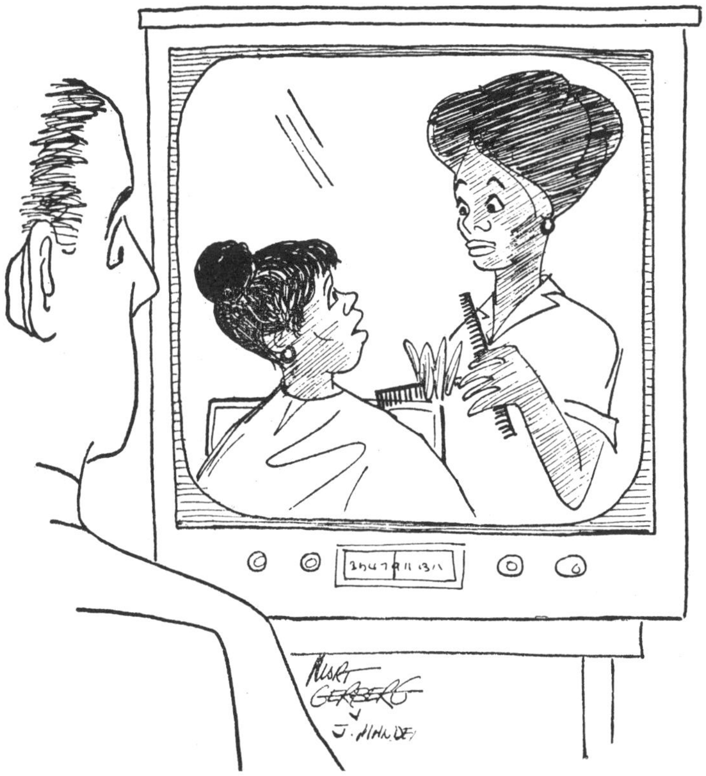
MORT GERBERG

"If I've only one life, let me live it as a blonde!"

MORT GERBERG. THE REALIST #41, JUNE 1963. *39

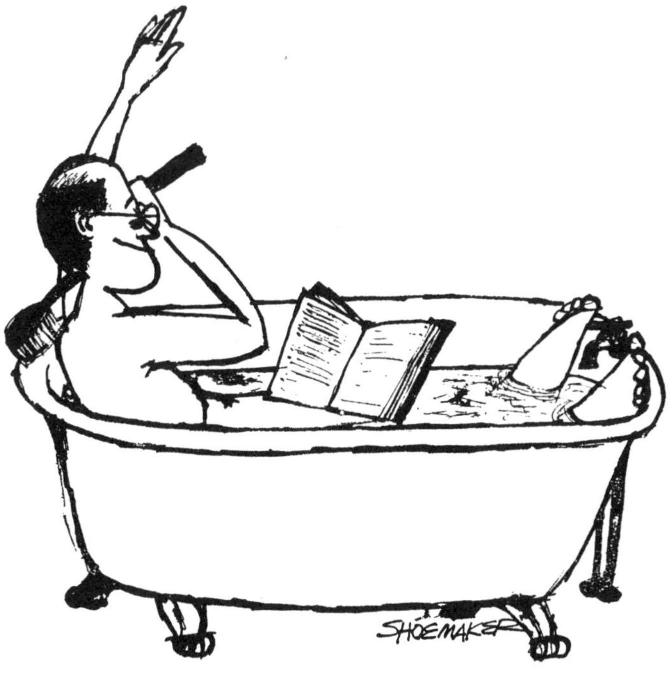
SHOEMAKER

HOWARD SHOEMAKER. THE REALIST #42, AUGUST 1963. *40

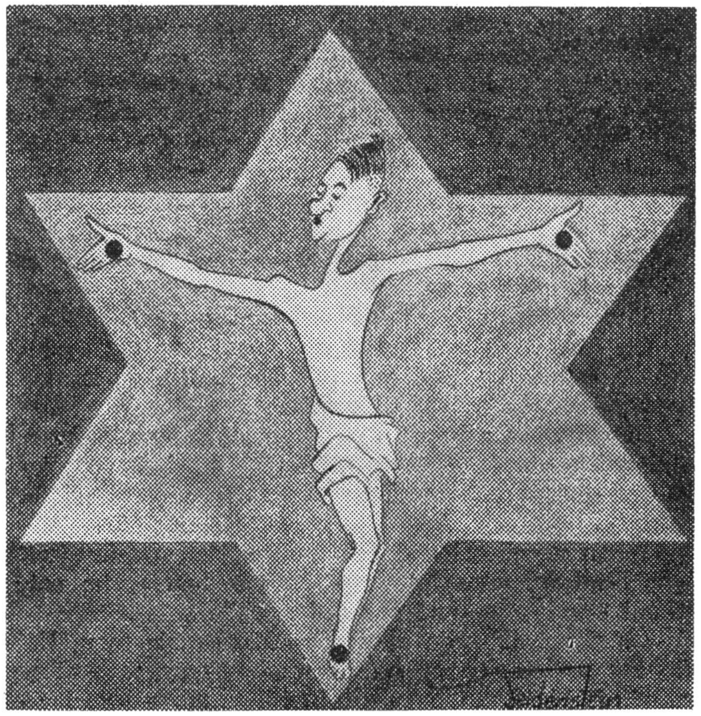

Lenny Bruce on George Lincoln Rockwell

Friends of mine are always showing me articles. "Look at what this bigoted bastard wrote!" And then I dug something. Liberals will buy anything a bigot writes. And they really support it. George Lincoln Rockwell, the head of the American Nazi Party, perhaps is a very knowledgeable businessman with no political convictions whatsoever. He gets three bucks a head and works the mass rallies of nothing but angry Jews, shaking their fists and wondering why there are so many Jews there. And he probably has two followers that are deaf. They think the swastika is an Aztec symbol.

THE REALIST #41, JUNE 1963. *41

①
②
③
PEPSI COLA
④
Koren

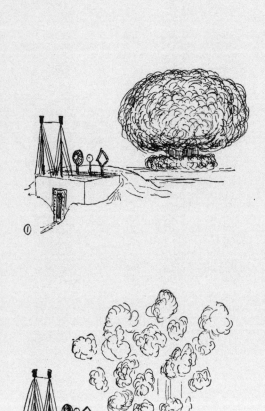

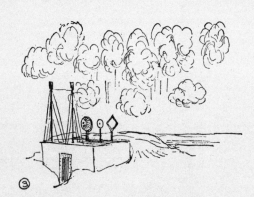

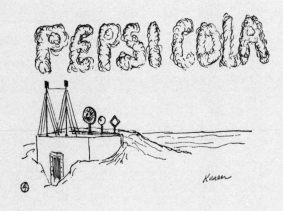

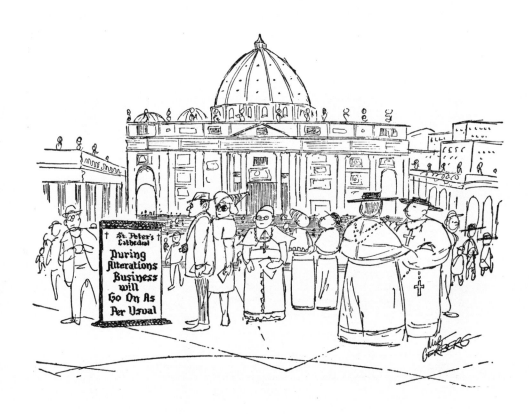

ED KOREN. THE REALIST #42, AUGUST 1963. *42

SAVE THE
MORE TESTS!
VIVA CASTRO!
DOWN WITH THE SYSTEM!
BAN THE BOMB!
UN STAY OUT!
BETTER RED THAN DEAD!
MORE BOMBS LESS PEACE!
DOWN WITH COMMUNISM!
BETTER DEAD THAN RED!
KENNE SI CASTRO NO!
YANKEE STAY OUT!
W. WOODMAN

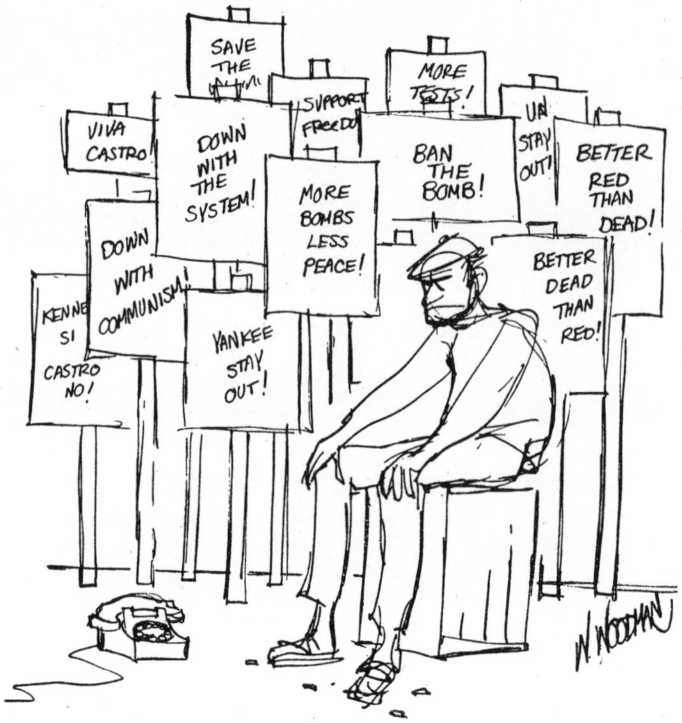

W. WOODMAN. THE REALIST #42, AUGUST 1963.

St. Peter's Cathedral
During Alterations Business will Go On As Per Usual
MORT GERBERG

MORT GERBERG. THE REALIST #42, AUGUST 1963.

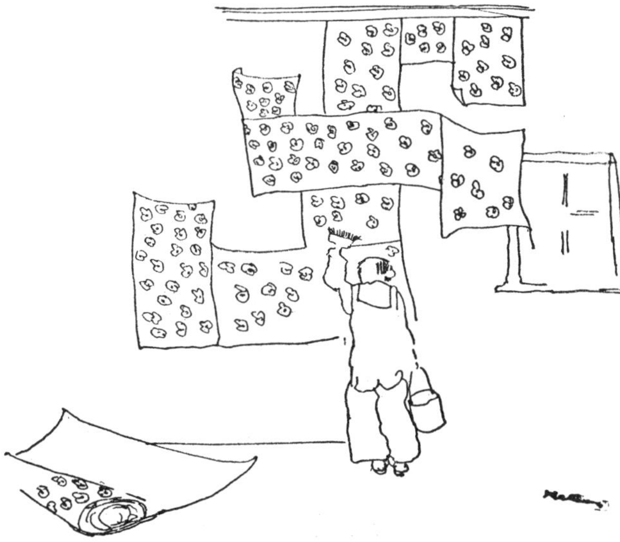

THE REALIST #42, AUGUST 1963.

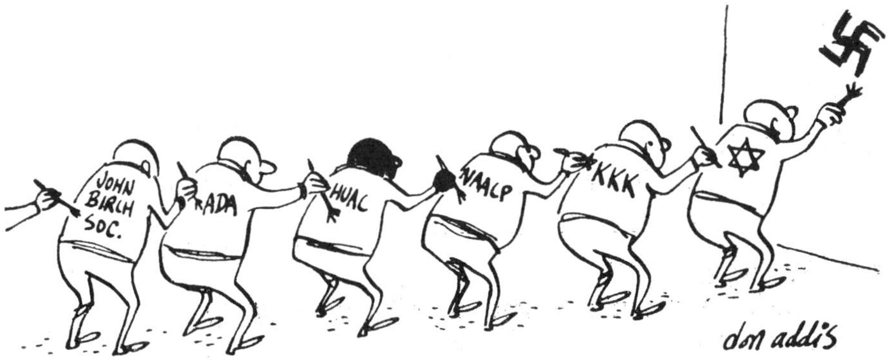
JOHN BIRCH SOC.
ADA
HUAC
NAACP
KKK
don addis

DON ADDIS. THE REALIST #43, SEPTEMBER 1963.

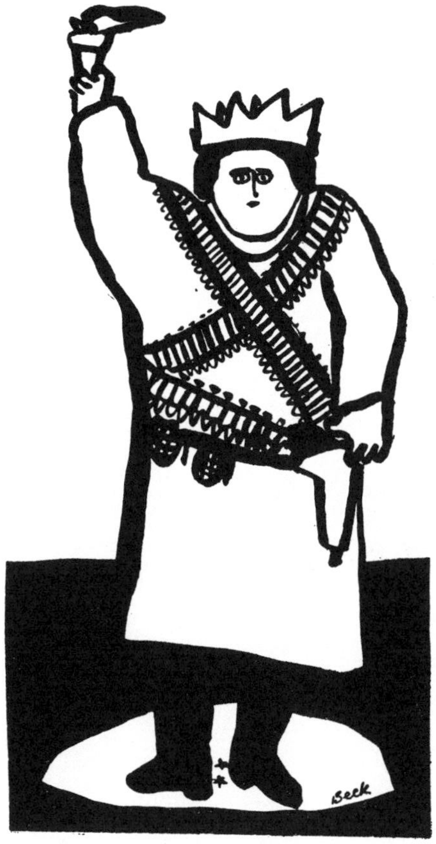
Beck

BECK. THE REALIST #42, AUGUST 1963. *43

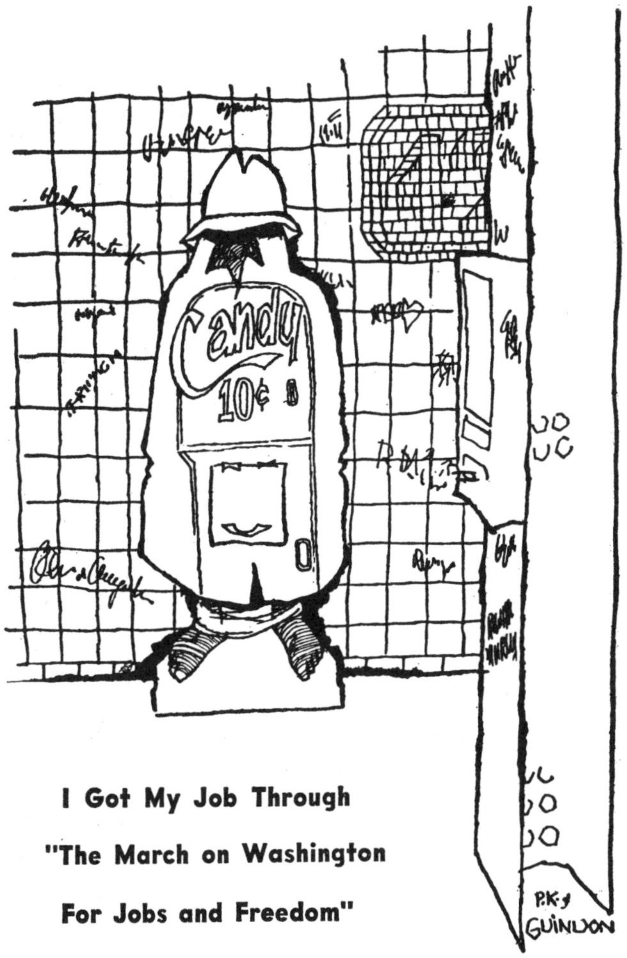
Candy
10¢
I Got My Job Through
"The March on Washington
For Jobs and Freedom"
GUINDON

RICHARD GUINDON. THE REALIST #43, SEPTEMBER 1963. *44

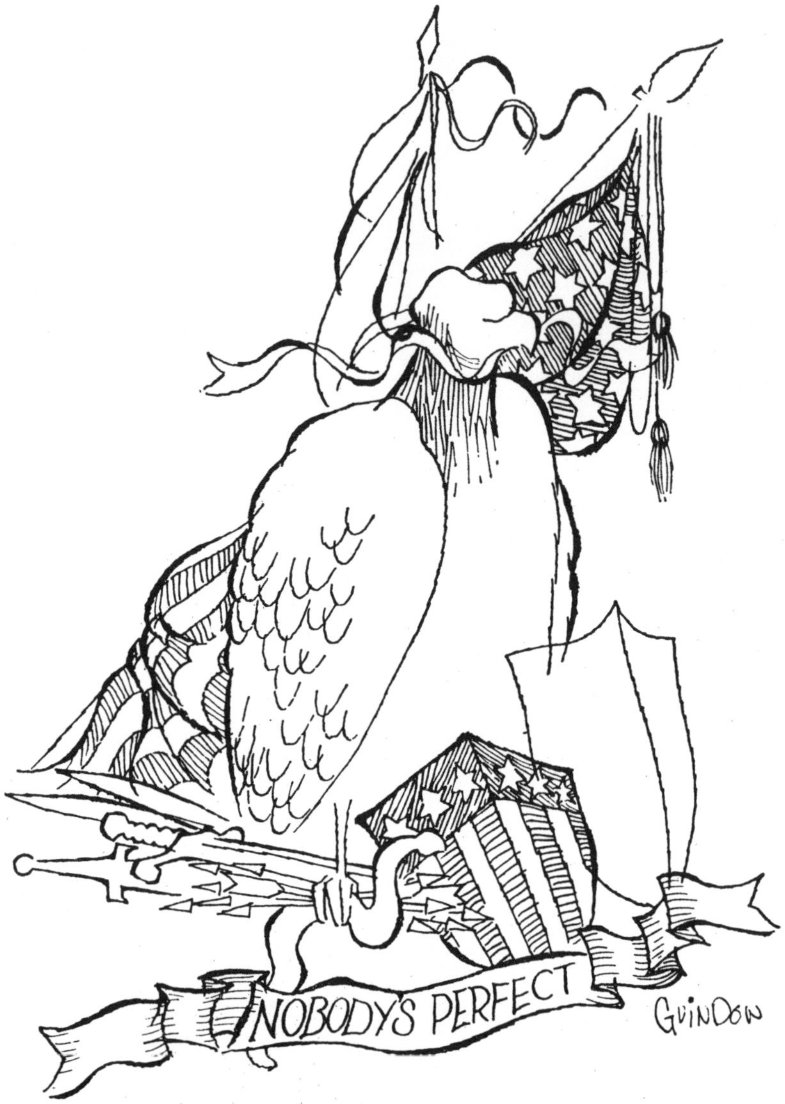
NOBODY'S PERFECT
GUINDON

RICHARD GUINDON. THE REALIST #47, FEBRUARY 1964. *45

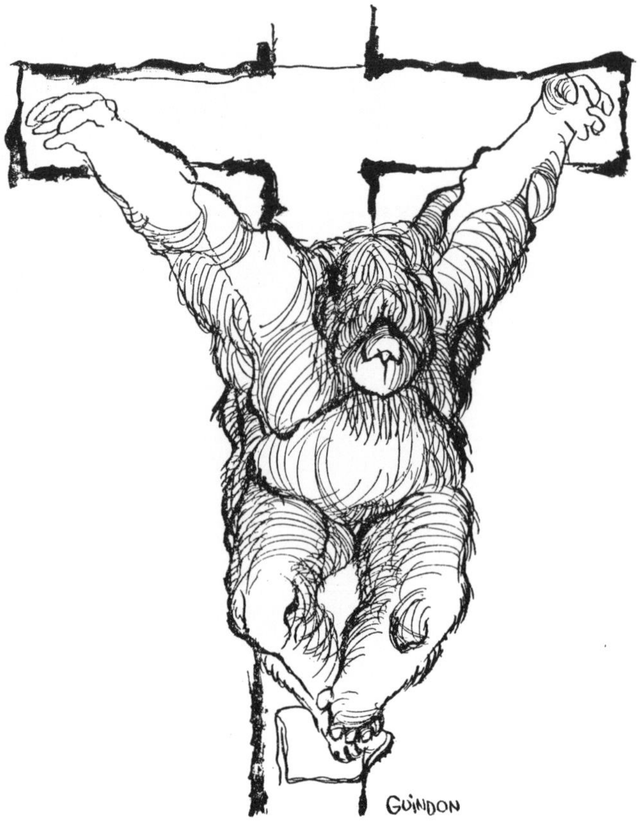
GUINDON

RICHARD GUINDON. THE REALIST #43, SEPTEMBER 1963. *46

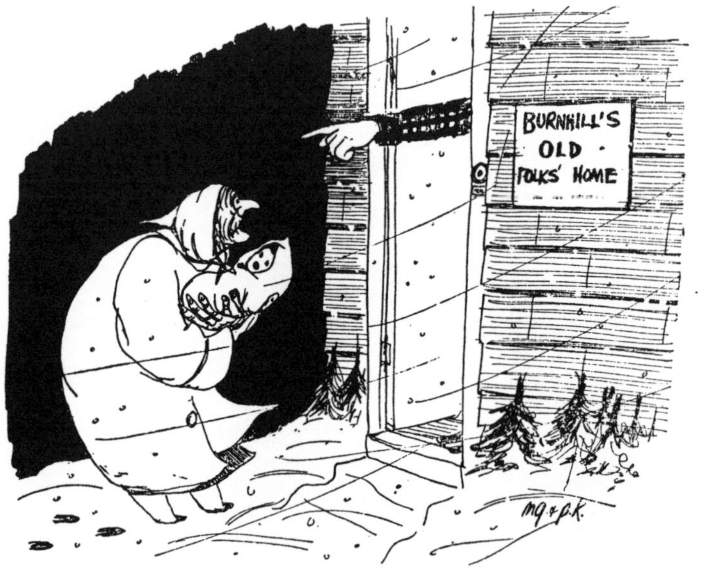
BURNHILL'S
OLD
FOLKS' HOME

NEWS ITEM: A doctor has warned the British Medical Association that — despite assurance that birth control pills are harmless — "evidence has been put before us that there is a possibility that they only delay ovulation." As a result, he said, women taking the pills for much of their life could find themselves pregnant at the age of 70.

MORT GERBERG. THE REALIST #43, SEPTEMBER 1963.

GUINDON

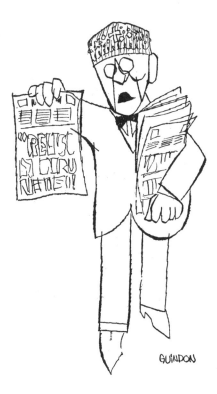

"GOLDWATER SPEAKS!"

RICHARD GUINDON. THE REALIST #43, SEPTEMBER 1963. *47

Cancer

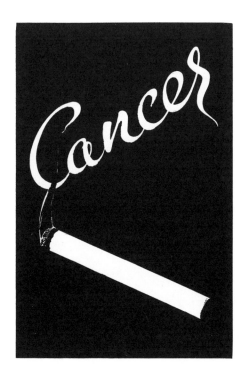

THE REALIST #45, NOVEMBER 1963.

There are 8500 members of the Communist Party of which 1500 are F.B.I. informants!
I would rather live on my knees than die on my knees
what if the Communist idea gets through to the the 1500 F.B.I. informants?
I would rather live lying down than die lying down.
....1500 agents for the Soviet Intellegence!
I would rather live standing up.
Marxism is lethal Philosophic dynamite. Can the F.B.I. withstand it?
I would rather be lying on my back, living, than on my knees.
If not then you'd have as the center of the Communist Party an armed federal Police and a communist take over!
I would rather live lying up than stand dying down.
You know what? J. Edgar Hoover's a Soviet agent!
I like it standing up or lying down on my knees.
LouMyers

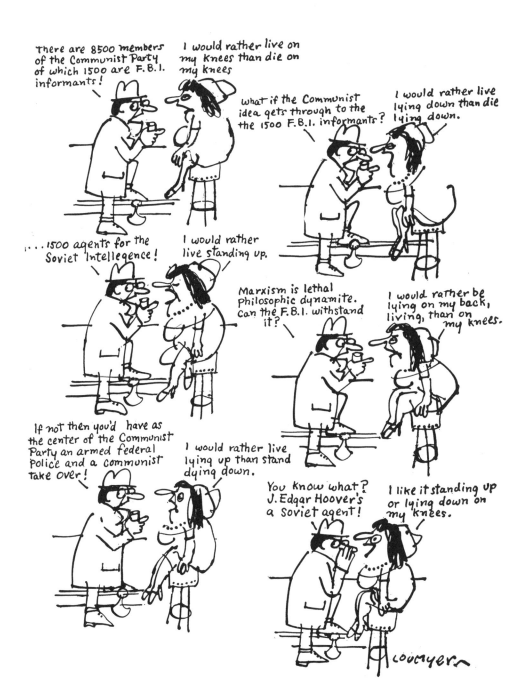

LOU MYERS. THE REALIST #47, FEBRUARY 1964.

BHOB STEWART/KEN SEAGLE.
THE REALIST #47, FEBRUARY 1964.

J.C.

by bhob stewart and Ken Seagle

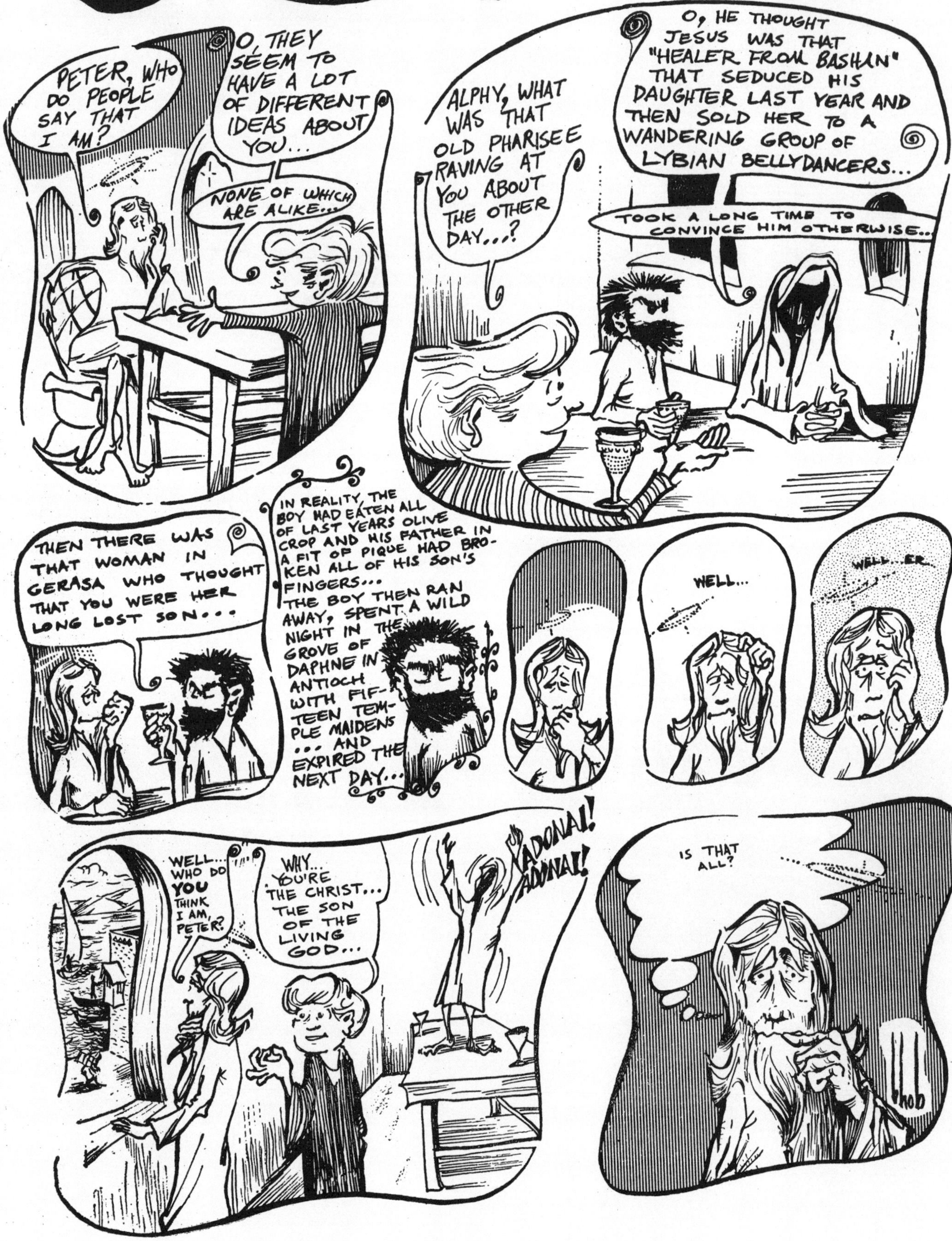
PETER, WHO DO PEOPLE SAY THAT I AM?
O, THEY SEEM TO HAVE A LOT OF DIFFERENT IDEAS ABOUT YOU...
NONE OF WHICH ARE ALIKE...
ALPHY, WHAT WAS THAT OLD PHARISEE RAVING AT YOU ABOUT THE OTHER DAY...?
O, HE THOUGHT JESUS WAS THAT "HEALER FROM BASHAN" THAT SEDUCED HIS DAUGHTER LAST YEAR AND THEN SOLD HER TO A WANDERING GROUP OF LYBIAN BELLYDANCERS...
TOOK A LONG TIME TO CONVINCE HIM OTHERWISE...
THEN THERE WAS THAT WOMAN IN GERASA WHO THOUGHT THAT YOU WERE HER LONG LOST SON...
IN REALITY, THE BOY HAD EATEN ALL OF LAST YEARS OLIVE CROP AND HIS FATHER IN A FIT OF PIQUE HAD BROKEN ALL OF HIS SON'S FINGERS... THE BOY THEN RAN AWAY, SPENT A WILD NIGHT IN THE GROVE OF DAPHNE IN ANTIOCH WITH FIFTEEN TEMPLE MAIDENS ... AND EXPIRED THE NEXT DAY...
WELL...
WELL...ER
WELL... WHO DO YOU THINK I AM, PETER?
WHY... YOU'RE THE CHRIST... THE SON OF THE LIVING GOD...
ADONAI! ADONAI!
IS THAT ALL?
bhob

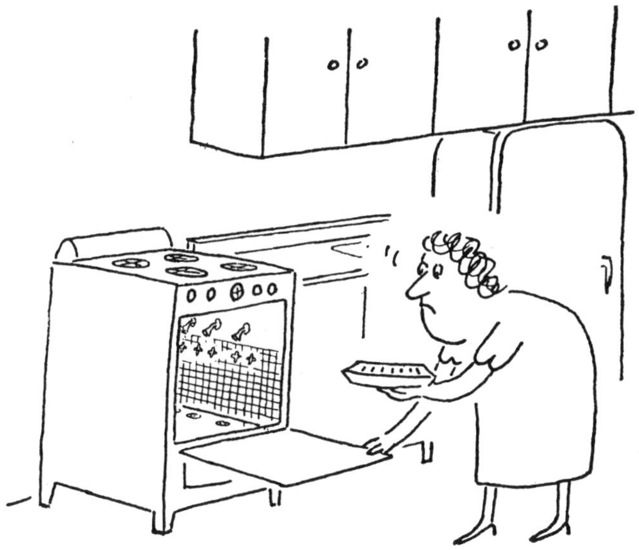

SAM GROSS. THE REALIST #47, FEBRUARY 1964. *48

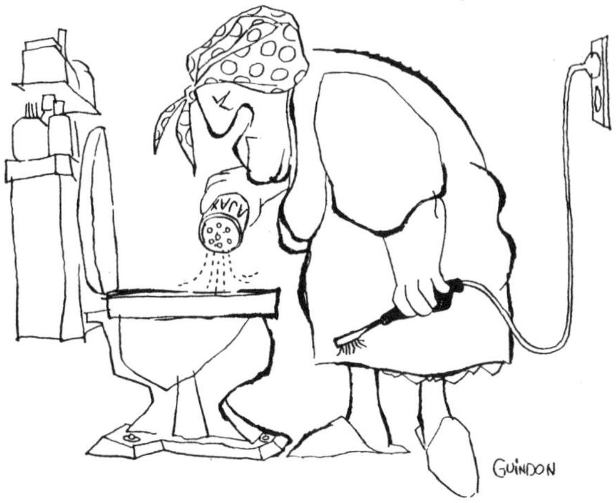
GUINDON

RICHARD GUINDON. THE REALIST #48, MARCH 1964.

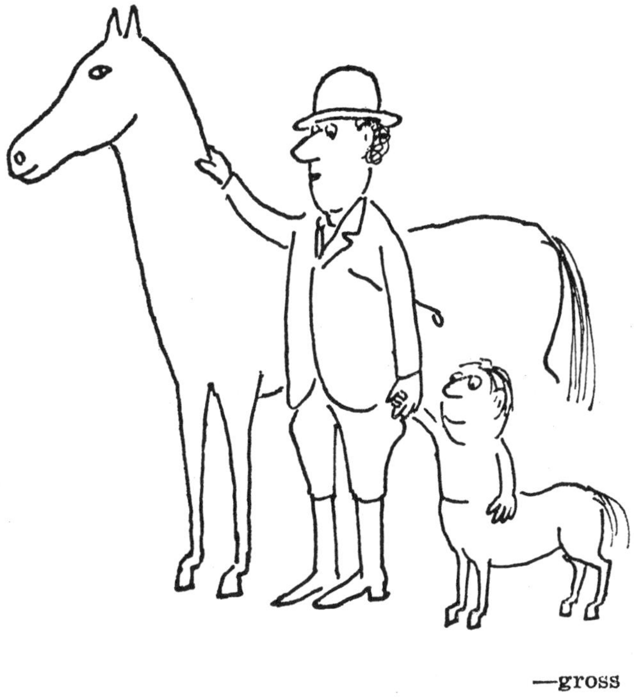
—gross

SAM GROSS. THE REALIST #48, MARCH 1964. *49

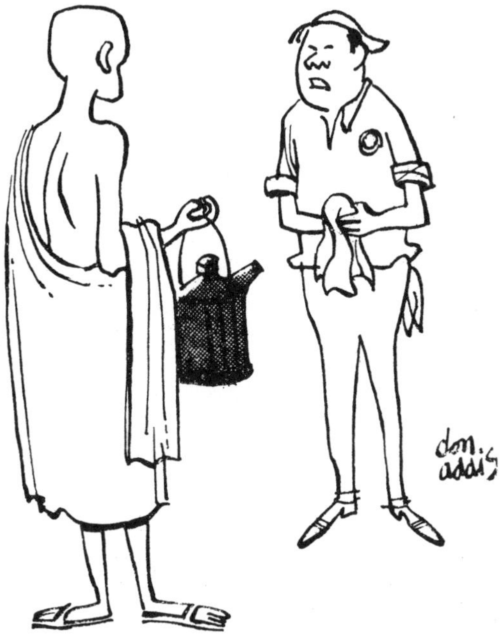
don addis

"Regular?"

DON ADDIS. THE REALIST #48, MARCH 1964. *50

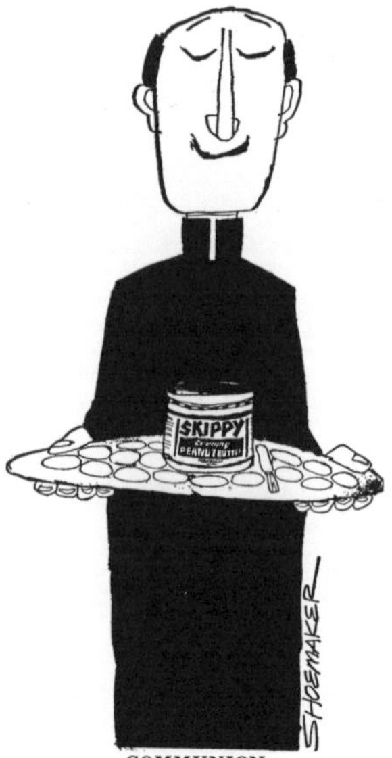
SKIPPY
SHOEMAKER

COMMUNION

HOWARD SHOEMAKER. THE REALIST #48, MARCH 1964. *51

Holly: An Introduction

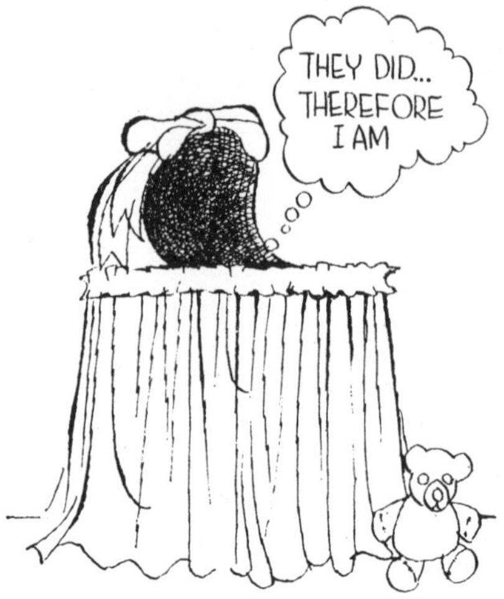
THEY DID...
THEREFORE
I AM

RICHARD GUINDON. THE REALIST #48, MARCH 1964. *52

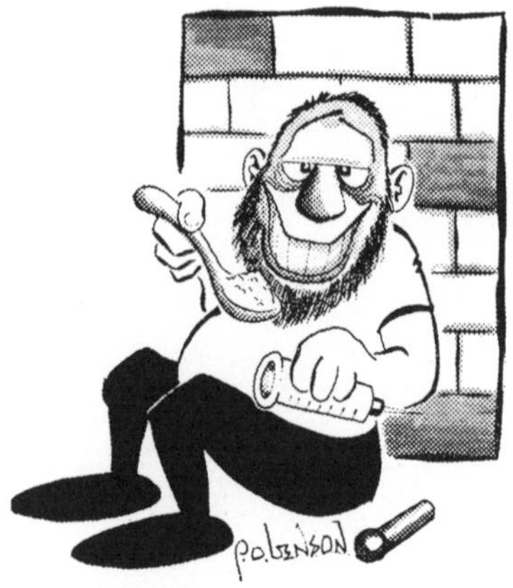
P.O. BENSON

"Say, buddy ... ya got a light?"

P.O. BENSON. THE REALIST #48, MARCH 1964.

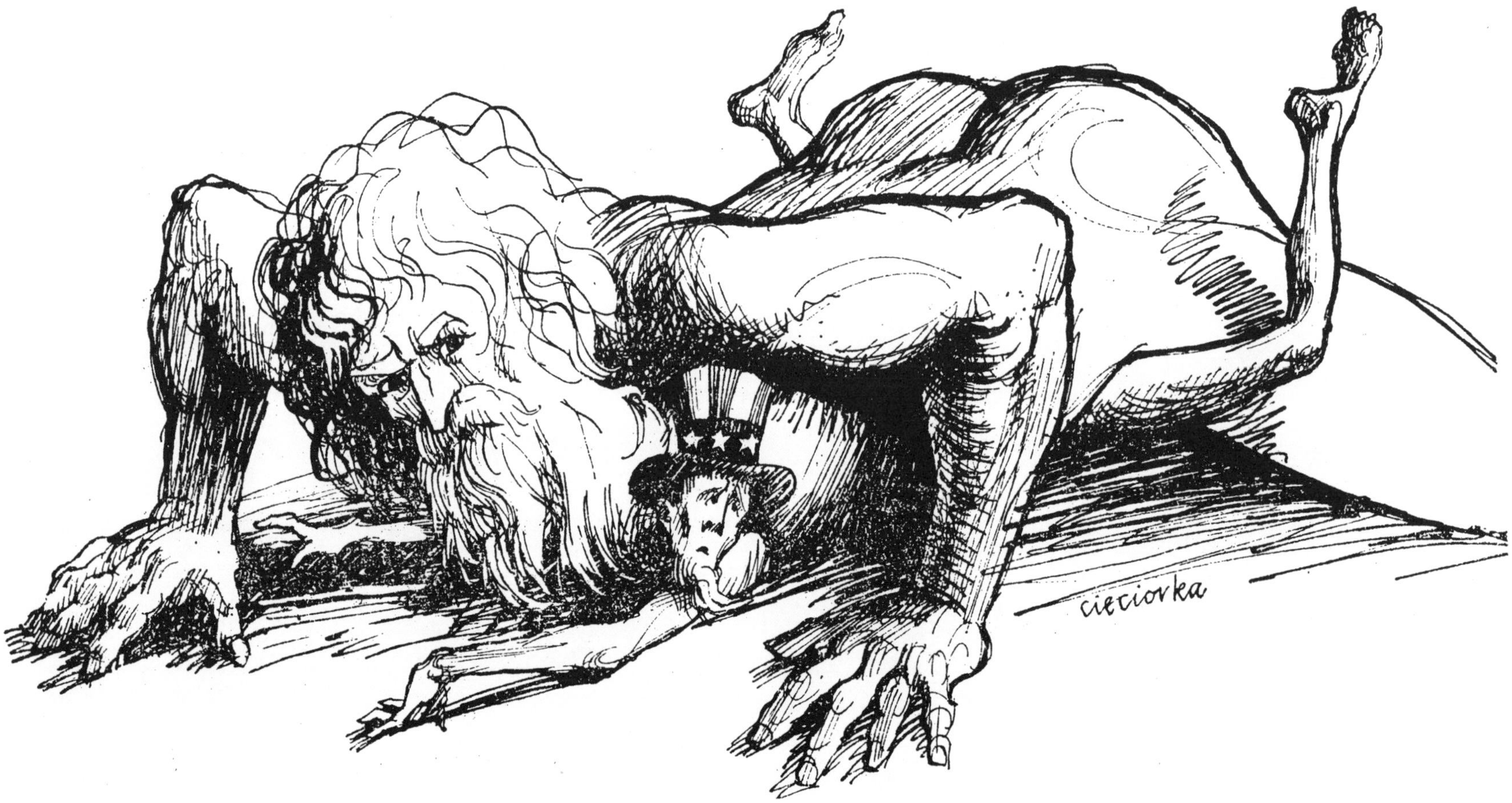
cieciorka

". . . one nation, under God . . ."

FRANK CIECIORKA. THE REALIST #48, MARCH 1964.

OUT TO LUNCH

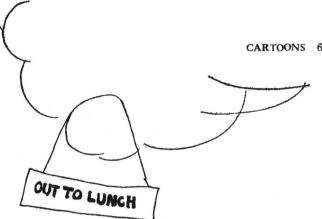

THE REALIST #49, APRIL 1964.

Me
Nice Doctor
Me

NEWS ITEM: A proposed program of mandatory sterilization for the feeble-minded is currently being sponsored by the Human Betterment Association.

RICHARD GUINDON. THE REALIST #48, MARCH 1964.

GUINDON

NEWS ITEM: The Delaware Supreme Court has upheld the right of its lower courts to invoke the whipping penalty.

RICHARD GUINDON. THE REALIST #48, MARCH 1964. *53

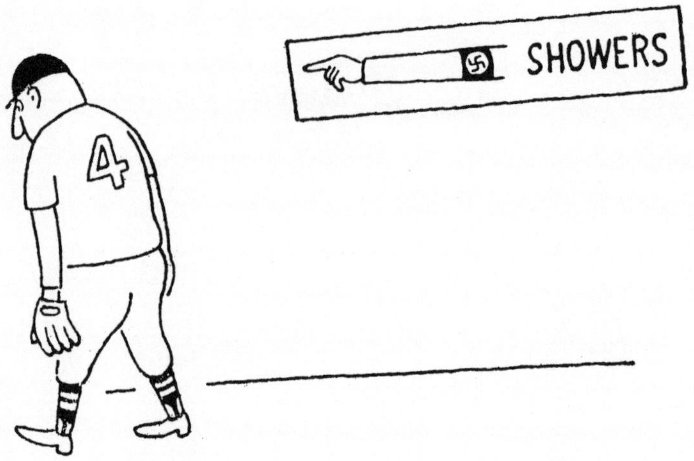
4
SHOWERS

SAM GROSS. THE REALIST #49, APRIL 1964. *54

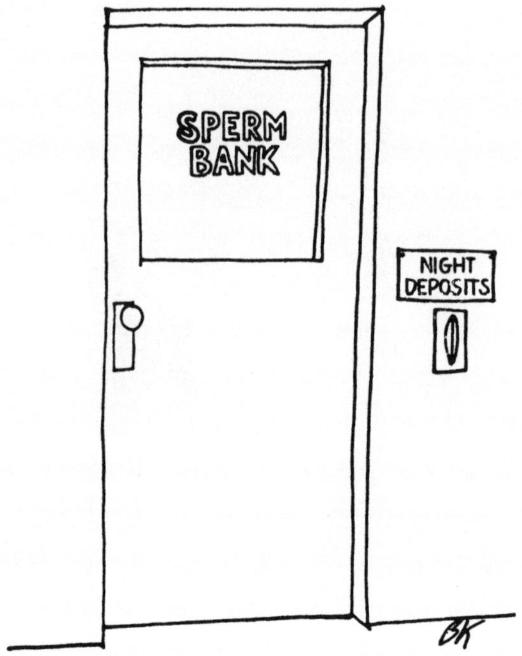
SPERM BANK
NIGHT DEPOSITS

B. KLIBAN. THE REALIST #49, APRIL 1964.

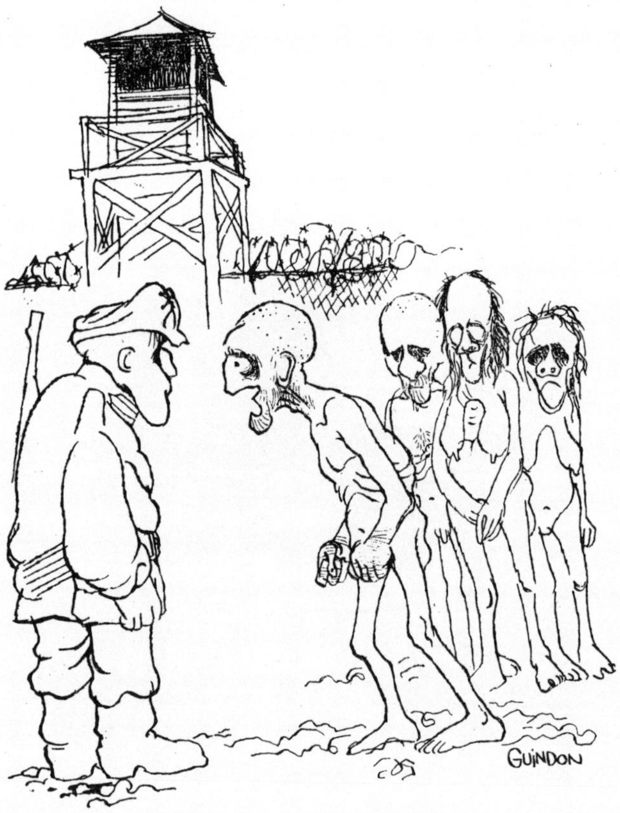
GUINDON

"You filthy swine — just wait till the Pope hears about this!"

RICHARD GUINDON. THE REALIST #50, MAY 1964.

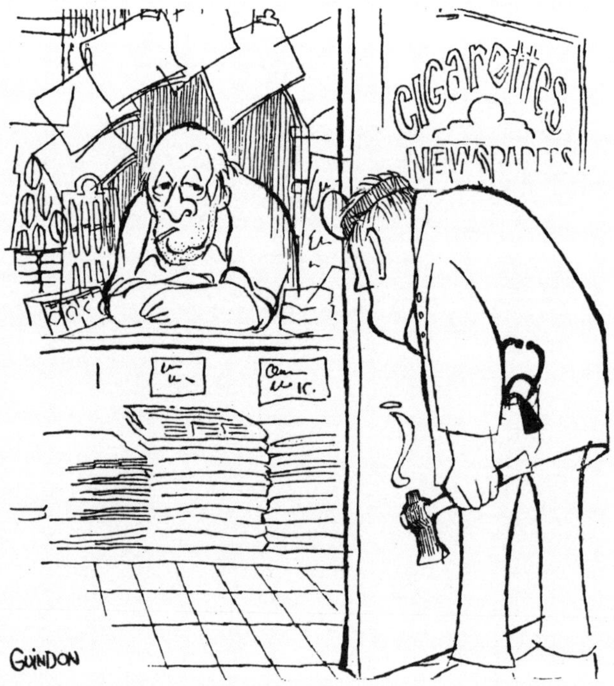
Cigarettes
GUINDON

RICHARD GUINDON. THE REALIST #49, APRIL 1964.

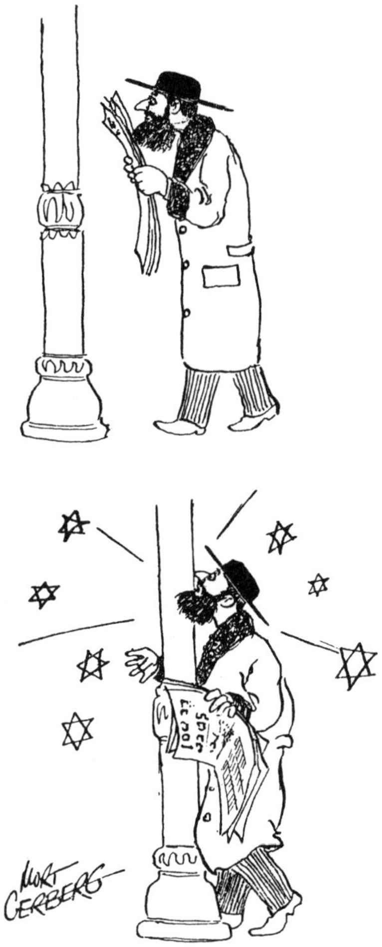
MORT GERBERG

MORT GERBERG. THE REALIST #49, APRIL 1964. *55

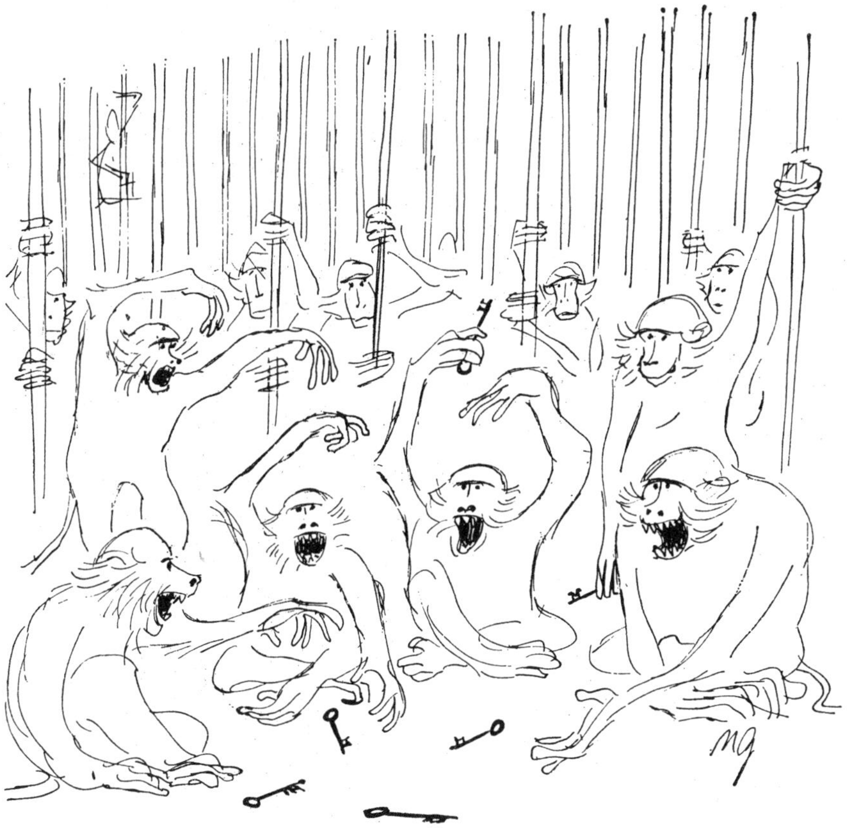

MORT GERBERG. THE REALIST #49, APRIL 1964. *56

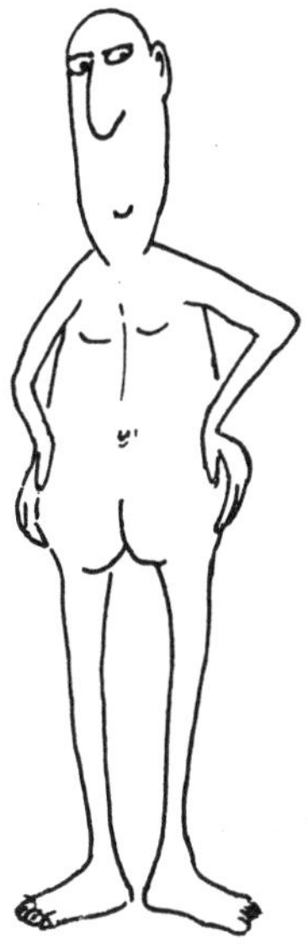

THE REALIST #49, APRIL 1964. 57

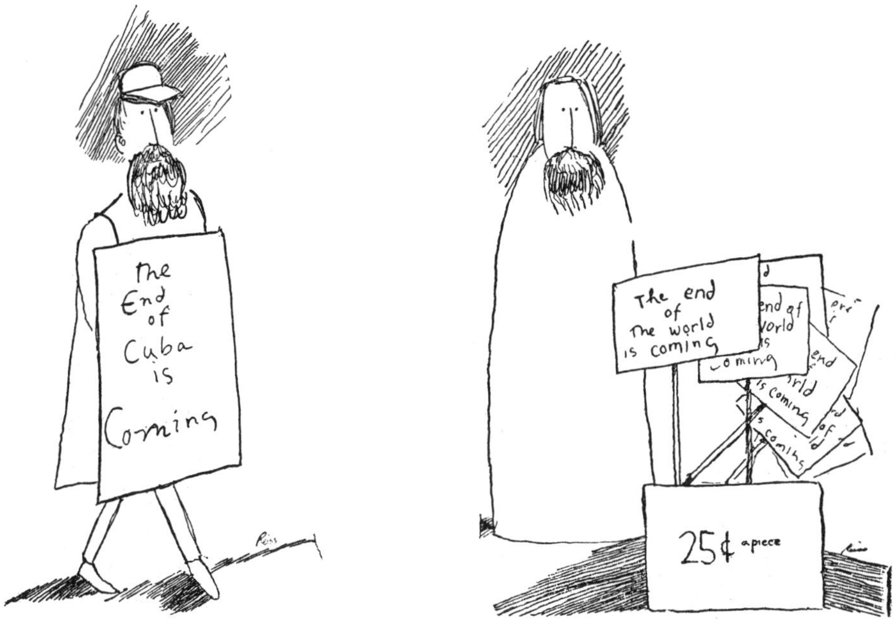
The End of Cuba is Coming
The end of The world is coming
25¢ apiece
Reiss

ANDY REISS. THE REALIST #49, APRIL 1964.

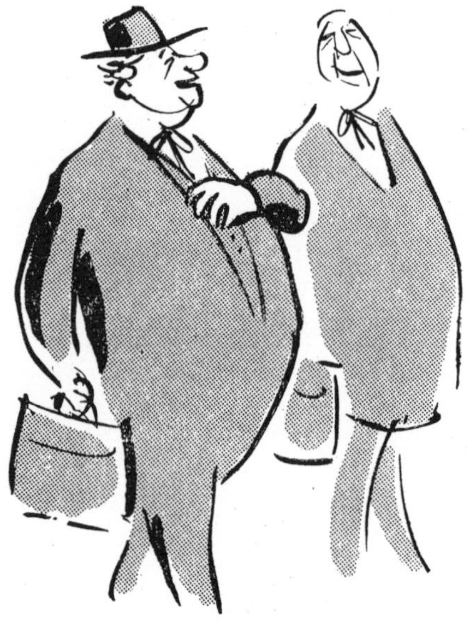

"Of course I'll vote for any bill our late, beloved John F. Kennedy wanted. But how do we know he really wanted disarmament, Medicare & civil rights?"

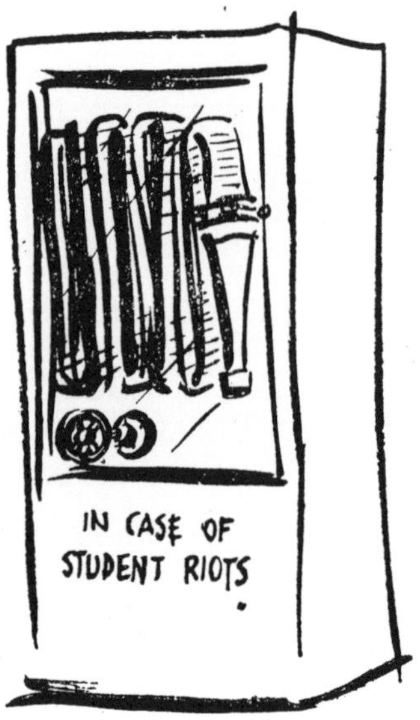
IN CASE OF
STUDENT RIOTS

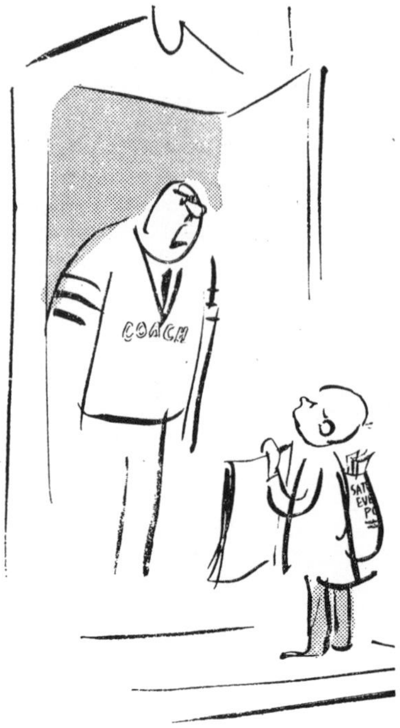
COACH

"Go peddle your filth elsewhere!"

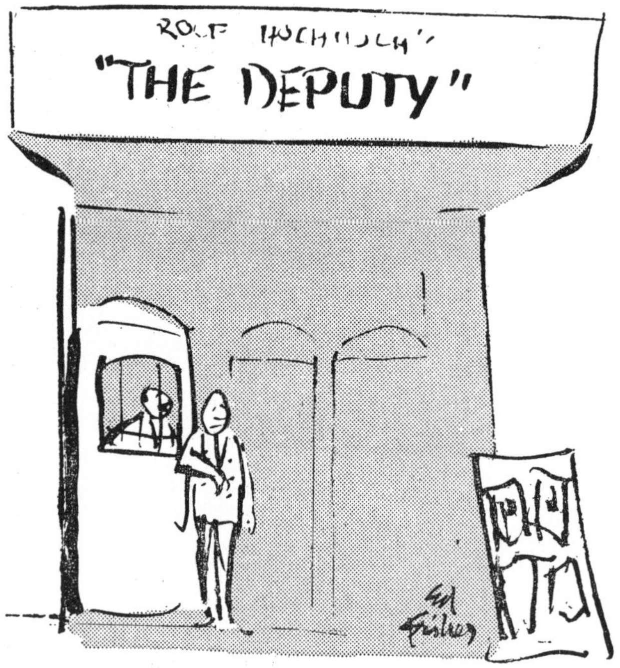
"THE DEPUTY"

"Don't worry, Mr. Shumlin — show business is always slow during Lent."

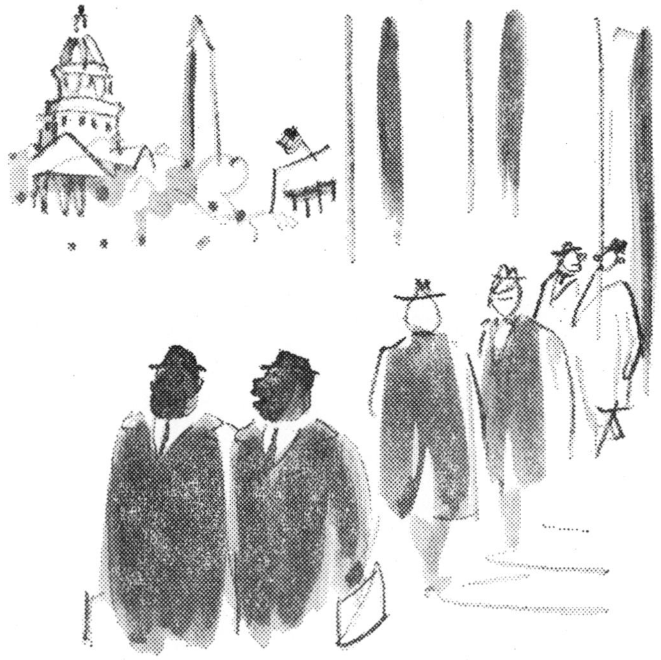

"Mark my words — when we do get into the Cabinet, it will probably only be in some menial capacity."

ED FISHER. THE REALIST #50, MAY 1964.

JOHN FRANCIS PUTNAM
AND MORT GERBERG.
THE REALIST #50, MAY 1964.

The World's Fair Poverty Pavilion

by John Francis Putnam and Mort Gerberg

About five years ago, the *Ladies Home Journal* ran a picture article in their "How America Lives" series on what a searing and dreadful thing it was to have to live in New York's Westchester County on $10,000 a year.

It was a brave story that told of tight-lipped young marrieds trying to put up a proper front under impossible circumstances. It was the first recognition in print that Poverty does exist in these United States. Which goes to show that you can be sitting right next to poor people on a commuter train and not even know it.

The poor, inconsiderately, are always with us. Don't let that 1949 Cadillac parked in front of the Negro sharecropper's cabin fool you for one instant.

Moreover, poverty now has official recognition—from the Administration, from TV comedians and from the pages of *Life* and *Look*—especially these latter "opinion molders," where the picture-article-spreads, usually aglow with "Leisure Living," now present a "Rural Resettlement Agency"—Depression scabrosity with indigent children peering out at the comfortable reader with haunting questions.

These are American kids, of course, so they are not quite as peaked and rickety as African or Asian kids, but they're still reproachful enough to nudge the suburban conscience to admit that the U.S. coin is not burnished bright on both sides.

Poverty, man, is *in* this year!

It is reasonable to assume that the New York World's Fair reflects the real America (Billy Graham Pavilion: "Come inside and pray with us . . . we have the only *safe* restrooms at the Fair"); therefore, as Paul Krassner points out in his letter to Robert Moses (still unanswered), a Poverty Pavilion is a must, if only to present this latest fashionable aspect of our way of life.

Since the purpose of the Fair is to entertain as it instructs and informs — the more amusing an unpalatable fact is made to seem, the more easily it is absorbed—our Poverty Pavilion will of necessity have an overt carnival-midway atmosphere.

The theme of the exhibit will be *"Poverty: Urban and Rural, 1964* or This - is - what - will - happen - to - you - lousy - kids - unless - you - buckle - down - and - face - the - facts - the - way - I - had - to - when - I - was - your - age!"

Here, then, are some excerpts from the *Official Guide Book to the World's Fair Poverty Pavilion.*

Hit the Beggar

Riot of fun ride where derelicts are loosed in simulated traffic. As they attempt to wipe your windshield, you attempt to run them down.

The Sweat Shop

Nearsighted Puerto Rican girls of six ply their trade by dim kerosene lamps, doing microscopic petit point embroidery. Beatings by foreman at 10 AM, 2 PM and 4 PM promptly.

Dust Bowl Ride

The Pavilion will provide free face masks. See Okies with hopeless expressions attempt to farm in six feet of fine, silicone dust.

The 24th Precinct

Basement obstacle race and police brutality demonstration; free bandaids.

Sleep Under a Bridge

Only 25¢ a night. Vermin-ridden blankets, 5¢ extra. Prices at this exhibit in no way reflect actual costs, which have been underwritten by various philanthropic organizations; they are set arbitrarily in order to give the layman an accurate conception of the poor man's idea of money.

Slumlord Symposium

Public may attend daily conferences of slum landlords flown in from Palm Beach and Las Vegas for discussions on how to fit one hundred Spanish-speaking people into small two-room apartments.

Daily Bread Riot

Horses are available so that visitors may join the mounted police in breaking it up.

Secaucus Pig Scramble

Admission 50¢. Watch starving Pennsylvania miner's children compete for luxury restaurant garbage with burly Secaucus (N.J.) pigs. Pari-mutual opens half hour before sty time.

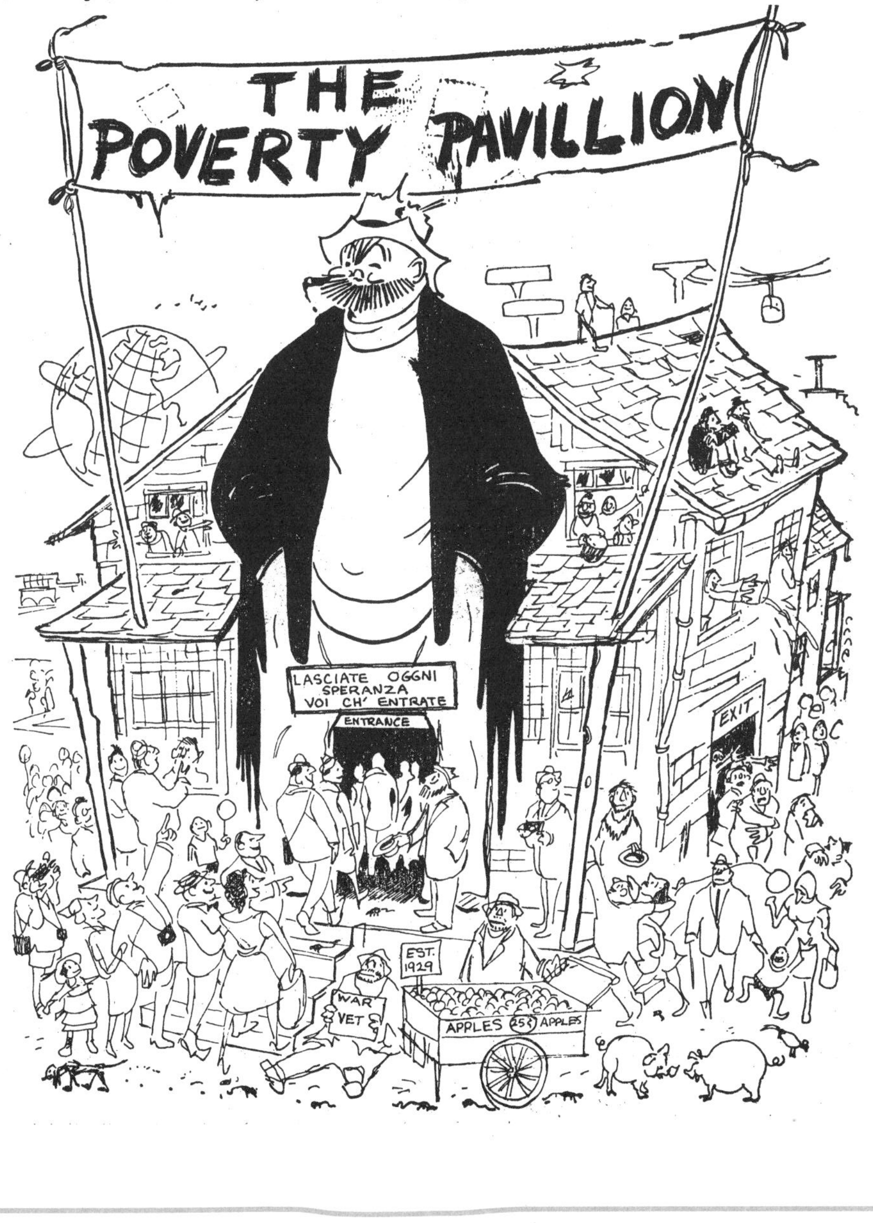
THE POVERTY PAVILLION
LASCIATE OGGNI SPERANZA VOI CH' ENTRATE
ENTRANCE
EXIT
EST. 1929
WAR VET
APPLES 25¢ APPLES

CONT'D

Souvenir Shoppe

An authentic Company Store setting. Features genuine cockroaches in laminated clear plastic key chains, miniature bags of government surplus flower with real weevils, plus such items as the bedbug breeder which allows one to *plant* bedbug eggs in the victim's bed, with riotous results.

Laugh with Joe Mitchell

Learn about the funny side of being on relief. Sit in with Newburgh (N.Y.) Commissioner Joseph Mitchell and join the hilarity as he turns down applications for home relief.

Barney's Shabbytown

Barney's goodwill outlet to clothe the needy at reasonable prices. Features government surplus military overcoats with World War I brass buttons, all sizes too big for any customer.

High School Dropoutsville

Administer a literacy test. You'll chortle at the way 20-year-old youths stutter and stammer their way through "See Ned run" first readers. Chuckle at their pathetic attempts to write (not print) their names. Receive the thrill of a lifetime as you grade them "Illiterate."

Graffiti Exhibit

Original drawings and text by ghetto youngsters. Only adults admitted.

Resettlement Roulette Booth

Here, for a modest 50¢, visitors may press a button and evict an impoverished family somewhere in the U.S. Identity of the evictees will be protected, but patrons will receive, within two weeks, a photograph of their heap of pathetic belongings piled on the street.

Replica of 125th Street

See the special backed-up-toilet fountain. Visit the Malnutrition Center. Sample the proud product of a Sneaky Pete Distillery.

Miniature Debtors Prison

The new State of Mississippi Debtors Prison is a model for Poverty Control, soon to be adopted by other Southern states.

Note: Visitors are reminded that there is a free Decontamination Station at every exit from the Poverty Pavilion. Nevertheless, the Bible says: "Ye have the poor always with you"—and we are honored to be carrying out the Word of God.

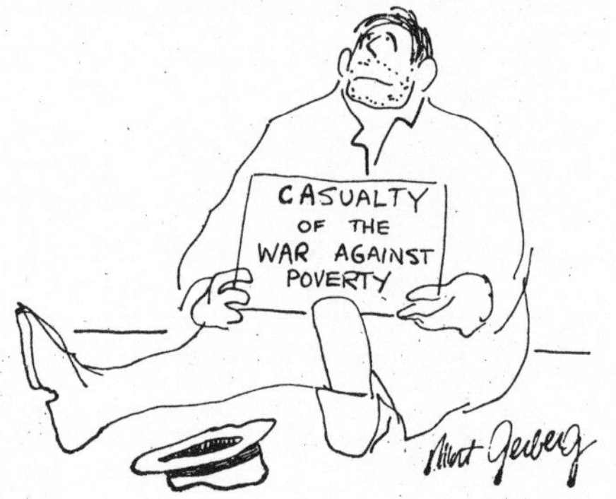
CASUALTY OF THE WAR AGAINST POVERTY
Mort Gerberg

Instant Uplift Booth

Talk to a plastic Sargent Shriver and ask any one of 50 questions on poverty in America, and he will give you any one of 50 straightforward, but reassuring, answers.

Mexican Wetback Dance

Our greasy little friends from South of the Border demonstrate how they slip past alert Texas Rangers and Border Patrol men.

Unplanned Parenthood

Sponsored by the Catholic Archdiocese of Brooklyn. Information on how large families on relief can get to be even larger.

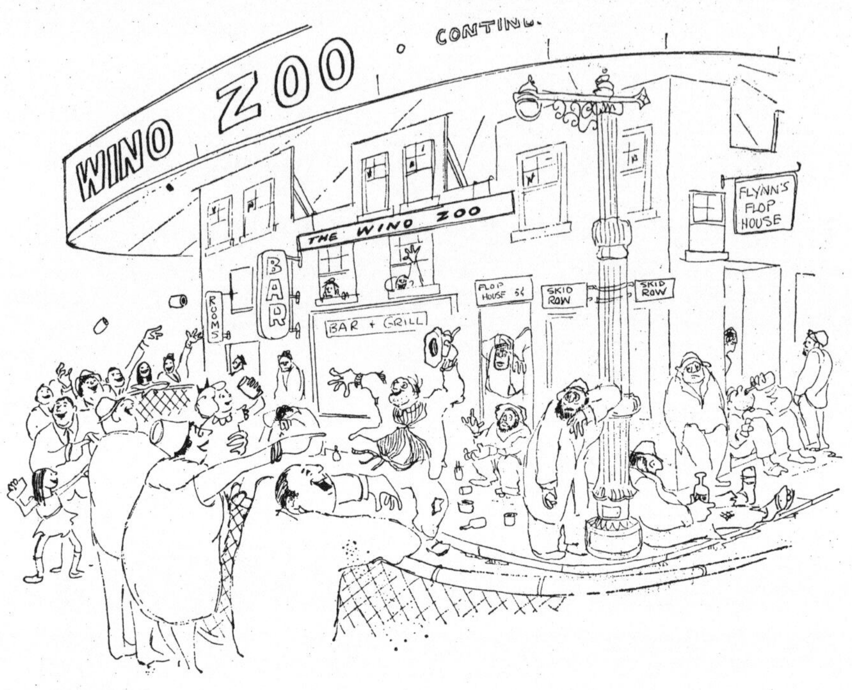
WINO ZOO
THE WINO ZOO
BAR
ROOMS
BAR + GRILL
SKID ROW
SKID ROW
FLYNN'S FLOP HOUSE

The Wino Zoo

Admission free. See authentic alcoholics disporting themselves in a realistic Bowery *cum* Skid Row setting. Visitors may purchase cans of Sterno and and toss them through the bars. Children love watching the funny antics of the inhabitants.

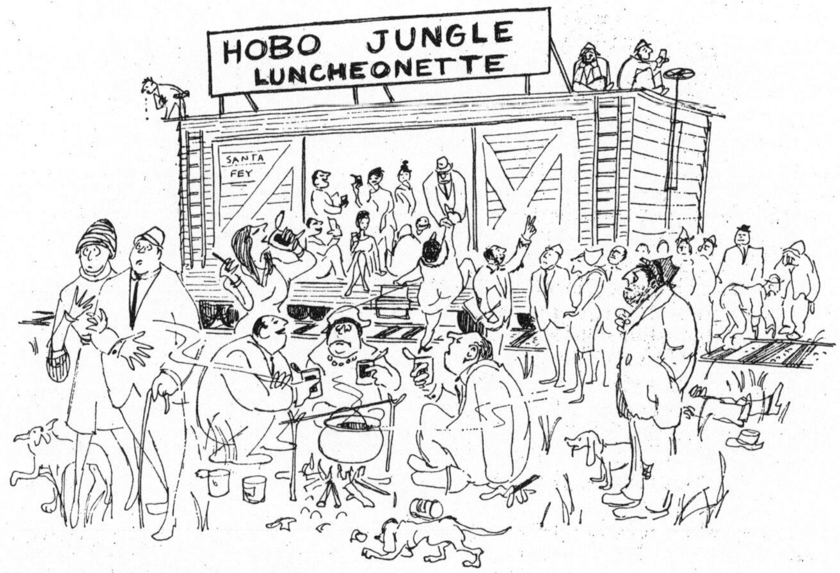
HOBO JUNGLE
LUNCHEONETTE
SANTA FEY

Hobo Jungle Luncheonette

Informal dining in a genuine boxcar setting. Mulligan Stew served in contaminated tin cans. Gourmet handouts. Family dinners from 6¢ up.

JOHN FRANCIS PUTNAM AND MORT GERBERG. THE REALIST #50, MAY 1964.

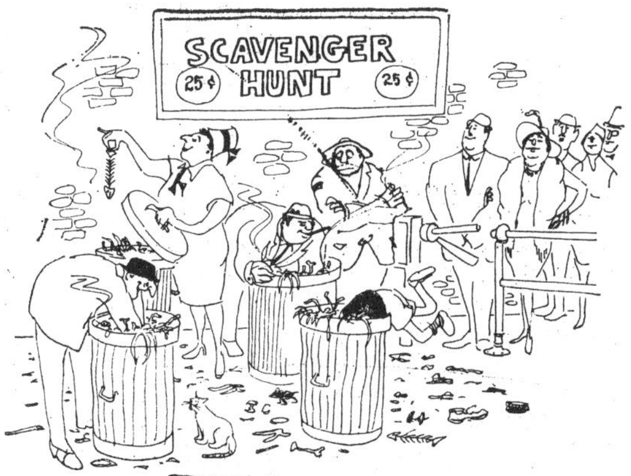
SCAVENGER HUNT
25¢
25¢

Scavenger Hunt

Forage through garbage cans and waste baskets, searching for something to eat, drink or smoke, just like the poor people do! More fun than Crackerjacks and twice as many surprises . . . such as maggot-ridden hambones or sweat-stiffened sweatsocks.

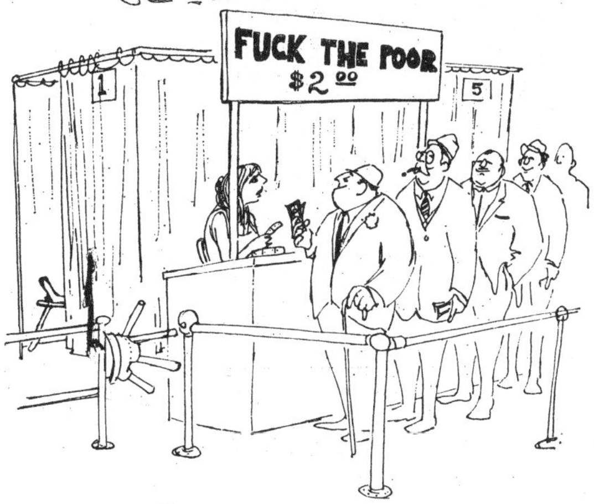
FUCK THE POOR
$2.00
1
5

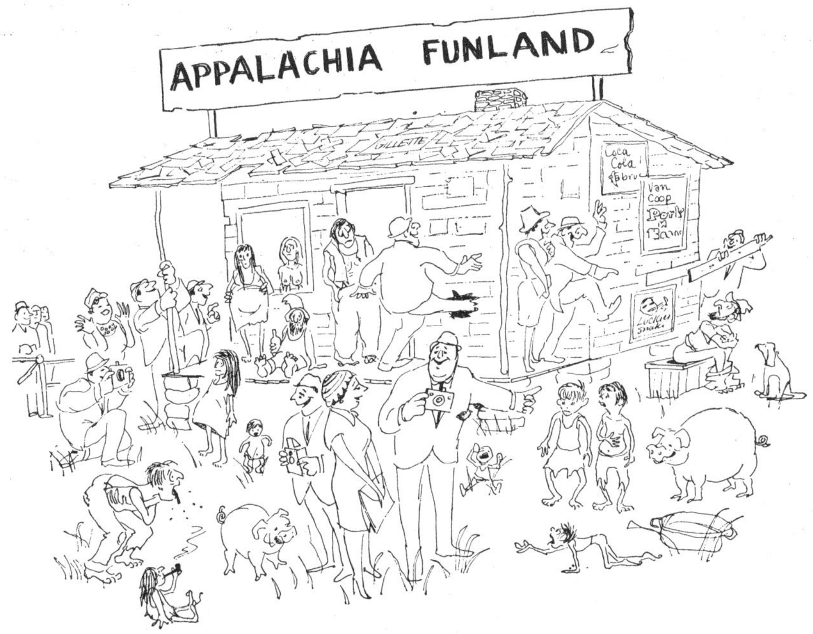
APPALACHIA FUNLAND

Appalachia Funland

Roar at the tobacco-chewing antics of a 5-year-old boy. Gawk at the pregnant 10-year-old girl. See the funny legs of the kids with rickets. Kick a hole in the wall of the splintering shacks. Open all day.

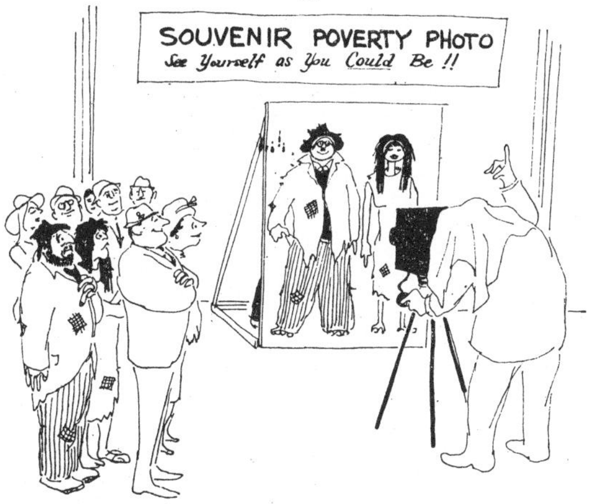
SOUVENIR POVERTY PHOTO
See Yourself as You Could Be !!

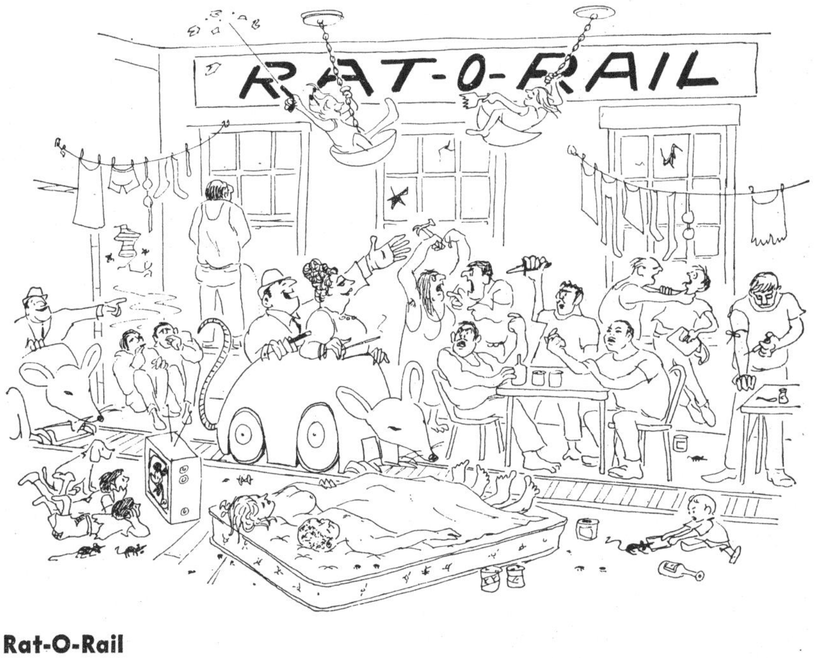
RAT-O-RAIL

Rat-O-Rail

Exciting tour through a West Side tenement. See the pot gardens on the fire escape. Watch the man urinating out the window. Listen while profanities are yelled up the air shaft. Observe the junkies in action. You are there as the Welfare caseworker is locked inside the hall toilet.

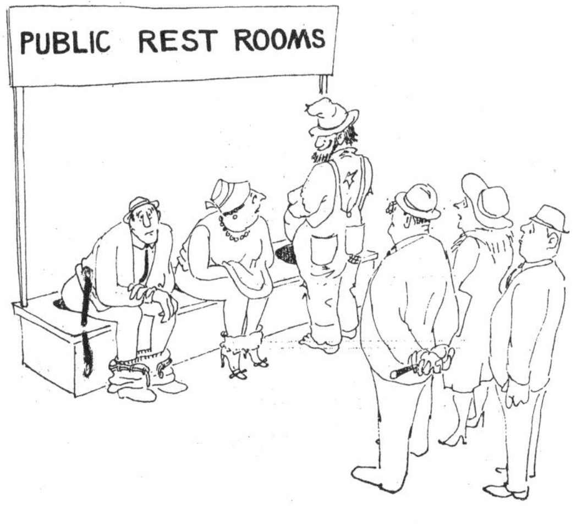
PUBLIC REST ROOMS

JOHN FRANCIS PUTNAM AND MORT GERBERG. THE REALIST #50, MAY 1964.

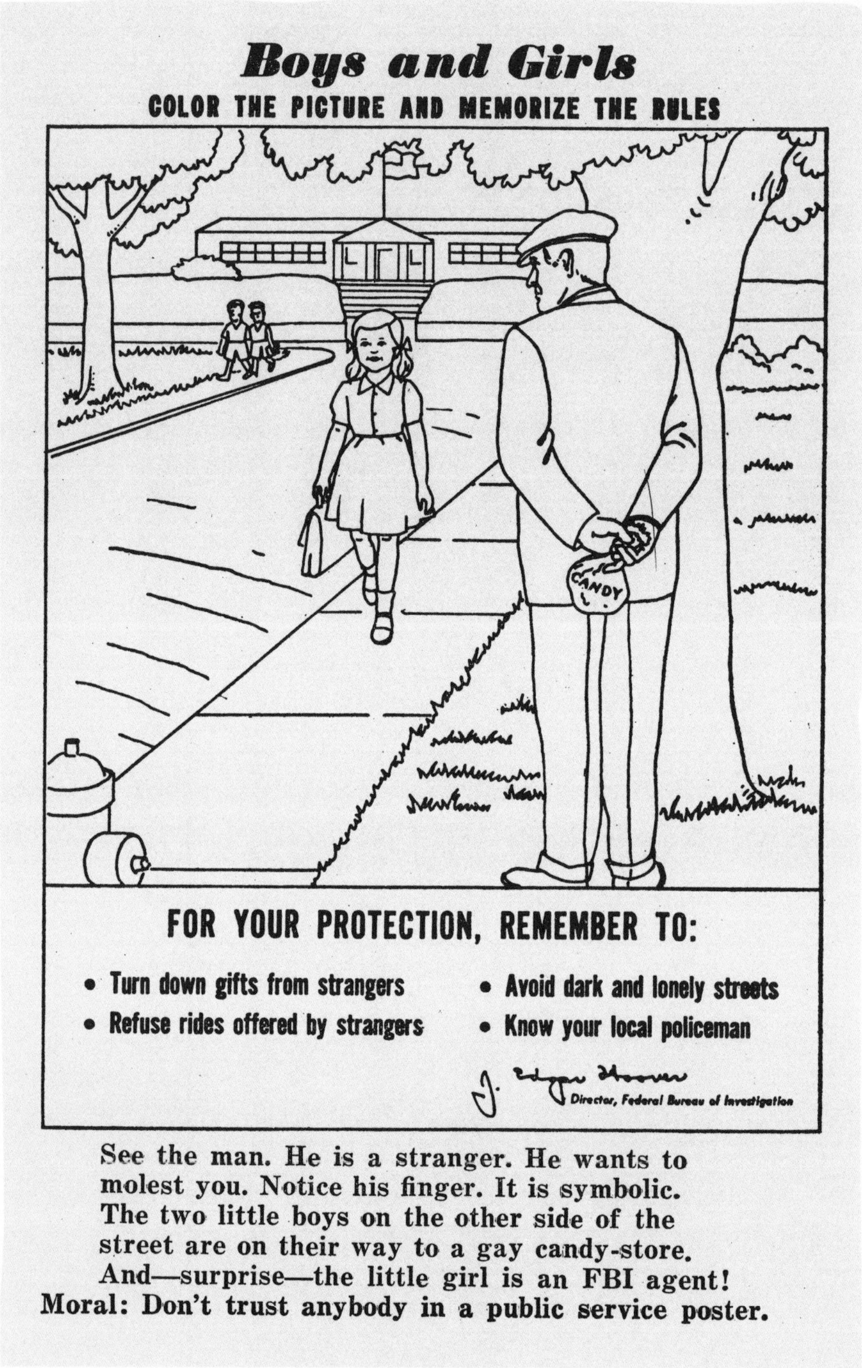
Boys and Girls
COLOR THE PICTURE AND MEMORIZE THE RULES
CANDY
FOR YOUR PROTECTION, REMEMBER TO:
• Turn down gifts from strangers
• Refuse rides offered by strangers
• Avoid dark and lonely streets
• Know your local policeman
J. Edgar Hoover
Director, Federal Bureau of Investigation
See the man. He is a stranger. He wants to molest you. Notice his finger. It is symbolic. The two little boys on the other side of the street are on their way to a gay candy-store. And—surprise—the little girl is an FBI agent!
Moral: Don't trust anybody in a public service poster.

THE REALIST #50, MAY 1964.

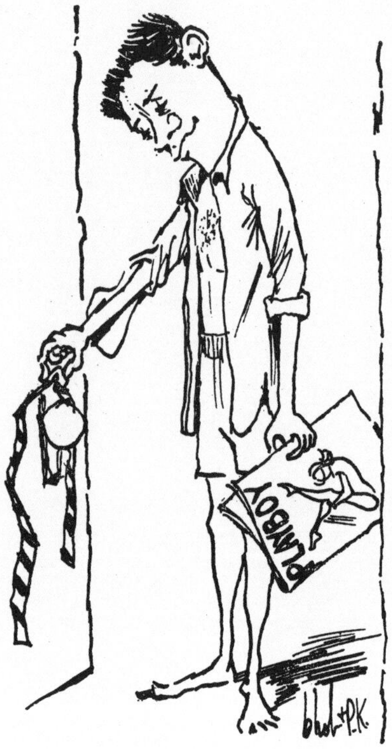
PLAYBOY

BHOB STEWART. THE REALIST #50, MAY 1964.

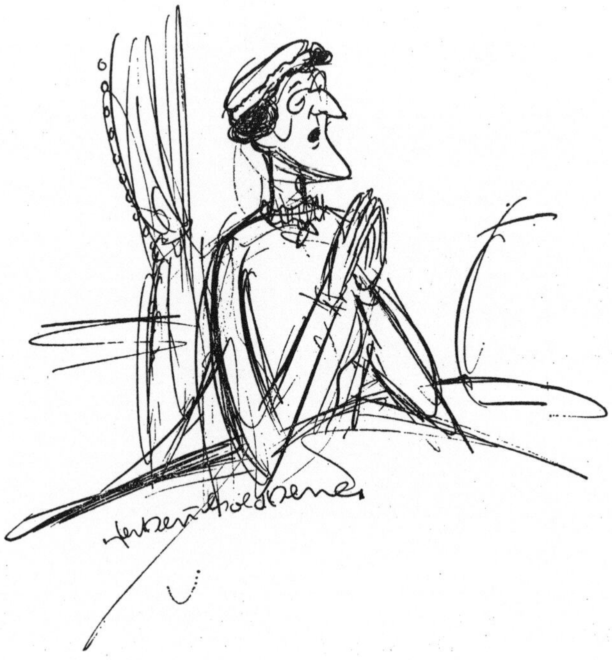

"... and dear God, let all those who are against school prayers be struck dead in their tracks ..."

HERBERT GOLDBERG. THE REALIST #50, MAY 1964.

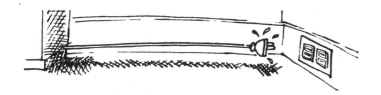

THE REALIST #50, MAY 1964.

cieciorka
The Cuban Crisis
Please Don't Bother the Rapist

FRANK CIECIORKA. THE REALIST #50, MAY 1964.

Are WICKED SPIRITS MISLEADING the WORLD ?
AB SENS

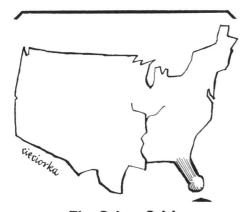

A.B. SENS. THE REALIST #51, JUNE 1964.

"Man is a monstrous farce ...
Present company excluded, of course!"

AL ROSS. THE REALIST #50, MAY 1964.

MEN

"Come on out, Lefty, we know you're in there!"

THE REALIST #50, MAY 1964.

"Of course, the strongest ticket of all would be: Grant
for President, and — if we could get him to run —
Lee for Vice-President ..."

"— And a special word to the ever-increasing number of you
who will go into the world of letters and write a novel based
on the experiences of these formative years: for God's sake,
set it in some anonymous, small Midwestern college!"

"Listen — they're shouting our slogan!"

"Well, there I was — a green recruit, see? — and General Hotch was
on the phone, asking me to come caddy for him, Mrs. Hotch wanted
me to serve canapés to the Bridge club, the wash was ready to be
Cloroxed, the General's dog needed to be walked ..."

ED FISHER. THE REALIST #51, JUNE 1964.

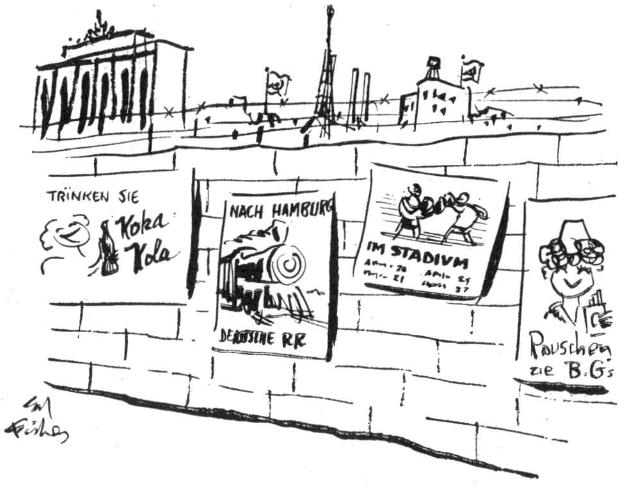
TRINKEN SIE
Koka Kola
NACH HAMBURG
DEUTSCHE RR
IM STADIUM

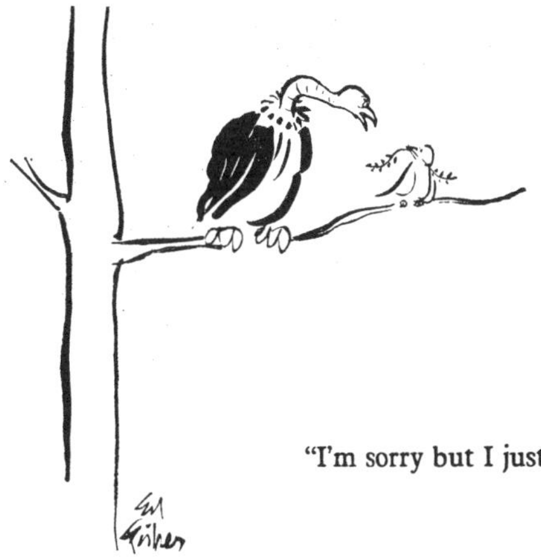

"I'm sorry but I just don't agree with you!"

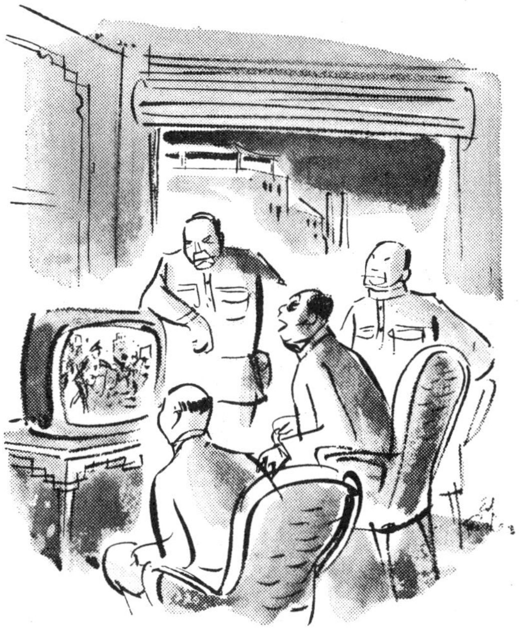

"Electric cattle-prodders! Now why didn't we think of that?"

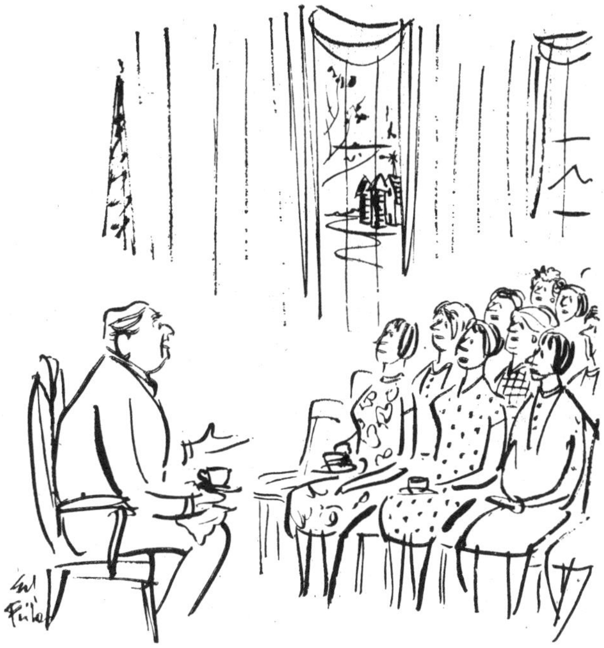

"So, you see, our only hope of staving off legislative reapportionment is a big boom in population ..."

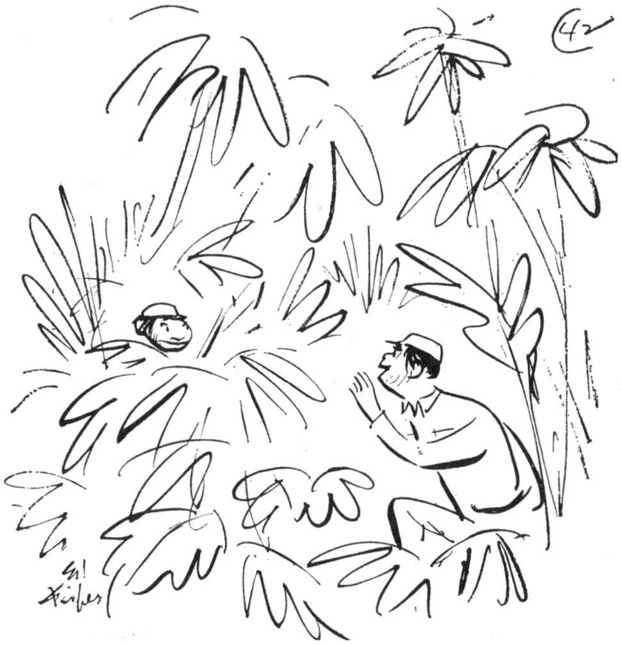

"Pssst — we've been ordered to bring back your local Viet Cong Commissioner at all costs! How about swapping him for our American Military Adviser?"

ED FISHER. THE REALIST #51, JUNE 1964.

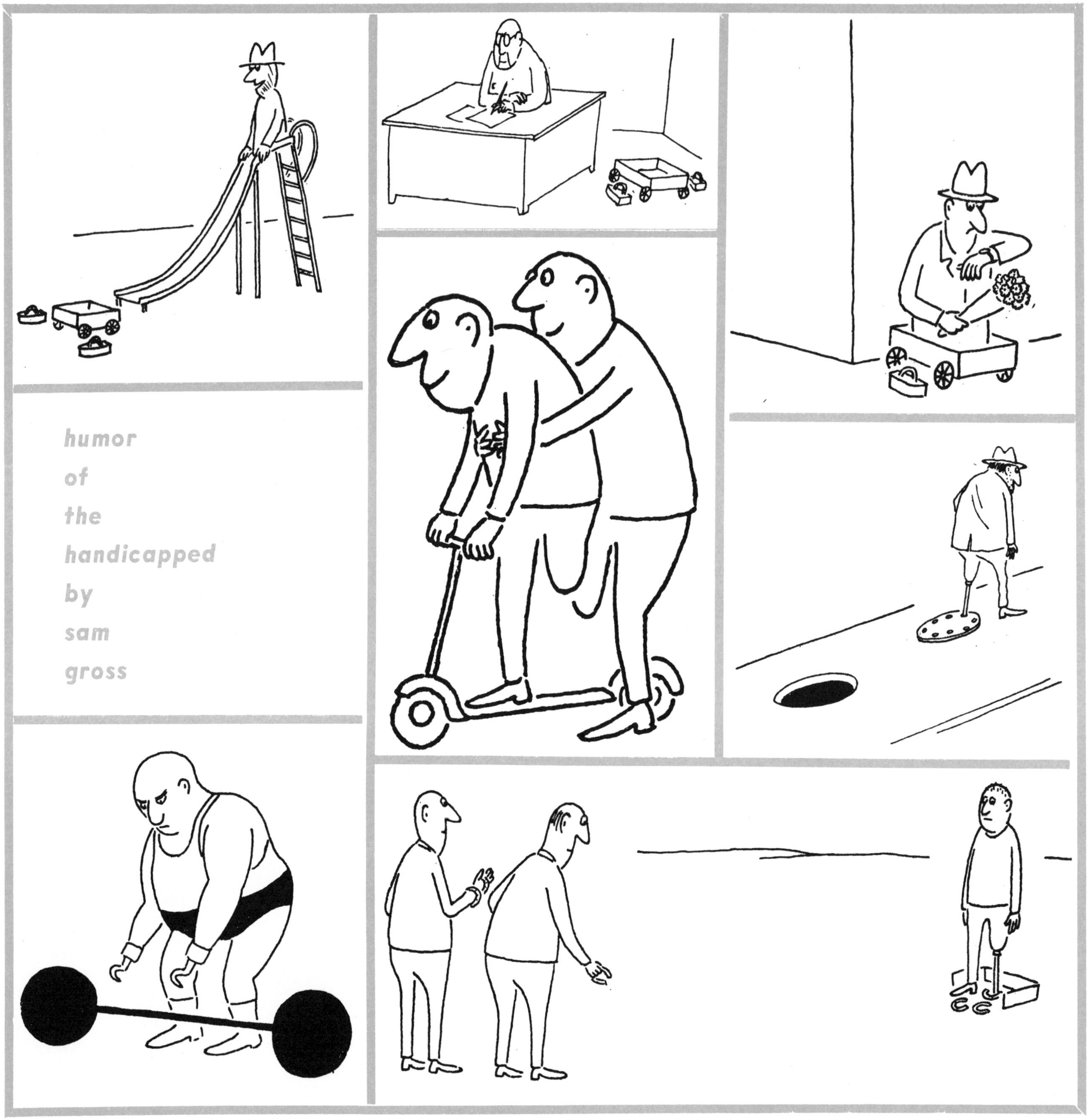
humor
of
the
handicapped
by
sam
gross

SAM GROSS. THE REALIST #51, JUNE 1964.

Terrace view
Apartments
Mort Gerberg

"You still interested in old man Burnhill's penthouse, sir?
I got word he's gonna die this week ..."

MORT GERBERG. THE REALIST #52, AUGUST 1964.

ALLIANCE FOR PROGRESS
IMPERIALISM
cieciorka

FRANK CIECIORKA. THE REALIST #51, JUNE 1964. *58

The Soviet Union's campaign to turn public opinion against Communist China has been so successful that Japanese citizens have complained that they are being abused by Russians mistaking them for Chinese.

Japanese sources report that their embassy in Moscow has been considering a proposal to require Japanese nationals to wear rising sun emblems so that they will not be taken as Chinese.

"The possibility is not excluded," said an embassy spokesman, "that such identification would become standard for Japanese in the U.S.S.R."

RICHARD GUINDON. THE REALIST #52, AUGUST 1964.

RICHARD GUINDON. THE REALIST #52, AUGUST 1964.

The Portable Goldwater

A BELIEVE-IT-OR-NOT COMPENDIUM OF **FACTS** THAT SHOULD BE READ BY **EVERY AMERICAN** WHO LOVES HIS COUNTRY.

FACT 1.

THE **FIRST** GOLDWATER ENTERPRISE IN AMERICA WAS A MINING TOWN SALOON DOWNSTAIRS FROM A **WHOREHOUSE!**

FACT 2. ONE **FOURTH OF JULY** AT THE AGE OF NINE, BARRY **EMPTIED A PISTOL** INTO THE CEILING OF HIS PARENTS BEDROOM!

FACT 3.

DURING THE SENATE CENSURE OF JOE MCCARTHY, **GOLDWATER**, IN AN EFFORT TO KEEP THE WISCONSIN SENATOR FROM MAKING ANY **FURTHER** INFLAMMATORY SPEECHES, WOULD **STEAL** THEM FROM HIS DESK!

FACT 4. BARRY GOLDWATER IS THE INVENTOR OF "ANTSY-PANTS" ANT-PATTERNED MENS SHORTS SOLD BY HIS DEPARTMENT STORE!

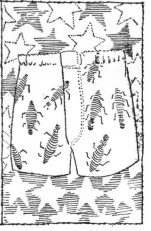

FACT 5.

SENATOR GOLDWATER HAS DEVISED A FLAGPOLE TO BE INSTALLED AT HIS HOME IN ARIZONA THAT RAISES AUTO-MATICALLY AT SUNRISE AND LOWERS ITSELF AT SUNSET PLAYING TAPS.

FACT 6.

SOMETIMES GOLDWATER CAN BE FOUND **SLEEPING** AT THE BOTTOM OF HIS **SWIMMING POOL** WITH AN AIR HOSE STUCK IN HIS MOUTH!

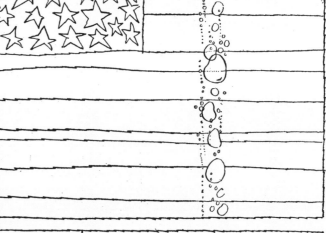

FACT 7.

SENATOR GOLDWATER HAS **FOUR DOTS** TATOOED ON HIS LEFT HAND WHICH IDENTIFY HIM AS A MEMBER OF A SMALL CLIQUE OF ARIZONA BUSINESSMEN CALLED THE SMOKI CLAN—INDIAN COSTUMED DANCERS WHO PERFORM WITH **LIVE BULL SNAKES!**

GUINDON

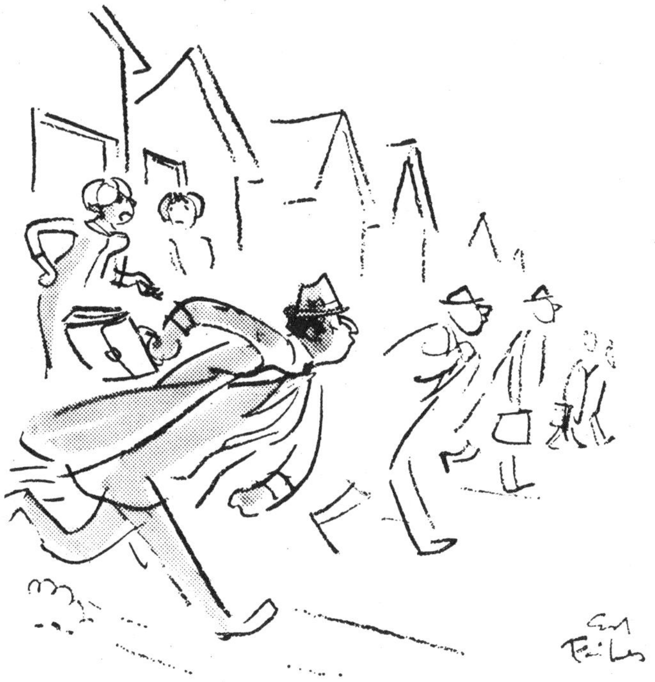

"I had thought that, being in the Mafia, he'd at least have different hours or something ..."

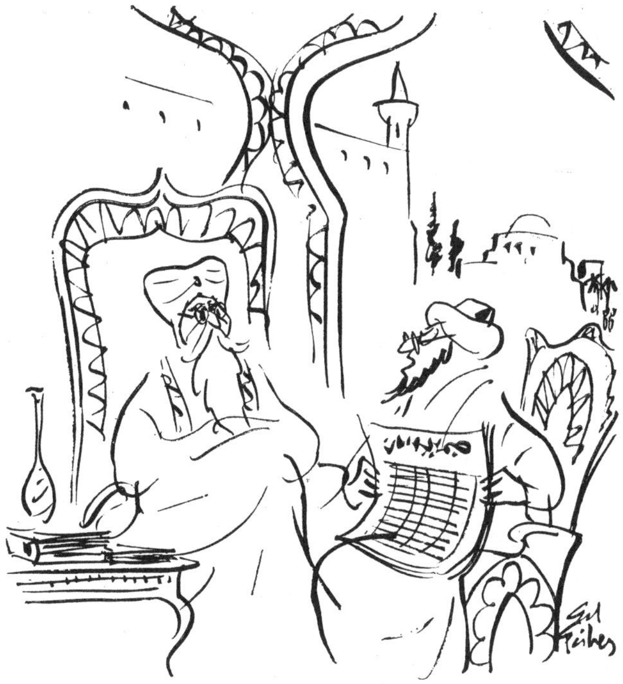

"Get this, Your Eminence — they're quitting the NAACP because they say it's 'white dominated.' Just what the hell do they think *we* are?"

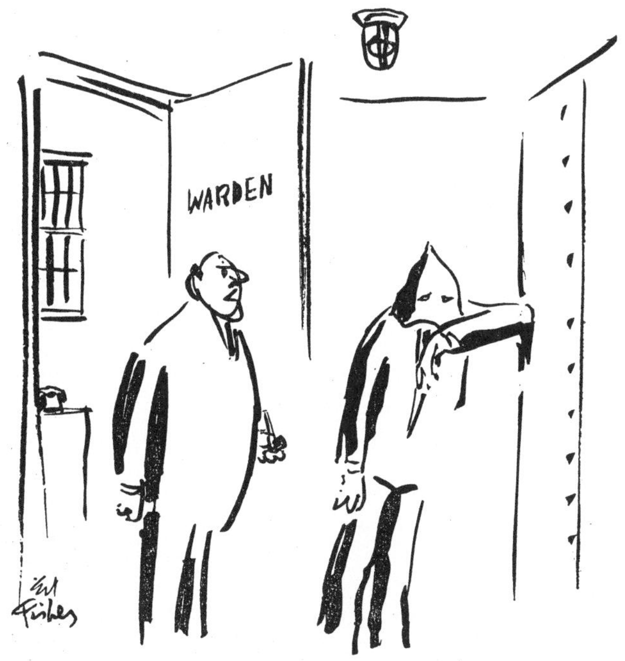
WARDEN

"You'll have to buck up, Swenson — there are lots of unemployed teen-agers who'd be happy to have your job!"

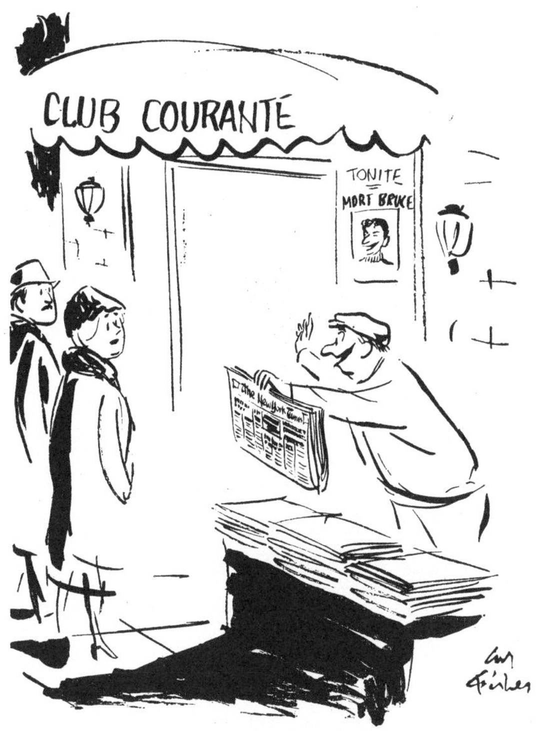
CLUB COURANTE
TONITE
MORT BRUKE

"Dig the topical humor in there, folks — buy the Times!"

ED FISHER. THE REALIST #52, AUGUST 1964.

". . . and therefore, my dear child, even though you have taken this drug not knowing that it would cause horrible deformities to your unborn baby, it is morally wrong for you to ask permission to be aborted and take this infant's life . . ."

". . . unfortunately, this state has abandoned drawing and quartering as punishment for a capital offense, but we do still have a way to deal with filthy, rotten, scum misfits like you, and I hereby sentence you to be hung by the neck until dead . . ."

HOWARD SHOEMAKER. THE REALIST #52, AUGUST 1964.

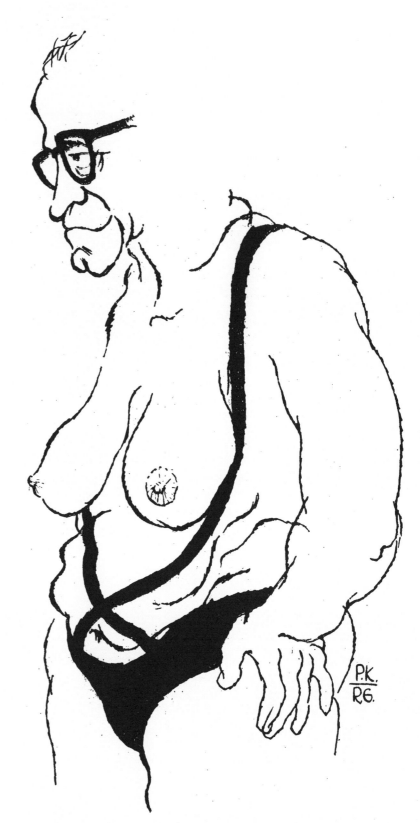

"I would remind you that extremism in the defense of liberty is no vice..."

RICHARD GUINDON. THE REALIST #53, SEPTEMBER 1964. *59

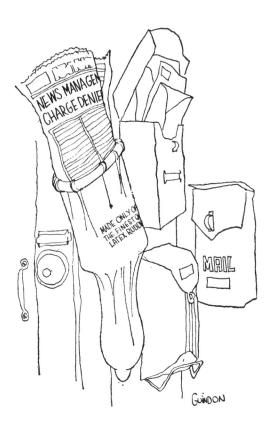

NEWS MANAGEN
CHARGE DENIE
MADE ONLY OF THE FINEST LATEX RUBB
MAIL
GUINDON

RICHARD GUINDON. THE REALIST #53, SEPTEMBER 1964.

PSYCHIATRIST
MORT GERBERG

MORT GERBERG. THE REALIST #53, SEPTEMBER 1964.

MISSOURI
GEORGIA
ILLINOIS
NEW YORK
ARIZO
FLORIDA
TEXAS
TODD

"Travel arrangements for participants on this program were made possible by American, Capitol, Eastern, TWA, BOAC, Pan-American Airlines; Pennsylvania, B. & O., New York Central, Union Pacific, Seaboard, Illinois Central Railroads, Greyhound, Trans-City Buses; Cunard, Grace Lines; Avis, Hertz Rent-a-Car. . . ."

TODD. THE REALIST #53, SEPTEMBER 1964.

A member of Israel's parliament says that the most serious problem confronting his nation is the integration of Oriental Jews into Israel's social, educational and economic life.

RICHARD GUINDON. THE REALIST #52, AUGUST 1964.

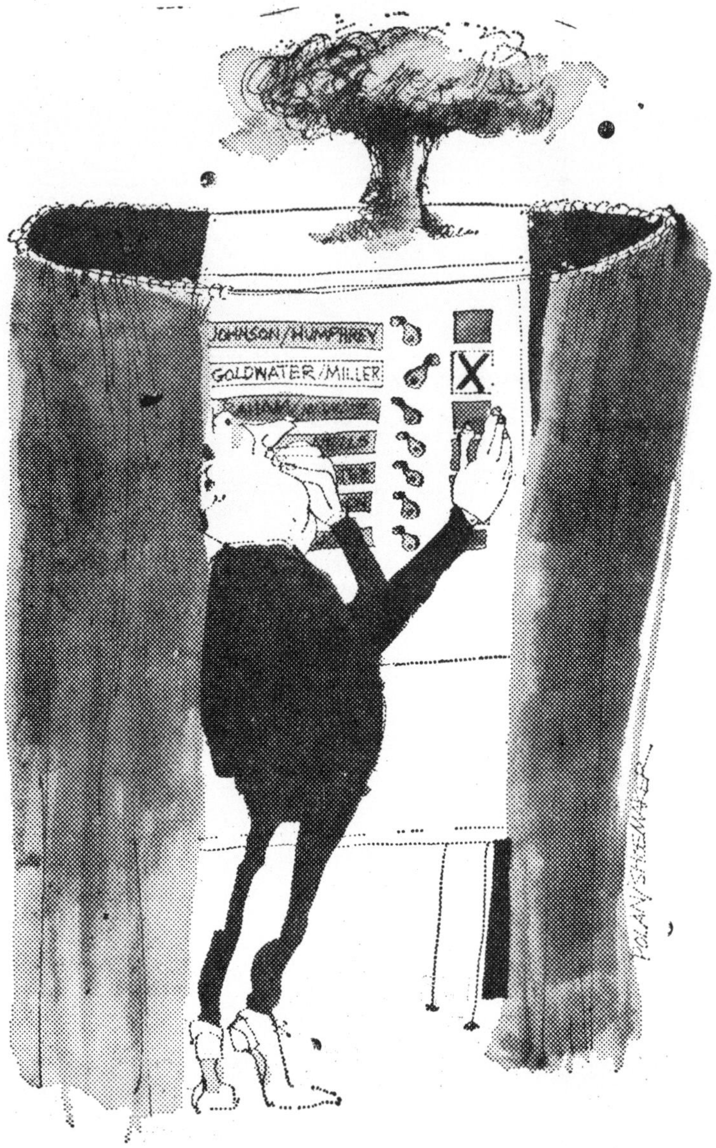
JOHNSON/HUMPHREY
GOLDWATER/MILLER

HOWARD SHOEMAKER. THE REALIST #54, NOVEMBER 1964. *60

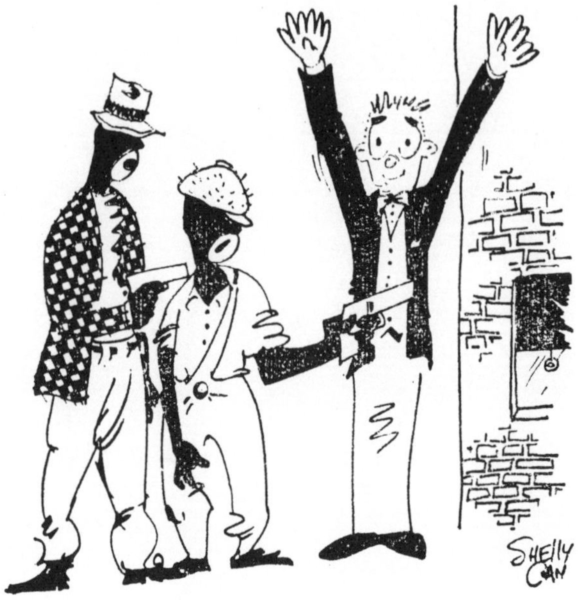
SHELLY CAN

"We shall overcome ..."

SHELLY CAN. THE REALIST #53, SEPTEMBER 1964.

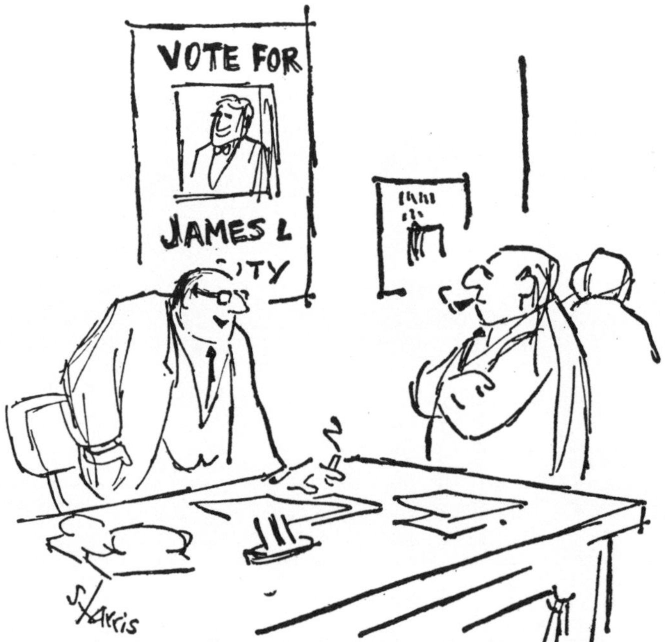
VOTE FOR
JAMES L

"Our boy has drive, ambition, know-how ...
he's a young Teddy Kennedy."

JOSEPH FARRIS. THE REALIST #54, NOVEMBER 1964.

RICHARD GUINDON.
THE REALIST #54,
NOVEMBER 1964.

Guindon Goes to a Reservation

This month there will be a dedication ceremony at the site of the recently completed Kinzua Dam, which is on the Allegheny River just over the New York State boundary into Pennsylvania. The Kinzua project is a scant 7½ miles downstream from a long, narrow piece of property which straddles the same river a mile wide for its 40-mile length called the Seneca Indian Reservation. The property is in the path of an artificial flood.

After the huge cement gates of the dam swing closed, the downward flow of the Allegheny will stop, back up and be sent spilling over its banks along its course, dispossessing some 482 Seneca Indians, turning their homesites into river bottom and their treaty into nothing more than a fine example of old government stationery.

The Pickering Treaty is not only the oldest Indian treaty in existence; it carried with it George Washington's personal guarantee, his word, that it would never be violated.

The Kinzua Dam was originally conceived as a flood control measure. At least that *was* the claim until the Seneca tribe brought in two engineers—Arthur E. Morgan, former president of the TVA, and Barton M. Jones, construction engineer for the same project—to see if some alternate plan couldn't be suggested. Their investigation found the Kinzua project to be something of a cement lemon. Perhaps more Tucker Torpedo than lemon, as it was incapable of filling its claims as a flood control device.

A new plan was submitted, estimated at half the cost of Kinzua. They had found a circle of hills, a natural reservoir that could control the water by simply diverting the river a short distance into the pocket. And, incidentally, no one need move his homesite to make way for the new plan. The treaty could be kept. *Could have been kept* is more correct, because the new

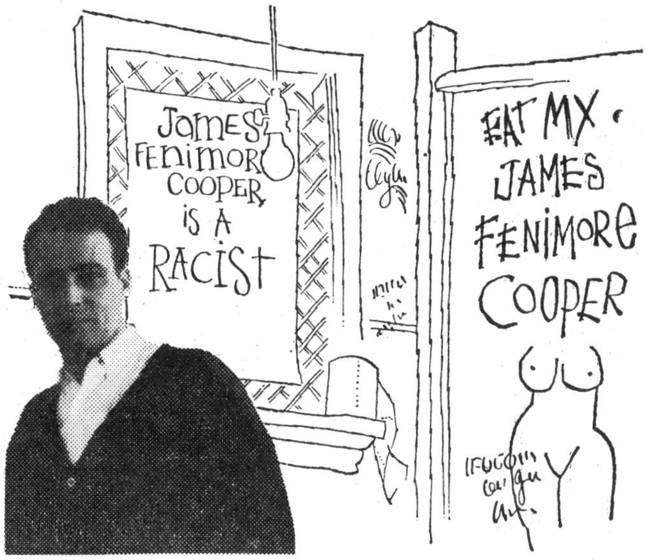
JAMES FENIMORE COOPER IS A RACIST
EAT MY JAMES FENIMORE COOPER

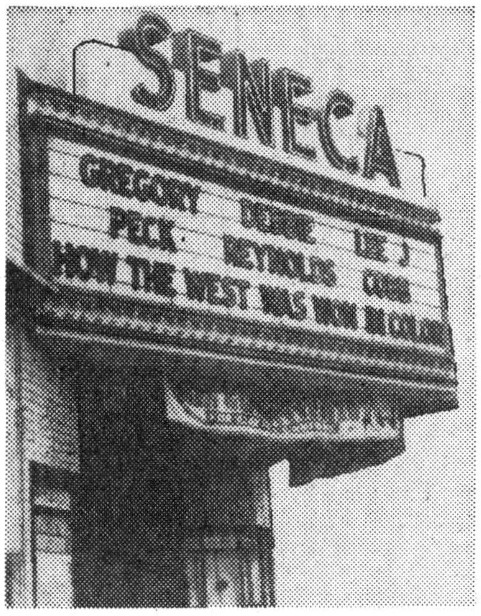
SENECA
GREGORY PECK DEBBIE REYNOLDS LEE J COBB
HOW THE WEST WAS WON IN COLOR

Salamanca, N. Y.: Built and occupied by whites on land leased from the Senecas. "Outsiders who have lived in the town say the whole place is rather neurotic, that is, suffers from a sense of frustration, on account of having Indians as landlords."—Edmund Wilson

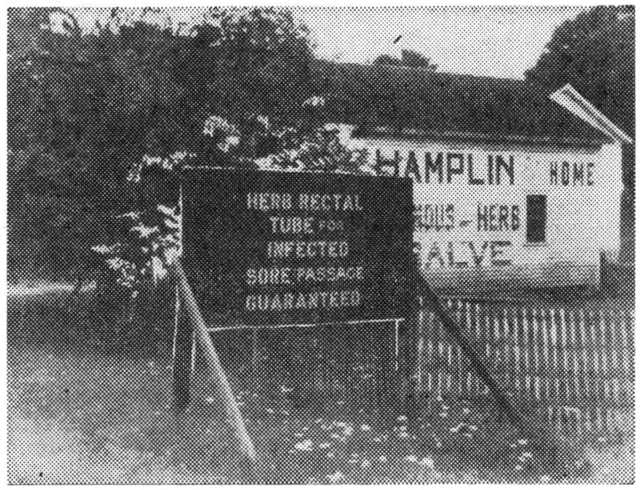
HERB RECTAL TUBE FOR INFECTED SORE PASSAGE GUARANTEED
HAMPLIN HOME
SALVE

Welcome to Salamanca

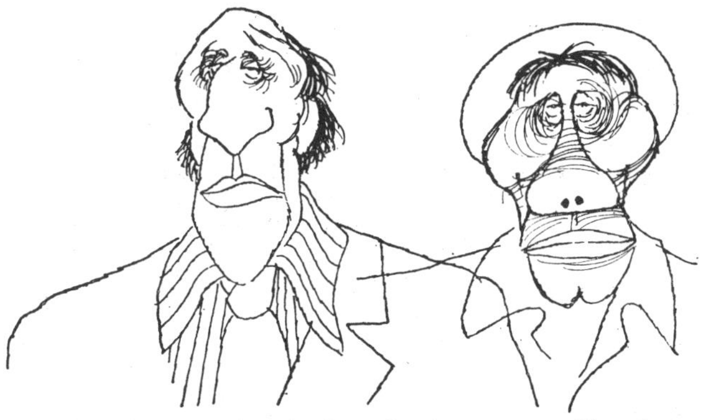

"I don't know how we'd feel about a cartoon like that—I guess we'd have to see it first. You say it would have the corps of Army engineers screwing an Indian?"

There are twice as many Negroes in Harlem as there are Indians in the United States

"We don't picket because it's un-Indian, that's why! How come the NAACP don't make somebody an honorary Negro?"

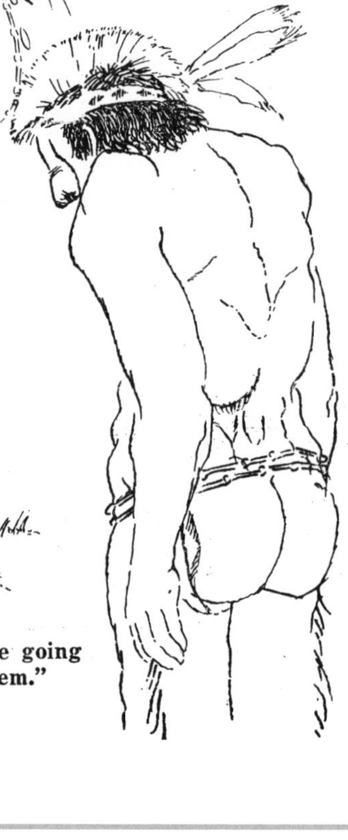

plan was rejected.

An ulterior motive was discovered by somebody* in the form of a lobby in Washington. The lobby represented a group of Pennsylvania coal mine owners who wanted to see the Kinzua Project go through. They had use for a dam. It seems they have a problem with sulfa drainage from their mines into the Allegheny River. Unless the water level is kept high enough to dilute it, the processing equipment pipes become corroded.

It has been estimated that the individual mines could install equipment to circumvent this problem at a cost of 3-to-4 thousand dollars. Our government was able to bring the Kinzua Dam project—ribbon, scissors and all—for $114,000,000. Now, about this problem of creeping socialism that private industry worries so much about. . . .

—DICK GUINDON

---

*Edmund Wilson in his book *Apologies to the Iroquois* mentioned that some "deeper digging" disclosed the lobby, but he didn't say who did the digging.

(Among a few of the Iroquois, however, there is a militant nationalist movement.)

"It's still not Indian, it's got to be a *real Indian* symbol!"

"The idea behind adopting, say, a Lady Bird Johnson into the tribe is that we hope when the word gets out she's an Indian, they'll grab some of *her* land."

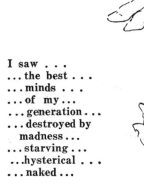

". . . Next year Herb and I are going to spend our two weeks in Harlem."

I saw . . .
. . . the best . . .
. . . minds . . .
. . . of my . . .
. . . generation . . .
. . . destroyed by
    madness . . .
. . . starving . . .
. . . hysterical . . .
. . . naked . . .

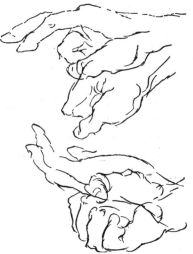

"White man's medicine has brought us many good things—treatment for measles . . . smallpox . . . syphilis. . . ."

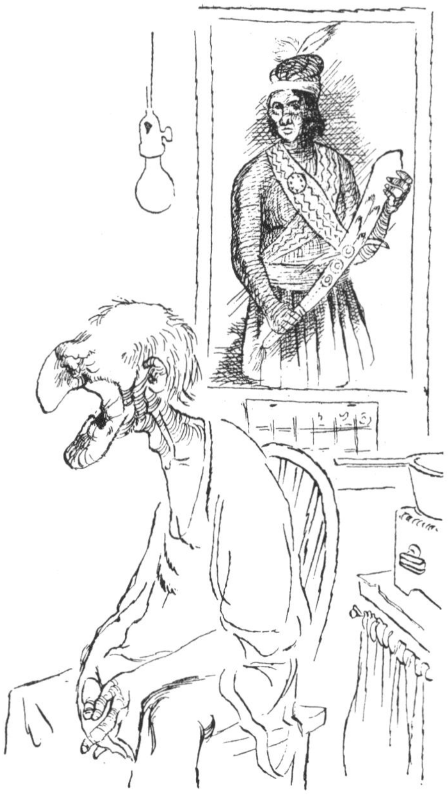

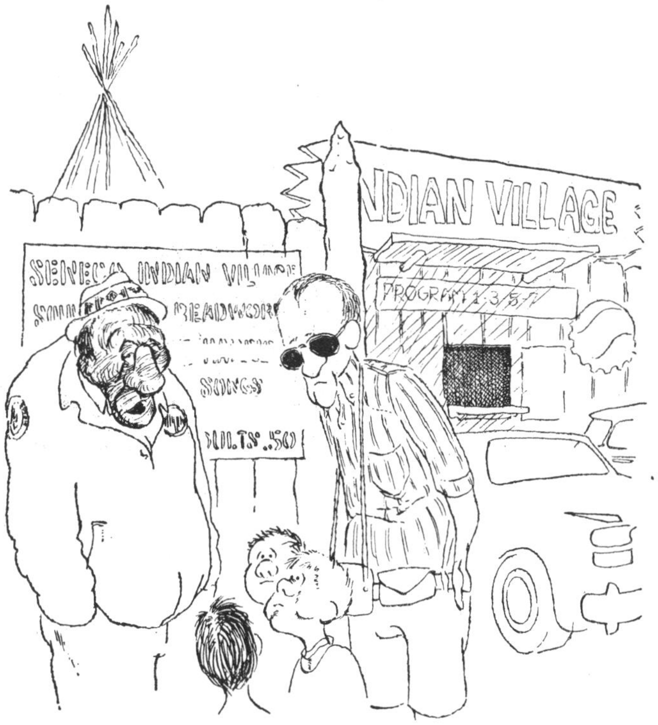
PROGRAM 1-3-5-7
SONGS

"An Indian reservation is where you reserve Indians, you never know when you might need one."

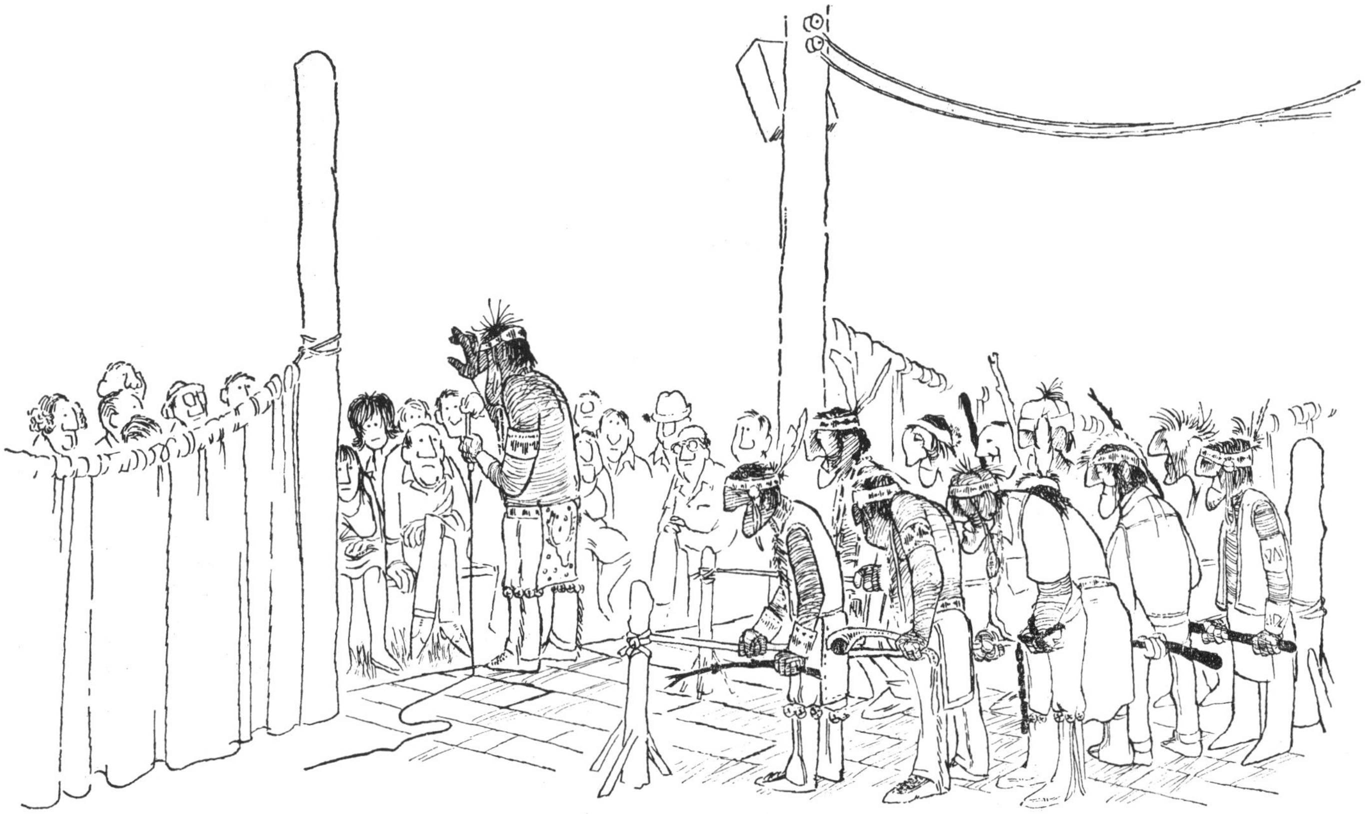

"We need a volunteer for the next number—a runner. . . . Have we got any runners out there?"

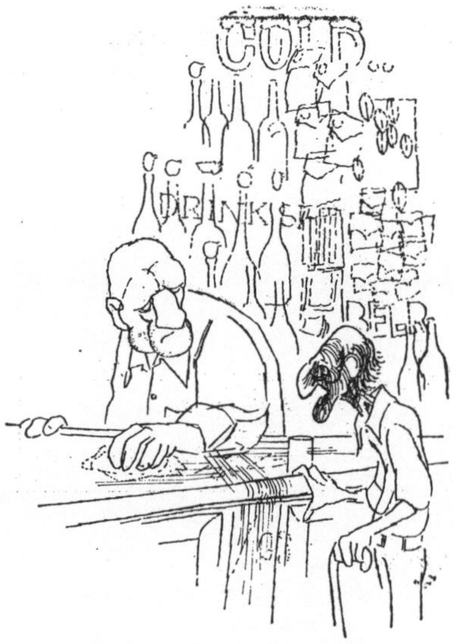

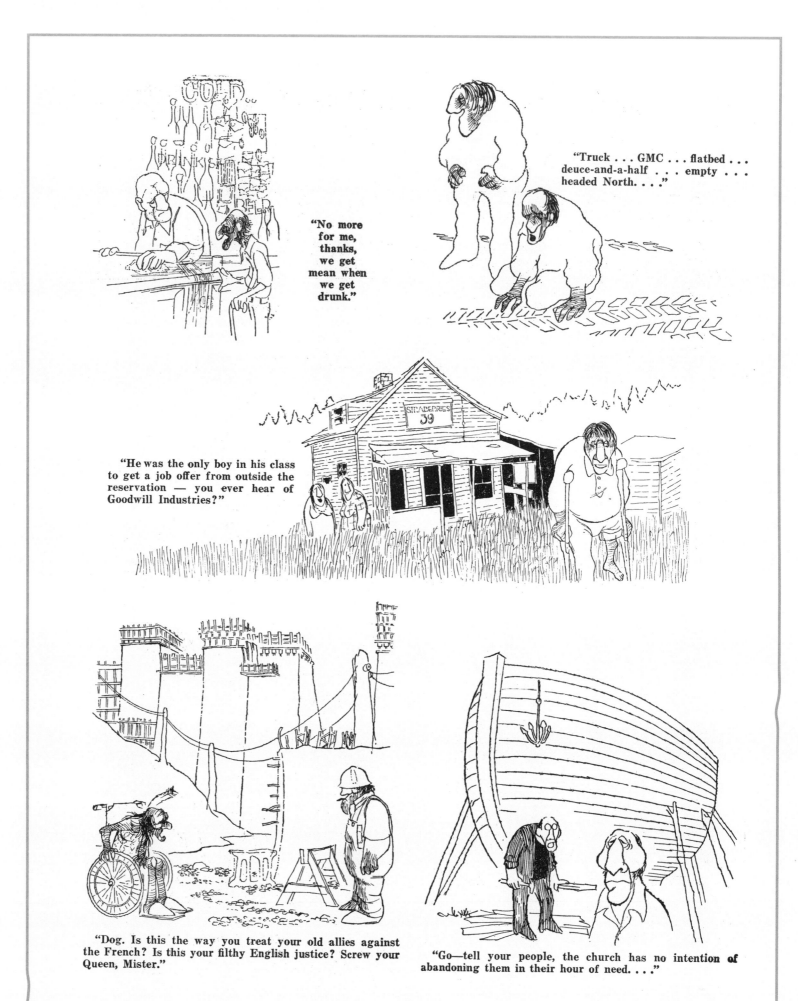

"No more for me, thanks, we get mean when we get drunk."

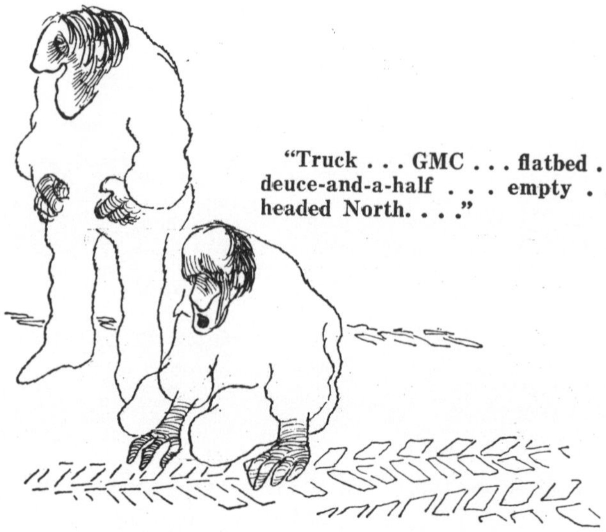

"Truck . . . GMC . . . flatbed . . . deuce-and-a-half . . . empty . . . headed North. . . ."

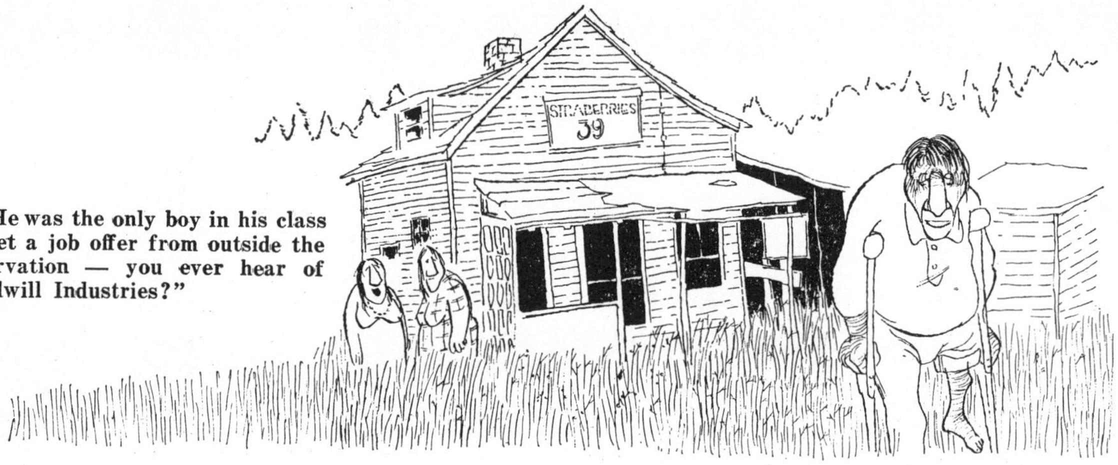
STRABERRIES
39

"He was the only boy in his class to get a job offer from outside the reservation — you ever hear of Goodwill Industries?"

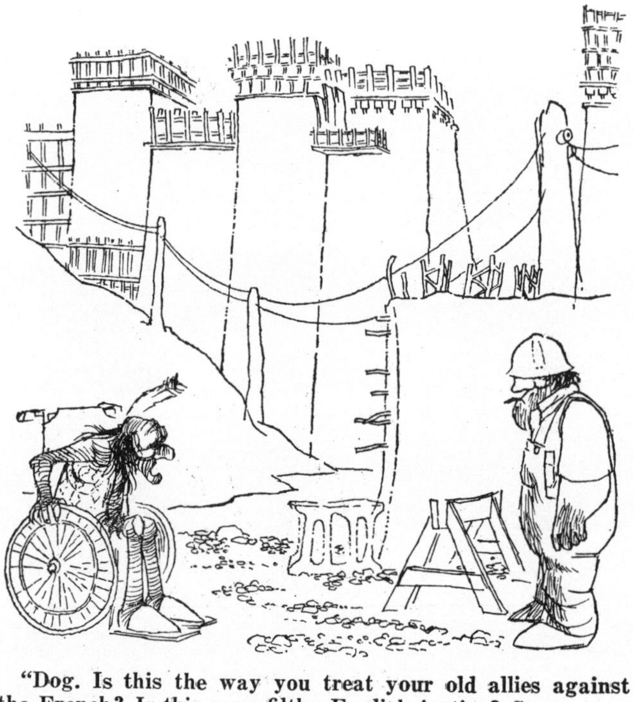

"Dog. Is this the way you treat your old allies against the French? Is this your filthy English justice? Screw your Queen, Mister."

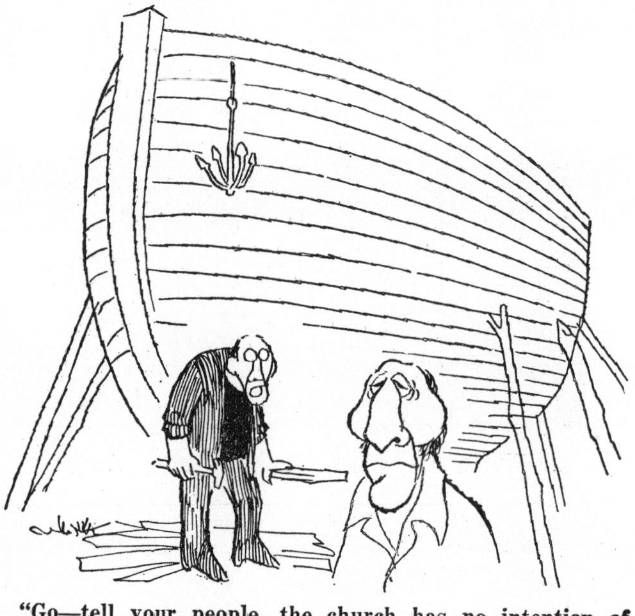

"Go—tell your people, the church has no intention of abandoning them in their hour of need. . . ."

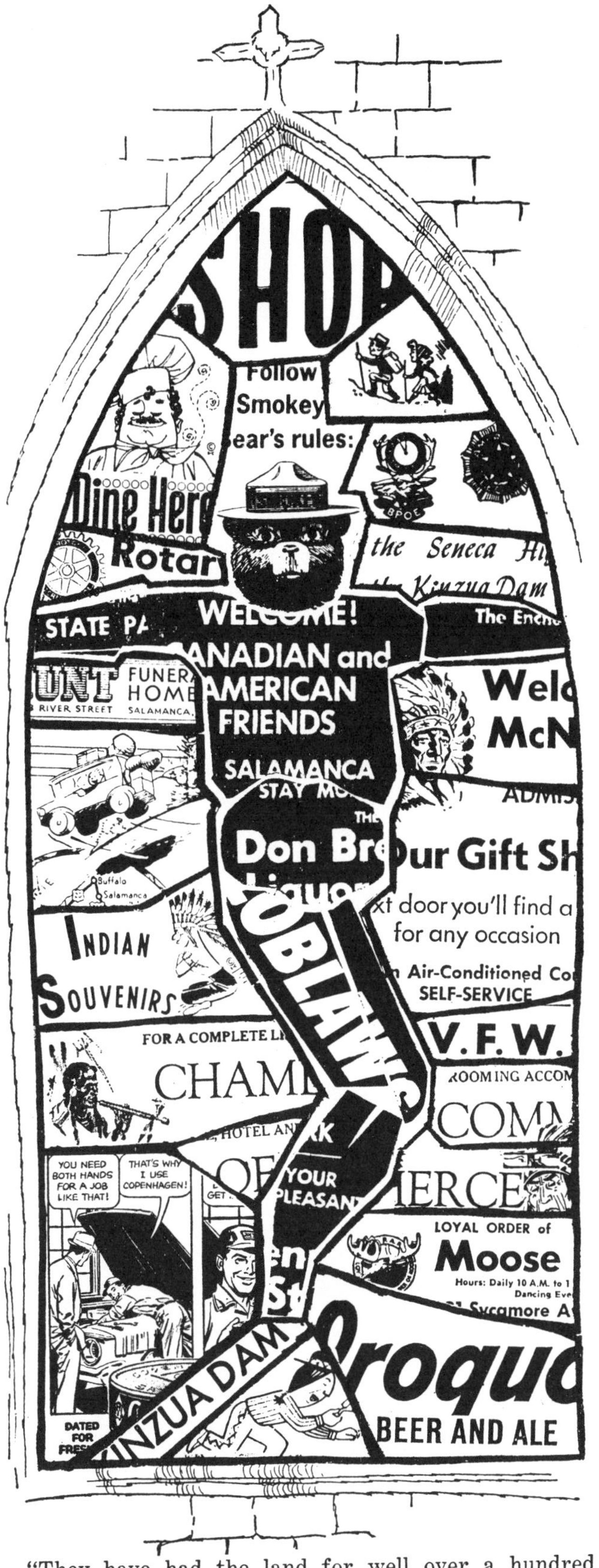
Follow
Smokey
ear's rules:
Dine Here
Rotar
the Seneca
WELCOME!
STATE PA
NADIAN and
AMERICAN
FRIENDS
SALAMANCA
FUNER
HOME
RIVER STREET
SALAMANCA
Welc
McN
Don Br
Our Gift Sh
xt door you'll find a
for any occasion
Air-Conditioned Co
SELF-SERVICE
INDIAN
SOUVENIRS
V. F. W.
FOR A COMPLETE LI
CHAM
COMM
HOTEL AN
ROOMING ACCOM
YOUR
PLEASAN
ERCE
YOU NEED BOTH HANDS FOR A JOB LIKE THAT!
THAT'S WHY I USE COPENHAGEN!
LOYAL ORDER of
Moose
Sycamore A
INZUA DAM
BEER AND ALE
DATED FOR

"They have had the land for well over a hundred years, and what have they done with it? Absolutely nothing."

—anonymous Salamanca resident
Salamanca Republican-Press

Women, children and Americans first

Everybody feels free to attack democracy:
"Up the Republic and down your semantic!"
"Send a Bishop to college."
"Put the 'Oligarch' back in 'Office.'"
"Wherever two or three are gathered together,
there Polity is."
"Democracy is the illusion of responsibility
built on the delusion of power."
Ah, they're endless.
I say go back to Russia
Go back to Germany, go back, go back all of you.
Leave me alone with the Indians a minute.
I think I can teach them how to repel
a beach landing.

—Paul Encimer

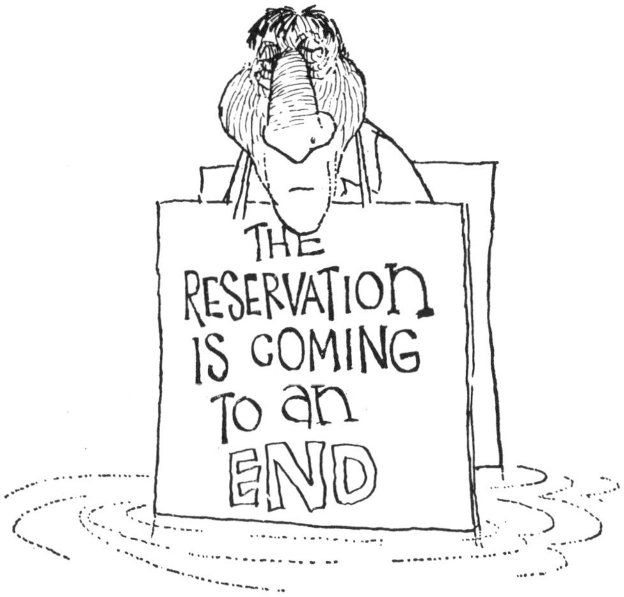
THE RESERVATION IS COMING TO AN END

"We, and they, are different in this respect. We keep our word. . . .

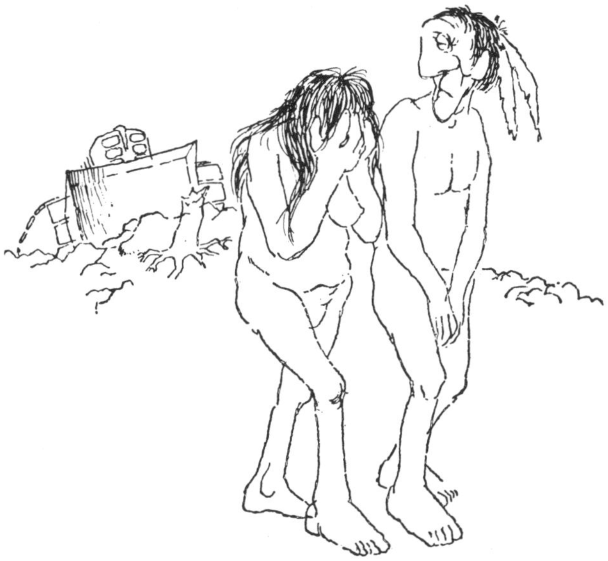

. . . The long and perfidious Communist record of breaking agreements and treaties proves that the Soviet Union will not keep any agreement that is not to its advantage to keep."

—Barry Goldwater

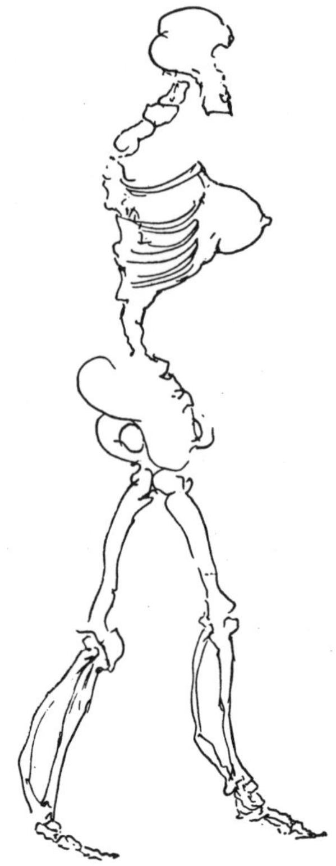

The Dying Star

RICHARD GUINDON. THE REALIST #54, NOVEMBER 1964.

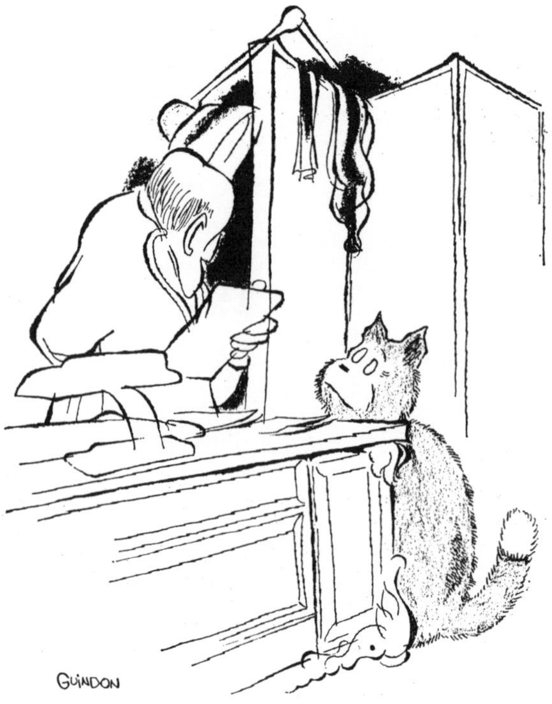
GUINDON

"Well, little lady ... today we learn
a new word — menopause."

RICHARD GUINDON. THE REALIST #54, NOVEMBER 1964.

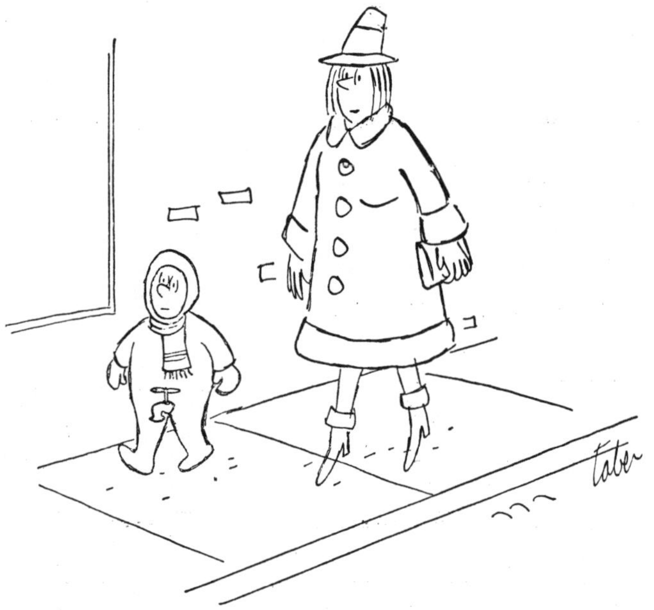

SAM GROSS. THE REALIST #54, NOVEMBER 1964.

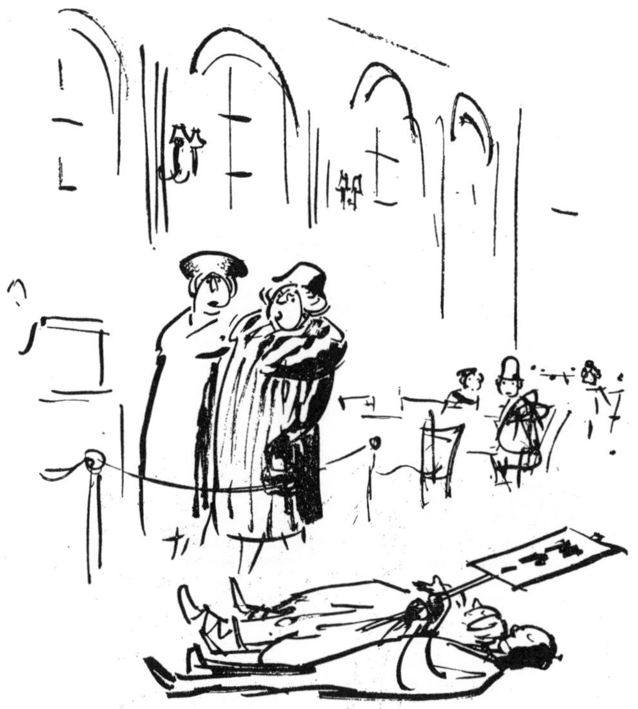

"Really! — in *Schrafft's?*"

ED FISHER. THE REALIST #54, NOVEMBER 1964.

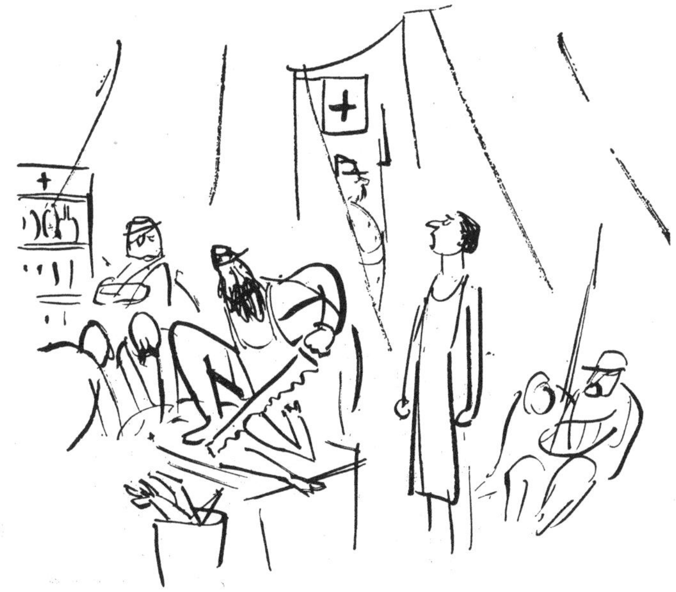

"Sir, as a conscientious objector I insist on being transferred out of the Medical Corps!"

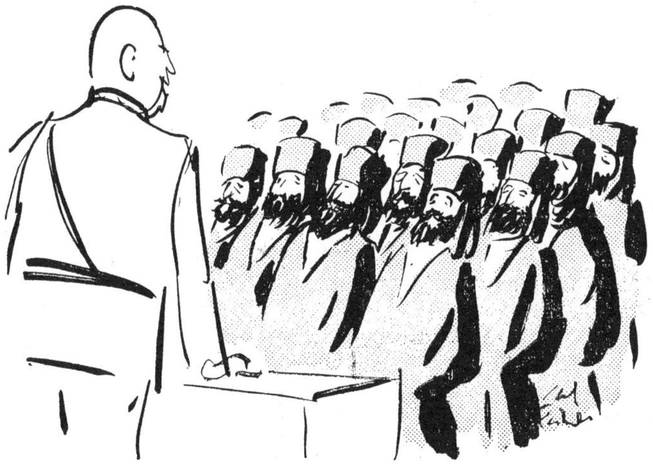

"Your job will be to sow confusion on the Cyprus Question ..."

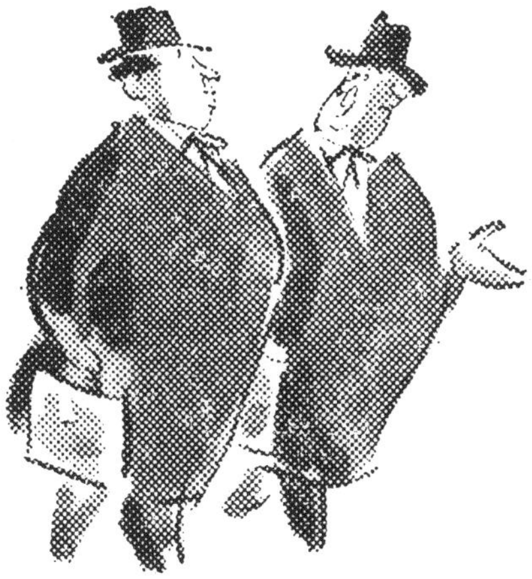

"The phone lobby has a great answer to the Religion in Schools controversy: Why not give each kid 15 minutes a day to dial-a-prayer?"

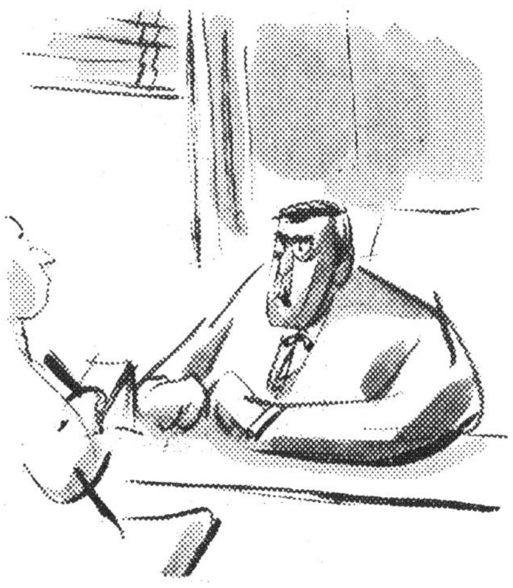

"I'll support him — provided he *doesn't* 'clarify' his views."

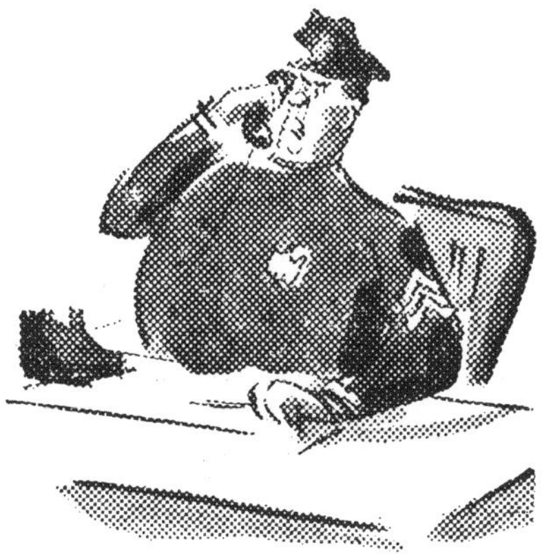

"What! Pick up Lenny Bruce again? G—*!!¢%! D—#*!●%M*F/ /S—=! ≈¢#½!!?. . . ."**

ED FISHER. THE REALIST #54, NOVEMBER 1964.

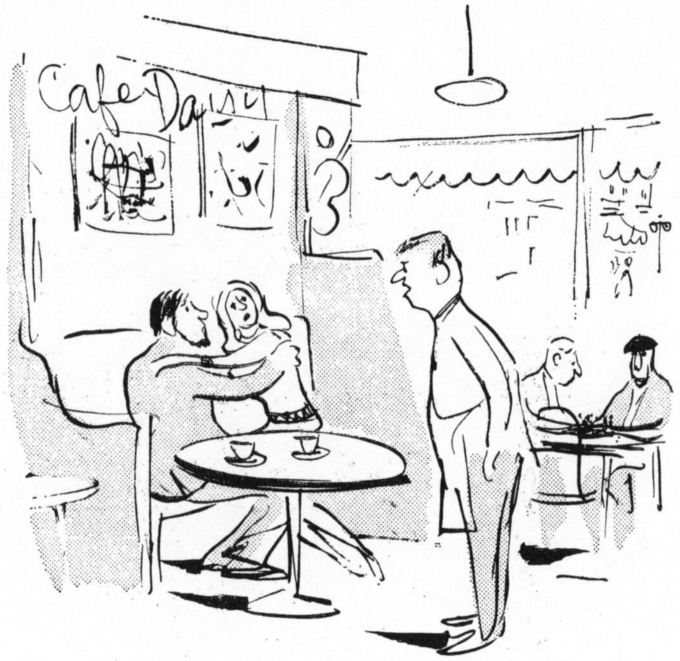

"Please, kids — I'm trying to get the place known as a homosexual hangout."

ED FISHER. THE REALIST #54, NOVEMBER 1964.

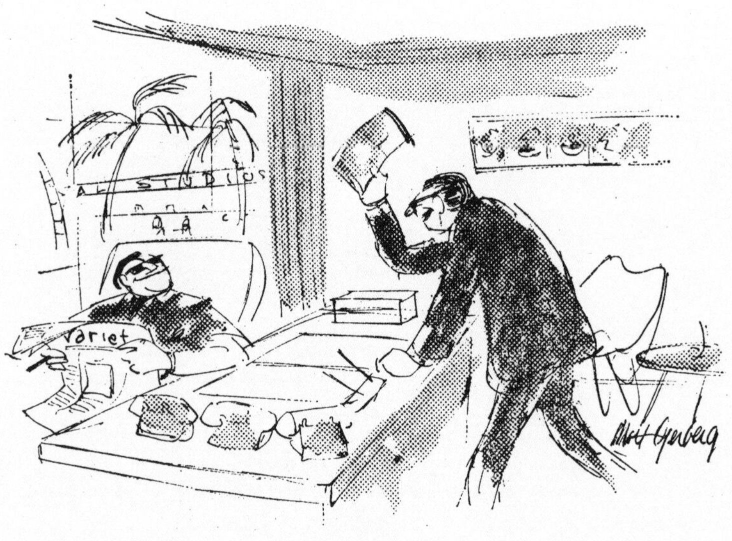
Variety
Mort Gerberg

"We've done it, B.J.! We got the option for a musical version of the Warren Report!"

MORT GERBERG. THE REALIST #55, DECEMBER 1964. *61

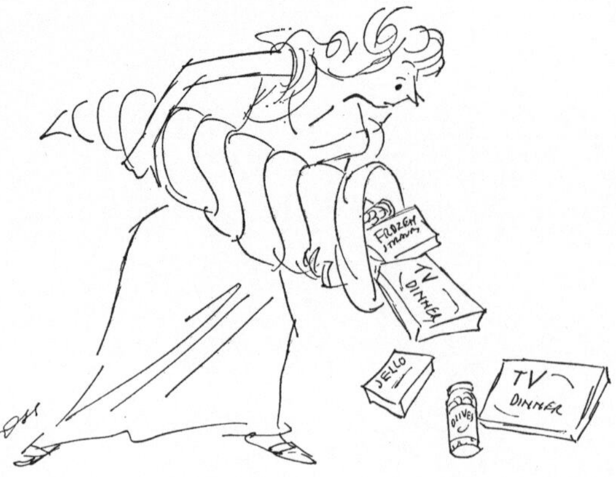
TV DINNER
JELLO
TV DINNER
Ross

AL ROSS. THE REALIST #55, DECEMBER 1964.

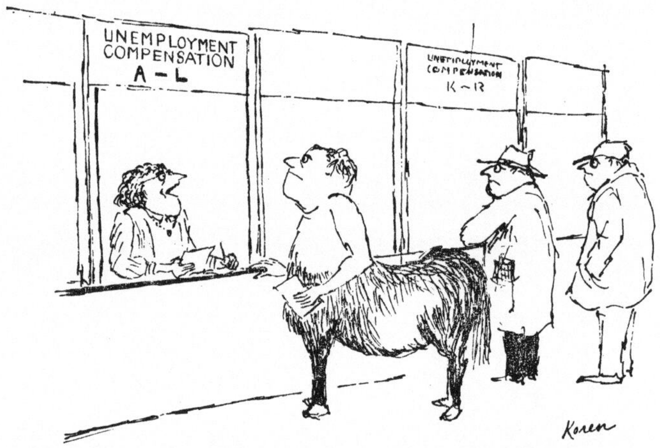
UNEMPLOYMENT COMPENSATION
A – L
UNEMPLOYMENT COMPENSATION
K – R
Koren

EDWARD KOREN. THE REALIST #55, DECEMBER 1964.

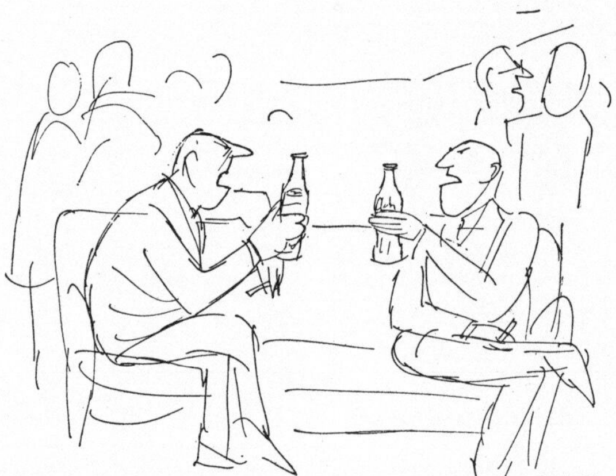
Ross

"Have a Pepsi!" "Have a Coke!"

AL ROSS. THE REALIST #55, DECEMBER 1964.

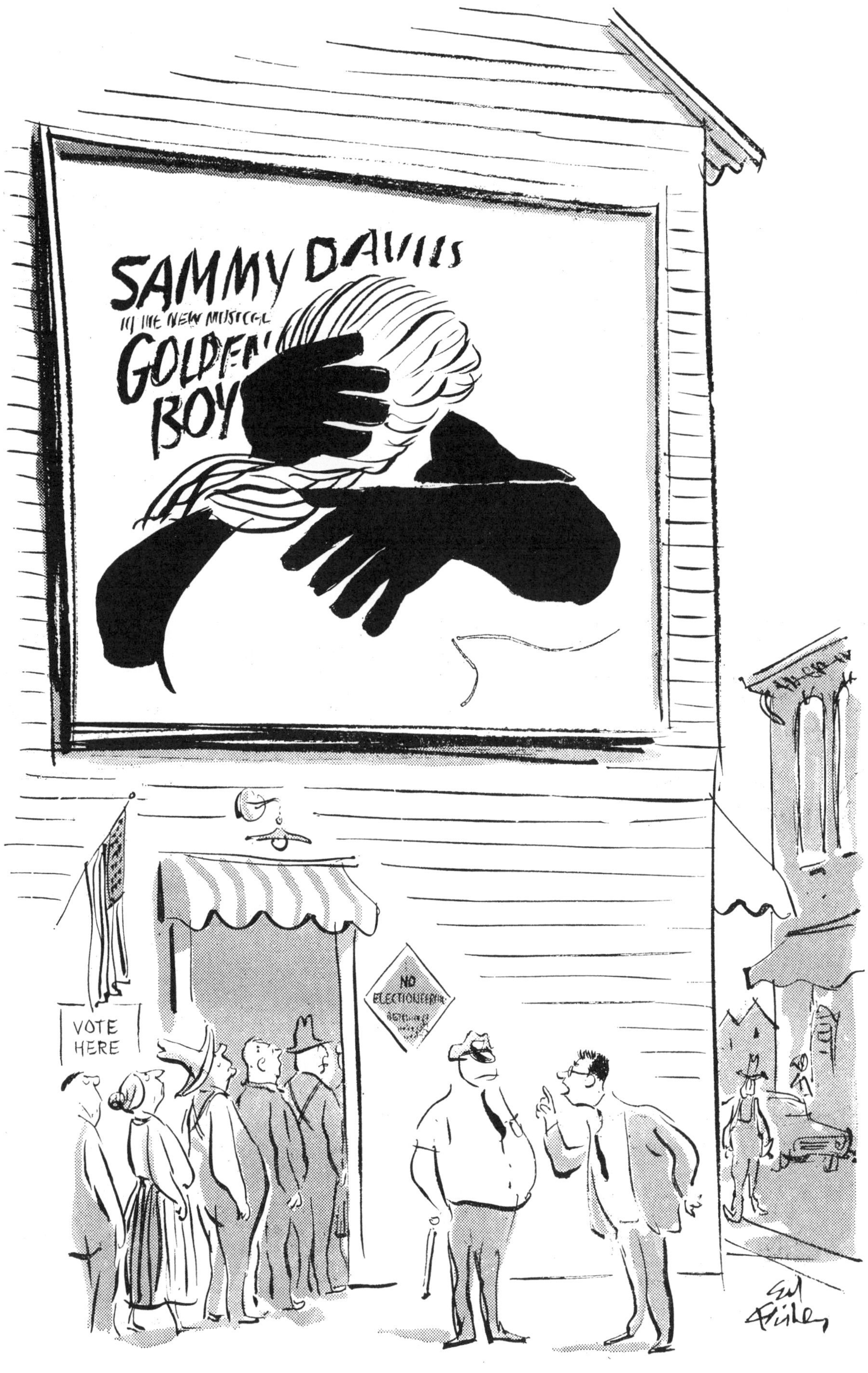
SAMMY DAVIS
VOTE
HERE
Ed Fisher

"—And I say it *is* electioneering!"

ED FISHER. THE REALIST #54, NOVEMBER 1964.

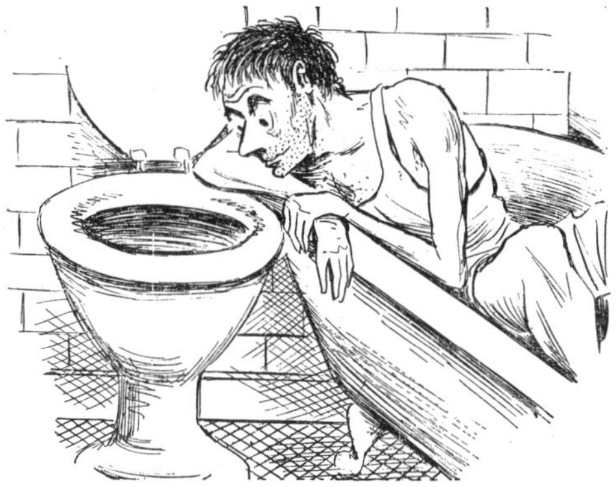

THE REALIST #54, NOVEMBER 1964.

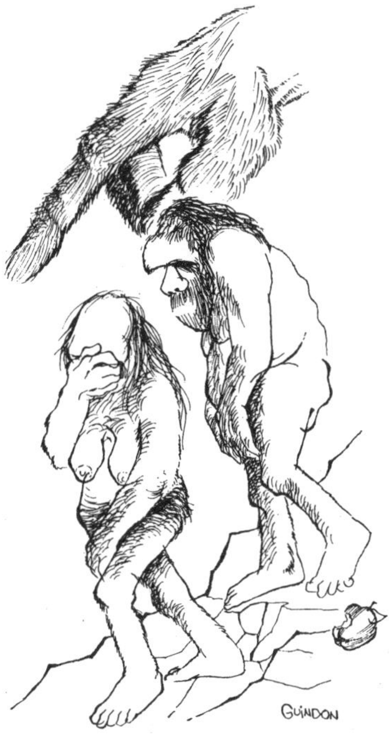
GUINDON

NEWS ITEM: In Texas a vote by the State Board of Education to adopt five controversial textbooks was in effect a rejection of charges that the books teach evolution in an atheistic manner.

RICHARD GUINDON. THE REALIST #55, DECEMBER 1964.

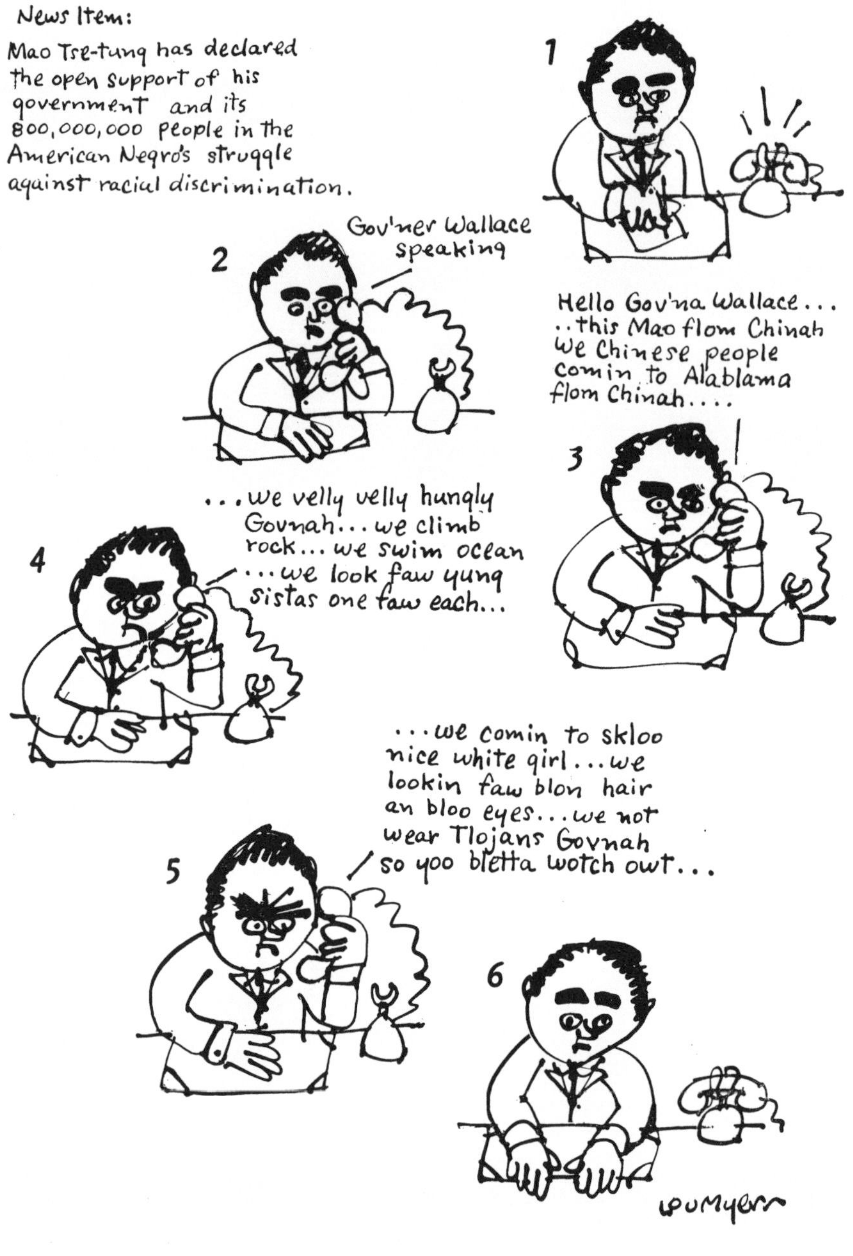
News Item:
Mao Tse-tung has declared the open support of his government and its 800,000,000 people in the American Negro's struggle against racial discrimination.
1
2
Gov'ner Wallace speaking
Hello Gov'na Wallace... ..this Mao flom Chinah We Chinese people comin to Alablama flom Chinah....
3
4
...we velly velly hungly Govnah... we climb rock... we swim ocean ...we look faw yung sistas one faw each...
5
...we comin to skloo nice white girl...we lookin faw blon hair an bloo eyes...we not wear Tlojans Govnah so yoo bletta wotch owt...
6
LouMyers

LOU MYERS. THE REALIST #55, DECEMBER 1964.

the inquiring cartoonist

QUESTION: How do you feel about Jean-Paul Sartre refusing the Nobel Prize and the $53,000 that goes with it?

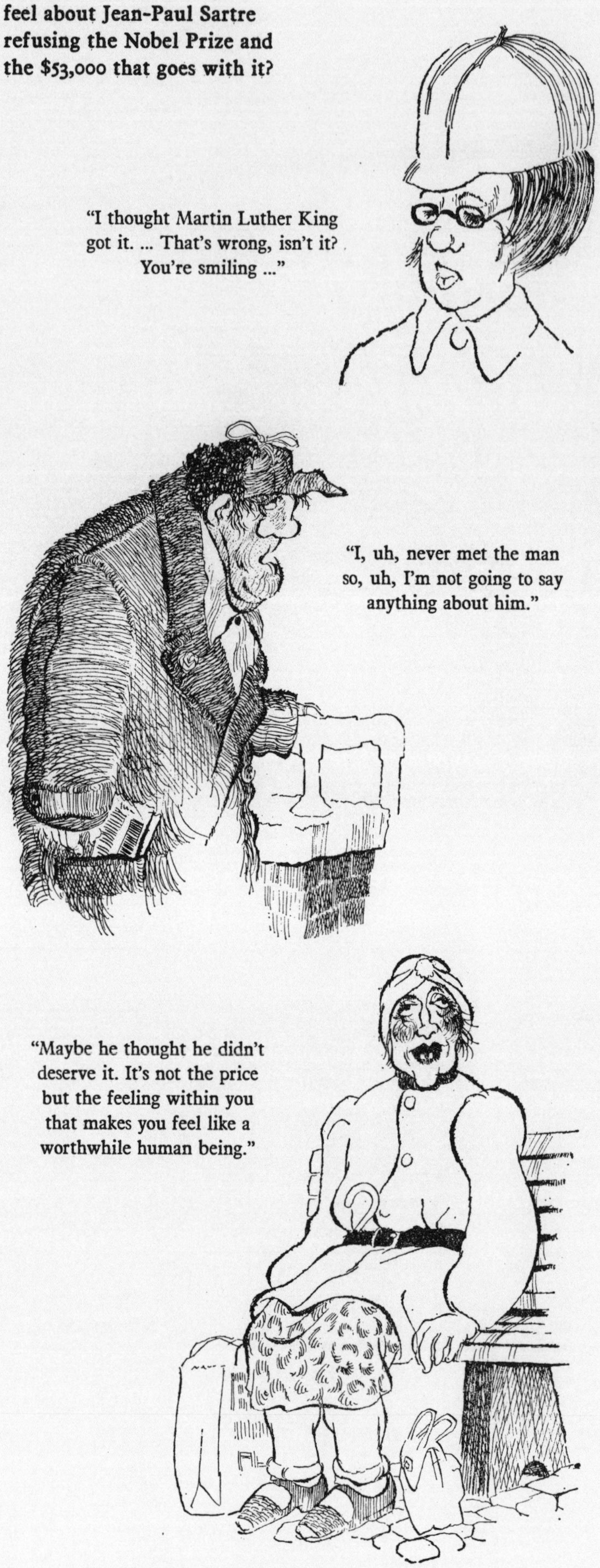
"I thought Martin Luther King got it. ... That's wrong, isn't it? You're smiling ..."
"I, uh, never met the man so, uh, I'm not going to say anything about him."
"Maybe he thought he didn't deserve it. It's not the price but the feeling within you that makes you feel like a worthwhile human being."

RICHARD GUINDON. THE REALIST #55, DECEMBER 1964.

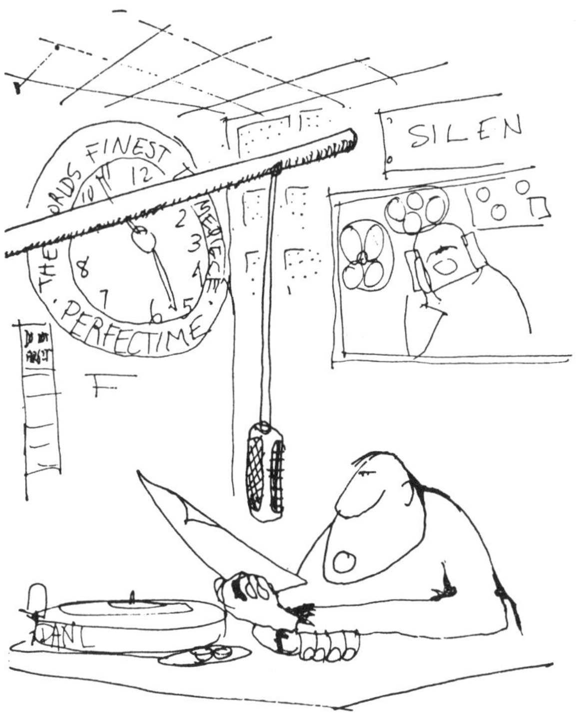
SILEN
FINEST
PERFECTIME

"Remember the real meaning of Christmas this year. Attend the church or synagogue of your choice."

THE REALIST #55, DECEMBER 1964.

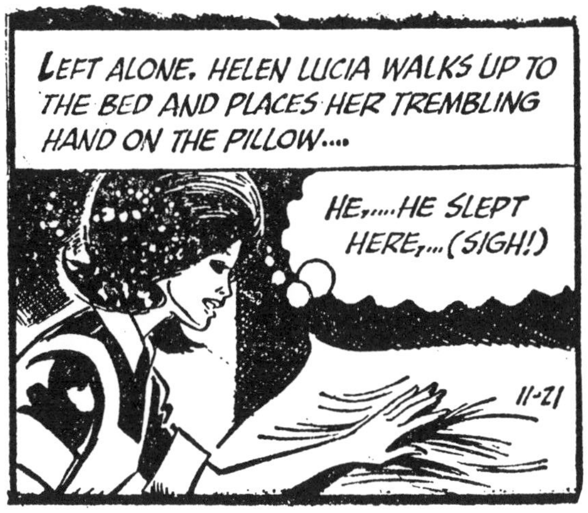
LEFT ALONE, HELEN LUCIA WALKS UP TO THE BED AND PLACES HER TREMBLING HAND ON THE PILLOW....
HE,...HE SLEPT HERE,...(SIGH!)
11-21

Pop Fetishism

DALE MESSICK. THE REALIST #55, DECEMBER 1964. *62

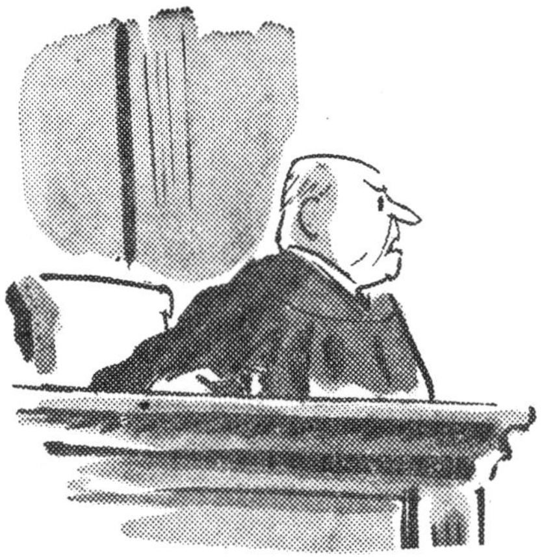

"Before I pass sentence on you, Lenny Bruce, is there anything you wish to say — anything printable, that is?"

ED FISHER. THE REALIST #55, DECEMBER 1964.

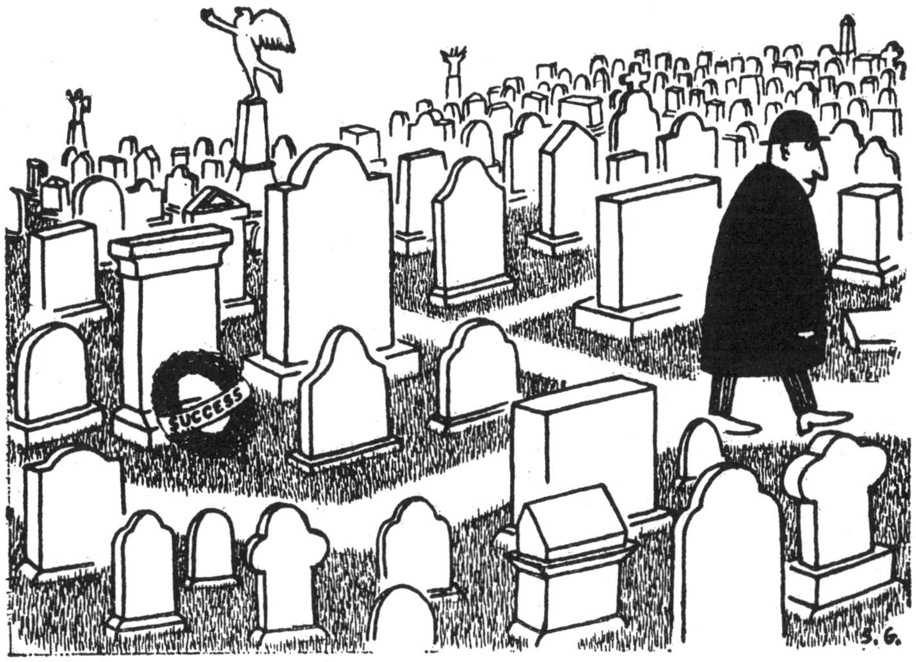
SUCCESS
S.G.

SAM GROSS. THE REALIST #55, DECEMBER 1964.

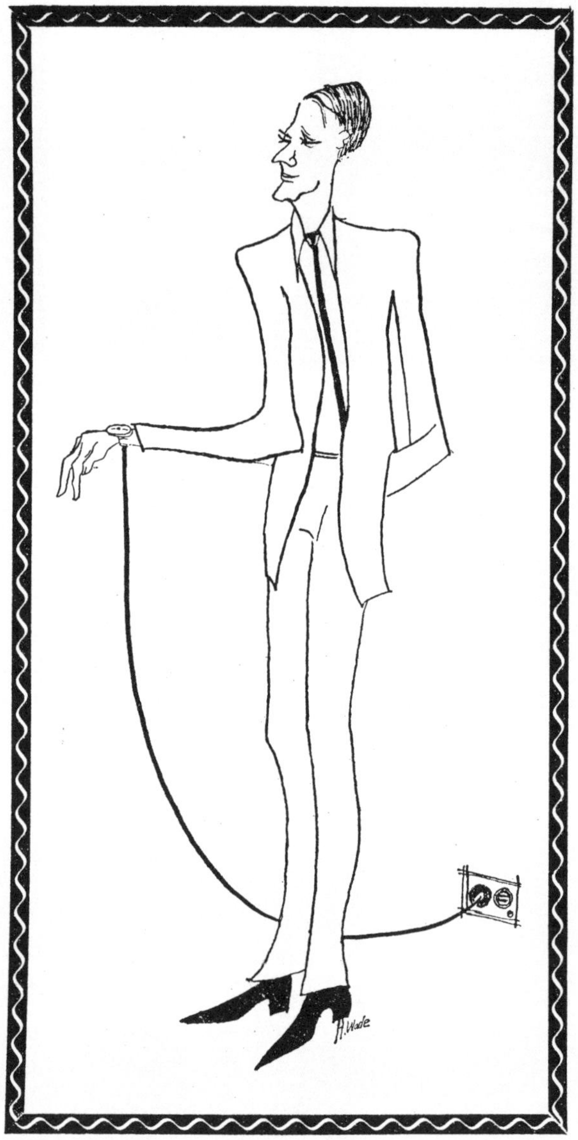

THE REALIST #55, DECEMBER 1964

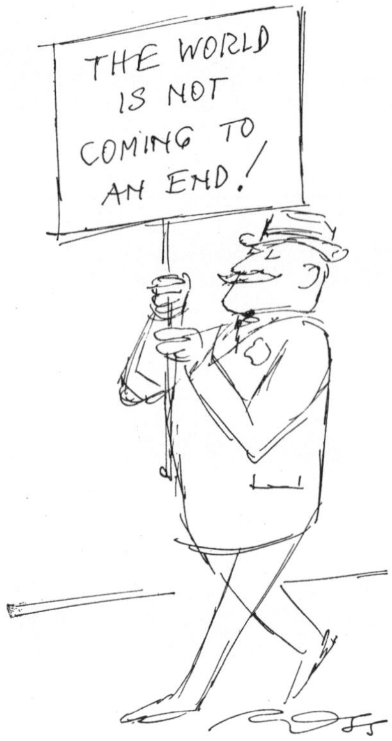
THE WORLD
IS NOT
COMING TO
AN END!

AL ROSS. THE REALIST #55, DECEMBER 1964.

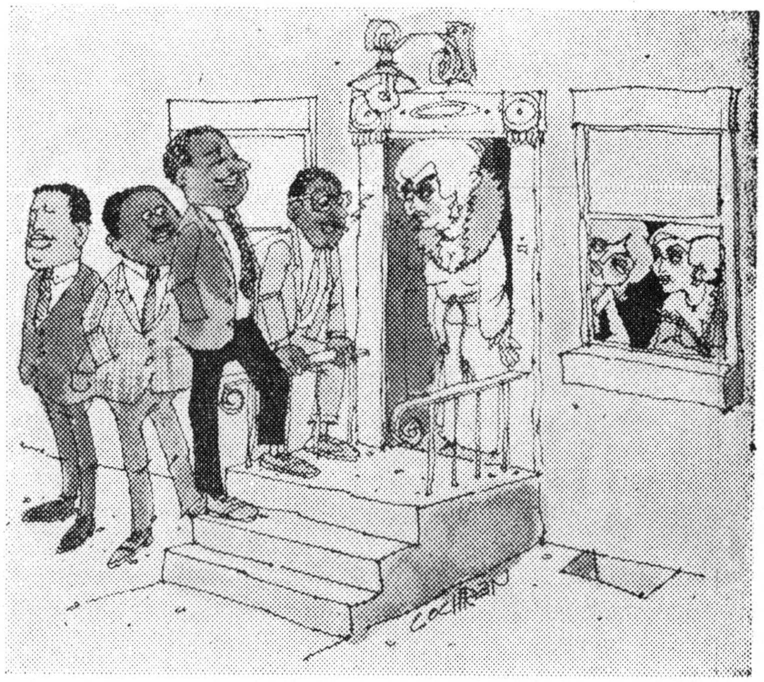

"No, ma'am—this isn't a *sit*-in..."

COCHRAN. THE REALIST #56, FEBRUARY 1965. *63

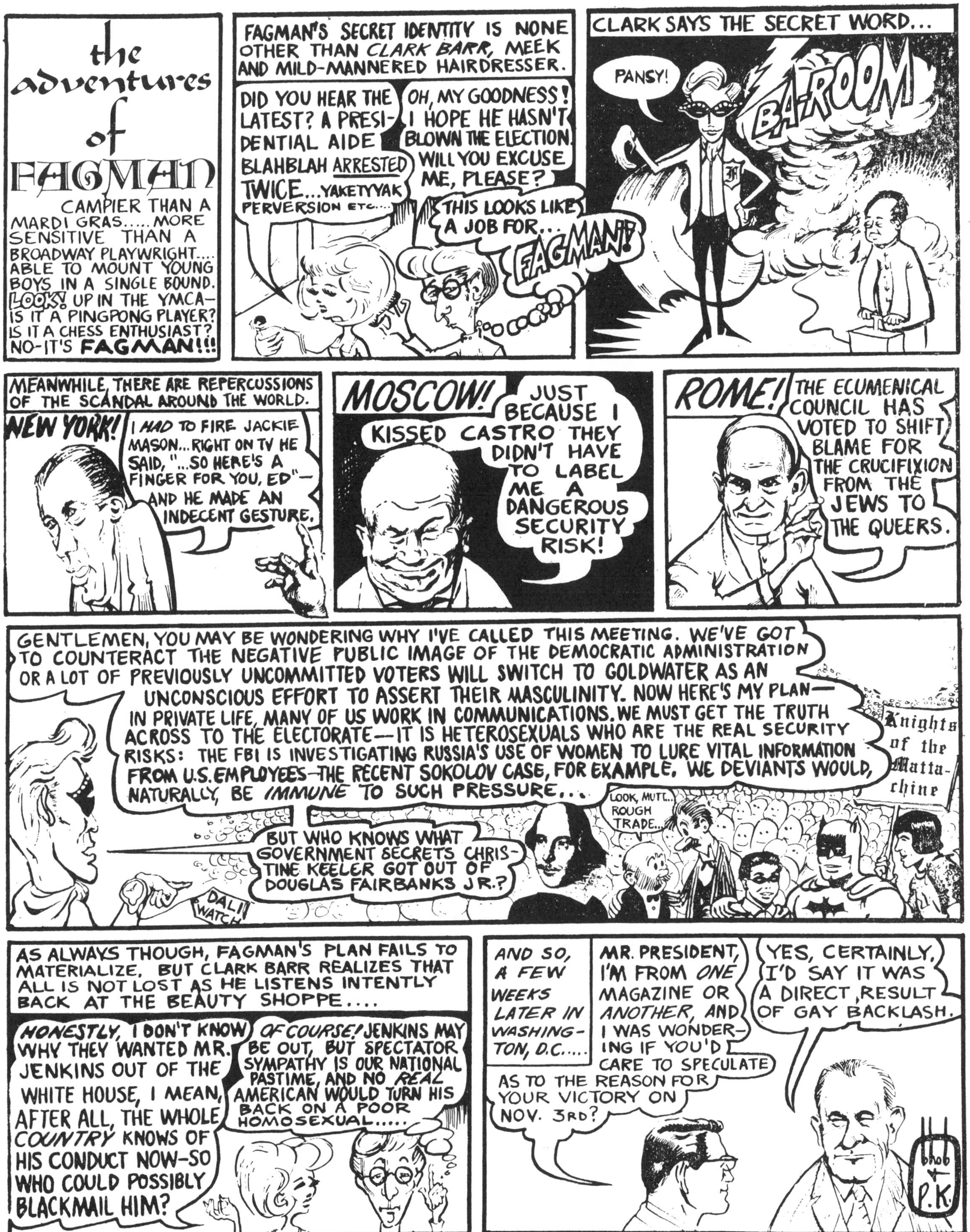
the adventures of FAGMAN
CAMPIER THAN A MARDI GRAS..... MORE SENSITIVE THAN A BROADWAY PLAYWRIGHT.... ABLE TO MOUNT YOUNG BOYS IN A SINGLE BOUND. LOOK! UP IN THE YMCA– IS IT A PINGPONG PLAYER? IS IT A CHESS ENTHUSIAST? NO–IT'S FAGMAN!!!
FAGMAN'S SECRET IDENTITY IS NONE OTHER THAN CLARK BARR, MEEK AND MILD-MANNERED HAIRDRESSER.
DID YOU HEAR THE LATEST? A PRESIDENTIAL AIDE BLAHBLAH ARRESTED TWICE...YAKETYYAK PERVERSION ETC....
OH, MY GOODNESS! I HOPE HE HASN'T BLOWN THE ELECTION. WILL YOU EXCUSE ME, PLEASE?
THIS LOOKS LIKE A JOB FOR... FAGMAN!
CLARK SAYS THE SECRET WORD...
PANSY!
BA-ROOM!
MEANWHILE, THERE ARE REPERCUSSIONS OF THE SCANDAL AROUND THE WORLD.
NEW YORK!
I HAD TO FIRE JACKIE MASON...RIGHT ON TV HE SAID, "...SO HERE'S A FINGER FOR YOU, ED"—AND HE MADE AN INDECENT GESTURE.
MOSCOW!
JUST BECAUSE I KISSED CASTRO THEY DIDN'T HAVE TO LABEL ME A DANGEROUS SECURITY RISK!
ROME!
THE ECUMENICAL COUNCIL HAS VOTED TO SHIFT BLAME FOR THE CRUCIFIXION FROM THE JEWS TO THE QUEERS.
GENTLEMEN, YOU MAY BE WONDERING WHY I'VE CALLED THIS MEETING. WE'VE GOT TO COUNTERACT THE NEGATIVE PUBLIC IMAGE OF THE DEMOCRATIC ADMINISTRATION OR A LOT OF PREVIOUSLY UNCOMMITTED VOTERS WILL SWITCH TO GOLDWATER AS AN UNCONSCIOUS EFFORT TO ASSERT THEIR MASCULINITY. NOW HERE'S MY PLAN— IN PRIVATE LIFE, MANY OF US WORK IN COMMUNICATIONS. WE MUST GET THE TRUTH ACROSS TO THE ELECTORATE—IT IS HETEROSEXUALS WHO ARE THE REAL SECURITY RISKS: THE FBI IS INVESTIGATING RUSSIA'S USE OF WOMEN TO LURE VITAL INFORMATION FROM U.S. EMPLOYEES—THE RECENT SOKOLOV CASE, FOR EXAMPLE. WE DEVIANTS WOULD, NATURALLY, BE IMMUNE TO SUCH PRESSURE...
BUT WHO KNOWS WHAT GOVERNMENT SECRETS CHRISTINE KEELER GOT OUT OF DOUGLAS FAIRBANKS JR.?
LOOK, MUTT... ROUGH TRADE...
Knights of the Mattachine
DALI WATCH
AS ALWAYS THOUGH, FAGMAN'S PLAN FAILS TO MATERIALIZE, BUT CLARK BARR REALIZES THAT ALL IS NOT LOST AS HE LISTENS INTENTLY BACK AT THE BEAUTY SHOPPE....
HONESTLY, I DON'T KNOW WHY THEY WANTED MR. JENKINS OUT OF THE WHITE HOUSE, I MEAN, AFTER ALL, THE WHOLE COUNTRY KNOWS OF HIS CONDUCT NOW–SO WHO COULD POSSIBLY BLACKMAIL HIM?
OF COURSE! JENKINS MAY BE OUT, BUT SPECTATOR SYMPATHY IS OUR NATIONAL PASTIME, AND NO REAL AMERICAN WOULD TURN HIS BACK ON A POOR HOMOSEXUAL.....
AND SO, A FEW WEEKS LATER IN WASHINGTON, D.C.....
MR. PRESIDENT, I'M FROM ONE MAGAZINE OR ANOTHER, AND I WAS WONDERING IF YOU'D CARE TO SPECULATE AS TO THE REASON FOR YOUR VICTORY ON NOV. 3RD?
YES, CERTAINLY, I'D SAY IT WAS A DIRECT RESULT OF GAY BACKLASH.
bhob + P.K.

PAUL KRASSNER AND BHOB STEWART. THE REALIST #55, DECEMBER 1964.

JOHN FRANCIS PUTNAM
AND SERGIO ARAGONÉS.
THE REALIST #58, APRIL 1965.

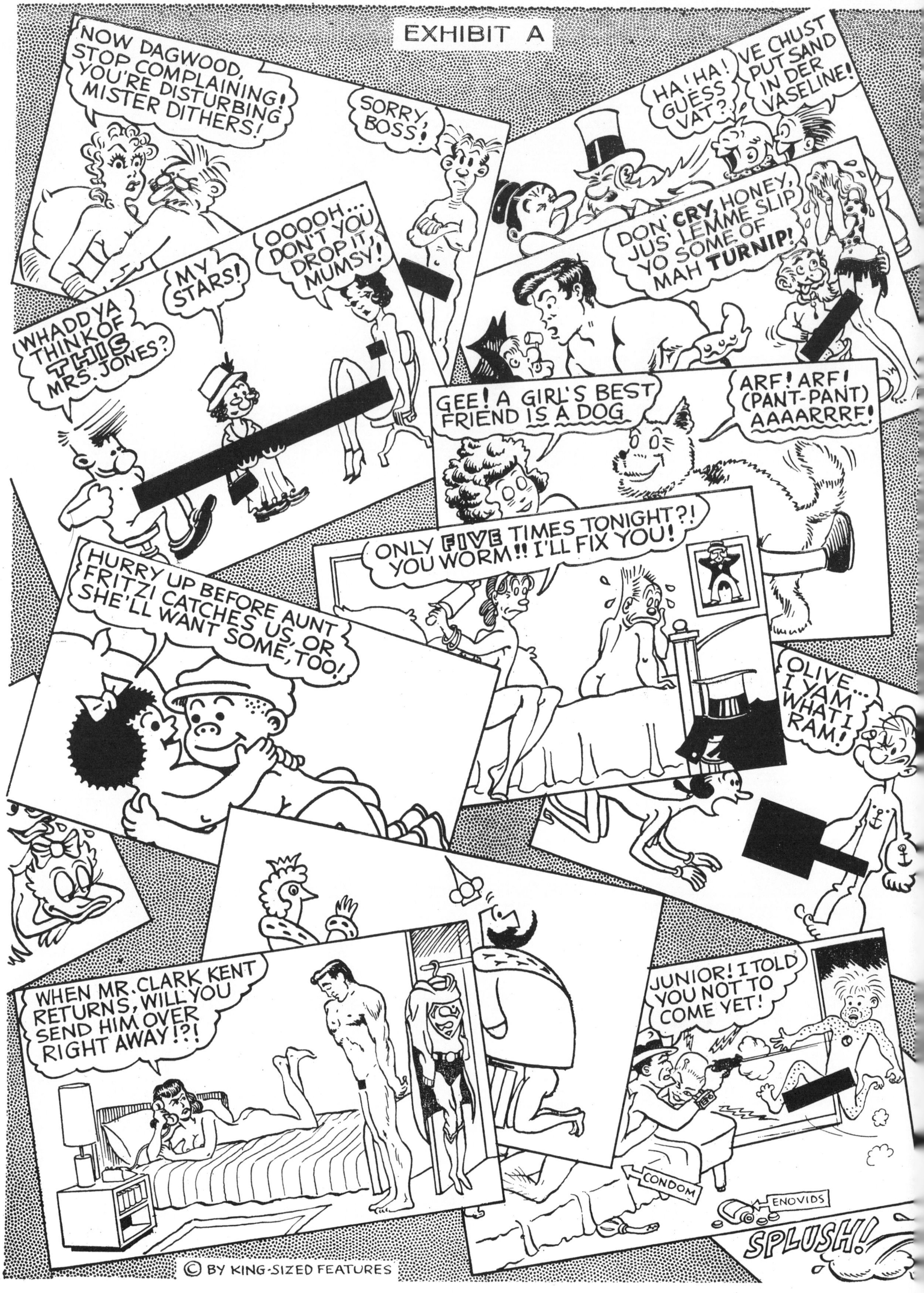
EXHIBIT A
NOW DAGWOOD, STOP COMPLAINING! YOU'RE DISTURBING MISTER DITHERS!
SORRY, BOSS!
HA! HA! GUESS VAT?
VE CHUST PUT SAND IN DER VASELINE!
DON' CRY HONEY, JUS' LEMME SLIP YO SOME OF MAH TURNIP!
WHADDYA THINK OF THIS MRS. JONES?
MY STARS!
OOOOH... DON'T YOU DROP IT, MUMSY!
GEE! A GIRL'S BEST FRIEND IS A DOG
ARF! ARF! (PANT-PANT) AAAARRRF!
ONLY FIVE TIMES TONIGHT?! YOU WORM!! I'LL FIX YOU!
HURRY UP BEFORE AUNT FRITZI CATCHES US, OR SHE'LL WANT SOME, TOO!
OLIVE... I YAM WHAT I RAM!
WHEN MR. CLARK KENT RETURNS, WILL YOU SEND HIM OVER RIGHT AWAY!?!
JUNIOR! I TOLD YOU NOT TO COME YET!
CONDOM
ENOVIDS
SPLUSH!
© BY KING-SIZED FEATURES

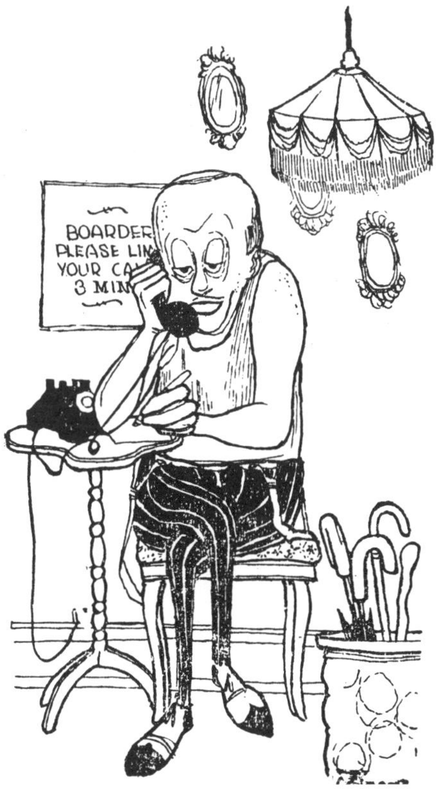
BOARDER
PLEASE LI
YOUR CA
3 MIN

"Hello, I'm contacting ladies in the neighborhood — would you be interested in receiving mash calls?"

RICHARD GUINDON. THE REALIST #57, MARCH 1965.

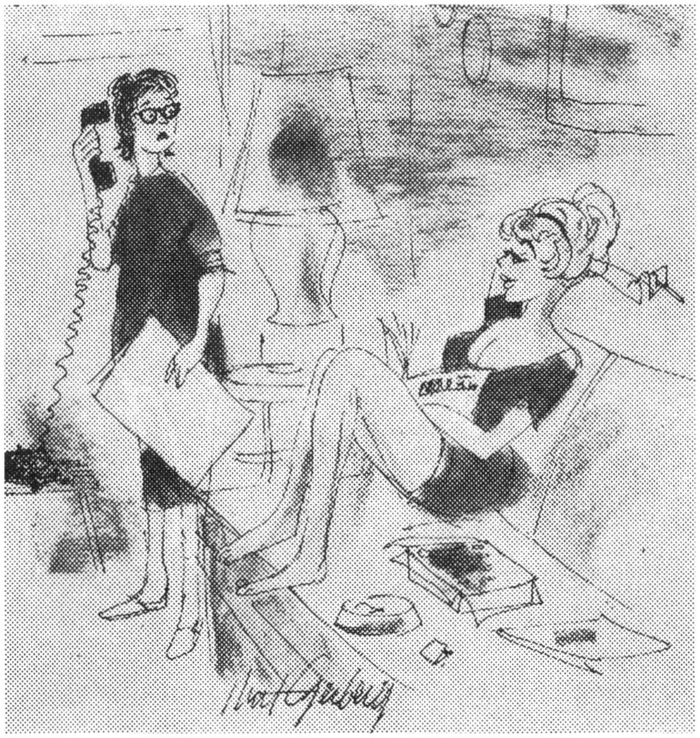

"— What? ... Oh, just a minute. ... It's for you — an obscene phone call!"

MORT GERBERG. THE REALIST #58, APRIL 1965.

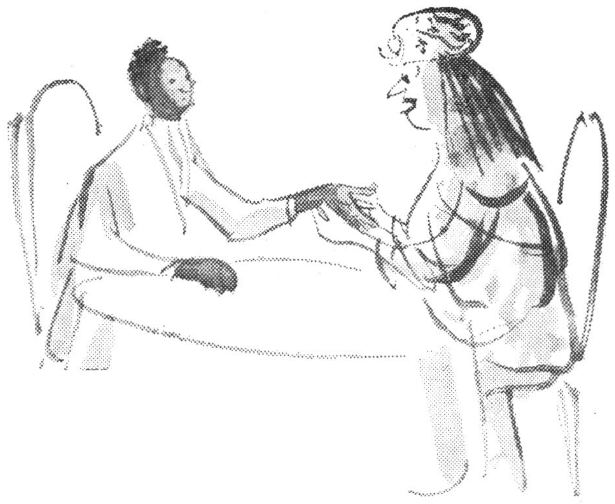

"You are underprivileged, bitter, culturally deprived, tired of being pushed around, determined to abolish the stigma of second-class citizenship ..."

ED FISHER. THE REALIST #58, APRIL 1965.

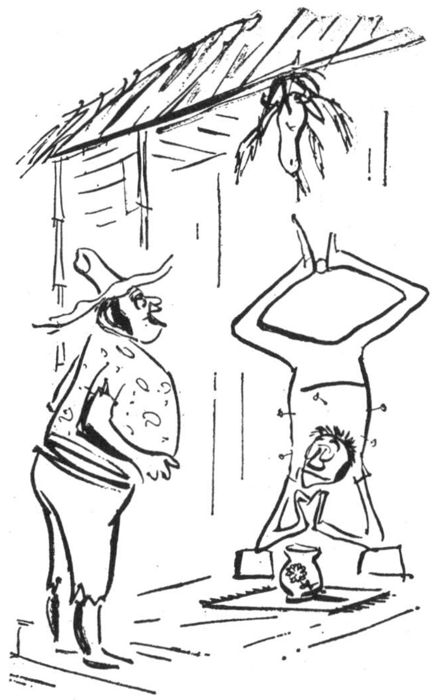

"Voodoo, Shinto and Yoga all rolled into one ... Man, that's ecumenism!"

ED FISHER. THE REALIST #58, APRIL 1965.

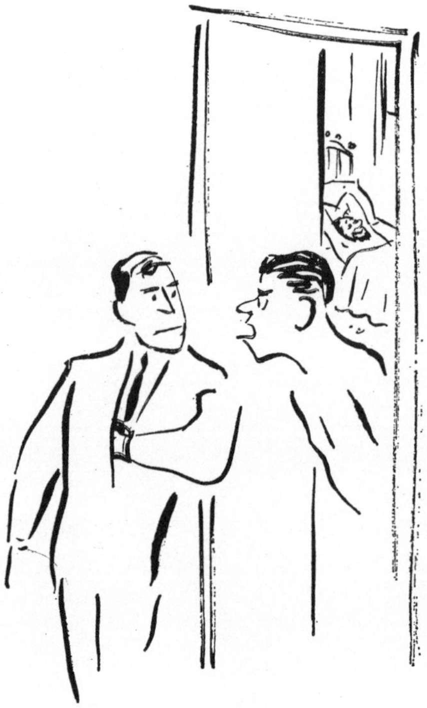

"By God, 007, I envy your luck — when *you* get into these situations, it's always with *girls!*"

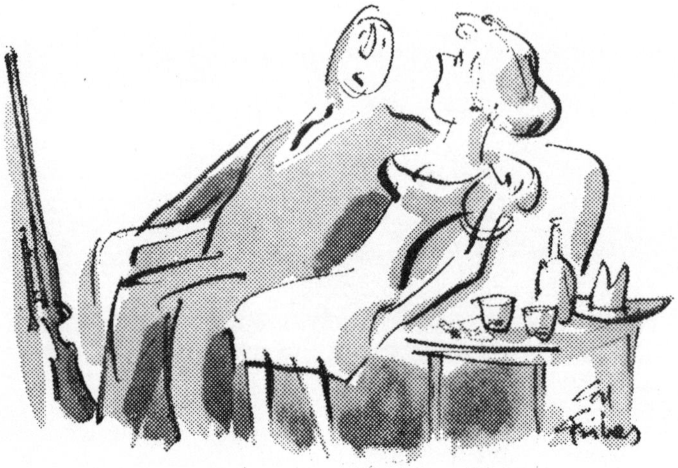

"I've got to go out now, honey, and fire a few rounds. My wife always sniffs the barrel when I tell her I've been to Minute Men practice."

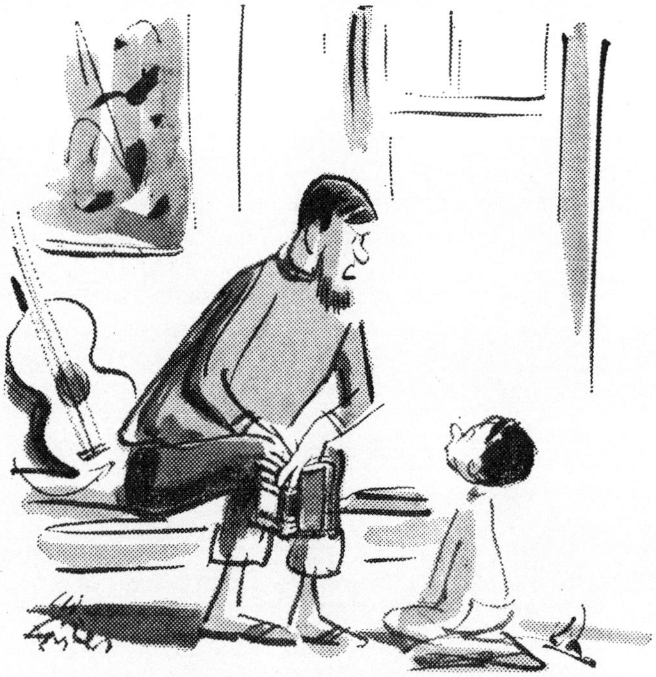

"— Afterward, Piglet grew up and became a dope-pusher, Owl sold out to IBM and Eeyore joined the John Birch Society!"

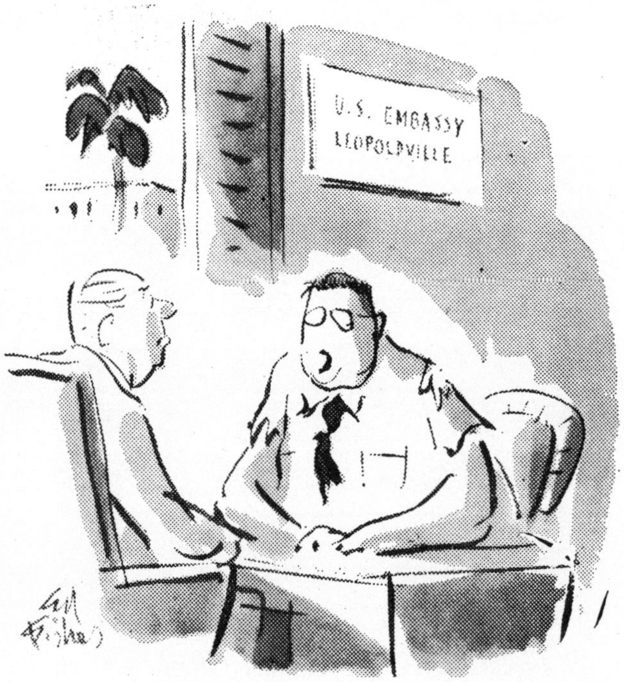
U.S. EMBASSY
LEOPOLDVILLE

"Not only did the rebels make us eat our flag; we had to eat our 'One nation under God' banner, too."

ED FISHER. THE REALIST #58, APRIL 1965.

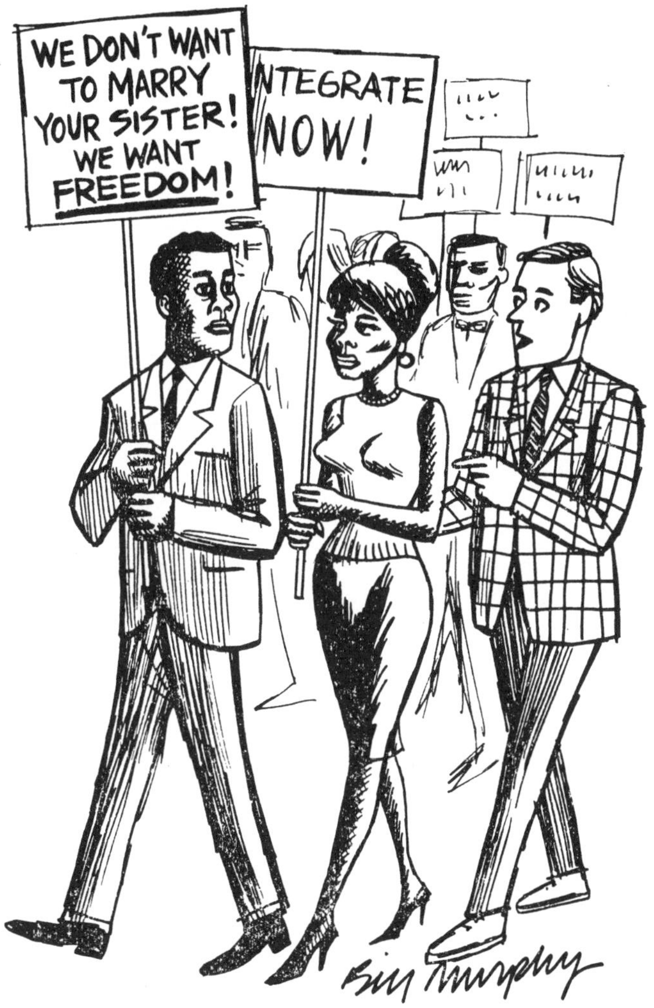
WE DON'T WANT TO MARRY YOUR SISTER! WE WANT FREEDOM!
NTEGRATE NOW!

"... Uh ... Ralph ... Your sister and I have something we'd like to talk to you about ..."

BILL MURPHY. THE REALIST #59, MAY 1965.

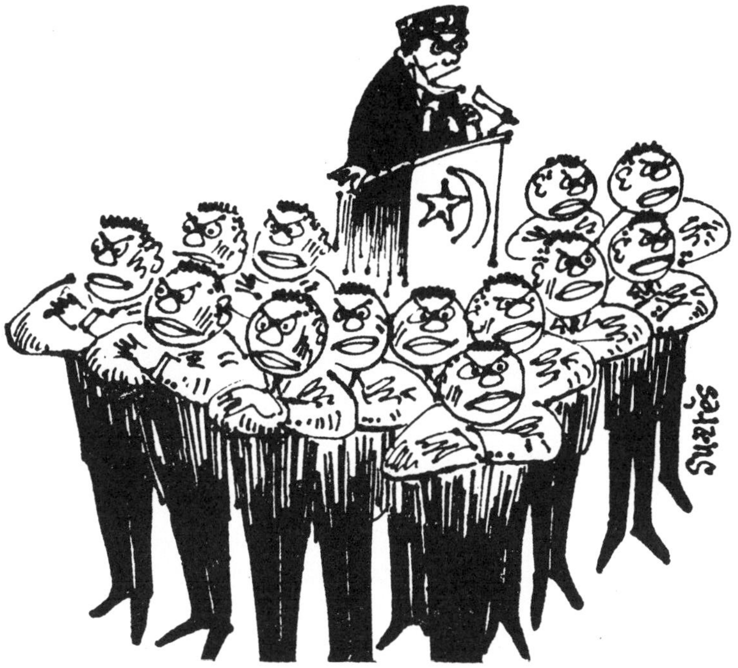

J.C. SUARES. THE REALIST #59, MAY 1965.

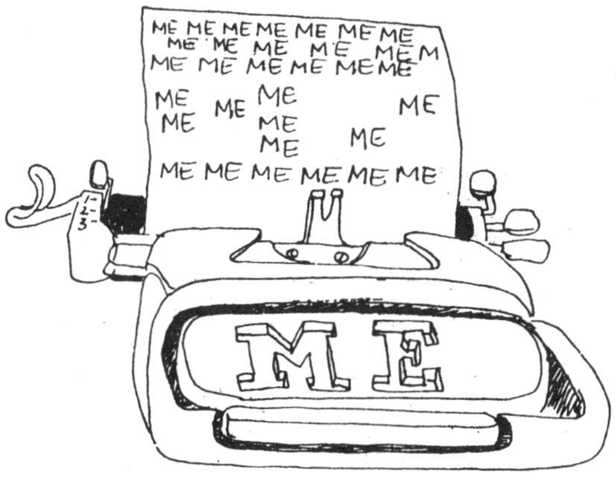
ME ME ME ME ME ME ME
ME ME ME ME ME ME ME ME ME ME ME ME ME
ME ME ME ME ME ME ME ME
ME ME ME ME ME ME
ME

PETER MARKUS. THE REALIST #59, MAY 1965.

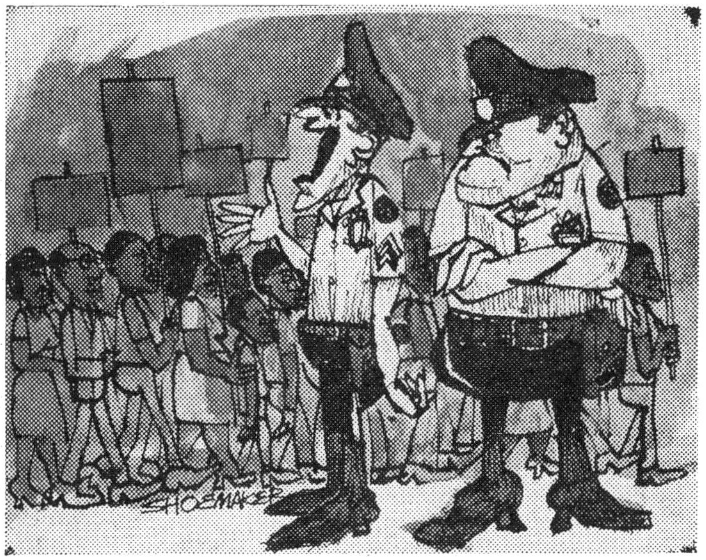

"Oh-oh-oh-oh-oh-oh — I ... love a parade!"

HOWARD SHOEMAKER. THE REALIST #59, MAY 1965.

BLOOM/LEONARD.

THE REALIST #59, MAY 1965. *64

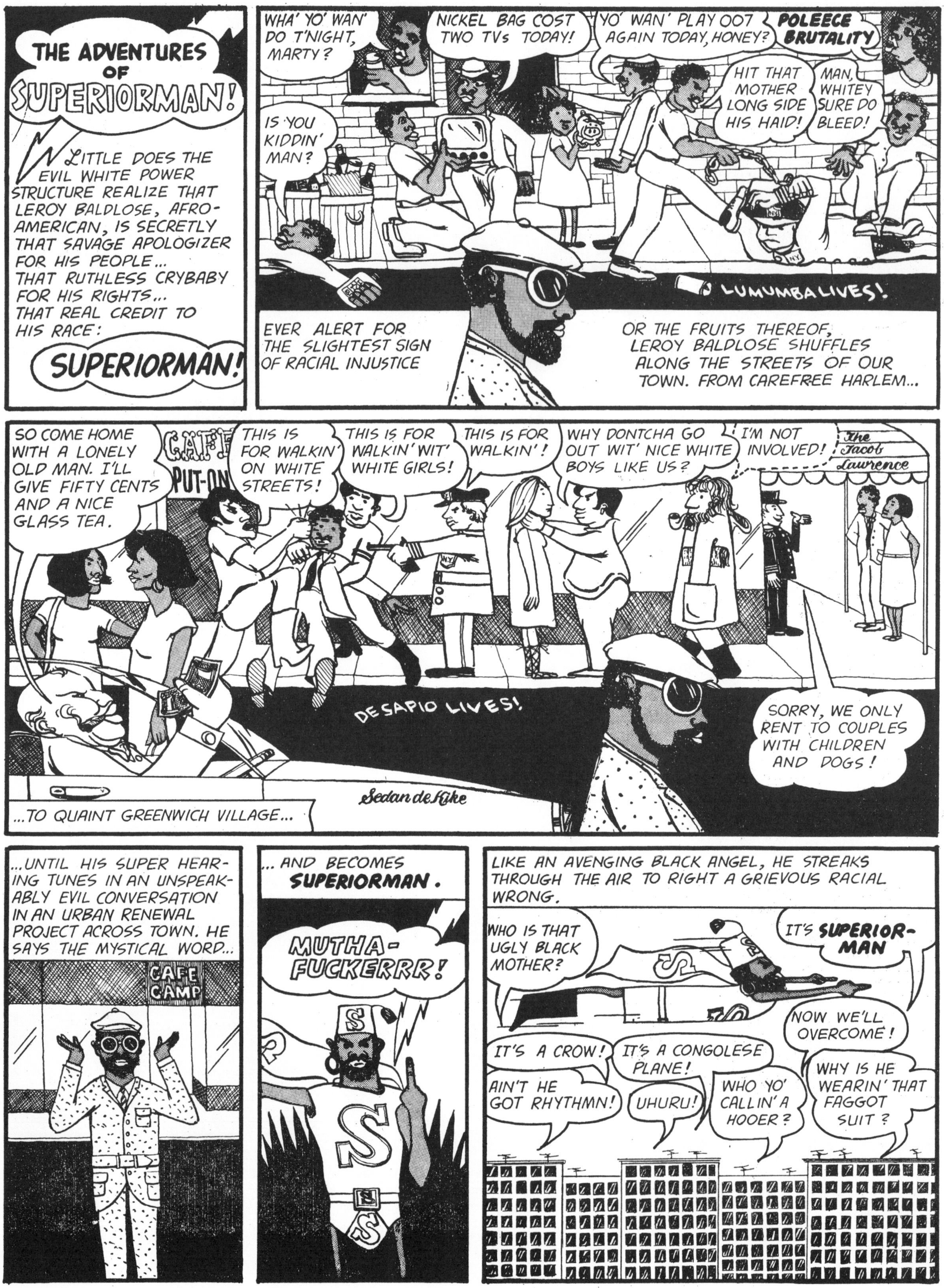
THE ADVENTURES OF SUPERIORMAN!
LITTLE DOES THE EVIL WHITE POWER STRUCTURE REALIZE THAT LEROY BALDLOSE, AFRO-AMERICAN, IS SECRETLY THAT SAVAGE APOLOGIZER FOR HIS PEOPLE... THAT RUTHLESS CRYBABY FOR HIS RIGHTS... THAT REAL CREDIT TO HIS RACE:
SUPERIORMAN!
WHA' YO' WAN' DO T'NIGHT, MARTY?
NICKEL BAG COST TWO TVs TODAY!
YO' WAN' PLAY 007 AGAIN TODAY, HONEY?
POLEECE BRUTALITY
IS YOU KIDDIN' MAN?
HIT THAT MOTHER LONG SIDE HIS HAID!
MAN, WHITEY SURE DO BLEED!
LUMUMBA LIVES!
EVER ALERT FOR THE SLIGHTEST SIGN OF RACIAL INJUSTICE
OR THE FRUITS THEREOF, LEROY BALDLOSE SHUFFLES ALONG THE STREETS OF OUR TOWN. FROM CAREFREE HARLEM...
SO COME HOME WITH A LONELY OLD MAN. I'LL GIVE FIFTY CENTS AND A NICE GLASS TEA.
PUT-ON
THIS IS FOR WALKIN' ON WHITE STREETS!
THIS IS FOR WALKIN' WIT' WHITE GIRLS!
THIS IS FOR WALKIN'!
WHY DONTCHA GO OUT WIT' NICE WHITE BOYS LIKE US?
I'M NOT INVOLVED!
The Jacob Laurence
DESAPIO LIVES!
SORRY, WE ONLY RENT TO COUPLES WITH CHILDREN AND DOGS!
Sedan de Kike
...TO QUAINT GREENWICH VILLAGE...
...UNTIL HIS SUPER HEARING TUNES IN AN UNSPEAKABLY EVIL CONVERSATION IN AN URBAN RENEWAL PROJECT ACROSS TOWN. HE SAYS THE MYSTICAL WORD...
CAFE CAMP
...AND BECOMES SUPERIORMAN.
MUTHA-FUCKERRR!
LIKE AN AVENGING BLACK ANGEL, HE STREAKS THROUGH THE AIR TO RIGHT A GRIEVOUS RACIAL WRONG.
WHO IS THAT UGLY BLACK MOTHER?
IT'S SUPERIOR-MAN
NOW WE'LL OVERCOME!
IT'S A CROW!
IT'S A CONGOLESE PLANE!
WHY IS HE WEARIN' THAT FAGGOT SUIT?
AIN'T HE GOT RHYTHMN!
UHURU!
WHO YO' CALLIN' A HOOER?

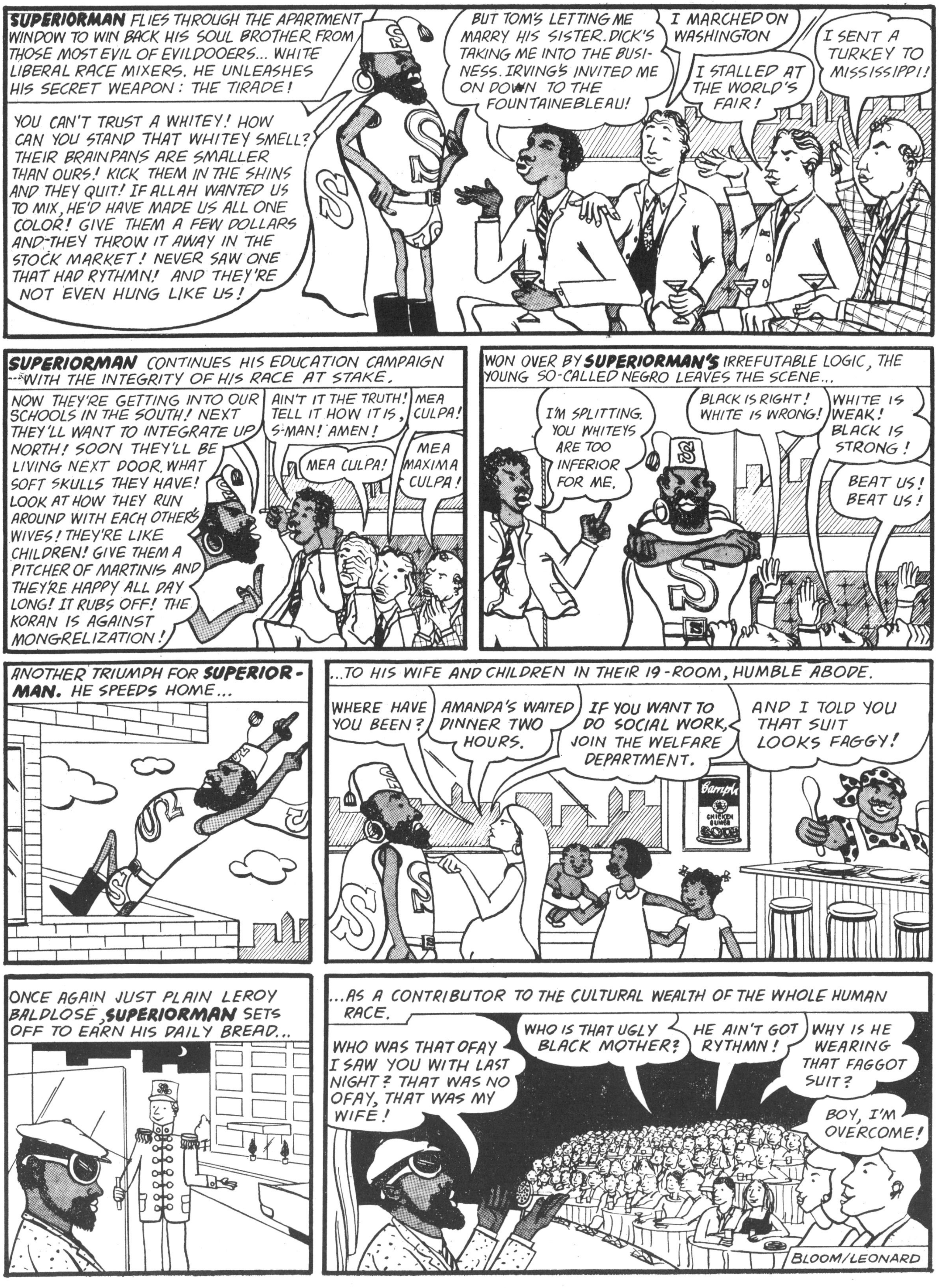
SUPERIORMAN FLIES THROUGH THE APARTMENT WINDOW TO WIN BACK HIS SOUL BROTHER FROM THOSE MOST EVIL OF EVILDOERS... WHITE LIBERAL RACE MIXERS. HE UNLEASHES HIS SECRET WEAPON: THE TIRADE!
YOU CAN'T TRUST A WHITEY! HOW CAN YOU STAND THAT WHITEY SMELL? THEIR BRAINPANS ARE SMALLER THAN OURS! KICK THEM IN THE SHINS AND THEY QUIT! IF ALLAH WANTED US TO MIX, HE'D HAVE MADE US ALL ONE COLOR! GIVE THEM A FEW DOLLARS AND THEY THROW IT AWAY IN THE STOCK MARKET! NEVER SAW ONE THAT HAD RYTHMN! AND THEY'RE NOT EVEN HUNG LIKE US!
BUT TOM'S LETTING ME MARRY HIS SISTER. DICK'S TAKING ME INTO THE BUSINESS. IRVING'S INVITED ME ON DOWN TO THE FOUNTAINEBLEAU!
I MARCHED ON WASHINGTON
I STALLED AT THE WORLD'S FAIR!
I SENT A TURKEY TO MISSISSIPPI!
SUPERIORMAN CONTINUES HIS EDUCATION CAMPAIGN --WITH THE INTEGRITY OF HIS RACE AT STAKE.
NOW THEY'RE GETTING INTO OUR SCHOOLS IN THE SOUTH! NEXT THEY'LL WANT TO INTEGRATE UP NORTH! SOON THEY'LL BE LIVING NEXT DOOR. WHAT SOFT SKULLS THEY HAVE! LOOK AT HOW THEY RUN AROUND WITH EACH OTHER'S WIVES! THEY'RE LIKE CHILDREN! GIVE THEM A PITCHER OF MARTINIS AND THEY'RE HAPPY ALL DAY LONG! IT RUBS OFF! THE KORAN IS AGAINST MONGRELIZATION!
AIN'T IT THE TRUTH! TELL IT HOW IT IS, S-MAN! AMEN!
MEA CULPA!
MEA CULPA!
MEA MAXIMA CULPA!
WON OVER BY SUPERIORMAN'S IRREFUTABLE LOGIC, THE YOUNG SO-CALLED NEGRO LEAVES THE SCENE...
I'M SPLITTING. YOU WHITEYS ARE TOO INFERIOR FOR ME.
BLACK IS RIGHT! WHITE IS WRONG!
WHITE IS WEAK! BLACK IS STRONG!
BEAT US! BEAT US!
ANOTHER TRIUMPH FOR SUPERIOR-MAN. HE SPEEDS HOME...
...TO HIS WIFE AND CHILDREN IN THEIR 19-ROOM, HUMBLE ABODE.
WHERE HAVE YOU BEEN?
AMANDA'S WAITED DINNER TWO HOURS.
IF YOU WANT TO DO SOCIAL WORK, JOIN THE WELFARE DEPARTMENT.
AND I TOLD YOU THAT SUIT LOOKS FAGGY!
Campbell's CHICKEN GUMBO SOUP
ONCE AGAIN JUST PLAIN LEROY BALDLOSE, SUPERIORMAN SETS OFF TO EARN HIS DAILY BREAD...
...AS A CONTRIBUTOR TO THE CULTURAL WEALTH OF THE WHOLE HUMAN RACE.
WHO WAS THAT OFAY I SAW YOU WITH LAST NIGHT? THAT WAS NO OFAY, THAT WAS MY WIFE!
WHO IS THAT UGLY BLACK MOTHER?
HE AIN'T GOT RYTHMN!
WHY IS HE WEARING THAT FAGGOT SUIT?
BOY, I'M OVERCOME!
BLOOM/LEONARD

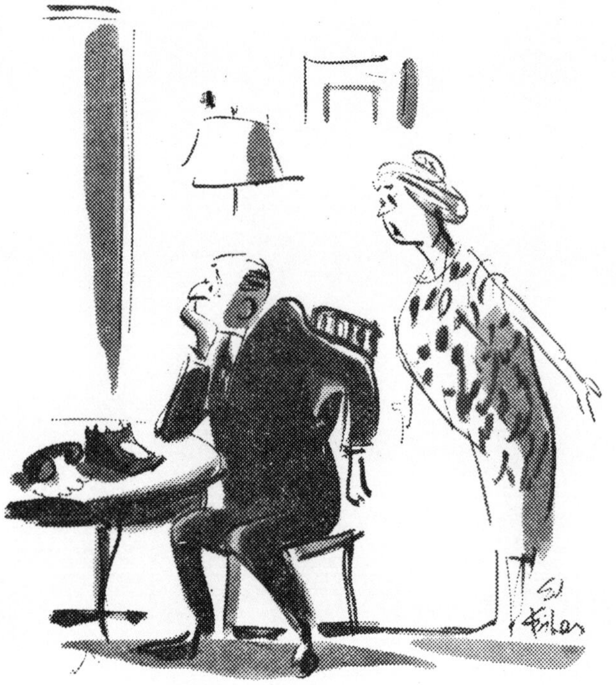

"It's just a loose wire or something —
Dial-a-prayer hasn't 'forsaken' you!"

ED FISHER. THE REALIST #59, MAY 1965.

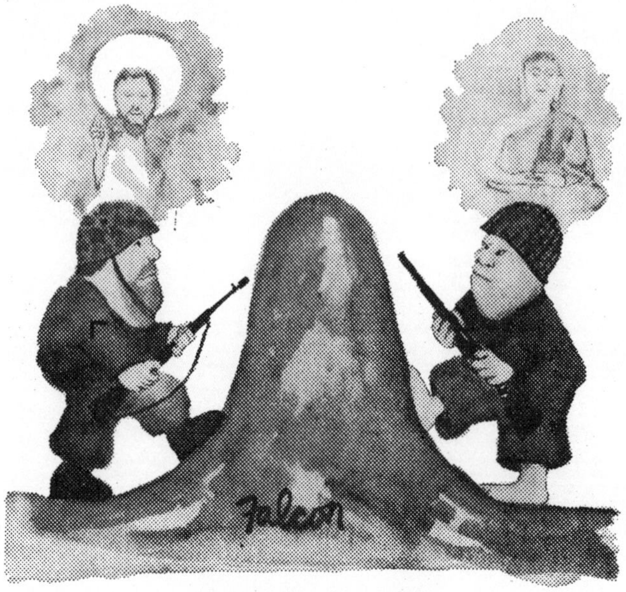
Falcon

God Is On Our Side

FALCON. THE REALIST #60, JUNE 1965.

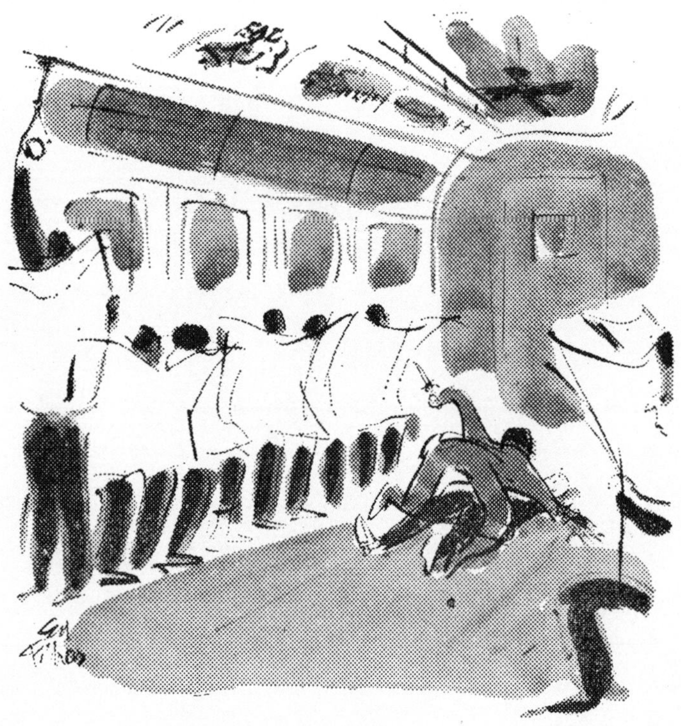

In New York Nearly Everyone Reads the Newspaper...

ED FISHER. THE REALIST #59, MAY 1965.

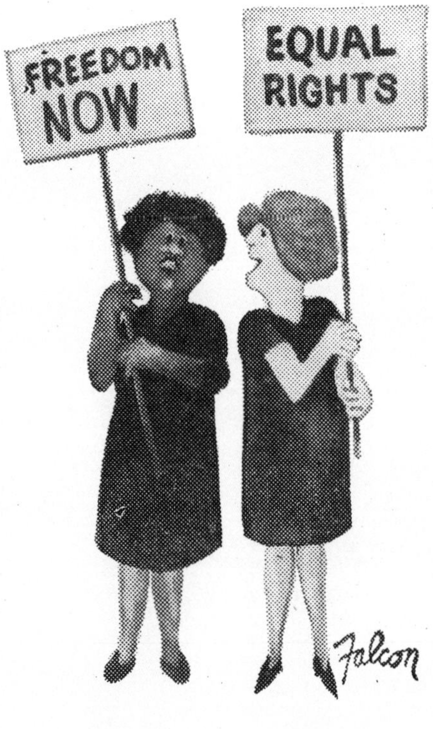
FREEDOM NOW
EQUAL RIGHTS
Falcon

"Excuse me, but would you have a
spare cleaning day available?"

FALCON. THE REALIST #59, MAY 1965.

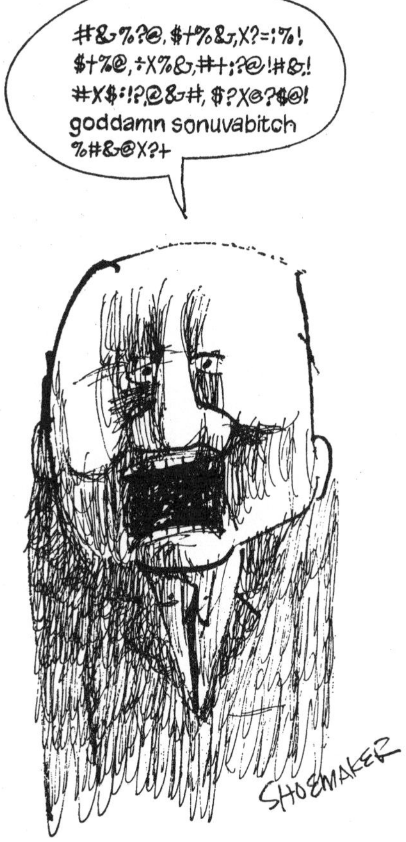
#&%?@, $+%&,X?=;%!
$+%@,÷X%&,#+;?@!#&!
#X$÷!?,@&#, $?X@?$@!
goddamn sonuvabitch
%#&@X?+
SHOEMAKER

HOWARD SHOEMAKER. THE REALIST #59, MAY 1965.

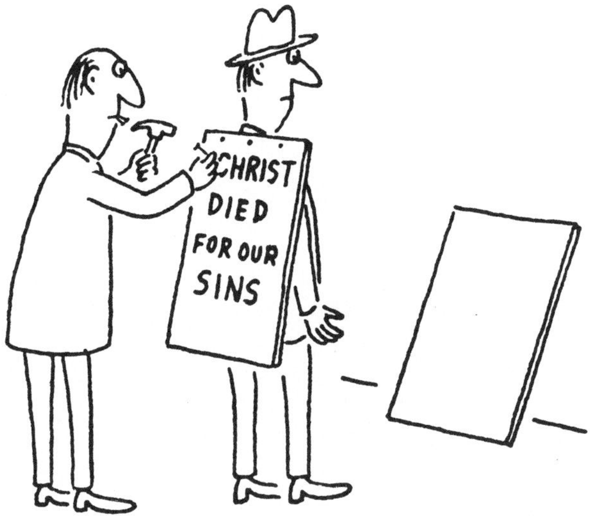
CHRIST
DIED
FOR OUR
SINS

SAM GROSS. THE REALIST #59, MAY 1965.

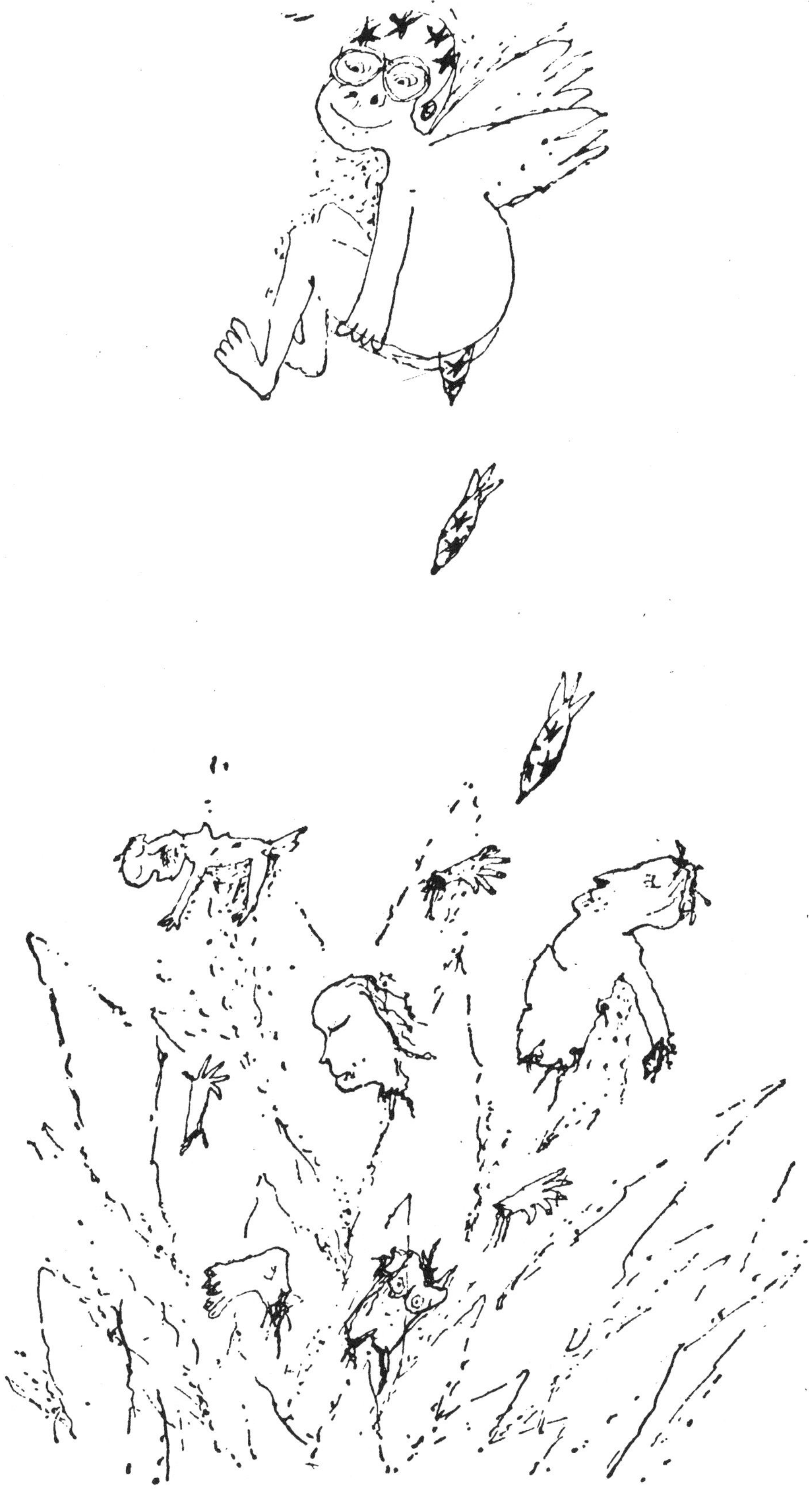

THE REALIST #59, MAY 1965.

RICHARD GUINDON.
THE REALIST #60, JUNE 1965.

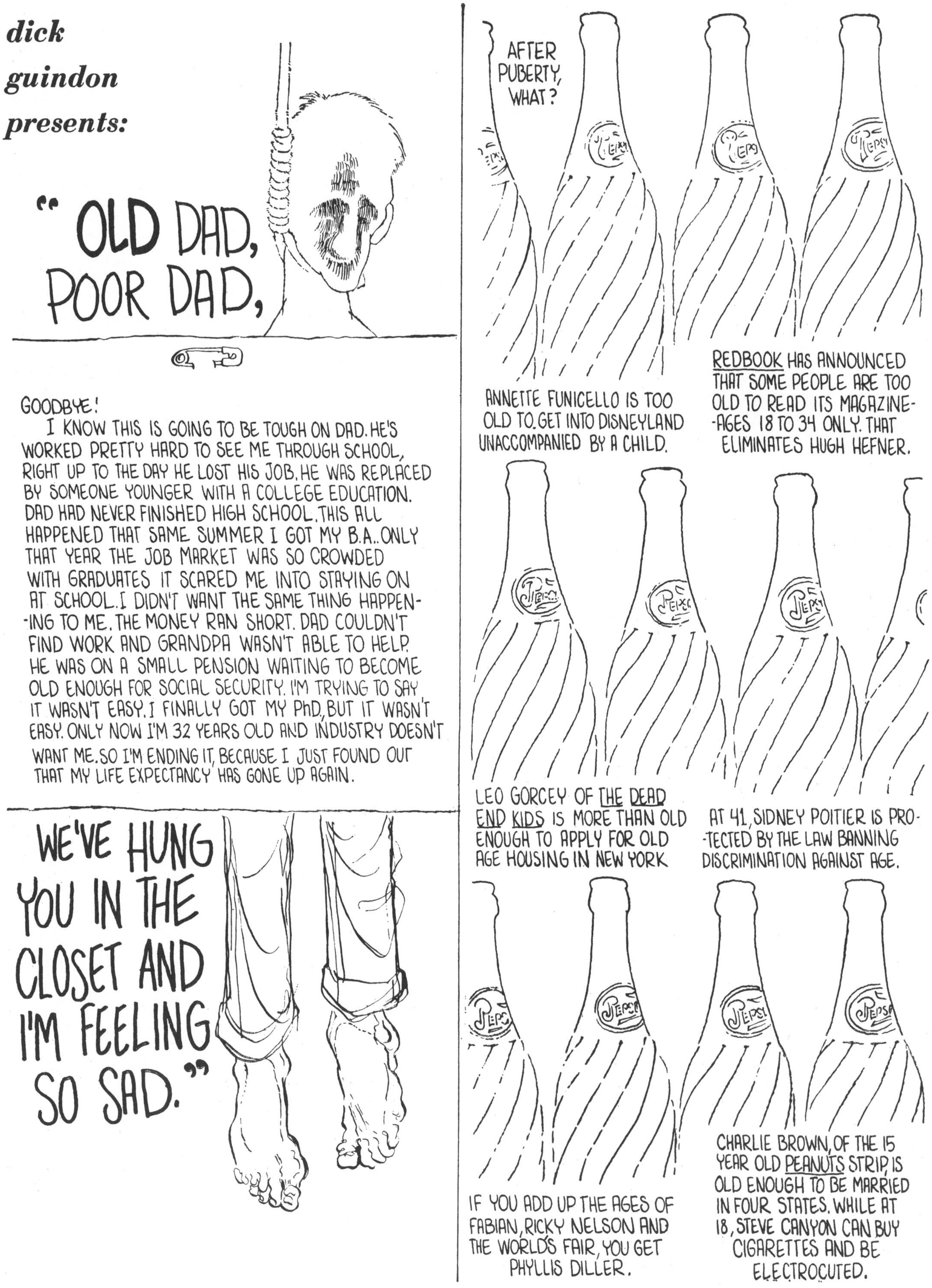
dick guindon presents:
"OLD DAD, POOR DAD,
GOODBYE!
I KNOW THIS IS GOING TO BE TOUGH ON DAD. HE'S WORKED PRETTY HARD TO SEE ME THROUGH SCHOOL, RIGHT UP TO THE DAY HE LOST HIS JOB. HE WAS REPLACED BY SOMEONE YOUNGER WITH A COLLEGE EDUCATION. DAD HAD NEVER FINISHED HIGH SCHOOL. THIS ALL HAPPENED THAT SAME SUMMER I GOT MY B.A.. ONLY THAT YEAR THE JOB MARKET WAS SO CROWDED WITH GRADUATES IT SCARED ME INTO STAYING ON AT SCHOOL. I DIDN'T WANT THE SAME THING HAPPEN-ING TO ME. THE MONEY RAN SHORT. DAD COULDN'T FIND WORK AND GRANDPA WASN'T ABLE TO HELP. HE WAS ON A SMALL PENSION WAITING TO BECOME OLD ENOUGH FOR SOCIAL SECURITY. I'M TRYING TO SAY IT WASN'T EASY. I FINALLY GOT MY PhD, BUT IT WASN'T EASY. ONLY NOW I'M 32 YEARS OLD AND INDUSTRY DOESN'T WANT ME. SO I'M ENDING IT, BECAUSE I JUST FOUND OUT THAT MY LIFE EXPECTANCY HAS GONE UP AGAIN.
WE'VE HUNG YOU IN THE CLOSET AND I'M FEELING SO SAD."
AFTER PUBERTY, WHAT?
ANNETTE FUNICELLO IS TOO OLD TO GET INTO DISNEYLAND UNACCOMPANIED BY A CHILD.
REDBOOK HAS ANNOUNCED THAT SOME PEOPLE ARE TOO OLD TO READ ITS MAGAZINE--AGES 18 TO 34 ONLY. THAT ELIMINATES HUGH HEFNER.
LEO GORCEY OF THE DEAD END KIDS IS MORE THAN OLD ENOUGH TO APPLY FOR OLD AGE HOUSING IN NEW YORK
AT 41, SIDNEY POITIER IS PRO-TECTED BY THE LAW BANNING DISCRIMINATION AGAINST AGE.
IF YOU ADD UP THE AGES OF FABIAN, RICKY NELSON AND THE WORLD'S FAIR, YOU GET PHYLLIS DILLER.
CHARLIE BROWN, OF THE 15 YEAR OLD PEANUTS STRIP, IS OLD ENOUGH TO BE MARRIED IN FOUR STATES. WHILE AT 18, STEVE CANYON CAN BUY CIGARETTES AND BE ELECTROCUTED.

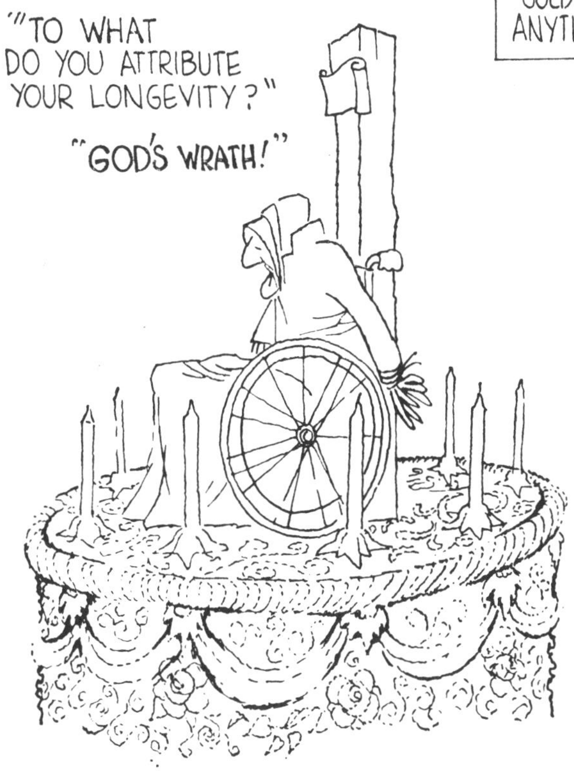
"'TO WHAT DO YOU ATTRIBUTE YOUR LONGEVITY?'"
"GOD'S WRATH!"

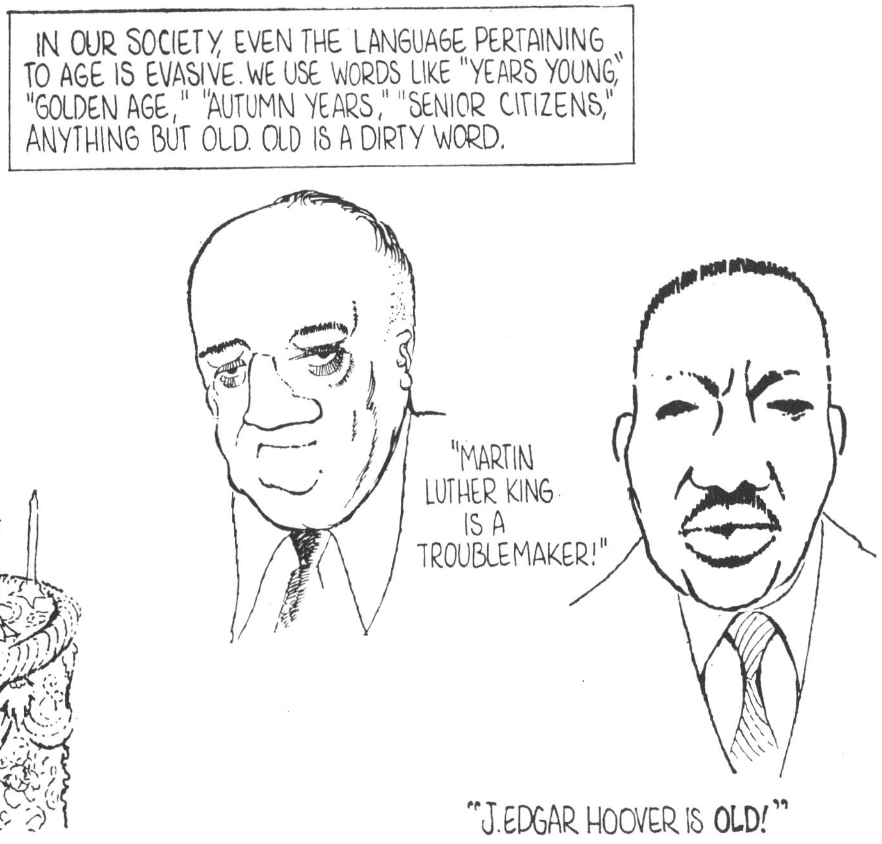
IN OUR SOCIETY, EVEN THE LANGUAGE PERTAINING TO AGE IS EVASIVE. WE USE WORDS LIKE "YEARS YOUNG," "GOLDEN AGE," "AUTUMN YEARS," "SENIOR CITIZENS," ANYTHING BUT OLD. OLD IS A DIRTY WORD.
"MARTIN LUTHER KING IS A TROUBLEMAKER!"
"J. EDGAR HOOVER IS OLD!"

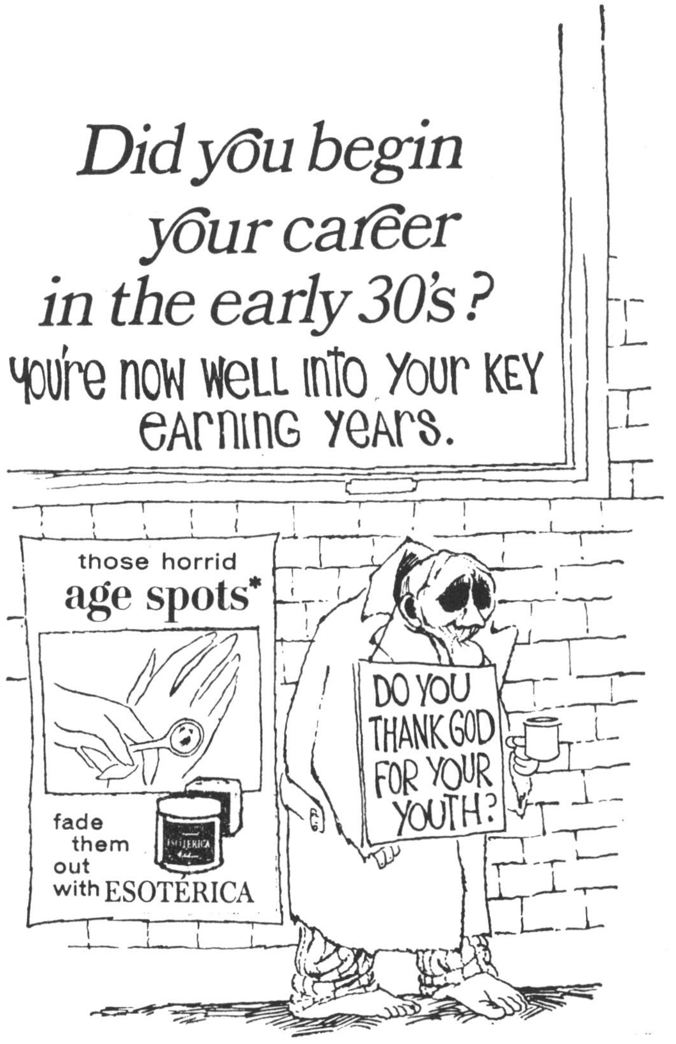
Did you begin your career in the early 30's?
you're now well into your key earning years.
those horrid age spots*
fade them out with ESOTÉRICA
DO YOU THANK GOD FOR YOUR YOUTH?

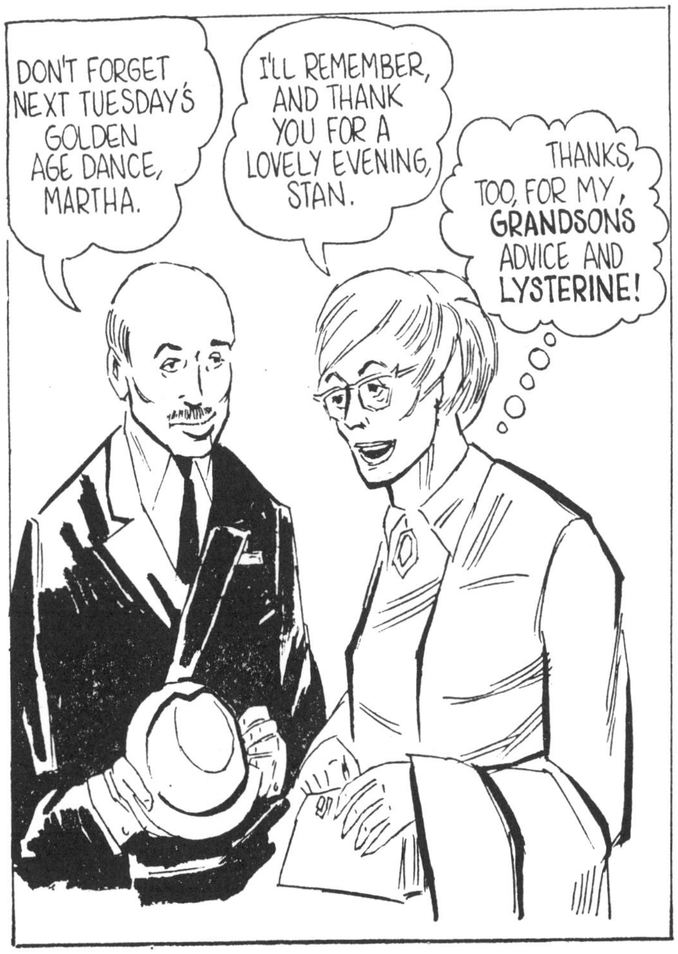
DON'T FORGET NEXT TUESDAY'S GOLDEN AGE DANCE, MARTHA.
I'LL REMEMBER, AND THANK YOU FOR A LOVELY EVENING, STAN.
THANKS, TOO, FOR MY GRANDSONS ADVICE AND LYSTERINE!

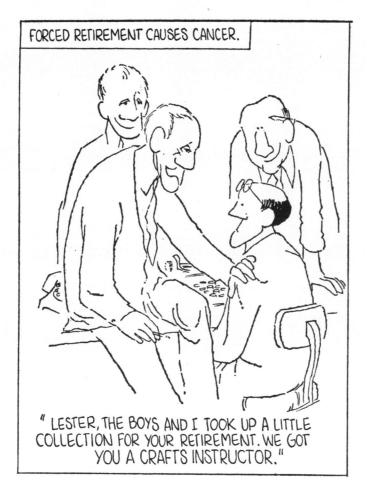

FORCED RETIREMENT CAUSES CANCER.

"LESTER, THE BOYS AND I TOOK UP A LITTLE COLLECTION FOR YOUR RETIREMENT. WE GOT YOU A CRAFTS INSTRUCTOR."

"FIRST OF ALL I WANT TO THANK THE ENTERTAINMENT COMMITTEE FOR GIVING ME THIS RETIREMENT BANQUET.

I ALSO WANT TO THANK AJAX AND SON FOR 30 WONDERFUL YEARS. MR. GORDON, MY IMMEDIATE SUPERVISOR...

...CERTAINLY DESERVES SOME MENTION HERE... AND... MENTION HERE... AND I.... I...

...I...AAAUGHHH!"

AND THEN WE RATIONALIZE BY HELPING WITH THE HOSPITAL BILL.

WOULDN'T IT BE EASIER TO GIVE HIM HIS JOB BACK?

SHUT UP AND OPEN THE WINDOW!

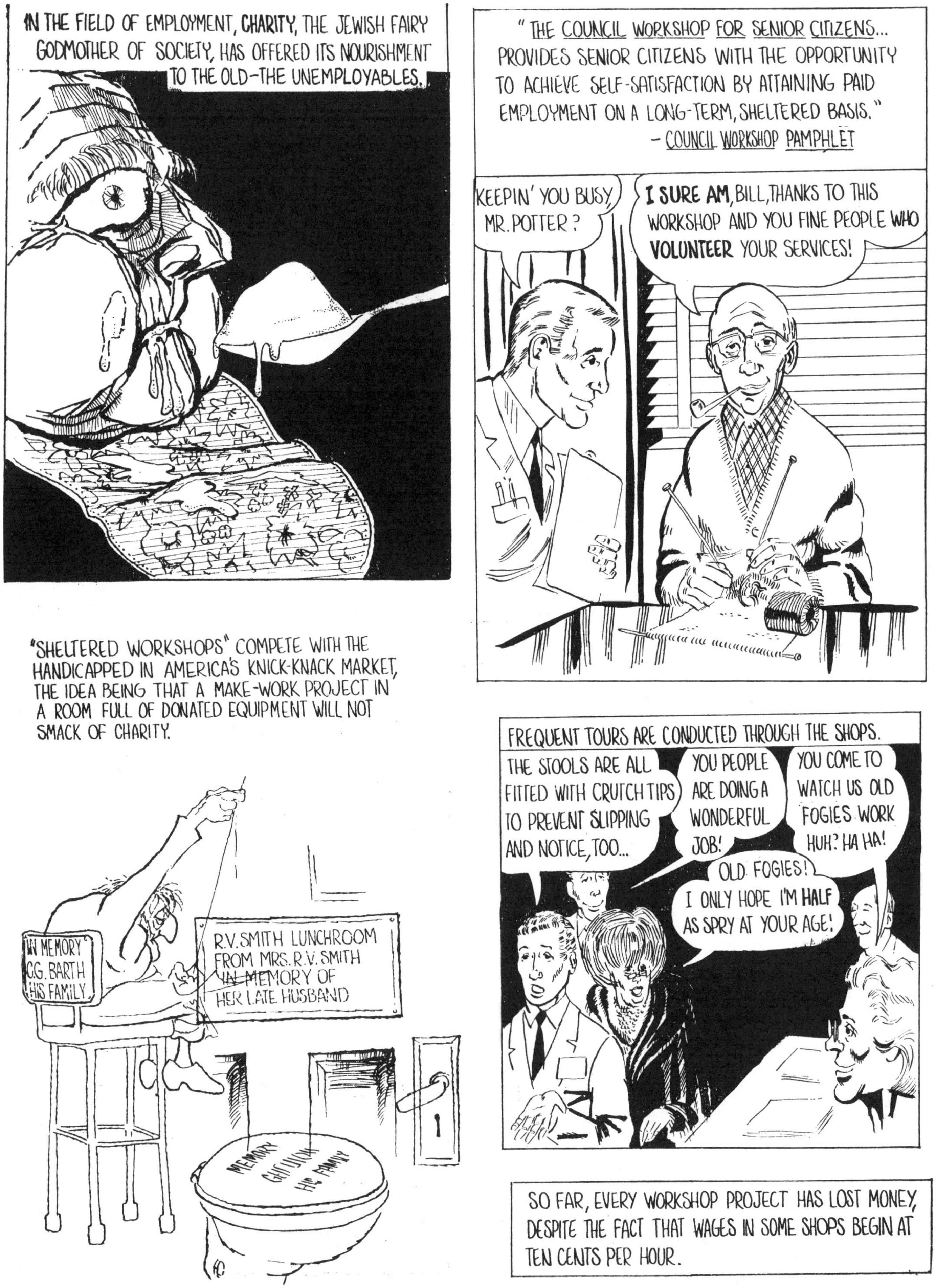
IN THE FIELD OF EMPLOYMENT, CHARITY, THE JEWISH FAIRY GODMOTHER OF SOCIETY, HAS OFFERED ITS NOURISHMENT TO THE OLD—THE UNEMPLOYABLES.
"THE COUNCIL WORKSHOP FOR SENIOR CITIZENS... PROVIDES SENIOR CITIZENS WITH THE OPPORTUNITY TO ACHIEVE SELF-SATISFACTION BY ATTAINING PAID EMPLOYMENT ON A LONG-TERM, SHELTERED BASIS."
—COUNCIL WORKSHOP PAMPHLET
KEEPIN' YOU BUSY, MR. POTTER?
I SURE AM, BILL, THANKS TO THIS WORKSHOP AND YOU FINE PEOPLE WHO VOLUNTEER YOUR SERVICES!
"SHELTERED WORKSHOPS" COMPETE WITH THE HANDICAPPED IN AMERICA'S KNICK-KNACK MARKET, THE IDEA BEING THAT A MAKE-WORK PROJECT IN A ROOM FULL OF DONATED EQUIPMENT WILL NOT SMACK OF CHARITY.
IN MEMORY C.G. BARTH HIS FAMILY
R.V. SMITH LUNCHROOM FROM MRS. R.V. SMITH IN MEMORY OF HER LATE HUSBAND
FREQUENT TOURS ARE CONDUCTED THROUGH THE SHOPS.
THE STOOLS ARE ALL FITTED WITH CRUTCH TIPS TO PREVENT SLIPPING AND NOTICE, TOO...
YOU PEOPLE ARE DOING A WONDERFUL JOB!
YOU COME TO WATCH US OLD FOGIES WORK HUH? HA HA!
OLD FOGIES! I ONLY HOPE I'M HALF AS SPRY AT YOUR AGE!
SO FAR, EVERY WORKSHOP PROJECT HAS LOST MONEY, DESPITE THE FACT THAT WAGES IN SOME SHOPS BEGIN AT TEN CENTS PER HOUR.

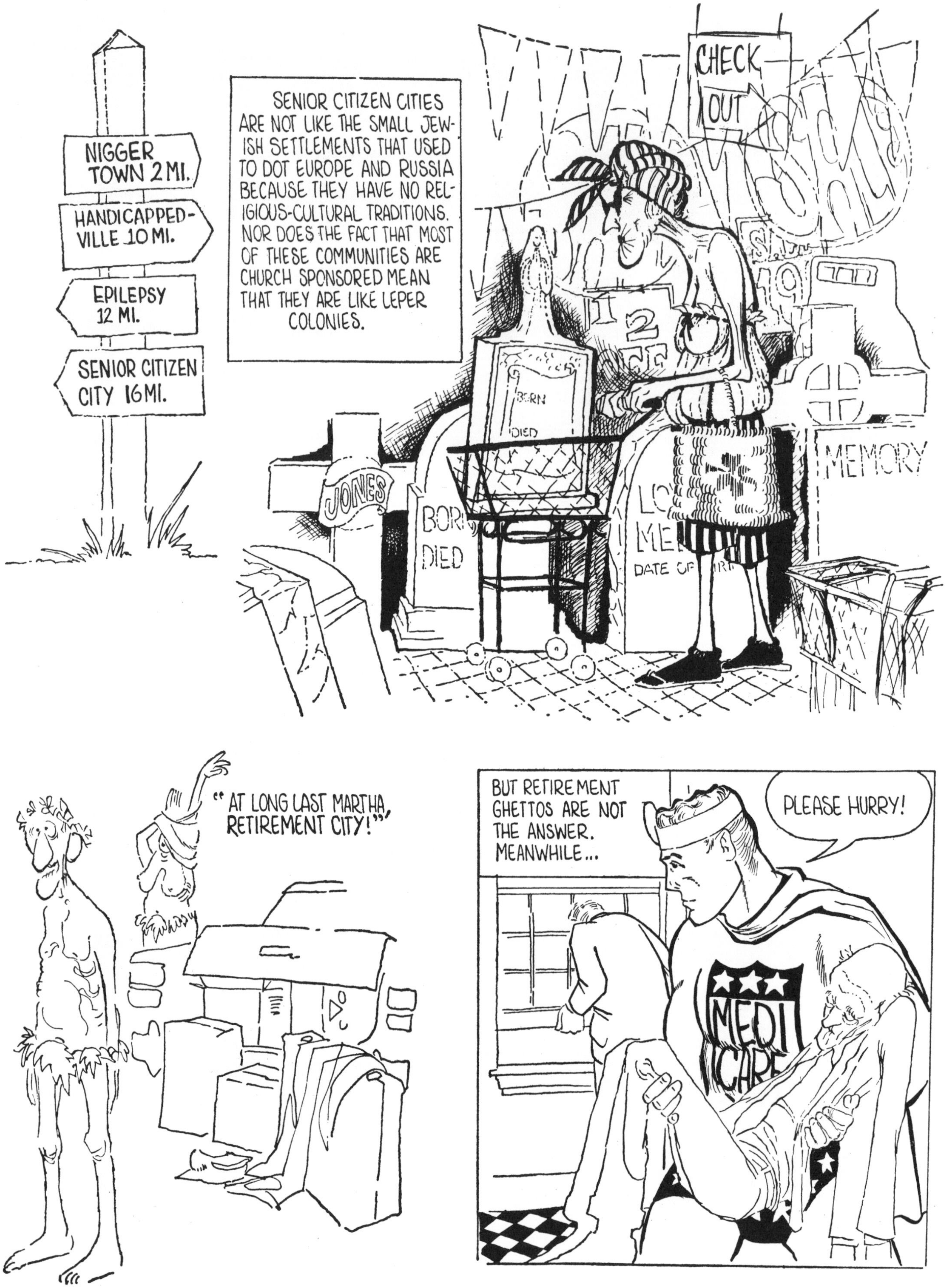
NIGGER TOWN 2 MI.
HANDICAPPED-VILLE 10 MI.
EPILEPSY 12 MI.
SENIOR CITIZEN CITY 16 MI.
SENIOR CITIZEN CITIES ARE NOT LIKE THE SMALL JEWISH SETTLEMENTS THAT USED TO DOT EUROPE AND RUSSIA BECAUSE THEY HAVE NO RELIGIOUS-CULTURAL TRADITIONS. NOR DOES THE FACT THAT MOST OF THESE COMMUNITIES ARE CHURCH SPONSORED MEAN THAT THEY ARE LIKE LEPER COLONIES.
CHECK OUT
BORN
DIED
JONES
MEMORY
"AT LONG LAST MARTHA, RETIREMENT CITY!"
BUT RETIREMENT GHETTOS ARE NOT THE ANSWER. MEANWHILE...
PLEASE HURRY!
MEDI CARE

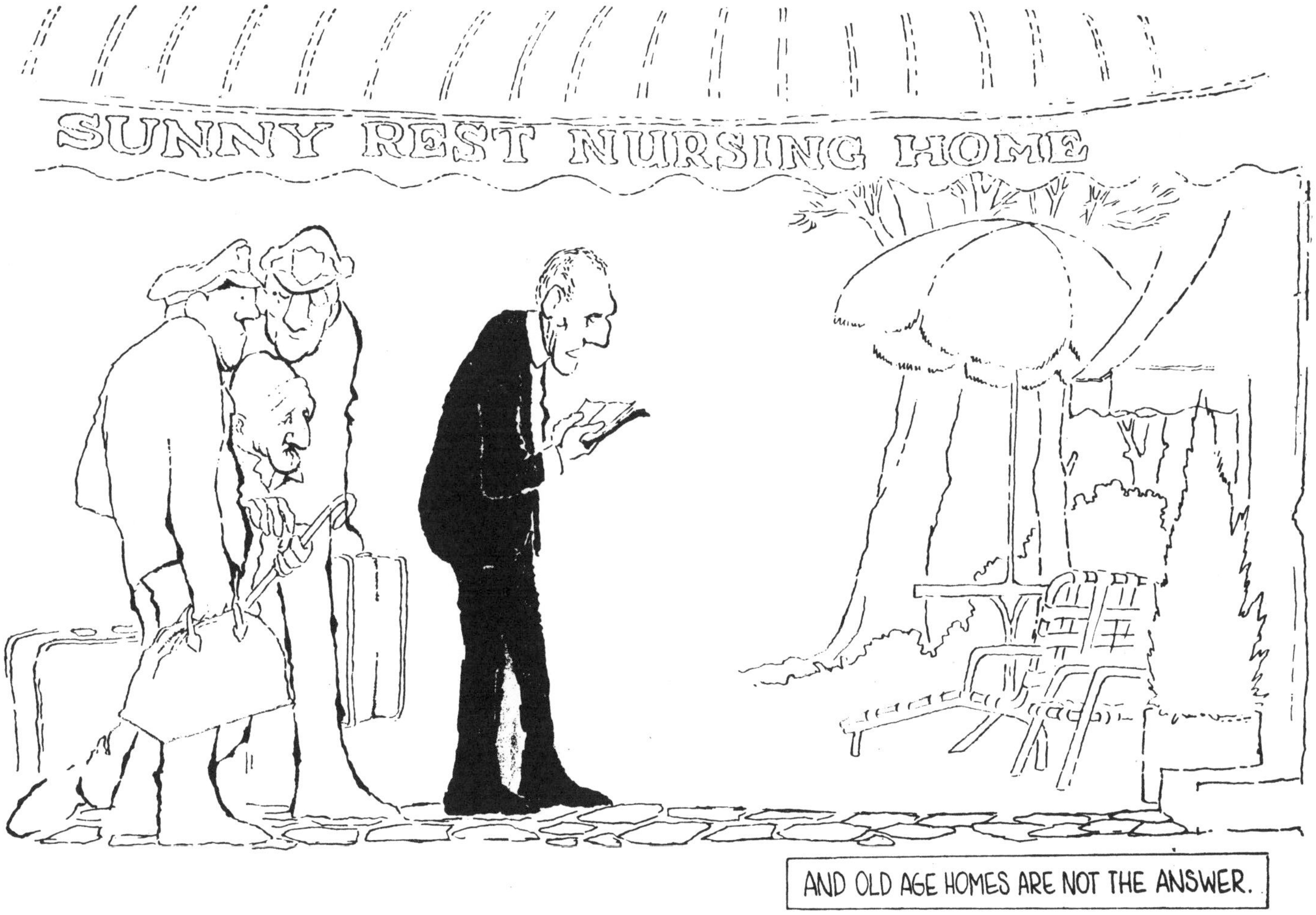
SUNNY REST NURSING HOME
AND OLD AGE HOMES ARE NOT THE ANSWER.

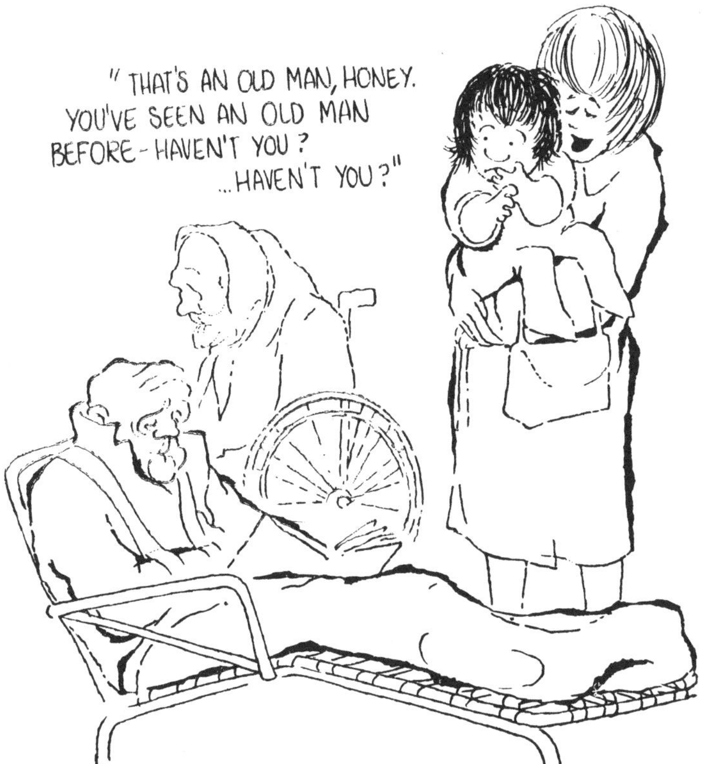
" THAT'S AN OLD MAN, HONEY.
YOU'VE SEEN AN OLD MAN
BEFORE - HAVEN'T YOU ?
...HAVEN'T YOU ?"

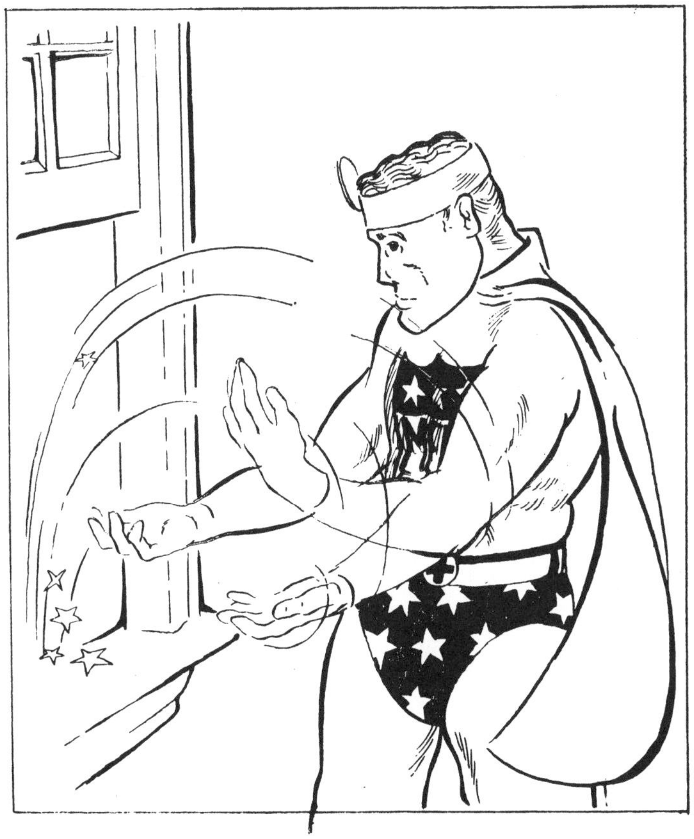

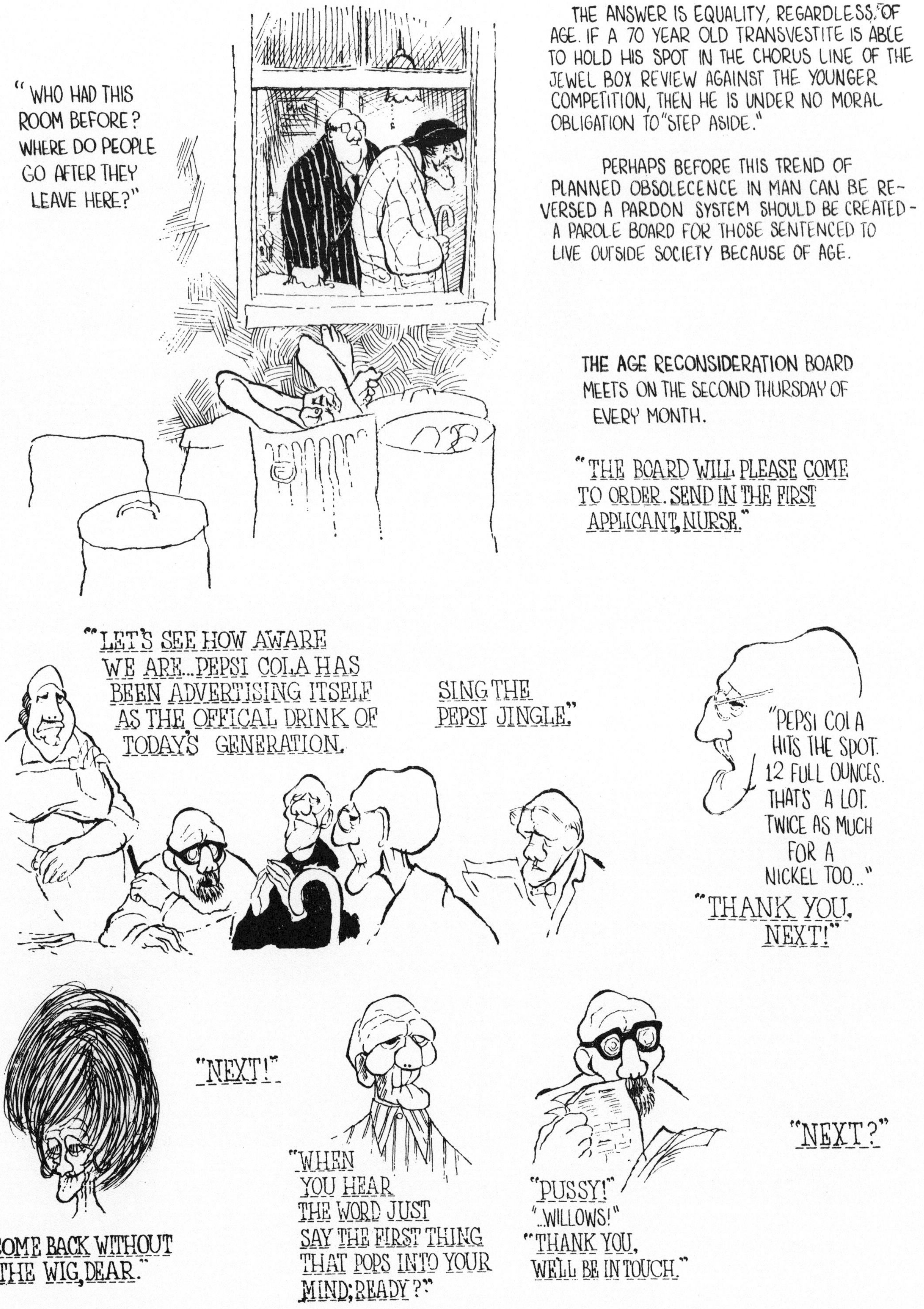
THE ANSWER IS EQUALITY, REGARDLESS OF AGE. IF A 70 YEAR OLD TRANSVESTITE IS ABLE TO HOLD HIS SPOT IN THE CHORUS LINE OF THE JEWEL BOX REVIEW AGAINST THE YOUNGER COMPETITION, THEN HE IS UNDER NO MORAL OBLIGATION TO "STEP ASIDE."
"WHO HAD THIS ROOM BEFORE? WHERE DO PEOPLE GO AFTER THEY LEAVE HERE?"
PERHAPS BEFORE THIS TREND OF PLANNED OBSOLECENCE IN MAN CAN BE REVERSED A PARDON SYSTEM SHOULD BE CREATED - A PAROLE BOARD FOR THOSE SENTENCED TO LIVE OUTSIDE SOCIETY BECAUSE OF AGE.
THE AGE RECONSIDERATION BOARD MEETS ON THE SECOND THURSDAY OF EVERY MONTH.
"THE BOARD WILL PLEASE COME TO ORDER. SEND IN THE FIRST APPLICANT, NURSE."
"LET'S SEE HOW AWARE WE ARE...PEPSI COLA HAS BEEN ADVERTISING ITSELF AS THE OFFICAL DRINK OF TODAY'S GENERATION.
SING THE PEPSI JINGLE."
"PEPSI COLA HITS THE SPOT. 12 FULL OUNCES. THAT'S A LOT. TWICE AS MUCH FOR A NICKEL TOO..."
"THANK YOU, NEXT!"
"COME BACK WITHOUT THE WIG, DEAR."
"NEXT!"
"WHEN YOU HEAR THE WORD JUST SAY THE FIRST THING THAT POPS INTO YOUR MIND; READY?"
"PUSSY!"
"...WILLOWS!"
"THANK YOU, WE'LL BE IN TOUCH."
"NEXT?"

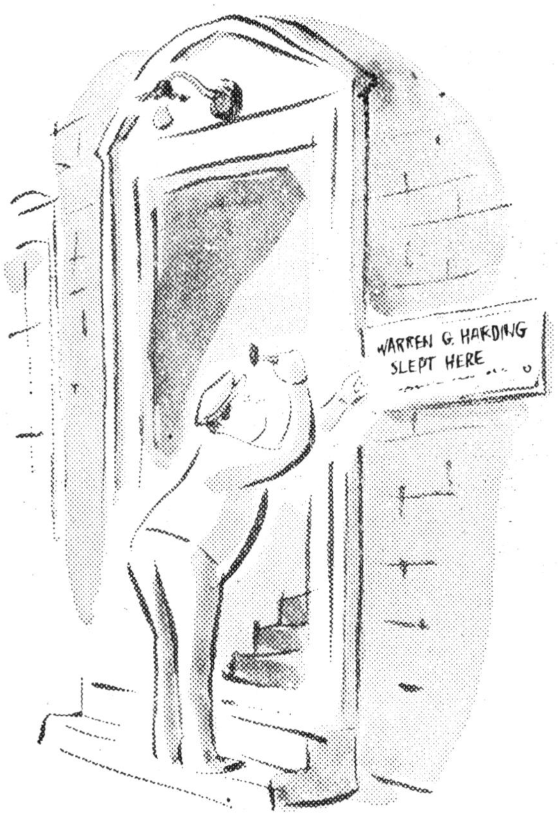
WARREN G. HARDING
SLEPT HERE

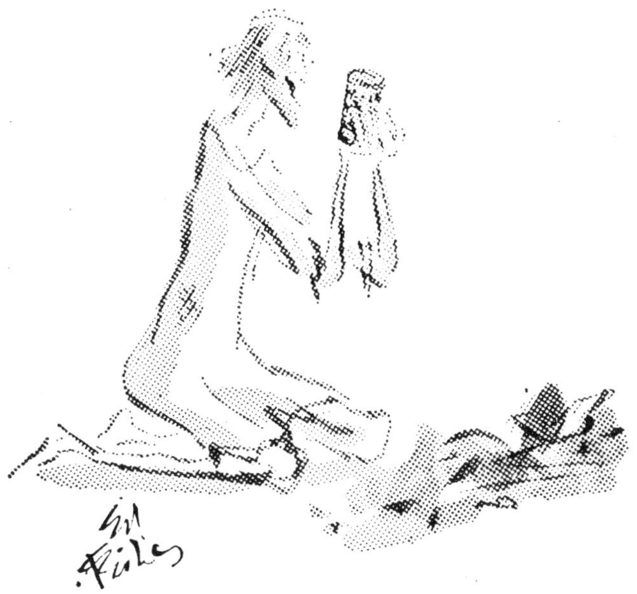

"Oh, boy — Laddie Boy!"

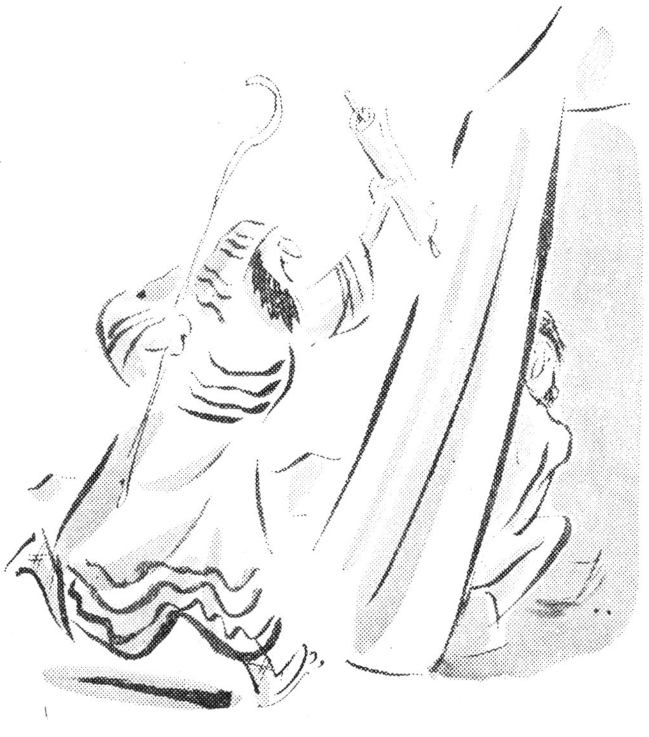

"Hay, Onan, you made The Bible!"

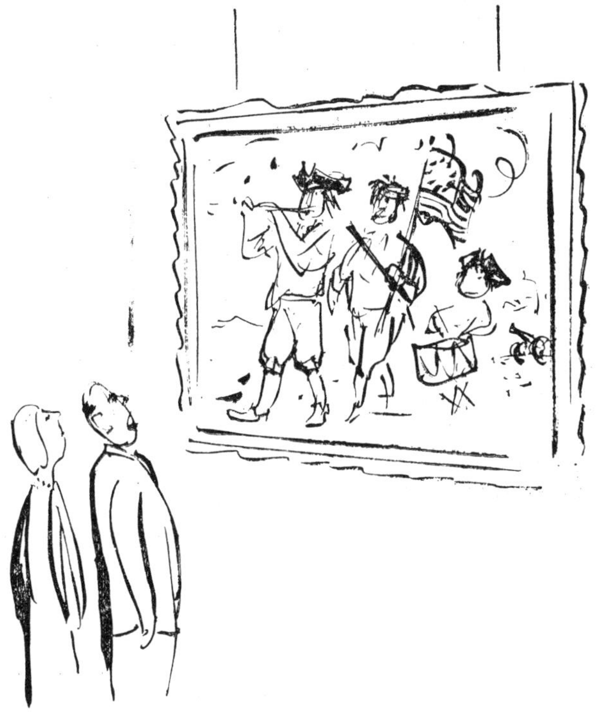

"One of them ought to be represented as a Negro."

ED FISHER. THE REALIST #60, JUNE 1965.

PHONE
DID YOU RISK A $25.00 FINE TODAY?
GUINDON

NEWS ITEM: A 25-year-old surgical intern from India was booked for 9 violations of the City Health Code after he confessed to dismembering the body of his wife.

RICHARD GUINDON. THE REALIST #61, AUGUST 1965.

GUINDON

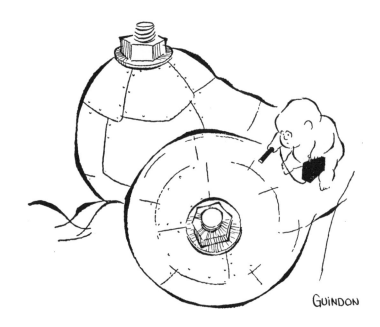

NEWS ITEM: Traces of radioactive Strontium 90 have been found in mother's milk.

RICHARD GUINDON. THE REALIST #61, AUGUST 1965.

"... Mrs. Braun, you've got a luvley daught-errr ... "

ED FISHER. THE REALIST #60, JUNE 1965. *65

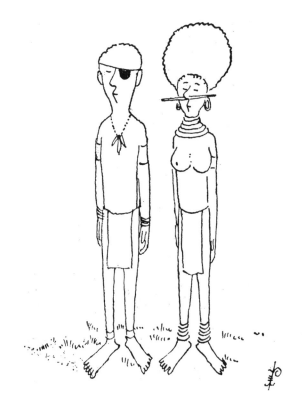

THE REALIST #60, JUNE 1965.

MIKE THALER.
THE REALIST #61, AUGUST 1965.

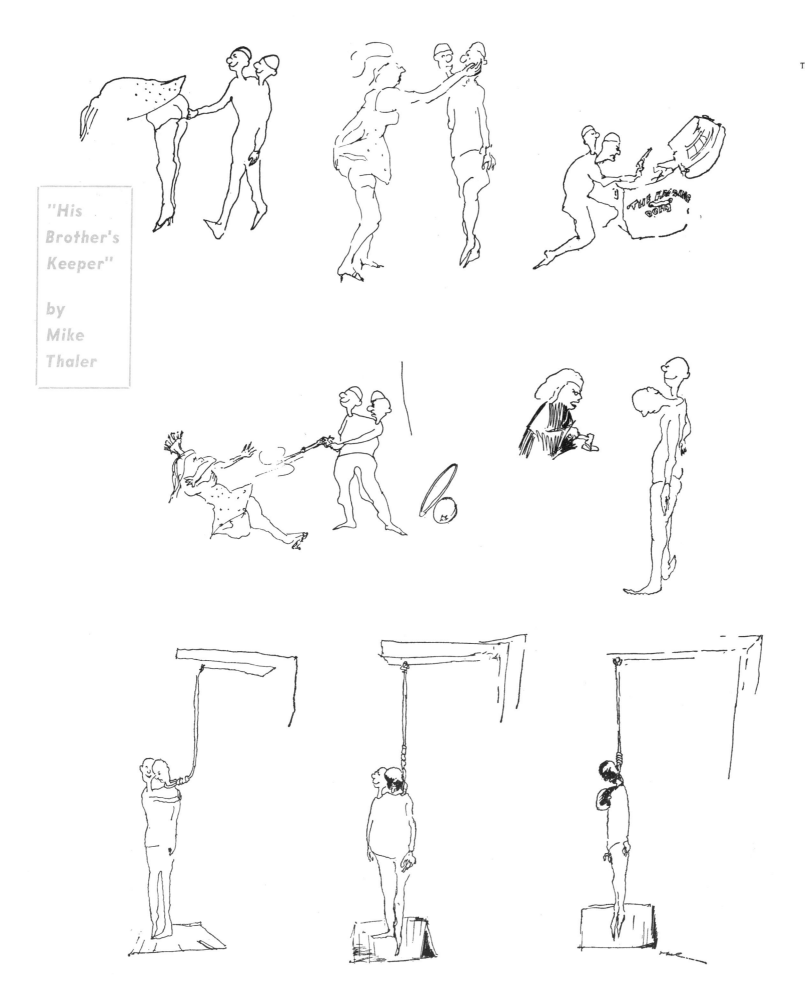

"His
Brother's
Keeper"

by
Mike
Thaler

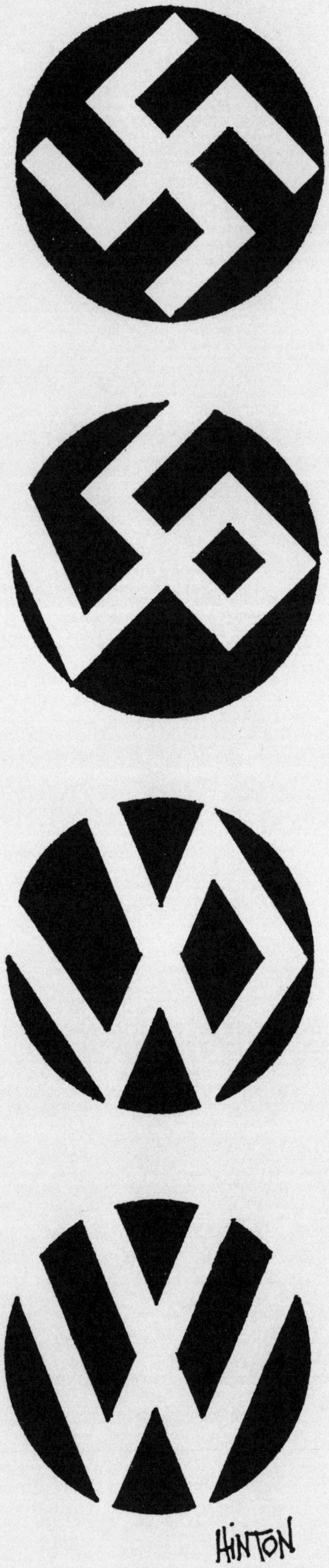
HINTON

HINTON. THE REALIST #61, AUGUST 1965.

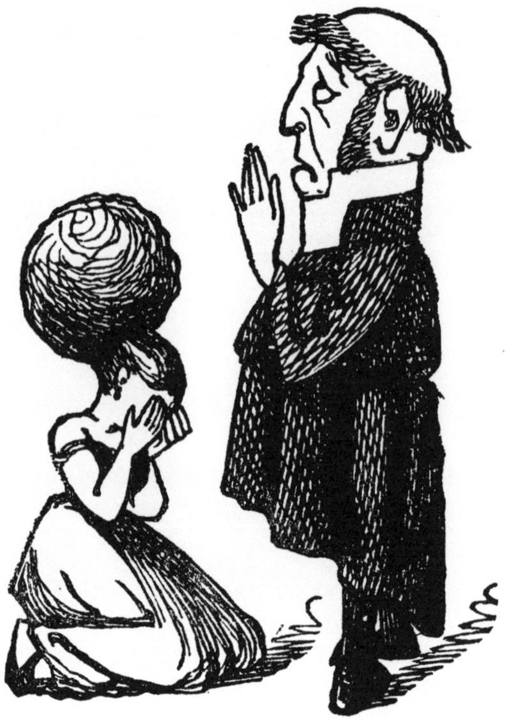

"Forgive her, Father, for she has had lustful thoughts about me — heh, heh, heh ..."

THE REALIST #61, AUGUST 1965.

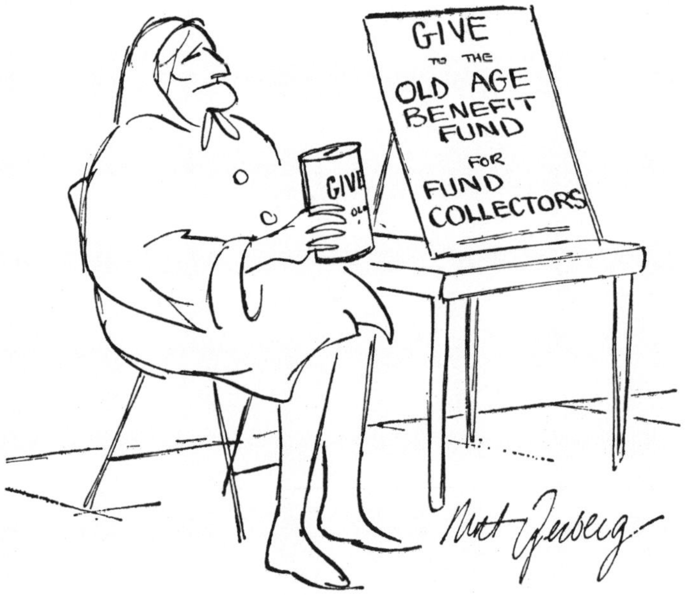
GIVE
TO THE
OLD AGE
BENEFIT
FUND
FOR
FUND
COLLECTORS
GIVE
Mort Gerberg

MORT GERBERG. THE REALIST #62, SEPTEMBER 1965.

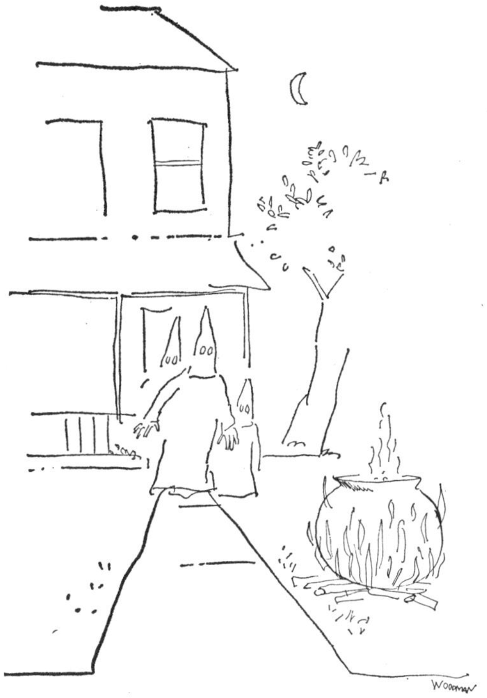
Woodman

WOODMAN. THE REALIST #62, SEPTEMBER 1965.

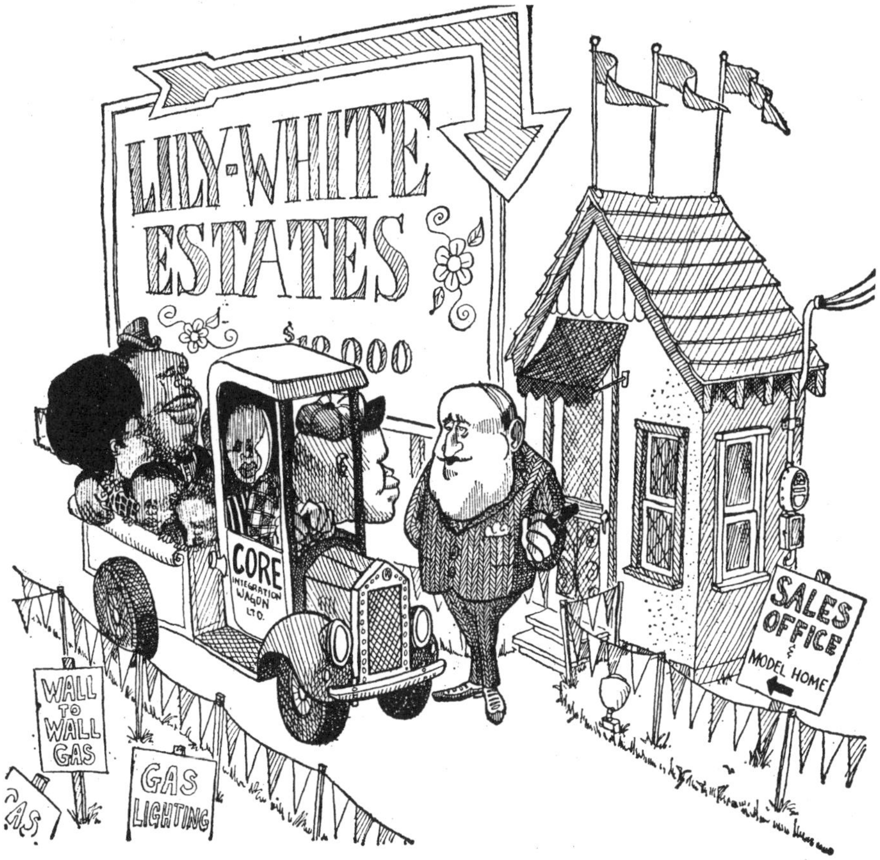
LILY-WHITE
ESTATES
CORE
INTEGRATION
WAGON
LTD.
SALES
OFFICE
&
MODEL HOME
WALL
TO
WALL
GAS
GAS
LIGHTING

"Sorry, we take from the NAACP."

TERRY GILLIAM. THE REALIST #62, SEPTEMBER 1965.

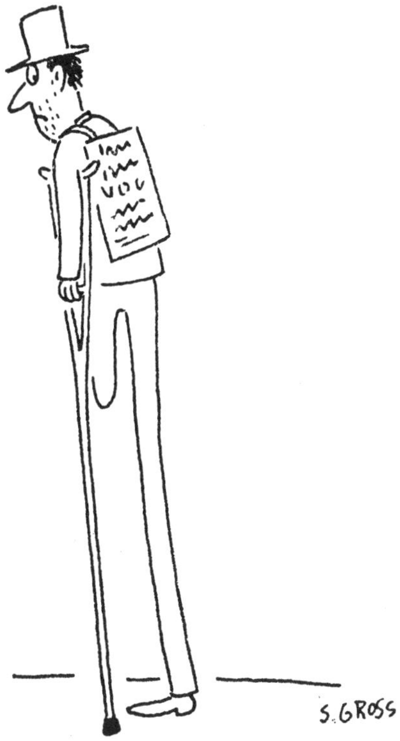
S. GROSS

SAM GROSS. THE REALIST #62, SEPTEMBER 1965.

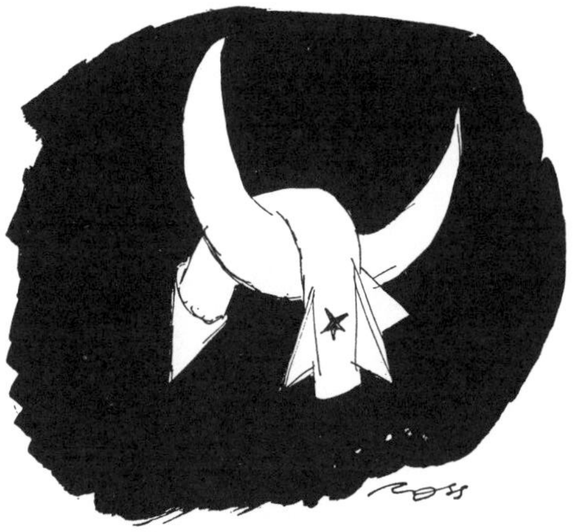
Ross

AL ROSS. THE REALIST #62, SEPTEMBER 1965.

RICHARD GUINDON. THE REALIST #63, OCTOBER 1963.

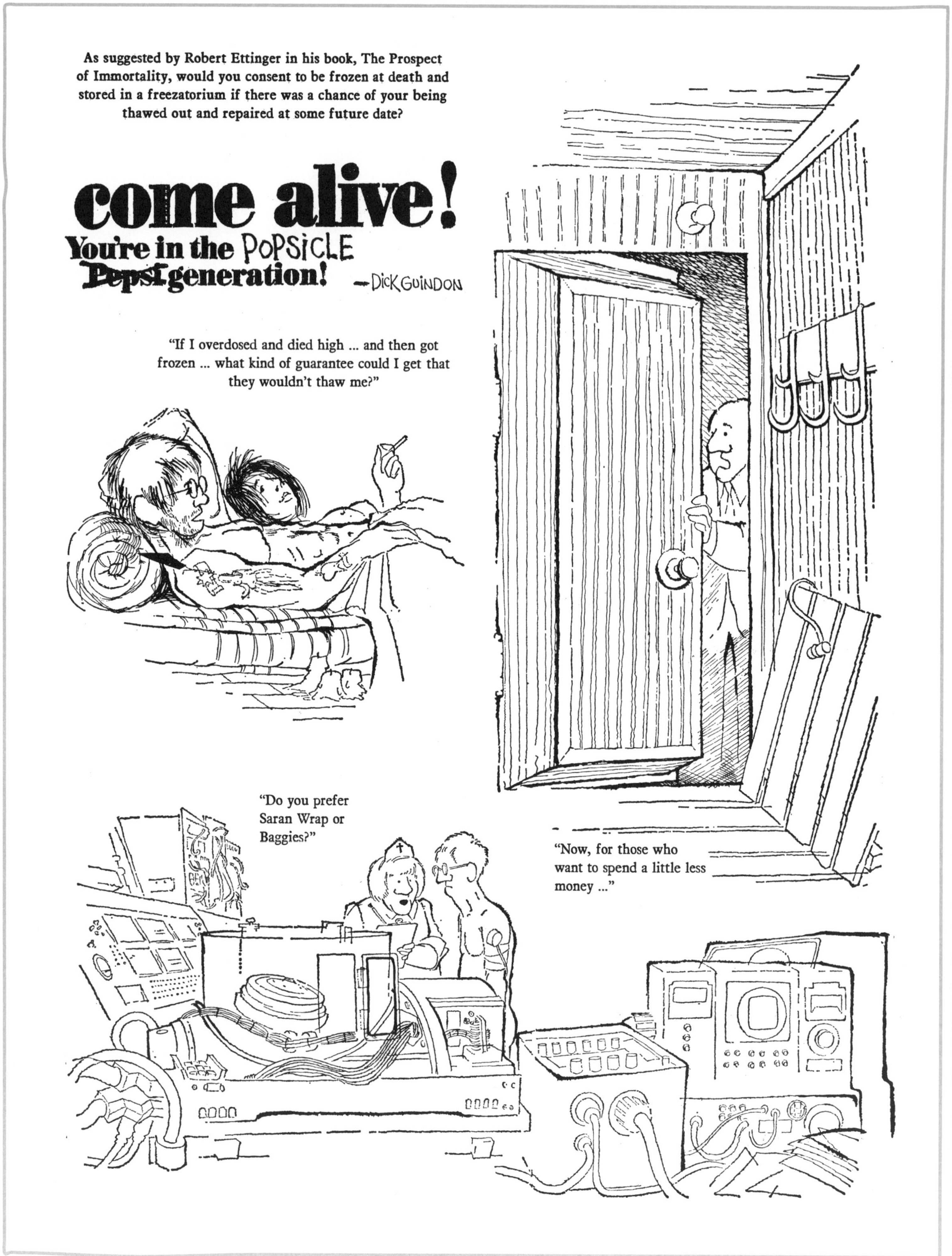
As suggested by Robert Ettinger in his book, The Prospect of Immortality, would you consent to be frozen at death and stored in a freezatorium if there was a chance of your being thawed out and repaired at some future date?
come alive!
You're in the POPSICLE
~~Pepsi~~ generation!
—DICK GUINDON
"If I overdosed and died high ... and then got frozen ... what kind of guarantee could I get that they wouldn't thaw me?"
"Do you prefer Saran Wrap or Baggies?"
"Now, for those who want to spend a little less money ..."

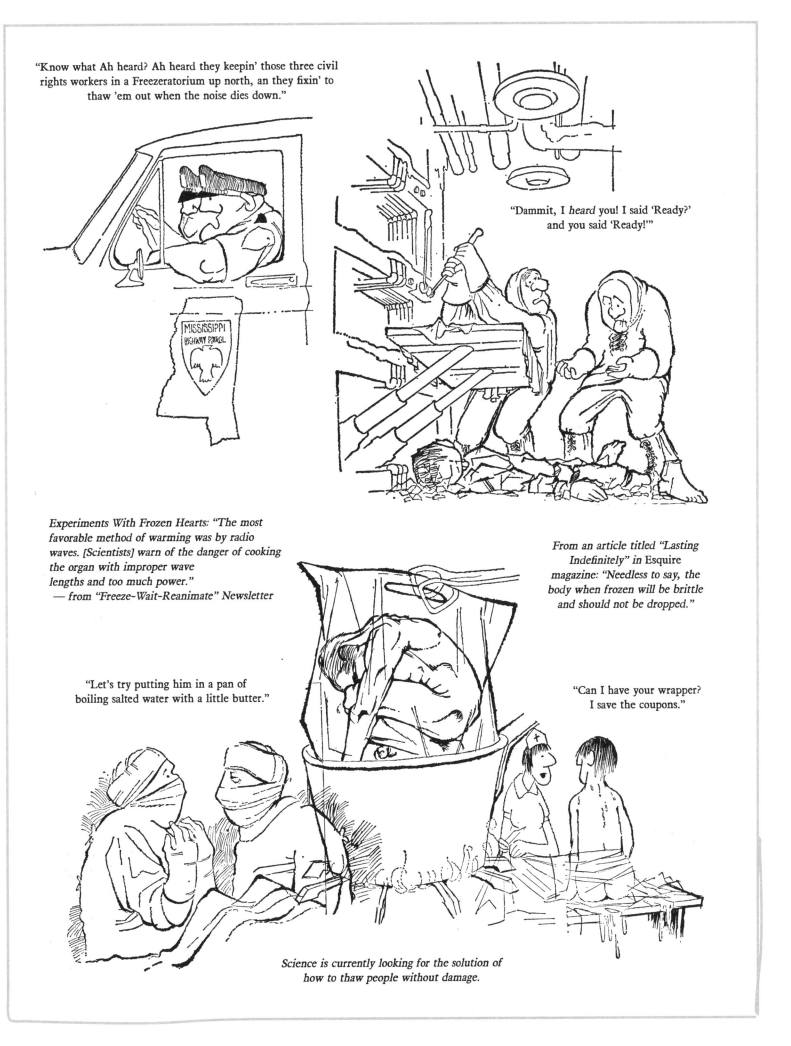

"Know what Ah heard? Ah heard they keepin' those three civil rights workers in a Freezeratorium up north, an they fixin' to thaw 'em out when the noise dies down."

MISSISSIPPI
HIGHWAY PATROL

"Dammit, I *heard* you! I said 'Ready?' and you said 'Ready!'"

Experiments With Frozen Hearts: "The most favorable method of warming was by radio waves. [Scientists] warn of the danger of cooking the organ with improper wave lengths and too much power."
— from "Freeze-Wait-Reanimate" Newsletter

From an article titled "Lasting Indefinitely" in Esquire *magazine: "Needless to say, the body when frozen will be brittle and should not be dropped."*

"Let's try putting him in a pan of boiling salted water with a little butter."

"Can I have your wrapper? I save the coupons."

Science is currently looking for the solution of how to thaw people without damage.

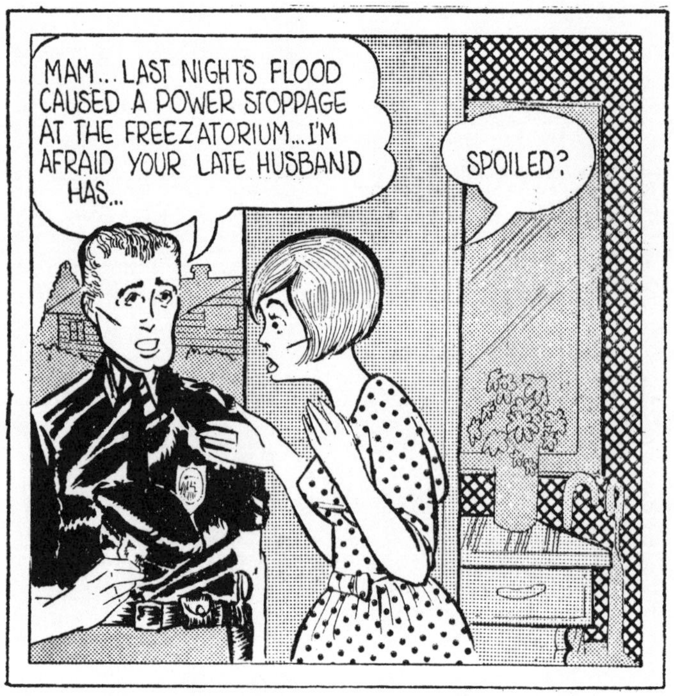
MAM... LAST NIGHTS FLOOD CAUSED A POWER STOPPAGE AT THE FREEZATORIUM...I'M AFRAID YOUR LATE HUSBAND HAS...
SPOILED?

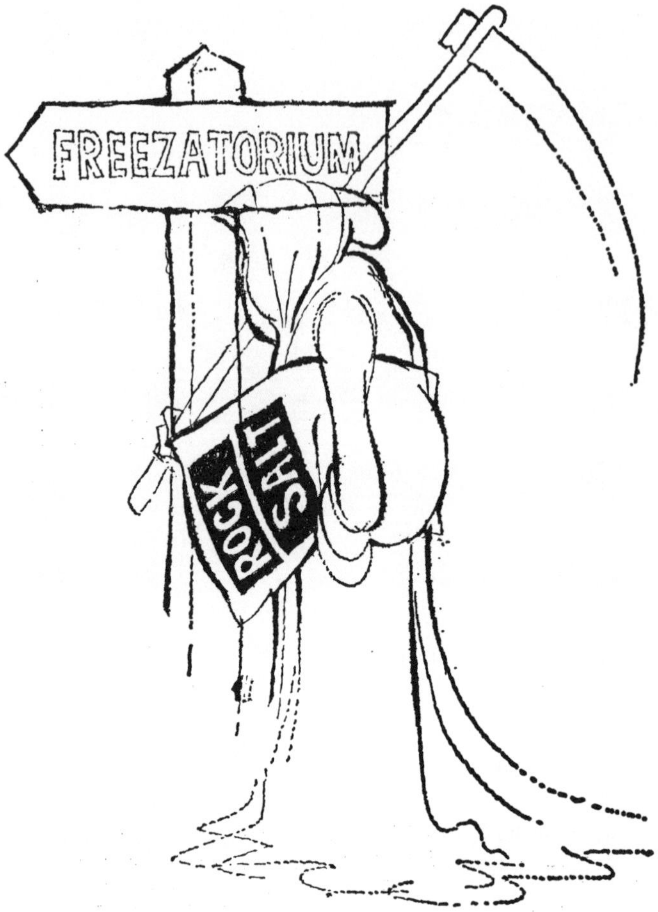
FREEZATORIUM
ROCK SALT

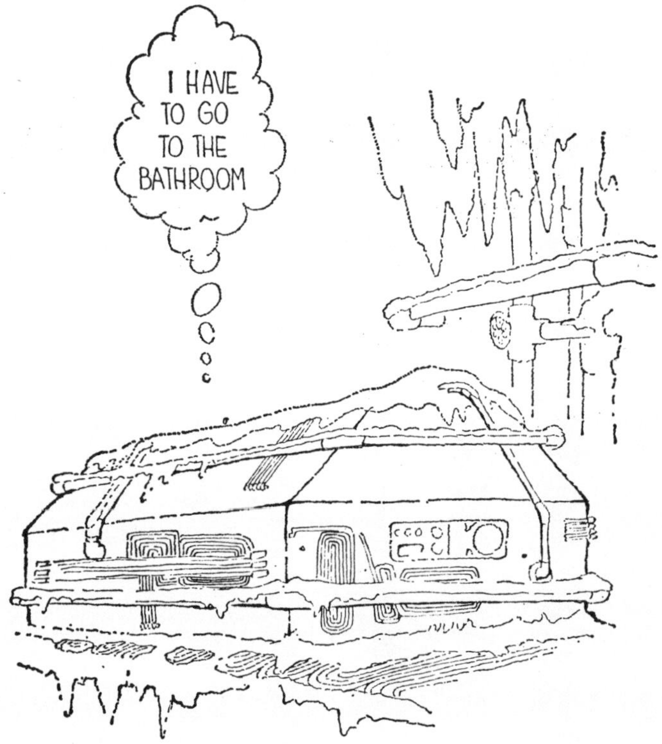
I HAVE TO GO TO THE BATHROOM

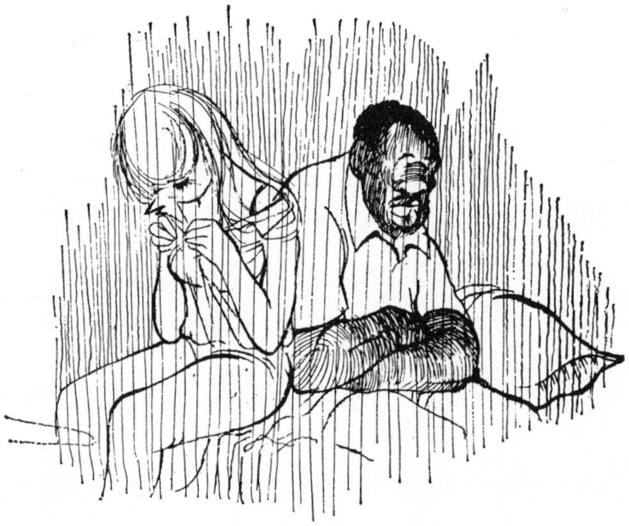

"You won't ball me be-cause
I'm a thawee."

On Death: "We will be pitting our brains against a ruthless and unremitting enemy."
— from a letter to the Life Extension Society.

WELL, HERE I AM, ONE OF THE LEADING SOCIAL CRITICS OF OUR TIME, SITTING HERE AT MY DRAWING BOARD, READY TO DELIVER A ANOTHER **ZINGER** TO THE LIBERAL PUBLIC AT LARGE.

TRUE, I'M NOT EXACTLY A MICHELANGELO—BUT THAT'S MORE THAN COMPENSATED FOR BY BOTH MY BITING SENSE OF HUMOR AND MY SHARP INSIGHT INTO CONTEMPORARY FOIBLES.

SO, LET'S SEE, WHAT HYPOCRISY SHALL I ATTACK IN MY STRIP **THIS** WEEK? ACCORDING TO RELIABLE AND/OR INFORMED SOURCES, MALAYSIA IS GOING TO BE THE NEXT VIET-NAM. ANOTHER INTERNATIONAL TRAGEDY IN THE MAKING. HMMM.... PERHAPS I CAN SUBTLY WORK SUKARNO'S PEDERASTY PROBLEM INTO THE STORYLINE. BOY, IF ALL THOSE SATISFIED READERS OUT THERE ONLY **KNEW** THE EFFORT I PUT INTO MY CREATIONS.

OH, YOU PEOPLE DON'T KNOW THE HALF OF IT. IN THE FIRST PLACE, I MUST HAVE EACH STRIP READY SEVEN WEEKS IN ADVANCE. THAT'S SYNDICATION BIZ, HEH HEH.

(...EXCEPT FOR MY PRURIENT DIALOGUES BE-TWEEN LITTLE LULU AND TUBBY ....I ALWAYS SEND THOSE TO PLAYBOY.)

AND THEN TOO, THERE'S THE PROBLEM OF THE GOOD GUYS VERSUS THE BAD GUYS. WHAT DO YOU SAY WHEN SOMEBODY LIKE DE GAULLE DOES THE **RIGHT** THING FOR THE **WRONG** REASON? IT'S A PARADOX.....OH, WELL, ENOUGH STALLING. I'VE GOT TO **REALLY SAY IT** THIS WEEK. SO WHAT IF I DID ONCE FAIL PENMANSHIP? THE BANK DOESN'T CARE IF I ENDORSE CHECKS BY PRINTING.

ANYWAY, ICON-OCLASTS CAN'T AFFORD TO BE GUILTY. AND SO TO WORK..... GOD, I ONLY HOPE THE CRISIS IN MALAYSIA LASTS ANOTHER SEVEN WEEKS.

©1965 PK-BHOB

PAUL KRASSNER AND BHOB STEWART. THE REALIST #63, OCTOBER 1963. *66

Why do Polacks have hunched-up shoulders and slope heads?
Because, when you ask them a question they go (see figure a)
and when you tell them the answer they go (see figure b).

ROGER PRICE. THE REALIST #63, OCTOBER 1963.

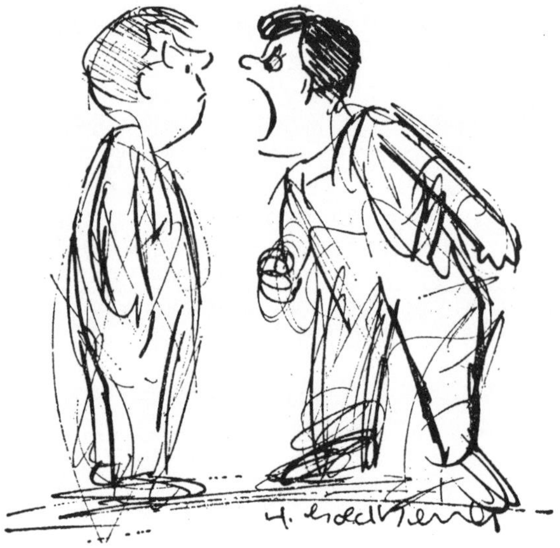
H. Goldberg

"You former Christ-killer!"

HERBERT GOLDBERG. THE REALIST #63, OCTOBER 1963.

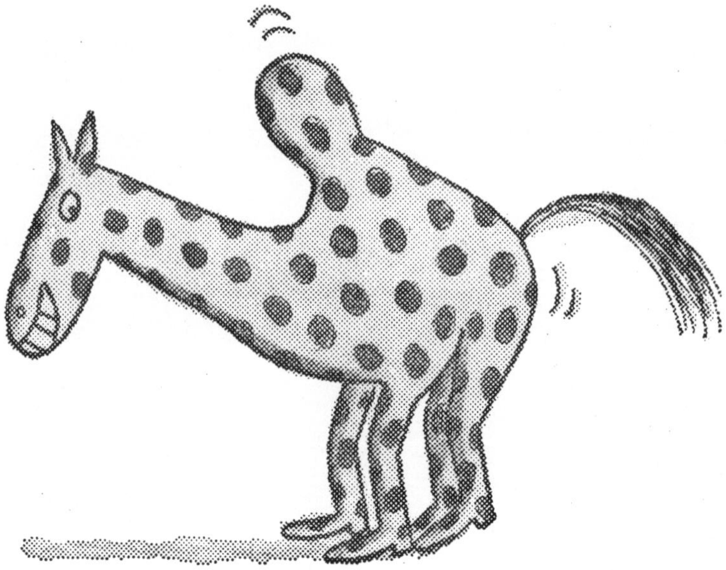

SAM GROSS. THE REALIST #63, OCTOBER 1963.

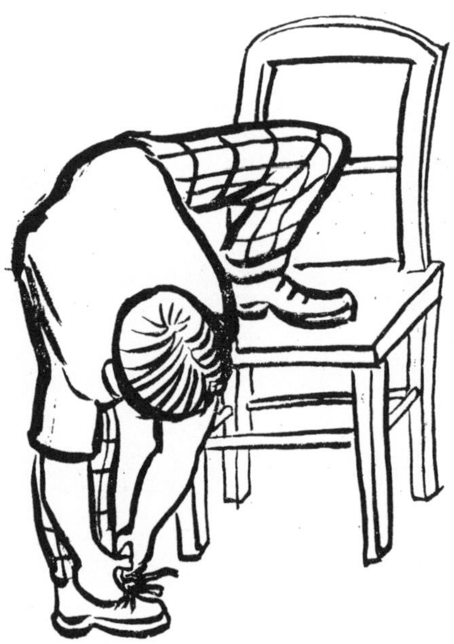

How does a Polack tie his shoelace?

ROGER PRICE. THE REALIST #63, OCTOBER 1963.

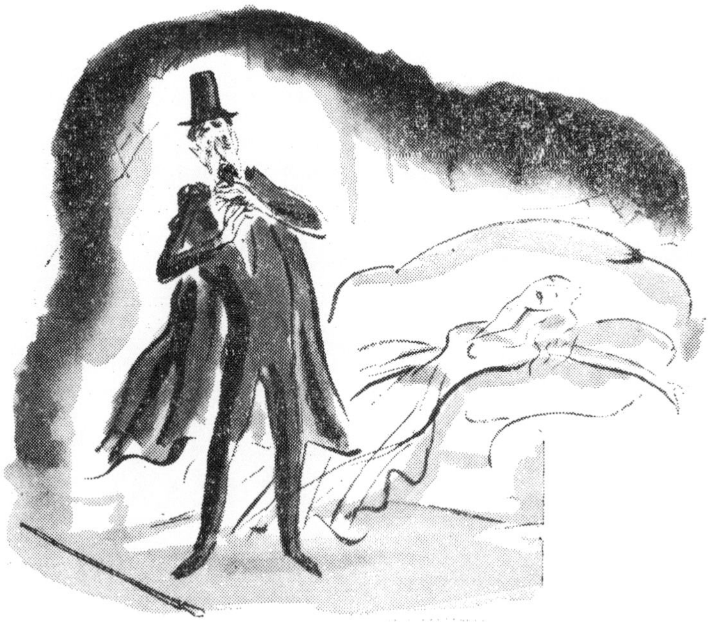

"Gaaaggghhh! — type 'O' negative!"

ED FISHER. THE REALIST #63, OCTOBER 1963.

"Preferential advancement?"

"Why, yes, I'll be glad to be on the Johnson Program's 'representative-of-the-poor' in this neighborhood. How much does the job pay?"

"— And stop calling me 'Pussycat'!"

"— Obscure symbols! ... Tricky word-play! ... Flashbacks-within-flashbacks! ... They just don't write plain, good hate literature any more!"

"— And you, Pfc. Andy Tuggle of A Company, 81st Infantry: If you weren't out here fighting us Vietnamese patriots you could be back home moving to a new neighborhood, going out with white girls, enjoying all those increased civil rights benefits your government has obtained for you ..."

ED FISHER. THE REALIST #63, OCTOBER 1963.

RICHARD GUINDON. THE REALIST #64,
FEBRUARY 1966.

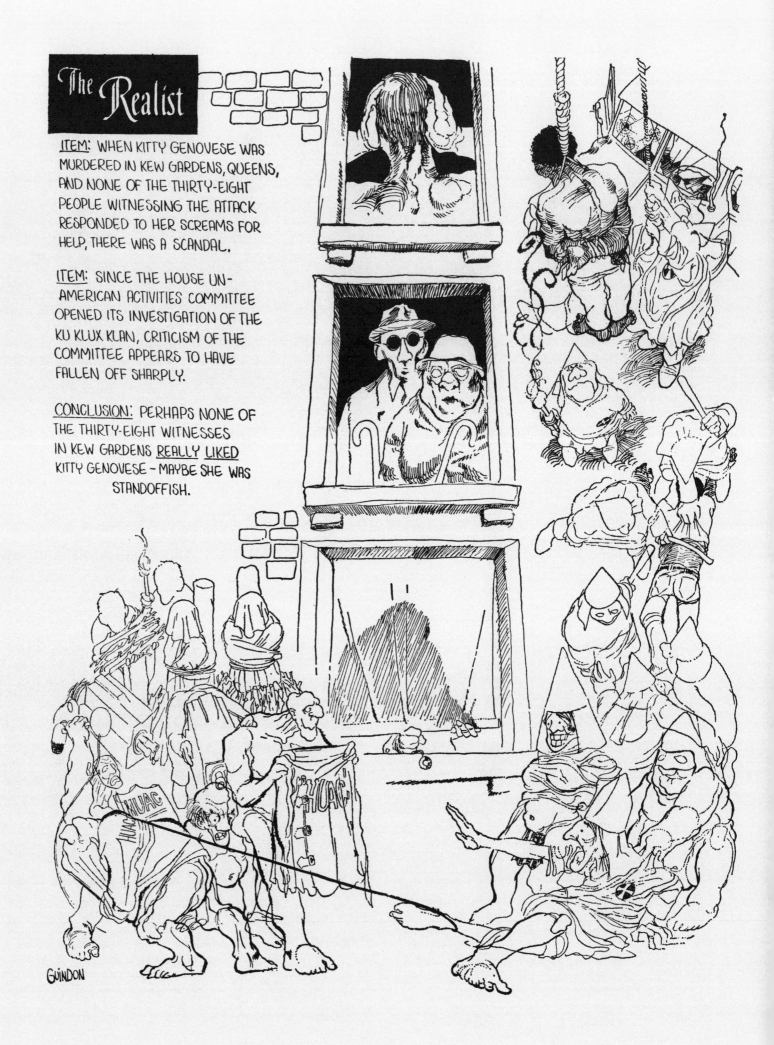

The Realist

ITEM: WHEN KITTY GENOVESE WAS MURDERED IN KEW GARDENS, QUEENS, AND NONE OF THE THIRTY-EIGHT PEOPLE WITNESSING THE ATTACK RESPONDED TO HER SCREAMS FOR HELP, THERE WAS A SCANDAL.

ITEM: SINCE THE HOUSE UN-AMERICAN ACTIVITIES COMMITTEE OPENED ITS INVESTIGATION OF THE KU KLUX KLAN, CRITICISM OF THE COMMITTEE APPEARS TO HAVE FALLEN OFF SHARPLY.

CONCLUSION: PERHAPS NONE OF THE THIRTY-EIGHT WITNESSES IN KEW GARDENS REALLY LIKED KITTY GENOVESE – MAYBE SHE WAS STANDOFFISH.

GUINDON

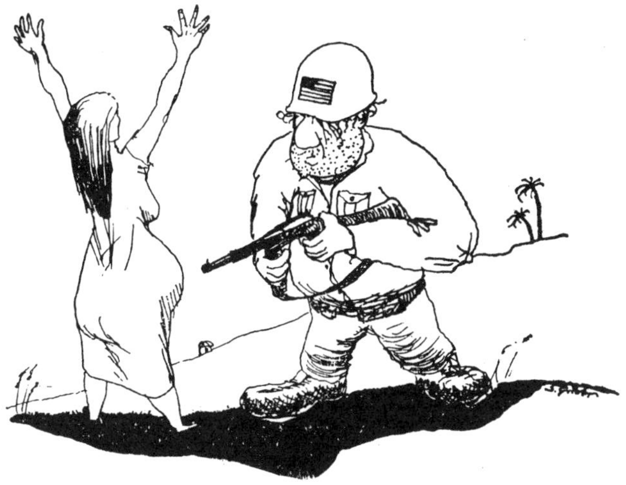

"Are you hiding a Viet Cong in there?"

THE REALIST #63, OCTOBER 1963.

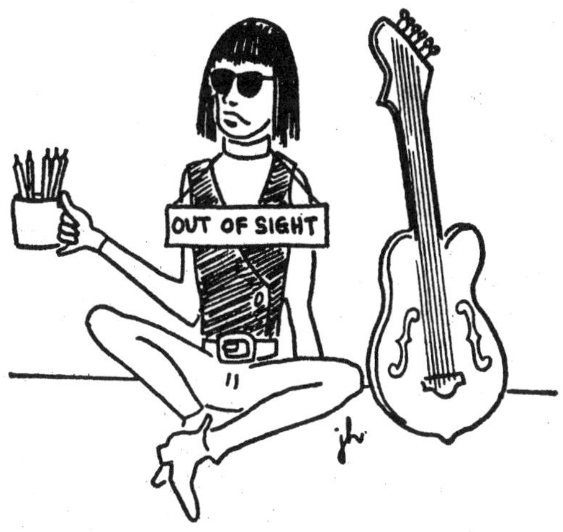
OUT OF SIGHT

JAMES "JAF" FRANKFORT. THE REALIST #64, FEBRUARY 1966.

The Day Barry Goldwater Immolated Himself in Support of LBJ's Vietnam Policy

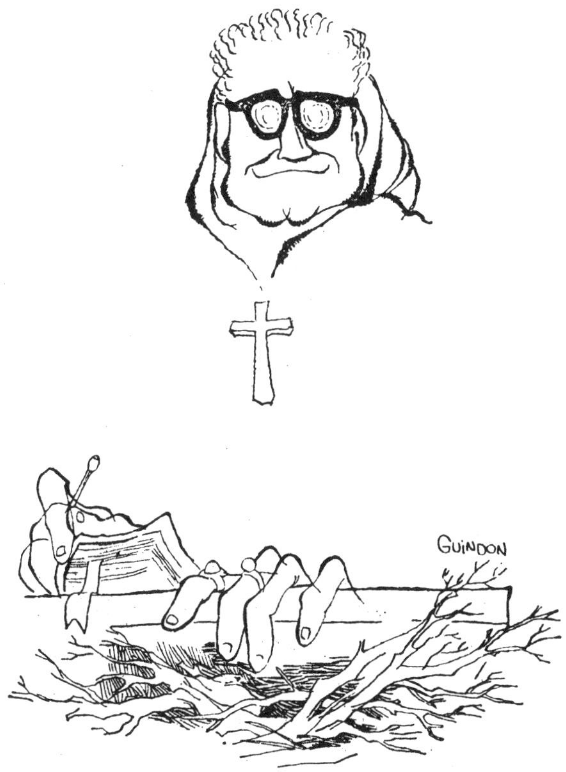
GUINDON

RICHARD GUINDON. THE REALIST #64, FEBRUARY 1966.

The Consecration of the Host

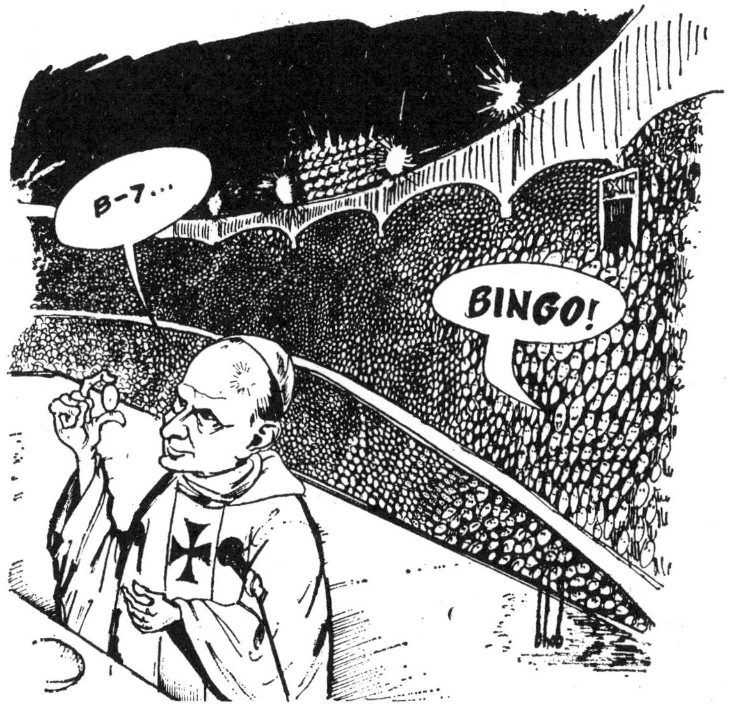
B-7...
BINGO!

BHOB STEWART. THE REALIST #64, FEBRUARY 1966.

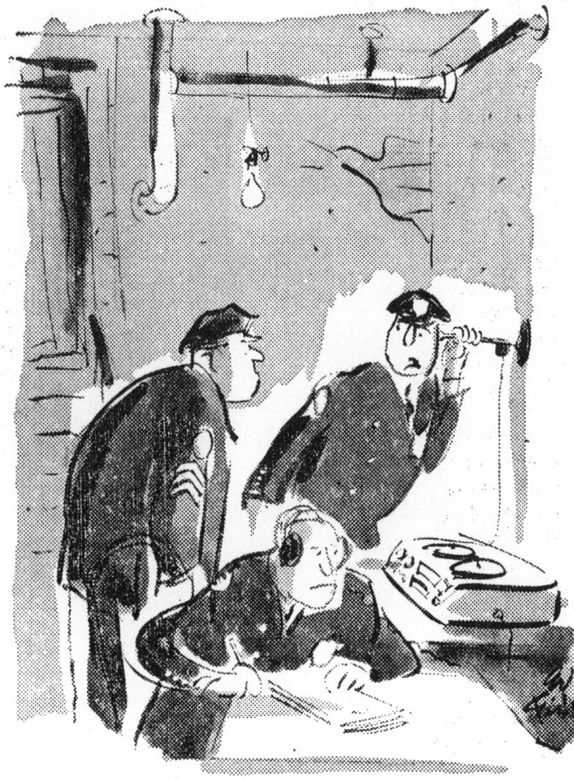

"Do we have to take it down word for word?
It's Dial-a-Prayer."

"So there's a war on in Vietnam! So you can here the guns sounding! ... But why must you be the one to leave your wife, home and child and go off to risk your life day after day, standing in front of troop trains?"

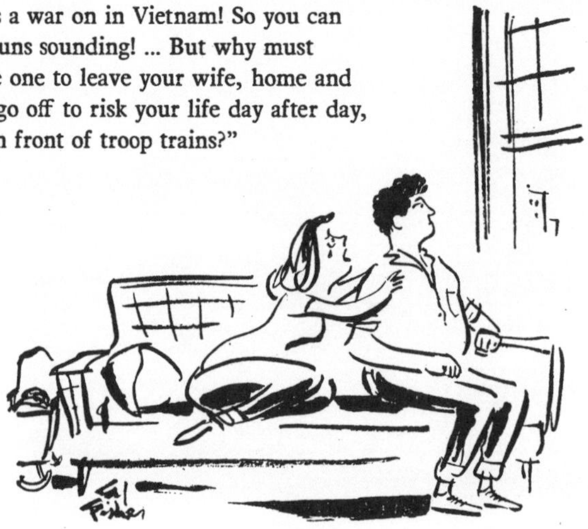

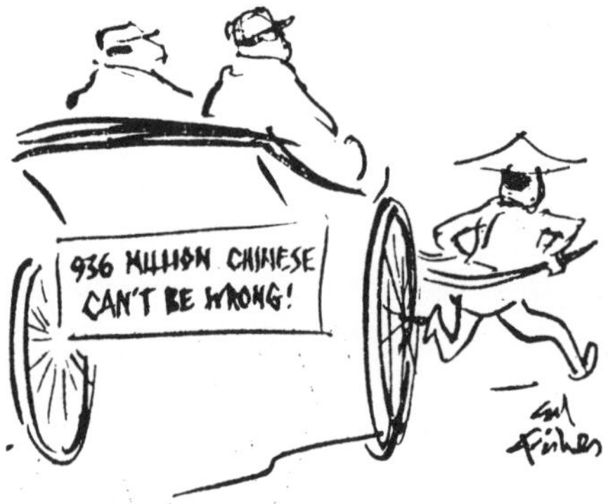
936 MILLION CHINESE
CAN'T BE WRONG!

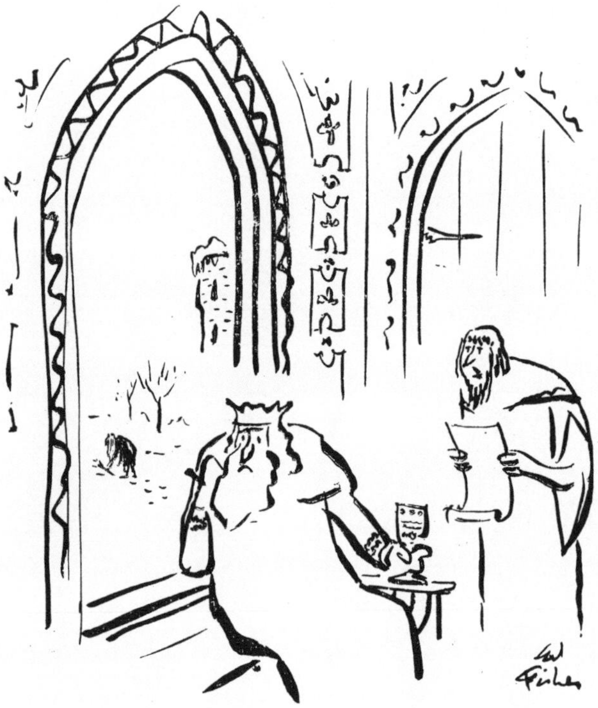

"The unemployment situation is getting very bad, King Wenceslas. You'll have to make some kind of a gesture ..."

"Look, honey, I don't mind your being a tree, part time — but what do you do while you're a tree? Whom do you see? ..."

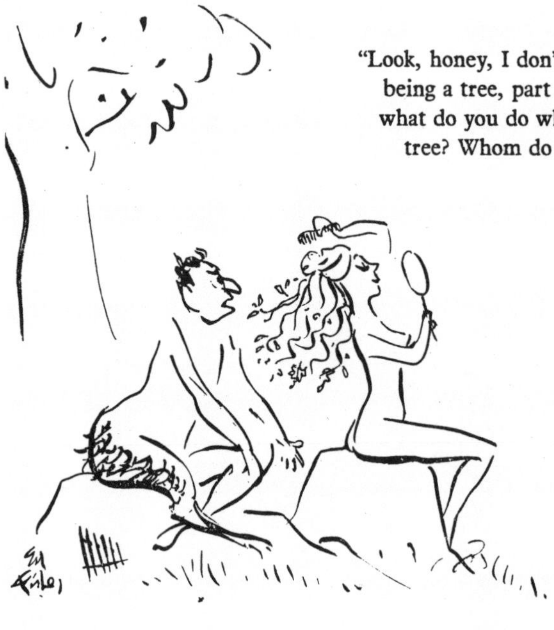

ED FISHER. THE REALIST #64, FEBRUARY 1966.

MORT GERBERG. THE REALIST #64, FEBRUARY 1966.

The Junkie Battalion
by Mort Gerberg

Washington, Oct. 20 (AP)—The Army should begin drafting the nation's "punks and young toughs," Rep. Paul A. Fino (R-N.Y.) said today. He introduced a bill which would amend the Selective Service Act to provide for drafting persons now considered deficient because of criminal records. He suggested special "junkie battalions" for those with narcotics records.

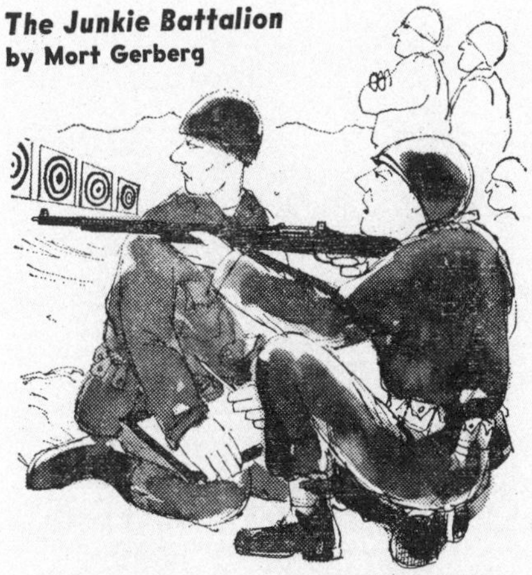

"*Bull's-eye?* Shit, man—I thought that bullet would never even *get* there . . ."

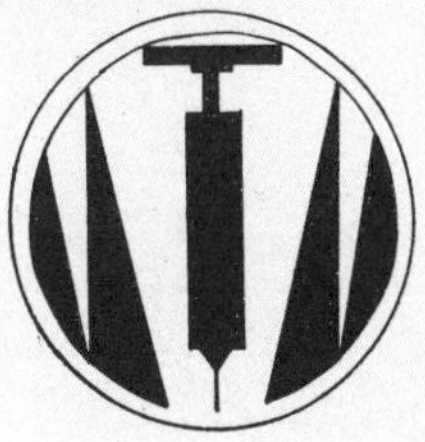

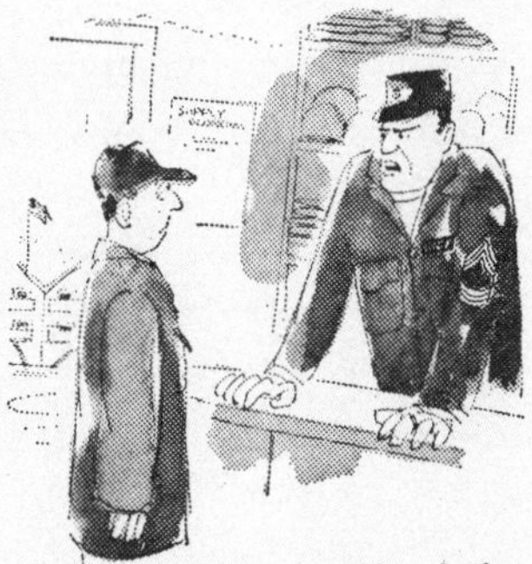

"You got it wrong, buddy—that's *not* what supply rooms are for . . ."

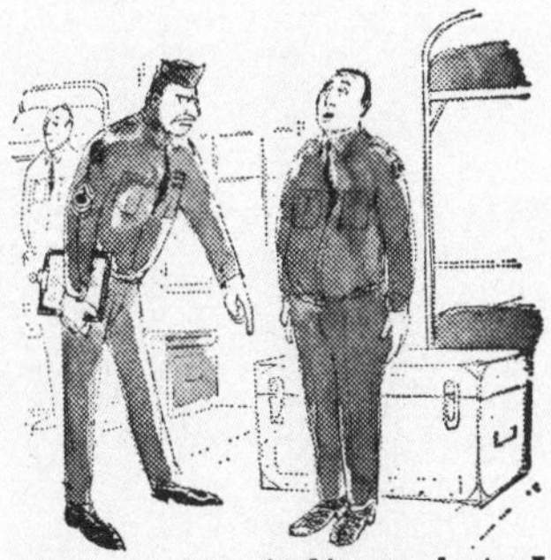

"Sarge, I *can't* spit-shine my boots. I ain't been able to spit in four years!"

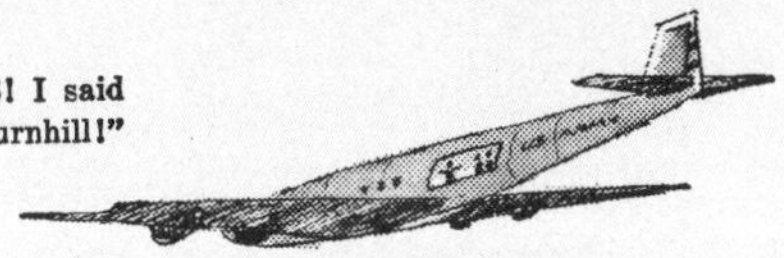

"*Now!* You want me to jump *now*? *Before* we take off?"

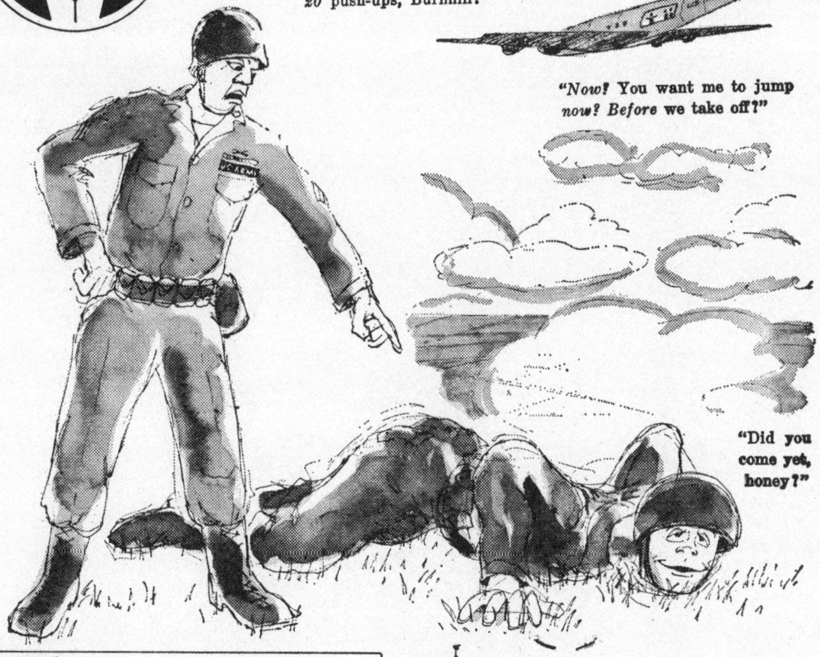

"That's only 16! I said *20* push-ups, Burnhill!"

"Did you come yet, honey?"

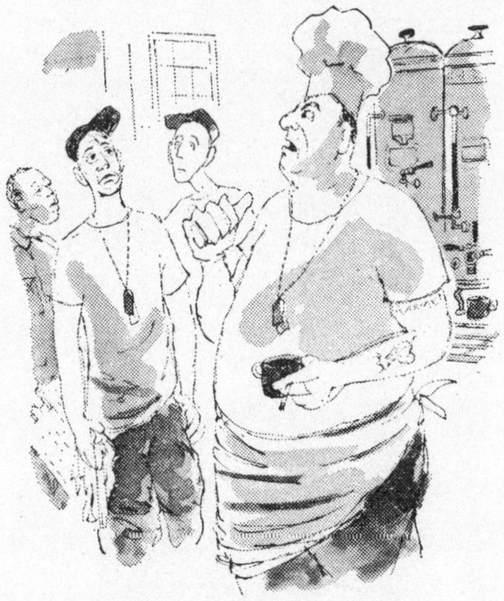

"*My* KP's? In *my* kitchen? In *my* Army? A *tea* break."

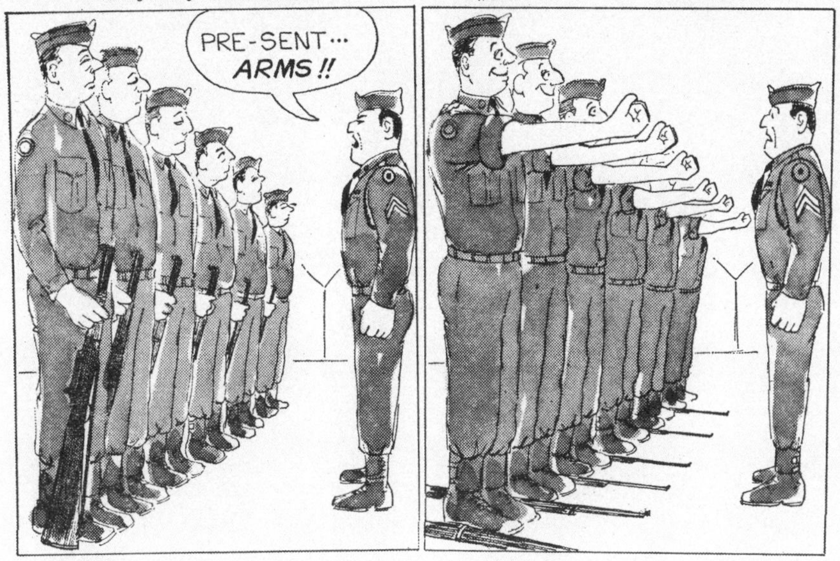
PRE-SENT...
ARMS !!

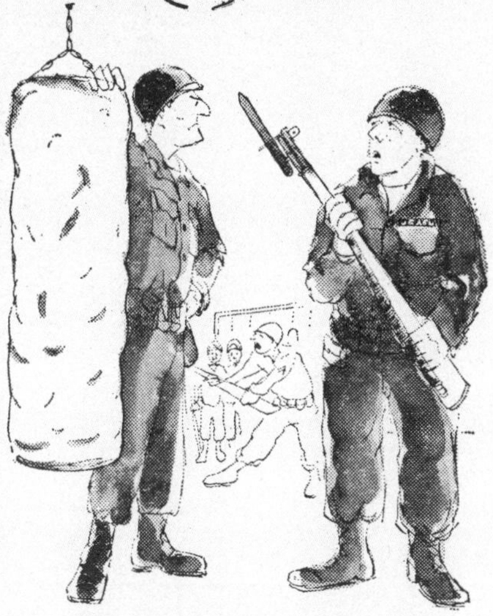

"Why can't I just tick him with a needle and sorta kill him with kindness?"

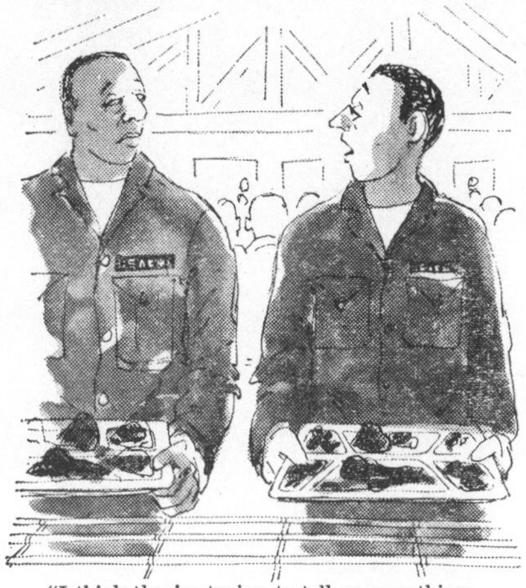

"I think they're trying to tell us something. This is the 18th straight day of cold turkey."

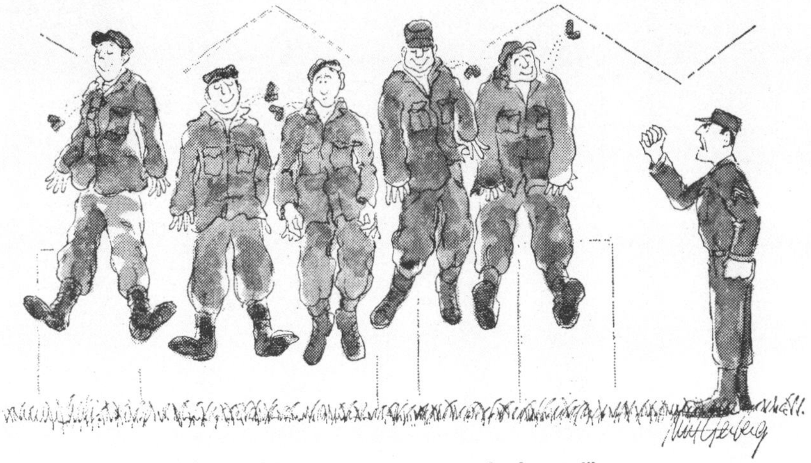

"All right, you guys—no more weekend passes!"

GANDHI
WANTS
YOU

ED FISHER. THE REALIST #64, FEBRUARY 1966.

PASSPORT
PHOTOS
IN 3 MINUTES
SPEE-DEE
PHOTO
SERVICE
1144 MAIN ST.
TEL - 842-6132

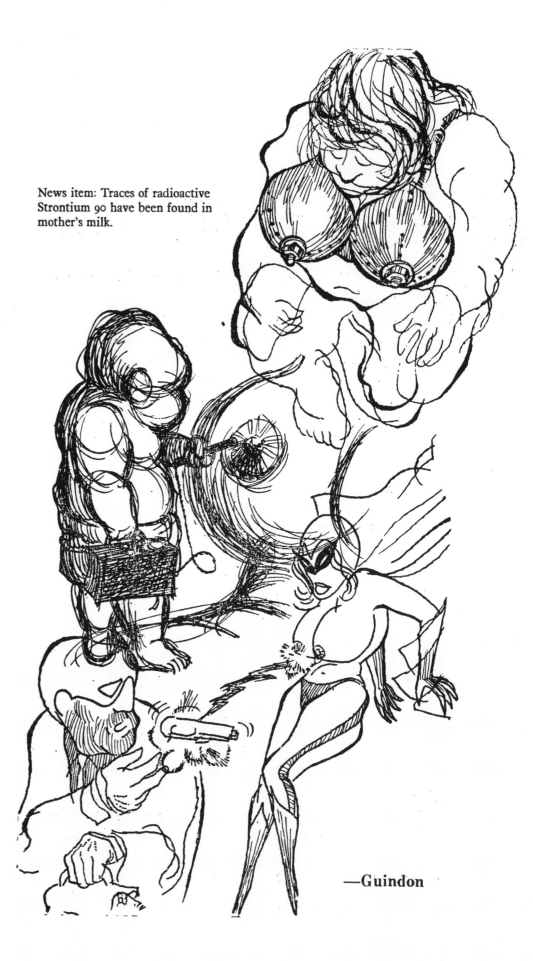

SAM GROSS. THE REALIST #65, MARCH 1966.

News item: Traces of radioactive Strontium 90 have been found in mother's milk.
—Guindon

RICHARD GUINDON. THE REALIST #64, FEBRUARY 1966.

AMERICANIZATION OF ZEN

K. POWERS. THE REALIST #64, FEBRUARY 1966.

"No, I'm not like the other Satyrs. Do you *mind*?"

ED FISHER. THE REALIST #65, MARCH 1966.

"When the guns boom, *our* art certainly doesn't die."

ED FISHER. THE REALIST #65, MARCH 1966.

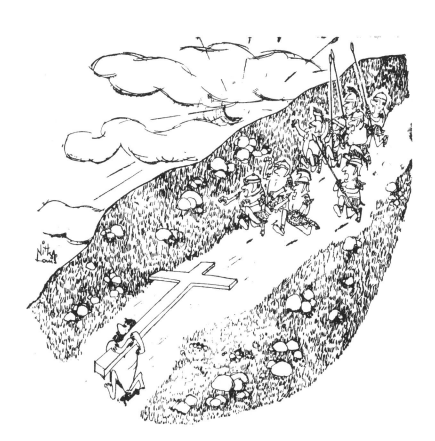

"Stop — thief!"

LOUIS NITKA. THE REALIST #65, MARCH 1966.

"— It's the one beer to have when you're having more than one!"

ED FISHER. THE REALIST #65, MARCH 1966.

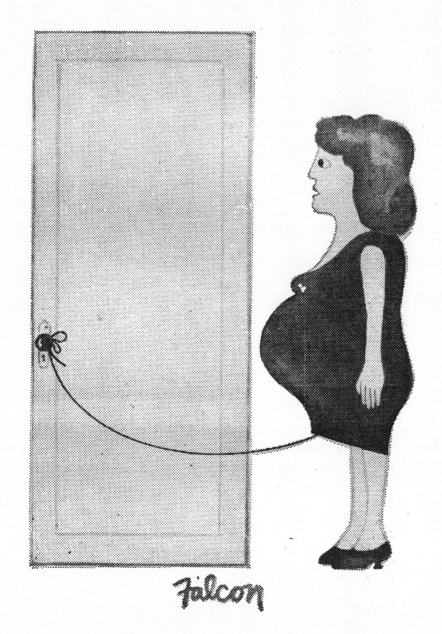

I WAS AN ABORTIONIST FOR THE FBI

FALCON. THE REALIST #66, APRIL 1966.

"— Yes, I switched to Islam because I found it a more satisfying religion than (*cuckoo!*) — or — (*cuckoo!*) ..."

ED FISHER. THE REALIST #65, MARCH 1966.

"Well, if it bothers you, remember — it's probably driving the FBI crazy, too!"

ED FISHER. THE REALIST #65, MARCH 1966.

LOUIS NITKA. THE REALIST #66, APRIL 1966.

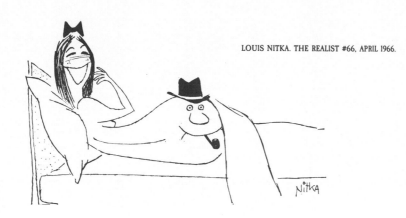

"Say 'Ah' ..."

LOUIS NITKA. THE REALIST #66, APRIL 1966.

J.C. SUARES. THE REALIST #65, MARCH 1966.

"THE SEARCH" by J. C. Suarez

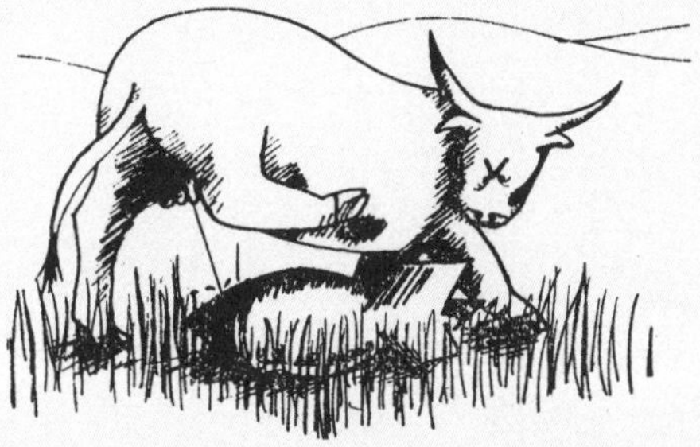

"Two weeks after the crash of a B-52 nuclear-armed bomber and a refueling jet tanker over the south-east tip of Spain, the U.S. Defense Dept. still refused to concede that one of its hydrogen bombs was missing (but) villagers of Palomares, near the crash site, were examined for radiation and many told to burn their clothing."
— *National Guardian*

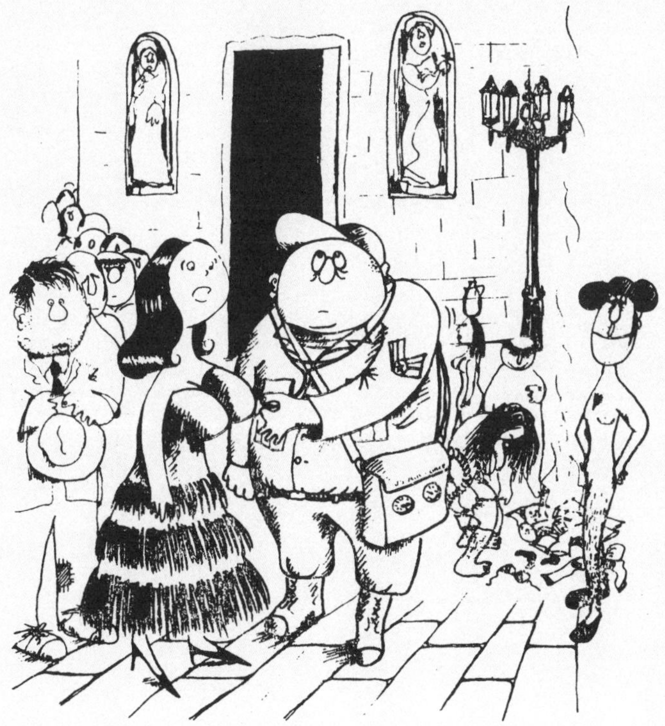

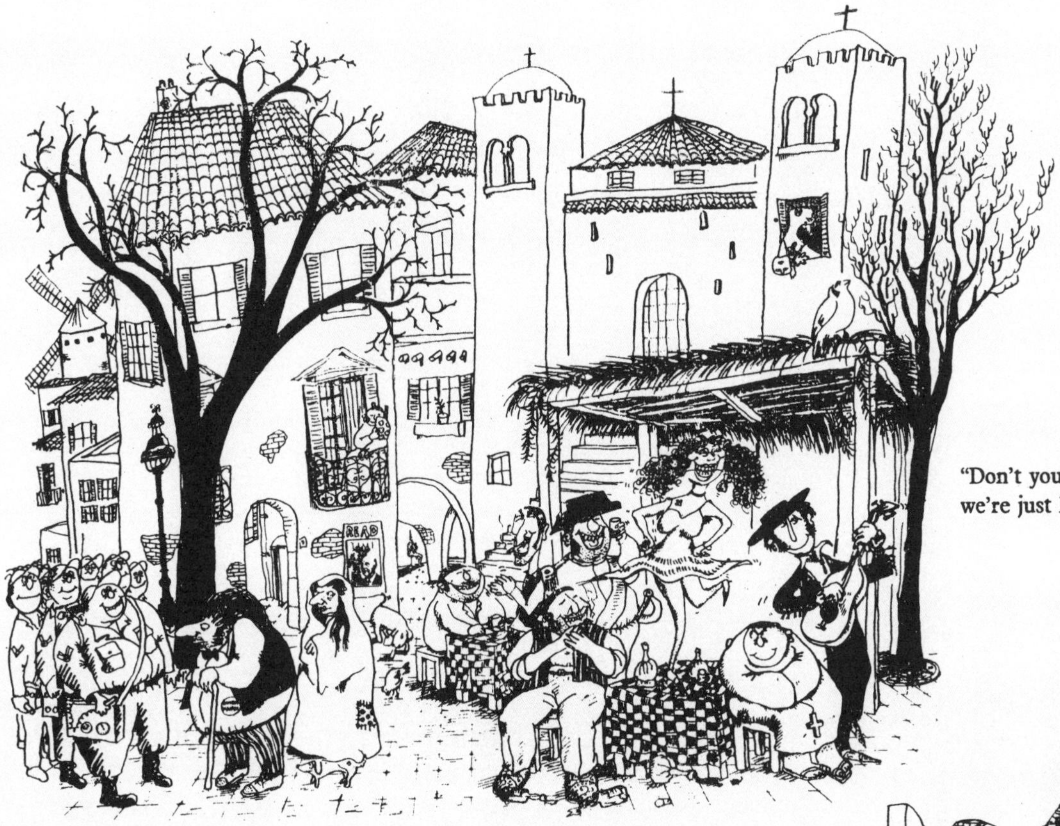
READ

"Don't you folks worry about us none — we're just looking for a hydrogen bomb."

"Hey, fellows, you're not going to believe this ..."

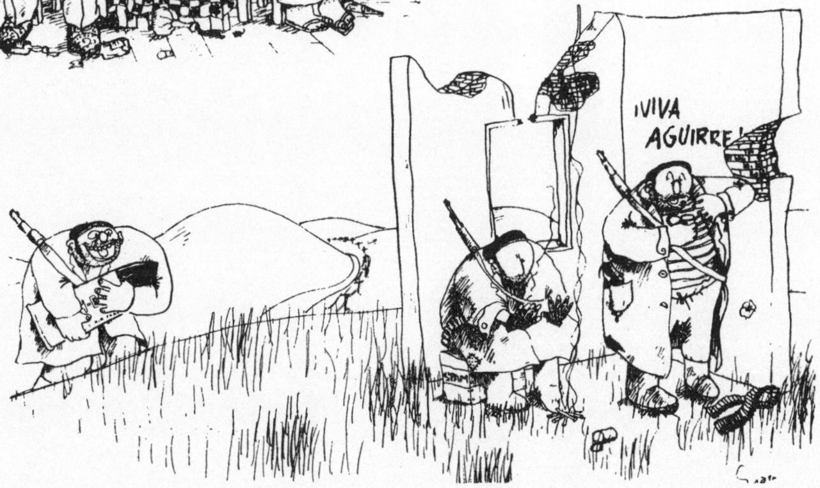
¡VIVA
AGUIRRE!

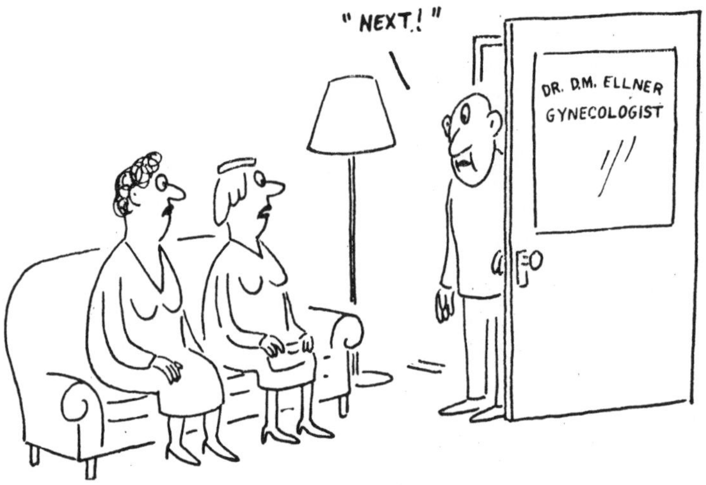
"NEXT!"
DR. D.M. ELLNER
GYNECOLOGIST

SAM GROSS. THE REALIST #66, APRIL 1966.

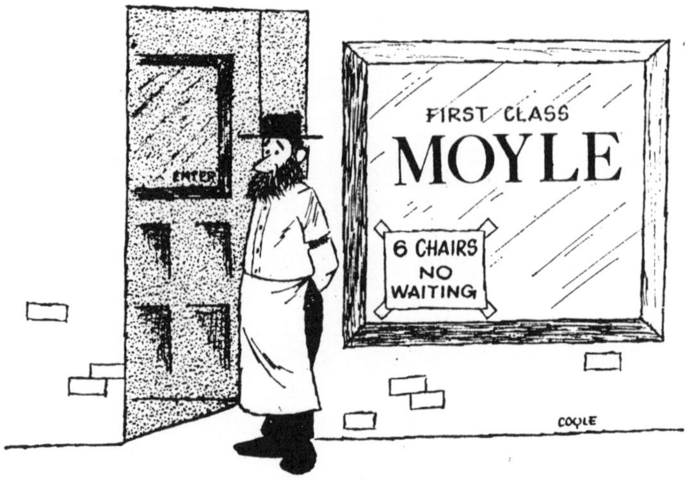
FIRST CLASS
MOYLE
6 CHAIRS
NO
WAITING

COYNE. THE REALIST #66, APRIL 1966.

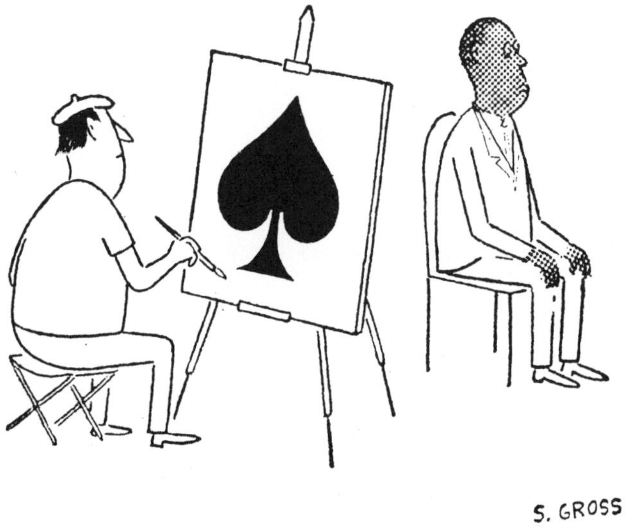
S. GROSS

SAM GROSS. THE REALIST #66, APRIL 1966.

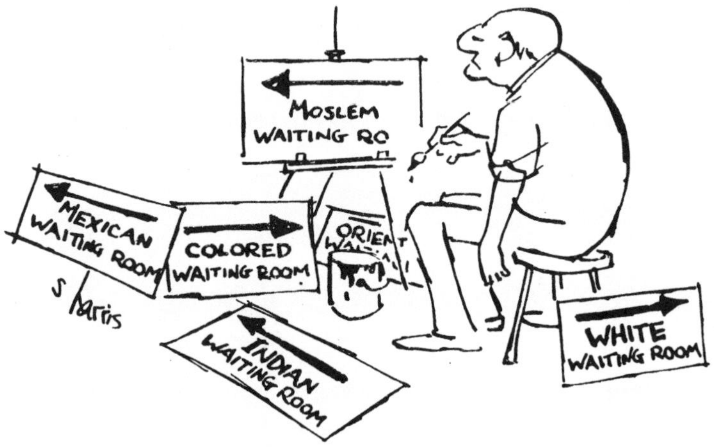
MOSLEM
WAITING RO
MEXICAN
WAITING ROOM
COLORED
WAITING ROOM
INDIAN
WAITING ROOM
WHITE
WAITING ROOM

SIDNEY HARRIS. THE REALIST #66, APRIL 1966.

"A Popsicle for me and a Fudgsicle for my brother."

THE REALIST #66, APRIL 1966.

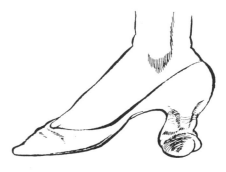

The Rape of the Foot

RICHARD GUINDON. THE REALIST #66, APRIL 1966.

"Please feel free to say anything at all that pops into your mind.
Unless, of course, it's Communist-inspired."

J.B. HANDELSMAN. THE REALIST #66, APRIL 1966.

SKIP WILLIAMSON. THE REALIST #66, APRIL 1966.

RICHARD GUINDON. THE REALIST #66, APRIL 1966.

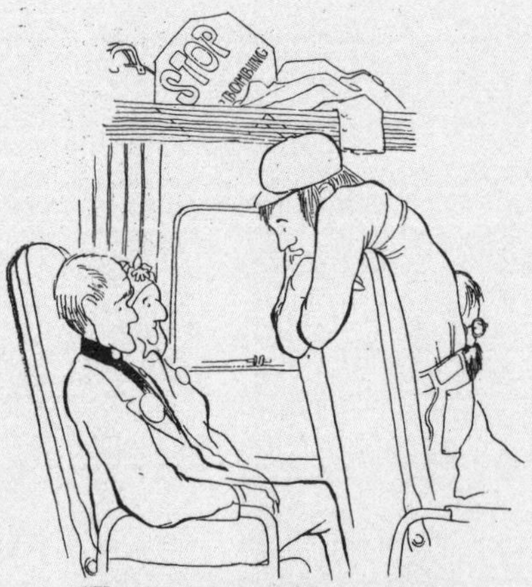
STOP

"You guys want to chip in with us on a motel room? We got some pot."

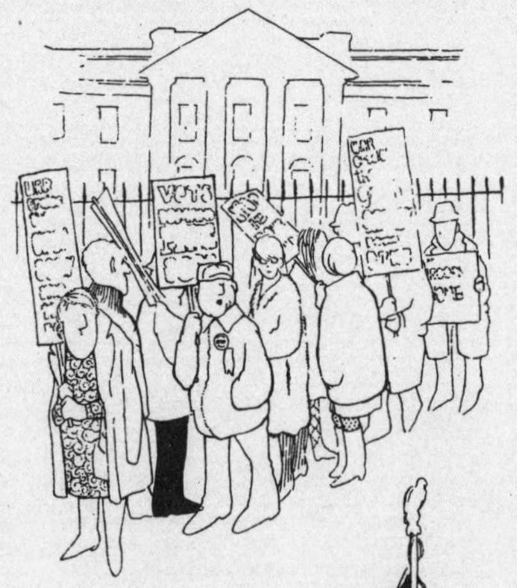
VOTE

"Isn't that our bus driver?"

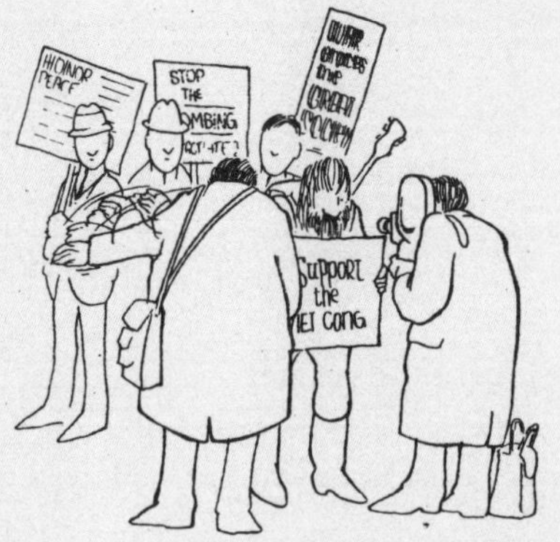
STOP THE BOMBING
WAR erodes the GREAT SOCIETY
SUPPORT the VIET CONG

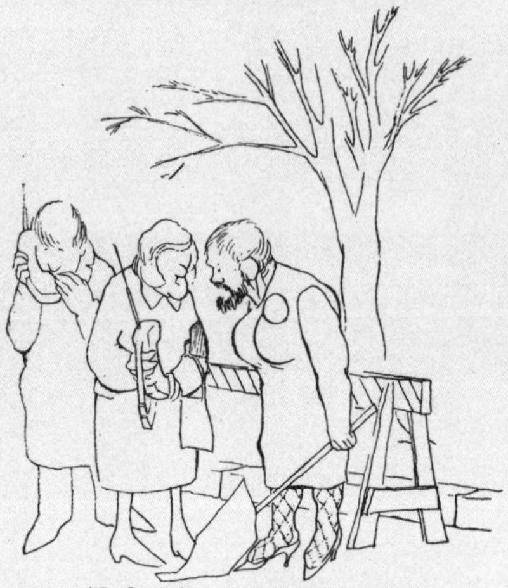

"Lady, I *have* to parade like this! Ten minutes after the train gets home, I report to my draft board."

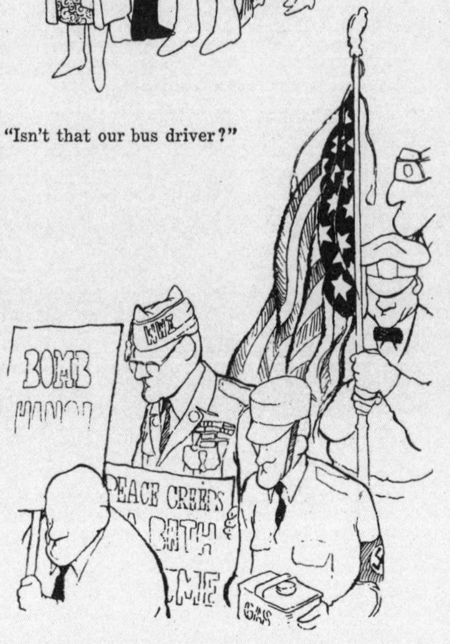
BOMB HANOI
PEACE CREEPS

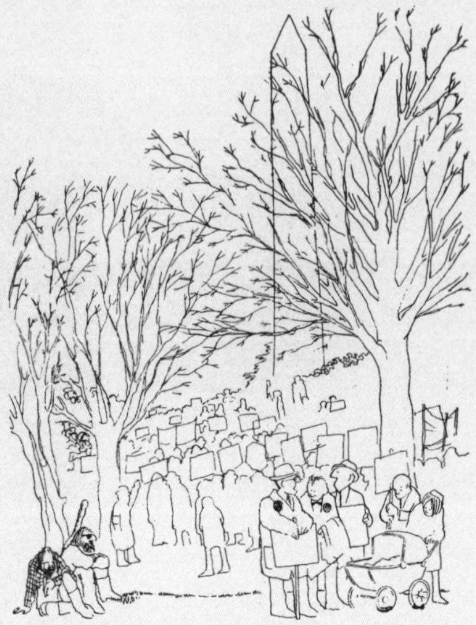

"Careful . . . they look like FBI agents."

Guindon Goes to the March on Washington For Peace in Vietnam

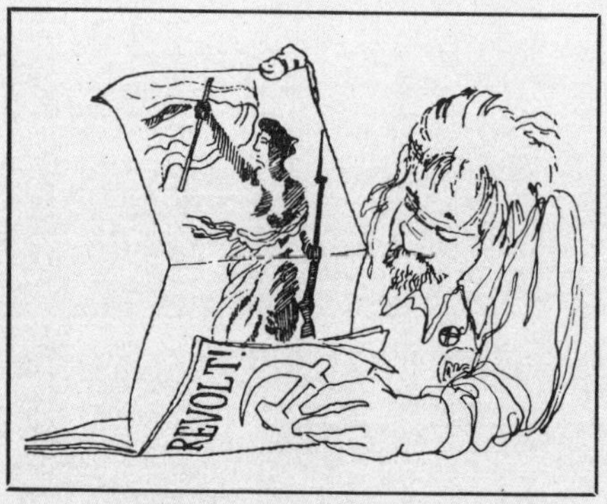
REVOLT!

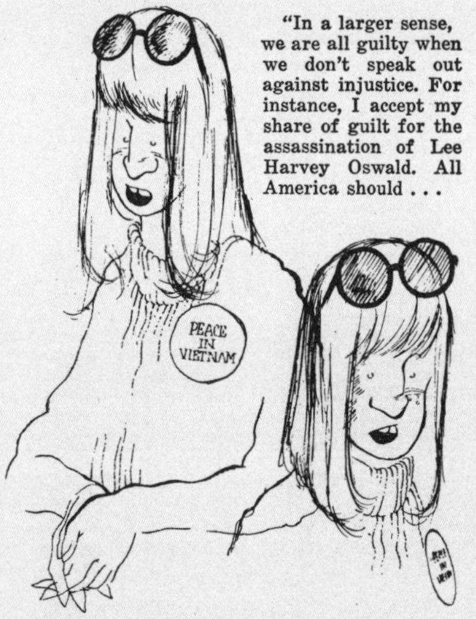
PEACE IN VIETNAM

"In a larger sense, we are all guilty when we don't speak out against injustice. For instance, I accept my share of guilt for the assassination of Lee Harvey Oswald. All America should . . .

. . . because one thing the Civil Rights movement proves is that we *must* stand up and be counted. I wonder why Martin Luther King didn't come to the march with his wife?"

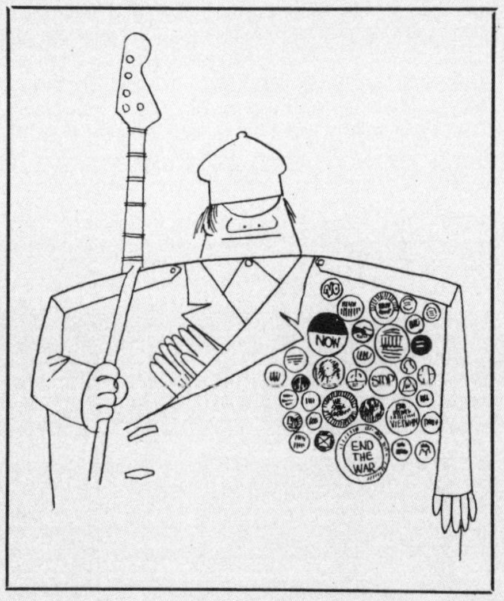
NOW
END THE WAR

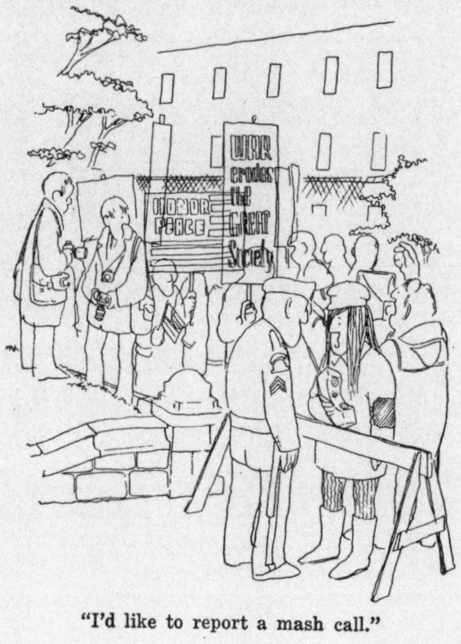
HONOR PEACE
WAR erodes the GREAT Society

"I'd like to report a mash call."

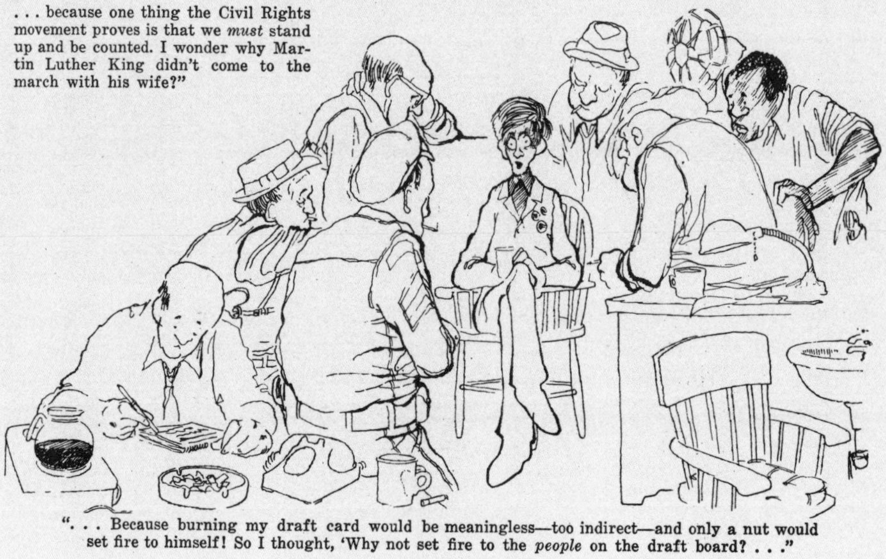

". . . Because burning my draft card would be meaningless—too indirect—and only a nut would set fire to himself! So I thought, 'Why not set fire to the *people* on the draft board? . . ."

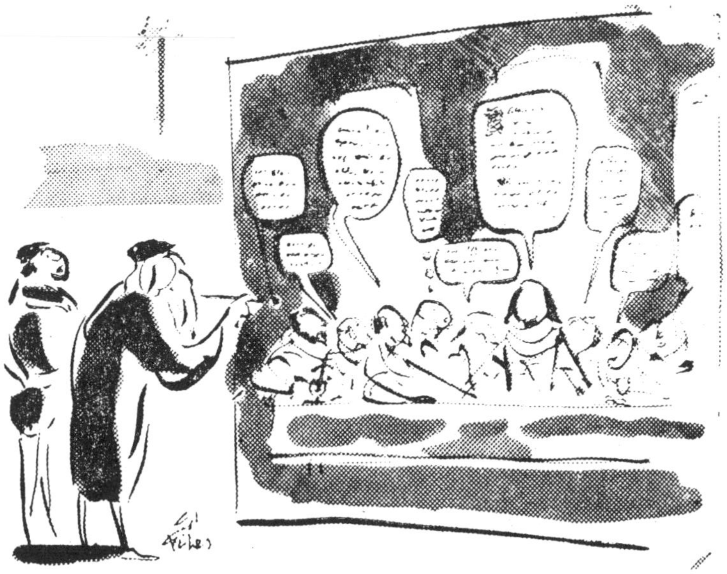

"As usual, Leonardo, you're ahead of your time."

ED FISHER. THE REALIST #66, APRIL 1966.

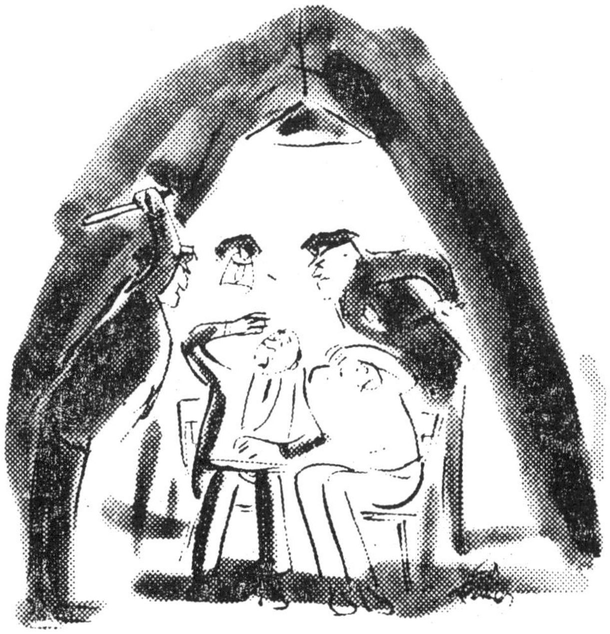

"Hey! — I'm the lawyer!"

ED FISHER. THE REALIST #66, APRIL 1966.

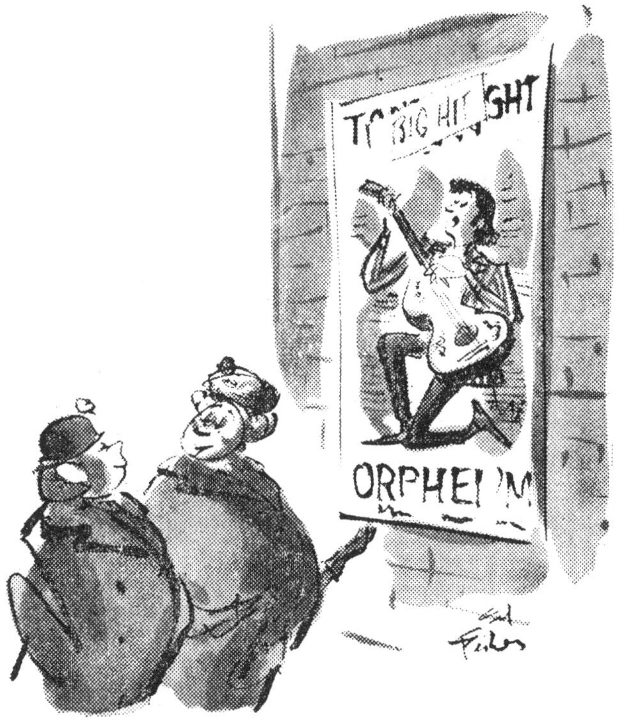
BIG HIT

"That's my son. It seems like only yesterday
he was just a little boy in pin curls."

ED FISHER. THE REALIST #66, APRIL 1966.

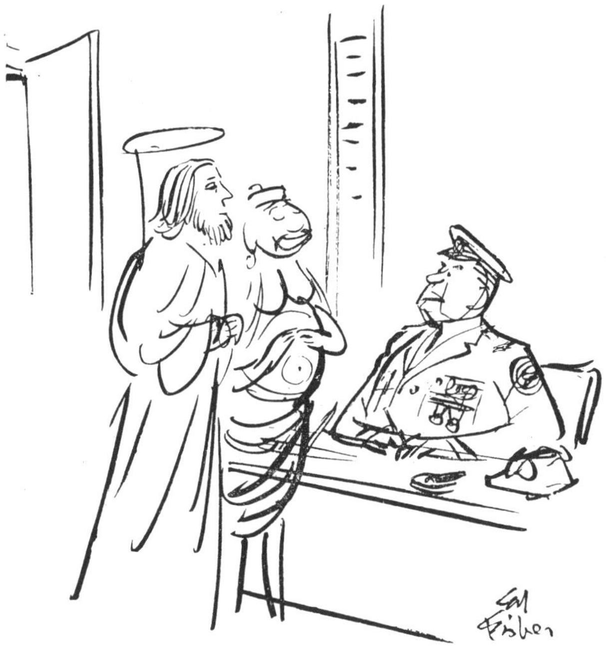

"— And *your* job, Crenshaw, will be to work
among the Vietnamese *Catholics*."

ED FISHER. THE REALIST #66, APRIL 1966.

Bobby Kennedy Contemplating the Bust of Garbage

NEWS ITEM: New York's Mayor John Lindsay vigorously shoveled trash on Saturday to help clean up a vacant lot which was scheduled to become the first of "hundreds of vest-pocket parks" throughout the city. Senator Robert F. Kennedy had been planning for more than a year to line up a bipartisan group of private benefactors to develop the plot into a playground.

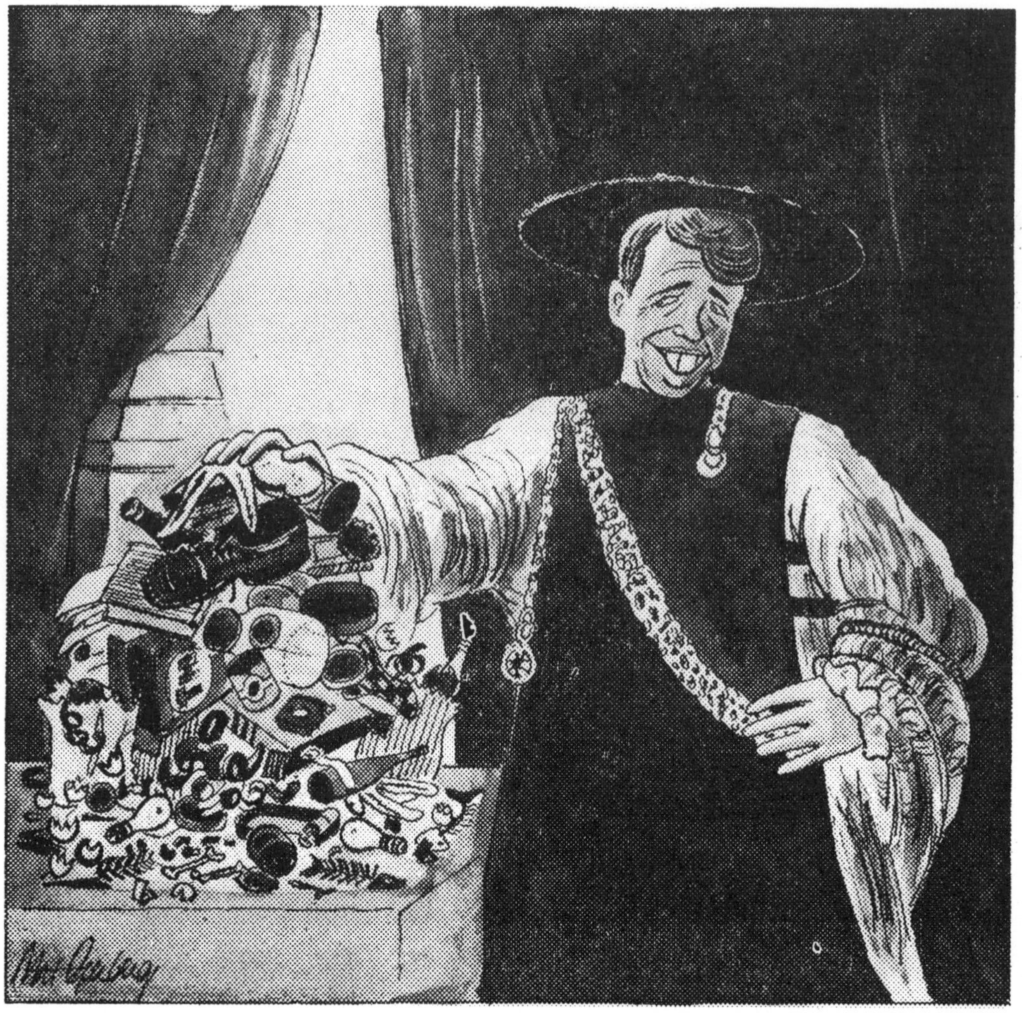

MORT GERBERG. THE REALIST #66, APRIL 1966.

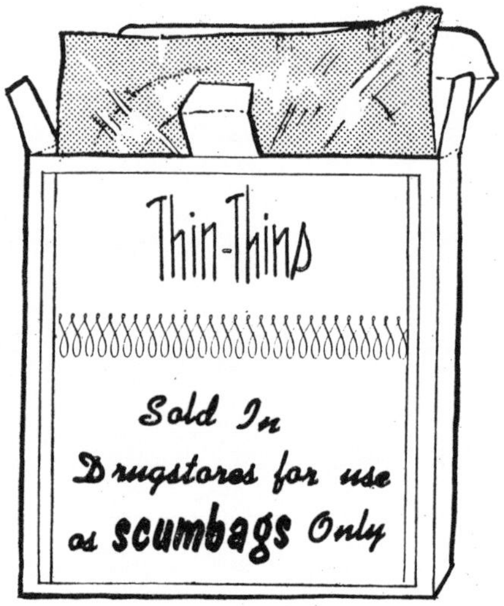
Thin-Thins
Sold In
Drugstores for use
as scumbags Only

RICHARD GUINDON. THE REALIST #66, APRIL 1966. *67

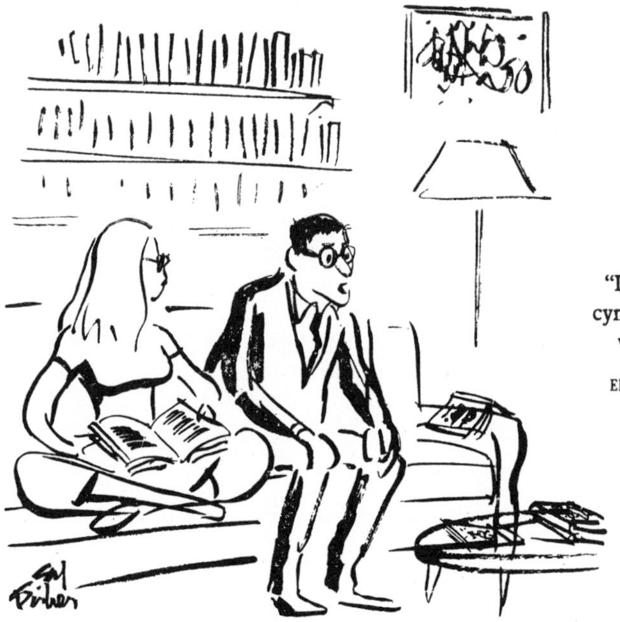

"I'm sorry — I'm not cowardly, cynical, effeminate, uninvolved ... we can't *all* be Anti-Heroes!"

ED FISHER. THE REALIST #66, APRIL 1966.

JOHN WILCOCK AND
HOWARD SHOEMAKER.
THE REALIST #66, APRIL 1966.

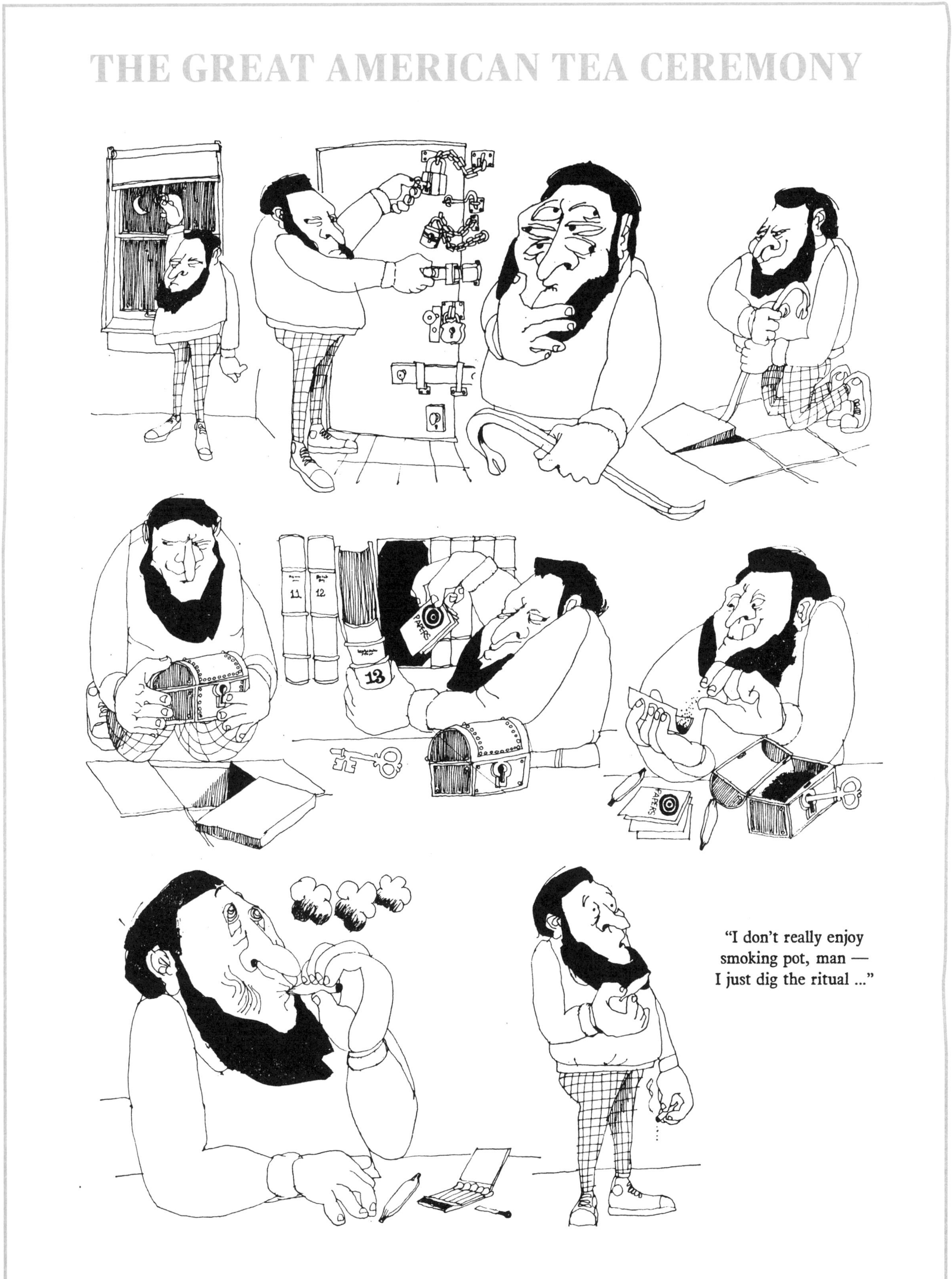
THE GREAT AMERICAN TEA CEREMONY
11
12
13
PAPERS
PAPERS
"I don't really enjoy
smoking pot, man —
I just dig the ritual ..."

RICHARD GUINDON.
THE REALIST #67, MAY 1966.

MR. EMPLOYER, DOES YOUR PERSONNEL DEPARTMENT USE A LIE DETECTOR? DO YOU HAVE THEFT DETECTION MIRRORS IN YOUR STORE? A CHECK CASHING CAMERA? CLOSED CIRCUIT T.V.? **ARE YOU PROTECTED?**

EXCERPTS FROM AN INDUSTRIAL SECURITY CATALOG.

"ORDINARY" TELEPHONE
WITH
BUILT-IN FM TRANSMITTER

- CHECK OUT YOUR BUSINESS TRAINESS "IN ACTION" WITHOUT MAKING THEM SELF CONSCIOUS OF YOUR "LISTENING IN" OR BEING IN THE SAME ROOM. $150.00

EVERY SUPERVISOR SHOULD HAVE ONE.

HERE'S YOUR TRANSMITTER, SIR. BY THE WAY, HOW DOES YOUR BOSS LIKE HIS?

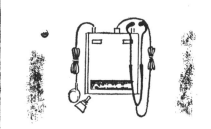

AUDIO ELECTRONIC STETHOSCOPE
- USES FOUR STANDARD BATTERIES LASTING TWO MONTHS!
- ULTRA-SENSITIVE! IT CAN PENETRATE THICK PLASTER!
- CAN EVEN DETECT THE HEARTBEAT OF UNBORN BABIES!

$100.00

- HEAR THE COUPLE IN THE NEXT ROOM MAKING A BABY!
- LISTEN TO ITS HEART BEAT BEFORE IT'S BORN!

- THE SECRETS OF LIFE!
- THE SOUNDS OF CREATION!

"IN THE BEGINNING THERE WAS THE WORD AND THE WORD WAS...

OHHHONEY!

AUDIO-WALL PROBE

- YOU SIMPLY PLACE AGAINST THE WALL AND THROUGH STETHOSCOPIC EARPHONES YOU DETECT THE VOICES AND SOUNDS IN THE NEXT ROOM! IDEAL AS AN ELECTRONIC BABY SITTER! $65.00

EARPHONES $9.95

BIG MOTHER IS WATCHING YOU.

JOKE: FROM THE TONIGHT SHOW

A NURSE IS TALKING THROUGH AN INTERCOM ON HER DESK TO A LITTLE BOY IN A HOSPITAL ROOM "JOHNNY, DID YOU TAKE YOUR MEDICINE?" NOBODY ANSWERS. "JOHNNY?" SILENCE. THE NURSE SAYS, "ANSWER ME JOHNNY, I KNOW YOU'RE IN THERE!"

AND THIS SMALL VOICE SAYS, "WHAT DO YOU WANT, WALL?"

HA-HA! WHAT DO YOU WANT, WALL? HA-HA!

HA! HA! GOODNIGHT, DEAR!

CLICK!

GOODNIGHT.

CLICK!

WHISPER LIGHT

- A BEAUTIFUL DECORATOR LAMP WITH A BUILT-IN TRANSMITTER. TRANSMITS ALL SOUNDS AND VOICES CLEARLY (WHETHER LAMP IS ON OR OFF TO) A MOBILE RECEIVER. $150.00

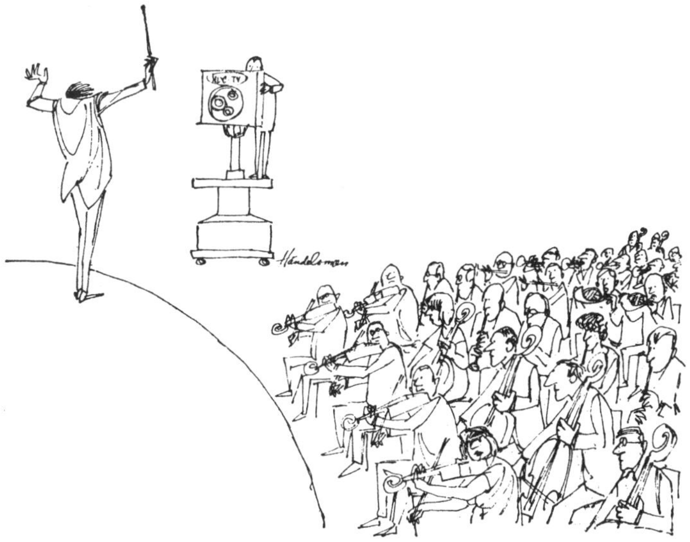

J.B. HANDELSMAN. THE REALIST #67, MAY 1966.

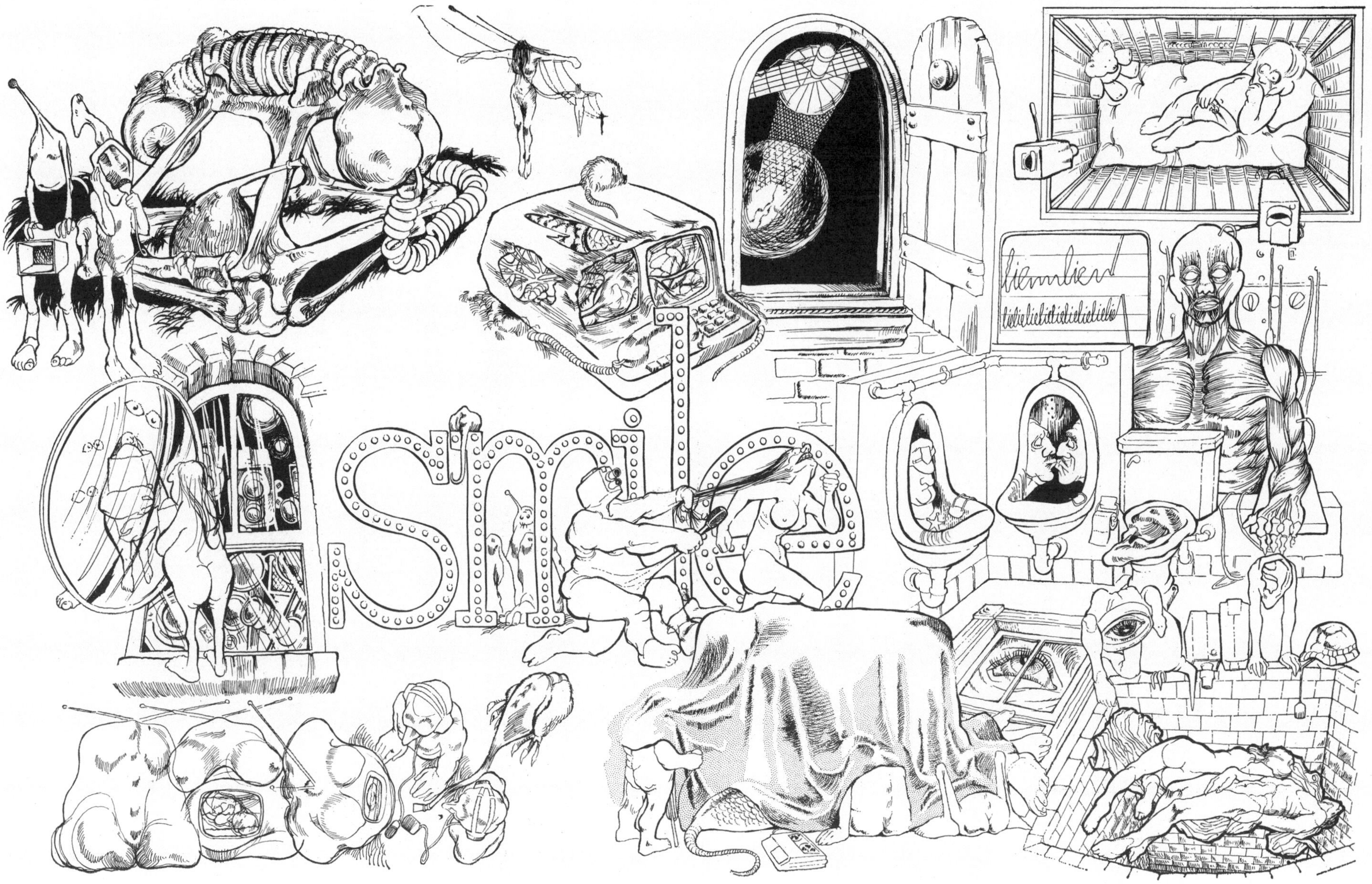

RICHARD GUINDON. THE REALIST #67, MAY 1966.

"Will the senior senator from Mississippi yield
to the junior senator from Mississippi?"

J.B. HANDELSMAN. THE REALIST #67-A, JUNE 1966.

SAM GROSS. THE REALIST #67-A, JUNE 1966.

B. KLIBAN. THE REALIST #67-A, JUNE 1966.

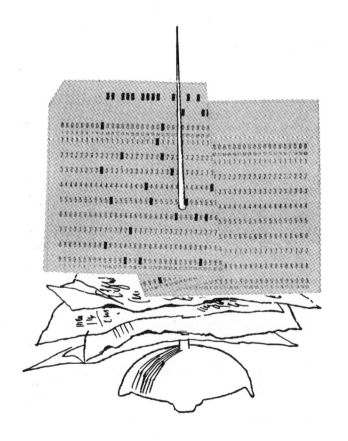

THE REALIST #68, AUGUST 1966. *68

RICHARD GUINDON. THE REALIST #68, AUGUST 1966.

IF GOD IS DEAD, WHAT DO YOU SAY WHEN SOMEBODY SNEEZES?

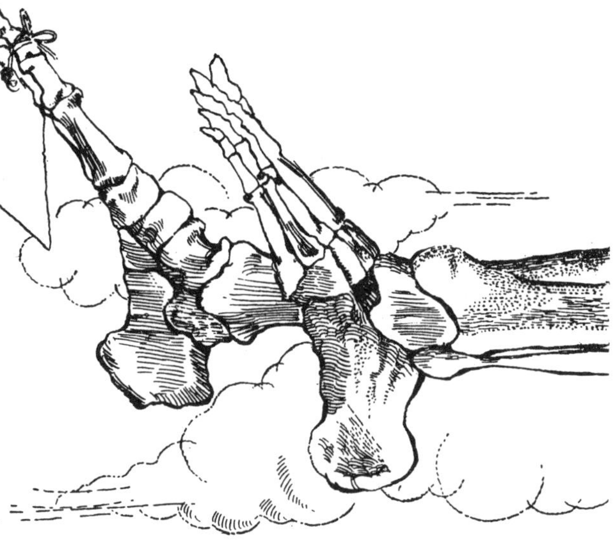

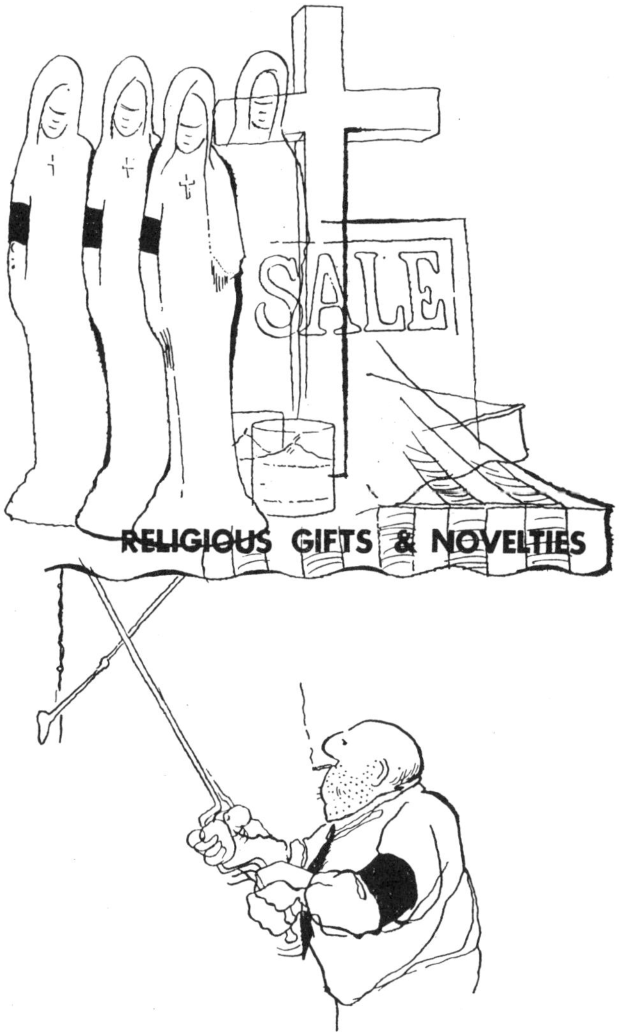
SALE
RELIGIOUS GIFTS & NOVELTIES

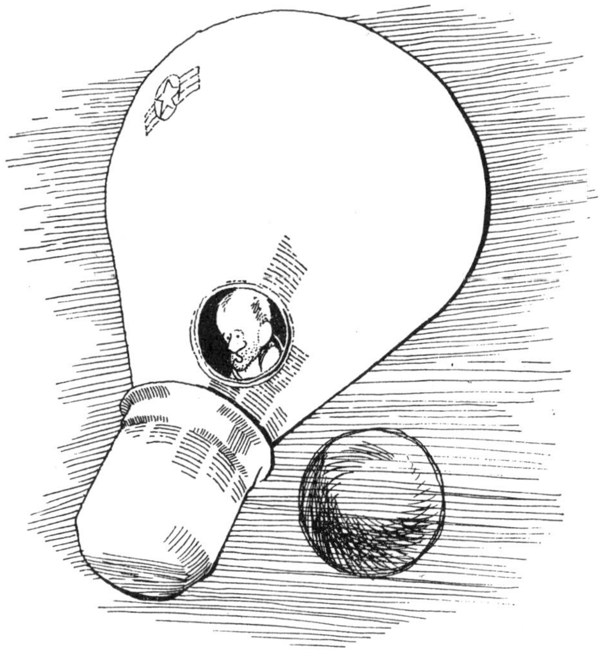

"On the other hand, I don't see any sign of Nietzsche either."

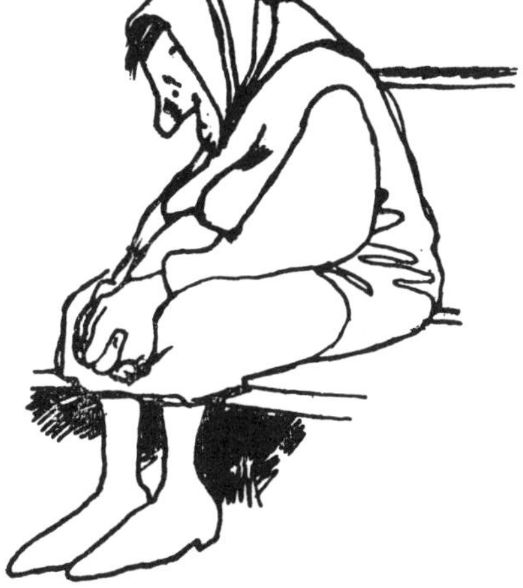

"Our Father ... who wert in heaven ..."

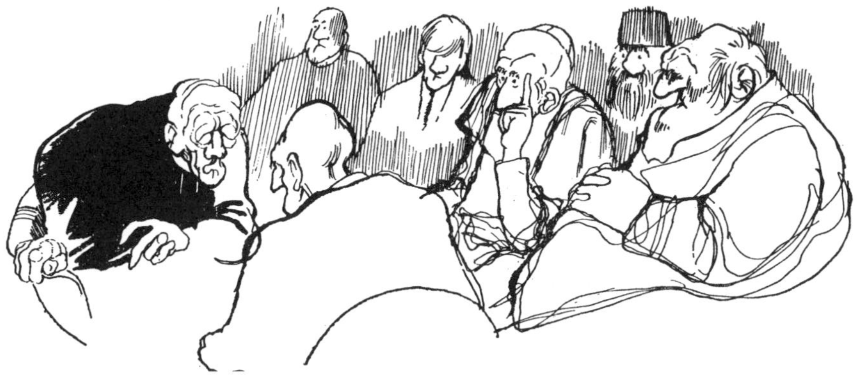

"Did Ford Motors quit just because Henry Ford died?"

"Next TV set they wheel in here, we shit on it!"

MORT GERBERG. THE REALIST #68, AUGUST 1966.

J.C. SUARES. THE REALIST #69, SEPTEMBER 1966. '69

Mr. Zip
Says:
Always
Use
Zip
Code

"Thanks!"

WOODMAN. THE REALIST #69, SEPTEMBER 1966.

ED FISHER. THE REALIST #69, SEPTEMBER 1966.

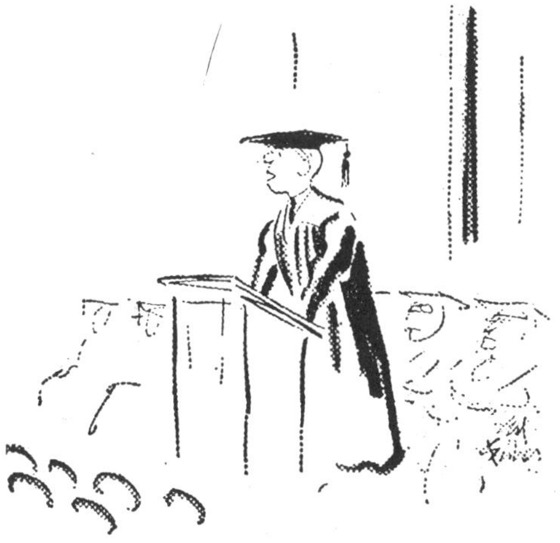

"—And, fellow students, in standing here before you, I am not selling out!"

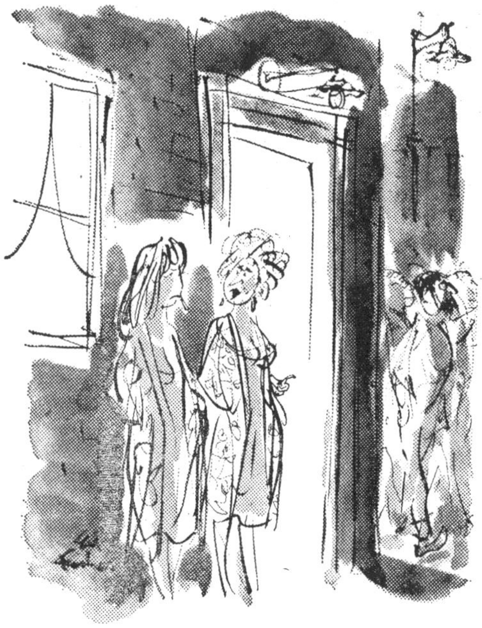

"As if things aren't bad enough, we need a dedicated, puritanical New Left?"

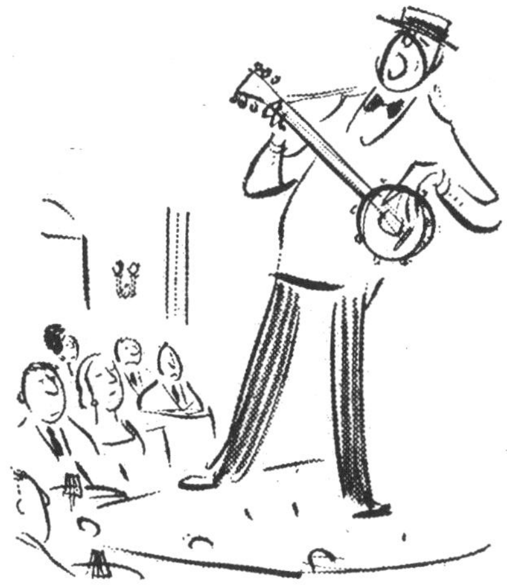

"—I'd walk a million miles for one of your smiles, Mam—I mean, Mother!"

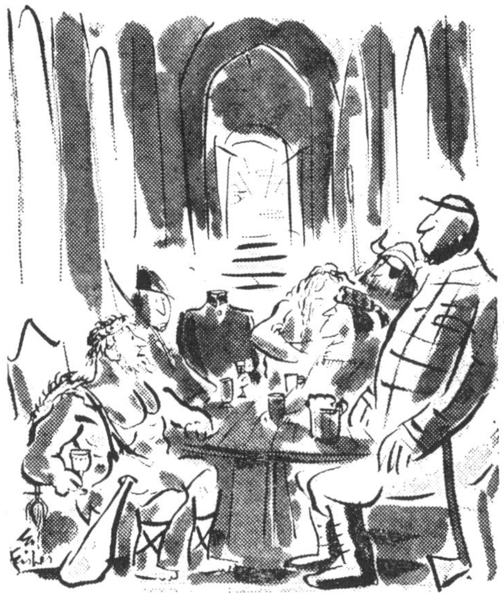

"Fellow folk-heroes, I'm afraid we're going to have to let in the John Henry legend."

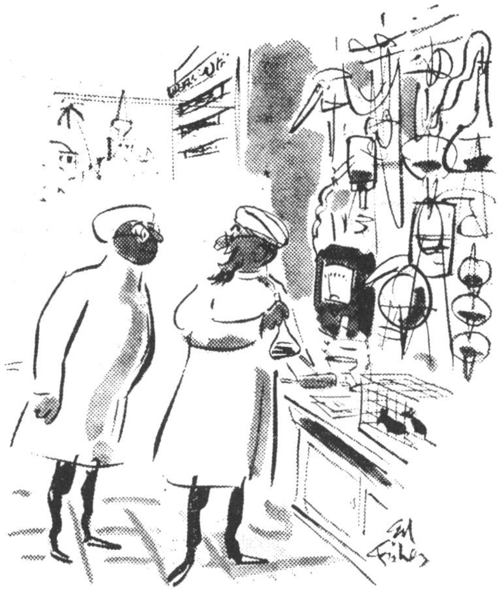

"Ha! I'd like to hear the U.S. Surgeon General's advice to the public on *this*! —a link between monogamy and cancer!"

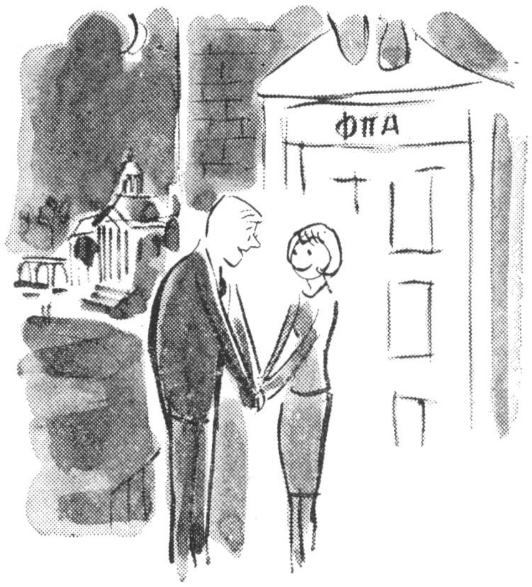
ΦΠΑ

"Sally—will you wear my Young-Progressives-Against-Lyndon's-Fascist-America pin?"

ED FISHER. THE REALIST #69, SEPTEMBER 1966.

MORT GERBERG.
THE REALIST #69, SEPTEMBER 1966.

The Fag Battalion

by MORT GERBERG

News item: An organization called the Committee to Fight Exclusion of Homosexuals from the Armed Forces contends that there are 17 million homosexuals in the nation, most of whom would be eager to fight for their country, and that an end to the ban on homosexuals would ease the shortage of manpower for Vietnam.

"A poodle cut, dear . . . and re-shape my bangs."

"I think shower time is the loveliest thing about the whole Army."

CLASSIFICATION
AND
ASSIGNMENT

"Frankly, I'd rather swish than fight."

"A soldier's work is never done . . ."

PARADE...
REST!!

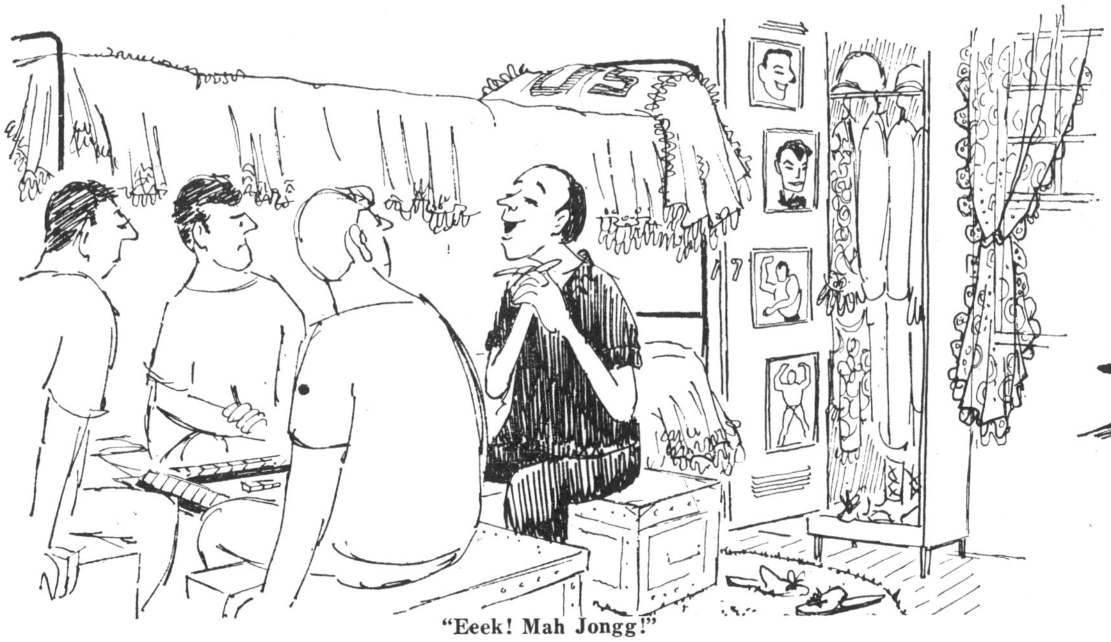

"Eeek! Mah Jongg!"

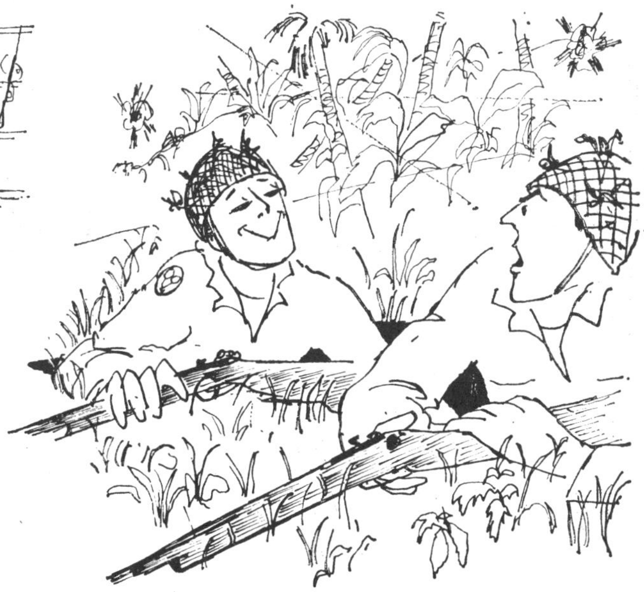

"*Please,* Walter—not here!"

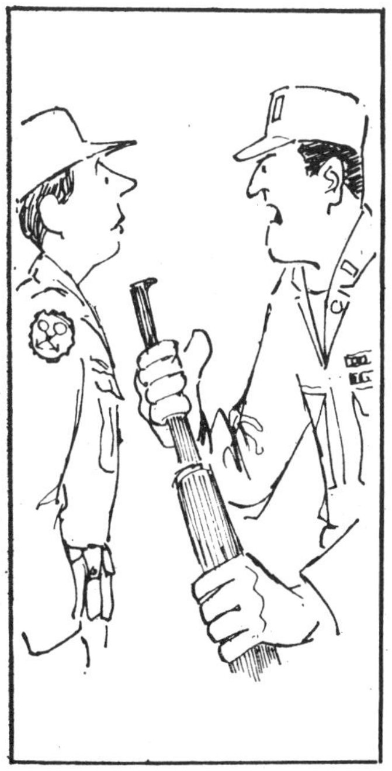

"Burnhill, how many times have I told you not to lubricate your rifle with K-Y Jelly!"

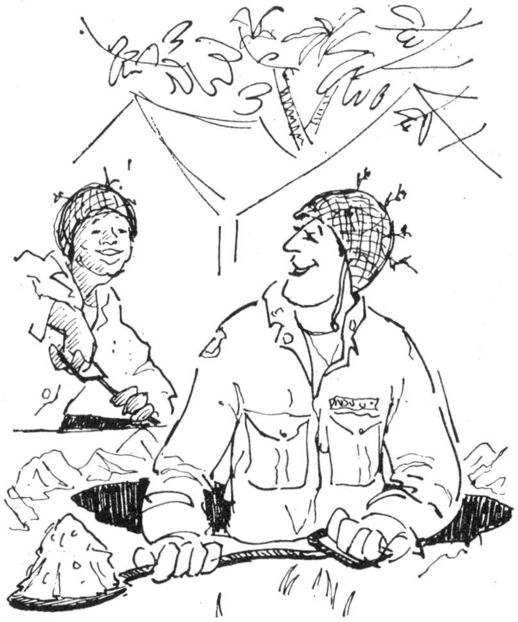

"I adore digging foxholes; it's so anal."

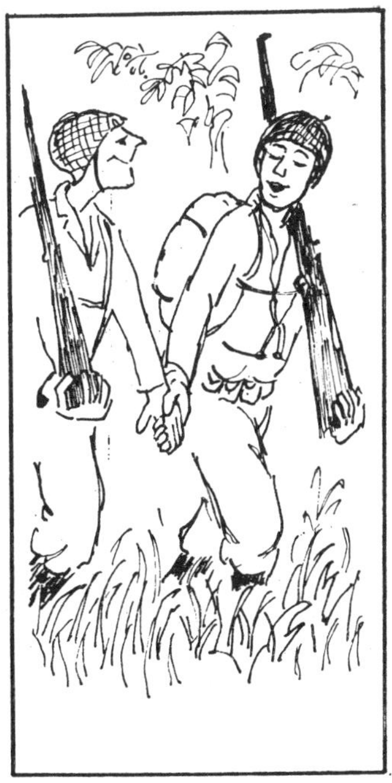

"I hope we take some prisoners. I'd love to see if it's true what they say about Oriental men."

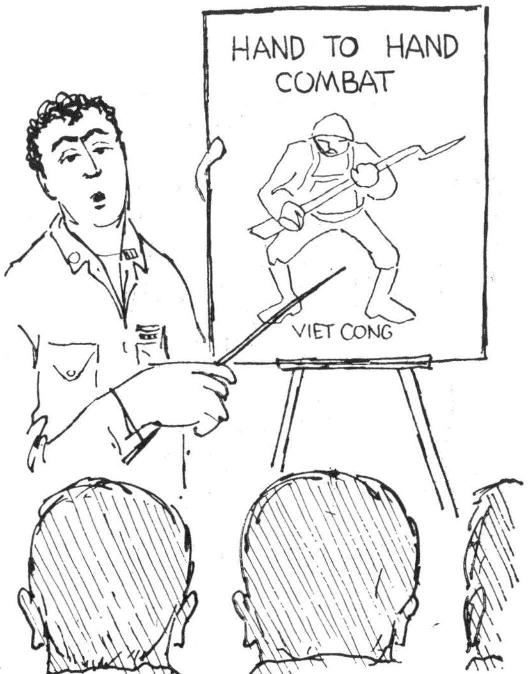
HAND TO HAND
COMBAT
VIET CONG

"...you sneak up quietly behind him, then *leap* on his back, *grab* him by the throat, and give him a *great* big kiss on the neck!"

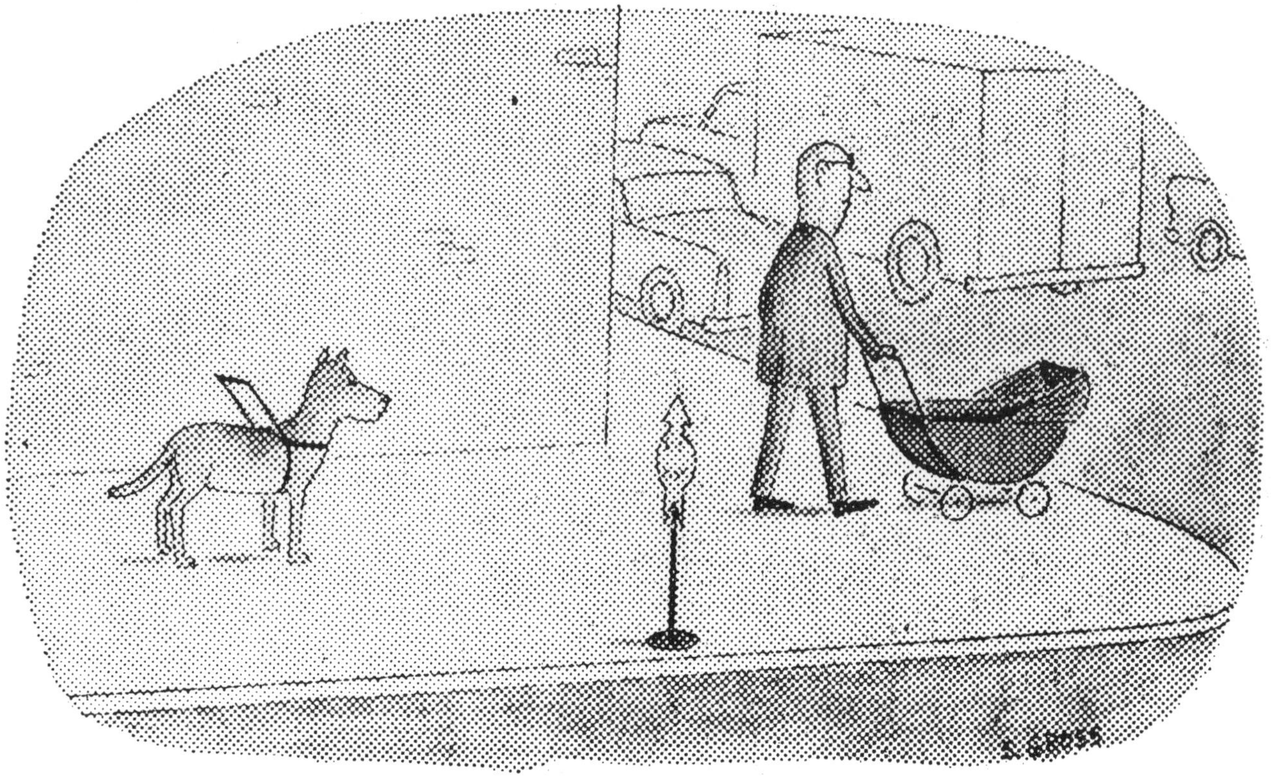
S. GROSS

SAM GROSS. THE REALIST #69, SEPTEMBER 1966.

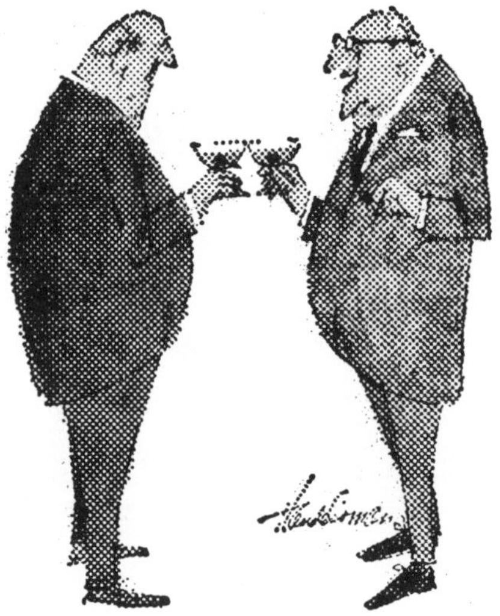

"I couldn't agree with you more. I don't hold with the Black Muslims, either."

J.B. HANDELSMAN. THE REALIST #69, SEPTEMBER 1966.

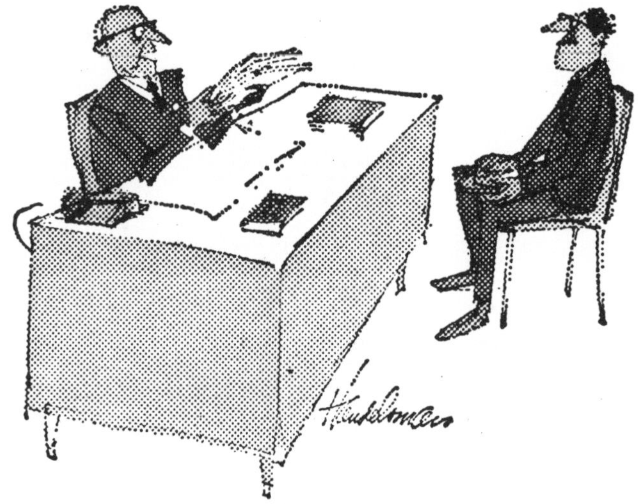

"These coincidences do occur in the writing game. I have no doubt you wrote 'Fanny Hill' in perfectly good faith."

J.B. HANDELSMAN. THE REALIST #69, SEPTEMBER 1966. *70

FRANKLY I DIDN'T GIVE A DAMN ABOUT IT!
TV
FRANKLY I DIDN'T GIVE A BLEEP ABOUT IT!
FUCK?
PISS?
SHIT?
CRAP?

THE REALIST #69, SEPTEMBER 1966.

"Cosmetics! ... A mirror!"

TELOS. THE REALIST #69, SEPTEMBER 1966.

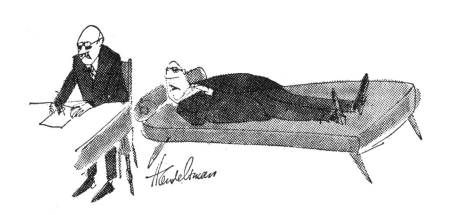

"I have some remarks here by Senator Dirksen that I'd like to insert into the record ..."

J.B. HANDELSMAN. THE REALIST #69, SEPTEMBER 1966. *71

A TRADITIONAL METHOD OF PROTECTING YOUR PERSONAL EFFECTS FROM THE DEPREDATIONS OF NEEDY NARCOTICS ADDICTS

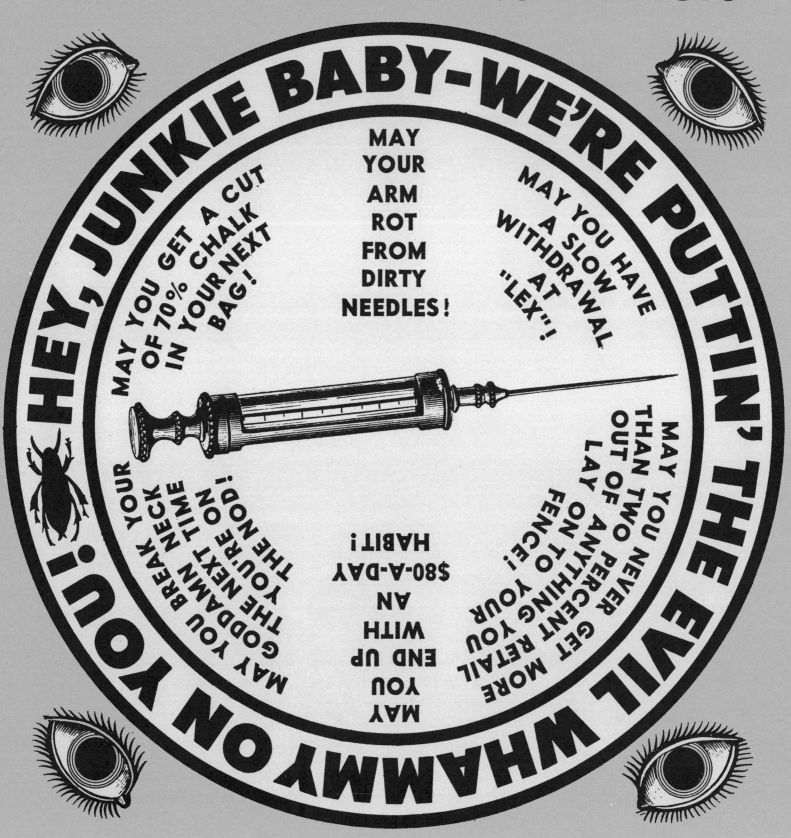

HEY, JUNKIE BABY-WE'RE PUTTIN' THE EVIL WHAMMY ON YOU!

MAY YOU GET A CUT OF 70% CHALK IN YOUR NEXT BAG!

MAY YOUR ARM ROT FROM DIRTY NEEDLES!

MAY YOU HAVE A SLOW WITHDRAWAL AT "LEX"!

MAY YOU NEVER GET MORE THAN TWO PERCENT RETAIL OUT OF ANYTHING YOU LAY ON TO YOUR FENCE!

MAY YOU END UP WITH AN $80-A-DAY HABIT!

MAY YOU GODDAMN BREAK YOUR NECK THE NEXT TIME YOU'RE ON THE NOD!

JOHN FRANCIS PUTNAM. THE REALIST #69, SEPTEMBER 1966.

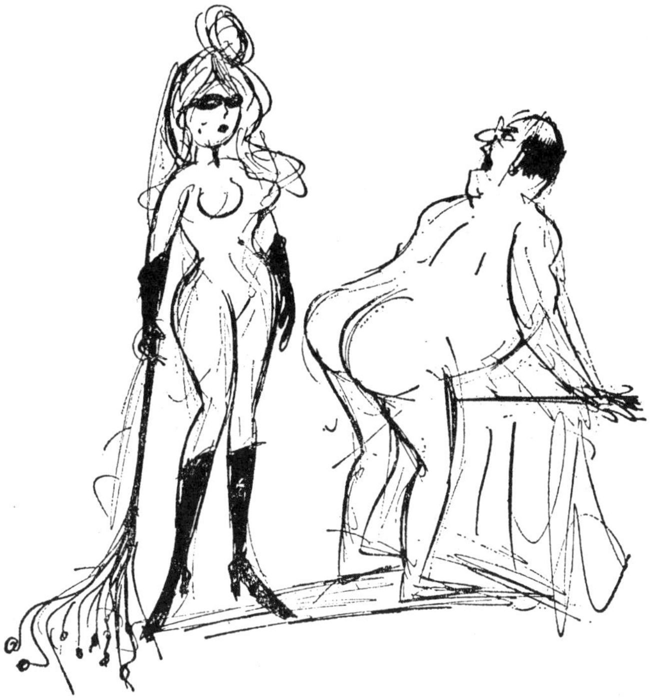

"Of course I think Ginzburg should be locked up."

ED FISHER. THE REALIST #69, SEPTEMBER 1966. '72

The Fanatics

Full-page ad:

"*Who cares* whether there are 200 tissues in the box—or only 199? Only some kind of fanatic would bother to count those tissues. But that's what we are: fanatics about the claims on labels. So—we count. And we don't stop at that. We'll measure the size of those tissues, analyze the quality, and critically judge the price. That's just one example of the *thousands* of product checks A&P

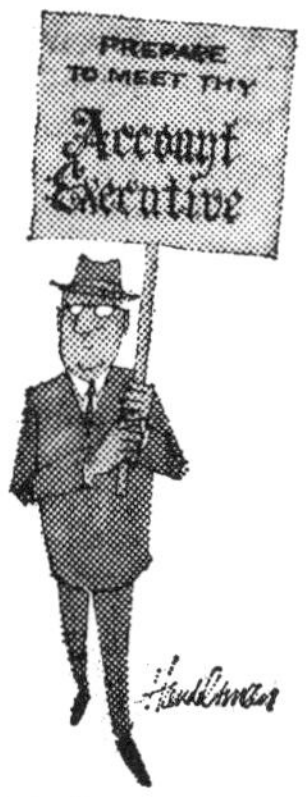
PREPARE TO MEET THY
Account Executive

Quality Testing Laboratories make every year—just one of the thousands of reasons you can count on the values at your A&P. *We care.*"

Tiny news item:

"The Great Atlantic and Pacific Tea Company pleaded guilty to short-weighting, ending two years of litigation. The charges originally included several employees as well as the A&P. The company was fined $100 on each of two charges resulting from discrepancies in the weight of pre-packaged meats."

J.B. HANDELSMAN. THE REALIST #69, SEPTEMBER 1966.

SUGAR COATING OF THE YEAR

"It is with infinite respect that I come among you and proclaim to each of you your nobility, your call to greatness, to the dignity of human life, to your transcendent destiny."

— Pope Paul VI, February 15, 1966, speaking to Rome's garbage collectors and street cleaners

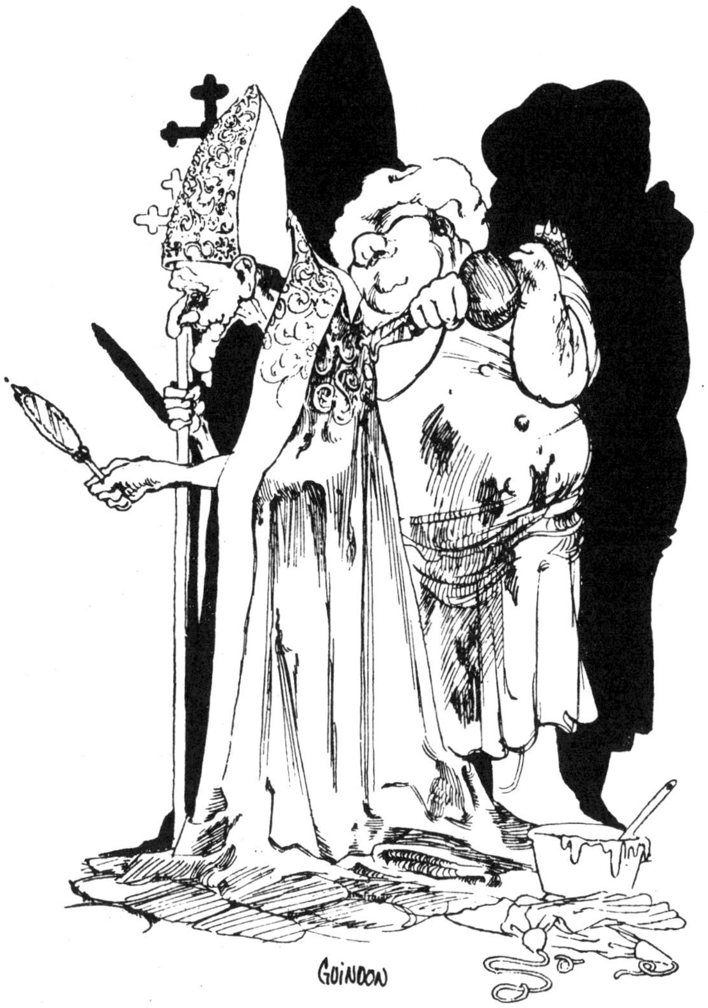

RICHARD GUINDON. THE REALIST #69, SEPTEMBER 1966.

BOUNCE

"Next time you be George and I'll be Lynda-Bird."

BOUNCE. THE REALIST #69, SEPTEMBER 1966. *73

GUINDON

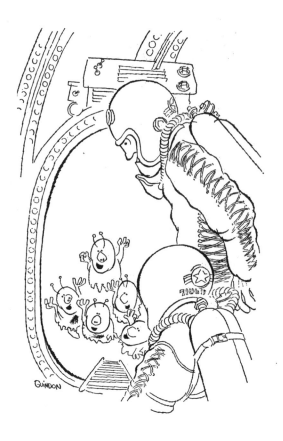

"Chocolate, G.I.? ... Cigarettes? ... Money? ..."

RICHARD GUINDON. THE REALIST #69, SEPTEMBER 1966.

PLANNED
CHILD
Koren

ED KOREN. THE REALIST #70, OCTOBER 1966.

"I quit!"
MSU
Suarès

Portrait of the A Team

J.C. SUARES. THE REALIST #69, SEPTEMBER 1966. *74

LOOK BACK IN APATHY

RICHARD GUINDON.
THE REALIST #71.
NOVEMBER 1966.

Should Dinky Town ever be noticed for any special characteristic making it stand out from the hundreds of other communities next to big universities, it will be because it is the largest, most apathetic bohemia that ever mushroomed.

Dinky Town and its sister neighborhood across the sprawling University of Minnesota campus, Seven Cornews, make up the student quarter in Minneapolis.

Even though Minnesota's is only the third largest university in the U.S., the Minneapolois campus, with its 49,000 enrollment, makes up the biggest single student population in the nation. More than twice the size of Berkeley, and with a much higher student-to-teacher ratio, you might expect trouble. Not true.

The concept that a student revolution is swapping the country is evidence only of the multitude of slow news days. During the recent nation-wide demonstrations against the war in Vietnam, 300 people marched in Minneapolis—that's almost the number of counter-pickets New York's 20,000 marchers drew.

—Richard Guindon

"Now stop being silly!
Come up here and take
your diplomas!"

"As I see it, our generation is fighting for the same
things our parents wanted at our age and have now.
We demand our place in the shade! Live slow!
Die old and have a good-looking corpse!"

"You must be Jim's parents,
right? ... Betty's parents?
... You're Lorna's parents,
aren't you? ... Close?"

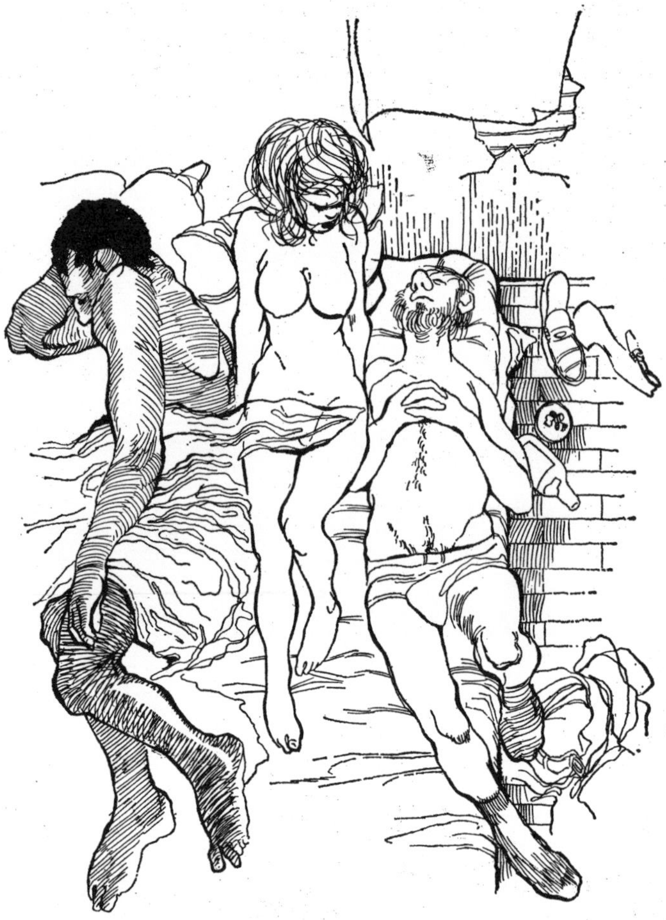

"Sometimes I think of Minnesota as one huge posse of screaming farmers who have surrounded Dinky Town with spotlights and sound trucks. And I hear them yelling, 'Throw your books down and come out with your hands up!'"

"Poor? You? Baby, until you start pretending you're an exchange student because all you've got to wear is the bedspread from a furnished room, you don't know the meaning of the word poor!"

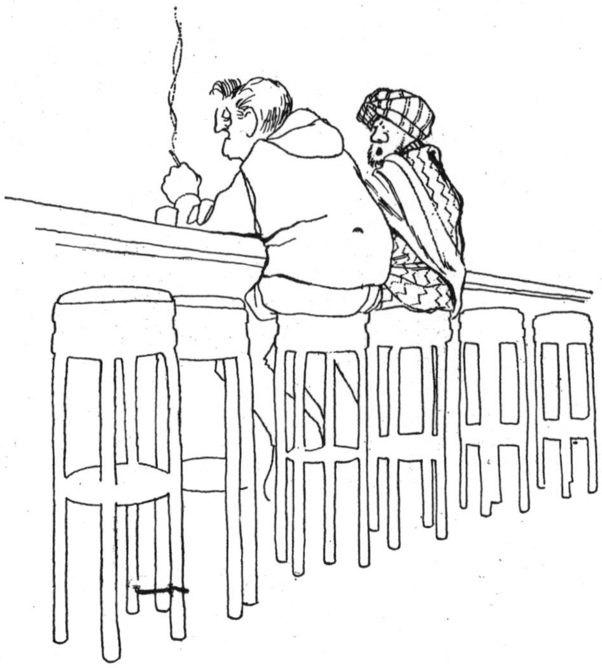

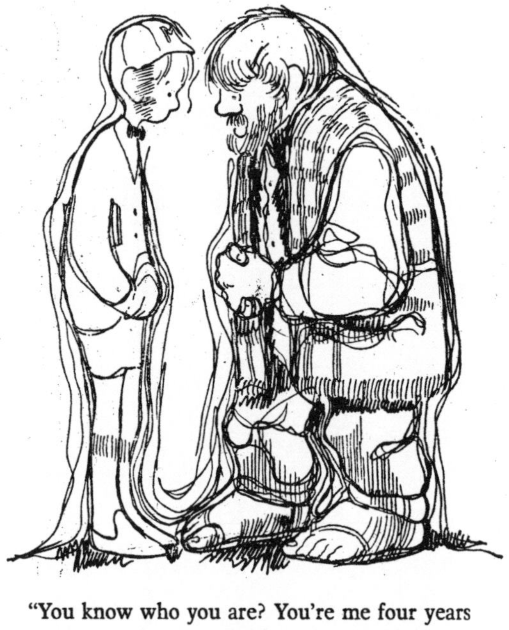

"You know who you are? You're me four years ago, come for an education, new to school, so clean, so neat — kiss me, for Chrissake!"

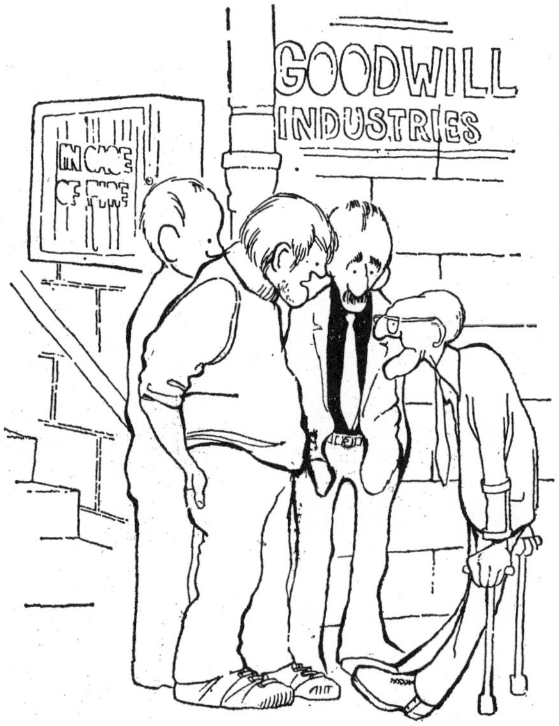
GOODWILL
INDUSTRIES

"But who hires us — the spiritually handicapped?"

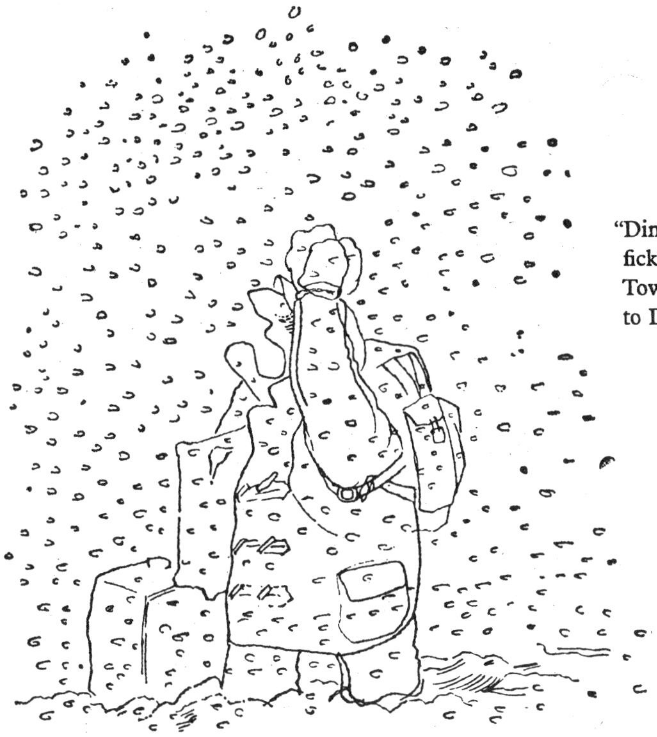

"Dinky Town, I'm going to beat you — you fickle bitch! I'm going to beat you, Dinky Town, and do you know how? I'm moving to Des Moises!"

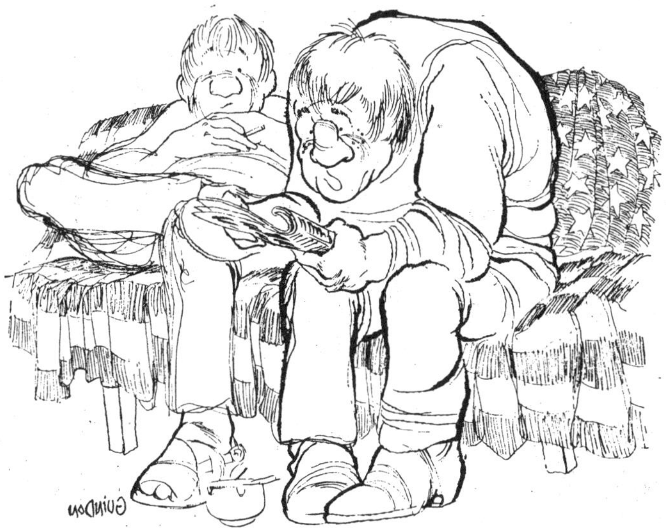

"Gee! *The Playboy Philosophy* sure makes good sense, don't it?"

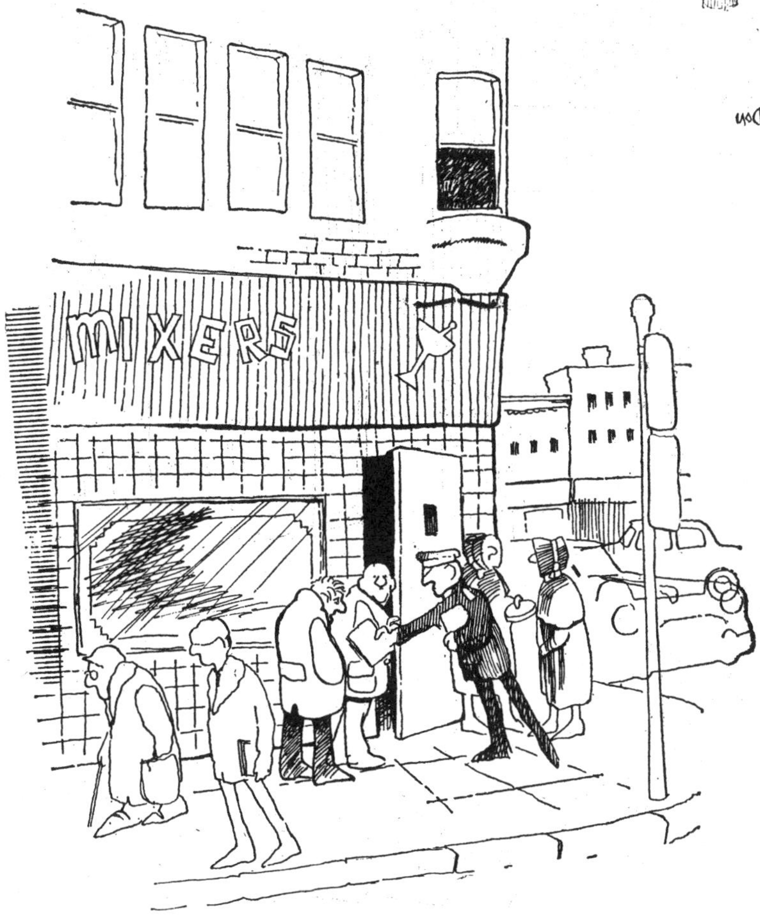
MIXERS

"Christianity? Sir, I haven't even accepted Western civilization yet."

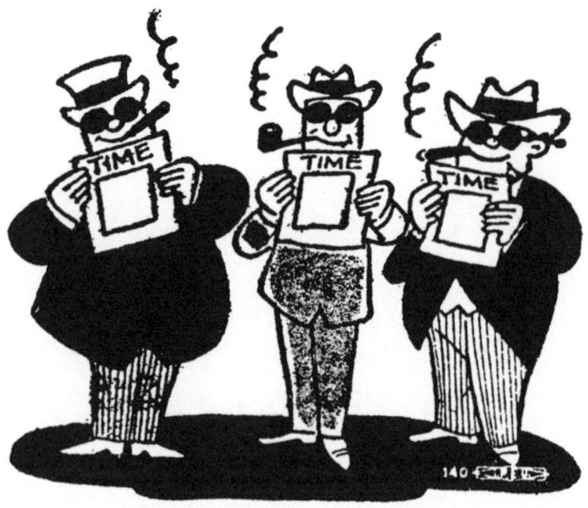
TIME
TIME
TIME

THE REALIST #72, DECEMBER 1966.

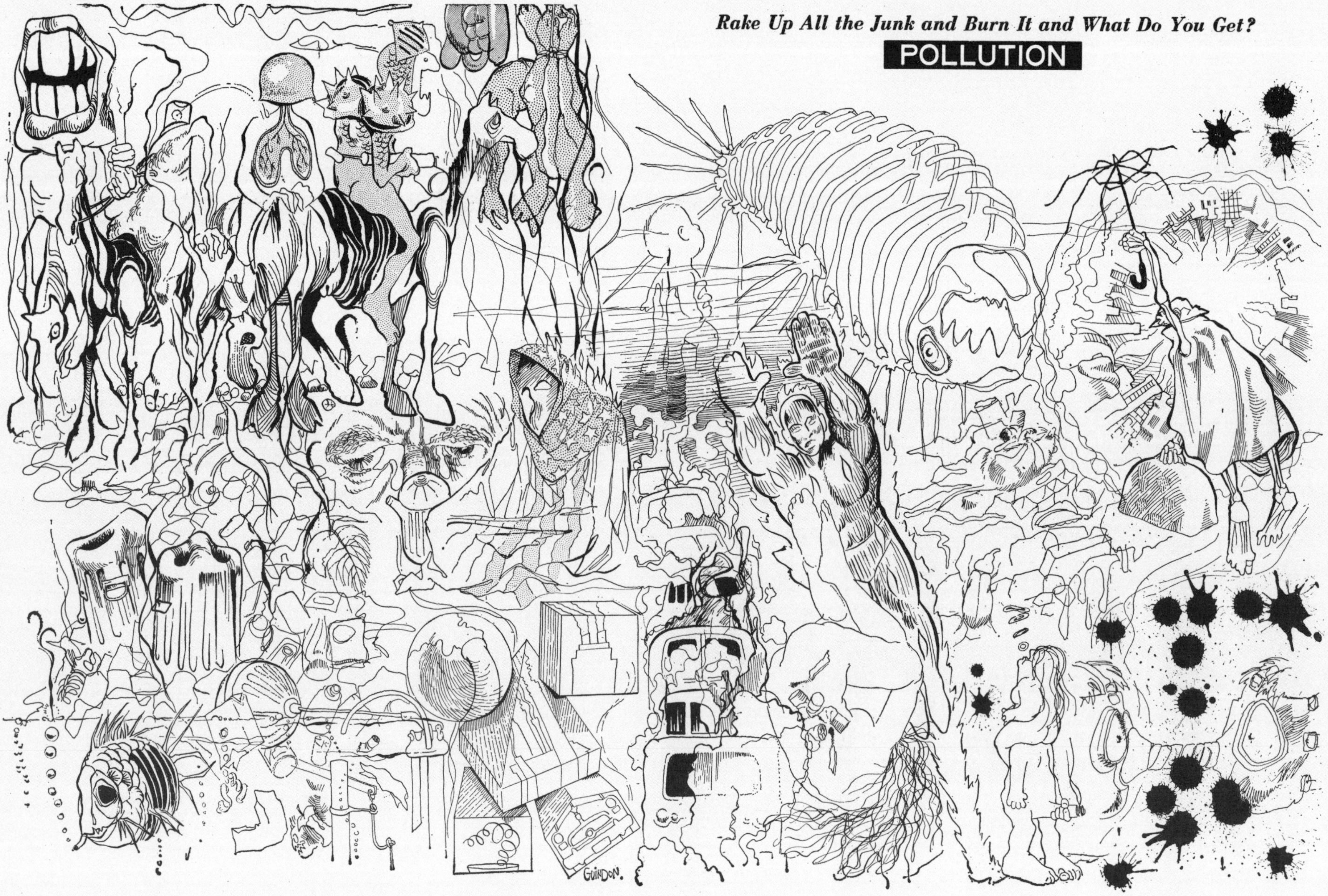
Rake Up All the Junk and Burn It and What Do You Get?
POLLUTION
GUINDON.

RICHARD GUINDON. THE REALIST #70, OCTOBER 1966.

"You're cute."

ED KOREN. THE REALIST #71, NOVEMBER 1966.

IBM

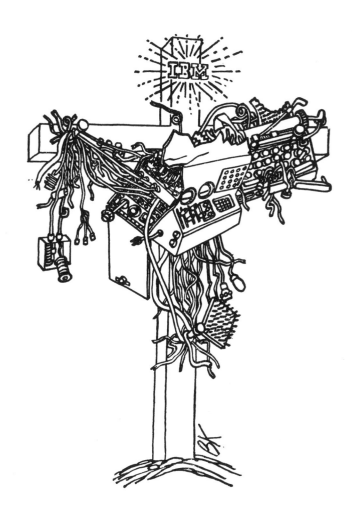

B. KLIBAN. THE REALIST #72, DECEMBER 1966.

REDDI-WHIP

RICHARD GUINDON. THE REALIST #72, DECEMBER 1966.

GIANT SIZE
BLACK POWER

RICHARD GUINDON. THE REALIST #71, NOVEMBER 1966.

THE BIG BAD BLACK POWER THREAT

J.C. SUARES. THE REALIST #72, DECEMBER 1966.

As the '66 Civil Rights Bill met its doom in Congress, Sen. Dirksen, who led the opposition, said it wasn't the color of Negroes he objected to, but their conduct. That same week a 12-year-old Negro schoolboy was beaten with chains and baseball bats and made to crawl away from the newly integrated school with a broken leg. — J. C. Suares

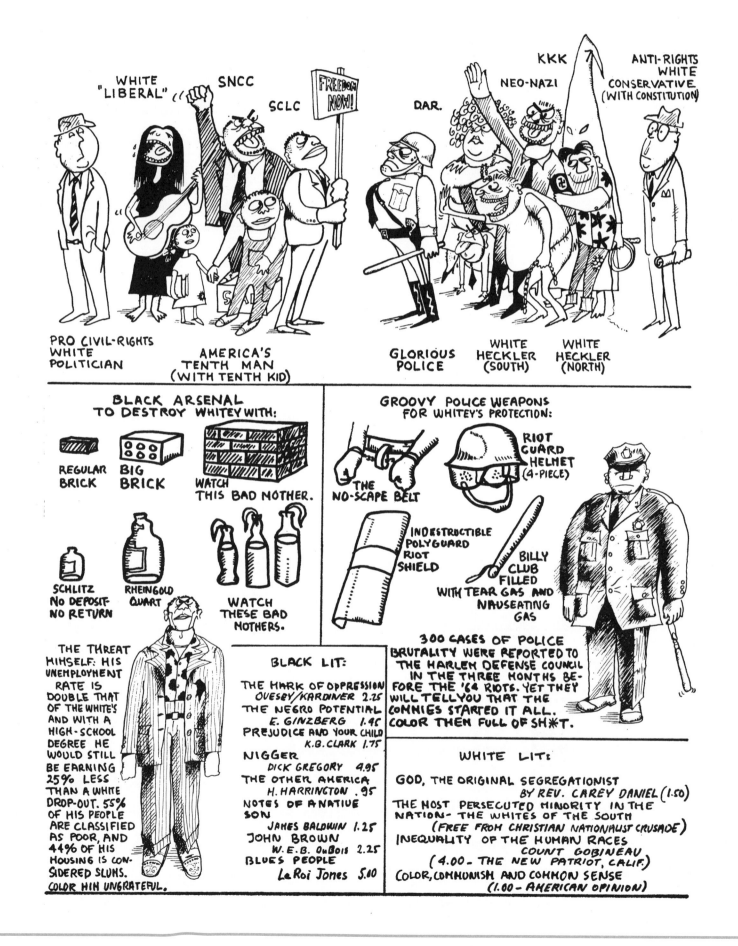

WHITE "LIBERAL"

SNCC

SCLC

FREEDOM NOW!

KKK

NEO-NAZI

D.A.R.

ANTI-RIGHTS WHITE CONSERVATIVE (WITH CONSTITUTION)

PRO CIVIL-RIGHTS WHITE POLITICIAN

AMERICA'S TENTH MAN (WITH TENTH KID)

GLORIOUS POLICE

WHITE HECKLER (SOUTH)

WHITE HECKLER (NORTH)

BLACK ARSENAL TO DESTROY WHITEY WITH:

REGULAR BRICK

BIG BRICK

WATCH THIS BAD MOTHER.

SCHLITZ NO DEPOSIT- NO RETURN

RHEINGOLD QUART

WATCH THESE BAD MOTHERS.

THE THREAT HIMSELF: HIS UNEMPLOYMENT RATE IS DOUBLE THAT OF THE WHITE'S AND WITH A HIGH-SCHOOL DEGREE HE WOULD STILL BE EARNING 25% LESS THAN A WHITE DROP-OUT. 55% OF HIS PEOPLE ARE CLASSIFIED AS POOR, AND 44% OF HIS HOUSING IS CON- SIDERED SLUMS. COLOR HIM UNGRATEFUL.

GROOVY POLICE WEAPONS FOR WHITEY'S PROTECTION:

THE NO-SCAPE BELT

RIOT GUARD HELMET (4-PIECE)

INDESTRUCTIBLE POLYGUARD RIOT SHIELD

BILLY CLUB FILLED WITH TEAR GAS AND NAUSEATING GAS

BLACK LIT:

THE MARK OF OPPRESSION
   OVESEY/KARDINER 2.25
THE NEGRO POTENTIAL
   E. GINZBERG 1.45
PREJUDICE AND YOUR CHILD
   K.B. CLARK 1.75
NIGGER
   DICK GREGORY 4.95
THE OTHER AMERICA
   H. HARRINGTON .95
NOTES OF A NATIVE SON
   JAMES BALDWIN 1.25
JOHN BROWN
   W.E.B. DuBois 2.25
BLUES PEOPLE
   LeRoi Jones 5.10

300 CASES OF POLICE BRUTALITY WERE REPORTED TO THE HARLEM DEFENSE COUNCIL IN THE THREE MONTHS BE- FORE THE '64 RIOTS. YET THEY WILL TELL YOU THAT THE COMMIES STARTED IT ALL. COLOR THEM FULL OF SH*T.

WHITE LIT:

GOD, THE ORIGINAL SEGREGATIONIST
   BY REV. CAREY DANIEL (1.50)
THE MOST PERSECUTED MINORITY IN THE NATION- THE WHITES OF THE SOUTH
   (FREE FROM CHRISTIAN NATIONALIST CRUSADE)
INEQUALITY OF THE HUMAN RACES
   COUNT GOBINEAU
   (4.00 - THE NEW PATRIOT, CALIF.)
COLOR, COMMUNISM AND COMMON SENSE
   (1.00 - AMERICAN OPINION)

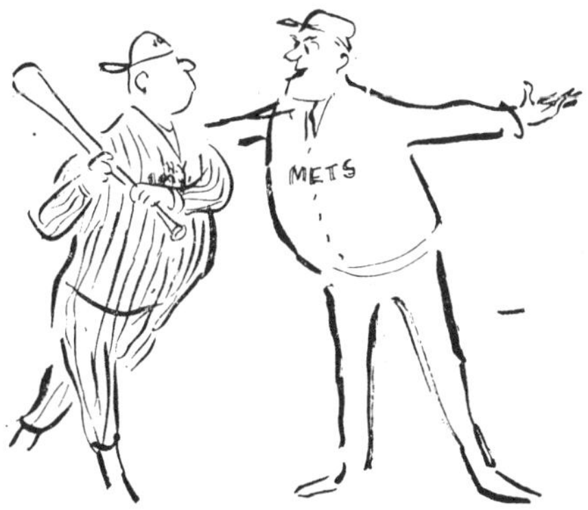
METS

"Get in there, Frankie, and show our New York boys in Vietnam that we're fully supporting them!"

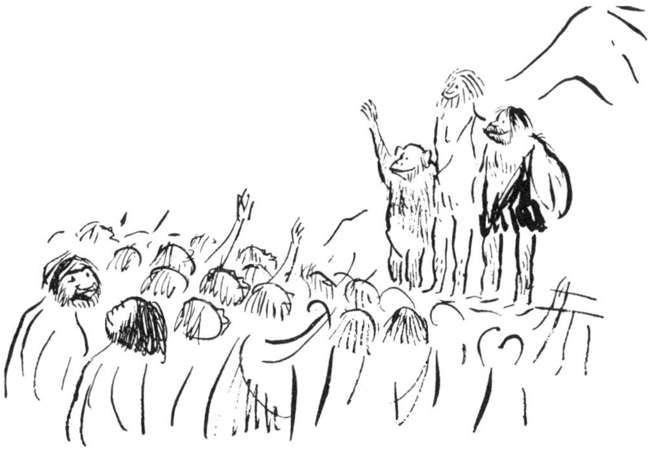

"The usual 'balanced ticket.'"

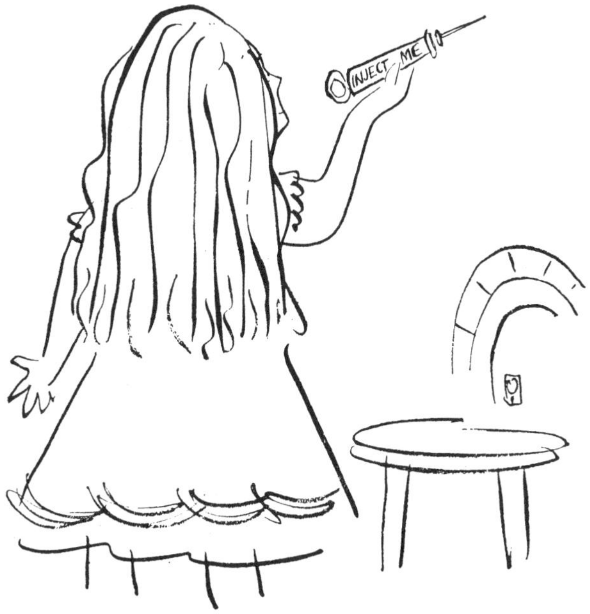
INJECT ME

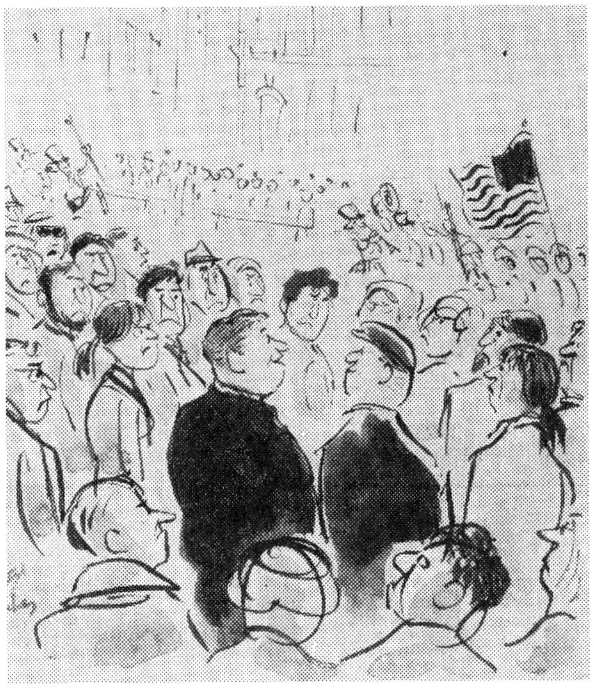

"It's a grand old flag."

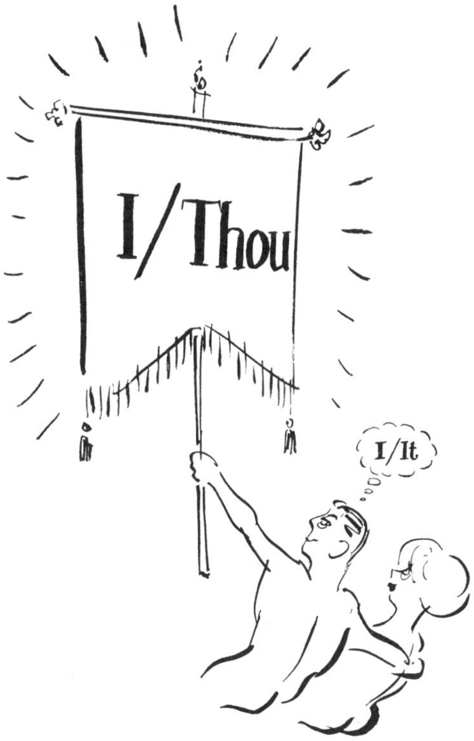
I/Thou
I/It

ED FISHER. THE REALIST #72, DECEMBER 1966.

RICHARD GUINDON.
THE REALIST #72, DECEMBER 1966.

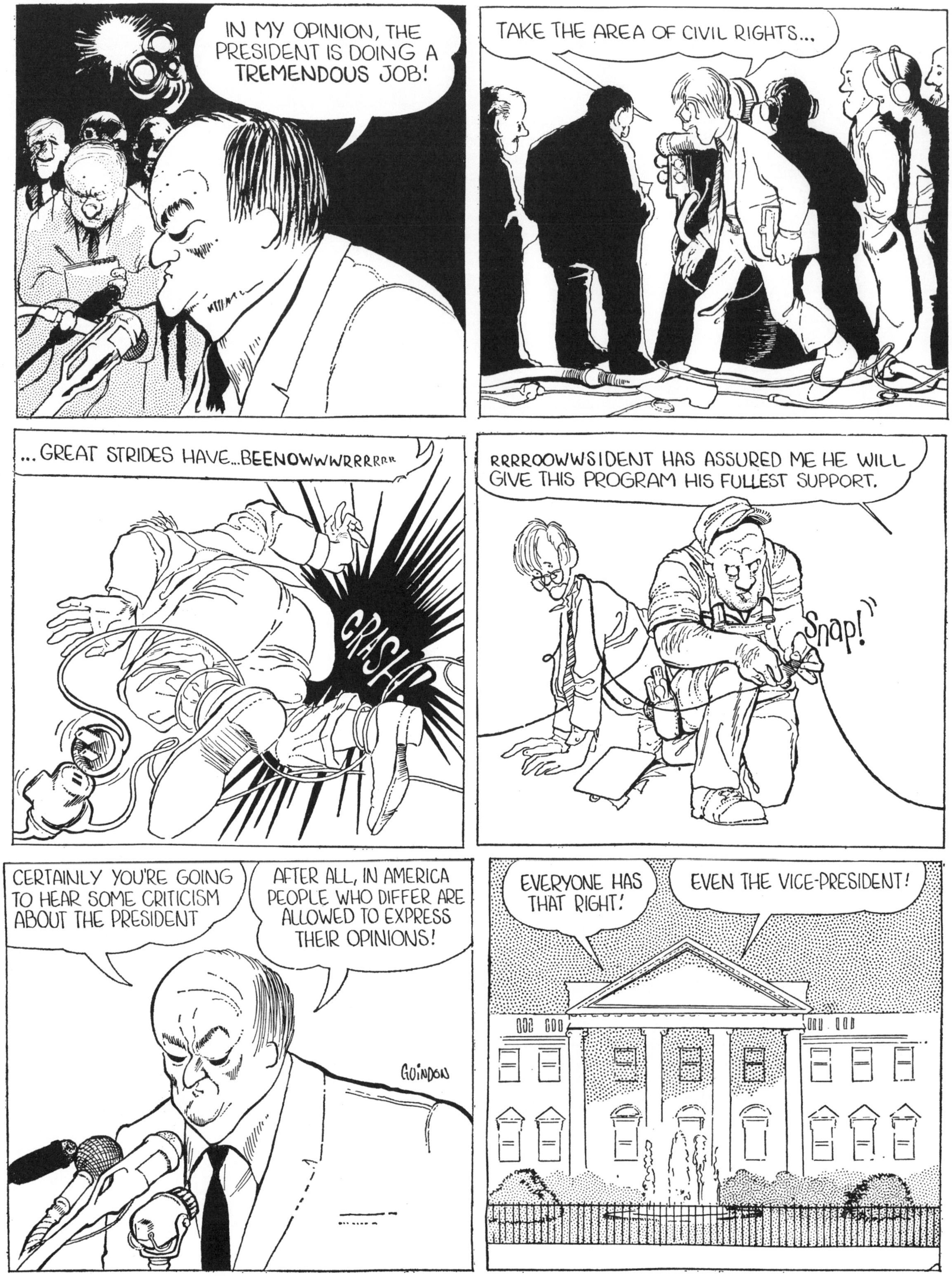
IN MY OPINION, THE PRESIDENT IS DOING A TREMENDOUS JOB!
TAKE THE AREA OF CIVIL RIGHTS...
...GREAT STRIDES HAVE...BEENOWWWRRRRRR
CRASH!!
RRRROOWWSIDENT HAS ASSURED ME HE WILL GIVE THIS PROGRAM HIS FULLEST SUPPORT.
Snap!
CERTAINLY YOU'RE GOING TO HEAR SOME CRITICISM ABOUT THE PRESIDENT
AFTER ALL, IN AMERICA PEOPLE WHO DIFFER ARE ALLOWED TO EXPRESS THEIR OPINIONS!
GUINDON
EVERYONE HAS THAT RIGHT!
EVEN THE VICE-PRESIDENT!

THE REPUBLICAN MACHINE IN THIS ELECTION HAS HURLED SOME PRETTY SERIOUS CHARGES AT ME!
THE QUESTION HAS BEEN RAISED AS TO WHETHER A DEMOCRATIC MACHINE CAN CONTINUE AS PRESIDENT! MY ANSWER TO YOU IS YES!
AS YOU KNOW MY OPPONENT WAS CONSTRUCTED ESPECIALLY FOR THIS ELECTION...
..BUT DID YOU KNOW THAT ALL THE PARTS AND MATERIAL USED IN THE REPUBLICAN MACHINE WERE MADE IN EUROPE?-BY FOREIGN LABOR?
IBM
I DON'T THINK ANYONE IS FOOLED BY THIS!
I'M SURE A DEMOCRATIC MACHINE CAN AND WILL BE ELECTED PRESIDENT!
THANK YOU
GUINDON
NOW IF YOU'LL FORM A LINE I'LL DISPENSE THE SOUP.

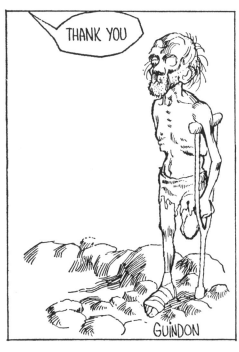

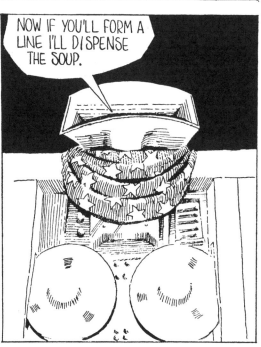

NEWS ITEM: Department stores are now hiring Puerto Ricans and Negroes to play Santa Claus.

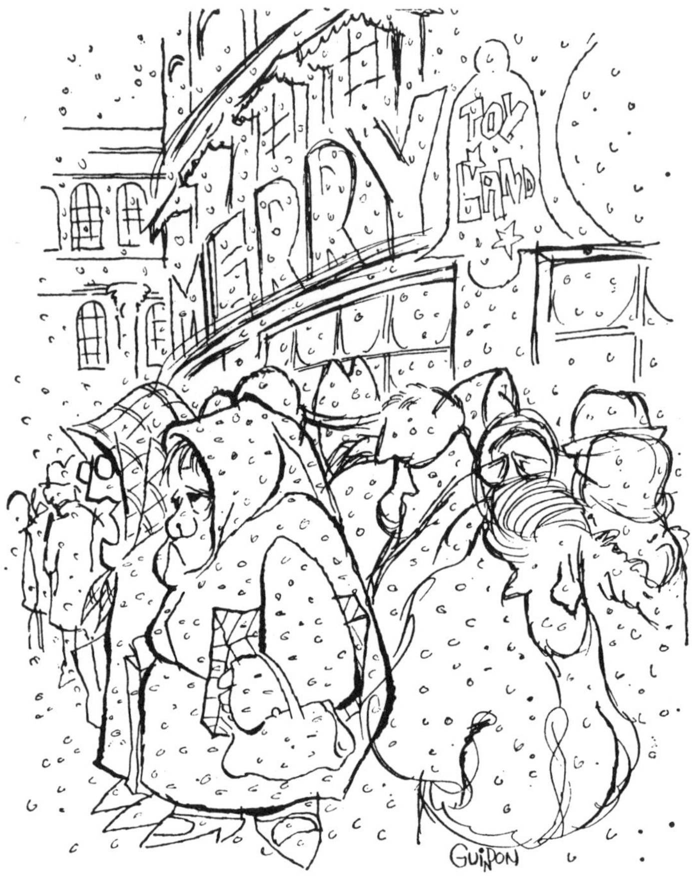
MERRY

"Look — there goes Santa Claus with a white woman!"

RICHARD GUINDON. THE REALIST #72, DECEMBER 1966.

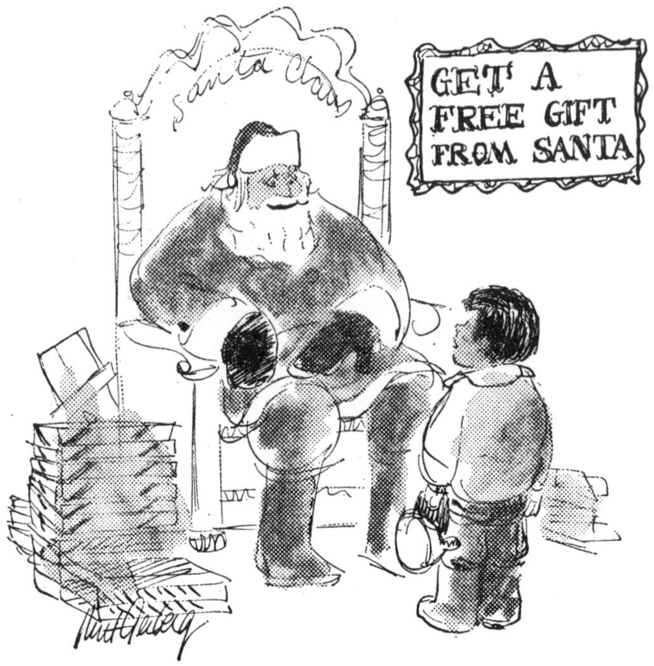
Santa Claus
GET A FREE GIFT FROM SANTA

"Toma Usted *dos* ..."

MORT GERBERG. THE REALIST #72, DECEMBER 1966.

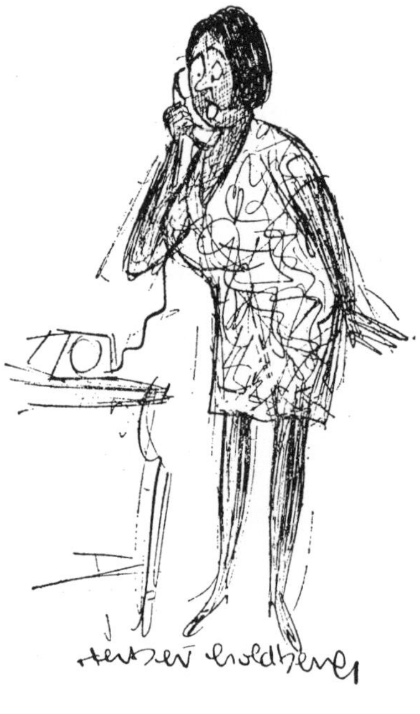

"Darling, my schwartza is threatening to quit!"

HERBERT GOLDBERG. THE REALIST #73, FEBRUARY 1967. '75

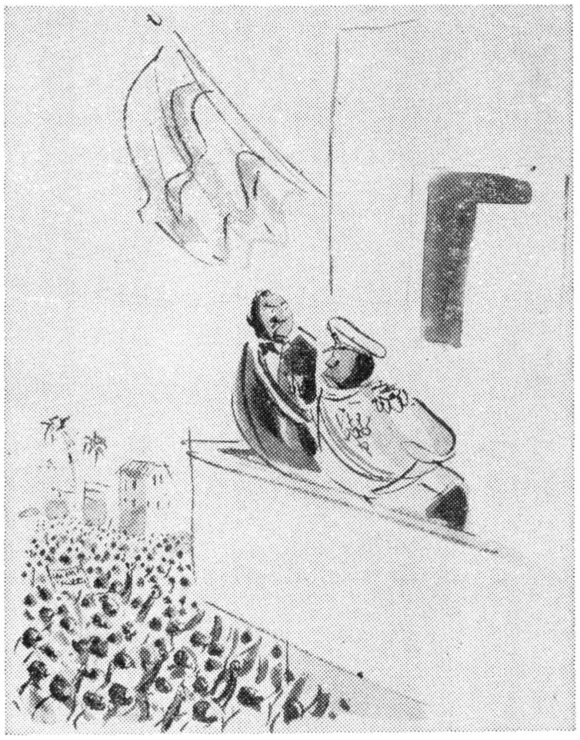

"What the hell do they mean, 'black power!' ..."

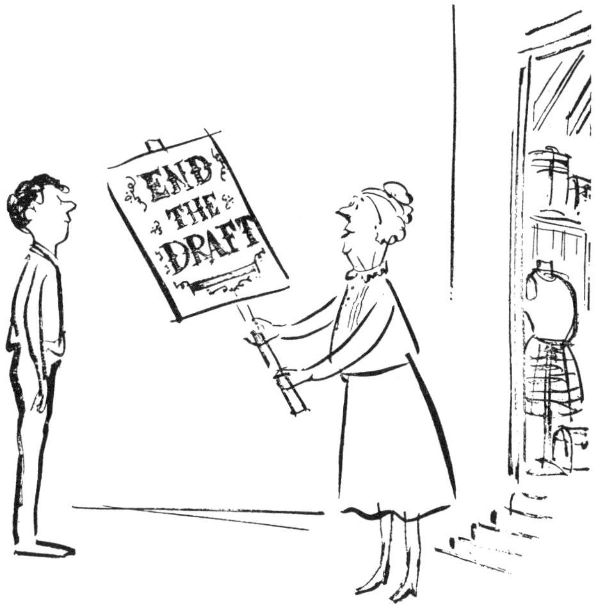
END
THE
DRAFT

"Take it, Norbert, and bear it well: your great-grandfather carried it against the Lincoln administration."

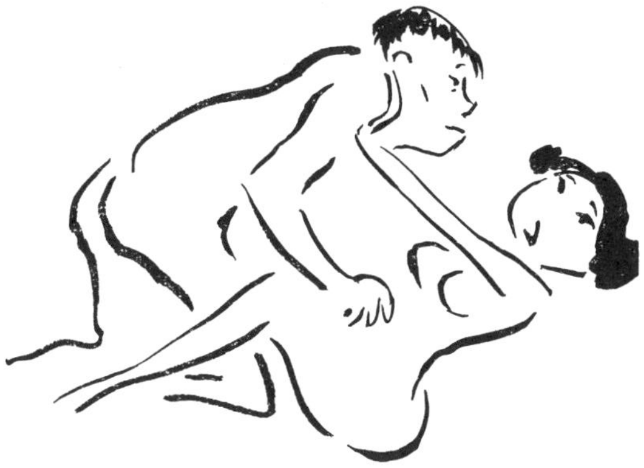

"But, Comrade Pao, what if we were to produce one of those 'flexible new leaders' Dean Rusk is counting on?"

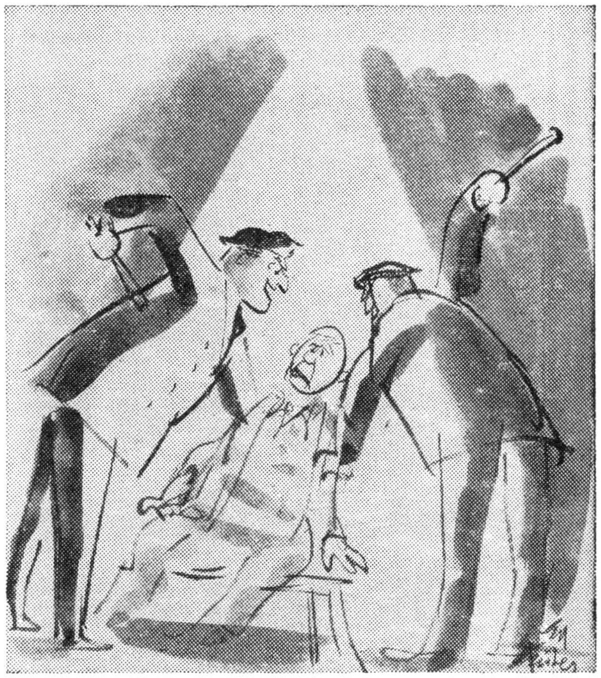

"We're not trying to get a confession. We're just beating you up."

ED FISHER. THE REALIST #73, FEBRUARY 1967.

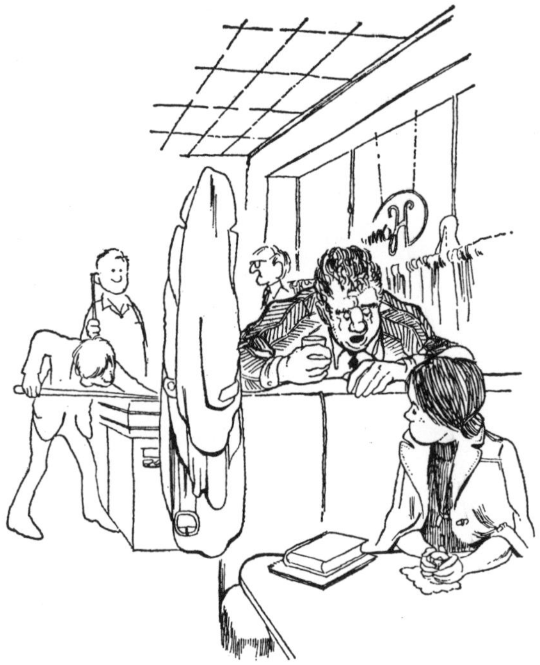

"Miss? Have you ever been so alienated that you wanted to take all of humanity and stomp it down a toilet while on the other hand you needed to get laid badly enough to kill?"

RICHARD GUINDON. THE REALIST #73, FEBRUARY 1967.

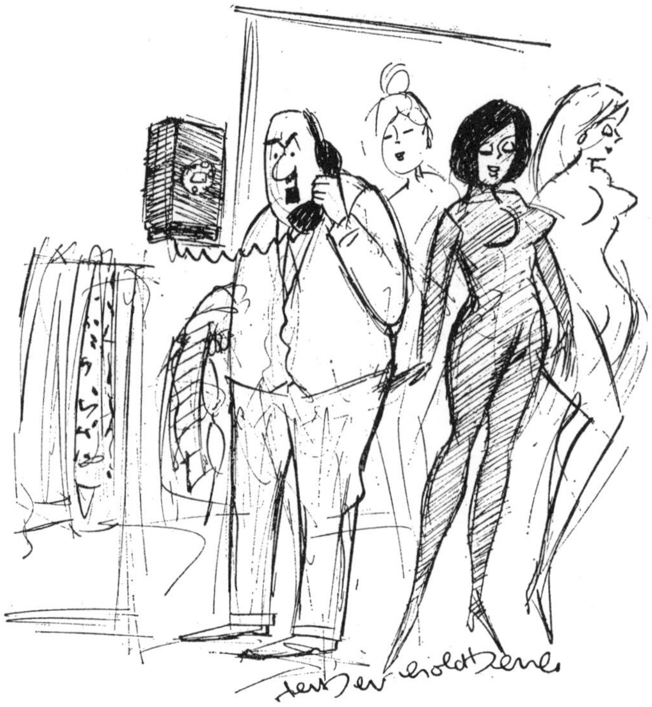

"Jerry, the Negro manikin — she's not light-skinned enough!"

HERBERT GOLDBERG. THE REALIST #73, FEBRUARY 1967.

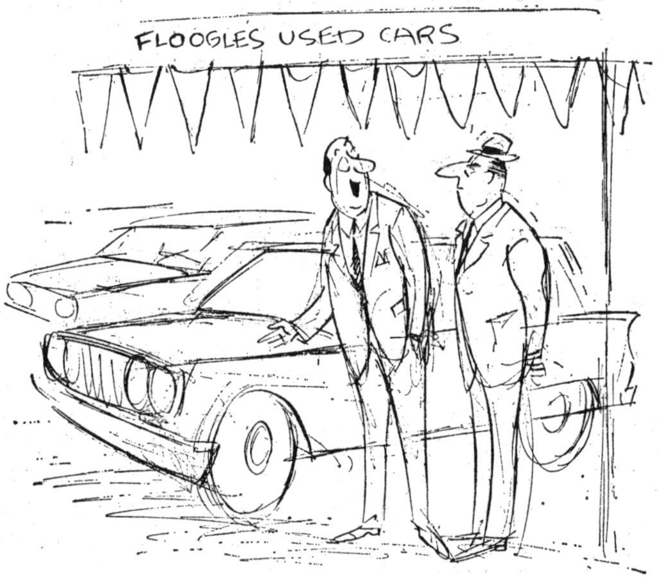
FLOOGLES USED CARS

"This one was owned by an elderly Negro who drove it under the speed limit for fear of some cop ticketing him."

ED FISHER. THE REALIST #73, FEBRUARY 1967.

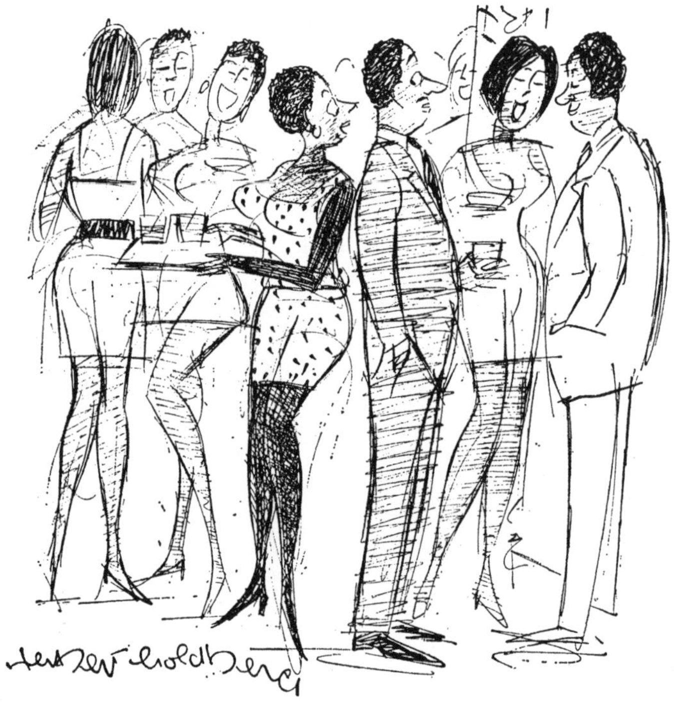

"Dear, we forgot to invite the necessary white liberal."

HERBERT GOLDBERG. THE REALIST #73, FEBRUARY 1967.

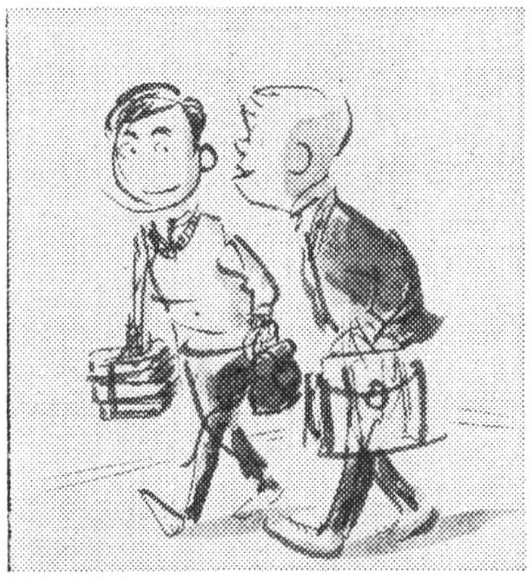

"If God is dead, how come we're not allowed to pray in school?"

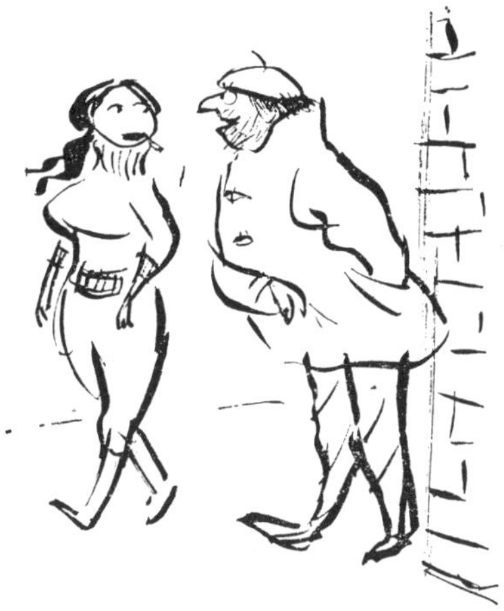

"— I can get you LSD in a sugar cube, or, if you're counting calories ..."

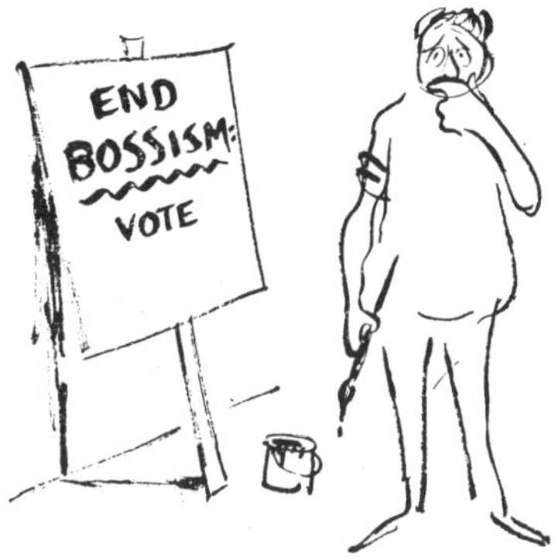
END
BOSSISM
VOTE

ED FISHER. THE REALIST #73, FEBRUARY 1967.

Soft-Core Pornography of the Month

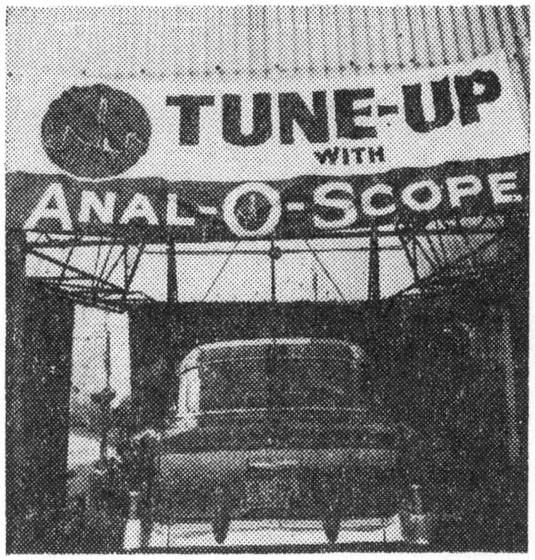
TUNE-UP
WITH
ANAL-O-SCOPE

—Photo by Bob Greger

A House of Homosexual Auto-Eroticism

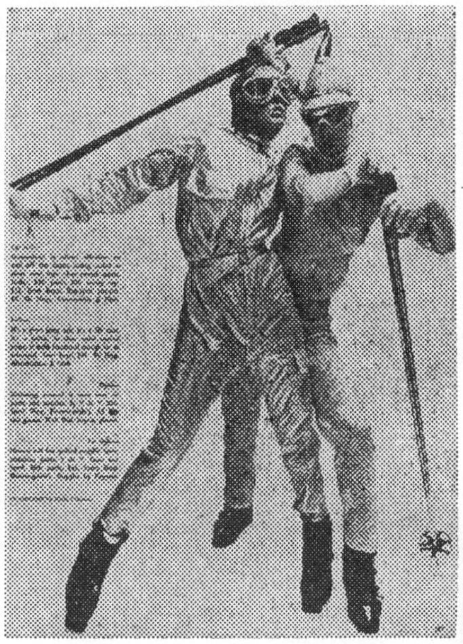

Lesbian Dry-Hump in the Times

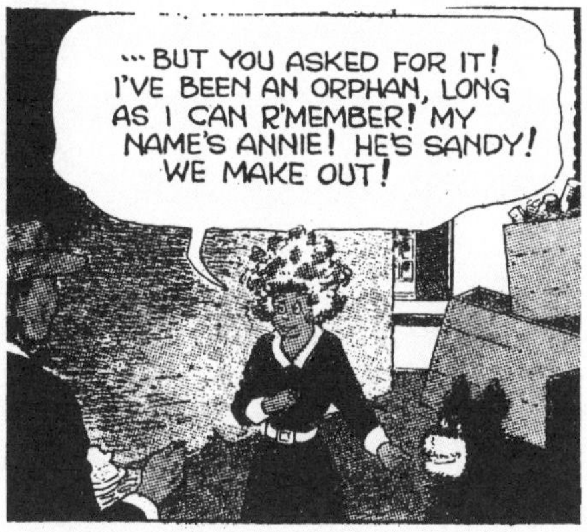
...BUT YOU ASKED FOR IT! I'VE BEEN AN ORPHAN, LONG AS I CAN R'MEMBER! MY NAME'S ANNIE! HE'S SANDY! WE MAKE OUT!

Bestiality in the Comic Section

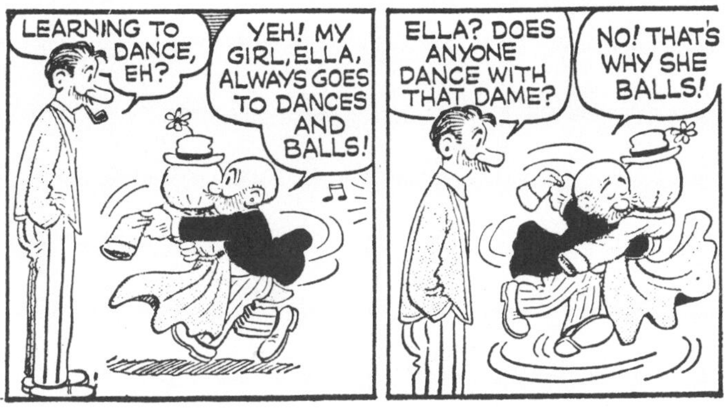
LEARNING TO DANCE, EH?
YEH! MY GIRL, ELLA, ALWAYS GOES TO DANCES AND BALLS!
ELLA? DOES ANYONE DANCE WITH THAT DAME?
NO! THAT'S WHY SHE BALLS!

Voyeurism, Male Fetishism and Female Promiscuity

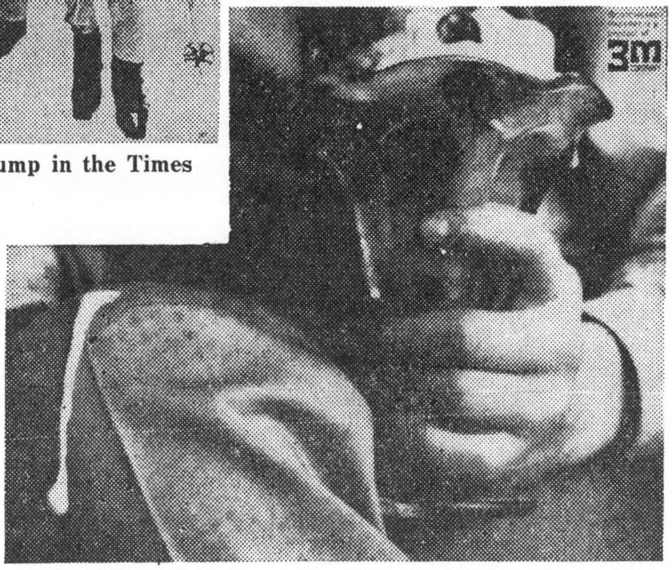
3m

Onanistic Success in the New Yorker's pages

THE REALIST #73, FEBRUARY 1967.

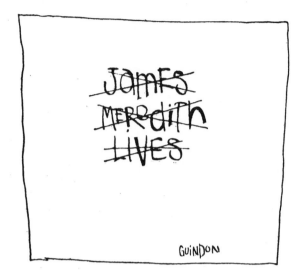

James
Meredith
Lives
GUINDON

RICHARD GUINDON. THE REALIST #73, FEBRUARY 1967.

CHICAGO
CHAMBER
OF
COMMERCE
S. GROSS

"Well, there go our chances for the nurses' convention."

RICHARD GUINDON. THE REALIST #73, FEBRUARY 1967.

"You can't argue with a Humanist because Humanism isn't based on reason. You know what they react with when you tell them that Man is dead? 'Well, you just got to have faith.'"

RICHARD GUINDON. THE REALIST #73, FEBRUARY 1967.

BUDDHA
IS
DEAD
JAY LYNCH

JAY LYNCH. THE REALIST #73, FEBRUARY 1967.

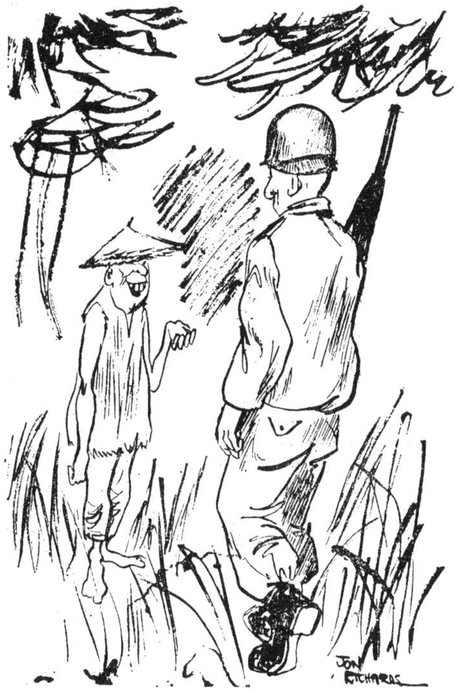
JON RICHARDS

"Hey, Joe — you got LSD?"

JON RICHARDS. THE REALIST #73, FEBRUARY 1967.

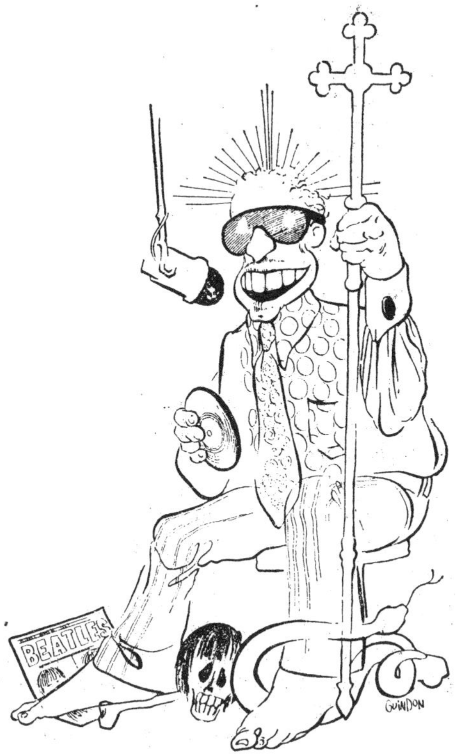
BEATLES
GUINDON

"And now — for Jesus, Mary and Joseph ..."

RICHARD GUINDON. THE REALIST #73, FEBRUARY 1967.

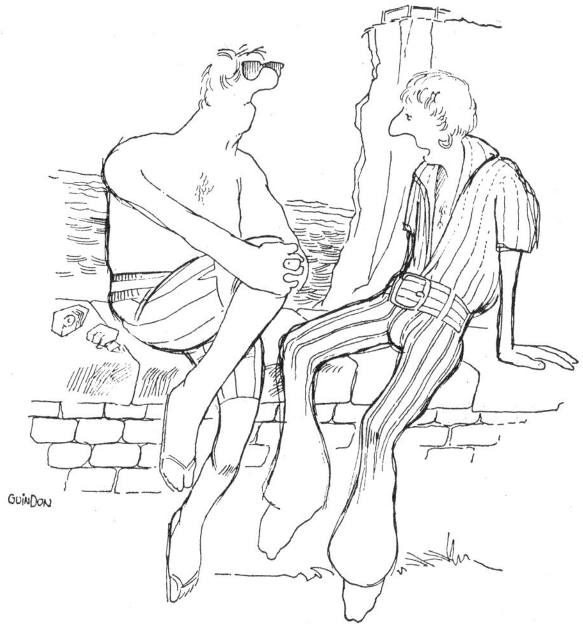
GUINDON

"Ronald Reagan was in this big crowd
and I copped a feel."

RICHARD GUINDON. THE REALIST #73, FEBRUARY 1967.

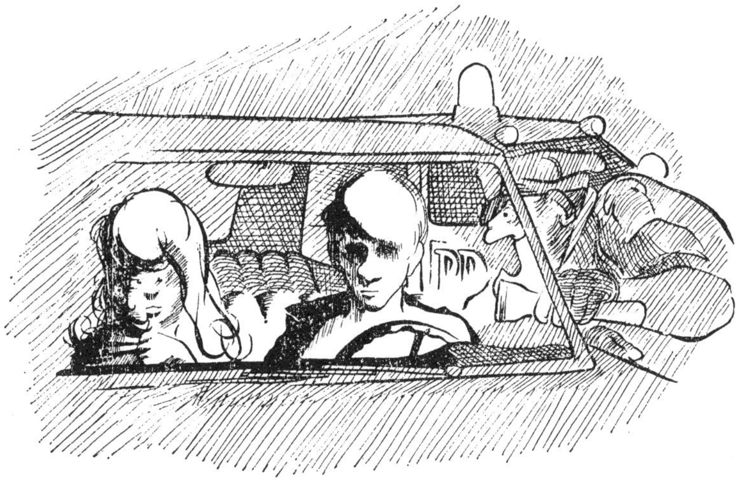

"Making love! Like hell! You were fucking — I saw you!"

RICHARD GUINDON. THE REALIST #73, FEBRUARY 1967.

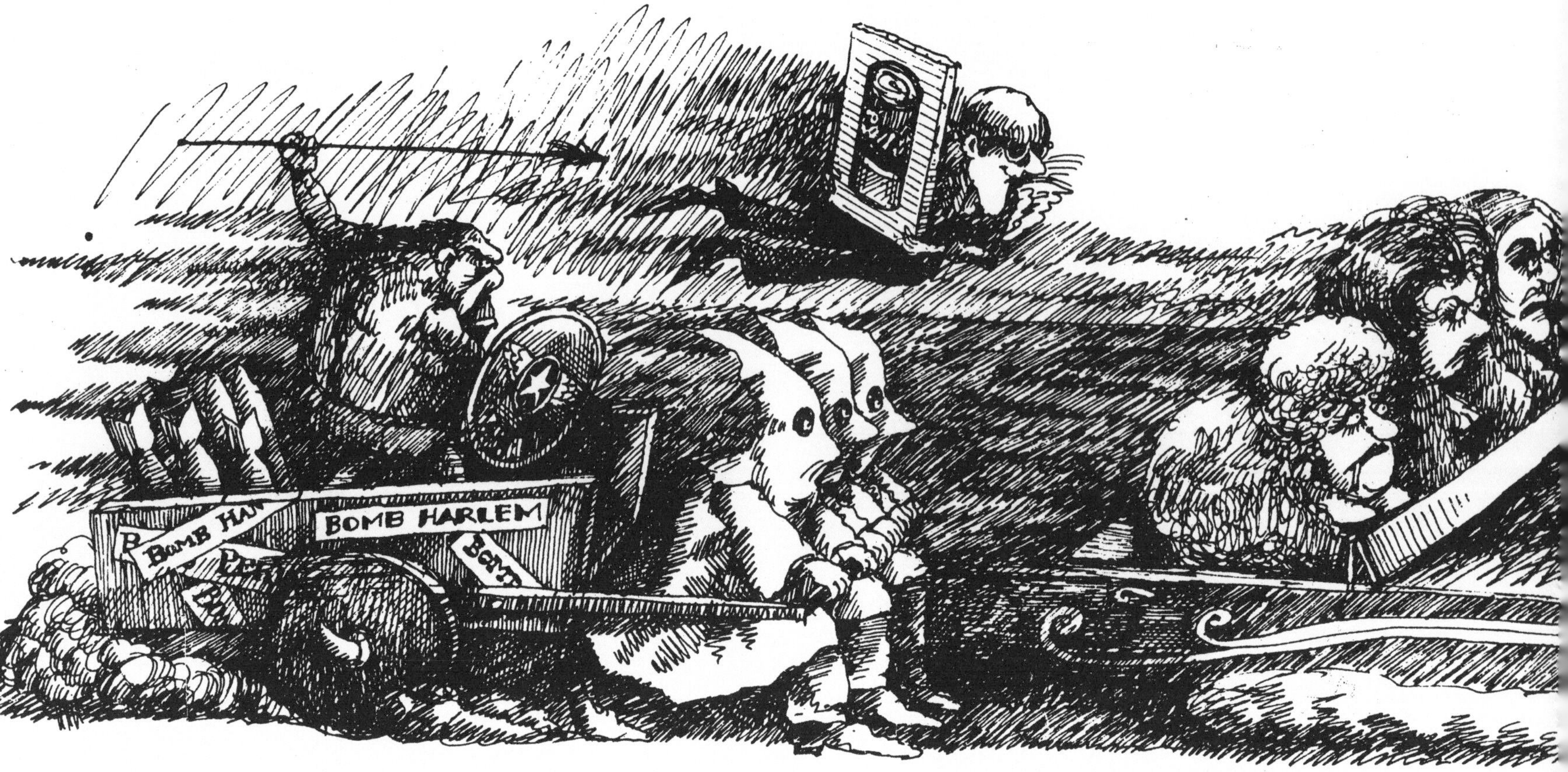
BOMB HARLEM

EDWARD SOREL. THE REALIST #74, MAY 1967.

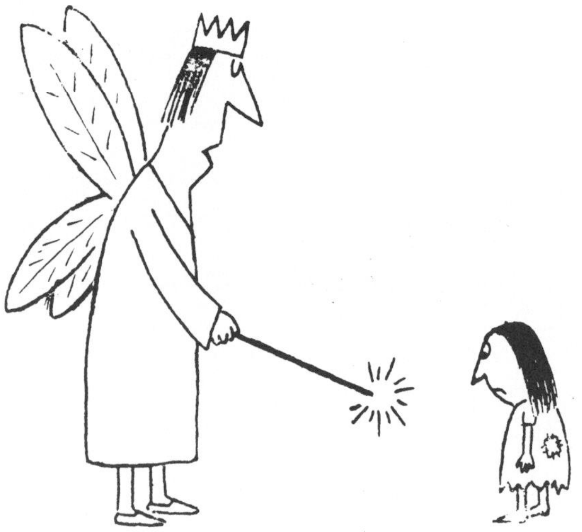

"No, my child, this is not a magic wand.
I just lit a fart."

SAM GROSS. THE REALIST #74, MAY 1967.

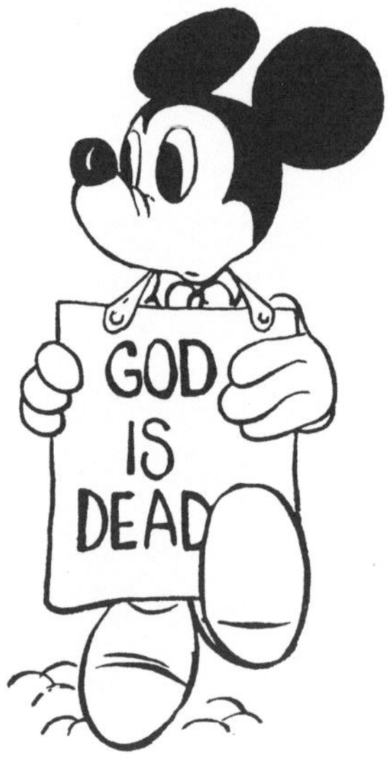
GOD
IS
DEAD

RICHARD GUINDON. THE REALIST #74, MAY 1967.

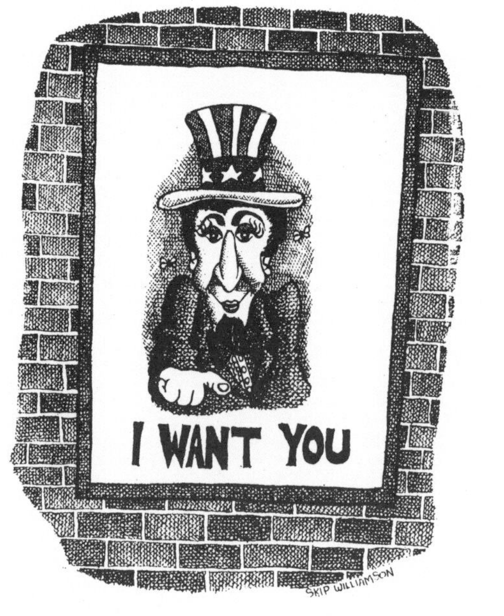
I WANT YOU
SKIP WILLIAMSON

SKIP WILLIAMSON. THE REALIST #74, MAY 1967.

"This war is, I believe, a war for civilization."
— Francis Cardinal Spellman

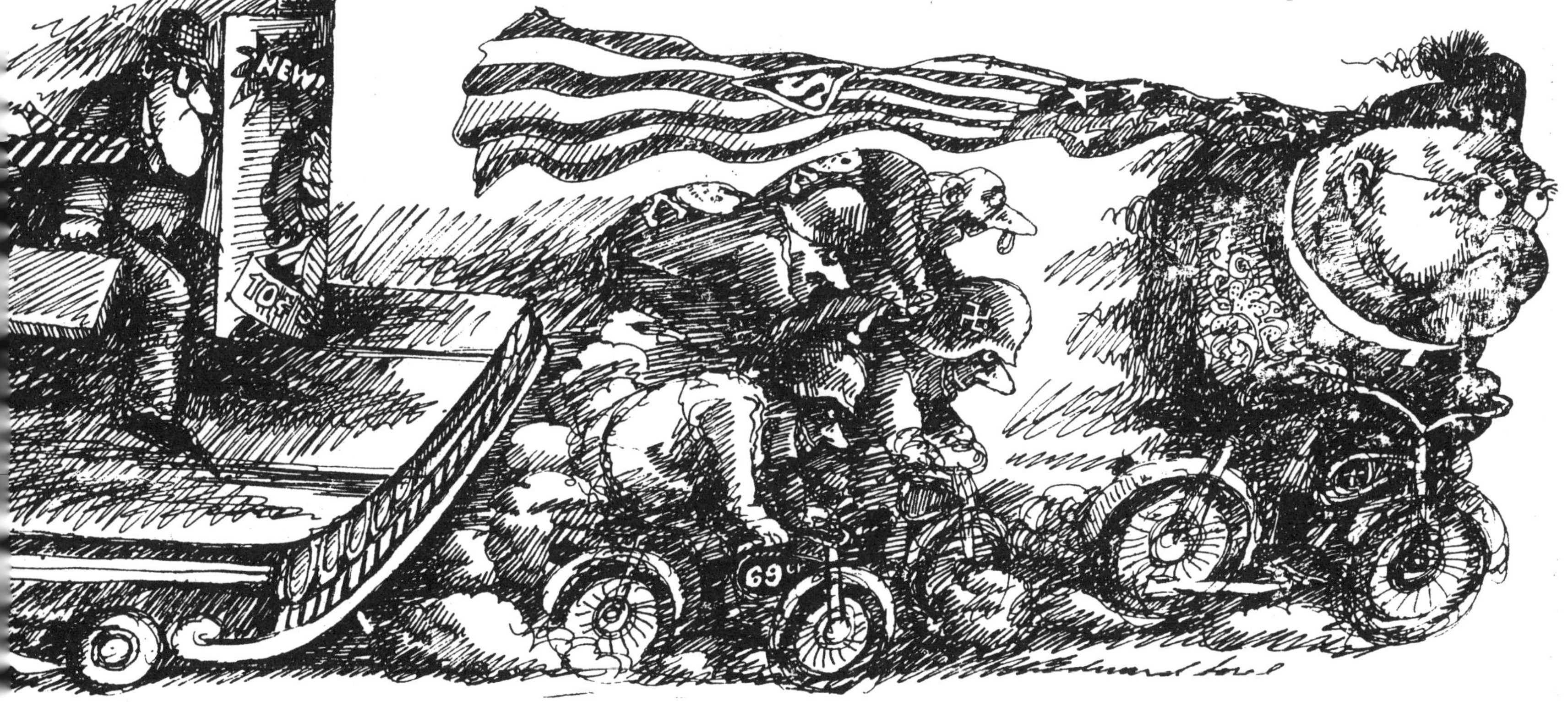

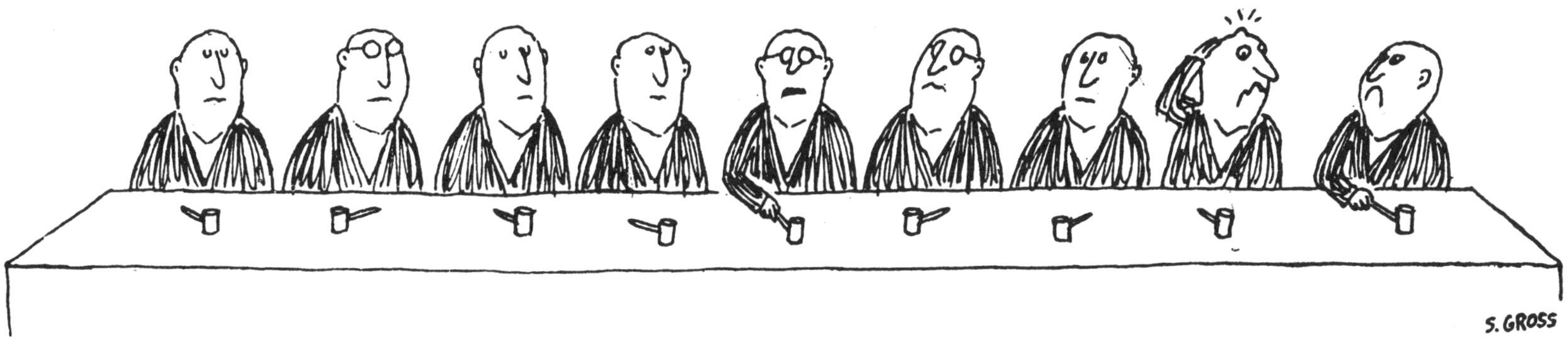
S. GROSS

"Eight for, and one against!"

SAM GROSS. THE REALIST #75, JUNE 1967.

WALLACE WOOD. THE REALIST #74, MAY 1967. *76

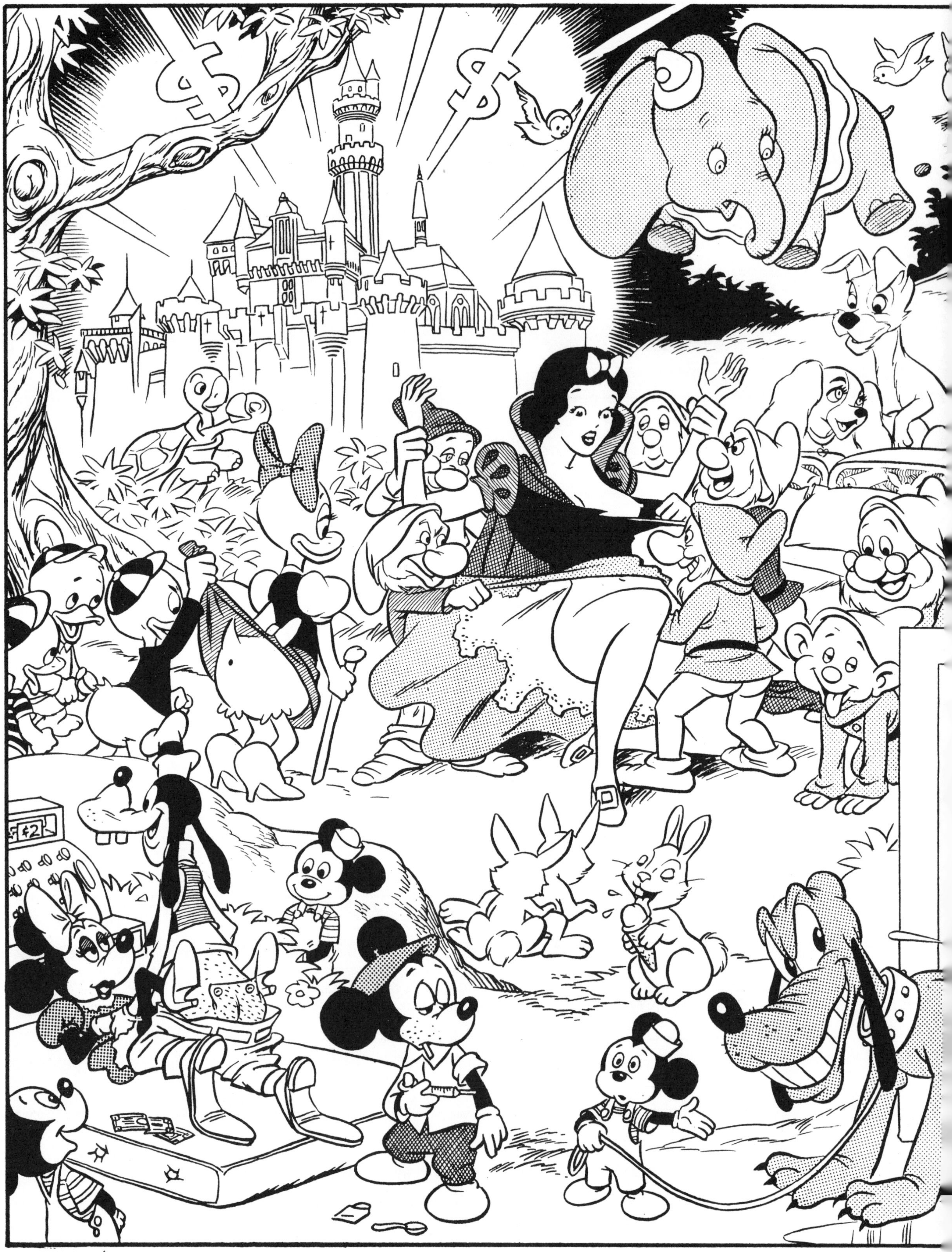

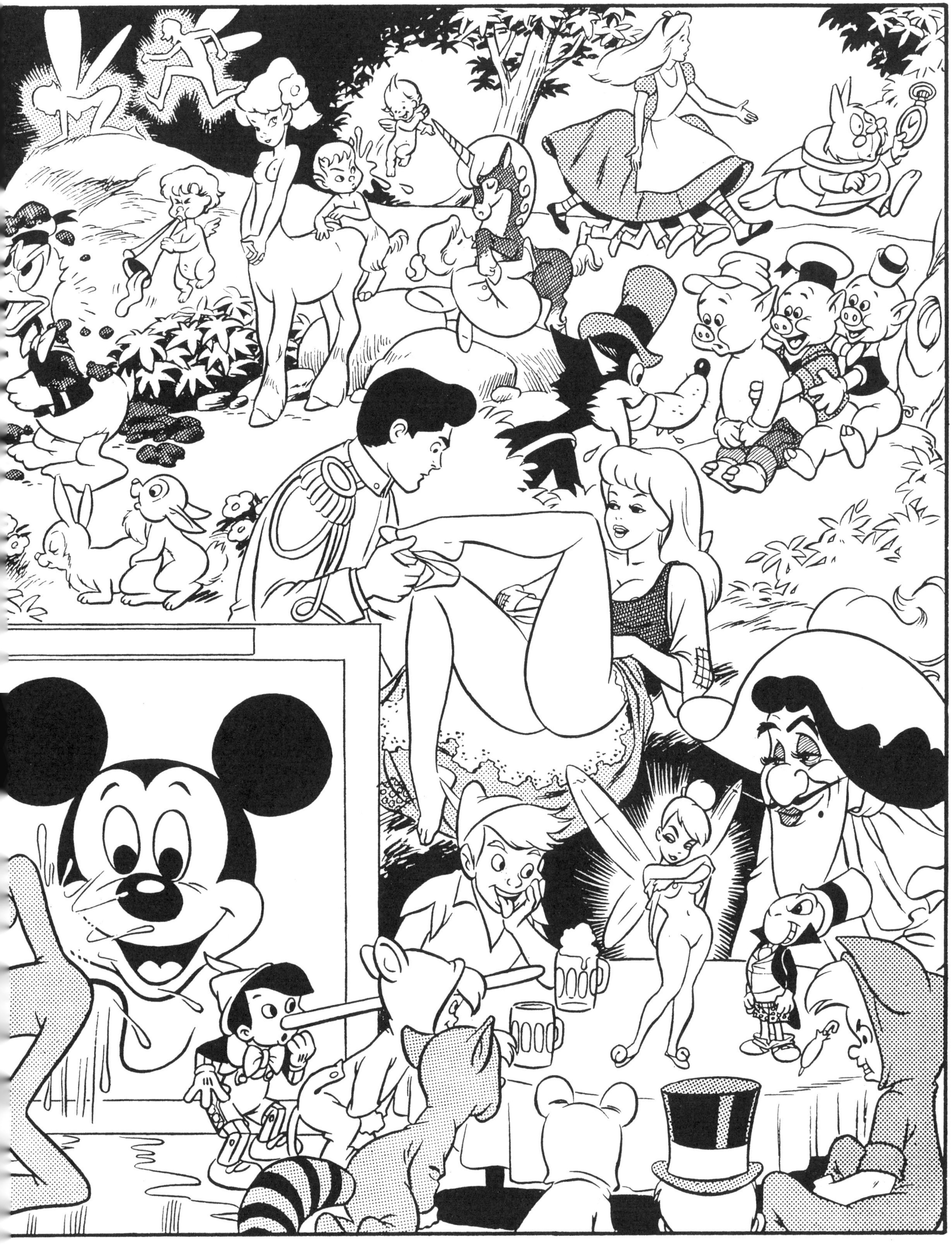

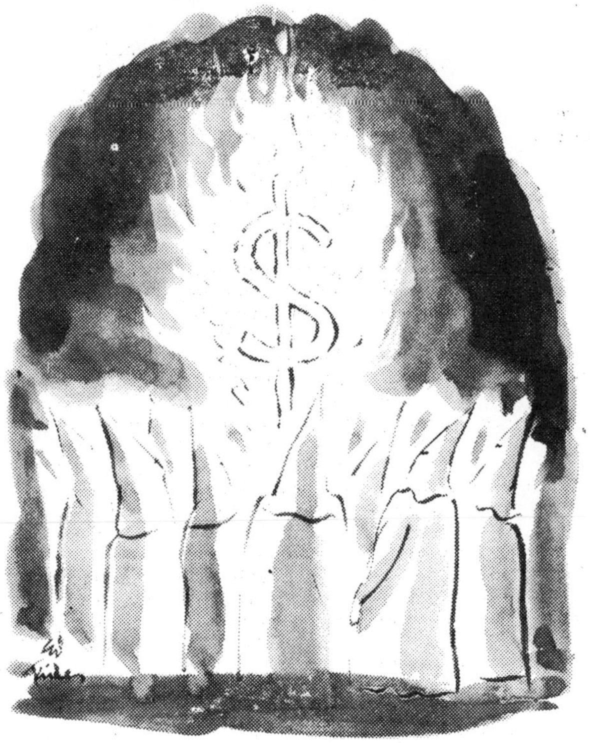

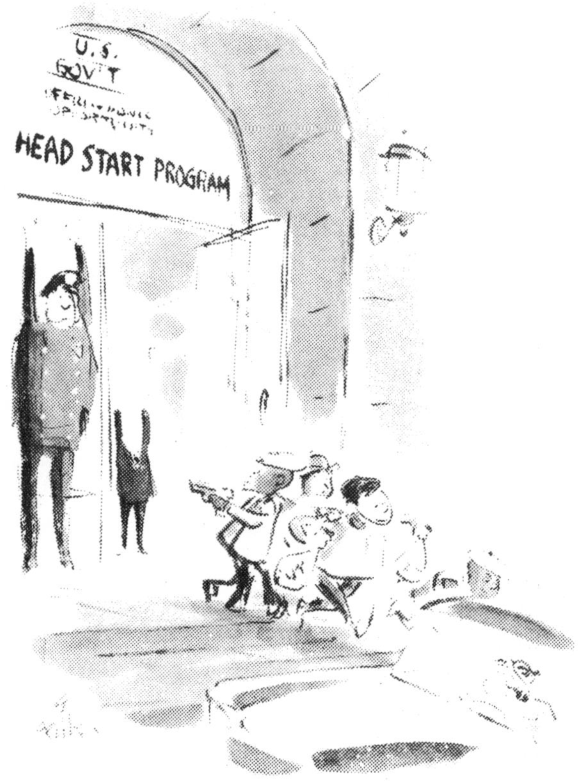
U.S. GOV'T
HEAD START PROGRAM

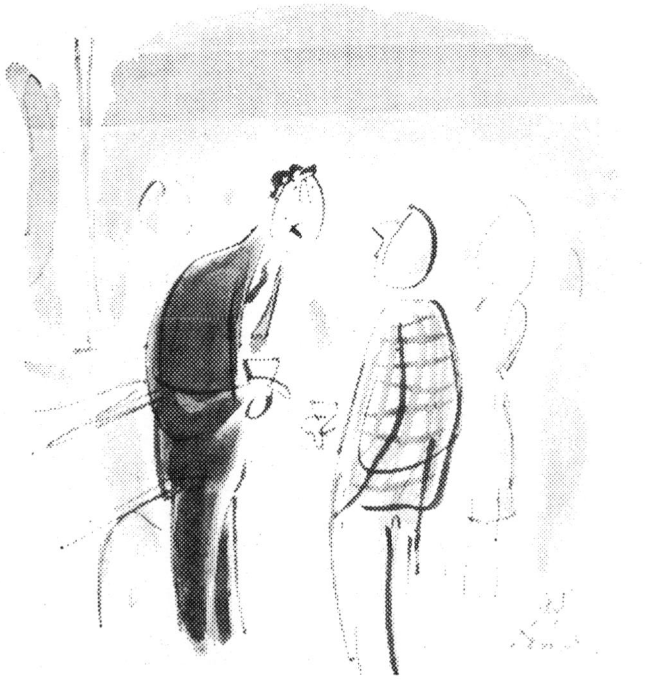

"What do I say about the Warren Commission? I say the Warren Commission was hasty in its judgment, devious, bigoted, guilty as hell of covering up, and inclined to make serious accusations without considering all the evidence. That's what I'd say; offhand."

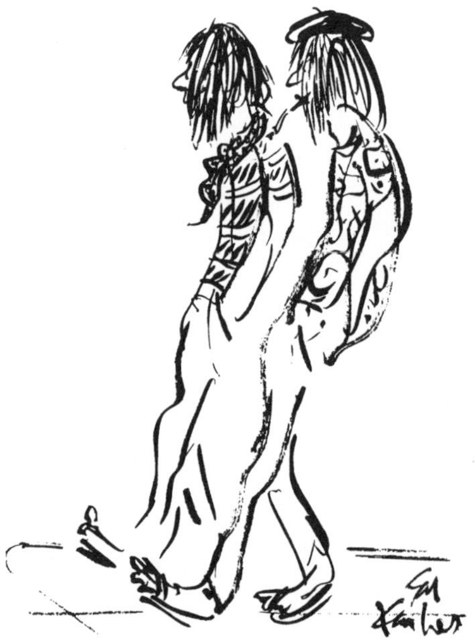

"It's simple. We use Vietcong tactics. Sneak into some little jerkwater Midwest town. Strike a blow against the Establishment. Then simply fade among the population."

ED FISHER. THE REALIST #74, MAY 1967.

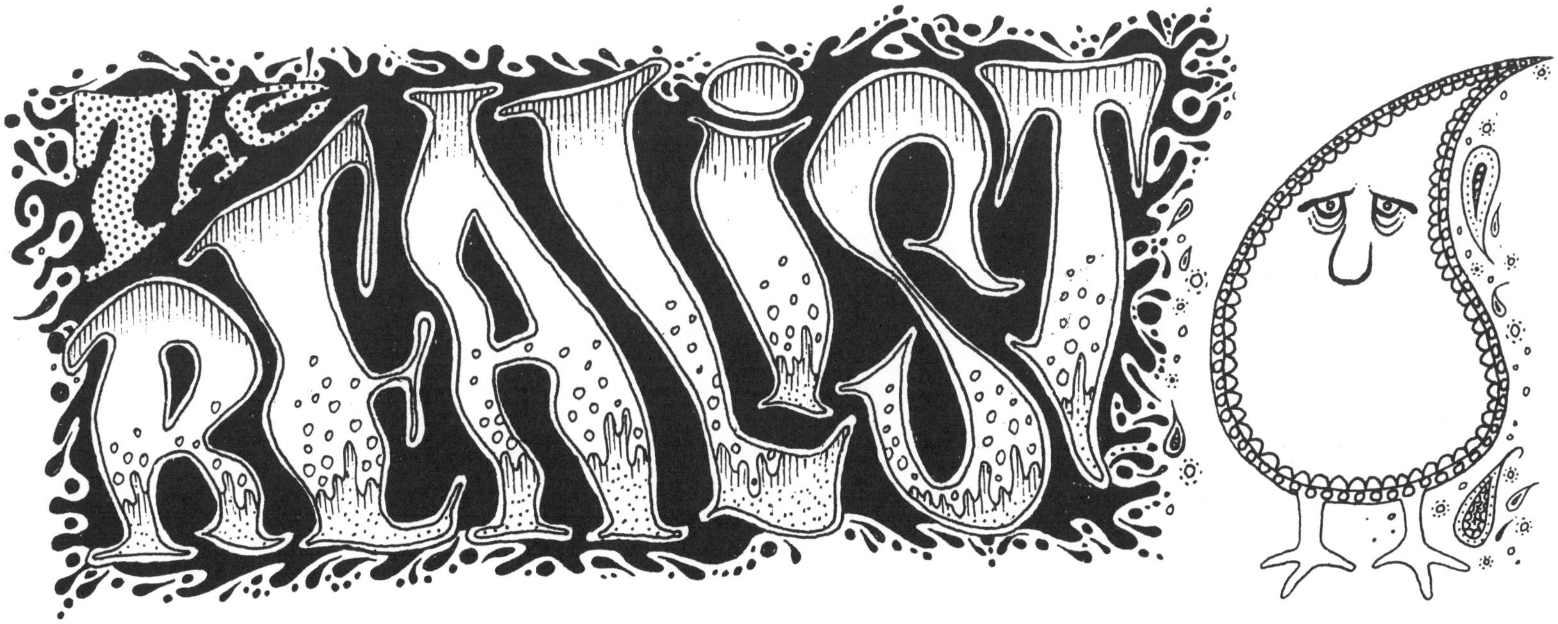
THE REALIST

JAY LYNCH. THE REALIST #75, JUNE 1967.

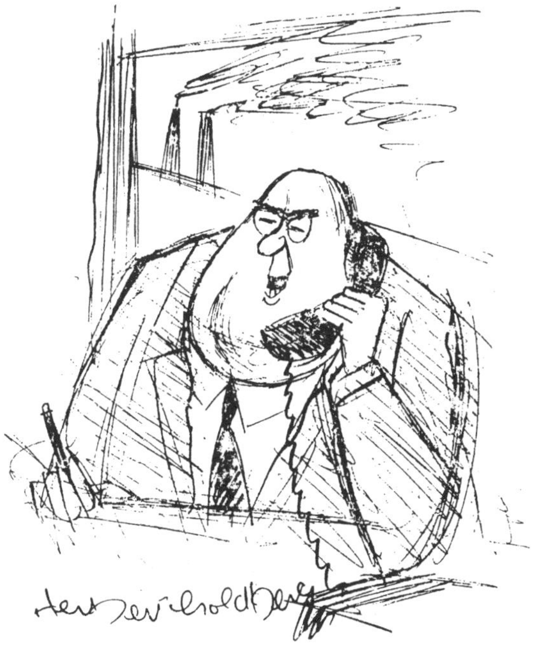

"So I thought it would be nice, Father, if you would bless the napalm."

HERBERT GOLDBERG. THE REALIST #74, MAY 1967. *77

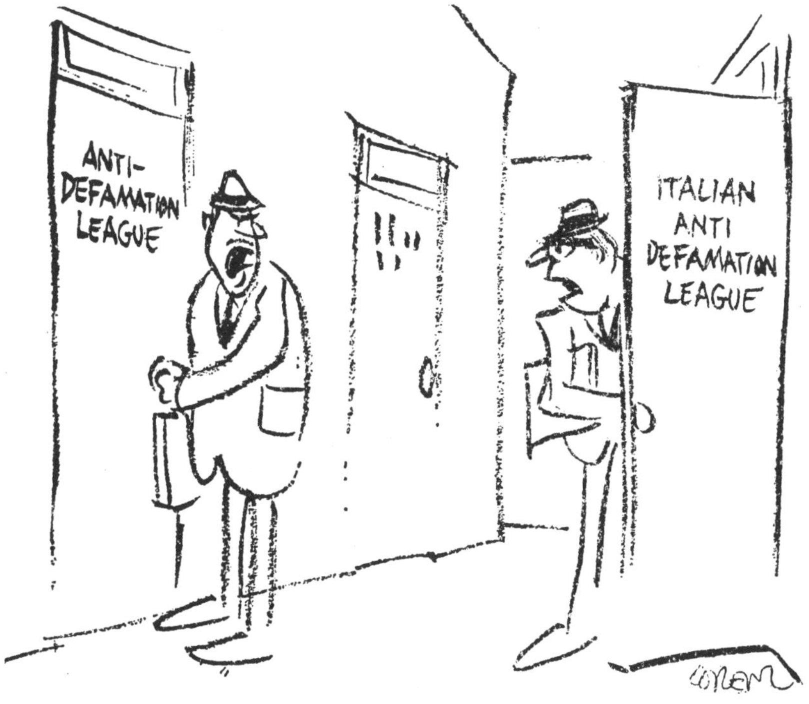
ANTI-DEFAMATION LEAGUE
ITALIAN ANTI DEFAMATION LEAGUE

"Wop!" "Kike!"

LEE LORENZ. THE REALIST #75, JUNE 1967.

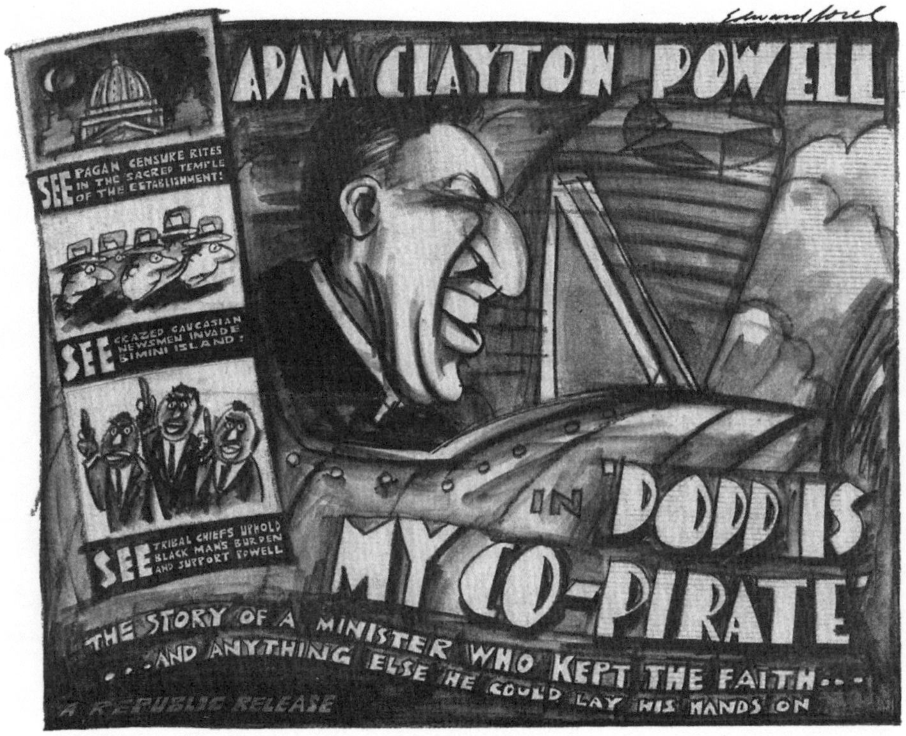
ADAM CLAYTON POWELL
SEE PAGAN CENSURE RITES IN THE SACRED TEMPLE OF THE ESTABLISHMENT!
SEE CRAZED CAUCASIAN NEWSMEN INVADE BIMINI ISLAND!
SEE TRIBAL CHIEFS UPHOLD BLACK MANS BURDEN AND SUPPORT POWELL
IN "DODD IS MY CO-PIRATE"
THE STORY OF A MINISTER WHO KEPT THE FAITH... ...AND ANYTHING ELSE HE COULD LAY HIS HANDS ON
A REPUBLIC RELEASE

ROBERT GROSSMAN. THE REALIST #76, AUGUST 1967-JANUARY 1968. *78

ROBERT GROSSMAN. THE REALIST #75, JUNE 1967.

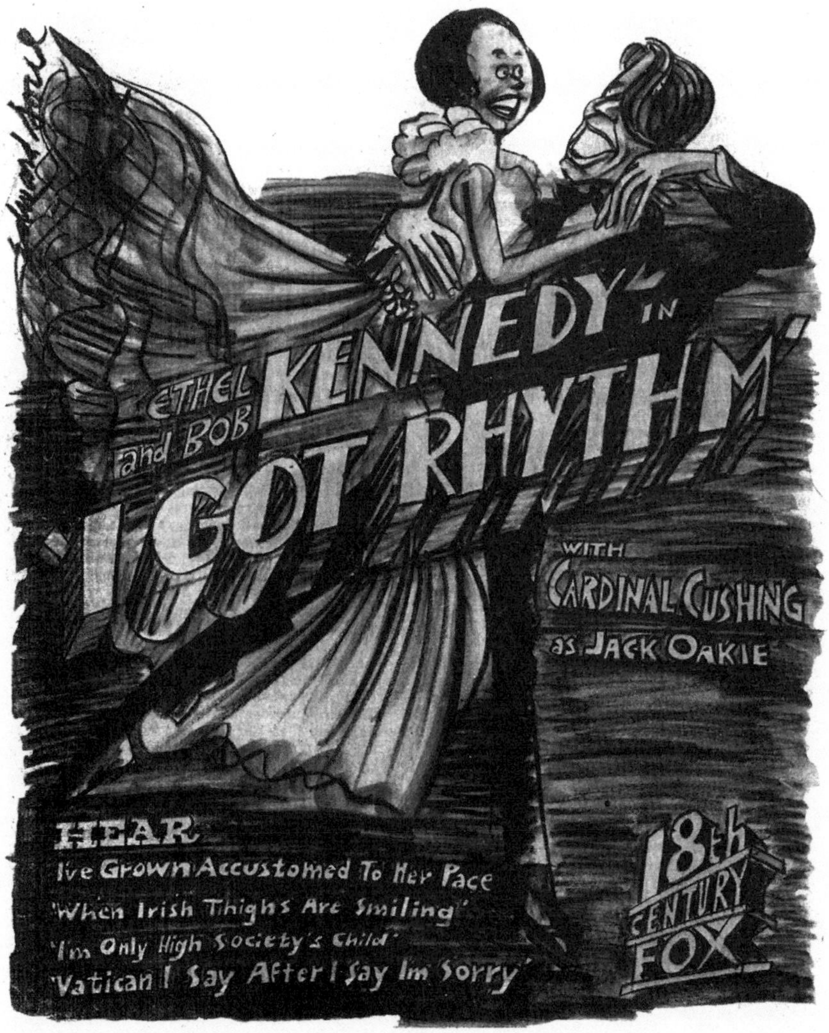
ETHEL and BOB KENNEDY IN
'I GOT RHYTHM'
WITH CARDINAL CUSHING as JACK OAKIE
HEAR
Ive Grown Accustomed To Her Pace
'When Irish Thighs Are Smiling'
'I'm Only High Society's Child'
'Vatican I Say After I Say Im Sorry'
18th CENTURY FOX

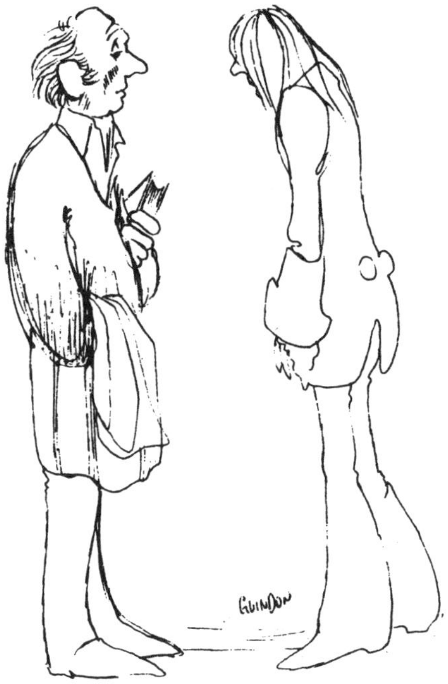

"No, I don't want a blow job — I'm a girl."

RICHARD GUINDON. THE REALIST #76, AUGUST 1967-JANUARY 1968.

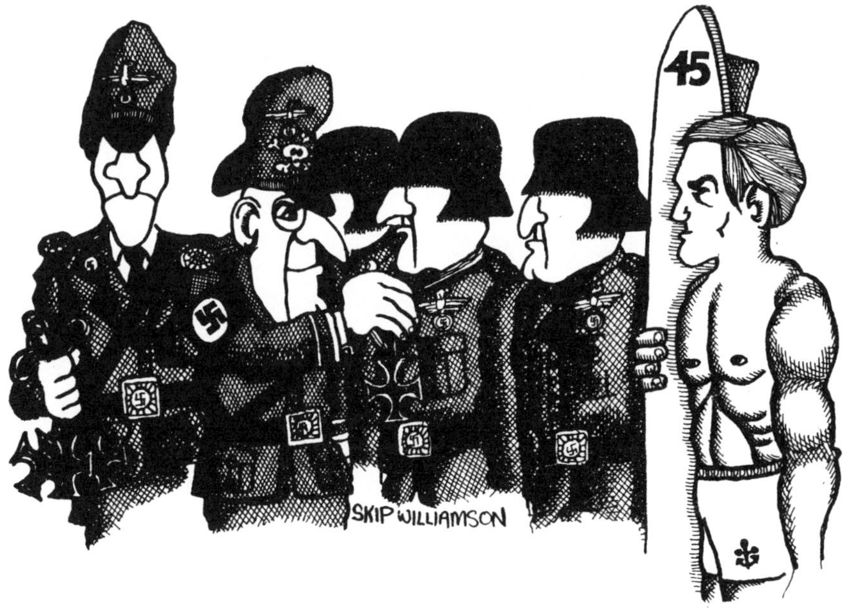
45
SKIP WILLIAMSON

SKIP WILLIAMSON. THE REALIST #75, JUNE 1967. *79

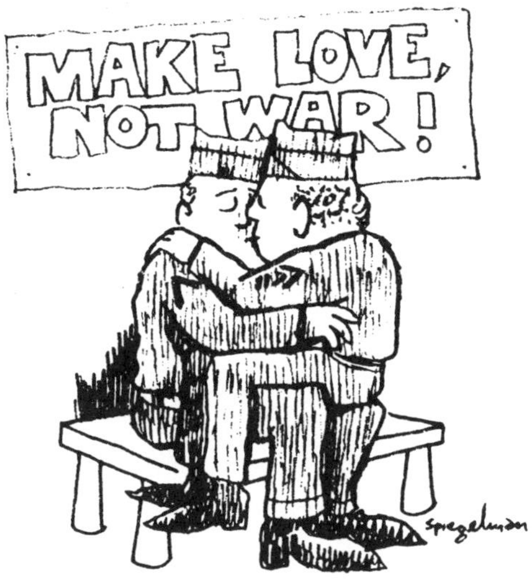
MAKE LOVE, NOT WAR!

ART SPIEGELMAN. THE REALIST #75, JUNE 1967.

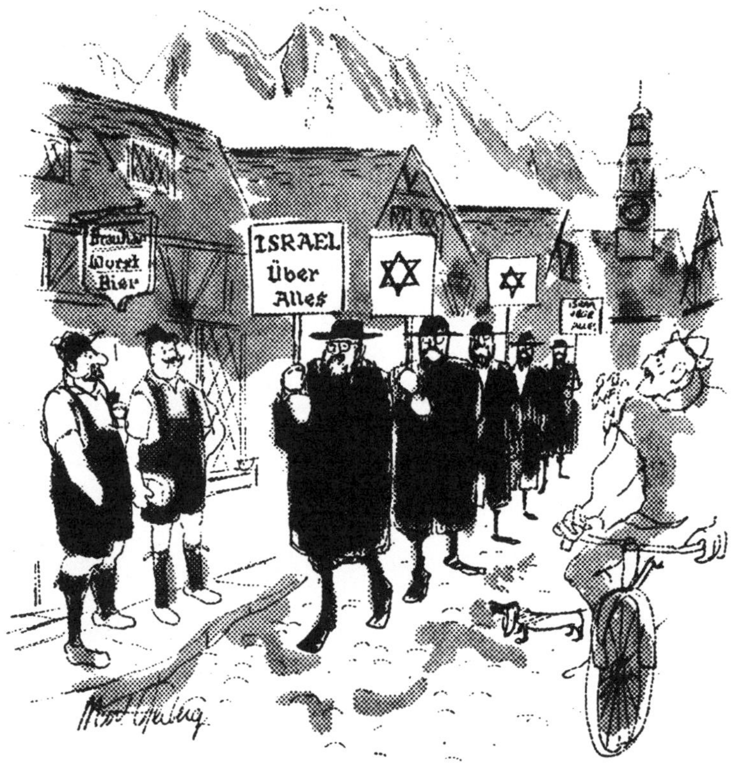
ISRAEL
Über
Alles

MORT GERBERG. THE REALIST #75, JUNE 1967. *80

PAUL KRASSNER AND
RICHARD GUINDON.
THE REALIST #76,
AUGUST 1967-JANUARY 1968.

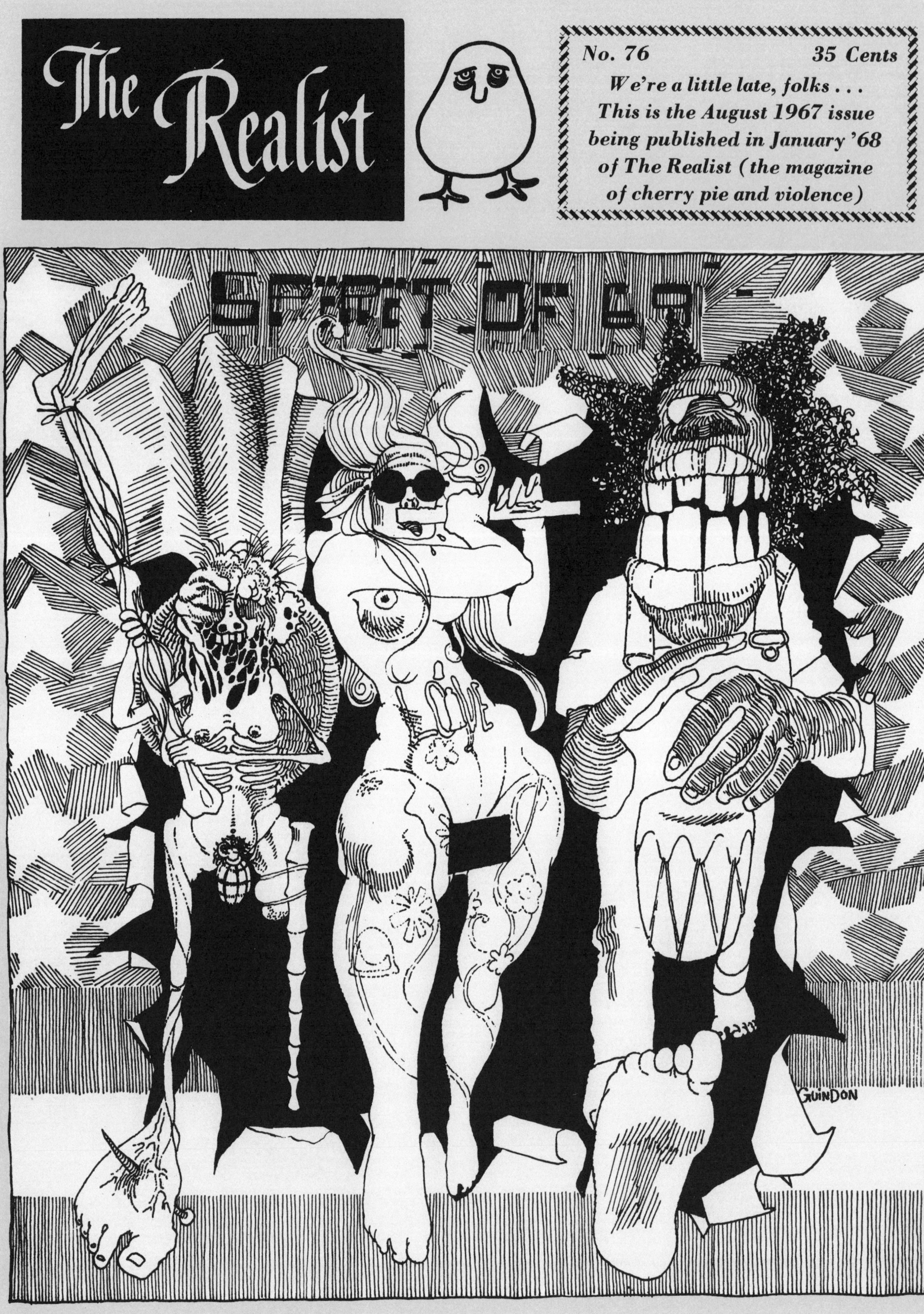
The Realist

No. 76 35 Cents

*We're a little late, folks . . .
This is the August 1967 issue
being published in January '68
of The Realist (the magazine
of cherry pie and violence)*

SPIRIT OF 69

GUINDON

"Everyone at the mortuary is out to lunch;
can you come back at two?"

RICHARD GUINDON. THE REALIST #78, APRIL 1968.

SAM GROSS. THE REALIST #77, MARCH 1968.

RICHARD GUINDON. THE REALIST #77, MARCH 1968.

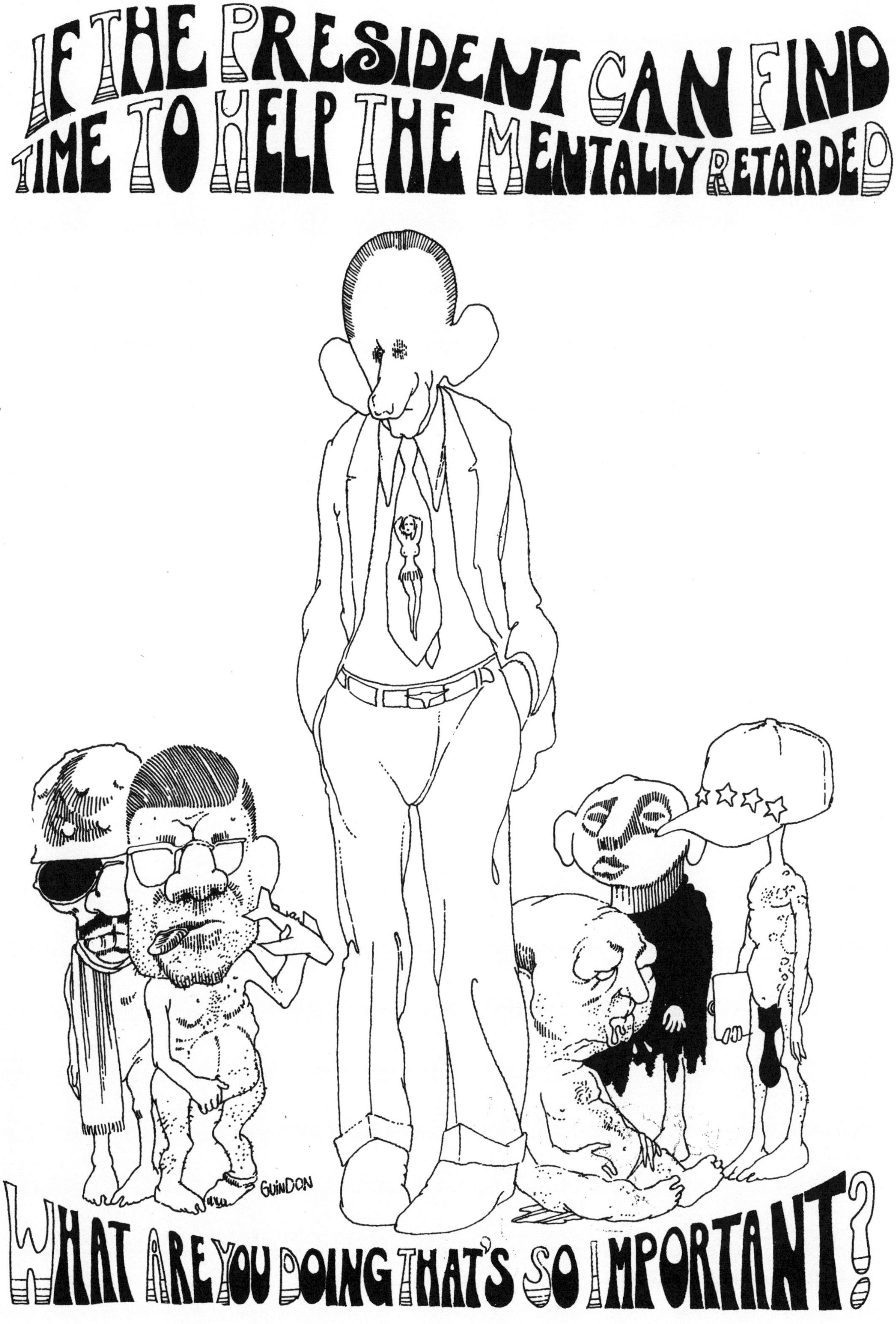
IF THE PRESIDENT CAN FIND TIME TO HELP THE MENTALLY RETARDED
GUINDON
WHAT ARE YOU DOING THAT'S SO IMPORTANT?

RICHARD GUINDON.
THE REALIST #77, MARCH 1968.

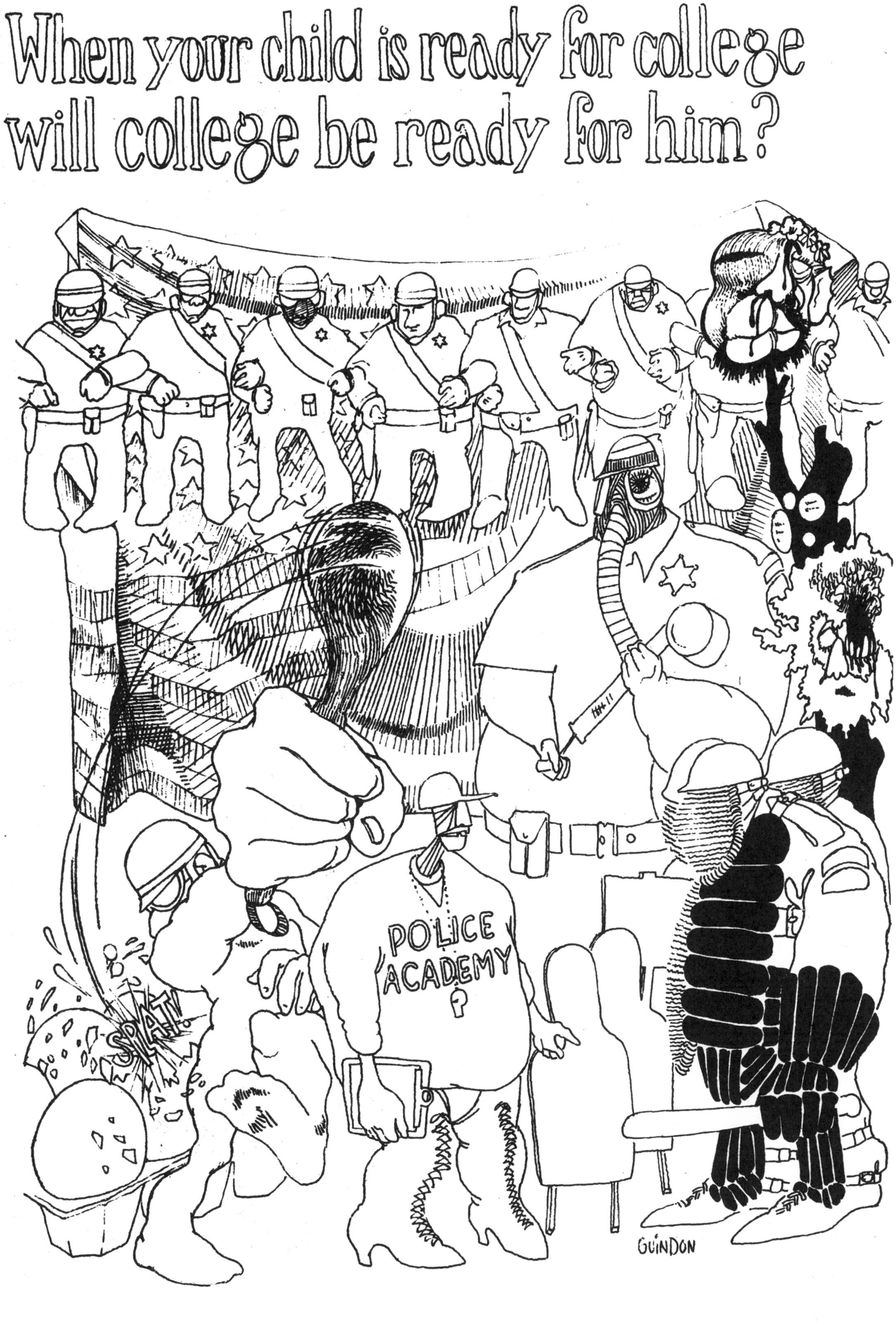
When your child is ready for college will college be ready for him?
POLICE ACADEMY
SPLAT!
GUINDON

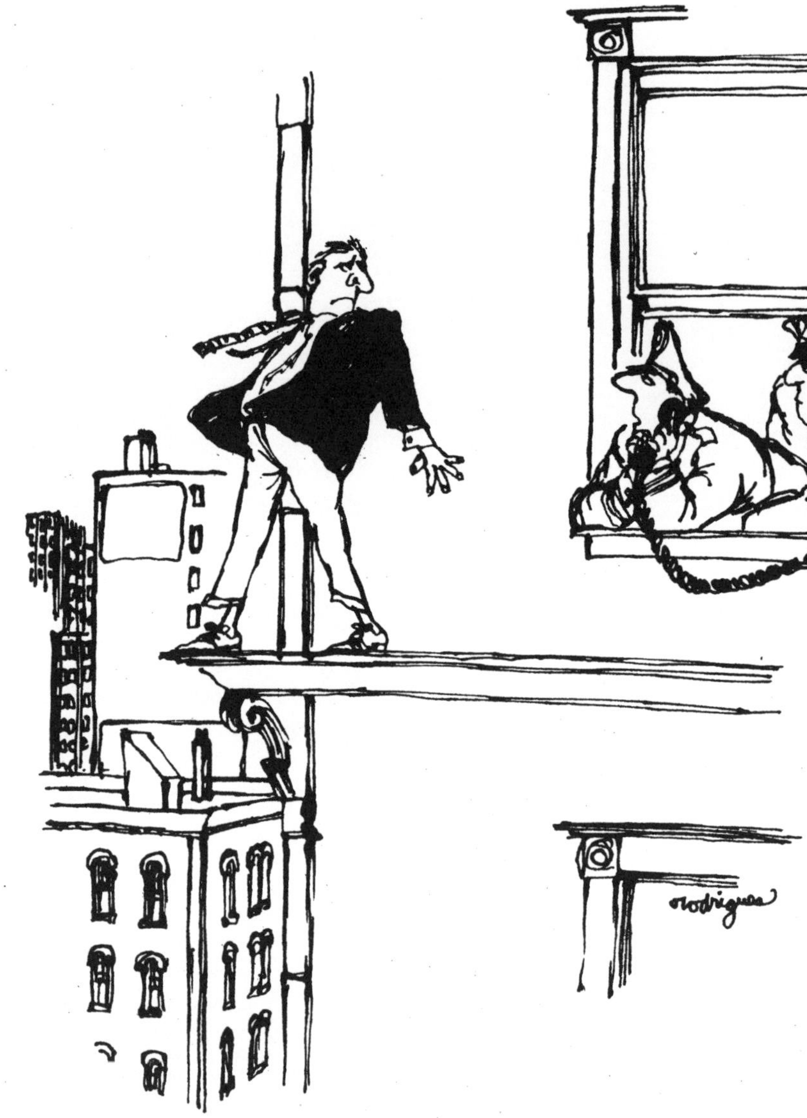
rodrigues

"... Okay, they've begun pulling out of Vietnam ..."

CHARLES RODRIGUES. THE REALIST #76, AUGUST 1967-JANUARY 1968.

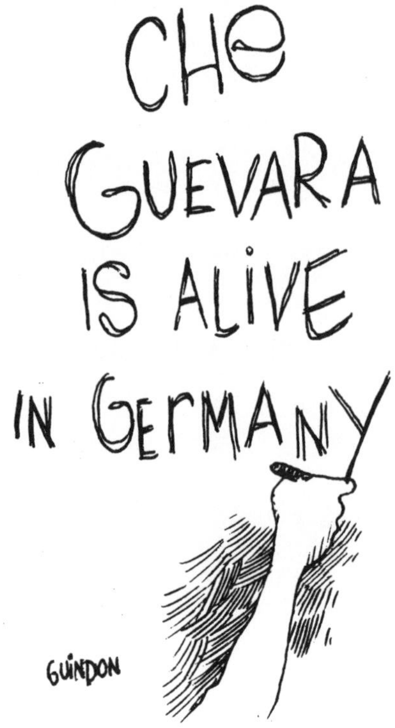
CHE GUEVARA IS ALIVE IN GERMANY
GUINDON

RICHARD GUINDON. THE REALIST #76, AUGUST 1967-JANUARY 1968.

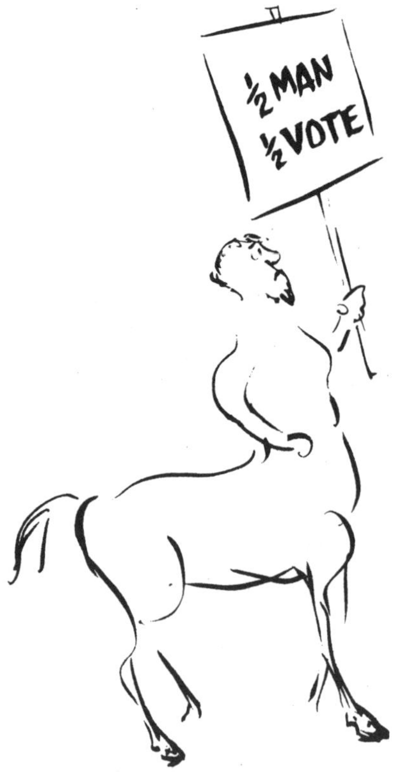
1/2 MAN
1/2 VOTE

ED FISHER. THE REALIST #78, APRIL 1968.

"— Moreover, peace in Vietnam would free enormous quantities of napalm for use in Yemen, Aden, Israel ..."

"He's in underground films. I know that foot!"

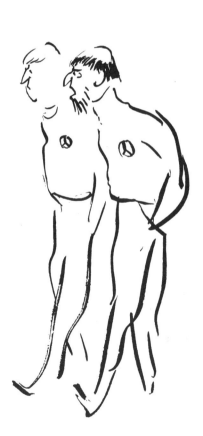

"— Don't you see, making the autos safe is just Ralph Nader's way of preserving a lot of guys so that the Establishment can send them to fight in Vietnam ... and Jonas Salk's a fink, too!"

"Wait till the Supreme Court hears how you got this confession!"

ED FISHER. THE REALIST #78, APRIL 1968.

RICHARD GUINDON. THE REALIST #79, MAY 1968.

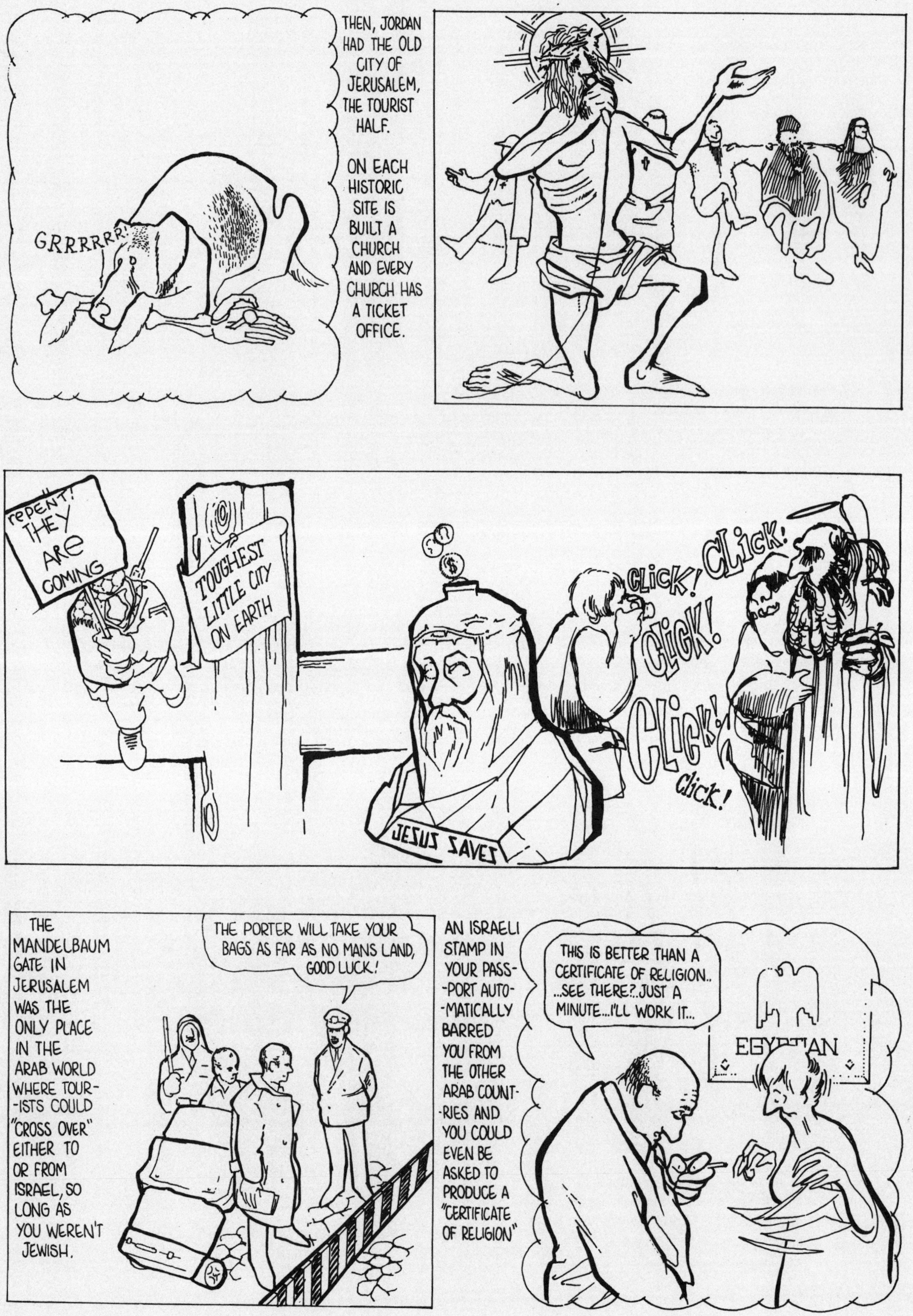
GRRRRRR!
THEN, JORDAN HAD THE OLD CITY OF JERUSALEM, THE TOURIST HALF.
ON EACH HISTORIC SITE IS BUILT A CHURCH AND EVERY CHURCH HAS A TICKET OFFICE.
repent! THEY ARE COMING
TOUGHEST LITTLE CITY ON EARTH
JESUS SAVES
CLICK! CLICK! CLICK! CLICK! Click!
THE MANDELBAUM GATE IN JERUSALEM WAS THE ONLY PLACE IN THE ARAB WORLD WHERE TOUR-ISTS COULD "CROSS OVER" EITHER TO OR FROM ISRAEL, SO LONG AS YOU WEREN'T JEWISH.
THE PORTER WILL TAKE YOUR BAGS AS FAR AS NO MANS LAND, GOOD LUCK!
AN ISRAELI STAMP IN YOUR PASS-PORT AUTO-MATICALLY BARRED YOU FROM THE OTHER ARAB COUNT-RIES AND YOU COULD EVEN BE ASKED TO PRODUCE A "CERTIFICATE OF RELIGION"
THIS IS BETTER THAN A CERTIFICATE OF RELIGION.. ...SEE THERE?..JUST A MINUTE...I'LL WORK IT...
EGYPTIAN

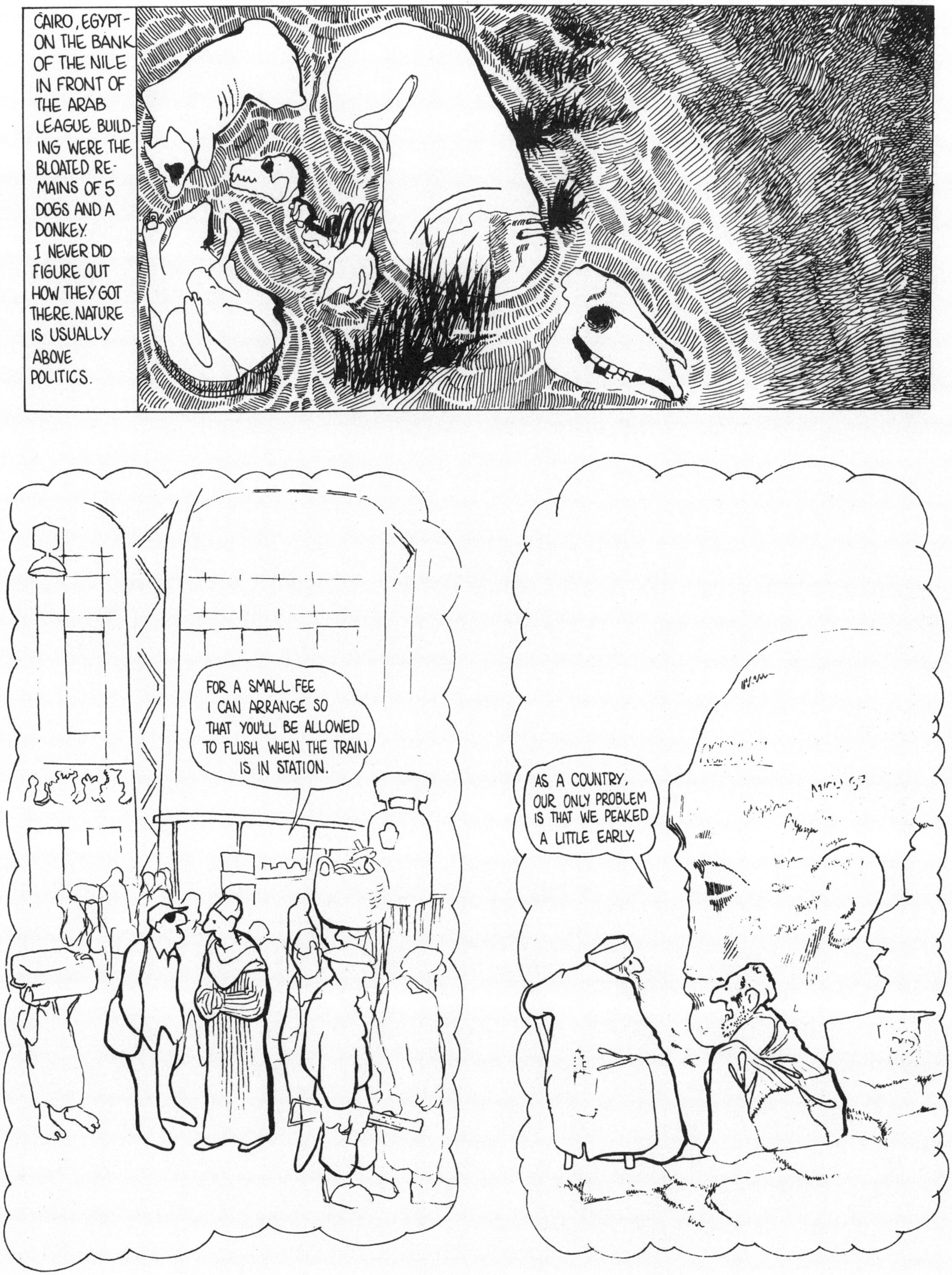
CAIRO, EGYPT-ON THE BANK OF THE NILE IN FRONT OF THE ARAB LEAGUE BUILDING WERE THE BLOATED REMAINS OF 5 DOGS AND A DONKEY. I NEVER DID FIGURE OUT HOW THEY GOT THERE. NATURE IS USUALLY ABOVE POLITICS.
FOR A SMALL FEE I CAN ARRANGE SO THAT YOU'LL BE ALLOWED TO FLUSH WHEN THE TRAIN IS IN STATION.
AS A COUNTRY, OUR ONLY PROBLEM IS THAT WE PEAKED A LITTLE EARLY.

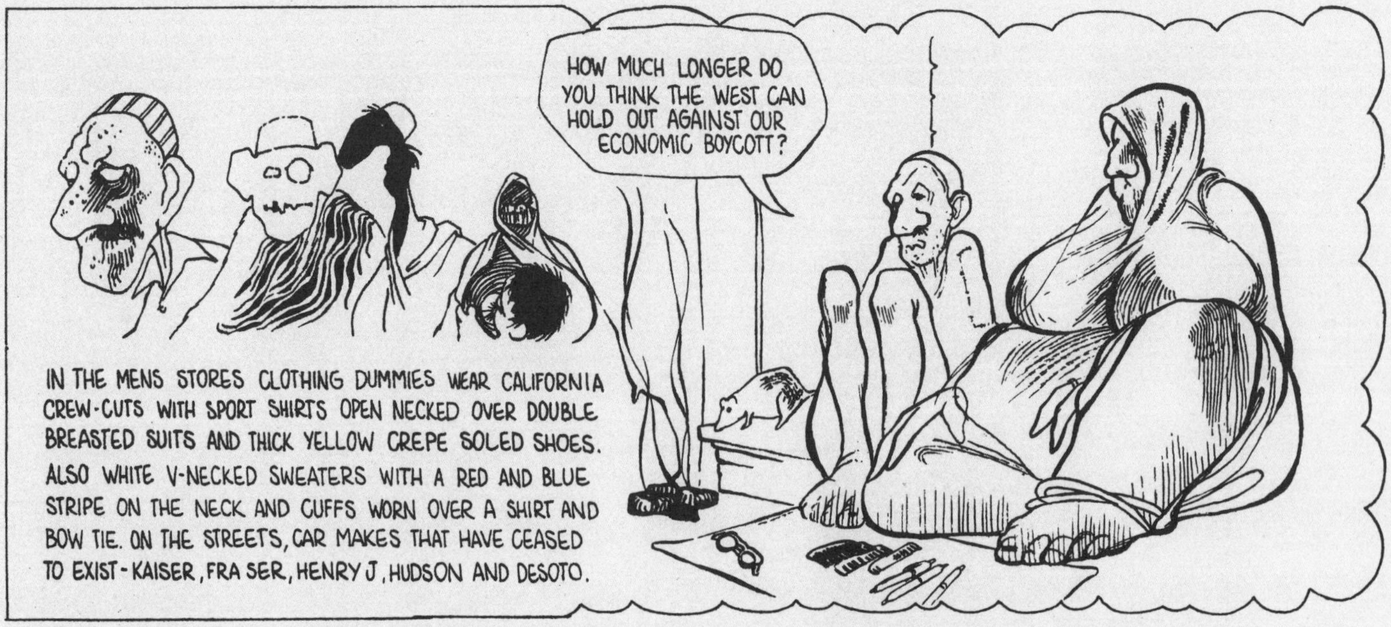
HOW MUCH LONGER DO YOU THINK THE WEST CAN HOLD OUT AGAINST OUR ECONOMIC BOYCOTT?
IN THE MENS STORES CLOTHING DUMMIES WEAR CALIFORNIA CREW-CUTS WITH SPORT SHIRTS OPEN NECKED OVER DOUBLE BREASTED SUITS AND THICK YELLOW CREPE SOLED SHOES. ALSO WHITE V-NECKED SWEATERS WITH A RED AND BLUE STRIPE ON THE NECK AND CUFFS WORN OVER A SHIRT AND BOW TIE. ON THE STREETS, CAR MAKES THAT HAVE CEASED TO EXIST - KAISER, FRA SER, HENRY J, HUDSON AND DESOTO.

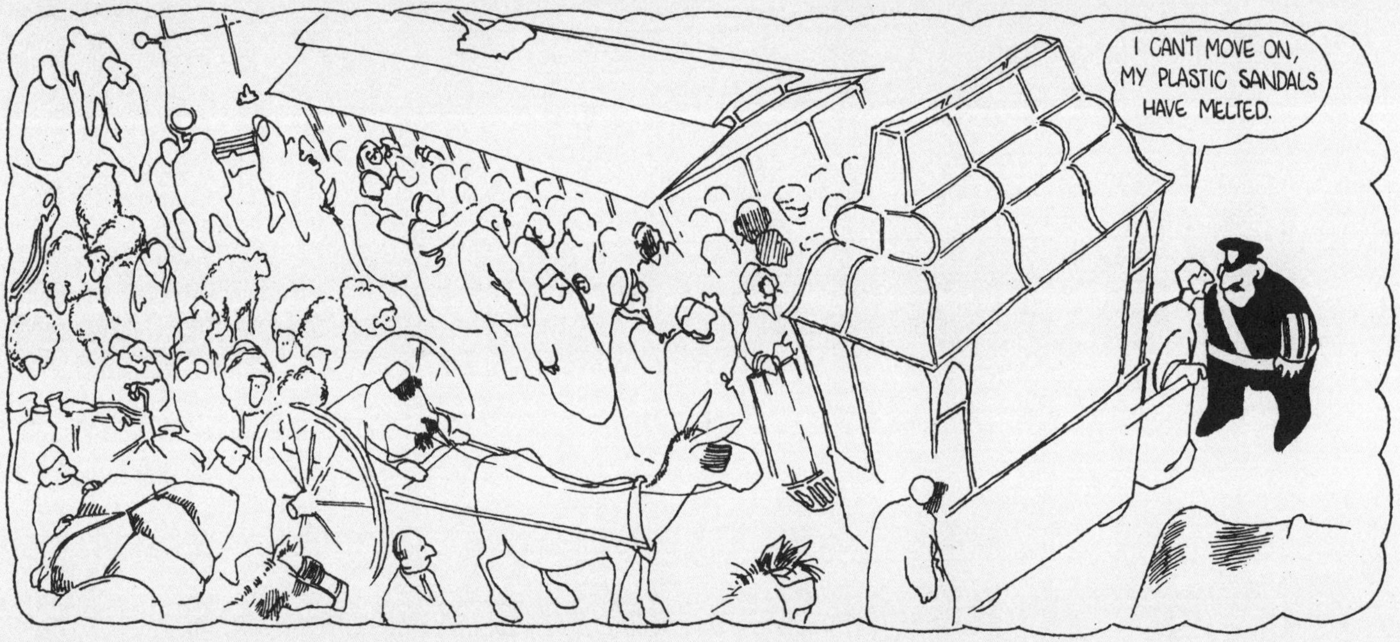
I CAN'T MOVE ON, MY PLASTIC SANDALS HAVE MELTED.

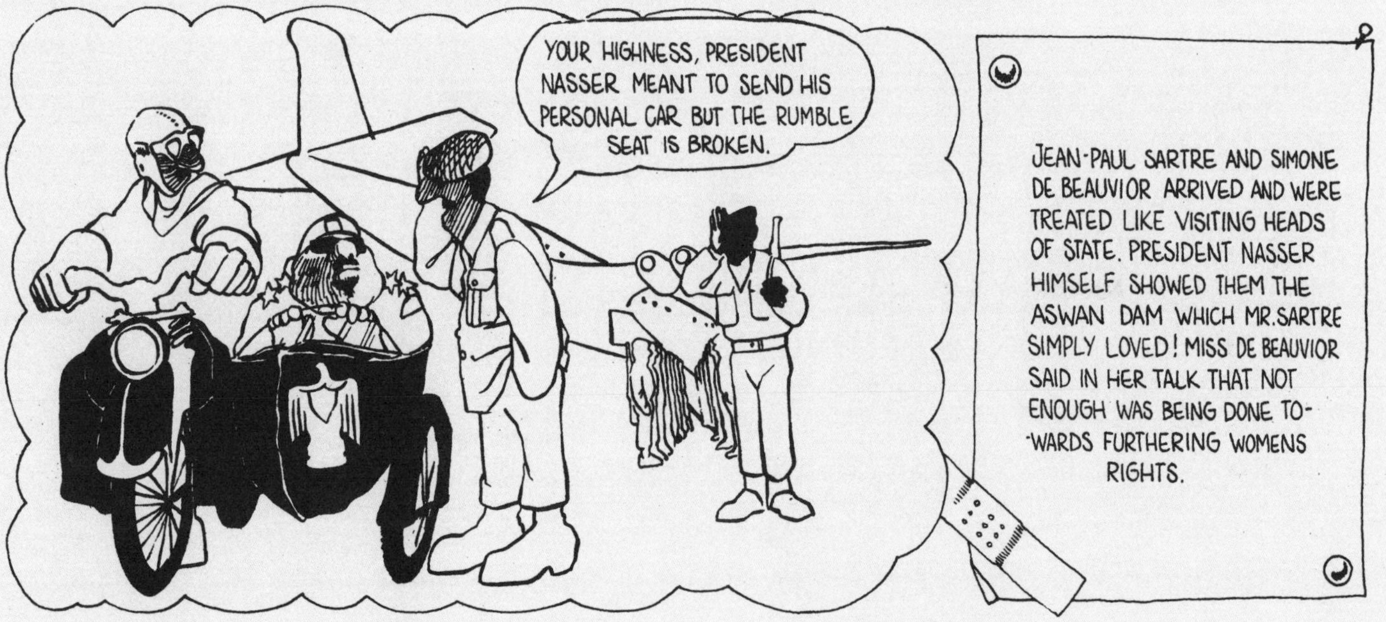
YOUR HIGHNESS, PRESIDENT NASSER MEANT TO SEND HIS PERSONAL CAR BUT THE RUMBLE SEAT IS BROKEN.
JEAN-PAUL SARTRE AND SIMONE DE BEAUVIOR ARRIVED AND WERE TREATED LIKE VISITING HEADS OF STATE. PRESIDENT NASSER HIMSELF SHOWED THEM THE ASWAN DAM WHICH MR.SARTRE SIMPLY LOVED! MISS DE BEAUVIOR SAID IN HER TALK THAT NOT ENOUGH WAS BEING DONE TO-WARDS FURTHERING WOMENS RIGHTS.

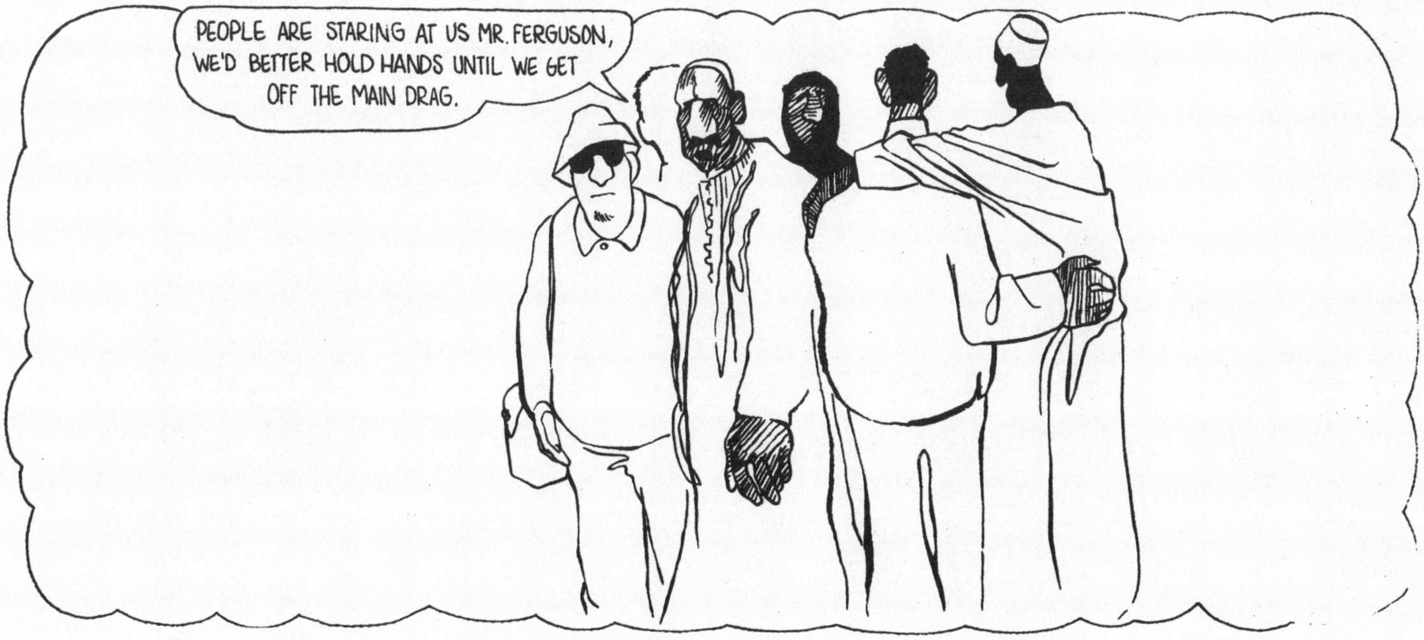
PEOPLE ARE STARING AT US MR. FERGUSON, WE'D BETTER HOLD HANDS UNTIL WE GET OFF THE MAIN DRAG.

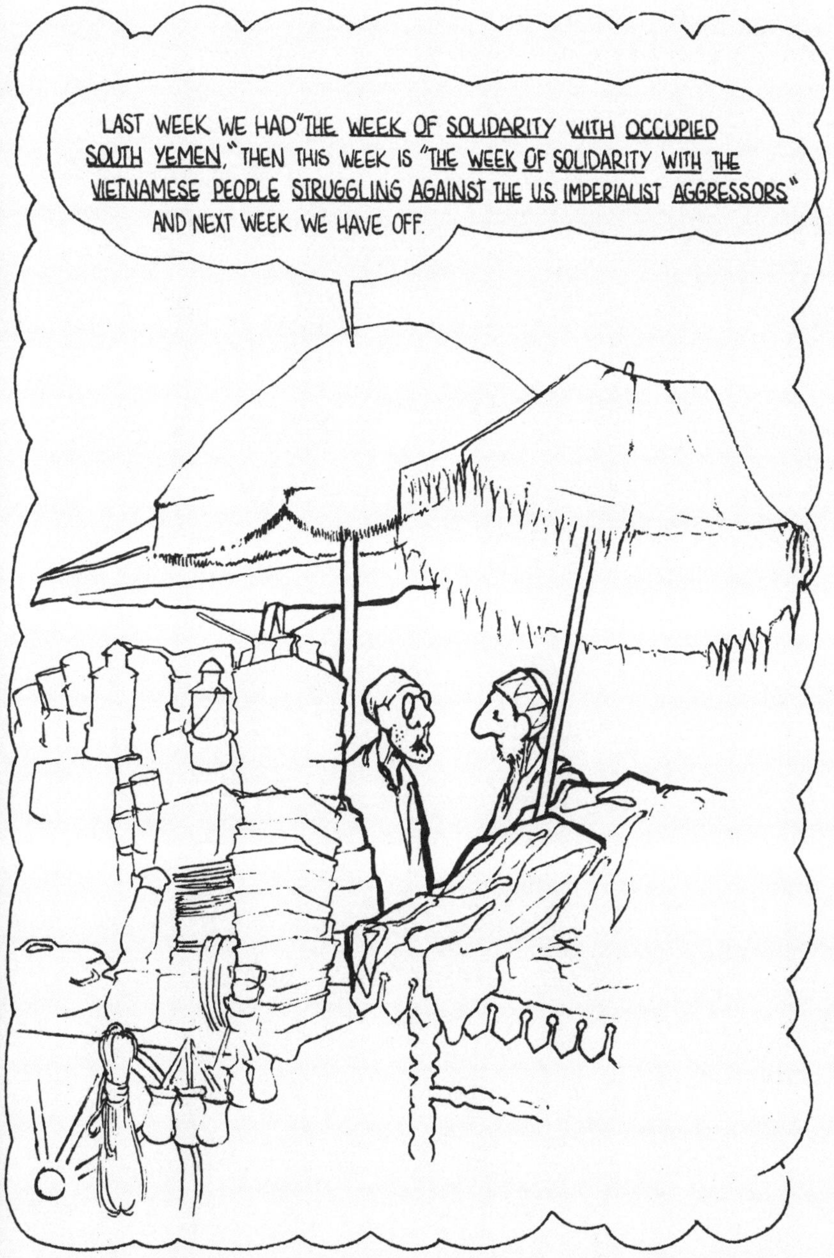
LAST WEEK WE HAD "THE WEEK OF SOLIDARITY WITH OCCUPIED SOUTH YEMEN," THEN THIS WEEK IS "THE WEEK OF SOLIDARITY WITH THE VIETNAMESE PEOPLE STRUGGLING AGAINST THE U.S. IMPERIALIST AGGRESSORS" AND NEXT WEEK WE HAVE OFF.

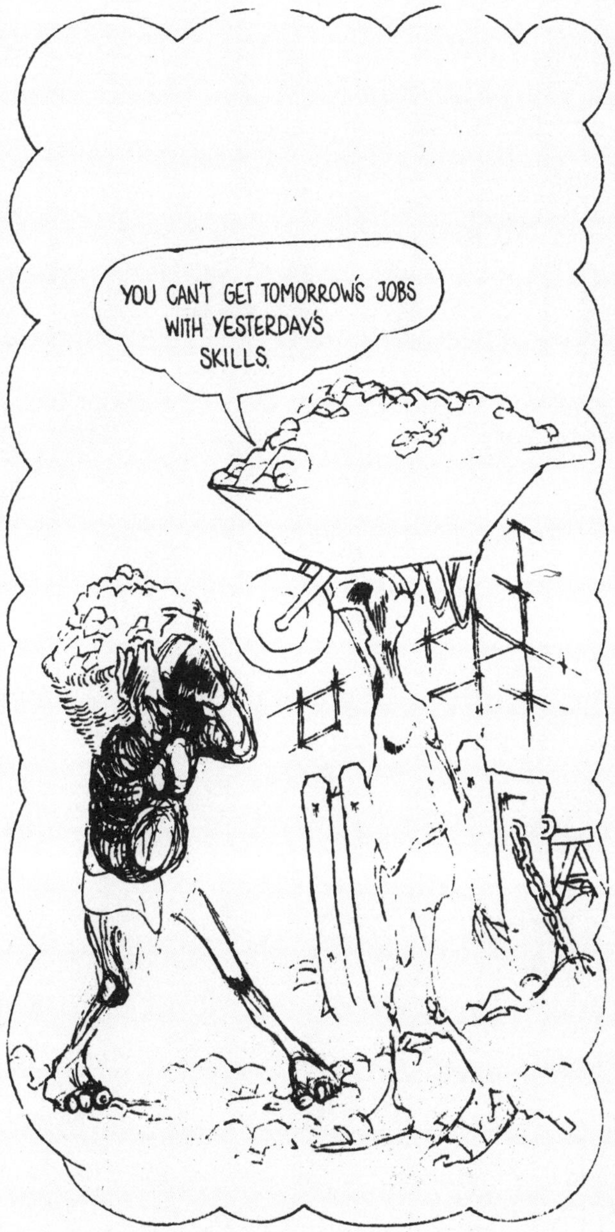
YOU CAN'T GET TOMORROW'S JOBS WITH YESTERDAY'S SKILLS.

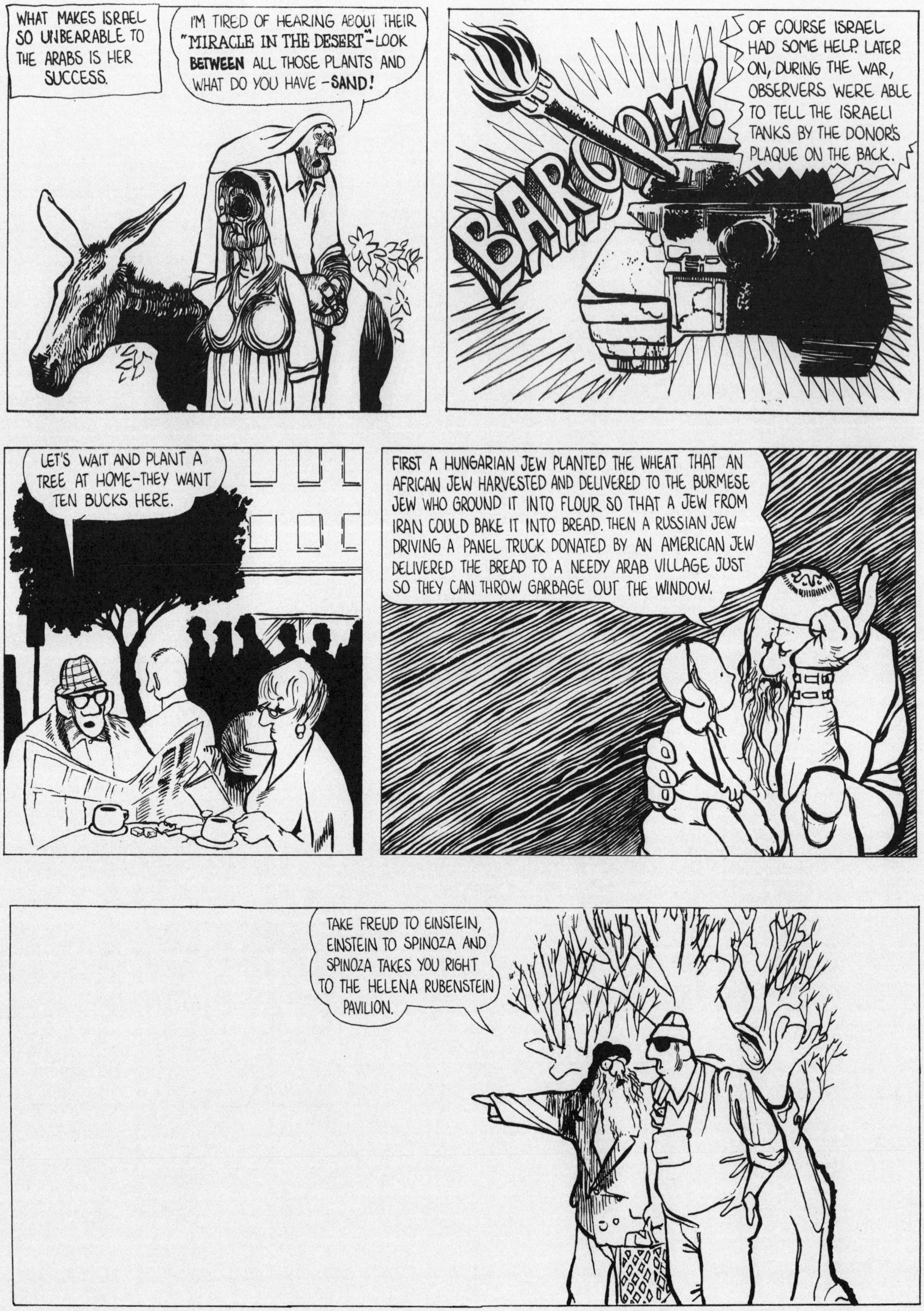
WHAT MAKES ISRAEL SO UNBEARABLE TO THE ARABS IS HER SUCCESS.
I'M TIRED OF HEARING ABOUT THEIR "MIRACLE IN THE DESERT"-LOOK BETWEEN ALL THOSE PLANTS AND WHAT DO YOU HAVE -SAND!
BAROOOM!
OF COURSE ISRAEL HAD SOME HELP. LATER ON, DURING THE WAR, OBSERVERS WERE ABLE TO TELL THE ISRAELI TANKS BY THE DONOR'S PLAQUE ON THE BACK.
LET'S WAIT AND PLANT A TREE AT HOME-THEY WANT TEN BUCKS HERE.
FIRST A HUNGARIAN JEW PLANTED THE WHEAT THAT AN AFRICAN JEW HARVESTED AND DELIVERED TO THE BURMESE JEW WHO GROUND IT INTO FLOUR SO THAT A JEW FROM IRAN COULD BAKE IT INTO BREAD. THEN A RUSSIAN JEW DRIVING A PANEL TRUCK DONATED BY AN AMERICAN JEW DELIVERED THE BREAD TO A NEEDY ARAB VILLAGE JUST SO THEY CAN THROW GARBAGE OUT THE WINDOW.
TAKE FREUD TO EINSTEIN, EINSTEIN TO SPINOZA AND SPINOZA TAKES YOU RIGHT TO THE HELENA RUBENSTEIN PAVILION.

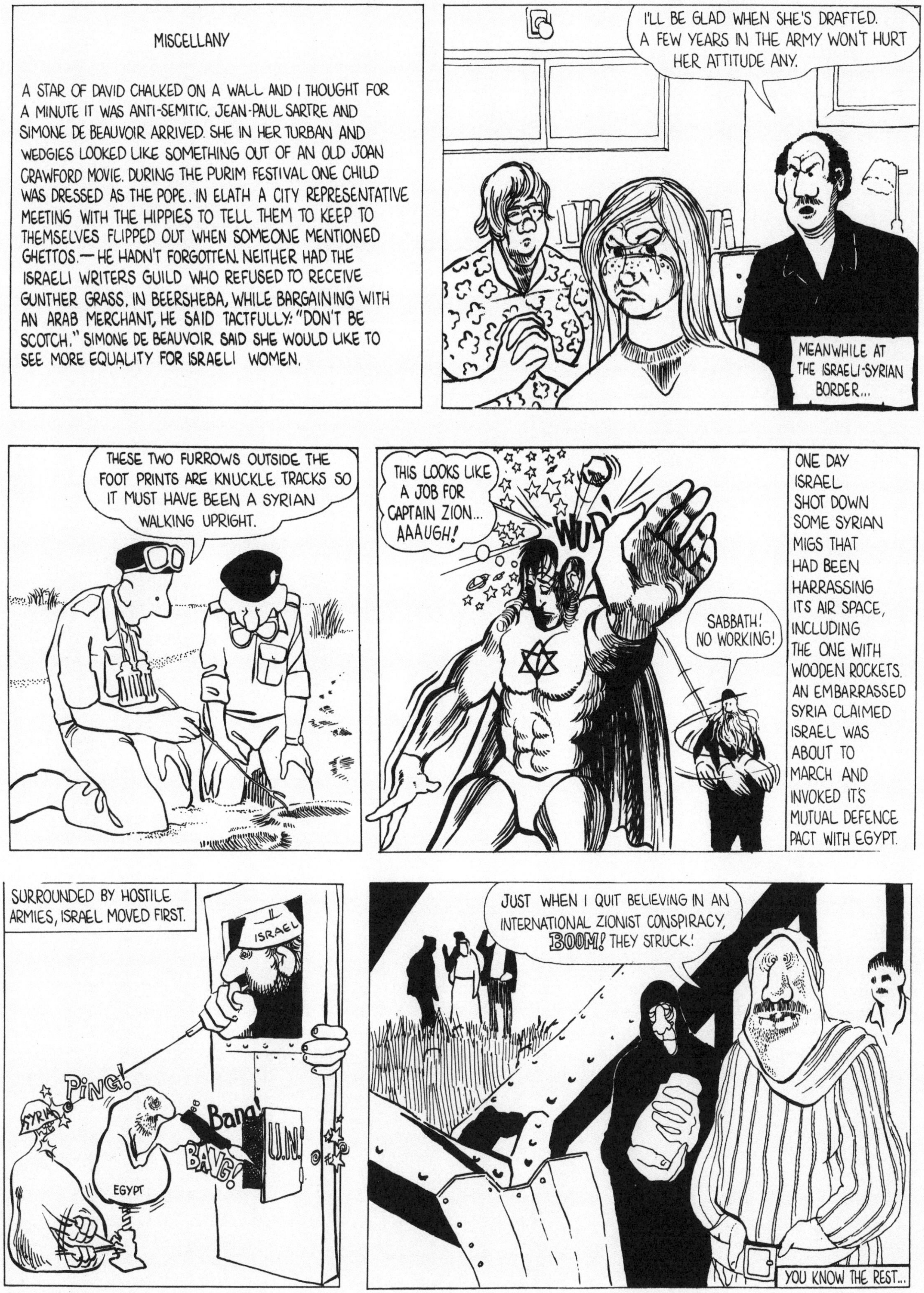
MISCELLANY
A STAR OF DAVID CHALKED ON A WALL AND I THOUGHT FOR A MINUTE IT WAS ANTI-SEMITIC. JEAN-PAUL SARTRE AND SIMONE DE BEAUVOIR ARRIVED. SHE IN HER TURBAN AND WEDGIES LOOKED LIKE SOMETHING OUT OF AN OLD JOAN CRAWFORD MOVIE. DURING THE PURIM FESTIVAL ONE CHILD WAS DRESSED AS THE POPE. IN ELATH A CITY REPRESENTATIVE MEETING WITH THE HIPPIES TO TELL THEM TO KEEP TO THEMSELVES FLIPPED OUT WHEN SOMEONE MENTIONED GHETTOS.— HE HADN'T FORGOTTEN. NEITHER HAD THE ISRAELI WRITERS GUILD WHO REFUSED TO RECEIVE GUNTHER GRASS. IN BEERSHEBA, WHILE BARGAINING WITH AN ARAB MERCHANT, HE SAID TACTFULLY: "DON'T BE SCOTCH." SIMONE DE BEAUVOIR SAID SHE WOULD LIKE TO SEE MORE EQUALITY FOR ISRAELI WOMEN.
I'LL BE GLAD WHEN SHE'S DRAFTED. A FEW YEARS IN THE ARMY WON'T HURT HER ATTITUDE ANY.
MEANWHILE AT THE ISRAELI-SYRIAN BORDER...
THESE TWO FURROWS OUTSIDE THE FOOT PRINTS ARE KNUCKLE TRACKS SO IT MUST HAVE BEEN A SYRIAN WALKING UPRIGHT.
THIS LOOKS LIKE A JOB FOR CAPTAIN ZION... AAAUGH!
WUD!
SABBATH! NO WORKING!
ONE DAY ISRAEL SHOT DOWN SOME SYRIAN MIGS THAT HAD BEEN HARRASSING ITS AIR SPACE, INCLUDING THE ONE WITH WOODEN ROCKETS. AN EMBARRASSED SYRIA CLAIMED ISRAEL WAS ABOUT TO MARCH AND INVOKED IT'S MUTUAL DEFENCE PACT WITH EGYPT.
SURROUNDED BY HOSTILE ARMIES, ISRAEL MOVED FIRST.
ISRAEL
PiNG!
SYRIA
Bang!
BANG!
U.N.
EGYPT
JUST WHEN I QUIT BELIEVING IN AN INTERNATIONAL ZIONIST CONSPIRACY, BOOM! THEY STRUCK!
YOU KNOW THE REST...

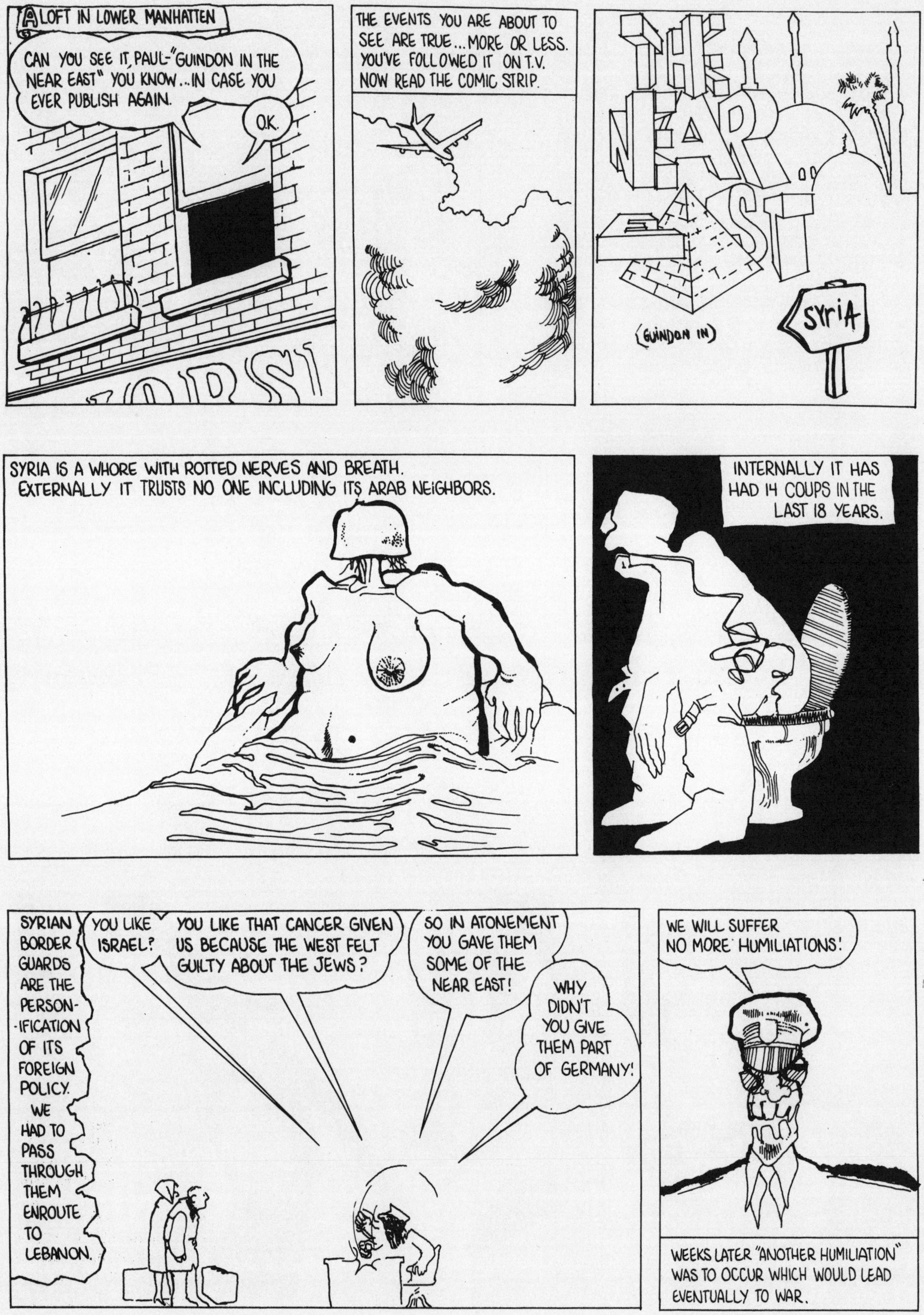
A LOFT IN LOWER MANHATTEN
CAN YOU SEE IT, PAUL- "GUINDON IN THE NEAR EAST" YOU KNOW...IN CASE YOU EVER PUBLISH AGAIN.
O.K.
THE EVENTS YOU ARE ABOUT TO SEE ARE TRUE... MORE OR LESS. YOU'VE FOLLOWED IT ON T.V. NOW READ THE COMIC STRIP.
THE NEAR EAST
(GUINDON IN)
SYRIA
SYRIA IS A WHORE WITH ROTTED NERVES AND BREATH. EXTERNALLY IT TRUSTS NO ONE INCLUDING ITS ARAB NEIGHBORS.
INTERNALLY IT HAS HAD 14 COUPS IN THE LAST 18 YEARS.
SYRIAN BORDER GUARDS ARE THE PERSON-IFICATION OF ITS FOREIGN POLICY. WE HAD TO PASS THROUGH THEM ENROUTE TO LEBANON.
YOU LIKE ISRAEL?
YOU LIKE THAT CANCER GIVEN US BECAUSE THE WEST FELT GUILTY ABOUT THE JEWS?
SO IN ATONEMENT YOU GAVE THEM SOME OF THE NEAR EAST!
WHY DIDN'T YOU GIVE THEM PART OF GERMANY!
WE WILL SUFFER NO MORE HUMILIATIONS!
WEEKS LATER "ANOTHER HUMILIATION" WAS TO OCCUR WHICH WOULD LEAD EVENTUALLY TO WAR.

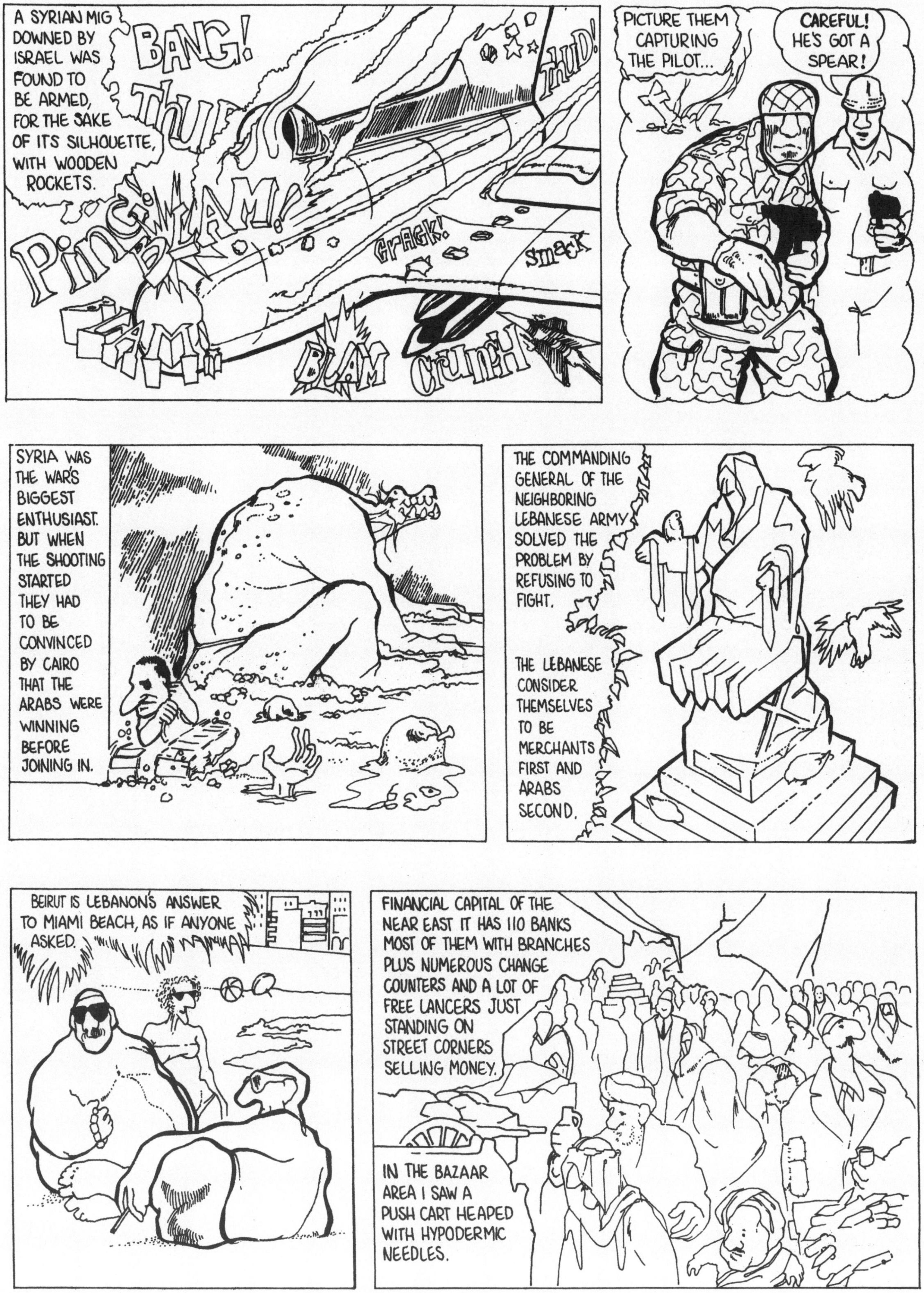
A SYRIAN MIG DOWNED BY ISRAEL WAS FOUND TO BE ARMED, FOR THE SAKE OF ITS SILHOUETTE, WITH WOODEN ROCKETS.
BANG!
THUD!
THUD!
PING
BLAM!
CRACK!
SMACK
BLAM
CRUNCH
PICTURE THEM CAPTURING THE PILOT...
CAREFUL! HE'S GOT A SPEAR!
SYRIA WAS THE WAR'S BIGGEST ENTHUSIAST. BUT WHEN THE SHOOTING STARTED THEY HAD TO BE CONVINCED BY CAIRO THAT THE ARABS WERE WINNING BEFORE JOINING IN.
THE COMMANDING GENERAL OF THE NEIGHBORING LEBANESE ARMY SOLVED THE PROBLEM BY REFUSING TO FIGHT.
THE LEBANESE CONSIDER THEMSELVES TO BE MERCHANTS FIRST AND ARABS SECOND.
BEIRUT IS LEBANON'S ANSWER TO MIAMI BEACH, AS IF ANYONE ASKED.
FINANCIAL CAPITAL OF THE NEAR EAST IT HAS 110 BANKS MOST OF THEM WITH BRANCHES PLUS NUMEROUS CHANGE COUNTERS AND A LOT OF FREE LANCERS JUST STANDING ON STREET CORNERS SELLING MONEY.
IN THE BAZAAR AREA I SAW A PUSH CART HEAPED WITH HYPODERMIC NEEDLES.

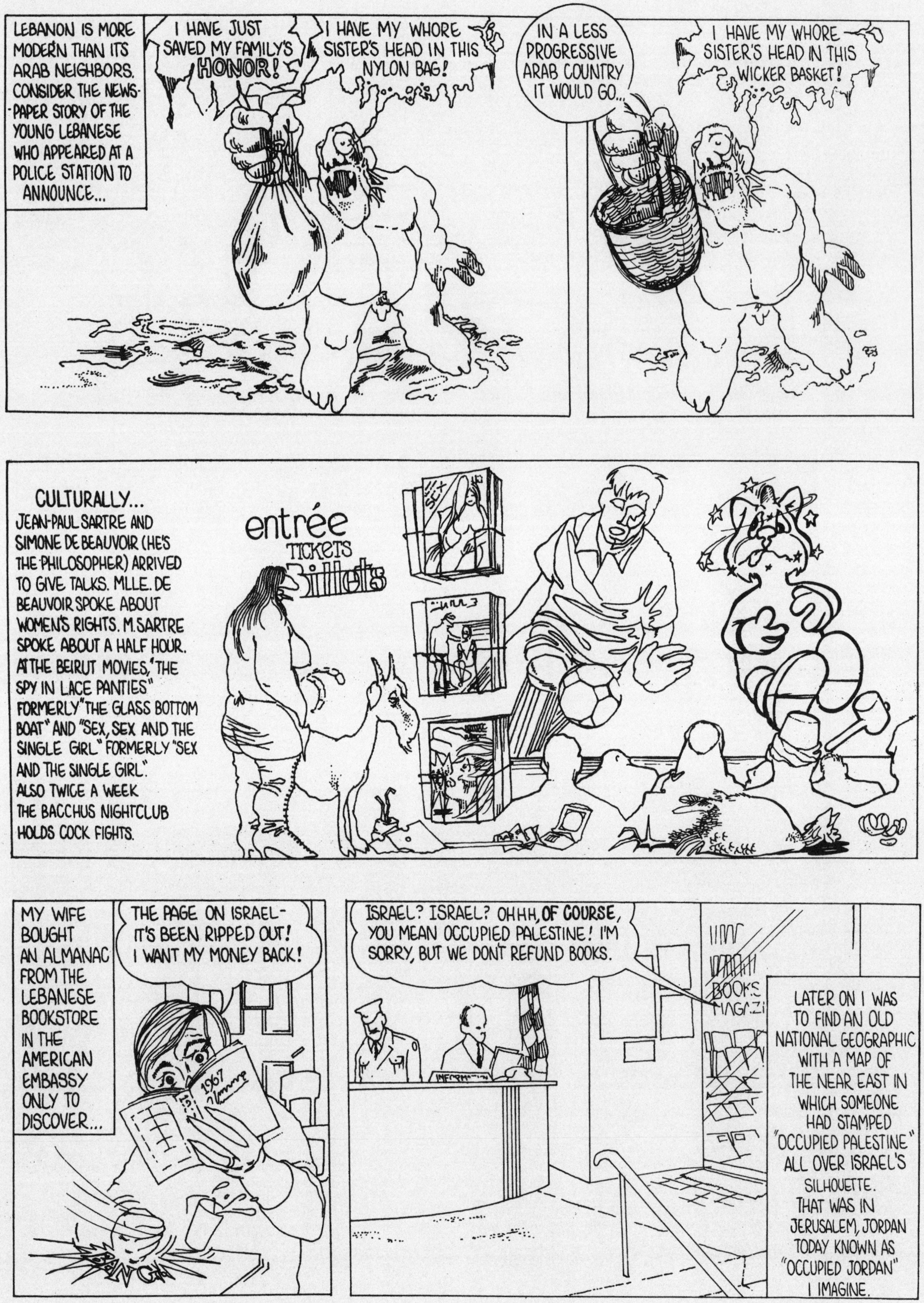
LEBANON IS MORE MODERN THAN ITS ARAB NEIGHBORS. CONSIDER THE NEWSPAPER STORY OF THE YOUNG LEBANESE WHO APPEARED AT A POLICE STATION TO ANNOUNCE...
I HAVE JUST SAVED MY FAMILY'S HONOR!
I HAVE MY WHORE SISTER'S HEAD IN THIS NYLON BAG!
IN A LESS PROGRESSIVE ARAB COUNTRY IT WOULD GO...
I HAVE MY WHORE SISTER'S HEAD IN THIS WICKER BASKET!
CULTURALLY...
JEAN-PAUL SARTRE AND SIMONE DE BEAUVOIR (HE'S THE PHILOSOPHER) ARRIVED TO GIVE TALKS. MLLE. DE BEAUVOIR SPOKE ABOUT WOMEN'S RIGHTS. M.SARTRE SPOKE ABOUT A HALF HOUR. AT THE BEIRUT MOVIES, "THE SPY IN LACE PANTIES" FORMERLY "THE GLASS BOTTOM BOAT" AND "SEX, SEX AND THE SINGLE GIRL" FORMERLY "SEX AND THE SINGLE GIRL". ALSO TWICE A WEEK THE BACCHUS NIGHTCLUB HOLDS COCK FIGHTS.
entrée
TICKETS
Billets
SEX
MY WIFE BOUGHT AN ALMANAC FROM THE LEBANESE BOOKSTORE IN THE AMERICAN EMBASSY ONLY TO DISCOVER...
THE PAGE ON ISRAEL- IT'S BEEN RIPPED OUT! I WANT MY MONEY BACK!
1967
BANG
ISRAEL? ISRAEL? OHHH, OF COURSE, YOU MEAN OCCUPIED PALESTINE! I'M SORRY, BUT WE DON'T REFUND BOOKS.
BOOKS
MAGAZI
LATER ON I WAS TO FIND AN OLD NATIONAL GEOGRAPHIC WITH A MAP OF THE NEAR EAST IN WHICH SOMEONE HAD STAMPED "OCCUPIED PALESTINE" ALL OVER ISRAEL'S SILHOUETTE. THAT WAS IN JERUSALEM, JORDAN TODAY KNOWN AS "OCCUPIED JORDAN" I IMAGINE.

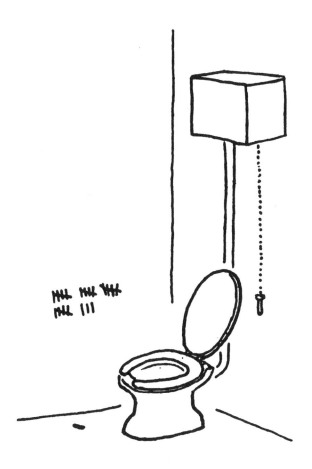

THE REALIST #80, JUNE 1968.

FALCON. THE REALIST #80, JUNE 1968.

"Move in, Uncle John, you're out of the picture ... Sis? That's better ... Mom, you're good ... Auntie May, you're blocking Dad's face with your ... Fine! Hold it, everyone!"

THE REALIST #80, JUNE 1968.

"This message will last just 60 seconds. The missiles are on their way. If you had started running at the beginning of this message, you might have made it."

THE REALIST #82, SEPTEMBER 1968.

CHARLES RODRIGUES.
THE REALIST #82,
SEPTEMBER 1968.

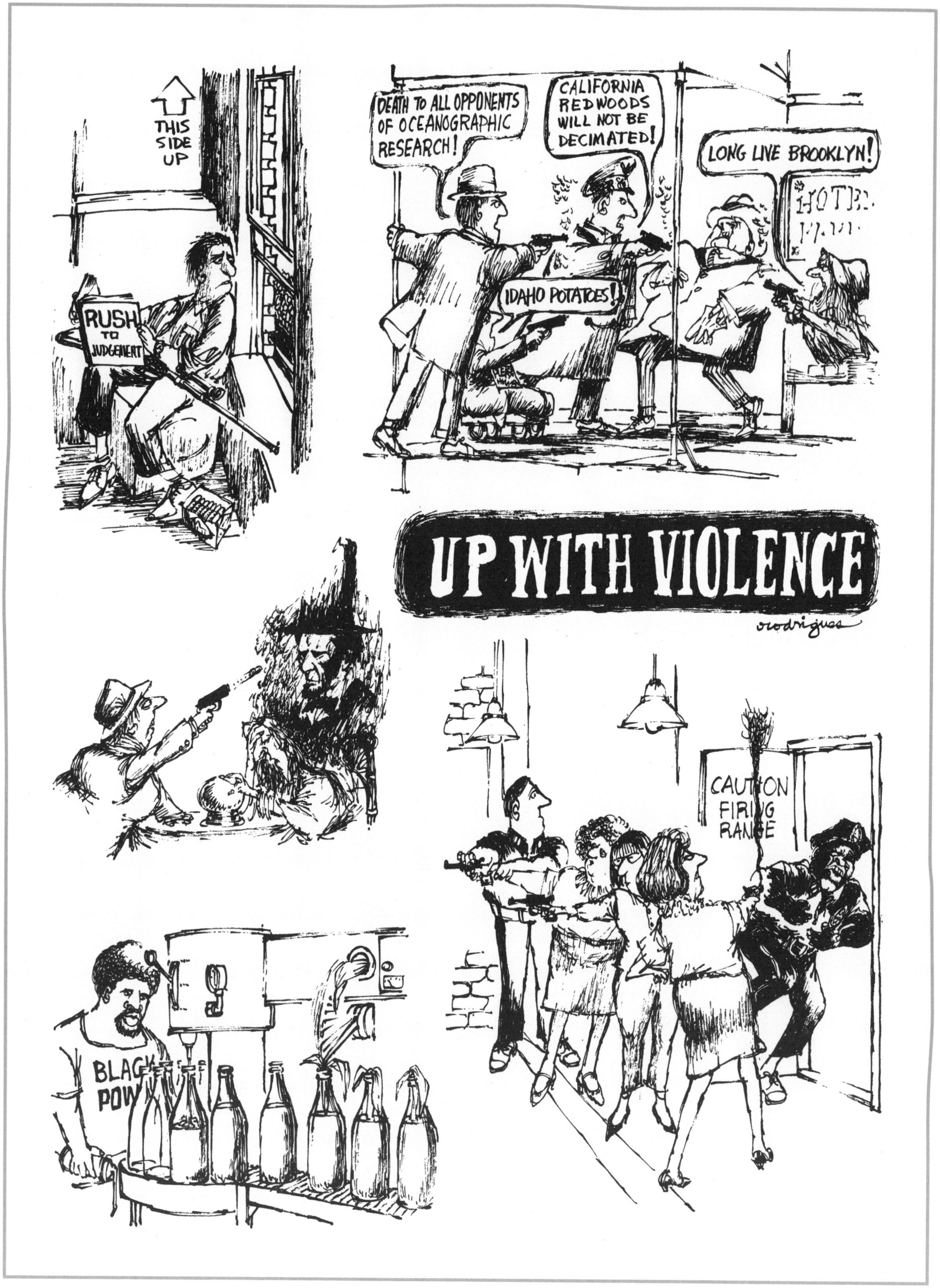
THIS SIDE UP
RUSH TO JUDGEMENT
DEATH TO ALL OPPONENTS OF OCEANOGRAPHIC RESEARCH!
CALIFORNIA REDWOODS WILL NOT BE DECIMATED!
LONG LIVE BROOKLYN!
IDAHO POTATOES!
UP WITH VIOLENCE
rodrigues
CAUTION FIRING RANGE
BLACK POW

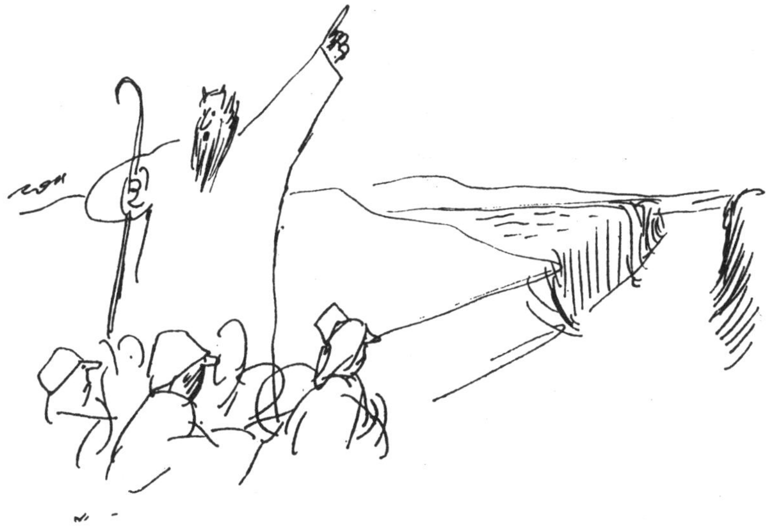

"Hurry, before it seeks its own level ..."

AL ROSS. THE REALIST #82, SEPTEMBER 1968.

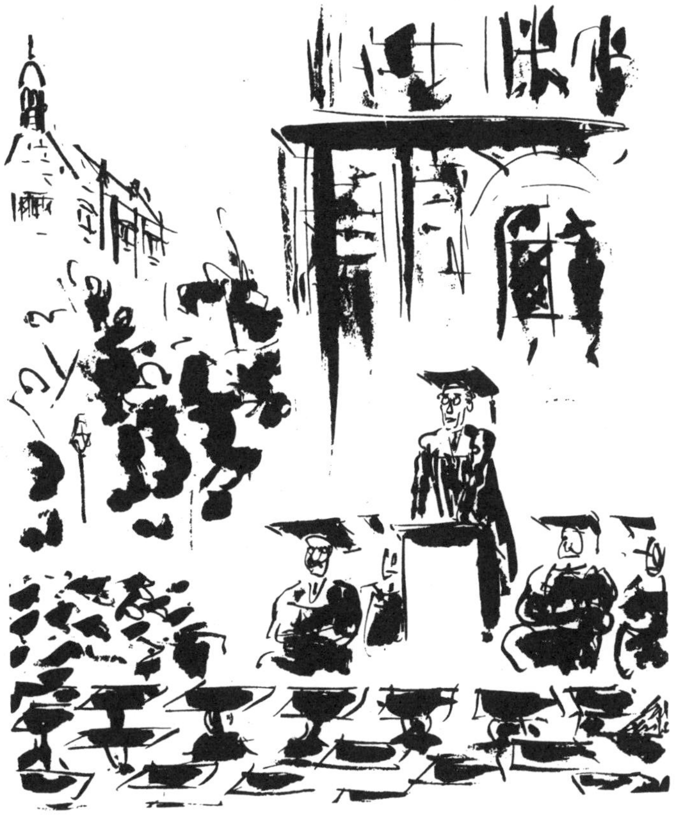

"And we, your teachers, will proudly be able to say, as we have said of each graduating class heretofore, that our lives have been made a little fuller, our tradition a little richer, by your presence — that is, as soon as the fire damage to North Hall has been repaired, the broken glass in the Administration Building swept up, the ..."

ED FISHER. THE REALIST #82, SEPTEMBER 1968.

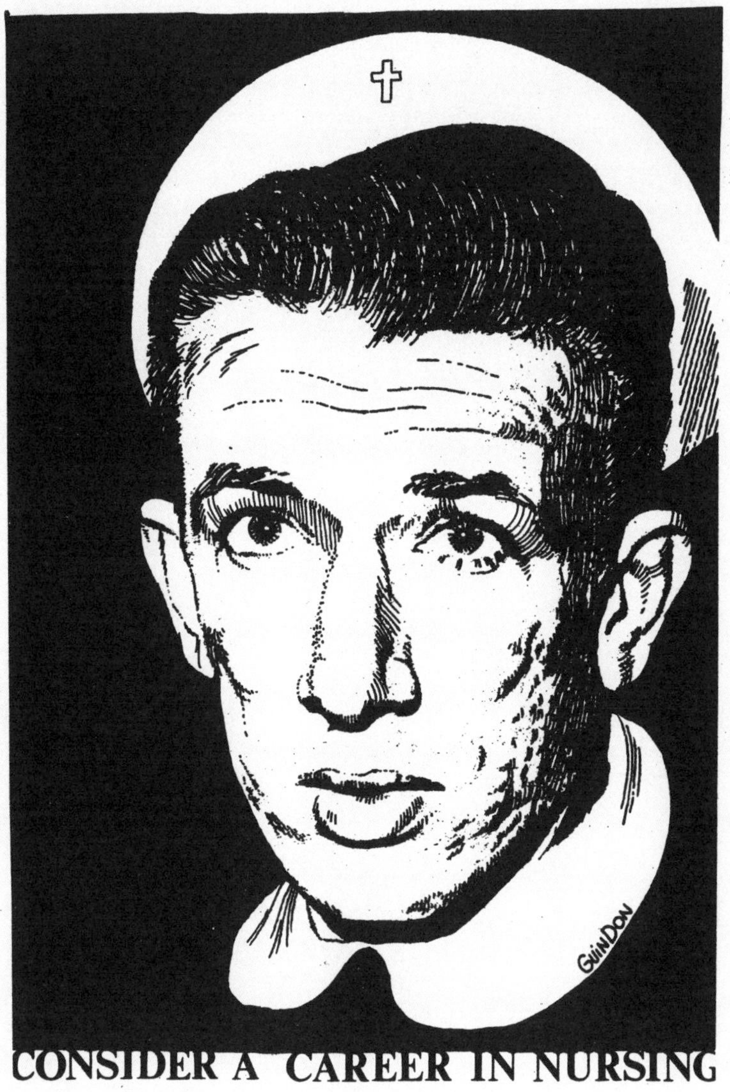
GUINDON
CONSIDER A CAREER IN NURSING

RICHARD GUINDON. THE REALIST #82, SEPTEMBER 1968. *81

"That's the fallacy! Throwing LeRoi Jones in jail won't silence him. It will only make him bitter."

ED FISHER. THE REALIST #82, SEPTEMBER 1968.

"Things fall apart, and the center cannot hold/ ... And some rough beast slouches toward Bethlehem to be born."

ED FISHER. THE REALIST #82, SEPTEMBER 1968.

"Don't worry, your new heart will be just like your old one. Full of Apartheid."

ED FISHER. THE REALIST #82, SEPTEMBER 1968.

"How can I burn, baby, burn if you won't *light*, baby, *light!*"

ED FISHER. THE REALIST #83, OCTOBER 1968.

1932

"... So, obviously — as I see it — the older people, who don't want any change in our sick society, will keep yelling for Law and Order and peaceful demonstrations, whereas if our youth movement *really* wants to accomplish anything ..."

ED FISHER. THE REALIST #82, SEPTEMBER 1968.

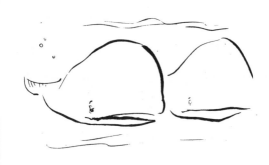

"I *can*, therefore I *do*, have this great big mammalian breast-fixation!"

ED FISHER. THE REALIST #83, OCTOBER 1968.

"Try to remember, eh, baby, that what you say and do can still be as traditional as you please. It's only our outward clerical garb and ceremonials that are laid down by the Church."

ED FISHER. THE REALIST #82, SEPTEMBER 1968.

ACME-COMFA.
LOUNGE-CHAIR CO.
THE SCIENTIFIC CHAIR
FOR ENDLESS RELAXATION

"They threaten that if we don't give in to their demands, they'll *end* their sit-in, claiming backache, tiredness, discomfort ..."

ED FISHER. THE REALIST #83, OCTOBER 1968.

"Damned Russian-made window catch! — No wonder we Czechs no longer practice defenestration!"

ED FISHER. THE REALIST #83, OCTOBER 1968.

"You don't know what a pleasure it is, Sir Henry, to meet someone in this town who isn't hysterically jabbering about crime in the streets!"

ED FISHER. THE REALIST #83, OCTOBER 1968.

THE SAMUEL AND SYLVIA FEINSTEIN ATOMIC REACTOR
RESTRICTED AREA ISRAEL GOVT.

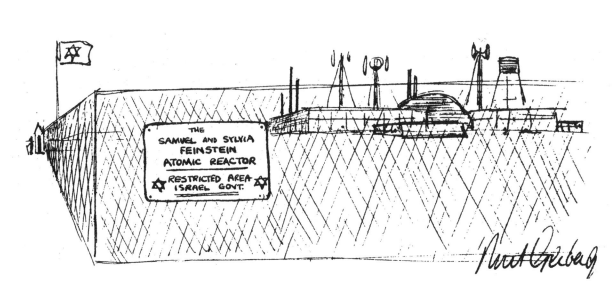

MORT GERBERG. THE REALIST #83, OCTOBER 1968.

ARMY INFORMATION SERVICE
"WE WRITE THE DIFFICULT. THE INCREDIBLE TAKES A LITTLE LONGER."

ED FISHER. THE REALIST #83, OCTOBER 1968.

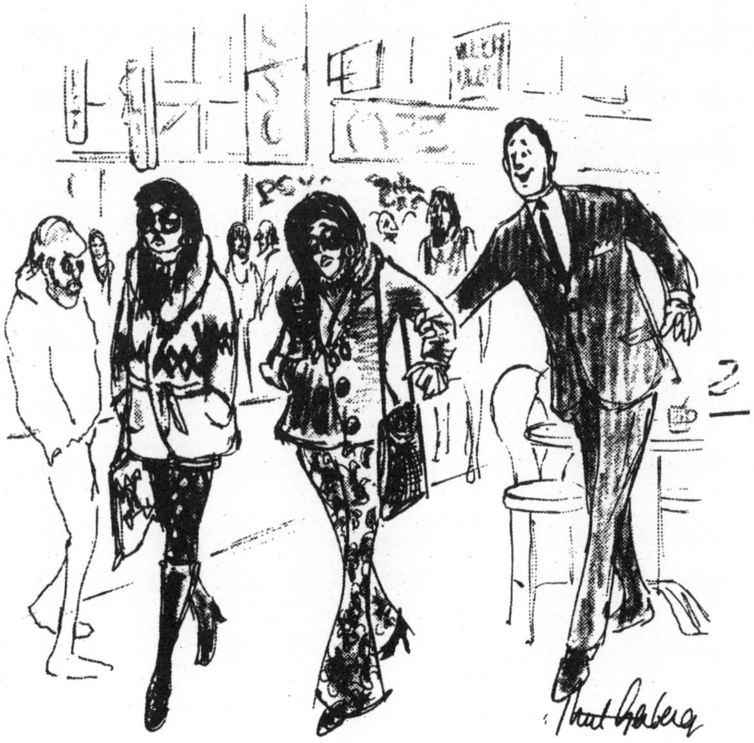

"Hey, it's me, Harriet — Woody — Clean for Gene!"

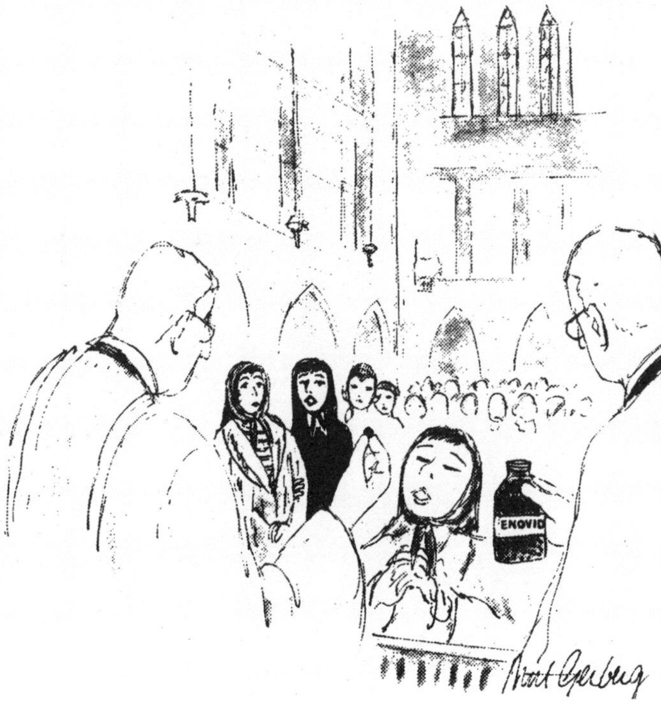
ENOVID

"See? Now *this* is what I call a progressive church."

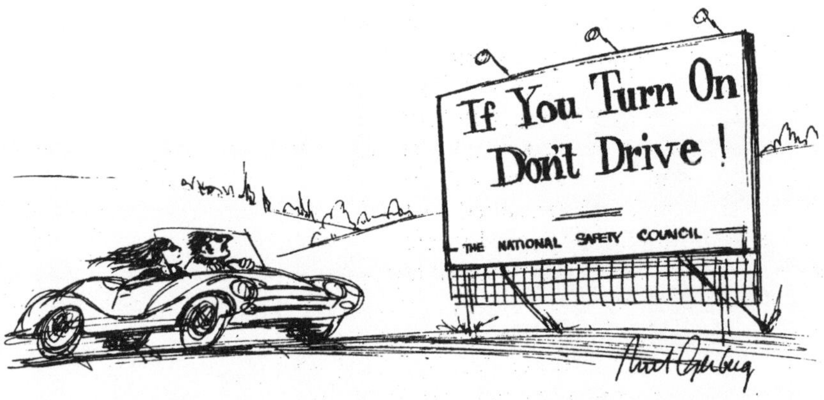
If You Turn On
Don't Drive !
THE NATIONAL SAFETY COUNCIL

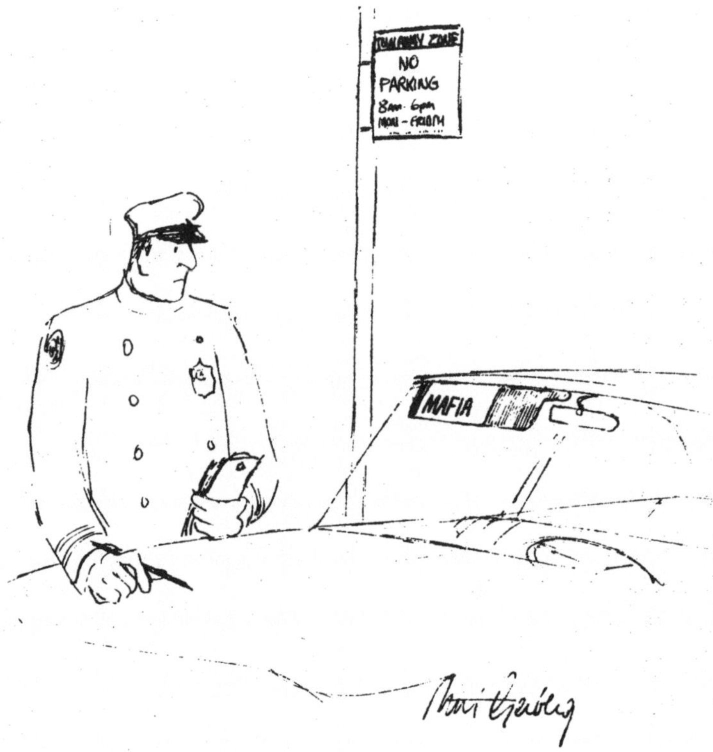
NO
PARKING
MAFIA

MORT GERBERG. THE REALIST #83, OCTOBER 1968.

CHARLES RODRIGUES.
THE REALIST #83, OCTOBER 1968.

INTERRACIAL marriage

rodrigues

"... I knew you'd like it, Barbara, it was dug by my people in South Africa."

"See, darling, I told you Mom would like you."

"... and that one from Uncle Fred in Detroit; the next one from my cousins Waverly and Tillie in Watts; that one from my Aunt Melissa in Newark; the tiny one from my Godfather in Bedford Stuyvesant ..."

CHARLES RODRIGUES.
THE REALIST #84, NOVEMBER 1968.

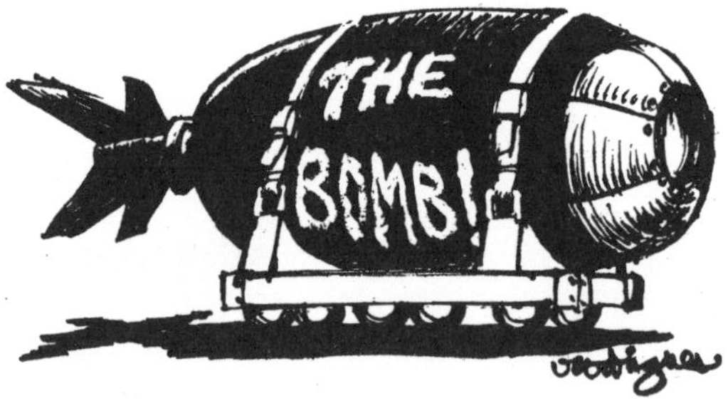
THE
BOMB!

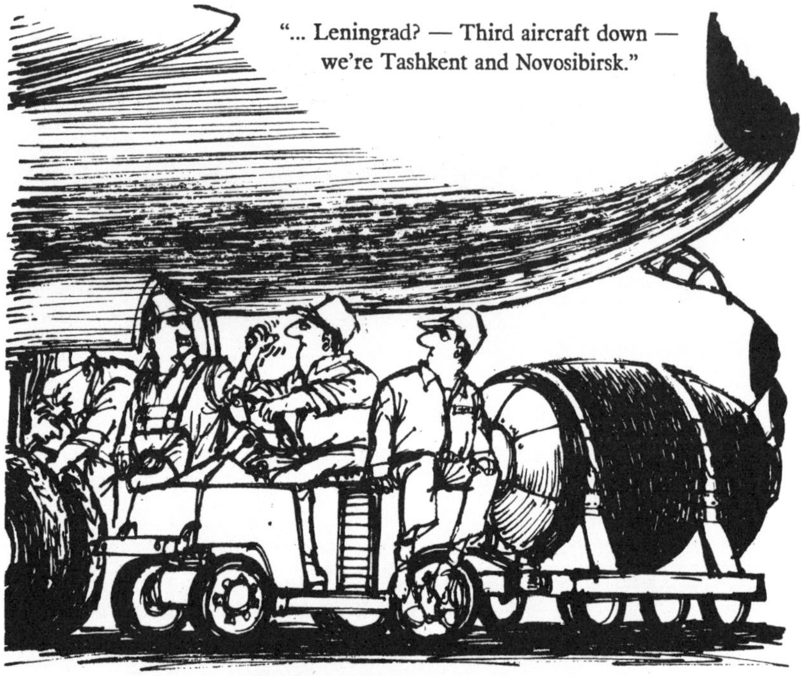

"... Leningrad? — Third aircraft down — we're Tashkent and Novosibirsk."

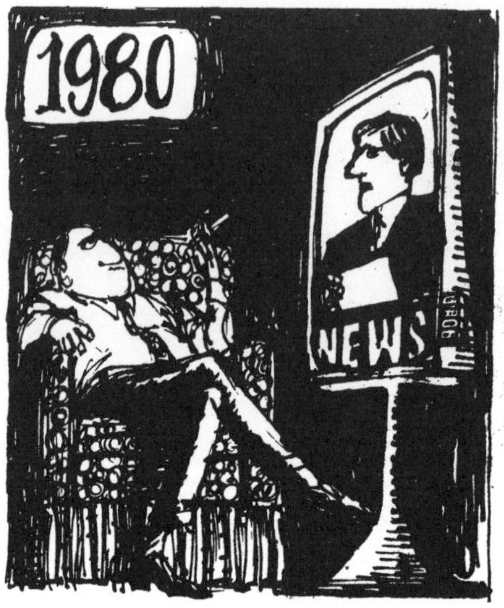
1980
NEWS

"... and finally in the news, the following countries reported detonating their first nuclear weapons today — Zambia, the Yemen, Gibraltar and the Falkland Islands. In addition, Cleveland, Ohio; Passaic, New Jersey; San Jose, California; Londonberry, Northern Ireland; and Durban, South Africa are in the process of exploding their first nuclear weapons at air time. Meanwhile in Las Vegas, a spokesman for Howard Hughes said the billionaire sportsman-industrialist would detonate his first H-bomb tomorrow, rain or shine."

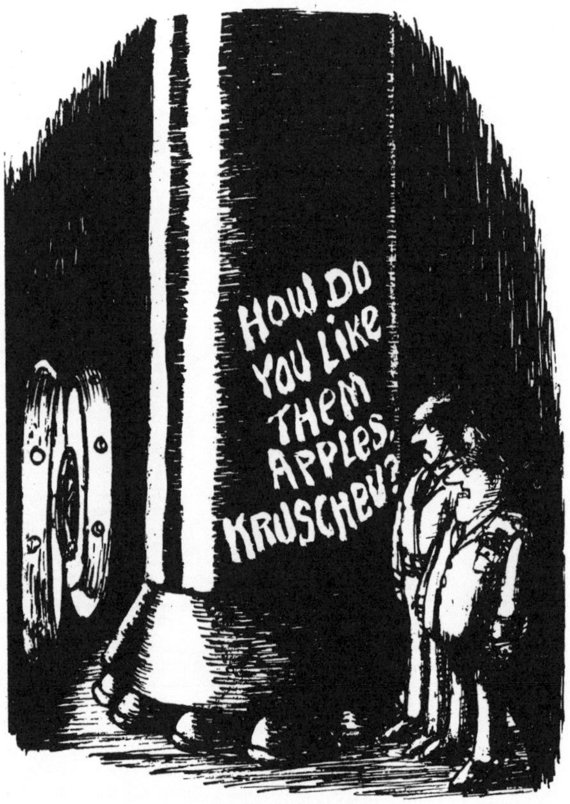
HOW DO
YOU LIKE
THEM
APPLES
KRUSCHEV?

"Dammit, Major, doesn't anybody around here read the papers?"

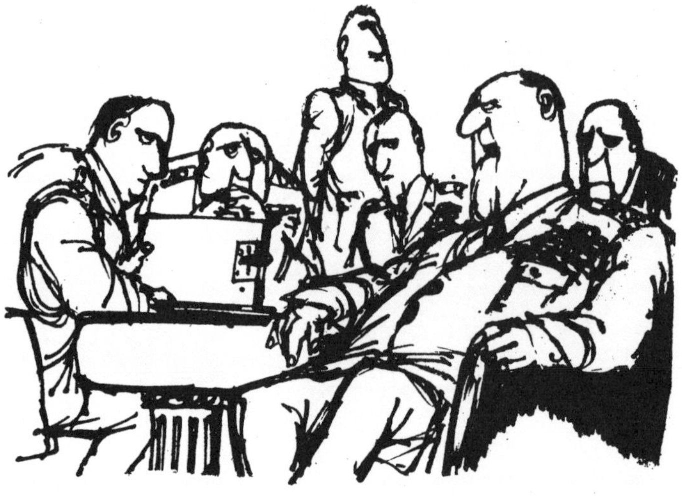

"... They SAY they'll never be the first to use their H-bomb, but who here feels that the Mafia can be trusted ..."

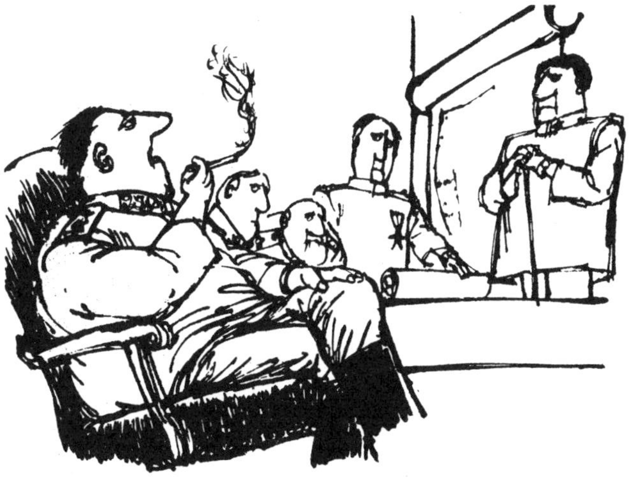

"... The grape growers attitude notwithstanding, Colonel Turgenev, I am against diverting the San Francisco missile to Delano ..."

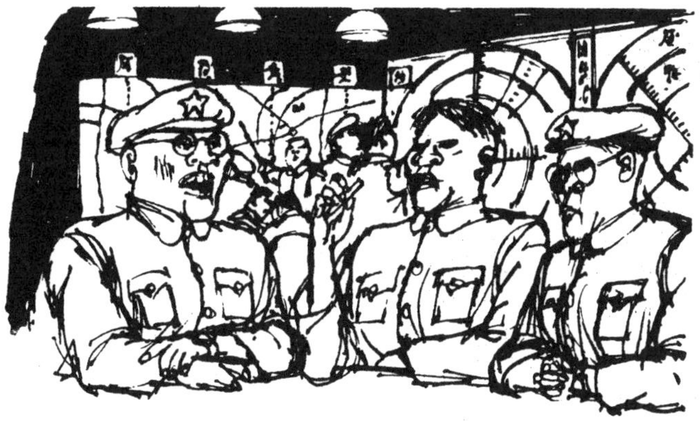

"Chairman Mao feels that the first strike strategy be Moscow, primary target — Washington, secondary ..."

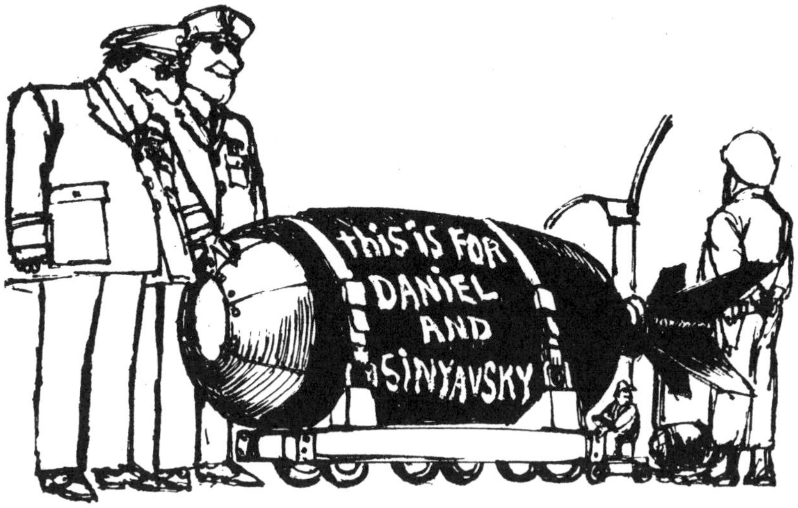
this is FOR DANIEL AND SINYAVSKY

"... Colonel Zent, it's damned heartwarming to know we've got cultured men in this outfit ..."

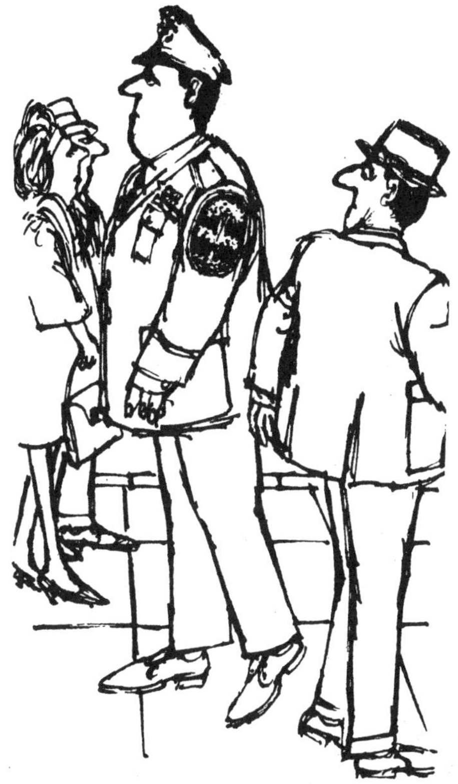

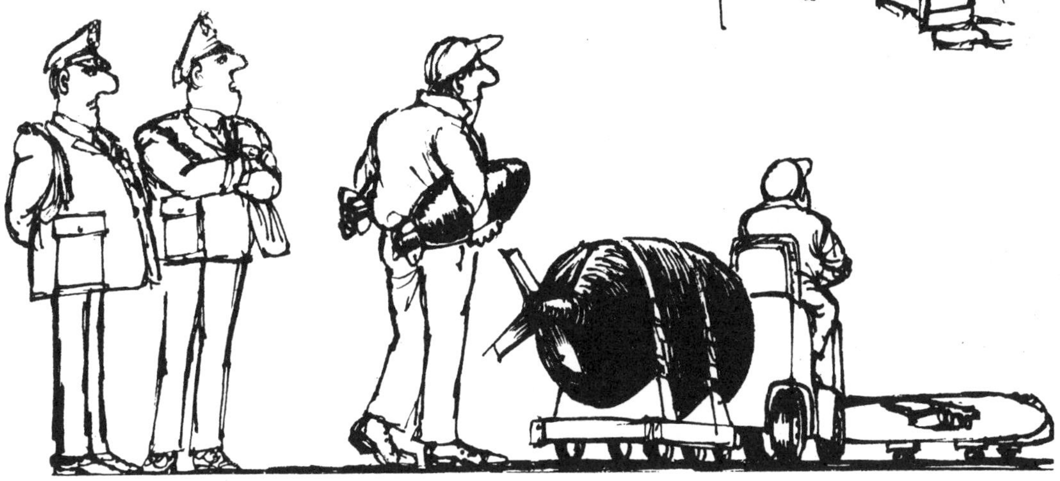

"... and those two conventional bombs bring up the total to an even ten million casualties."

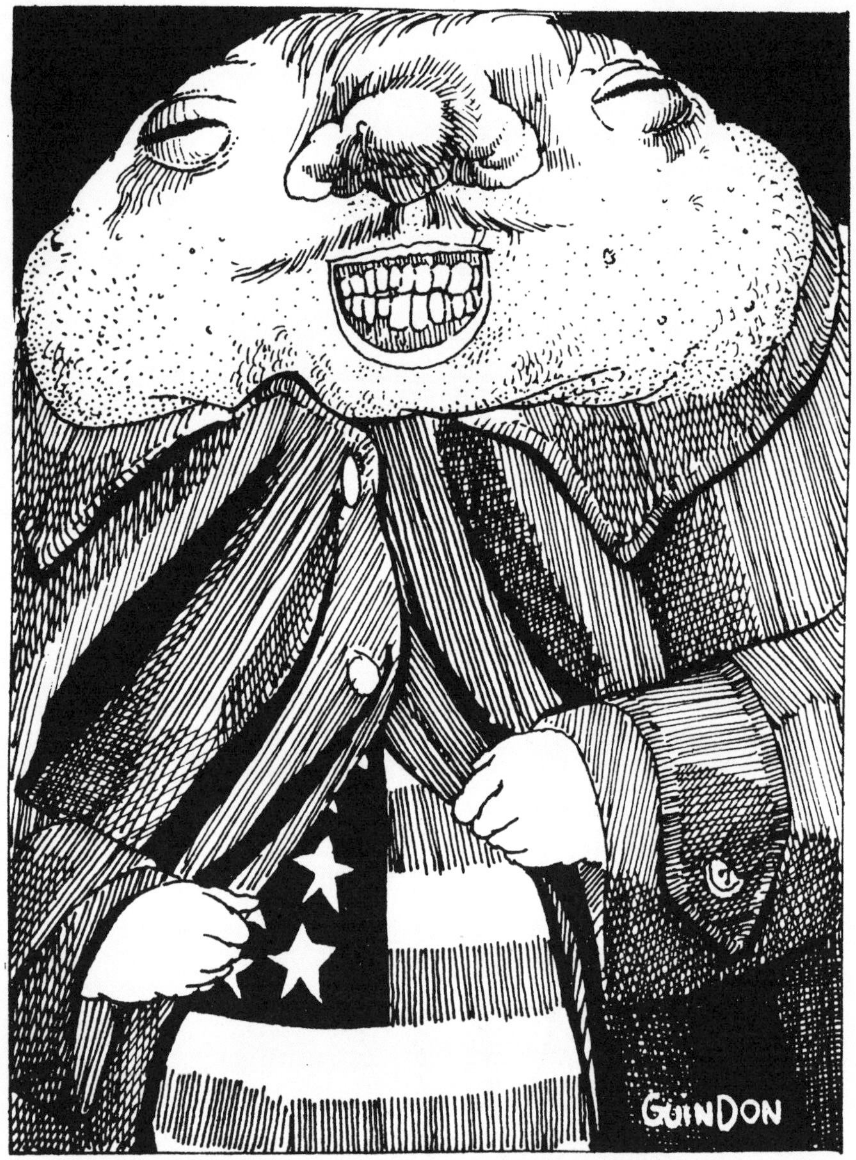
GUINDON

THE TRIAL OF ABBIE HOFFMAN'S SHIRT

RICHARD GUINDON. THE REALIST #84, NOVEMBER 1968. *82

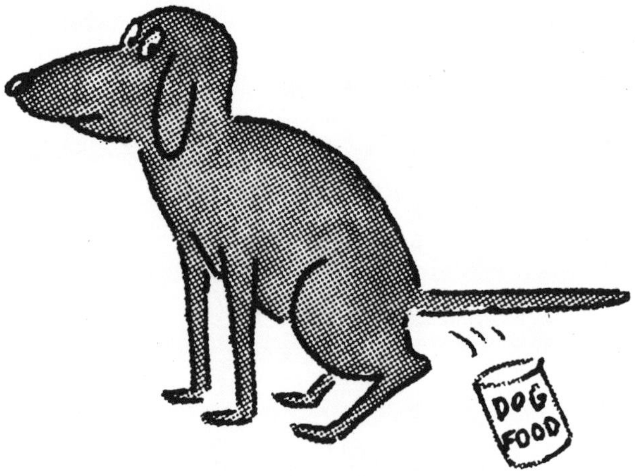
DOG FOOD

SAM GROSS. THE REALIST #83, OCTOBER 1968.

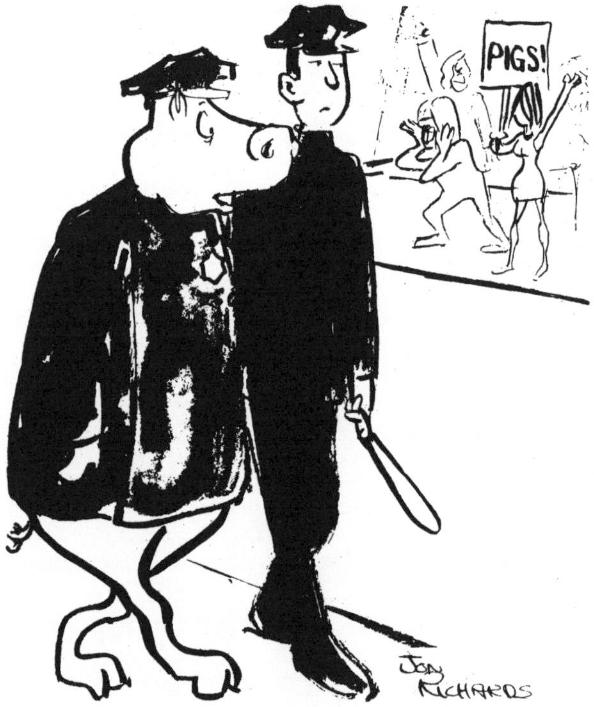
PIGS!
JON RICHARDS

"I don't know... it never struck me as such a terrible insult."

JON RICHARDS. THE REALIST #84, NOVEMBER 1968.

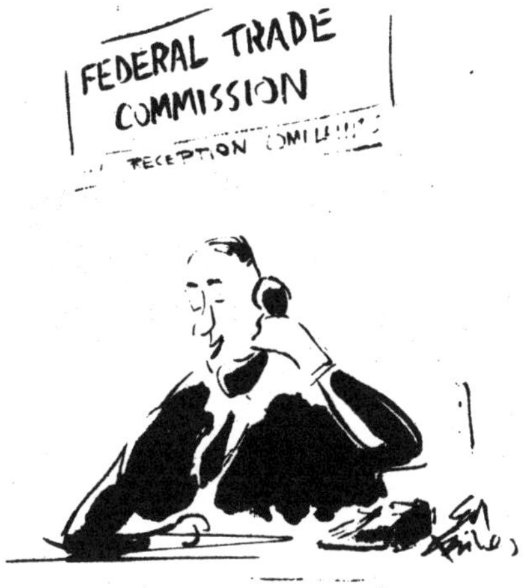
FEDERAL TRADE
COMMISSION

"... No, madame, we are NOT shocked by the current Nude Look, See-Through, Peak-a-Boo, Backless and Topless styles. On the contrary; remember, we administer the recently passed Truth-in-Packaging law."

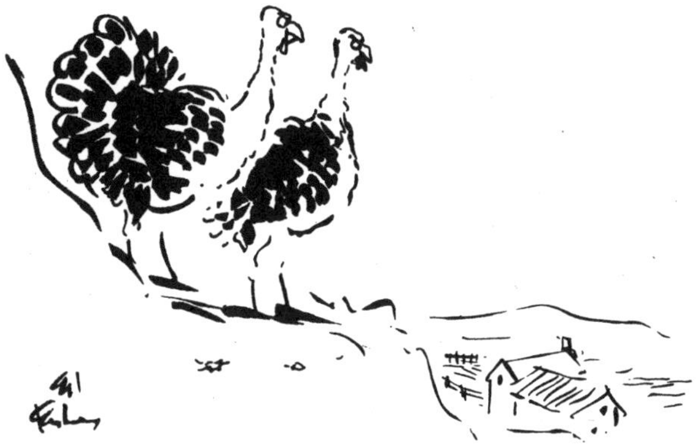

"The 175th anniversary of our Resistance! — And still no sign that the other side is willing to stop the slaughter, or negotiate!"

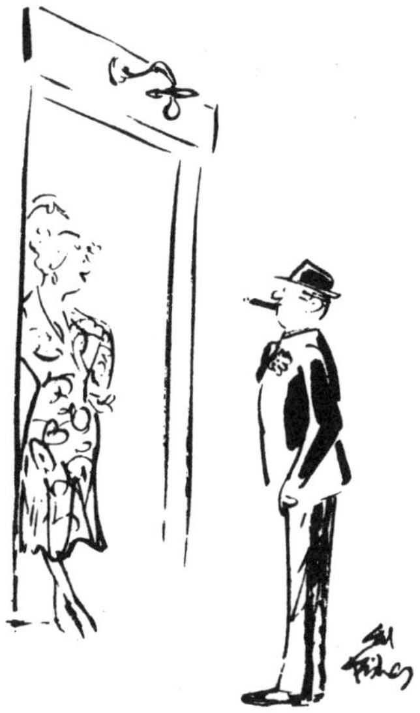

"You'll have to wait. The girls are conducting a slow-down."

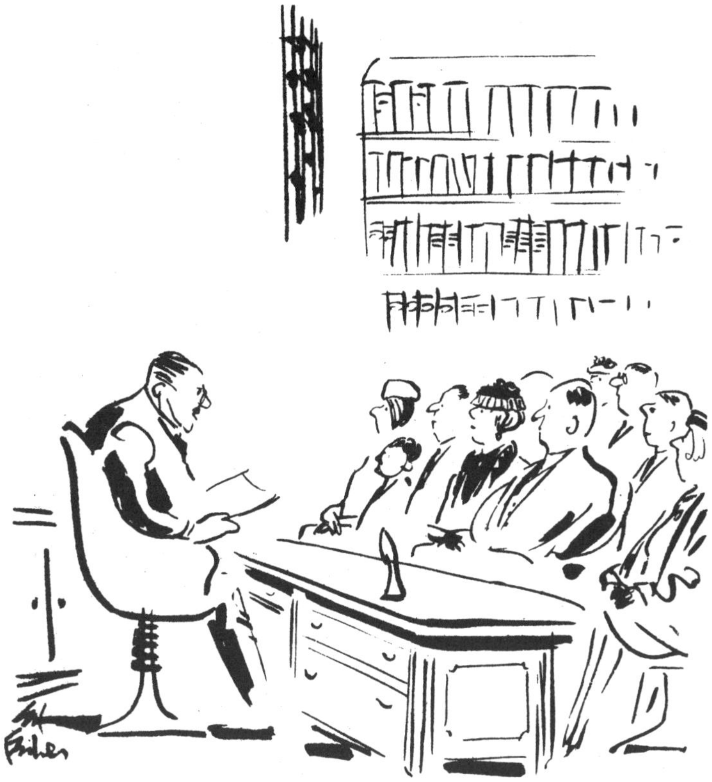

"— And to my brother, James, I leave my newer kidney and both ventricles; to my nephew William, 4 feet of small intestine and an excellently working cornea; to my sister-in-law Millicent ..."

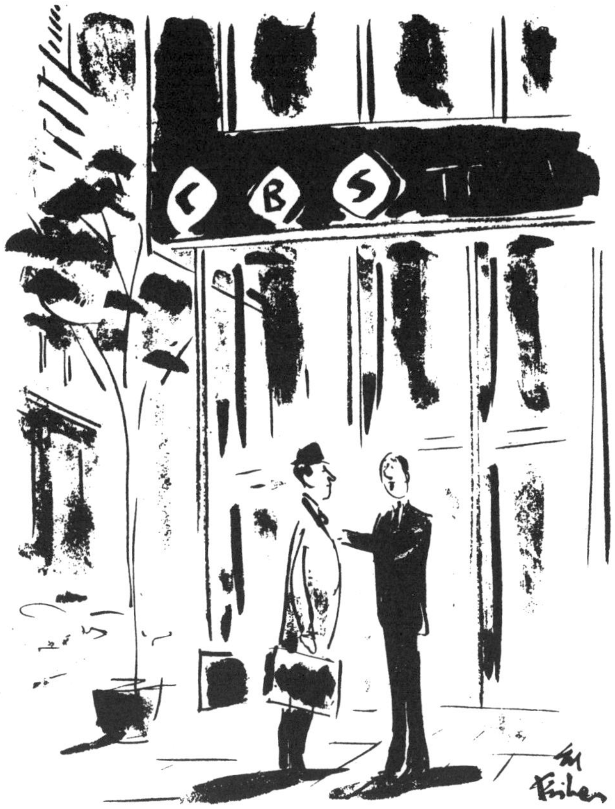
CBS

"Be careful how you introduce the Nostalgia Show over in Germany, Japan, Italy ..."

ED FISHER. THE REALIST #84, NOVEMBER 1968.

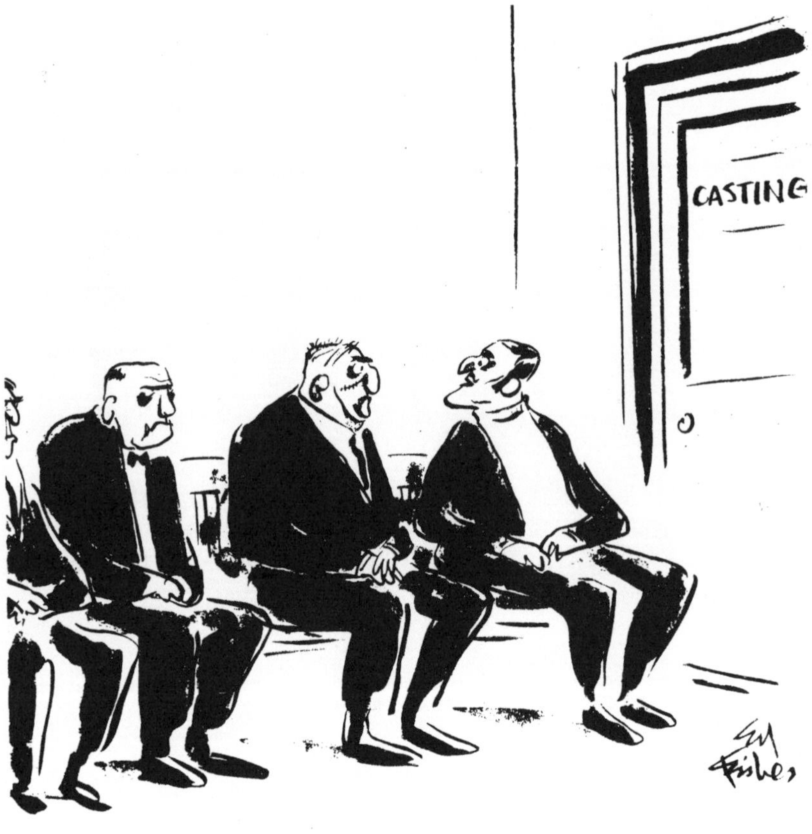
CASTING

"— I understand it's for a drama about the founding of the Republic, by LeRoi Jones."

*83

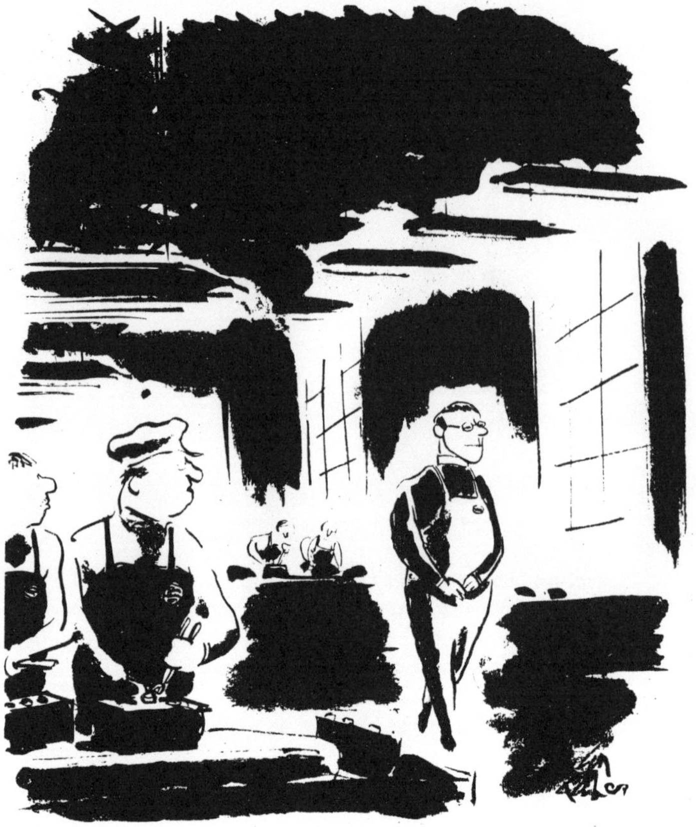

"He started here as a worker-priest, worked his way up to foreman-priest, and now he's hand-in-glove with the management-priests."

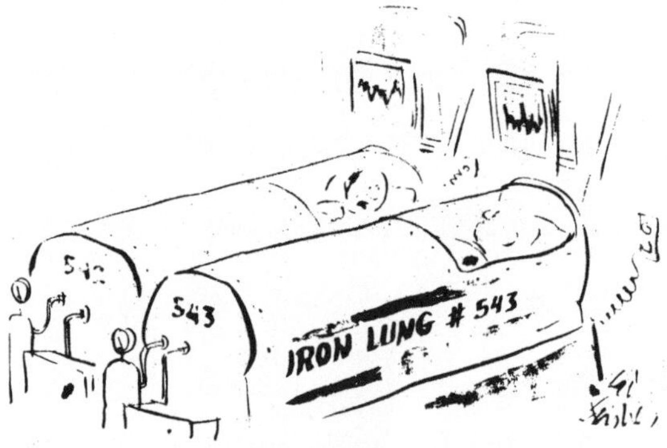
542
543
IRON LUNG # 543

"— And if the Establishment denies us our rights as a special minority, we start thinking up costly little ways to harass it, disrupt it, even if necessary smash it! ..."

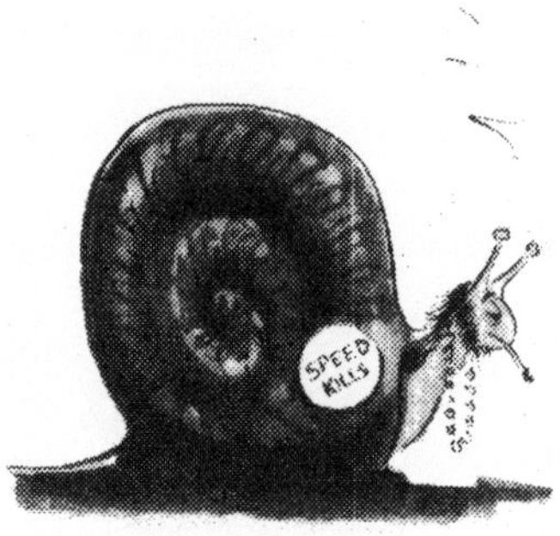
SPEED KILLS

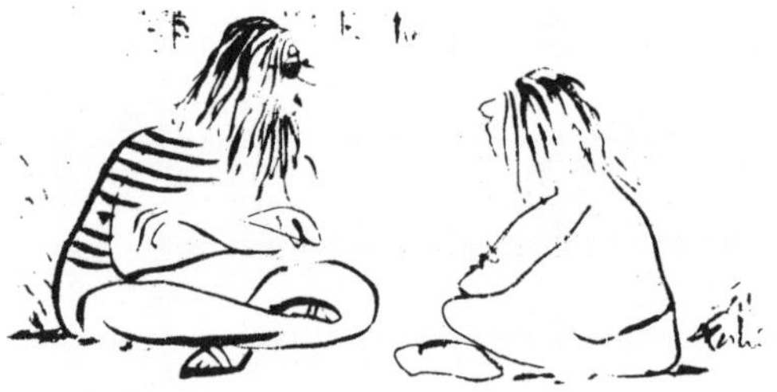

"When I told you to question everything, I didn't mean question Herbert Marcuse!"

*84

ED FISHER. THE REALIST #84, NOVEMBER 1968.

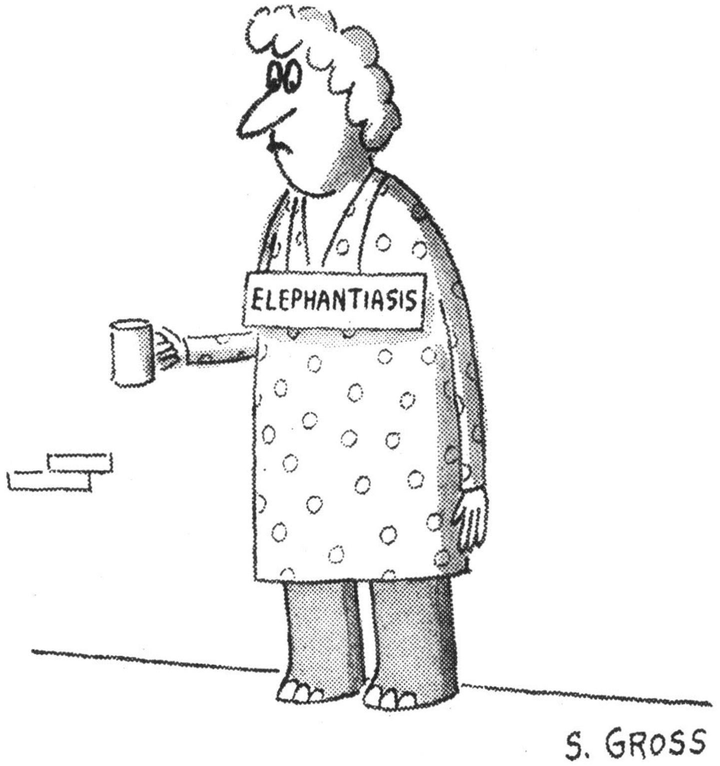
ELEPHANTIASIS
S. GROSS

SAM GROSS. THE REALIST #84, NOVEMBER 1968.

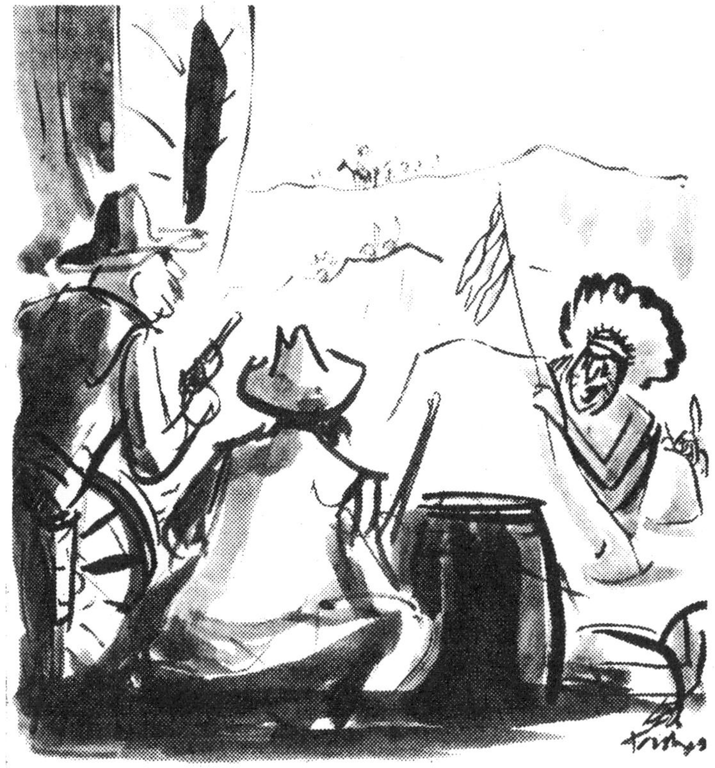

"If you boys are counting on any last-minute rescue, forget it — the Seventh Cavalry's been paid off!"

ED FISHER. THE REALIST #86, NOVEMBER-DECEMBER 1969.

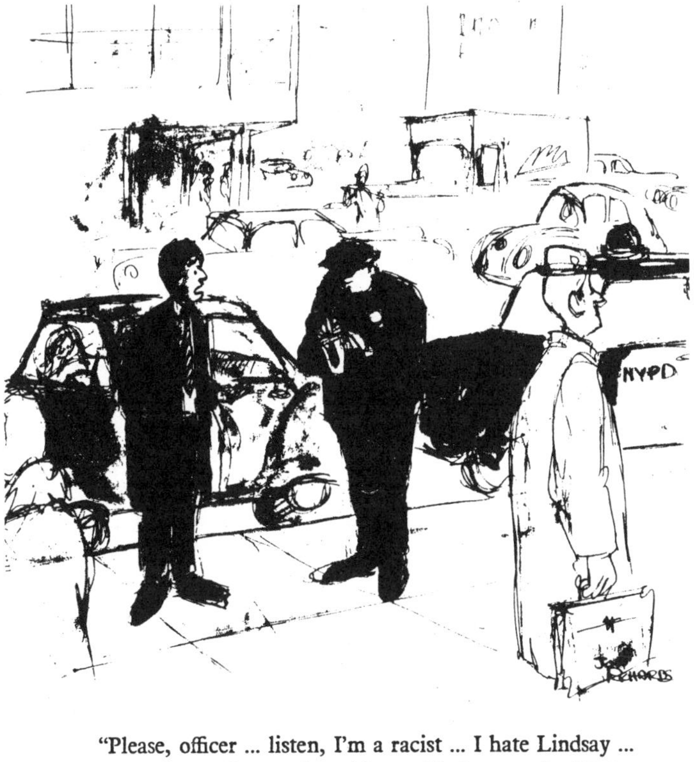
NYPD
RICHARDS

"Please, officer ... listen, I'm a racist ... I hate Lindsay ... I voted for Wallace and Buckley ... I belong to the NRA ... I'm for victory in Vietnam ... I ..."

JON RICHARDS. THE REALIST #84, NOVEMBER 1968.

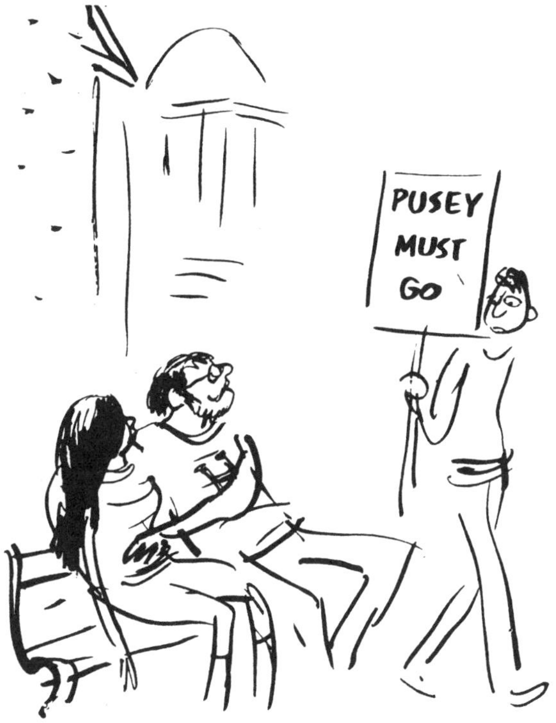
PUSEY MUST GO

"Pusey ... oh ... you startled me."

ED FISHER. THE REALIST #86, NOVEMBER-DECEMBER 1969.

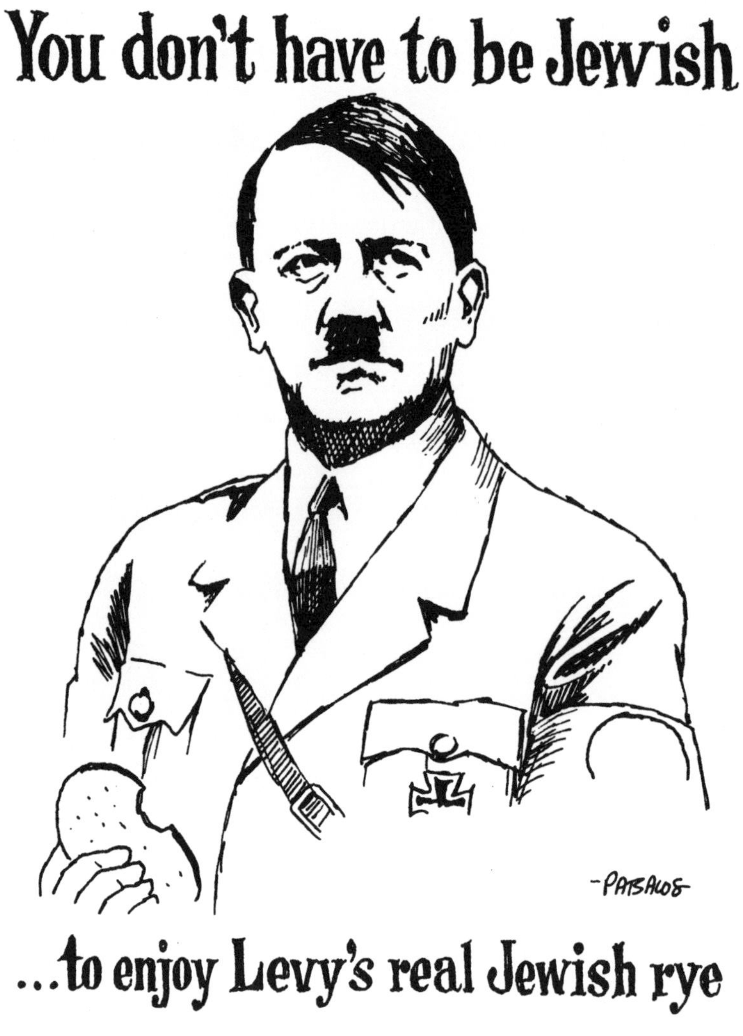
You don't have to be Jewish
-PATSALOS
...to enjoy Levy's real Jewish rye

JOHN PATLER. THE REALIST #85-FEBRUARY, DECEMBER 1968-JUNE 1969. *85

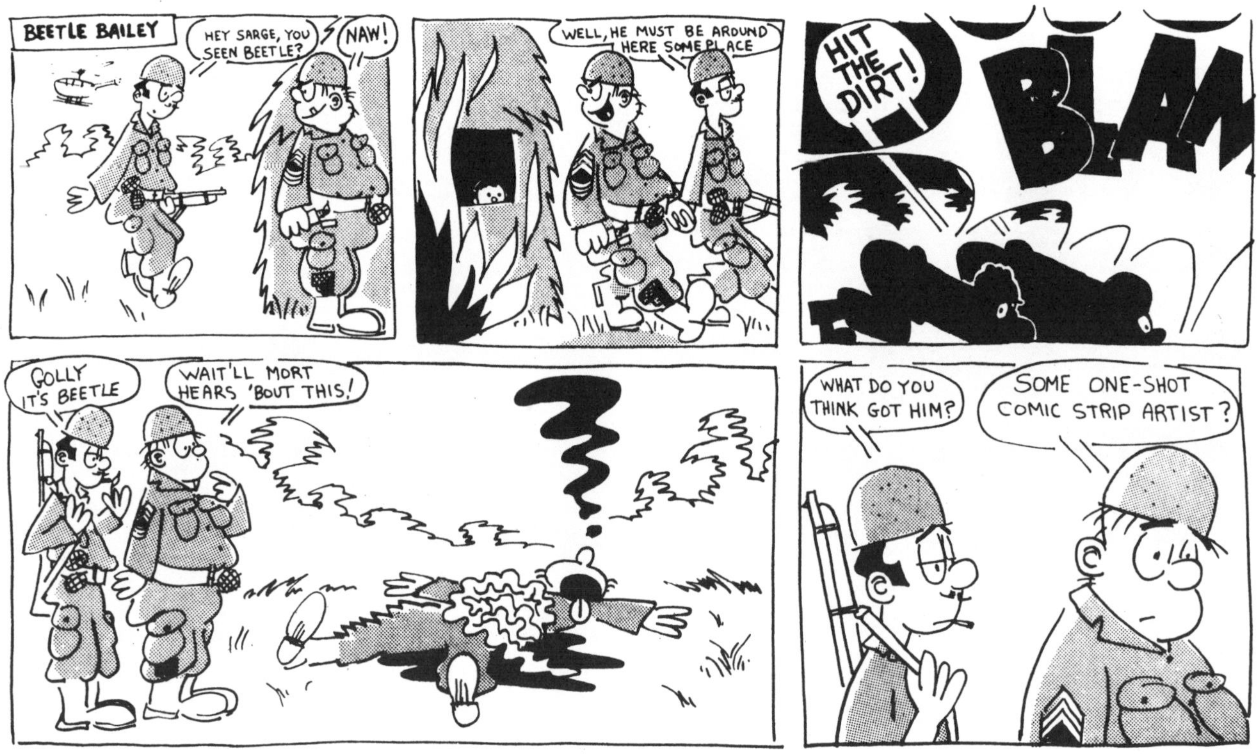
BEETLE BAILEY
HEY SARGE, YOU SEEN BEETLE?
NAW!
WELL, HE MUST BE AROUND HERE SOMEPLACE
HIT THE DIRT!
BLAM
GOLLY IT'S BEETLE
WAIT'LL MORT HEARS 'BOUT THIS!
WHAT DO YOU THINK GOT HIM?
SOME ONE-SHOT COMIC STRIP ARTIST?

DOMENICK CAPOBIANCO. THE REALIST #86, NOVEMBER-DECEMBER 1969.

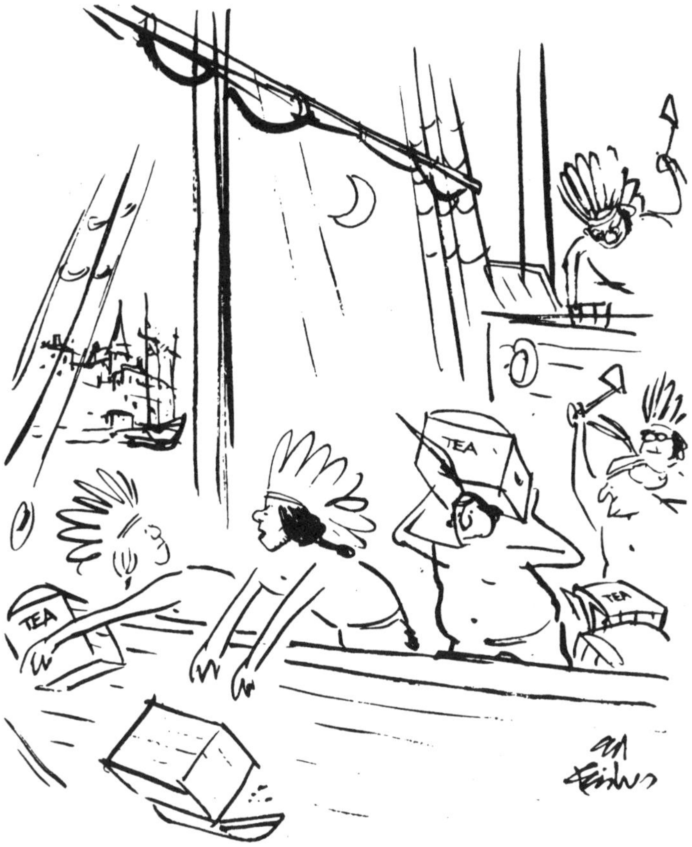
TEA
TEA
TEA

"Oh, knock off the balderdash, man! If we really thought it was legal to use violence in a rightful cause, how come we're all dressed up like Indians?"

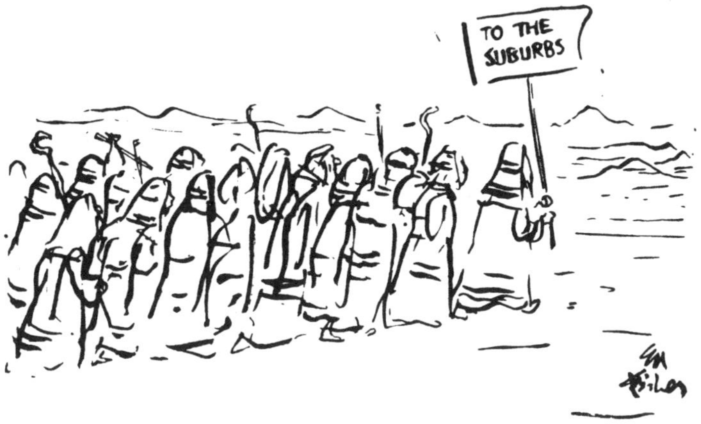
TO THE SUBURBS

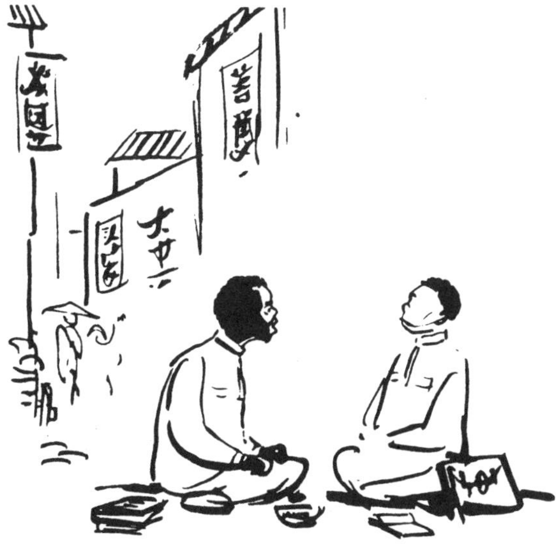

"What we want is our own autonomous department inside Peking University, where we can relate the black experience combined with special needs and relevances of minority culture, and apply it fully — in all its unique potential — to the whole range of our study ... which will, of course, continue to be The Thoughts of Chairman Mao."

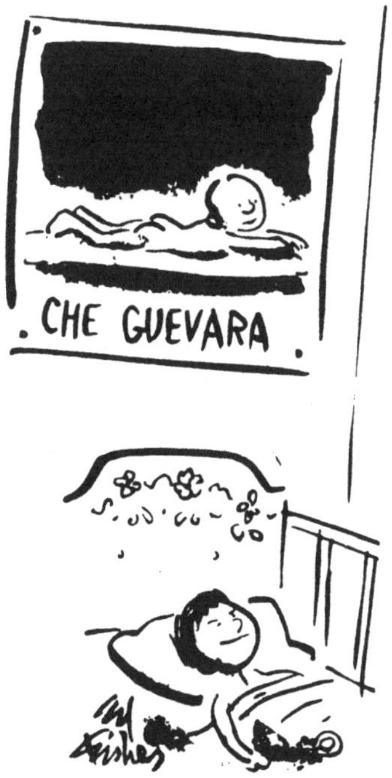
CHE GUEVARA

ED FISHER. THE REALIST #86, NOVEMBER-DECEMBER 1969.

CHARLES RODRIGUES.
THE REALIST #86,
NOVEMBER-DECEMBER 1969.

SOME OF MY BEST FRIENDS ARE...

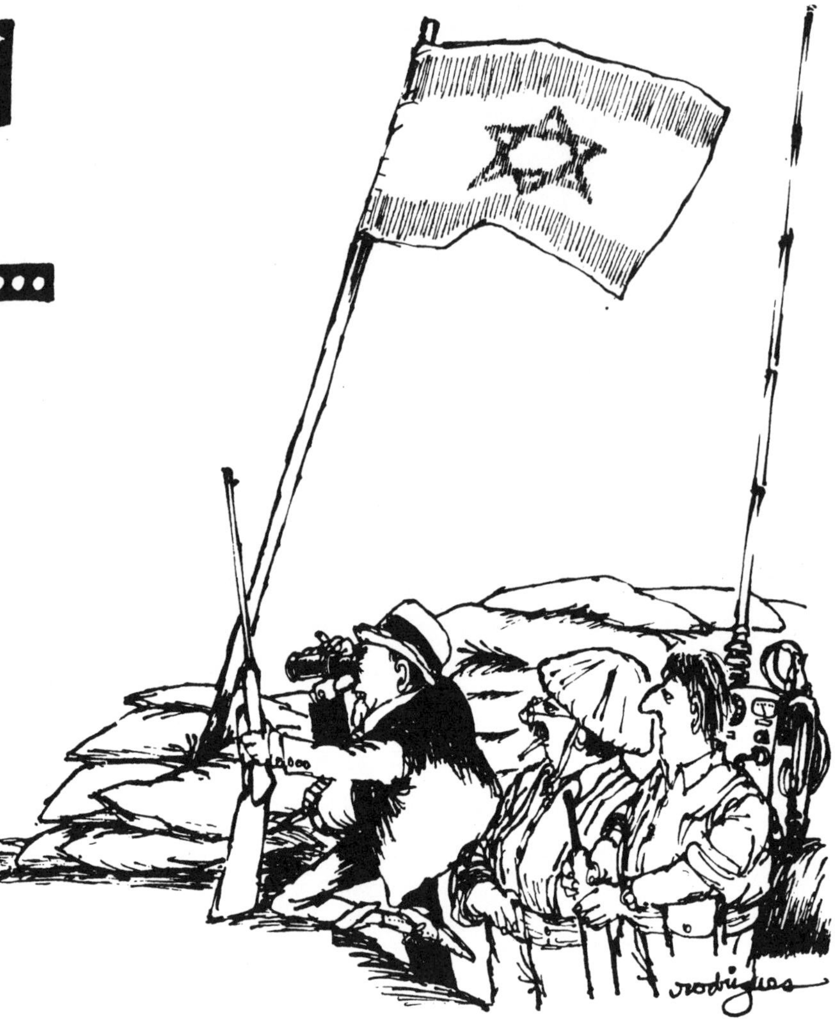
rodrigues

"All I know is he's Sidney Beserosky from Chicago and he's concerned about his $2,500 in Israel bonds ..."

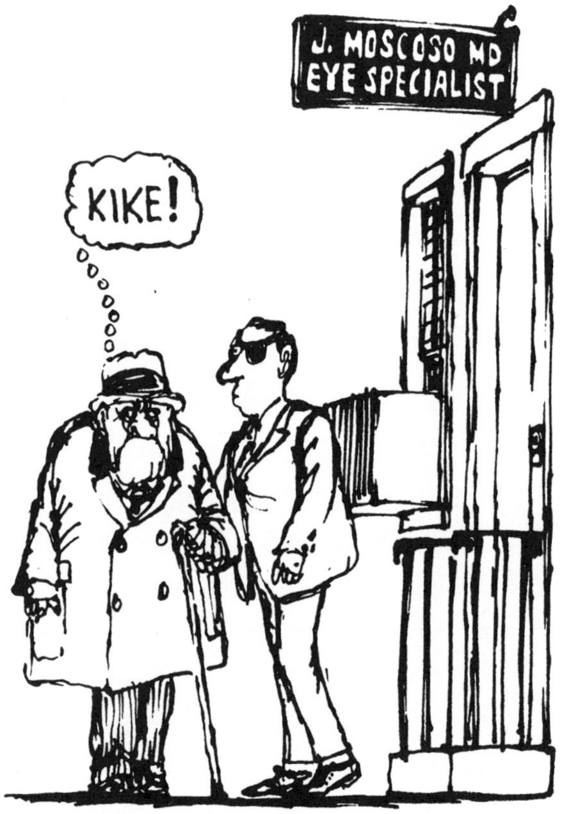
J. MOSCOSO MD
EYE SPECIALIST
KIKE!

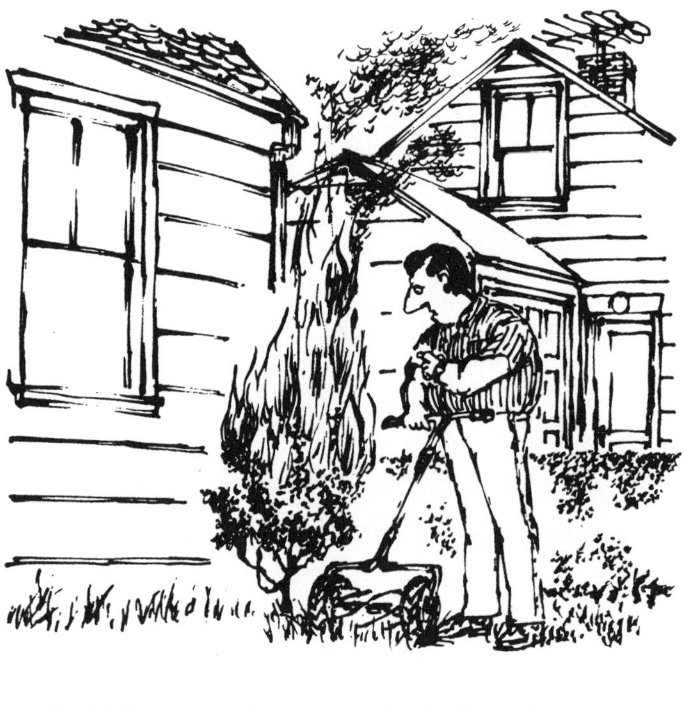

"... I think you have the wrong party. I'm Tony Nunzio — you want Marry Moses next door."

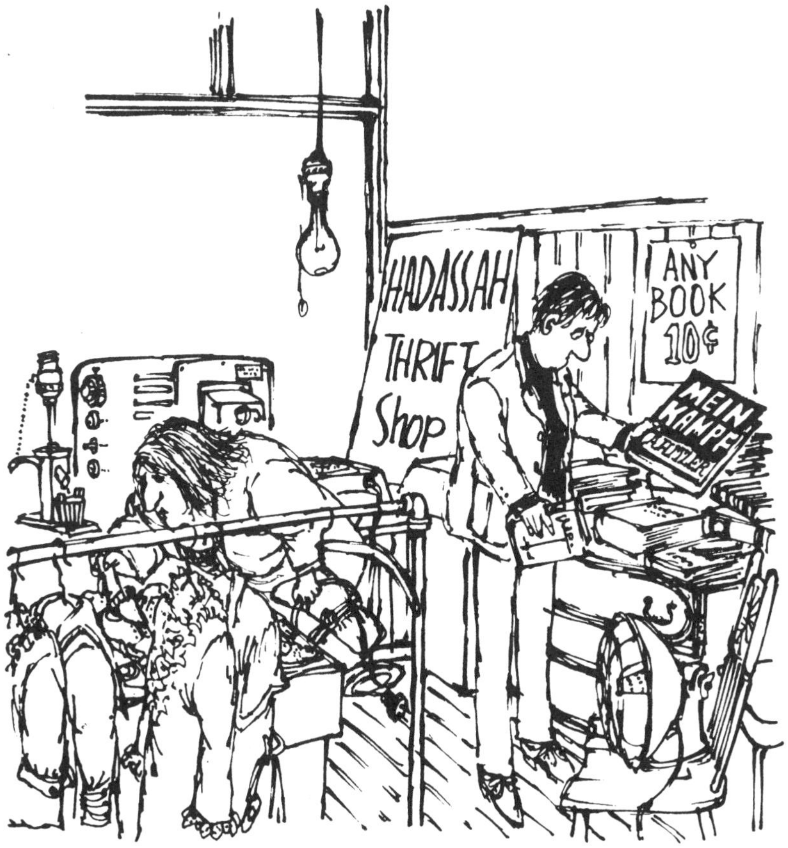
HADASSAH
THRIFT
Shop
ANY
BOOK
10¢
MEIN
KAMPF

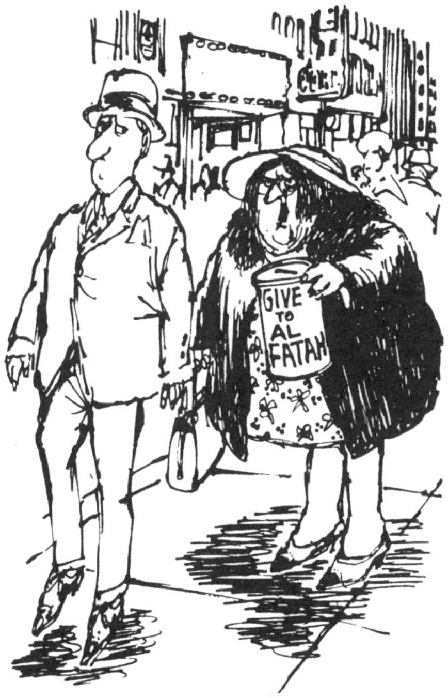
GIVE
TO
AL
FATAH

"Goddam Jew!"

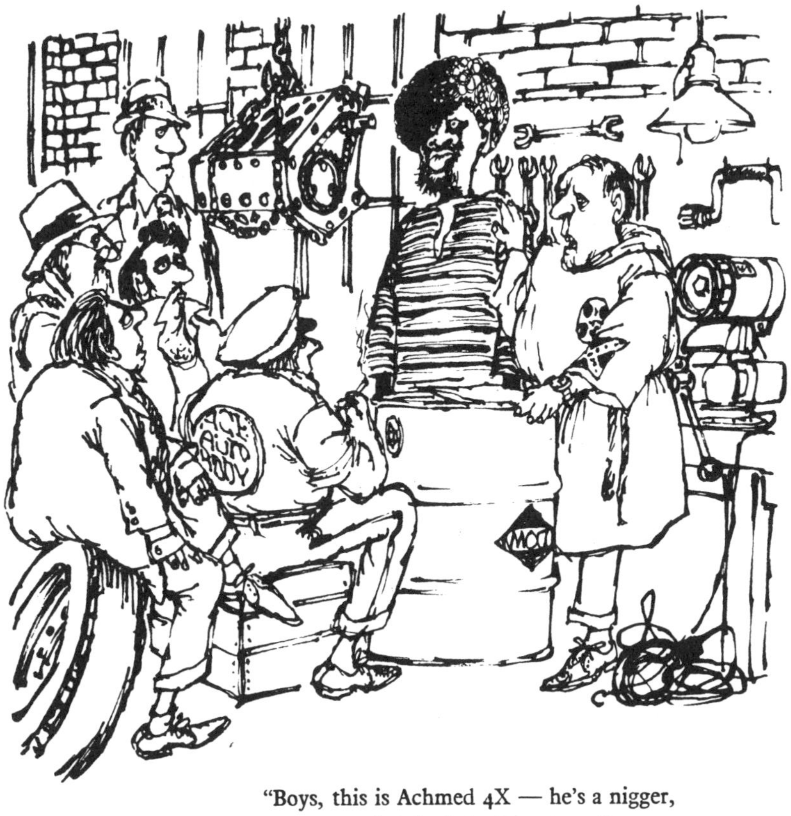

"Boys, this is Achmed 4X — he's a nigger, yes, but he hates Jews too ..."

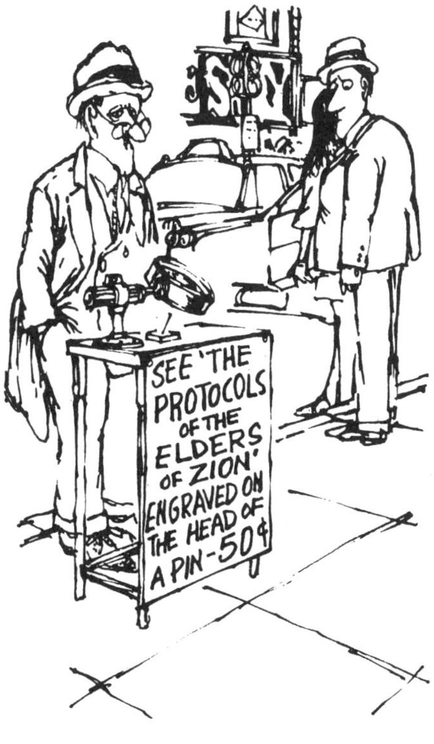
SEE 'THE PROTOCOLS OF THE ELDERS OF ZION' ENGRAVED ON THE HEAD OF A PIN - 50¢

"I'm a woman! I'm a woman!"

AMAZING
KISSING
DOLL
$5.95
Amazing
Kissing
Doll
Amazing
Kissing
Doll
Amazing
Kissing
Doll

"Don't bother to wrap it — I'll kiss it here."

Guindon's Burlap Underground

RICHARD GUINDON. THE REALIST #86, NOVEMBER-DECEMBER 1969.

"Under the circumstances, mister, I'm sure the telephone company will credit you for a wrong number."

"I'm sorry, madam, but the Shetland pony *must* have some luggage."

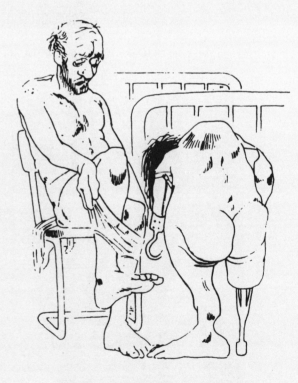

"Oh, no — I like you for your mind too."

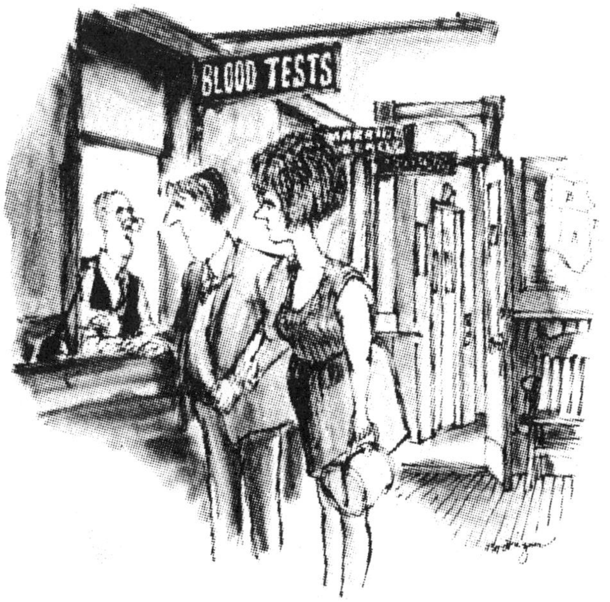
BLOOD TESTS

"... I don't like bringing this up after giving you the bad news, but the County Health Director wants to know if you would be available as a source for vaccine ..."

CHARLES RODRIGUES. THE REALIST #88, JANUARY-FEBRUARY 1971.

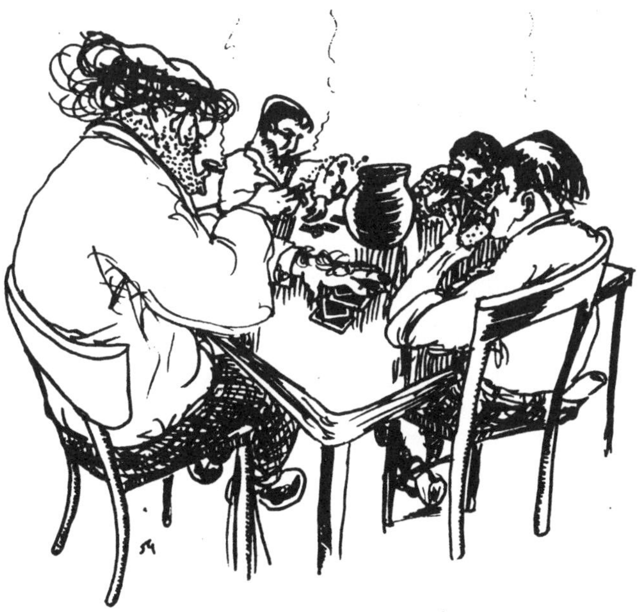

"Raise ya two thorazines an' a dexie!"

JAMES "JAF" FRANKFORT. THE REALIST #86-B, MARCH-APRIL 1970.

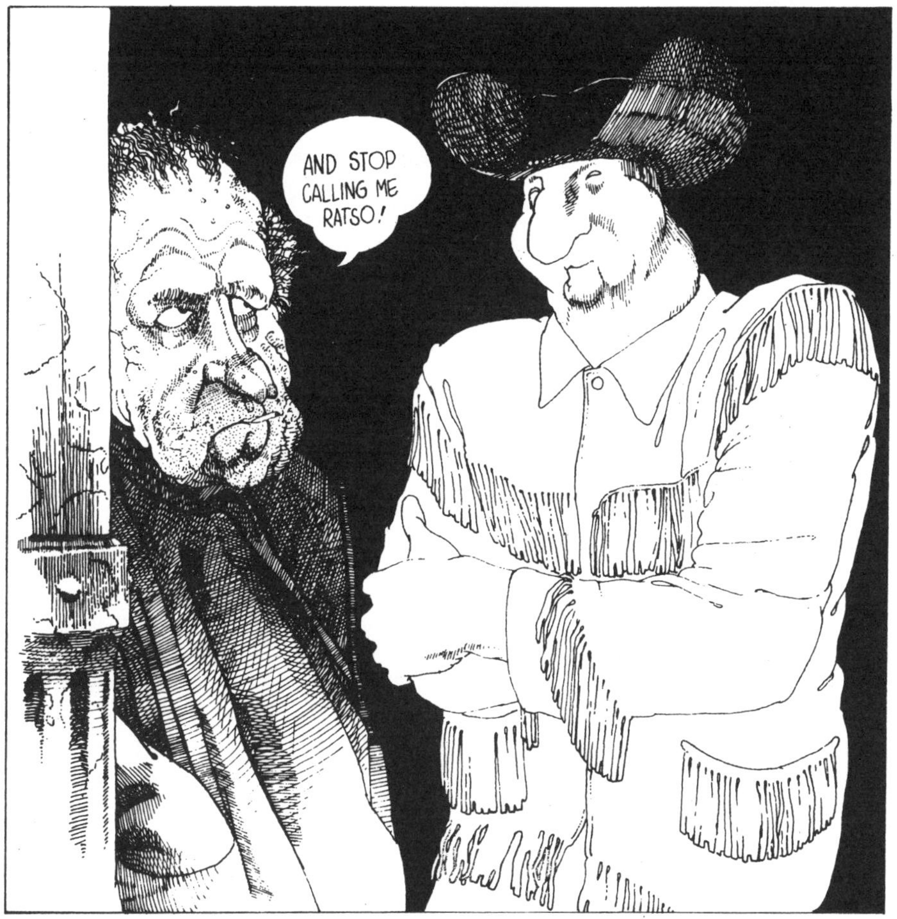
AND STOP CALLING ME RATSO!

RICHARD GUINDON. THE REALIST #86-B, MARCH-APRIL 1970. *86

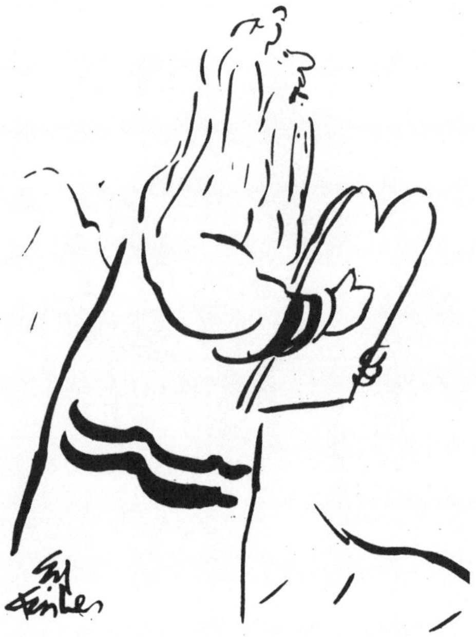

"But don't you feel the people of Israel
will reject this as an imposed solution?"

ED FISHER. THE REALIST #88, JANUARY-FEBRUARY 1971.

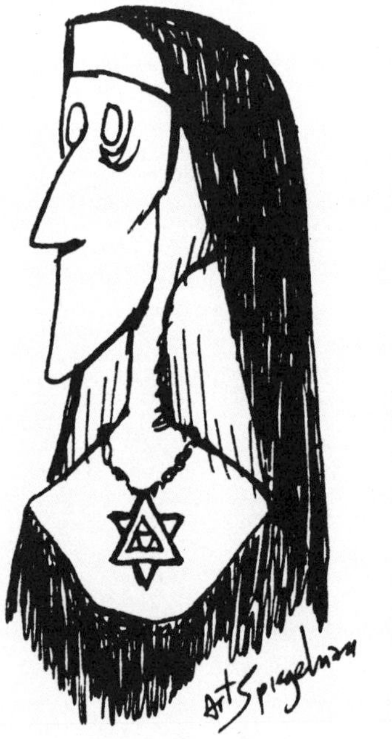

ART SPIEGELMAN. THE REALIST #86, NOVEMBER-DECEMBER 1969.

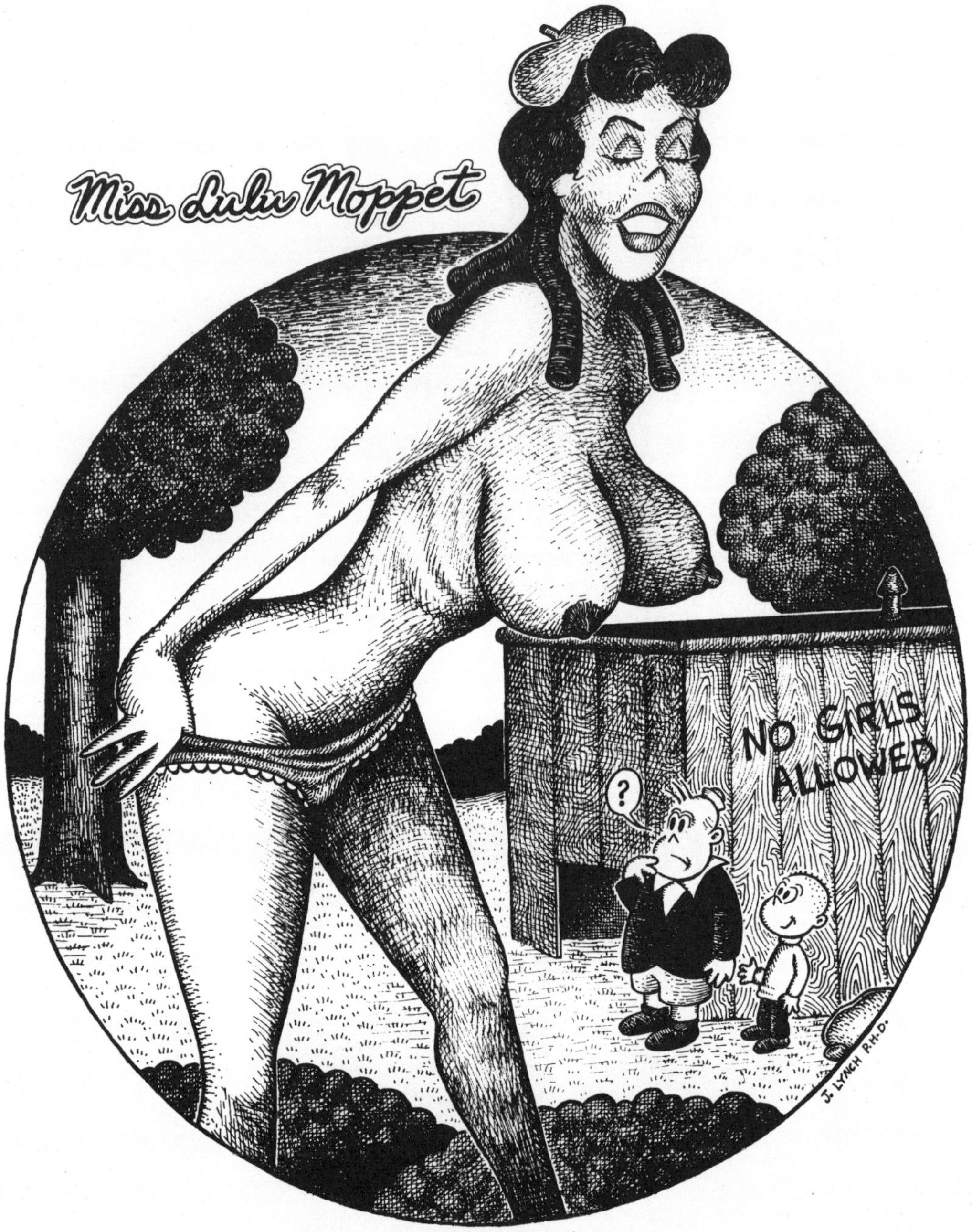
Miss Lulu Moppet
?
NO GIRLS ALLOWED

"Ban the bra!" is the battle cry of Miss Lulu Moppett, a cutie for the cause of feminine independence. But we'd say this magnificently mammaried militant has her sister suffragettes outranked. In Lulu's home town of Deerfield, Ill., there is an exclusive men's club which no female has ever before invaded. In a "stand-in" demonstration, prim but principled Miss Moppett "steps out"—of her panties—to expose to club officers her impassioned belief that a woman is more than a sex object. "I am an intellectual as well as a woman," erupts Lulu, "and I'll get those stoopid boys to give in yet!" We can hardly accuse her of skirting the issue!!!

JAY LYNCH. THE REALIST #87, MAY-JUNE 1970.

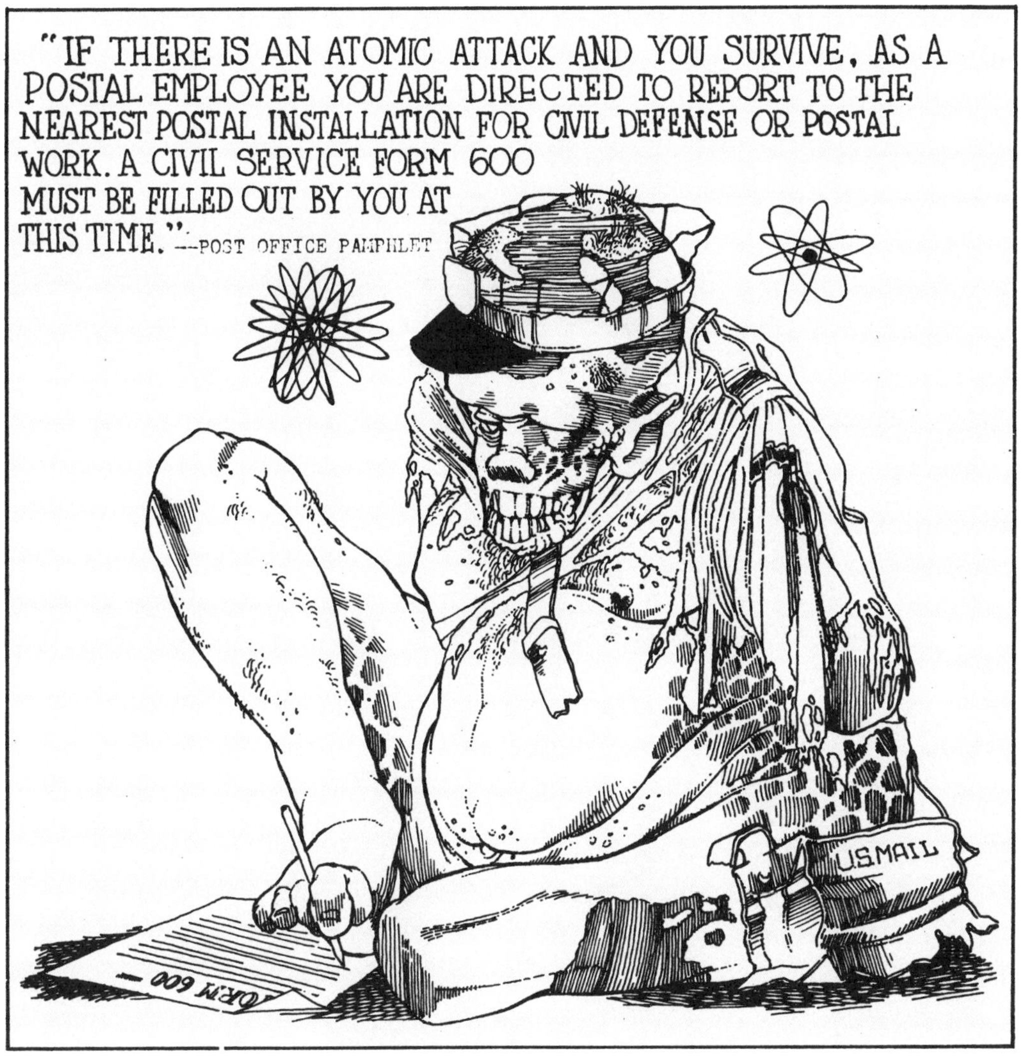
"IF THERE IS AN ATOMIC ATTACK AND YOU SURVIVE, AS A POSTAL EMPLOYEE YOU ARE DIRECTED TO REPORT TO THE NEAREST POSTAL INSTALLATION FOR CIVIL DEFENSE OR POSTAL WORK. A CIVIL SERVICE FORM 600 MUST BE FILLED OUT BY YOU AT THIS TIME." —POST OFFICE PAMPHLET
U.S. MAIL
FORM 600

RICHARD GUINDON. THE REALIST #87, MAY-JUNE 1970.

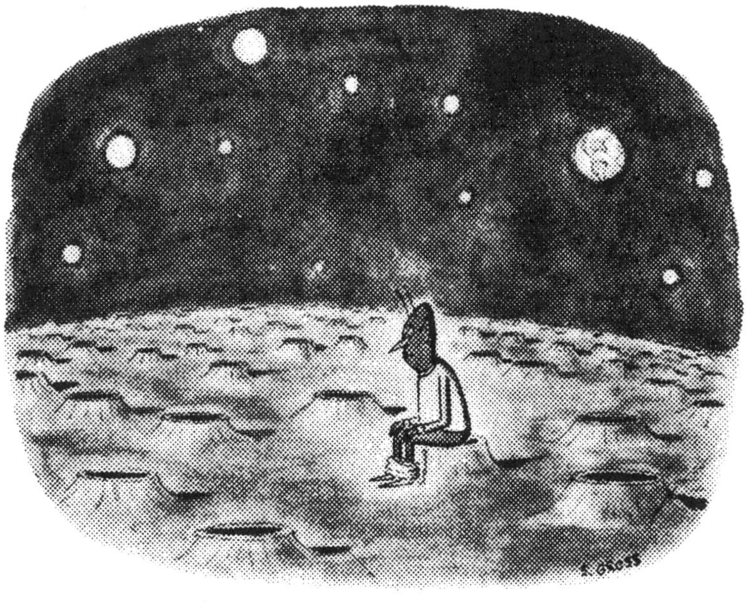
S. GROSS

SAM GROSS. THE REALIST #86-B, MARCH-APRIL 1970.

The Realist
50 ¢
Jan. - Feb.
1971
No. 88
MARTHA MITCHELL
IS A SPEED FREAK
" Tim and Rosemary and Eldridge and Kathleen "
(... consider the possibilities)

ROBERT GROSSMAN. THE REALIST #88, JANUARY-FEBRUARY 1971. *87

THE REALIST presents:
March
1971
The Last
Supplement
to the WHOLE EARTH CATALOG
$1.00
"HE WHO SHITS IN THE ROAD WILL MEET FLIES ON HIS RETURN"
THAT'S AN OLD SOUTH AFRICAN PARABLE, GANG!
HUH!
TAKE HEED!
TSK! PLEASE I'M EATING!
OH WOW!
P-PHAW HAW HAW RAT ON!
FREE BOBBY, ANGELA, JOHN, ALL OTHERS
$
OW!
OFF OUR BACKS
I STAND GUARD!
HEART
DRAWN BY R. "SOUTHPAW" CRUMB

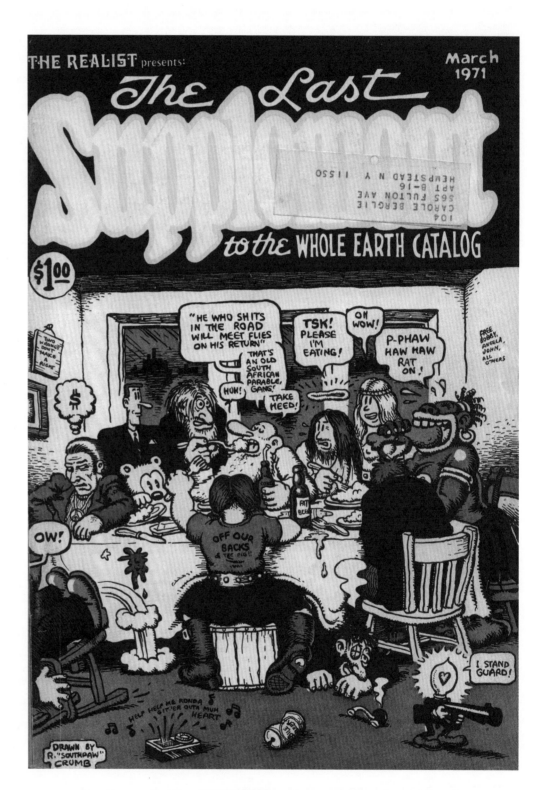

ROBERT CRUMB. THE REALIST #89, MARCH-APRIL 1971.

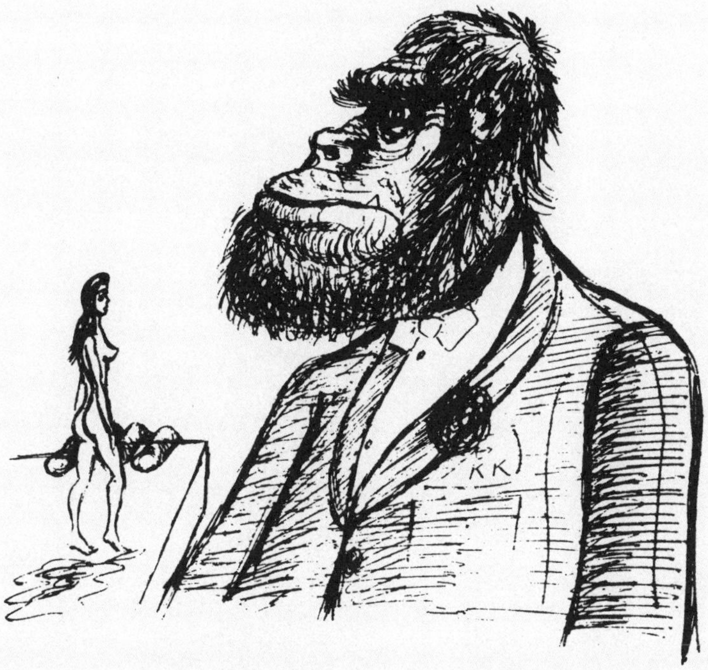
KK

King Kong Died For Our Sins

He was just a kid when
They got 'im.

(It was a Spad wasn't it?
Wasn't he nailed by a Spad?)

Who didn't know about it?
Why doesn't anyone speak of it?

So what if he would of
Married the broad?

What buildings he could have
Climbed.
Bucky Fuller would have
Built him a world to swing in.

--Yabe Yablonsky

JOHN PATLER. THE REALIST #89, MARCH-APRIL 1971.

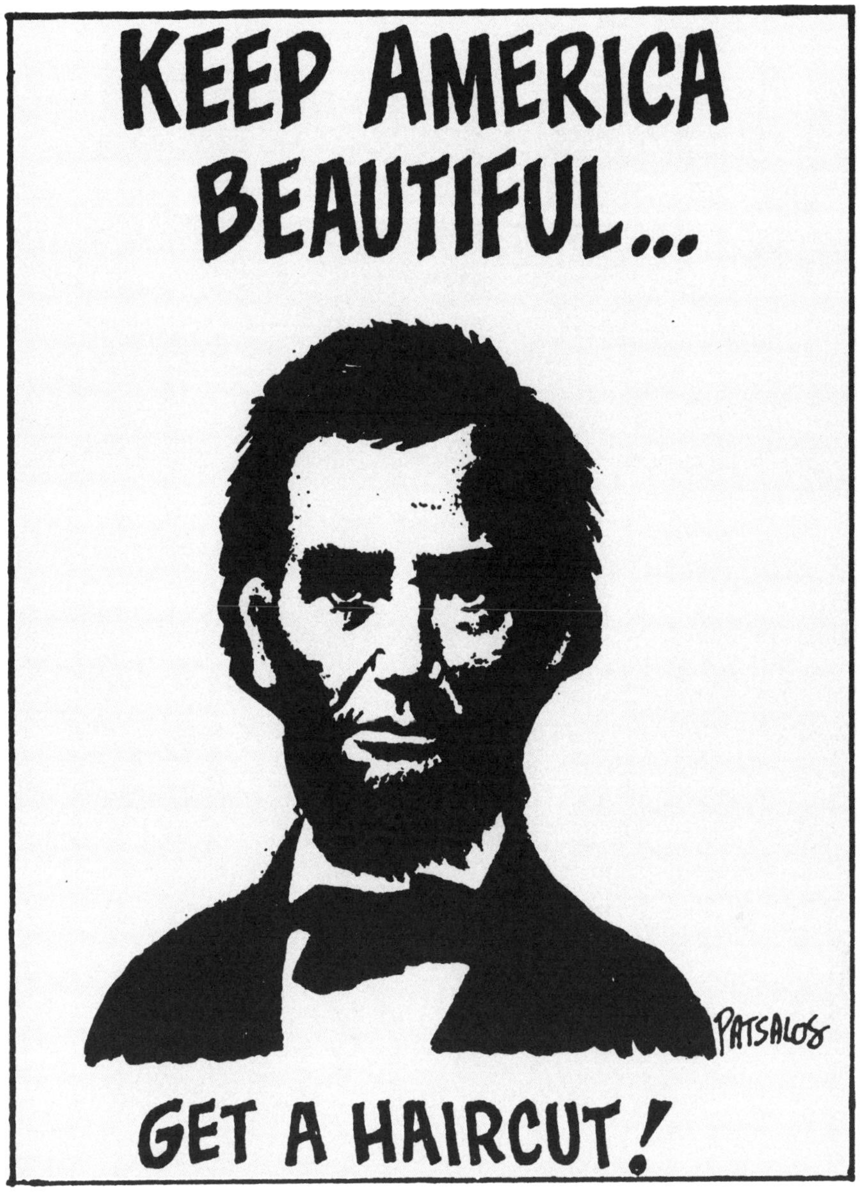
KEEP AMERICA
BEAUTIFUL...
PATSALOS
GET A HAIRCUT!

JOHN PATLER. THE REALIST #89, MARCH-APRIL 1971.

DUMB BIRD
I CAN SEE THE OCEAN! I CAN SEE THE SUN AND THE MOON!!
FRED CAN SEE US, SUN!!
FRED HAS BEEN KNOWN TO SCARF A MAGIC COOKIE..
WHAT DOES A BIRD KNOW ABOUT BEING IRISH!
YOU WANT A CONVERSATION WITH SOMETHING NO ONE CAN SEE!!
ODD Bodkins
it's not all colorful
and it's not like a comic book
and it's not very funny.
why I like it
because some of it is colorful.
because the sun and the moon and the ocean talk.
because Fred knows where a magic cookie bush is.
--Jed

DAN O'NEILL. THE REALIST #89, MARCH-APRIL 1971.

cieciorka

THE LAST JUDGMENT

FRANK CIECIORKA. THE REALIST #89, MARCH-APRIL 1971.

JERRY MAYER

"Oh my goodness! The sky is falling!"

JERRY MAYER. THE REALIST #89, MARCH-APRIL 1971.

PLANETARY PEOPLE BY ED ROSENFELD

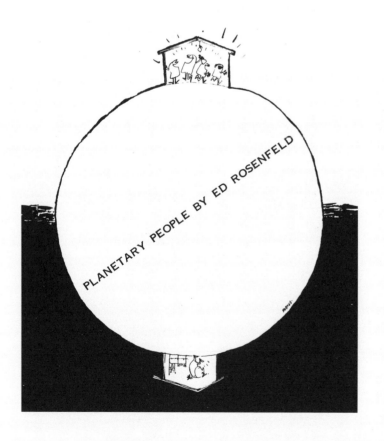

BARNES. THE REALIST #89, MARCH-APRIL 1971.

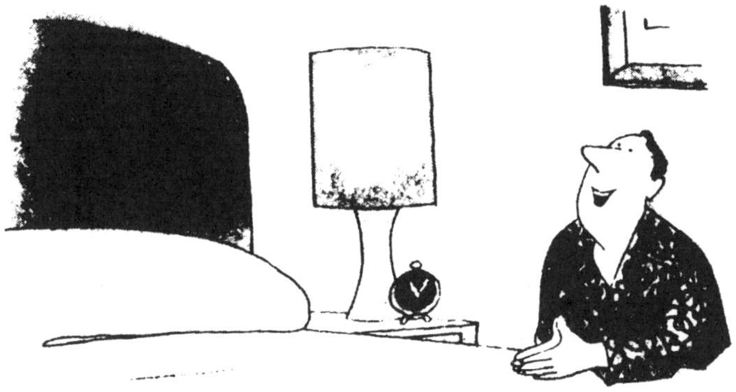

"Nothing special tonight. Just saying hello."

THE REALIST #89, MARCH-APRIL 1971.

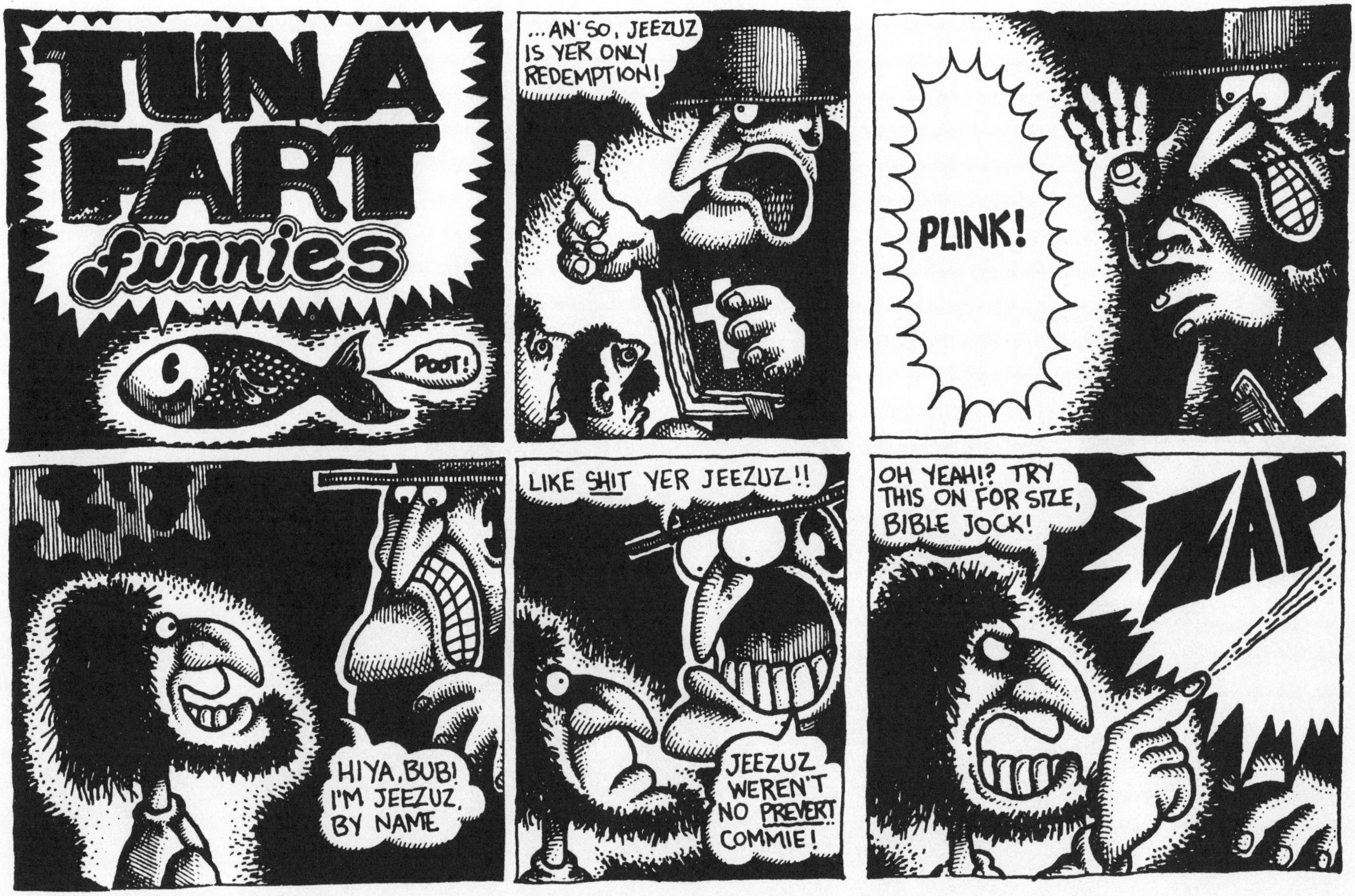
TUNA FART funnies
POOT!
...AN' SO, JEEZUZ IS YER ONLY REDEMPTION!
PLINK!
HIYA, BUB! I'M JEEZUZ, BY NAME
LIKE SHIT YER JEEZUZ!!
JEEZUZ WEREN'T NO PREVERT COMMIE!
OH YEAH!? TRY THIS ON FOR SIZE, BIBLE JOCK!
ZAP

SKIP WILLIAMSON. THE REALIST #89, MARCH-APRIL 1971.

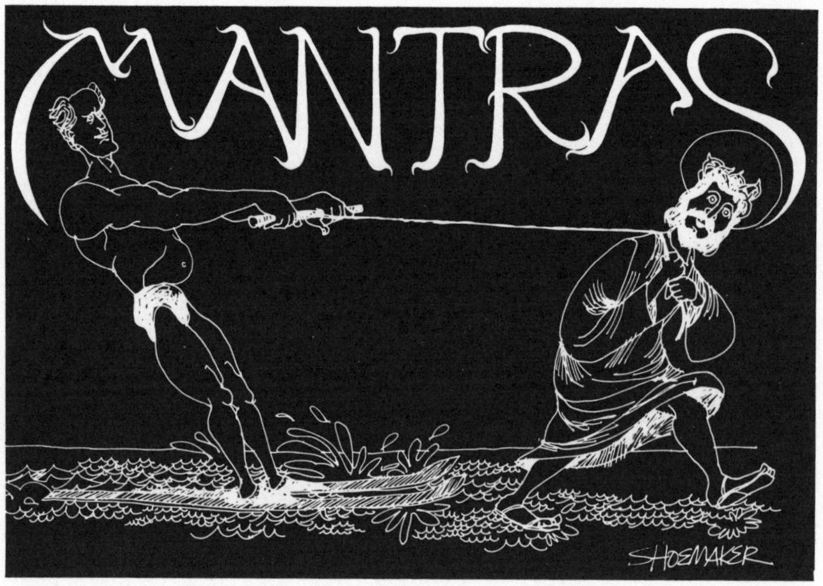
MANTRAS
SHOEMAKER

HOWARD SHOEMAKER. THE REALIST #89, MARCH-APRIL 1971.

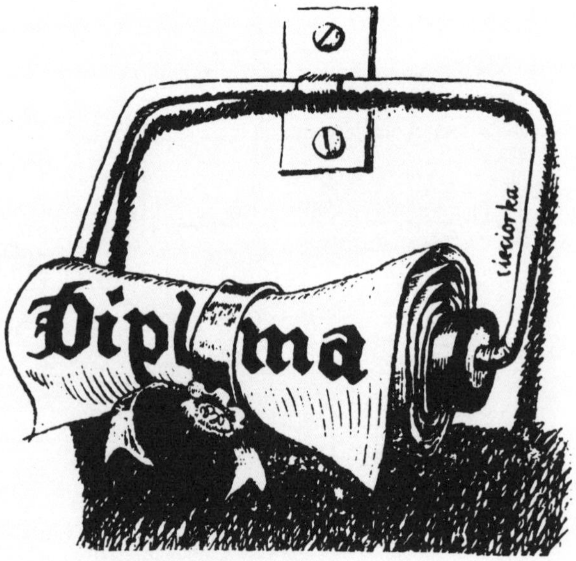
Diploma
cieciorka

FRANK CIECIORKA. THE REALIST #89, MARCH-APRIL 1971.

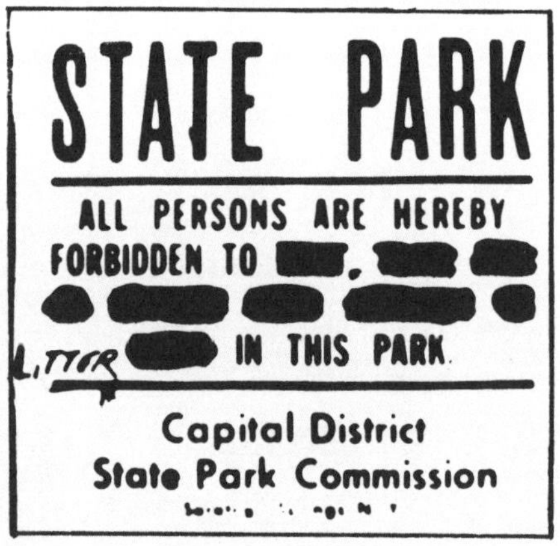
STATE PARK
ALL PERSONS ARE HEREBY
FORBIDDEN TO [redacted], [redacted]
LITTER [redacted] IN THIS PARK
Capital District
State Park Commission

THE REALIST #89, MARCH-APRIL 1971.

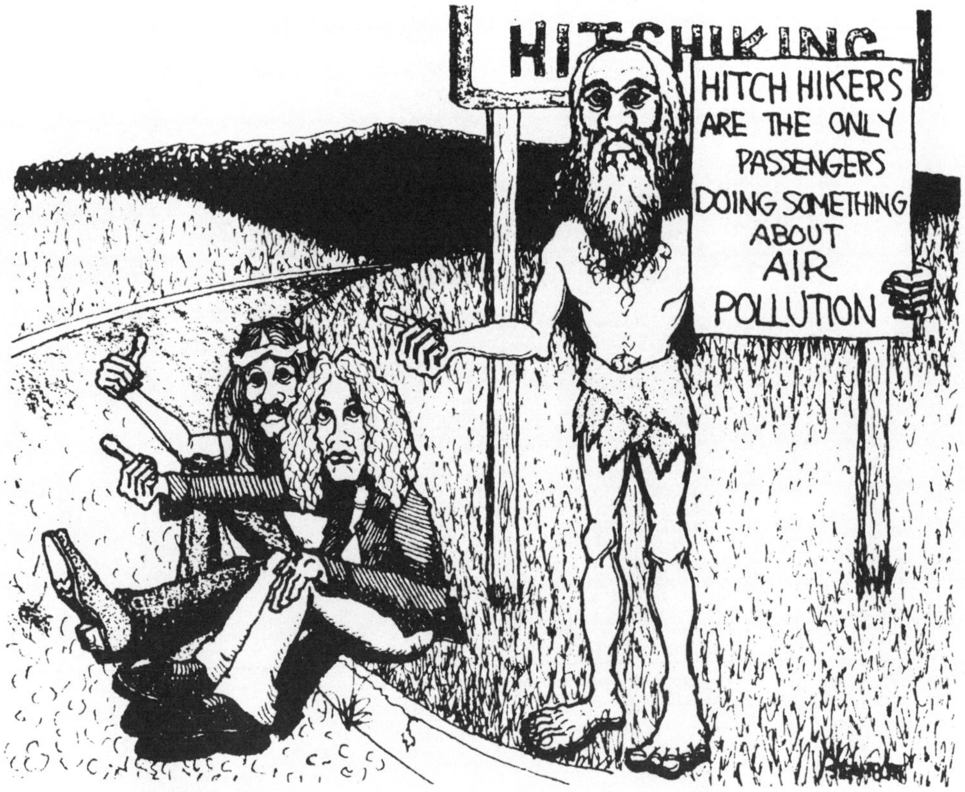
HITCH HIKERS
ARE THE ONLY
PASSENGERS
DOING SOMETHING
ABOUT
AIR
POLLUTION

STEAMBOAT. THE REALIST #89, MARCH-APRIL 1971.

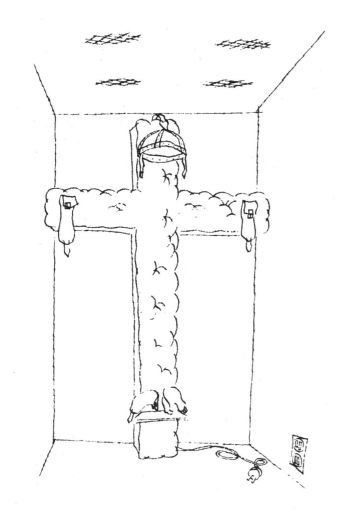

THE REALIST #89, MARCH-APRIL 1971.

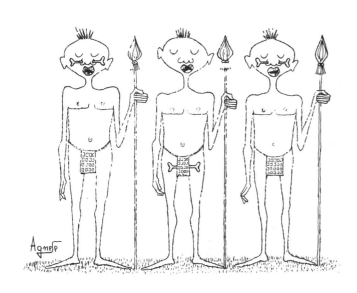

THE REALIST #89, MARCH-APRIL 1971.

RICHARD GUINDON. THE REALIST #89, MARCH-APRIL 1971.

ED BADAJOS. THE REALIST #89, MARCH-APRIL 1971.

FILIPINO FOOD

After swearing we won't take anything else into the Last Supplement--no more time! no more room! No more!--we arrive at the office and discover these nice little wooden-covered packages tied with hemp cord, and a note "Dear Ken and Paul: Gene Schoenfeld thought you might appreciate these. Ed Badajos drew 'FILIPINO FOOD'. This is a limited edition 1000, though the paperback will be out shortly. ($1.25) Yours, David Dawdly."

We united the string, figuring it's a cookbook, some kind of esoteric food trip, then, BAM we're into this fantastic saga of Modern Man in Search of a Soul, any soul at all! Done entirely in ink drawings, this book takes you on a series of trips that makes your eyes pop and your brain burn. Badajos is like a cross between Kafka and Burroughs gifted with the sustained precision of Escher. The book is a joy and I thank whoever sent it our way.

—Ken Kesey

It made me say "Far out!" for the first time.

—Paul Krassner

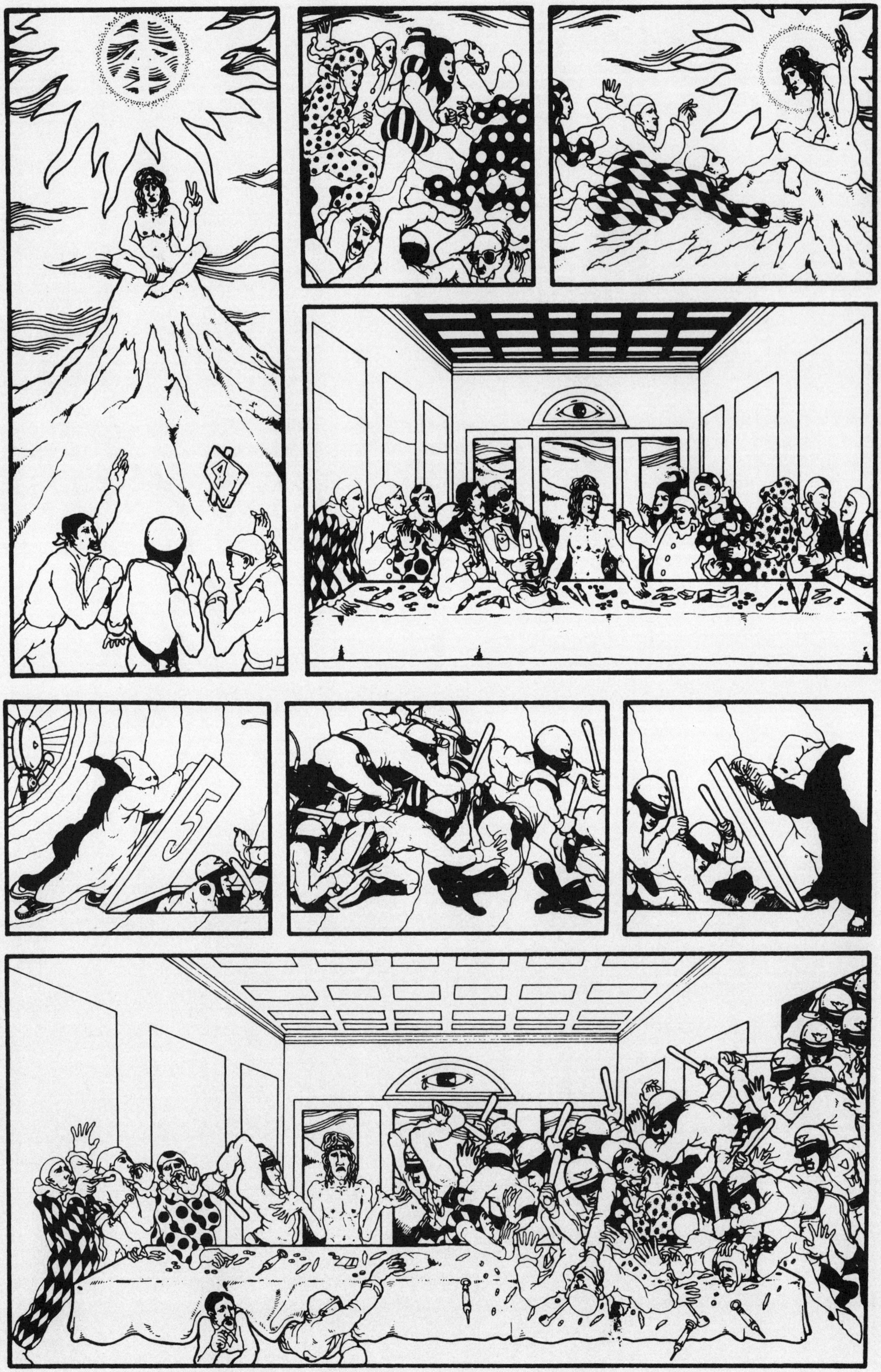
4
5

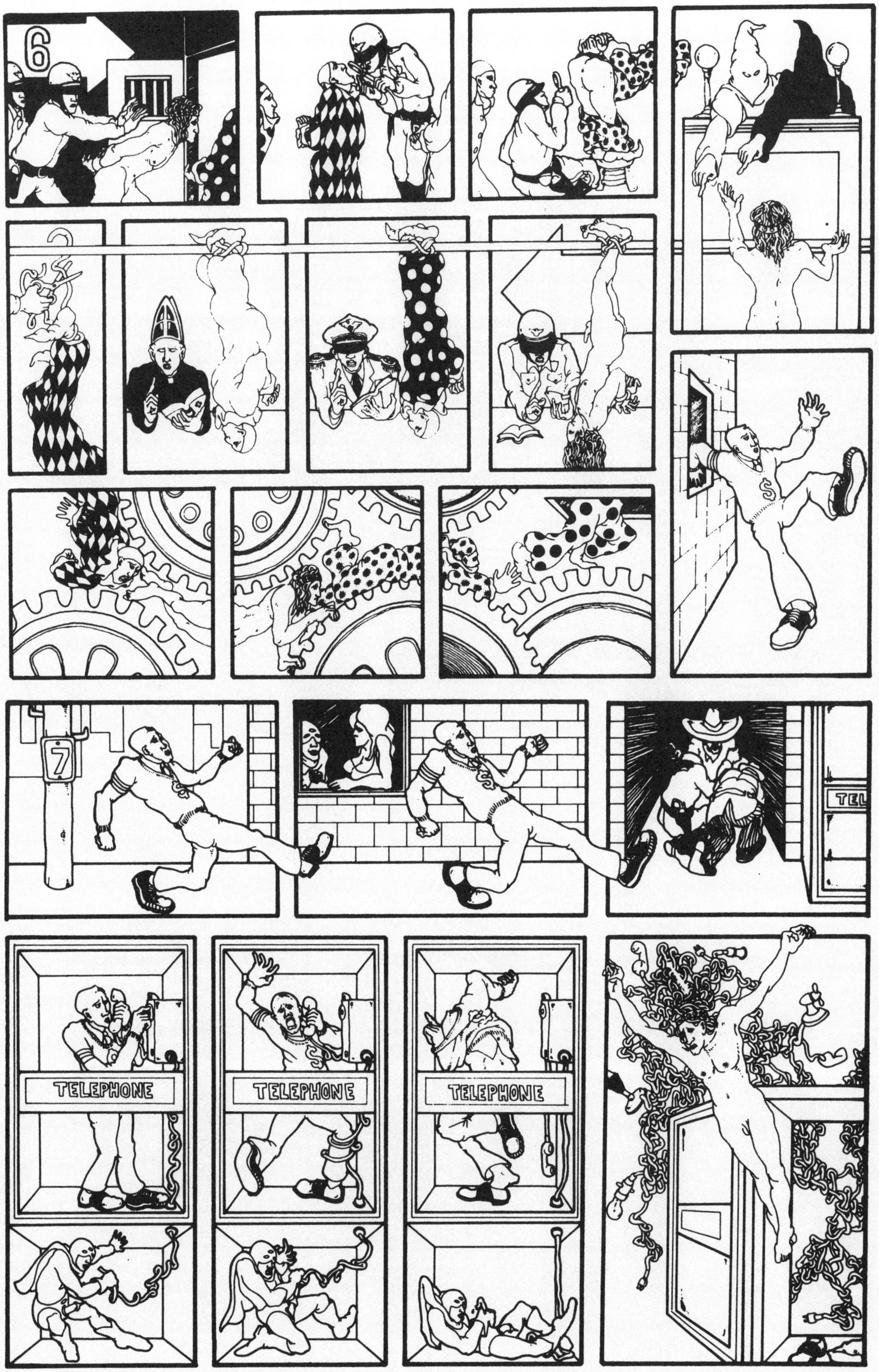
6
7
TELEPHONE
TELEPHONE
TELEPHONE

TOOLS FROM MY CHEST
FIRE DEPT

THE REALIST #89, MARCH-APRIL 1971.

THE POPE'S INCENSED
THE CLERGY RAVES
BUT NEVERTHELESS
JESUS SHAVES!

THE REALIST #89, MARCH-APRIL 1971.

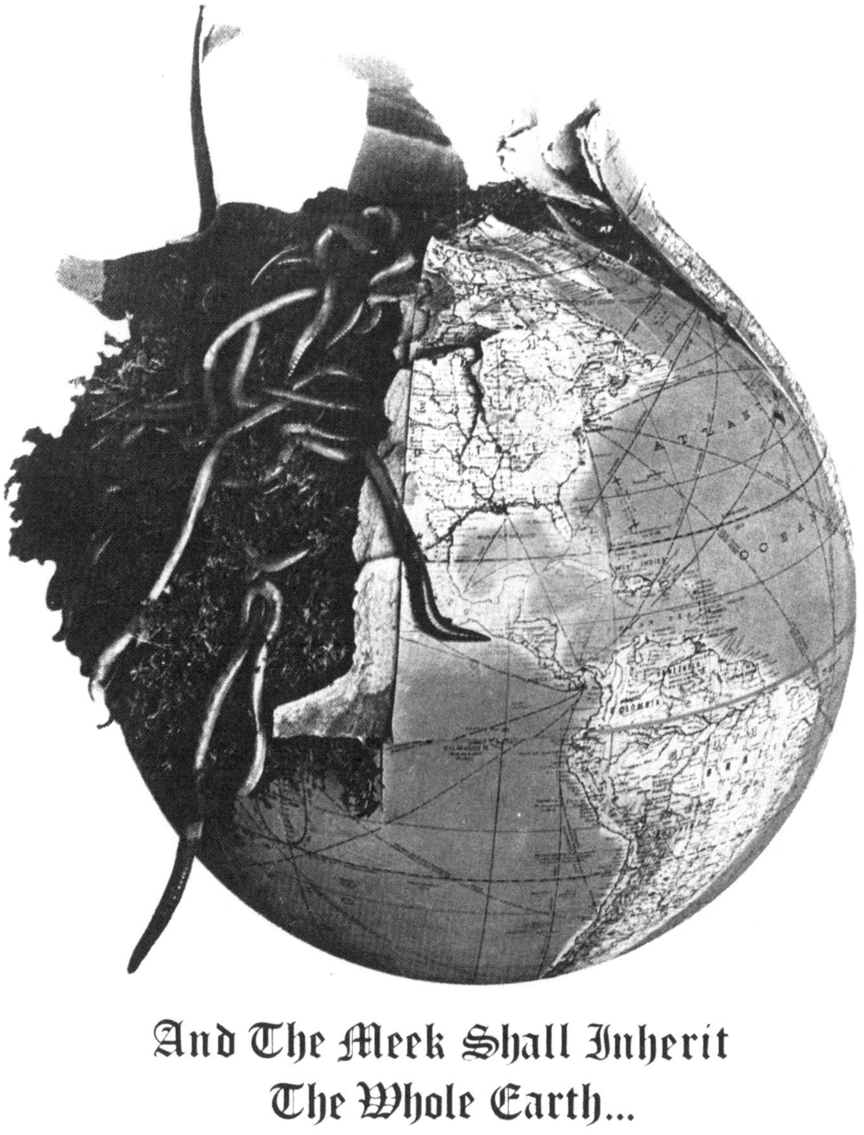
And The Meek Shall Inherit
The Whole Earth...

THE REALIST #89, MARCH-APRIL 1971.

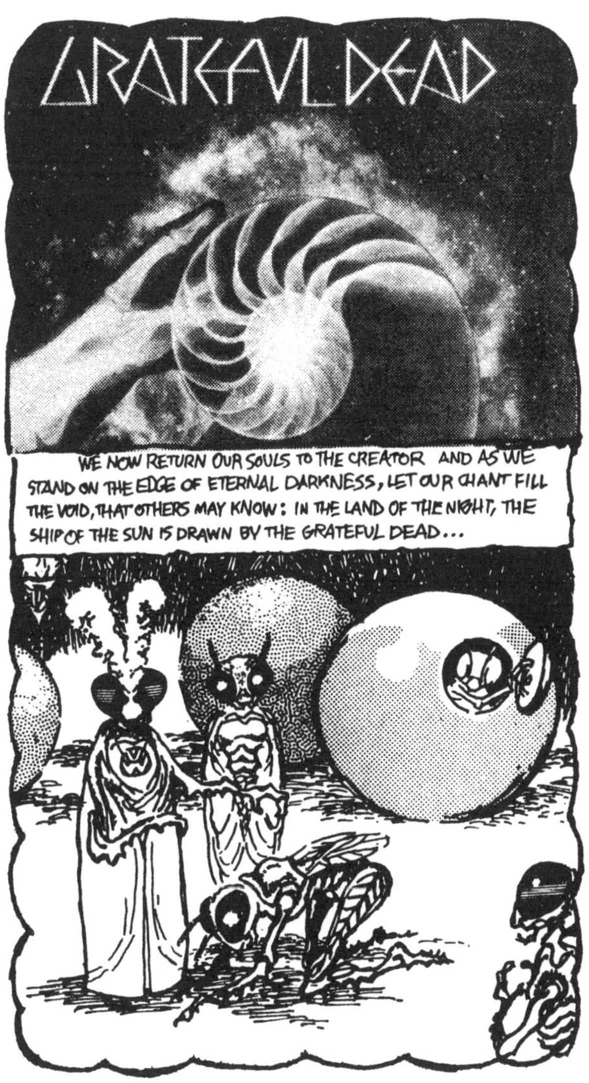
GRATEFUL DEAD
WE NOW RETURN OUR SOULS TO THE CREATOR AND AS WE STAND ON THE EDGE OF ETERNAL DARKNESS, LET OUR CHANT FILL THE VOID, THAT OTHERS MAY KNOW: IN THE LAND OF THE NIGHT, THE SHIP OF THE SUN IS DRAWN BY THE GRATEFUL DEAD...

THE REALIST #89, MARCH-APRIL 1971.

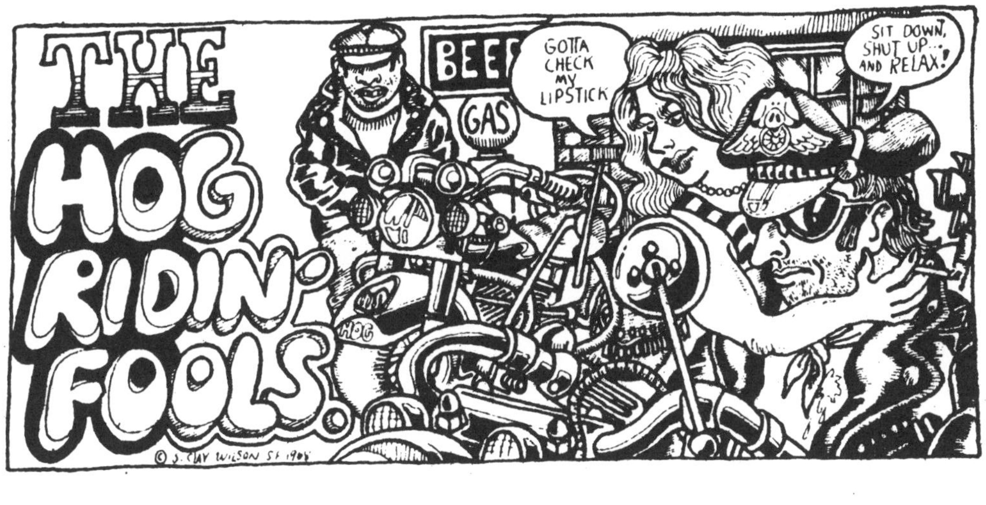
THE HOG RIDIN' FOOLS.
BEER
GAS
GOTTA CHECK MY LIPSTICK
SIT DOWN, SHUT UP... AND RELAX!

S. CLAY WILSON. THE REALIST #89, MARCH-APRIL 1971.

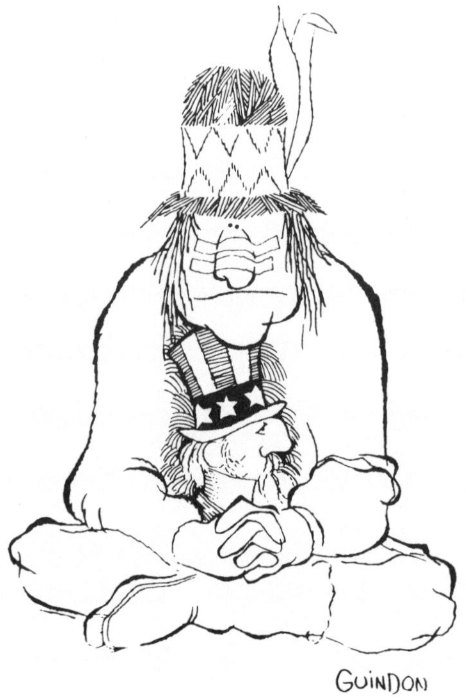
GUINDON

"Any people anywhere, being inclined and having the power, have the right to rise up, and shake off the existing government, and form a new one that suits them better. This is a most valuable, a most sacred right--a right, which we hope and believe, is to liberate the world."
—Abraham Lincoln

RICHARD GUINDON. THE REALIST #89, MARCH-APRIL 1971.

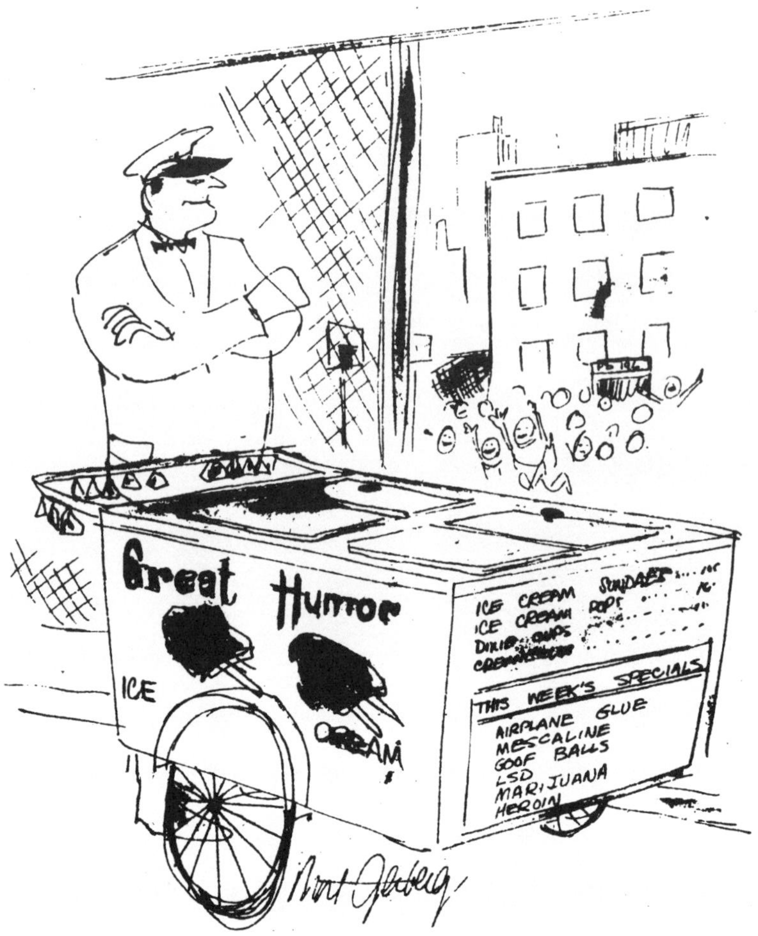
Great Humor
ICE CREAM
ICE CREAM SUNDAES
ICE CREAM POPS
THIS WEEK'S SPECIALS
AIRPLANE GLUE
MESCALINE
GOOF BALLS
LSD
MARIJUANA
HEROIN
Mort Gerberg

MORT GERBERG. THE REALIST #89, MARCH-APRIL 1971.

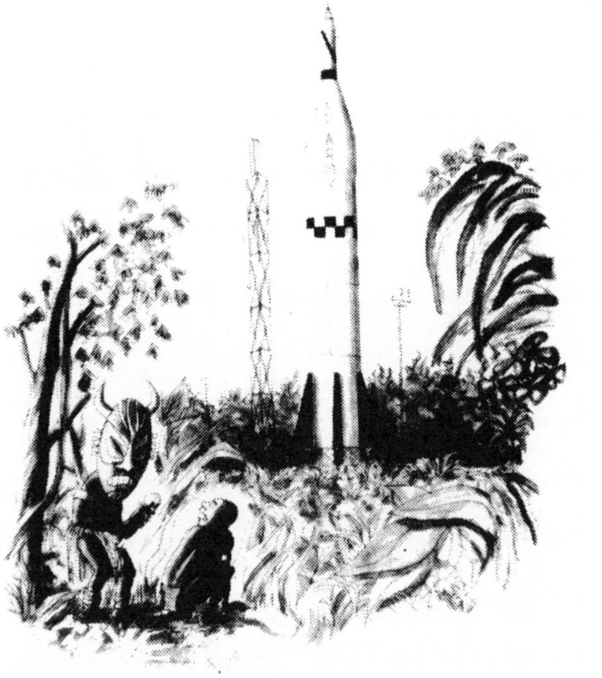

"Wait till they light the fire. It's the most fantastic fertility rite you've ever seen."

THE REALIST #89, MARCH-APRIL 1971.

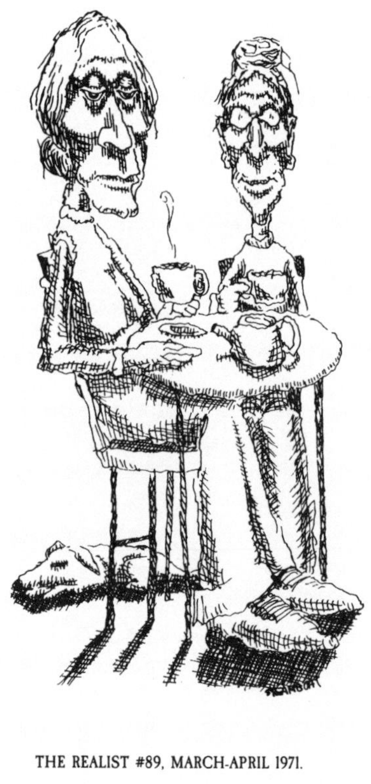

THE REALIST #89, MARCH-APRIL 1971.

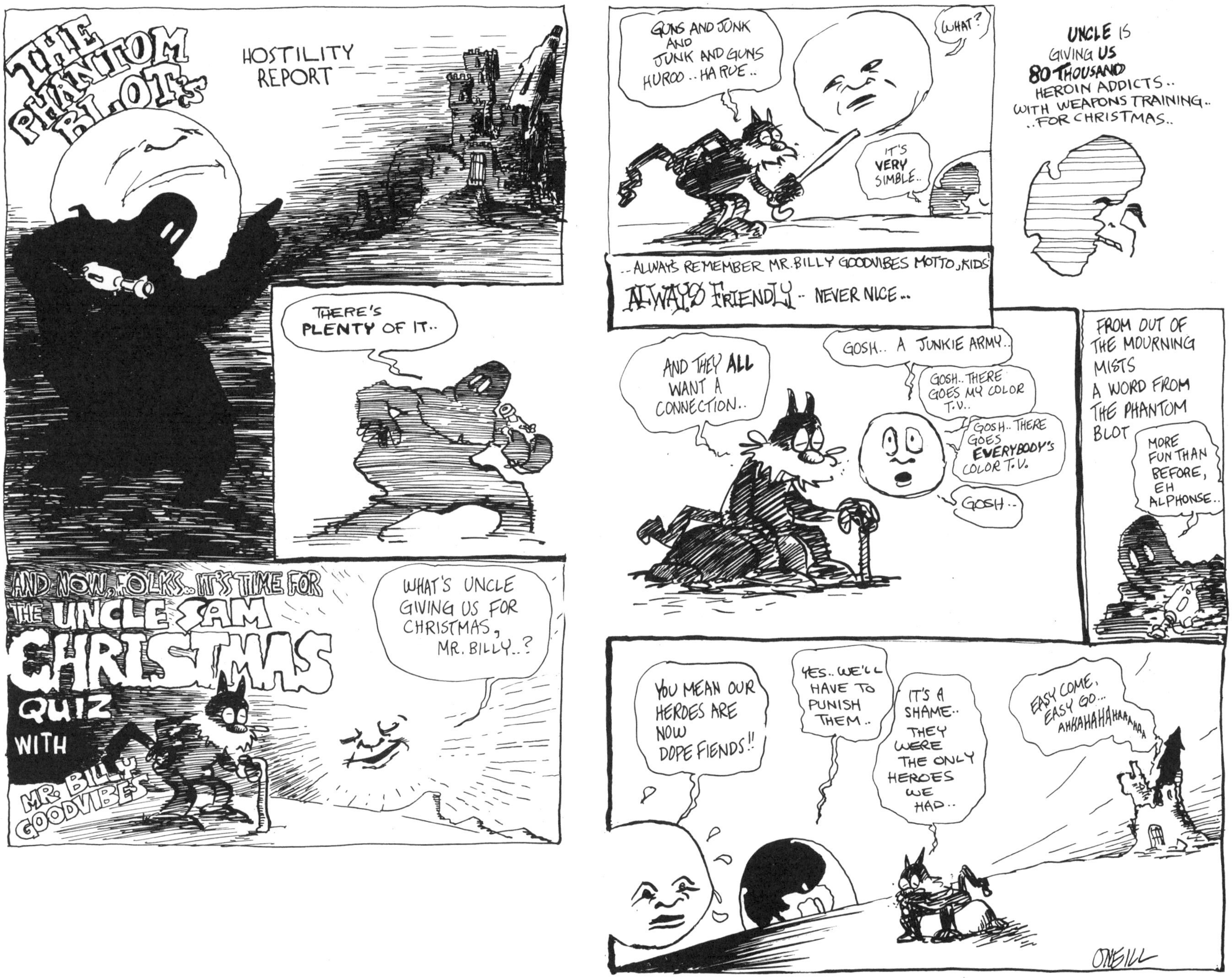
THE PHANTOM BLOT's
HOSTILITY REPORT
THERE'S PLENTY OF IT..
AND NOW, FOLKS.. IT'S TIME FOR THE UNCLE SAM CHRISTMAS QUIZ WITH MR. BILLY GOODVIBES
WHAT'S UNCLE GIVING US FOR CHRISTMAS, MR. BILLY..?
GUNS AND JUNK AND JUNK AND GUNS HUROO.. HA RUE..
WHAT?
IT'S VERY SIMBLE..
UNCLE IS GIVING US 80 THOUSAND HEROIN ADDICTS.. WITH WEAPONS TRAINING.. ..FOR CHRISTMAS..
..ALWAYS REMEMBER MR. BILLY GOODVIBES MOTTO, KIDS: ALWAYS FRIENDLY.. NEVER NICE..
AND THEY ALL WANT A CONNECTION..
GOSH.. A JUNKIE ARMY..
GOSH.. THERE GOES MY COLOR T.V..
GOSH.. THERE GOES EVERYBODY'S COLOR T.V.
GOSH..
FROM OUT OF THE MOURNING MISTS A WORD FROM THE PHANTOM BLOT
MORE FUN THAN BEFORE, EH ALPHONSE..
YOU MEAN OUR HEROES ARE NOW DOPE FIENDS!!
YES.. WE'LL HAVE TO PUNISH THEM..
IT'S A SHAME.. THEY WERE THE ONLY HEROES WE HAD..
EASY COME, EASY GO... AHHAHAHAHAHAHAHA
O'NEILL

DAN O'NEILL. THE REALIST #90, MAY-JUNE 1971.

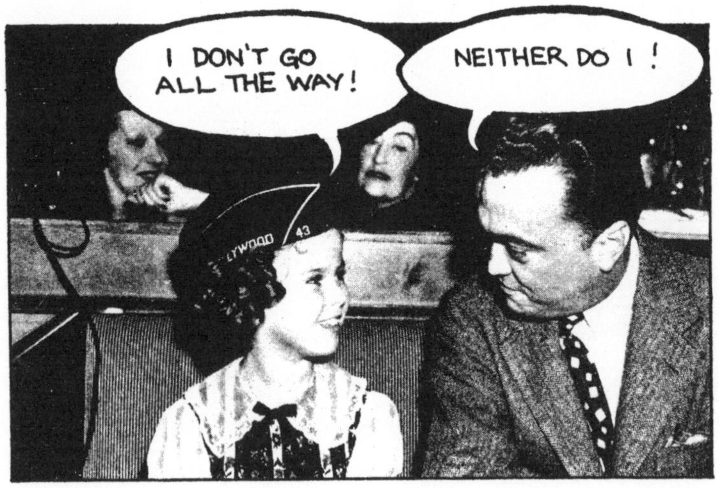
I DON'T GO ALL THE WAY!
NEITHER DO I!

THE REALIST #90, MAY-JUNE 1971.

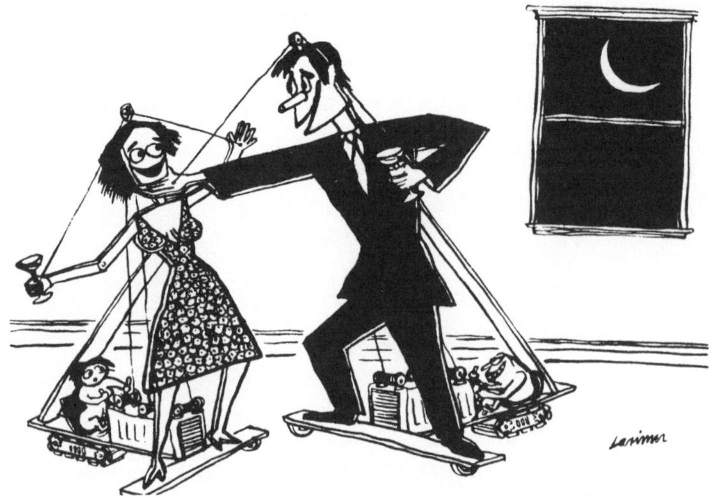

ILLEGIBLE SIGNATURE. THE REALIST #90, MAY-JUNE 1971.

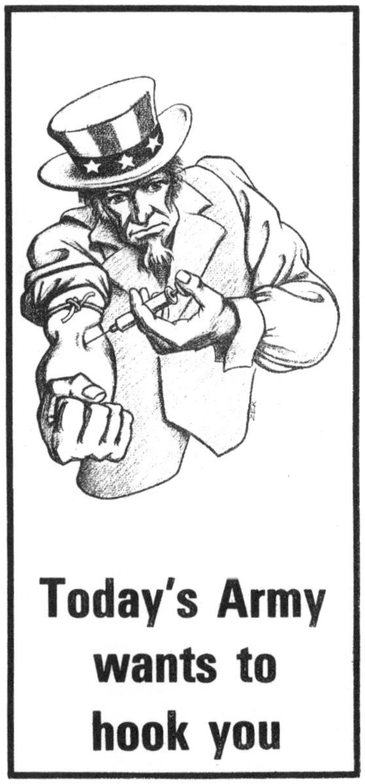
Today's Army
wants to
hook you

ZEK. THE REALIST #90, MAY-JUNE 1971.

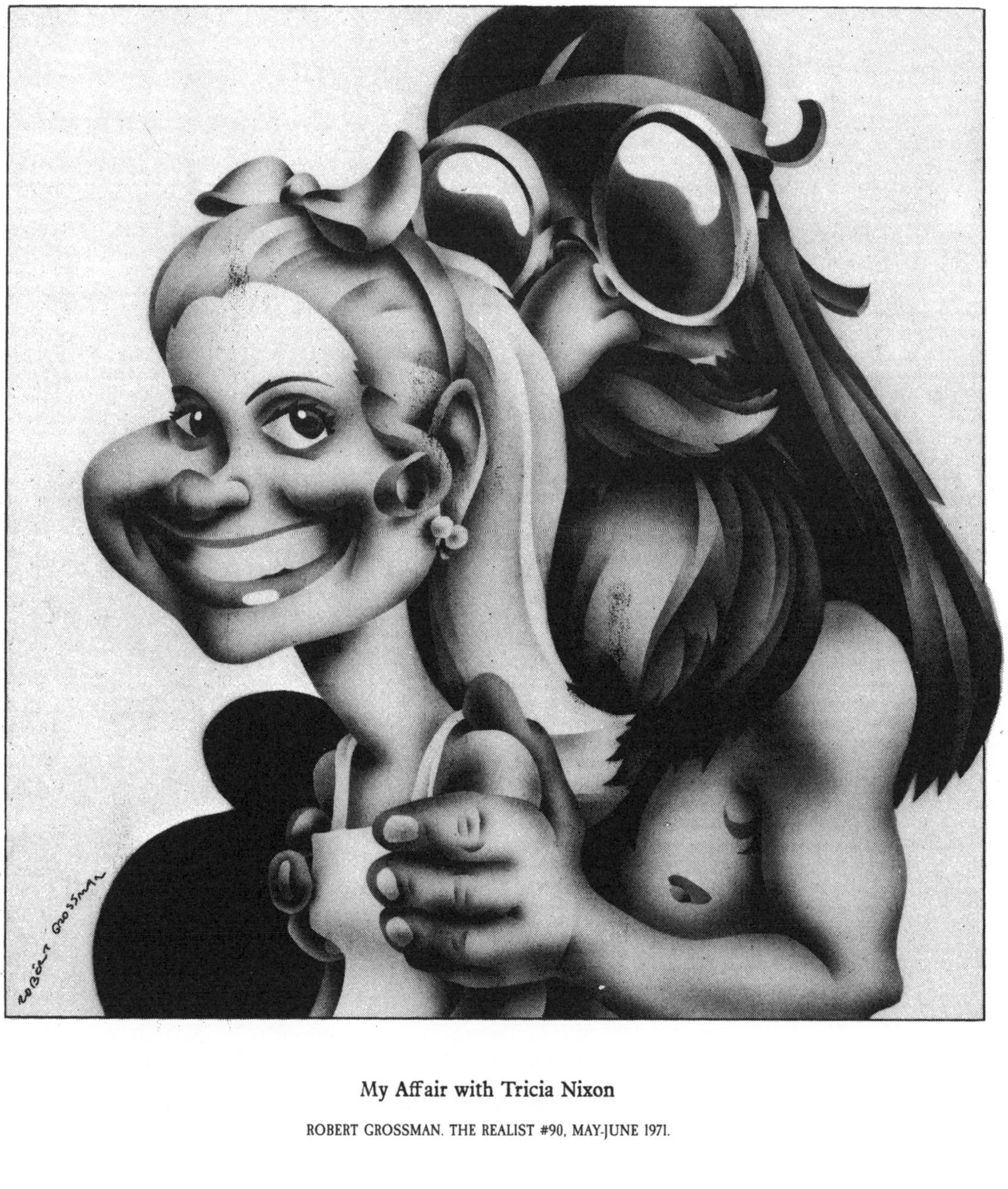

My Affair with Tricia Nixon

ROBERT GROSSMAN. THE REALIST #90, MAY-JUNE 1971.

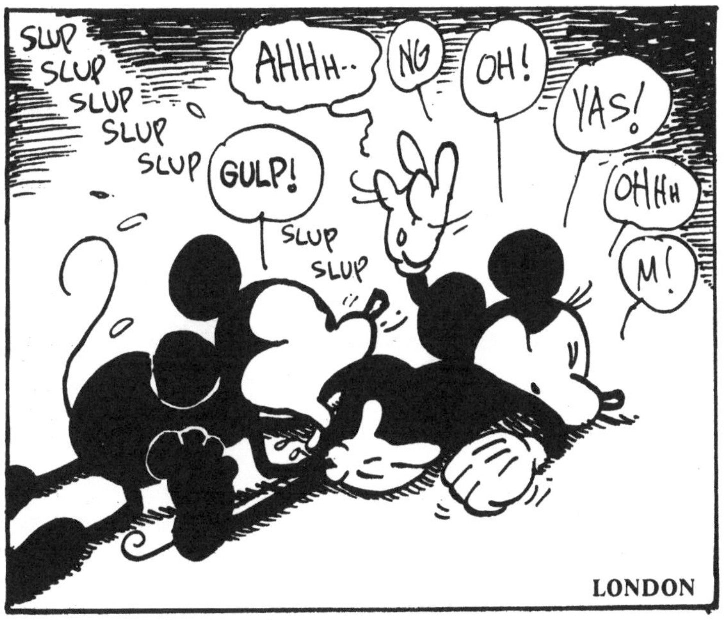
SLUP
SLUP
SLUP
SLUP
SLUP
AHHH..
NG
OH!
YAS!
GULP!
SLUP
SLUP
OHHH
M!
LONDON

BOBBY LONDON. THE REALIST #90, MAY-JUNE 1971.

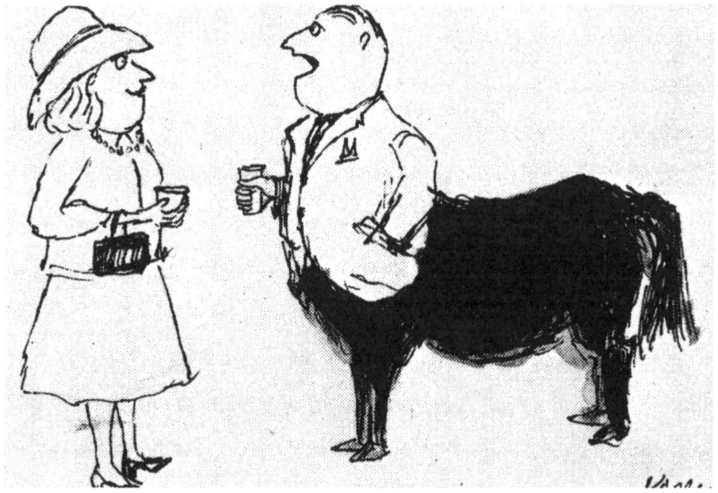

"I find it very difficult to be an intellectual
in the United States."

ED KOREN. THE REALIST #90, MAY-JUNE 1971.

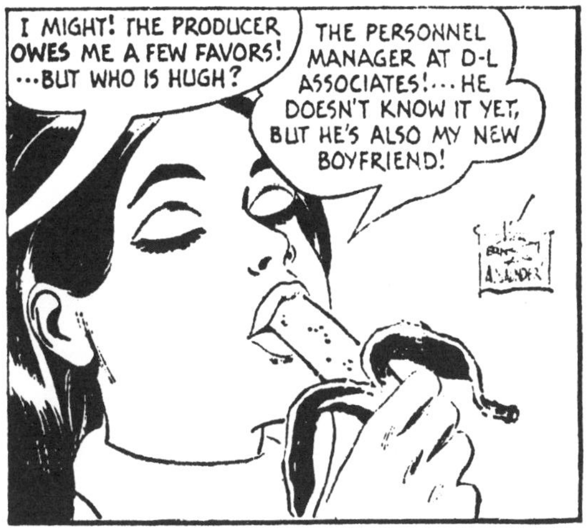
I MIGHT! THE PRODUCER OWES ME A FEW FAVORS! ...BUT WHO IS HUGH?
THE PERSONNEL MANAGER AT D-L ASSOCIATES!... HE DOESN'T KNOW IT YET, BUT HE'S ALSO MY NEW BOYFRIEND!

Fellatio Comes to Mary Worth

ALLEN SAUNDERS/KEN ERNST. THE REALIST #90, MAY-JUNE 1971.

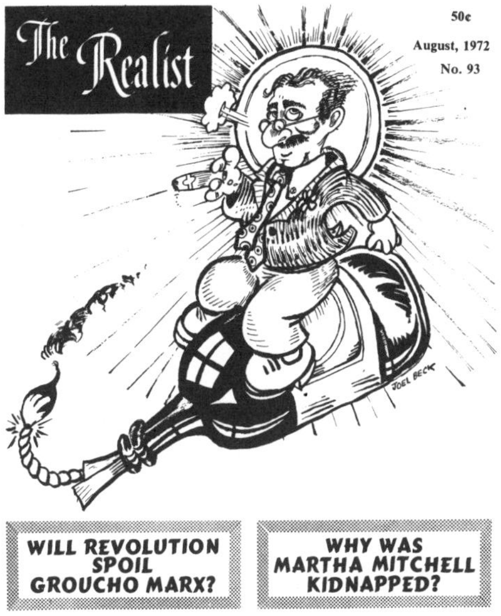
The Realist
50¢
August, 1972
No. 93
WILL REVOLUTION SPOIL GROUCHO MARX?
WHY WAS MARTHA MITCHELL KIDNAPPED?

JOEL BECK. THE REALIST #93, AUGUST 1972.

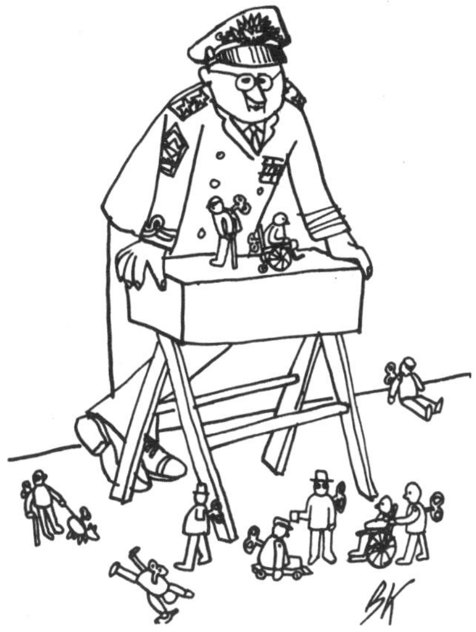

B. KLIBAN. THE REALIST #90, MAY-JUNE 1971.

RICHARD GUINDON.
THE REALIST #92-B.
MARCH-APRIL 1972.

ADVERTISING

EVERY PRODUCT IN AMERICA IS MEANINGFUL AND "TODAY"—

THERE WAS THE DODGE REBELLION,

THEN FLAIR WROTE IT LIKE IT IS.

LYSOL NOW KILLS "ENVIRONMENTAL" GERMS.—

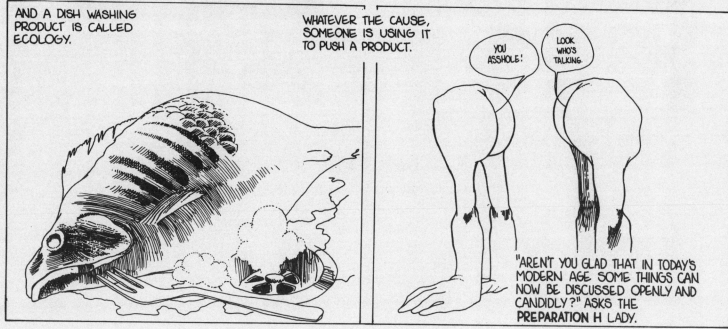

AND A DISH WASHING PRODUCT IS CALLED ECOLOGY.

WHATEVER THE CAUSE, SOMEONE IS USING IT TO PUSH A PRODUCT.

YOU ASSHOLE!

LOOK WHO'S TALKING.

"AREN'T YOU GLAD THAT IN TODAY'S MODERN AGE SOME THINGS CAN NOW BE DISCUSSED OPENLY AND CANDIDLY?" ASKS THE PREPARATION H LADY.

THE OIL SPILLS WERE AN ADVERTISING STUNT. WITH EVERY FULL TANK OF GAS YOUR GULF DEALER GIVES YOU FREE AN OIL COVERED DUCK.
NOW GULF HAS MADE IT POSSIBLE FOR YOU TO DO SOMETHING ABOUT ECOLOGY!
TAKE IT HOME, CLEAN IT AND THEN SET IT FREE!
IT'S GULF'S REVENGE FOR OUR USING THEIR GAS STATIONS AS TOILETS ALL THESE YEARS.
CONSIDER THE FACT THAT PEOPLE ARE BIO-DEGRADABLE...
AND NOW THIS MESSAGE FROM FERGUSON'S FUNERAL HOME WITH SOME THOUGHTS ABOUT RECYCLING.
THE DAY AFTER THIS PANEL WAS FINISHED, A NEWBORN INFANT WAS FOUND DEAD IN A GOODWILL INDUSTRIES COLLECTION BOX IN ST. PAUL, MINNESOTA.
WHADAYA GOT IN BACK?
SECTION B
6 NIGGERS, 12 HIPPIES AND SOME CRIPPLES

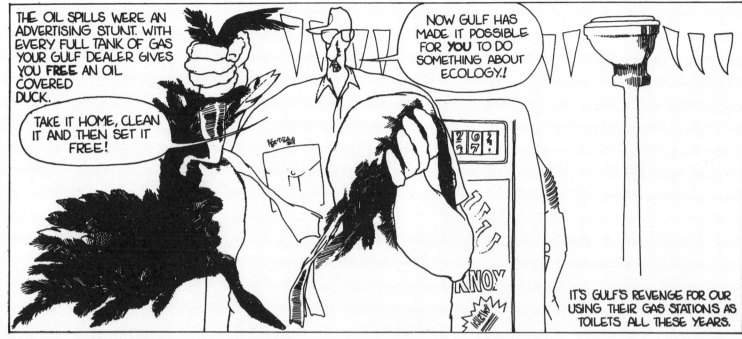

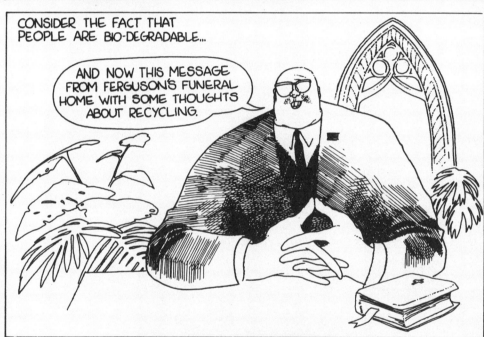

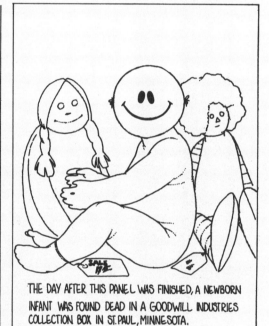

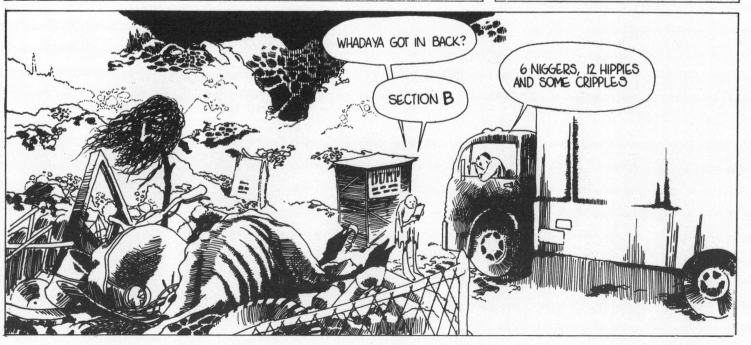

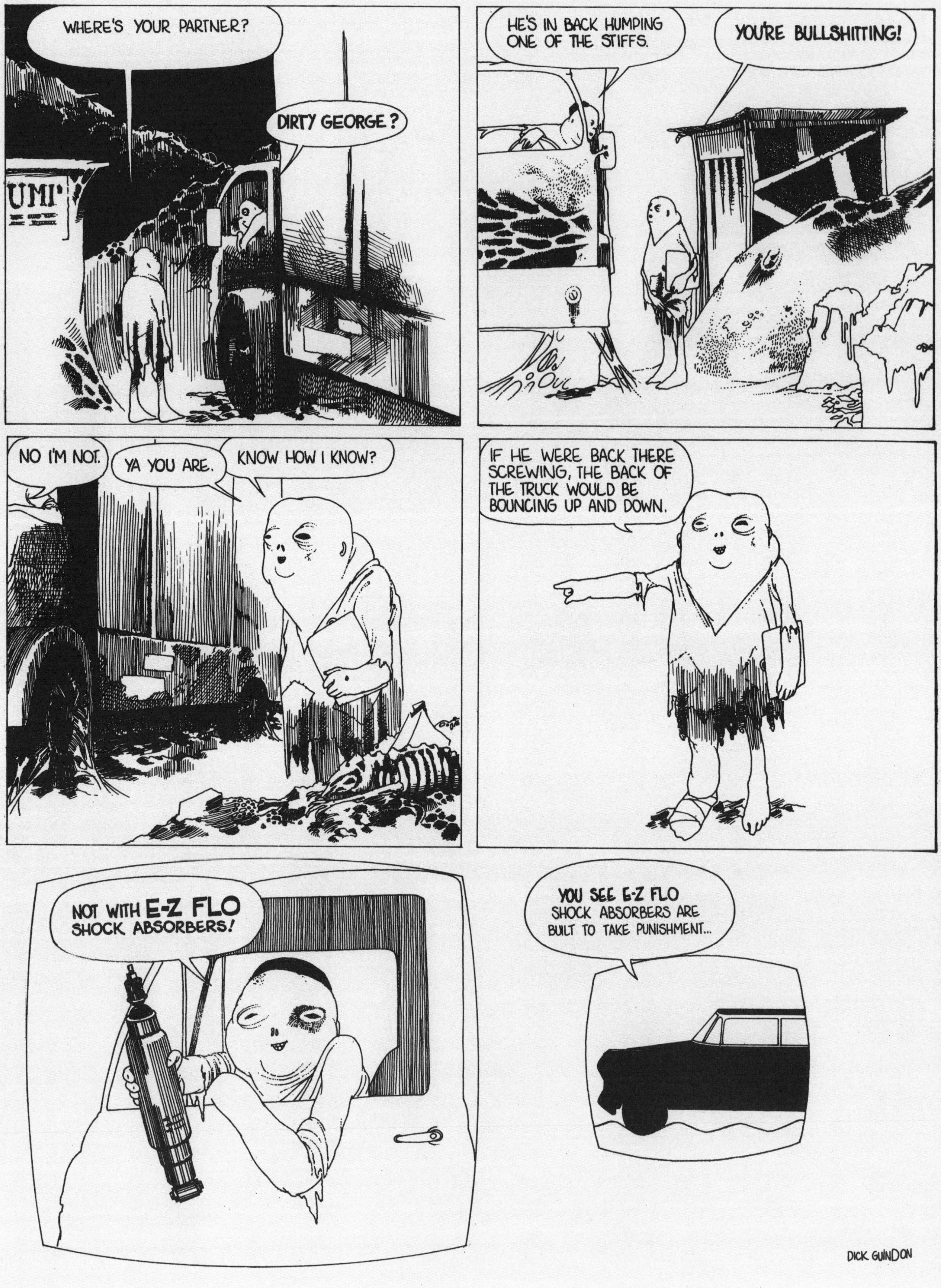
WHERE'S YOUR PARTNER?
DIRTY GEORGE?
UMP
HE'S IN BACK HUMPING ONE OF THE STIFFS.
YOU'RE BULLSHITTING!
NO I'M NOT.
YA YOU ARE.
KNOW HOW I KNOW?
IF HE WERE BACK THERE SCREWING, THE BACK OF THE TRUCK WOULD BE BOUNCING UP AND DOWN.
NOT WITH E-Z FLO SHOCK ABSORBERS!
YOU SEE E-Z FLO SHOCK ABSORBERS ARE BUILT TO TAKE PUNISHMENT...
DICK GUINDON

BOOGIE and BONS
GET AWAY FROM THAT TIT..
NO.
S. CLAY WILSON 1971-72
THE YEAR IS 1762... TWO BOOGIE MEN FIGHT ABOUT A CAPTIVE DUMPLING.
NUK..
HFF
CNK
FEEESH
YARRGH
YOUR FRILLY BLOWS FAIL TO STOP ME.. IM GONNA SCARF BOTH GAMS.
DIDNT KNOW I HAD MY EYE-SCREW DID YA?
THAT FOUL CREATURE IS NUZZLIN MY SHOE BOW.
THE FETISH SAVIOR SUDDENLY CONJURED UP....
PARF
VIT
VIT
LET NO BOOGIE MAN TOUCH HIS LIPS TO THESE FRILLY BOWS.
CUT THESE ROPES!
SNURT

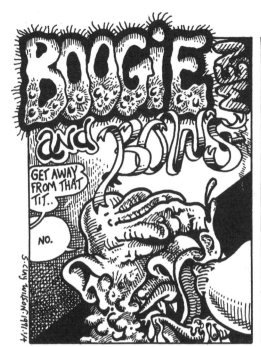

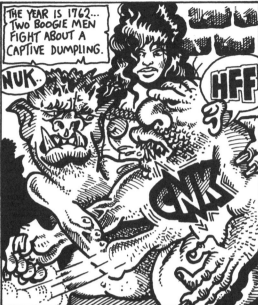

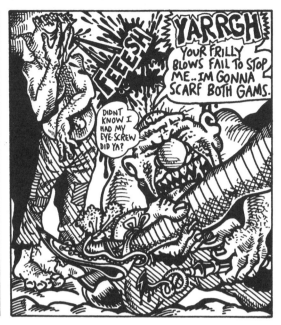

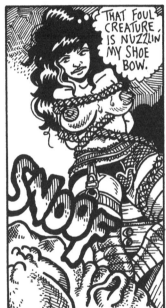

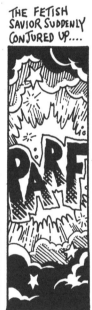

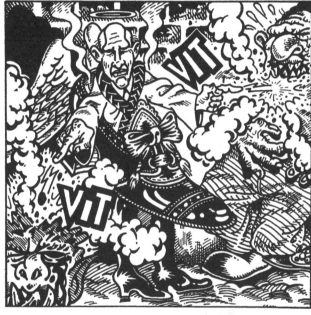

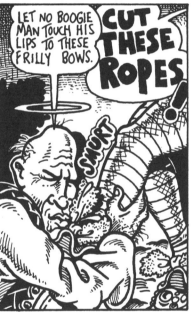

S. CLAY WILSON. THE REALIST #93, AUGUST 1972.

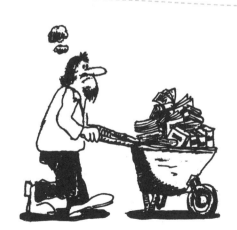

THE REALIST #92-B, MARCH-APRIL 1972.

DAN O'NEILL. THE REALIST #93, AUGUST 1972.

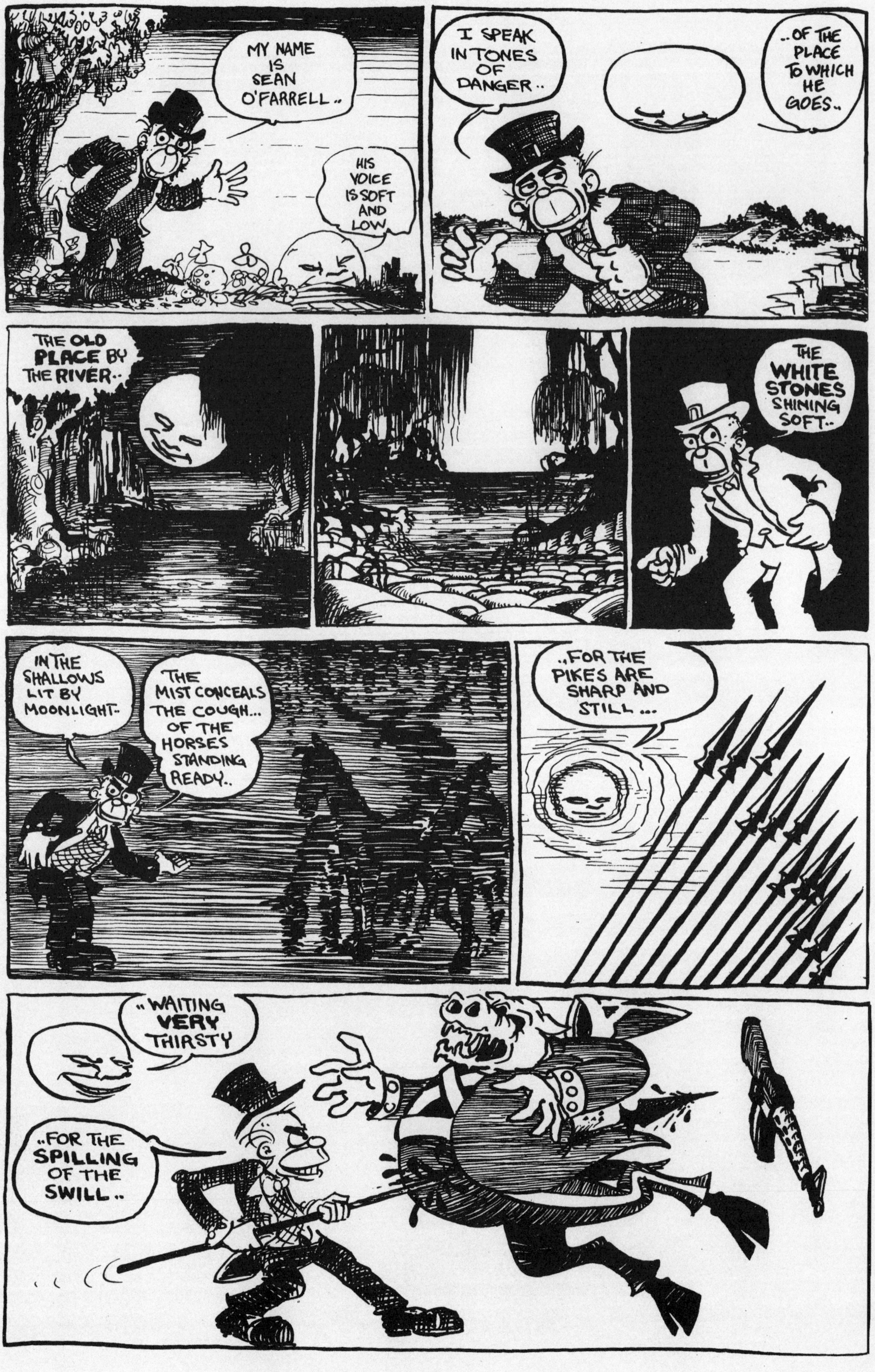
MY NAME IS SEAN O'FARRELL..
HIS VOICE IS SOFT AND LOW
I SPEAK IN TONES OF DANGER..
..OF THE PLACE TO WHICH HE GOES..
THE OLD PLACE BY THE RIVER..
THE WHITE STONES SHINING SOFT..
IN THE SHALLOWS LIT BY MOONLIGHT..
THE MIST CONCEALS THE COUGH... OF THE HORSES STANDING READY..
..FOR THE PIKES ARE SHARP AND STILL ...
..WAITING VERY THIRSTY
..FOR THE SPILLING OF THE SWILL..

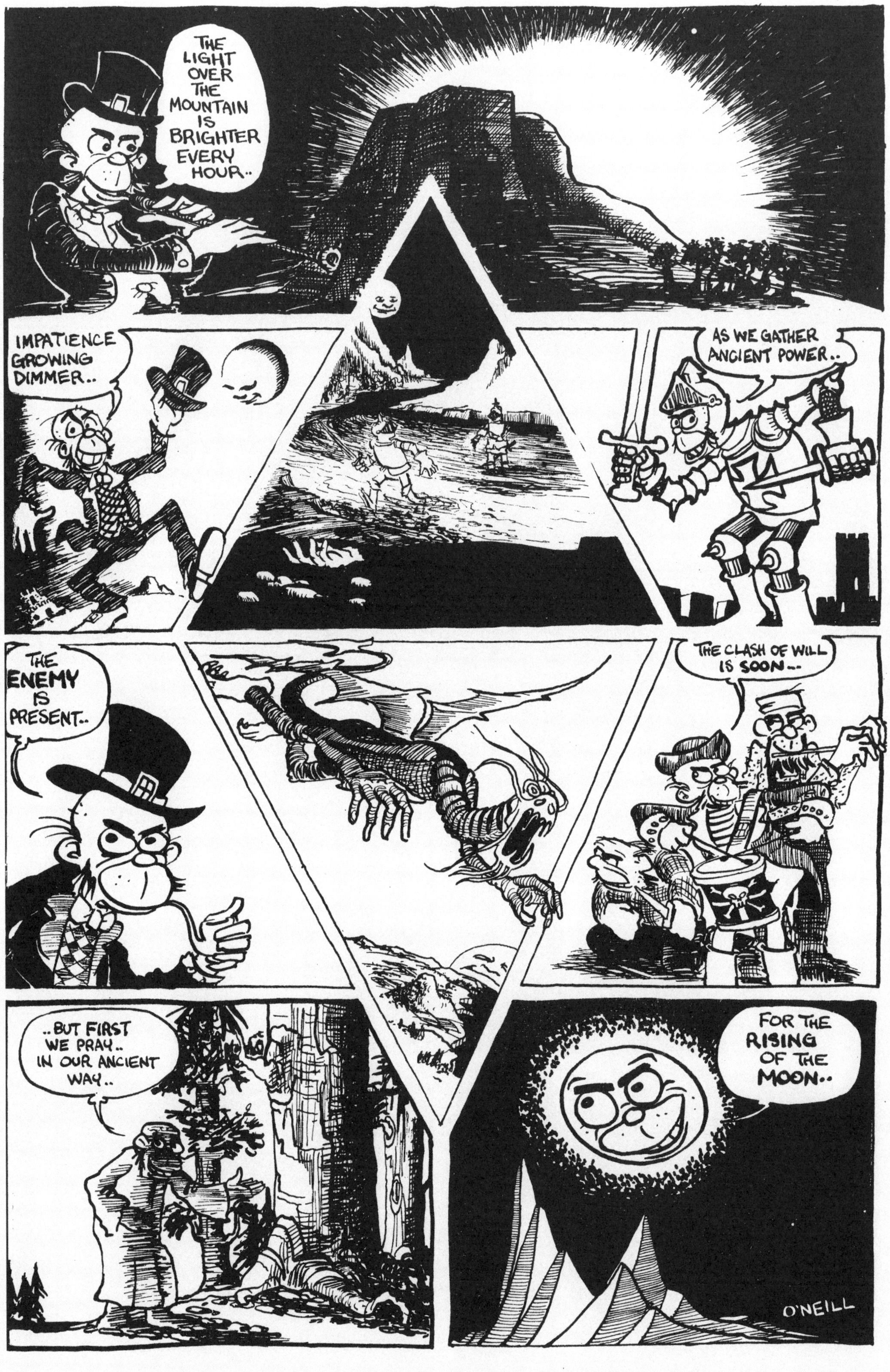
THE LIGHT OVER THE MOUNTAIN IS BRIGHTER EVERY HOUR..
IMPATIENCE GROWING DIMMER..
AS WE GATHER ANCIENT POWER..
THE ENEMY IS PRESENT..
THE CLASH OF WILL IS SOON...
..BUT FIRST WE PRAY.. IN OUR ANCIENT WAY..
FOR THE RISING OF THE MOON..
O'NEILL

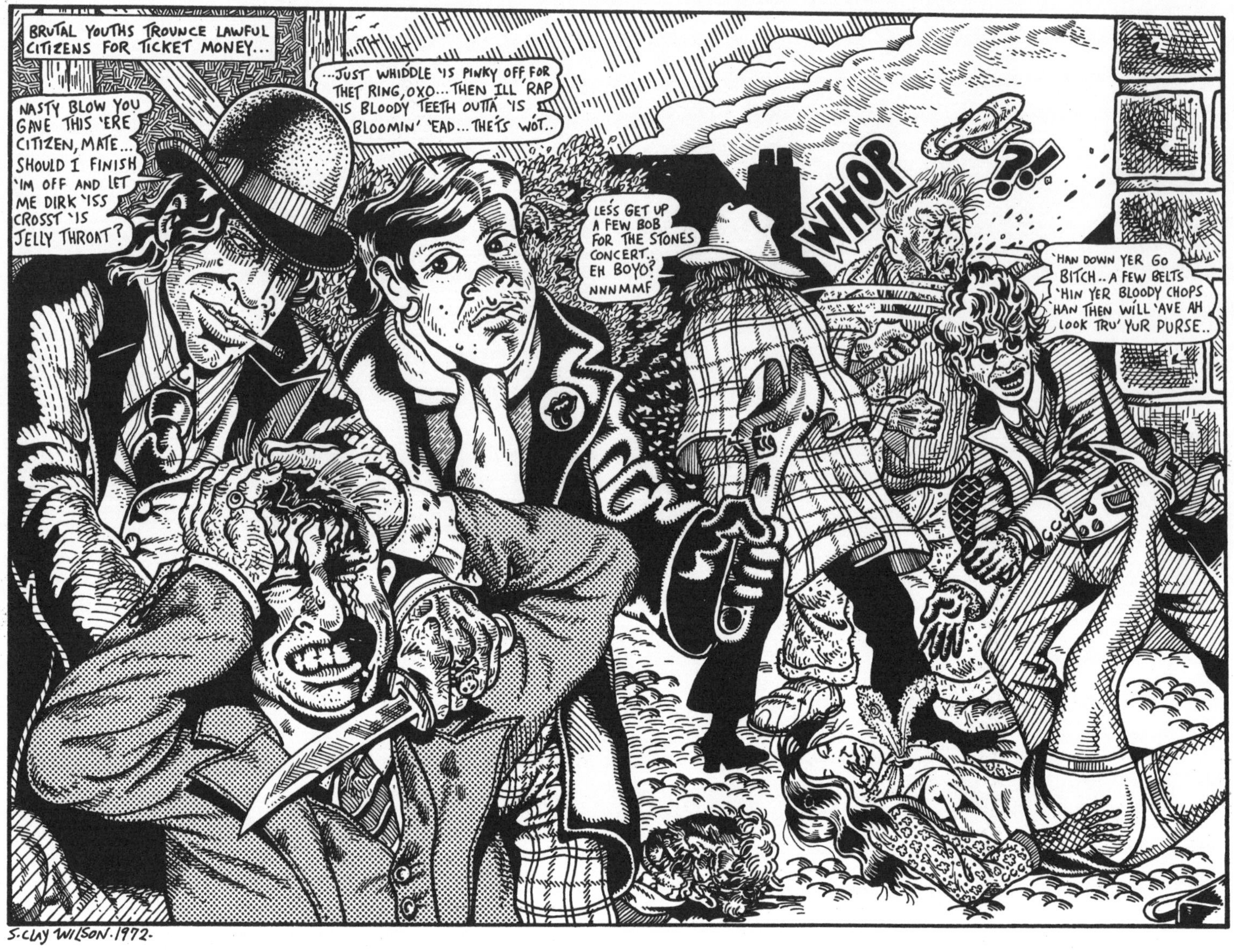
BRUTAL YOUTHS TROUNCE LAWFUL CITIZENS FOR TICKET MONEY...
NASTY BLOW YOU GAVE THIS 'ERE CITIZEN, MATE... SHOULD I FINISH 'IM OFF AND LET ME DIRK 'ISS CROSST 'IS JELLY THROAT?
...JUST WHIDDLE 'IS PINKY OFF FOR THET RING, OXO... THEN ILL 'RAP 'IS BLOODY TEETH OUTTA 'IS BLOOMIN' 'EAD... THET'S WOT..
LESS GET UP A FEW BOB FOR THE STONES CONCERT.. EH BOYO? NNNMMF
WHOP
?!
'HAN DOWN YER GO BITCH.. A FEW BELTS 'HIN YER BLOODY CHOPS HAN THEN WILL 'AVE AH LOOK TRU' YUR PURSE..
S. CLAY WILSON. 1972.

S. CLAY WILSON. THE REALIST #93, AUGUST 1972.

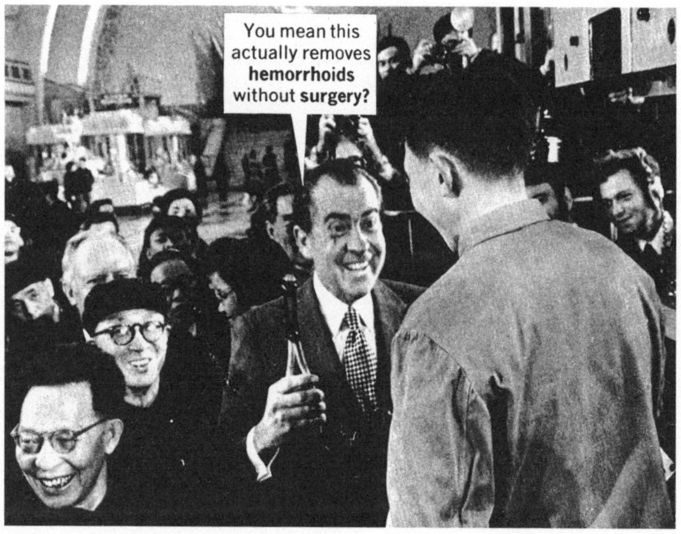
You mean this actually removes **hemorrhoids** without **surgery?**

THE REALIST #93, AUGUST 1972.

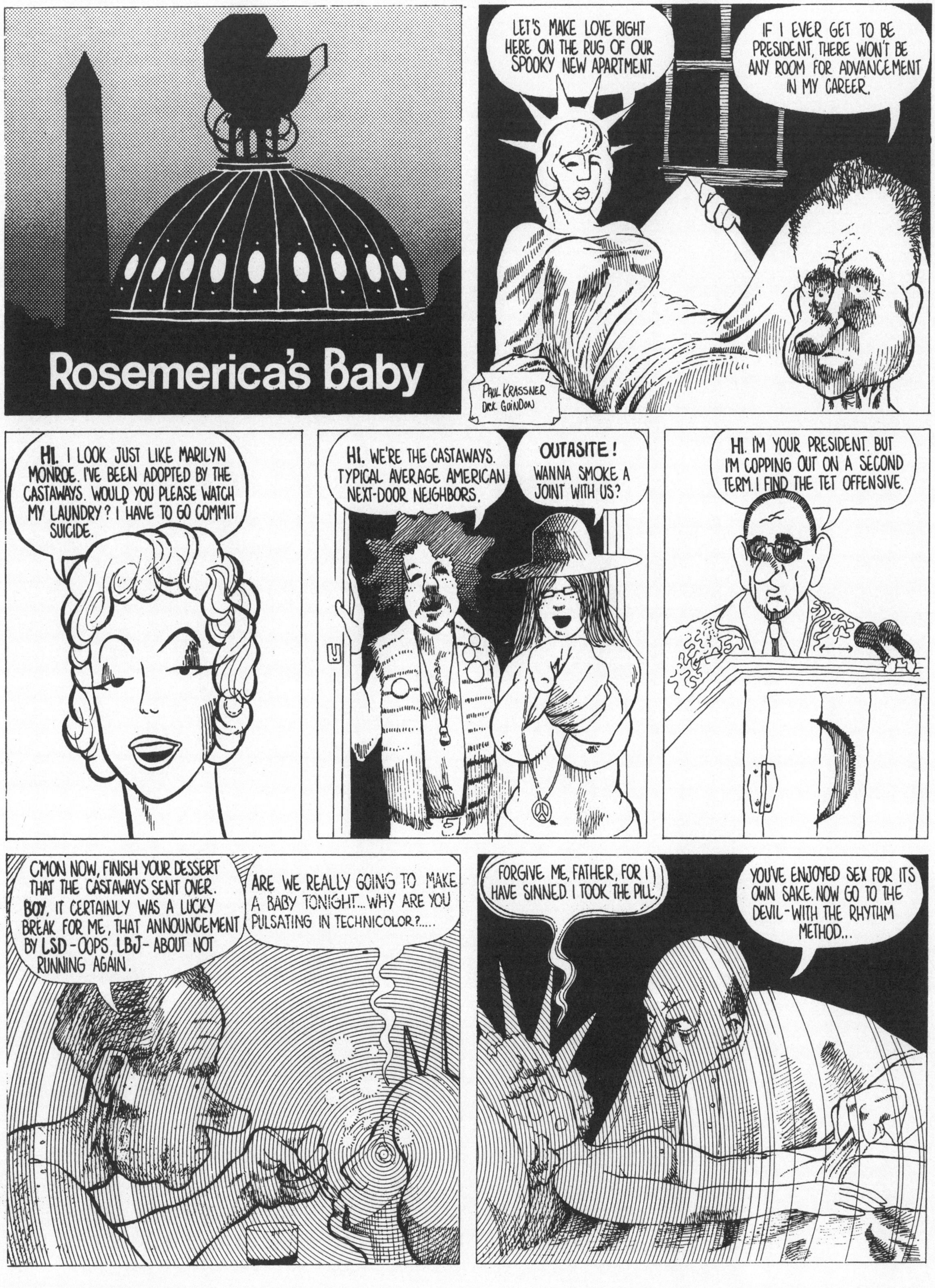
Rosemerica's Baby
LET'S MAKE LOVE RIGHT HERE ON THE RUG OF OUR SPOOKY NEW APARTMENT.
IF I EVER GET TO BE PRESIDENT, THERE WON'T BE ANY ROOM FOR ADVANCEMENT IN MY CAREER.
PAUL KRASSNER DICK GUINDON
HI. I LOOK JUST LIKE MARILYN MONROE. I'VE BEEN ADOPTED BY THE CASTAWAYS. WOULD YOU PLEASE WATCH MY LAUNDRY? I HAVE TO GO COMMIT SUICIDE.
HI. WE'RE THE CASTAWAYS. TYPICAL AVERAGE AMERICAN NEXT-DOOR NEIGHBORS.
OUTASITE! WANNA SMOKE A JOINT WITH US?
HI. I'M YOUR PRESIDENT. BUT I'M COPPING OUT ON A SECOND TERM. I FIND THE TET OFFENSIVE.
C'MON NOW, FINISH YOUR DESSERT THAT THE CASTAWAYS SENT OVER. BOY, IT CERTAINLY WAS A LUCKY BREAK FOR ME, THAT ANNOUNCEMENT BY LSD-OOPS, LBJ- ABOUT NOT RUNNING AGAIN.
ARE WE REALLY GOING TO MAKE A BABY TONIGHT...WHY ARE YOU PULSATING IN TECHNICOLOR?.....
FORGIVE ME, FATHER, FOR I HAVE SINNED. I TOOK THE PILL.
YOU'VE ENJOYED SEX FOR ITS OWN SAKE. NOW GO TO THE DEVIL-WITH THE RHYTHM METHOD...

PAUL KRASSNER AND RICHARD GUINDON.
THE REALIST #93, AUGUST 1972. *88

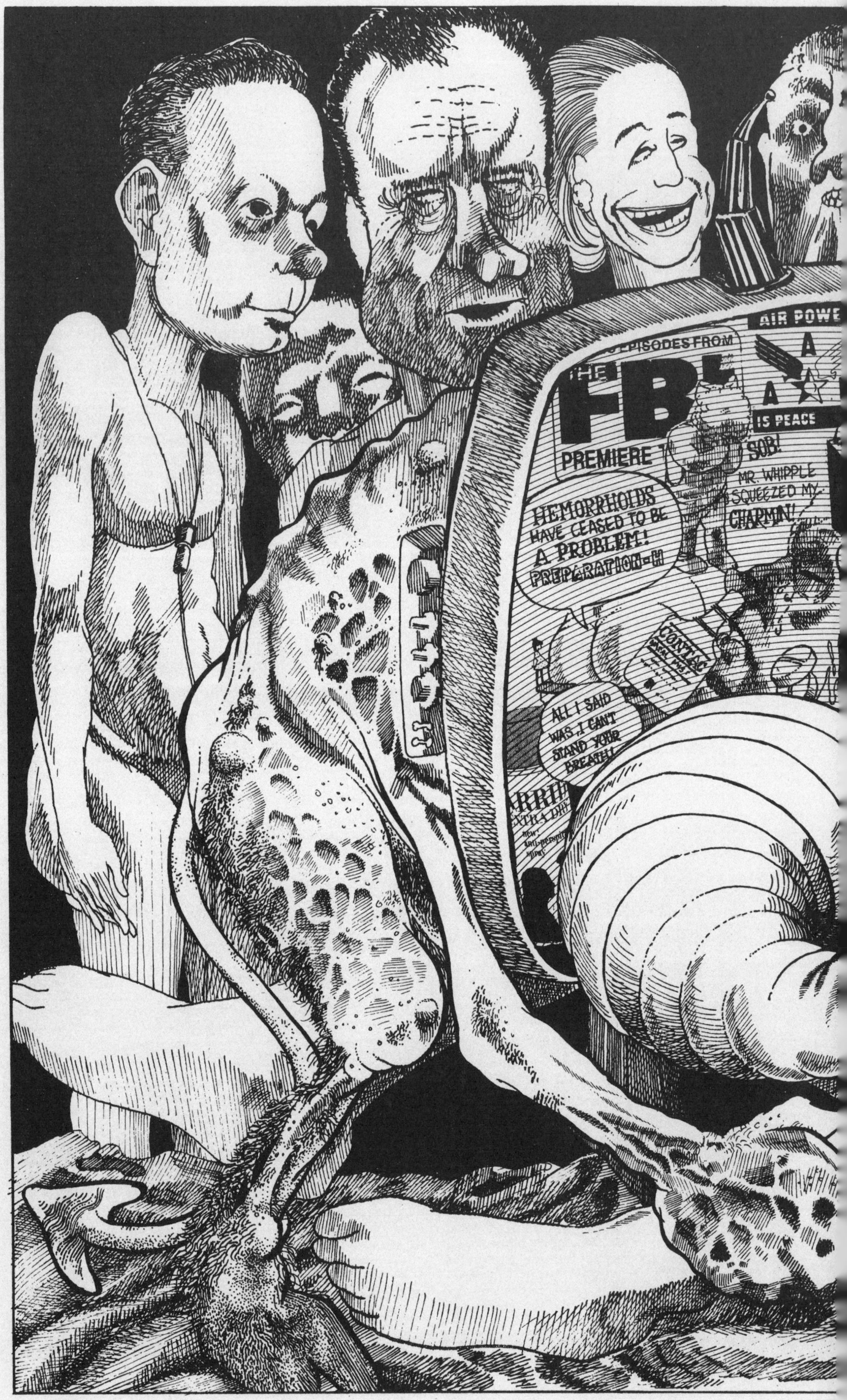
AIR POWE
IS PEACE
EPISODES FROM
THE FB
PREMIERE
SOB!
MR. WHIPPLE SQUEEZED MY CHARMIN!
HEMORRHOIDS HAVE CEASED TO BE A PROBLEM!
PREPARATION-H
CONTAC
ALL I SAID WAS I CANT STAND YOUR BREATH!

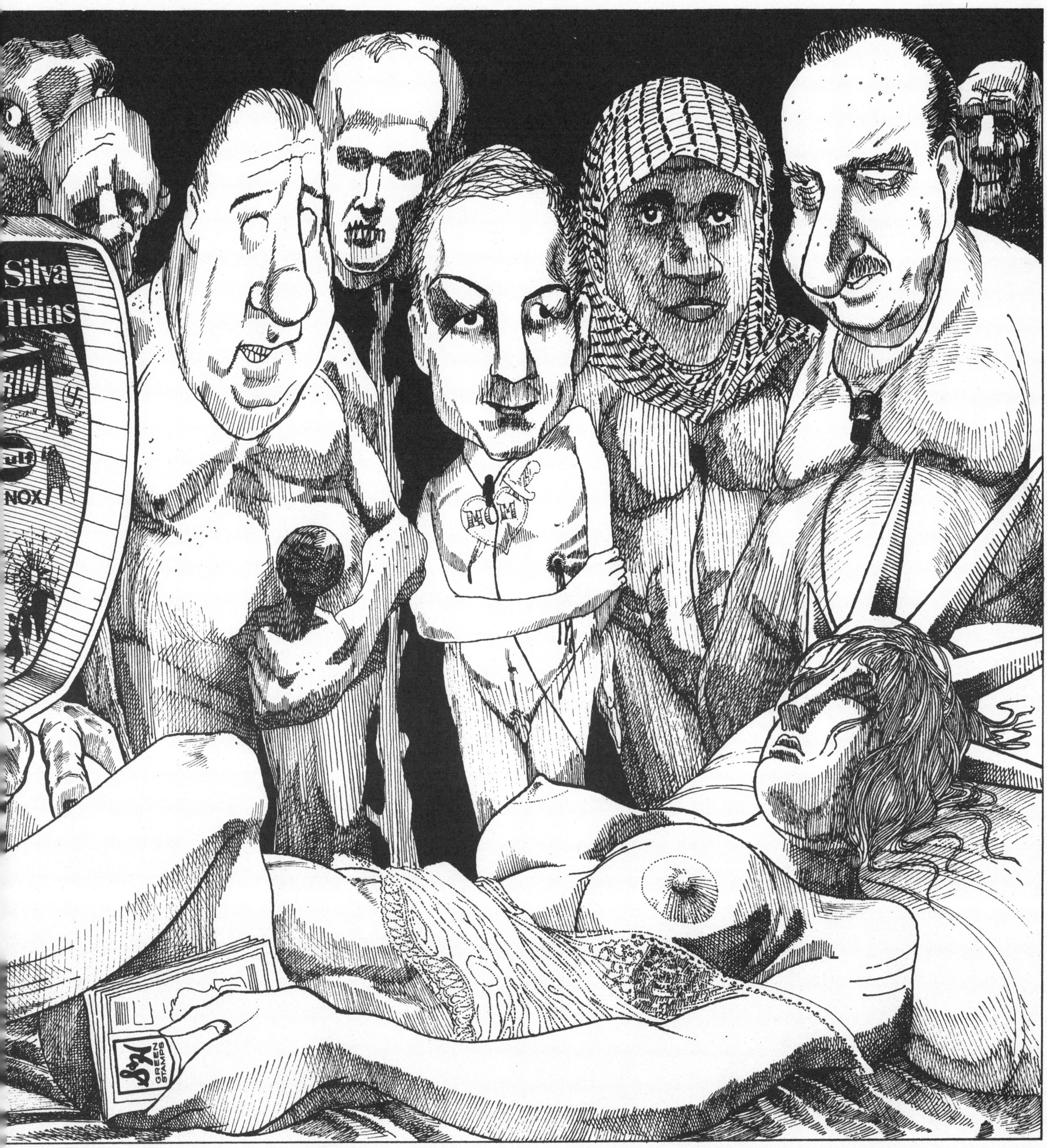
Silva
NOX
MOM
GREEN STAMPS

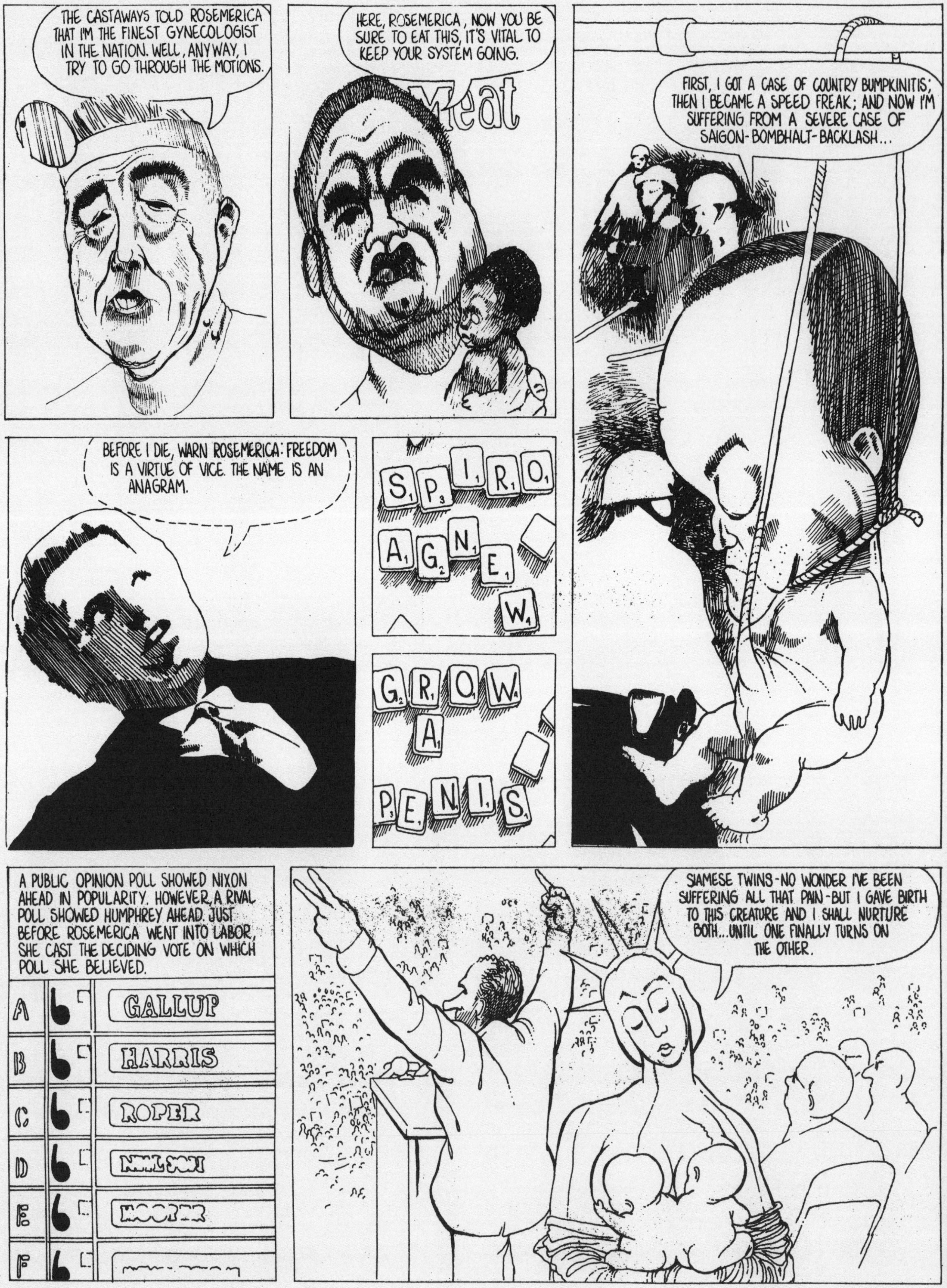
THE CASTAWAYS TOLD ROSEMERICA THAT I'M THE FINEST GYNECOLOGIST IN THE NATION. WELL, ANYWAY, I TRY TO GO THROUGH THE MOTIONS.
HERE, ROSEMERICA, NOW YOU BE SURE TO EAT THIS, IT'S VITAL TO KEEP YOUR SYSTEM GOING.
Meat
FIRST, I GOT A CASE OF COUNTRY BUMPKINITIS; THEN I BECAME A SPEED FREAK; AND NOW I'M SUFFERING FROM A SEVERE CASE OF SAIGON-BOMBHALT-BACKLASH...
BEFORE I DIE, WARN ROSEMERICA: FREEDOM IS A VIRTUE OF VICE. THE NAME IS AN ANAGRAM.
SPIRO
AGNEW
GROW
A
PENIS
A PUBLIC OPINION POLL SHOWED NIXON AHEAD IN POPULARITY. HOWEVER, A RIVAL POLL SHOWED HUMPHREY AHEAD. JUST BEFORE ROSEMERICA WENT INTO LABOR, SHE CAST THE DECIDING VOTE ON WHICH POLL SHE BELIEVED.
A GALLUP
B HARRIS
C ROPER
D
E
F
SIAMESE TWINS-NO WONDER I'VE BEEN SUFFERING ALL THAT PAIN-BUT I GAVE BIRTH TO THIS CREATURE AND I SHALL NURTURE BOTH...UNTIL ONE FINALLY TURNS ON THE OTHER.

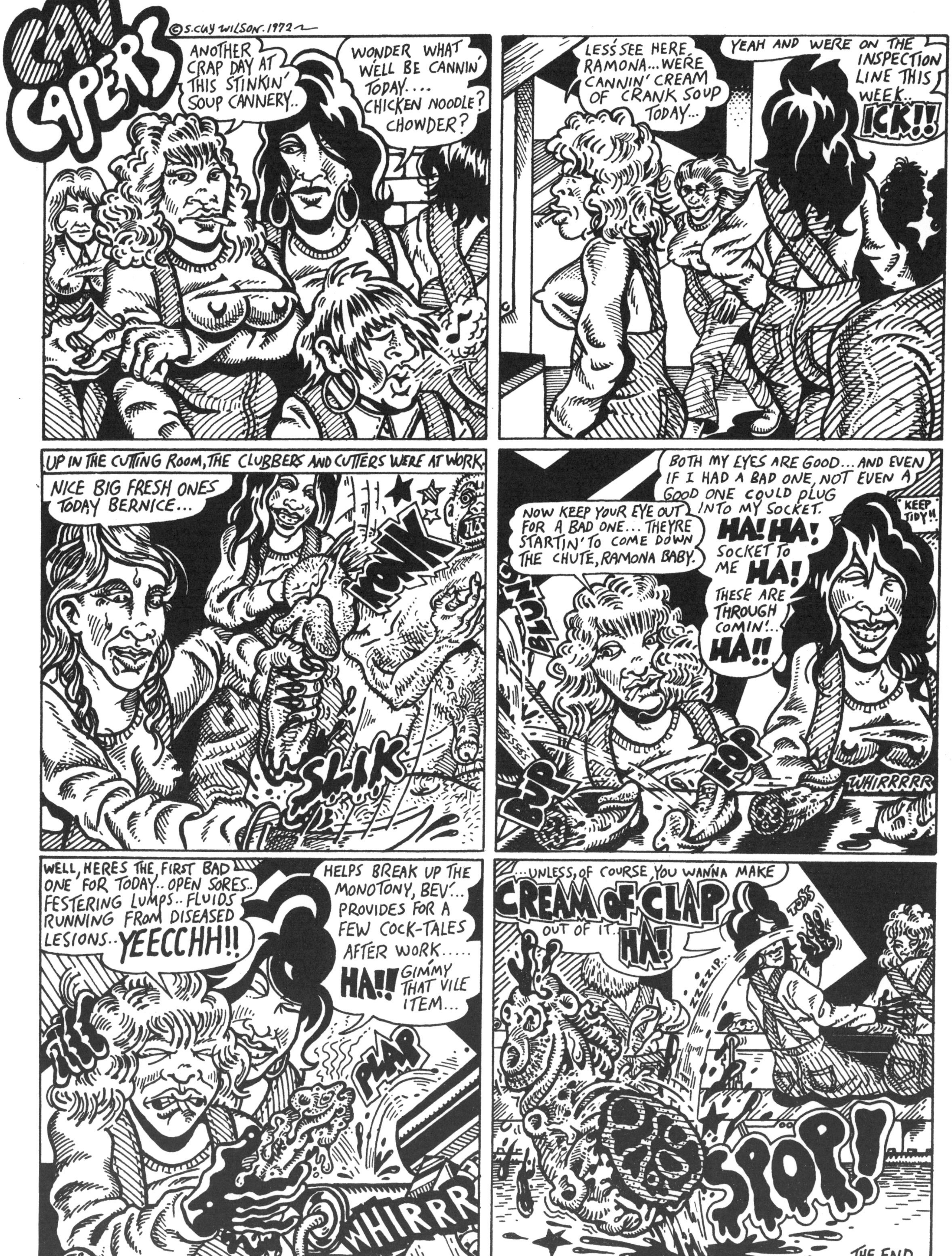
CAN CAPERS
©S.CLAY WILSON.1972
ANOTHER CRAP DAY AT THIS STINKIN' SOUP CANNERY..
WONDER WHAT WE'LL BE CANNIN' TODAY.... CHICKEN NOODLE? CHOWDER?
LESS SEE HERE, RAMONA... WERE CANNIN' CREAM OF CRANK SOUP TODAY...
YEAH AND WERE ON THE INSPECTION LINE THIS WEEK.. ICK!!
UP IN THE CUTTING ROOM, THE CLUBBERS AND CUTTERS WERE AT WORK.
NICE BIG FRESH ONES TODAY BERNICE...
KONK
SLIK
NOW KEEP YOUR EYE OUT FOR A BAD ONE... THEYRE STARTIN' TO COME DOWN THE CHUTE, RAMONA BABY.
BOTH MY EYES ARE GOOD... AND EVEN IF I HAD A BAD ONE, NOT EVEN A GOOD ONE COULD PLUG INTO MY SOCKET.
HA! HA! SOCKET TO ME HA! THESE ARE THROUGH COMIN'... HA!!
KEEP TIDY!!
BUP
FOP
WHIRRRRR
WELL, HERES THE FIRST BAD ONE FOR TODAY.. OPEN SORES.. FESTERING LUMPS.. FLUIDS RUNNING FROM DISEASED LESIONS.. YEECCHH!!
HELPS BREAK UP THE MONOTONY, BEV... PROVIDES FOR A FEW COCK-TALES AFTER WORK..... HA!! GIMMY THAT VILE ITEM...
PLAP
WHIRRR
...UNLESS, OF COURSE, YOU WANNA MAKE CREAM OF CLAP OUT OF IT. HA!
TOSS
SPOP!
THE END...
AND DONT FORGET TO STICK IT.

S. CLAY WILSON. THE REALIST #93, AUGUST 1972.

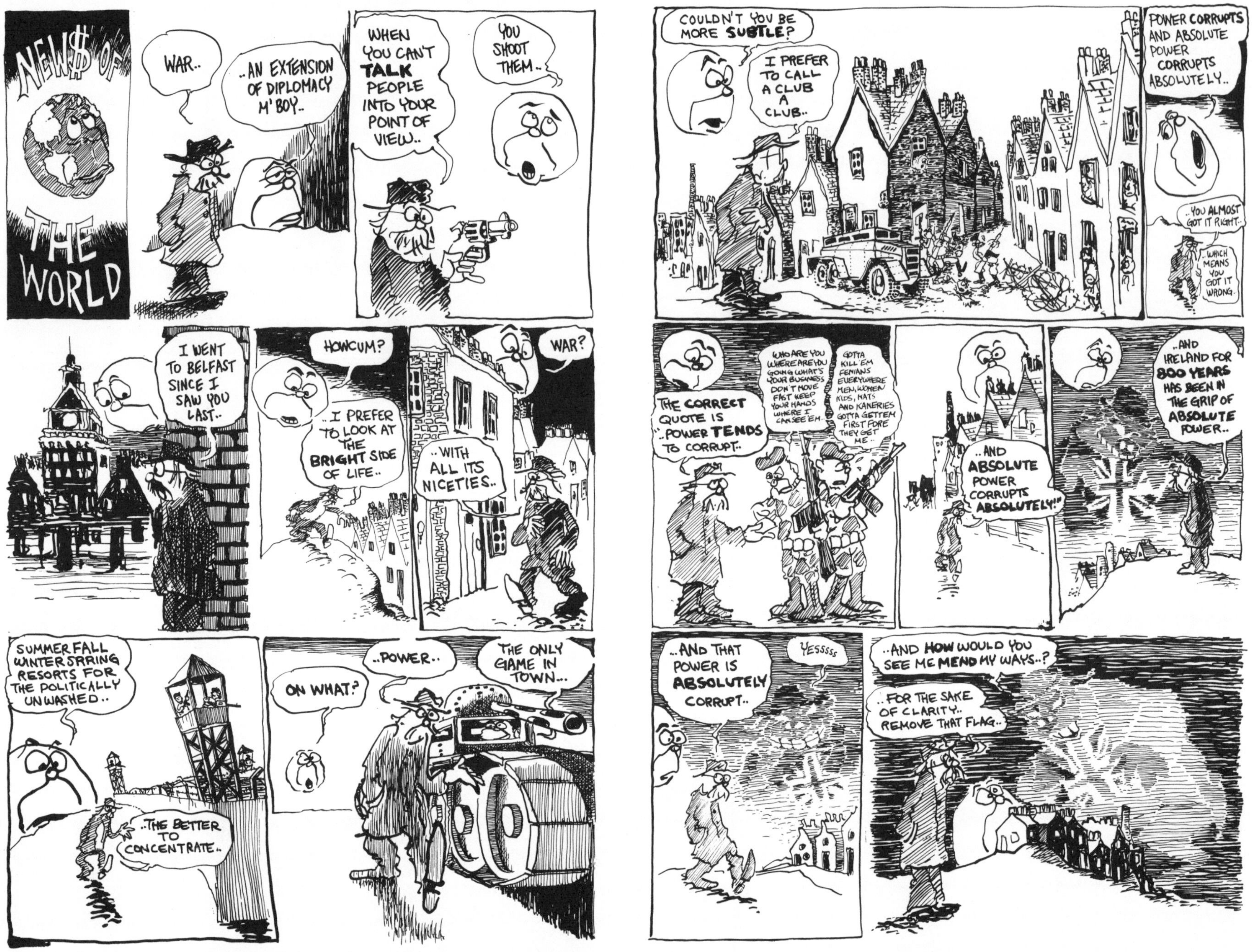
NEW$ OF THE WORLD
WAR..
..AN EXTENSION OF DIPLOMACY M' BOY..
WHEN YOU CAN'T TALK PEOPLE INTO YOUR POINT OF VIEW..
YOU SHOOT THEM..
COULDN'T YOU BE MORE SUBTLE?
I PREFER TO CALL A CLUB A CLUB..
POWER CORRUPTS AND ABSOLUTE POWER CORRUPTS ABSOLUTELY..
..YOU ALMOST GOT IT RIGHT..
..WHICH MEANS YOU GOT IT WRONG.
I WENT TO BELFAST SINCE I SAW YOU LAST..
HOWCUM?
..I PREFER TO LOOK AT THE BRIGHT SIDE OF LIFE..
WAR?
..WITH ALL ITS NICETIES..
THE CORRECT QUOTE IS "..POWER TENDS TO CORRUPT..
WHO ARE YOU WHERE ARE YOU GOING WHAT'S YOUR BUSINESS DON'T MOVE FAST KEEP YOUR HANDS WHERE I CAN SEE 'EM..
GOTTA KILL 'EM FENIANS EVERYWHERE MEN, WOMEN KIDS, KATS AND KANERIES GOTTA GETTEM FIRST FORE THEY GET ME..
..AND ABSOLUTE POWER CORRUPTS ABSOLUTELY!"
..AND IRELAND FOR 800 YEARS HAS BEEN IN THE GRIP OF ABSOLUTE POWER..
SUMMER FALL WINTER SPRING RESORTS FOR THE POLITICALLY UNWASHED..
..THE BETTER TO CONCENTRATE..
ON WHAT?
..POWER..
THE ONLY GAME IN TOWN...
..AND THAT POWER IS ABSOLUTELY CORRUPT..
YESSSSS
..AND HOW WOULD YOU SEE ME MEND MY WAYS..?
..FOR THE SAKE OF CLARITY.. REMOVE THAT FLAG..

DAN O'NEILL. THE REALIST #94, OCTOBER 1972.

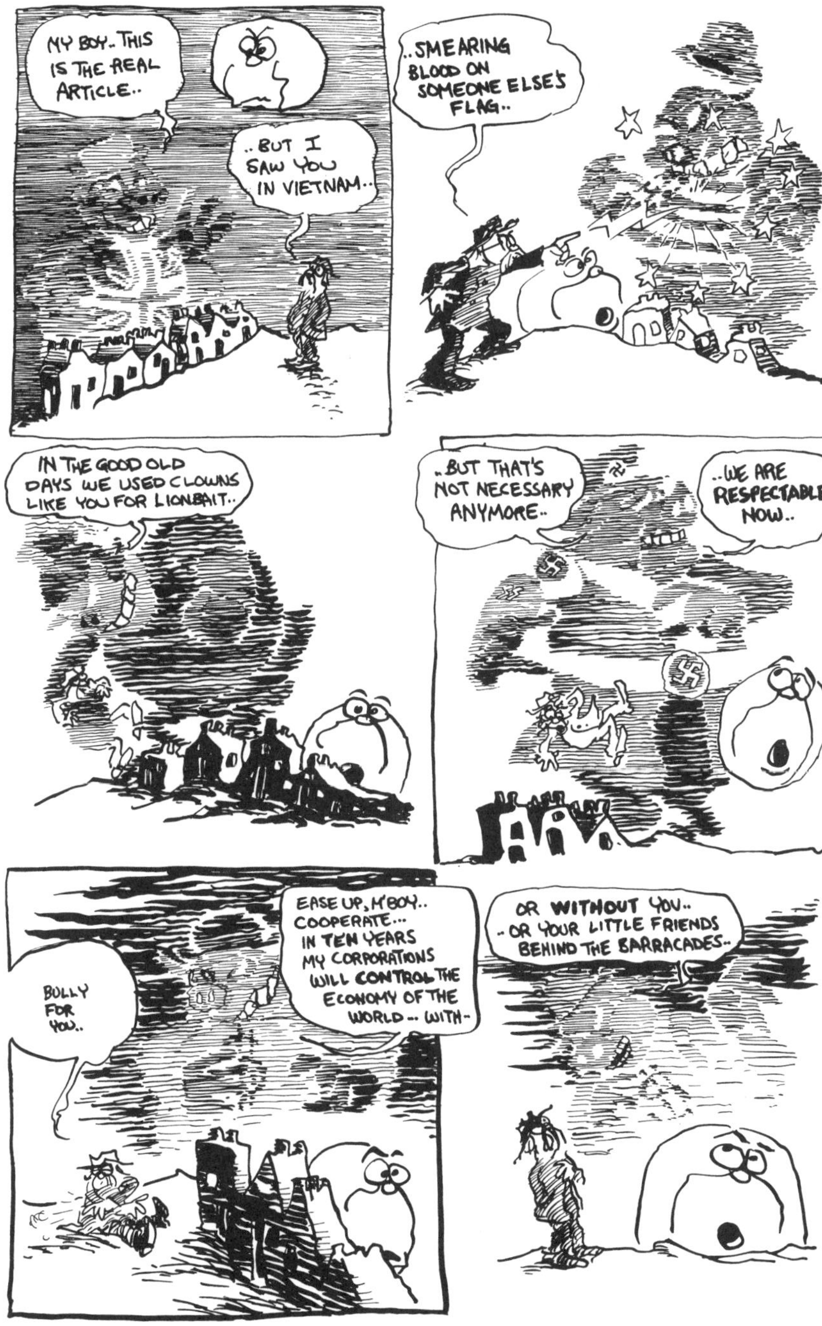
MY BOY.. THIS IS THE REAL ARTICLE..
..BUT I SAW YOU IN VIETNAM..
..SMEARING BLOOD ON SOMEONE ELSE'S FLAG..
IN THE GOOD OLD DAYS WE USED CLOWNS LIKE YOU FOR LIONBAIT..
..BUT THAT'S NOT NECESSARY ANYMORE..
..WE ARE RESPECTABLE NOW..
BULLY FOR YOU..
EASE UP, M'BOY.. COOPERATE... IN TEN YEARS MY CORPORATIONS WILL CONTROL THE ECONOMY OF THE WORLD.. WITH-
OR WITHOUT YOU.. ..OR YOUR LITTLE FRIENDS BEHIND THE BARRACADES..

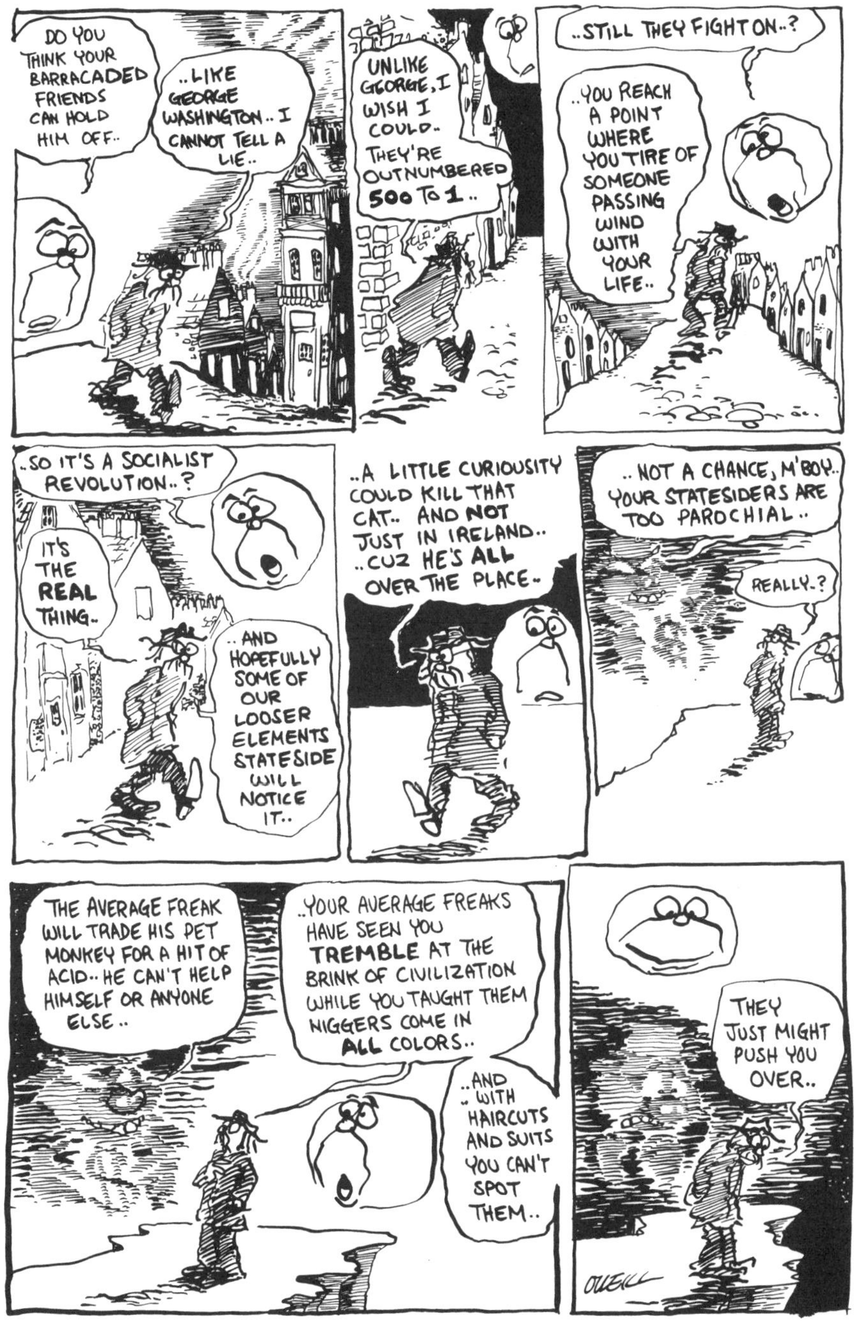
DO YOU THINK YOUR BARRACADED FRIENDS CAN HOLD HIM OFF..
..LIKE GEORGE WASHINGTON.. I CANNOT TELL A LIE..
UNLIKE GEORGE, I WISH I COULD.. THEY'RE OUTNUMBERED 500 TO 1..
..STILL THEY FIGHT ON..?
..YOU REACH A POINT WHERE YOU TIRE OF SOMEONE PASSING WIND WITH YOUR LIFE..
..SO IT'S A SOCIALIST REVOLUTION..?
IT'S THE REAL THING..
..AND HOPEFULLY SOME OF OUR LOOSER ELEMENTS STATESIDE WILL NOTICE IT..
..A LITTLE CURIOUSITY COULD KILL THAT CAT.. AND NOT JUST IN IRELAND.. ..CUZ HE'S ALL OVER THE PLACE..
.. NOT A CHANCE, M'BOY.. YOUR STATESIDERS ARE TOO PAROCHIAL..
REALLY..?
THE AVERAGE FREAK WILL TRADE HIS PET MONKEY FOR A HIT OF ACID.. HE CAN'T HELP HIMSELF OR ANYONE ELSE..
..YOUR AVERAGE FREAKS HAVE SEEN YOU TREMBLE AT THE BRINK OF CIVILIZATION WHILE YOU TAUGHT THEM NIGGERS COME IN ALL COLORS..
..AND ..WITH HAIRCUTS AND SUITS YOU CAN'T SPOT THEM..
THEY JUST MIGHT PUSH YOU OVER..
O'NEILL

DAN O'NEILL. THE REALIST #94, OCTOBER 1972.

"Im glad you dig it, man. ... It's nostril hairs."

FORD. THE REALIST #94, OCTOBER 1972.

The Odd Couple

ROBERT GROSSMAN. THE REALIST #94, OCTOBER 1972.

"Children do not believe in God. It is when they have to learn to suppress the sexual excitation that goes hand in hand with masturbation that the belief in God generally becomes embedded in them. Owing to this suppression, they acquire a fear of pleasure. Now they begin to blieve in God in earnest and to develop a fear of him. On the one hand they fear him as an omniscient and omnipotent being, and on the other hand they invoke his protection against their own sexual excitation. All of this has the function of avoiding masturbation. Thus, it is in early childhood that religious ideas become embedded."

—Wilhelm Reich
The Mass Psychology of Fascism

ART SPIEGELMAN. THE REALIST #94, OCTOBER 1972.

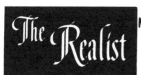

50¢
The Realist
Mae Brussell's Conspiracy Newsletter:
The Senate Committee
Is Part of the Cover-Up

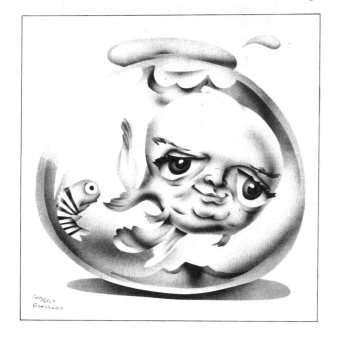

Why Truman Capote Went to Jail

ROBERT GROSSMAN. THE REALIST #95, DECEMBER 1972.

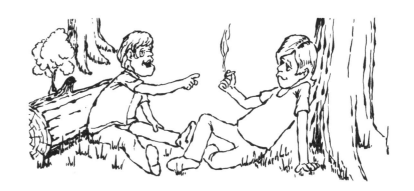

"My Dad's grass is stronger than your Dad's grass."

THE REALIST #94, OCTOBER 1972.

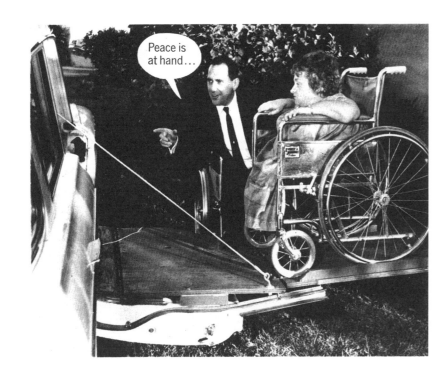

Peace is
at hand...

THE REALIST #95, DECEMBER 1972.

GARDEN
CLUB
JON RICHARDS

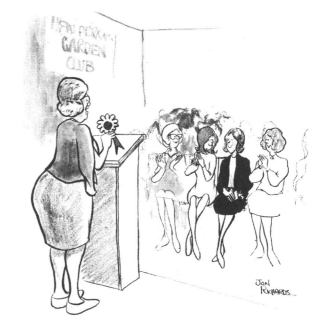

"And a special prize to Norma Burnhill
for her marvelous Cannabis!"

JON RICHARDS. THE REALIST #96-C, JUNE 1973.

S. CLAY WILSON.
THE REALIST #95, DECEMBER 1972.

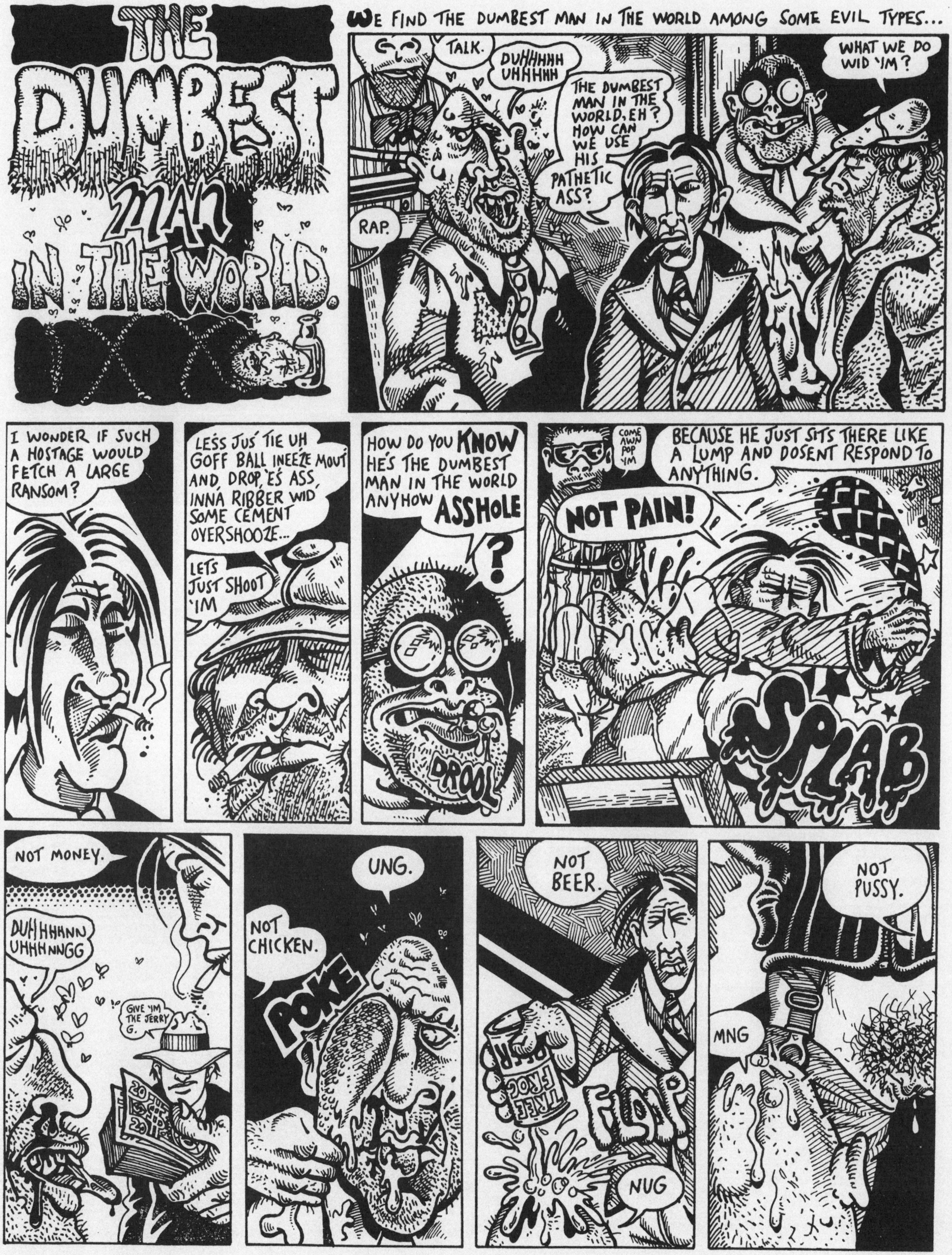
THE DUMBEST MAN IN THE WORLD.
WE FIND THE DUMBEST MAN IN THE WORLD AMONG SOME EVIL TYPES...
TALK.
DUHHHHH UHHHHH
THE DUMBEST MAN IN THE WORLD, EH? HOW CAN WE USE HIS PATHETIC ASS?
WHAT WE DO WID 'IM?
RAP.
I WONDER IF SUCH A HOSTAGE WOULD FETCH A LARGE RANSOM?
LESS JUS' TIE UH GOFF BALL INEEZE MOUT AND DROP 'ES ASS INNA RIBBER WID SOME CEMENT OVERSHOOZE...
LETS JUST SHOOT 'IM
HOW DO YOU KNOW HE'S THE DUMBEST MAN IN THE WORLD ANYHOW ASSHOLE
?
DROOL
COME AWN POP 'IM
BECAUSE HE JUST SITS THERE LIKE A LUMP AND DOSENT RESPOND TO ANYTHING.
NOT PAIN!
SPLAB
NOT MONEY.
DUHHHHNN UHHHNNGG
GIVE 'IM THE JERRY G.
UNG.
NOT CHICKEN.
POKE
NOT BEER.
TREE FROG BEER
FLOP
NUG
NOT PUSSY.
MNG

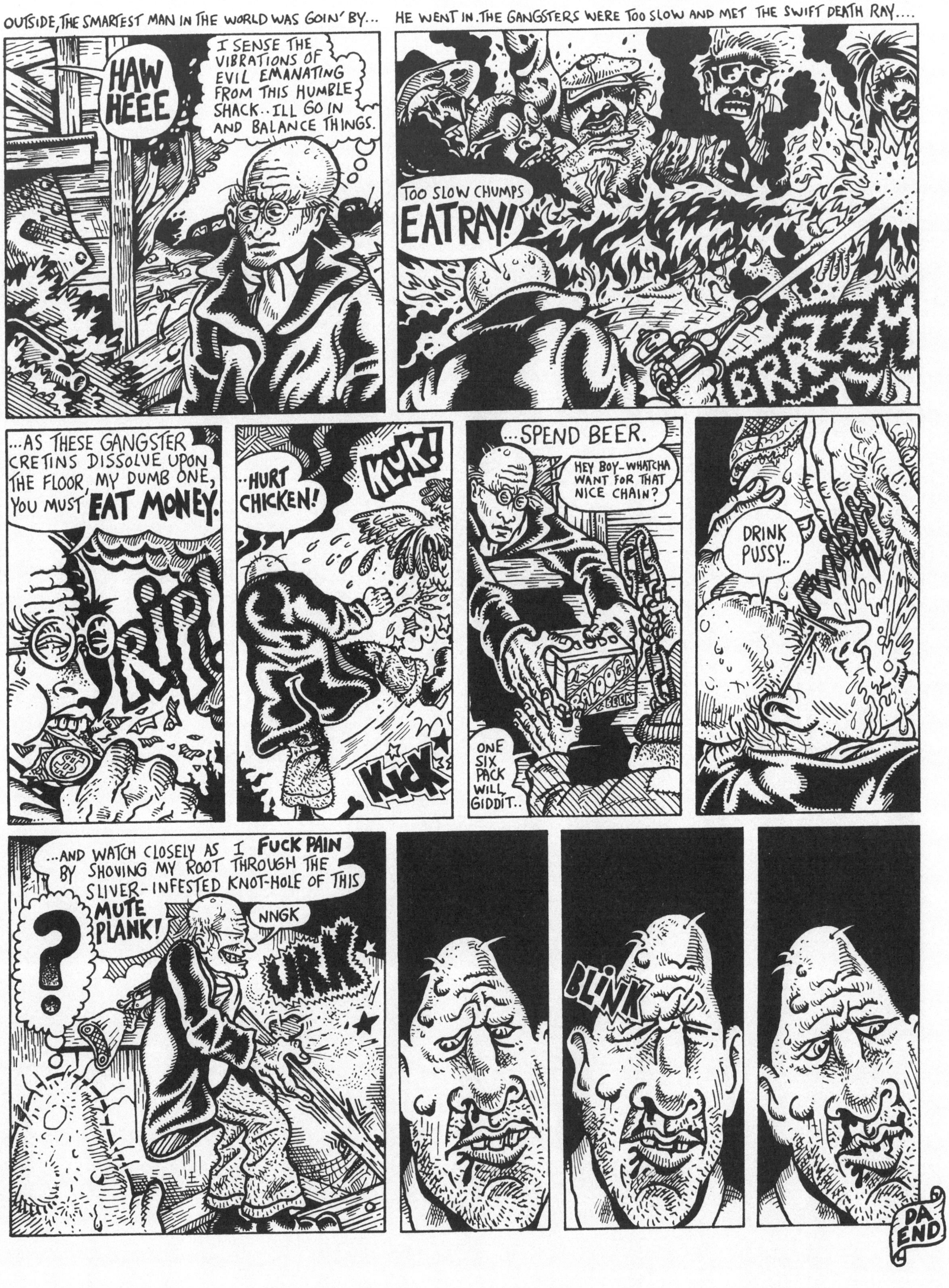
OUTSIDE, THE SMARTEST MAN IN THE WORLD WAS GOIN' BY...
HAW HEEE
I SENSE THE VIBRATIONS OF EVIL EMANATING FROM THIS HUMBLE SHACK.. ILL GO IN AND BALANCE THINGS.
HE WENT IN. THE GANGSTERS WERE TOO SLOW AND MET THE SWIFT DEATH RAY....
TOO SLOW CHUMPS EATRAY!
...AS THESE GANGSTER CRETINS DISSOLVE UPON THE FLOOR, MY DUMB ONE, YOU MUST EAT MONEY.
RIP!
..HURT CHICKEN!
KLUK!
KICK
...SPEND BEER.
HEY BOY- WHATCHA WANT FOR THAT NICE CHAIN?
ONE SIX PACK WILL GIDDIT..
DRINK PUSSY..
...AND WATCH CLOSELY AS I FUCK PAIN BY SHOVING MY ROOT THROUGH THE SLIVER-INFESTED KNOT-HOLE OF THIS MUTE PLANK!
?
NNGK
URK
BLINK
DA END

CIA Surplus Items

UNO
BANCO CENTRAL DE LA REPUBLICA DOMINICANA
B981537F
UN PESO ORO
B981537F
UN PESO ORO
UN PESO ORO

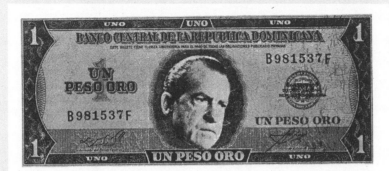

Military Occupation Scrip. Unlimited quantities of this scrip, attractively printed in the language and currency of every Non-Aligned Nation in the world. These are fresh, crisp bills, suitable for adding to your money collection. Think of it, you can own one billion inflationary United States Military Occupation Dollars from any Third World country of your choice for only $3.00, post paid. Add 35¢ for a selection of plastic "small-change" token coins.

Canvas Bags Filled with Live Cats. Effective psychological preparation of emotionally unstable military recruits when they are faced with their first session of bayonet practice, has been cleverly met by the introduction of this device which allows the un-tested soldier the completely realistic "simulation" of actual battle conditions experienced when thrusting a sharp bayonet into a living adversary, complete with screams and gushing blood. Each bag comes complete with 20 live cats. Designed for one time use only. $30.00 each.

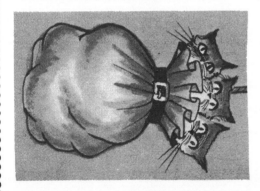

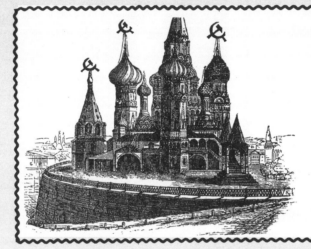

A Complete Russian Small Town, Authentic in Every Detail, reconstructed in a secret mountain retreat near Green River, Wyoming. This settlement duplicates a Typical Soviet Russian Village, complete with a Park of Culture and Rest with statues of Lavrenti Bereia, Krupskaya and an Anonymous Hero of Soviet Labor; an NKVD office; a Komsomol Basketball Court, two Worker's Children's Creches, A Museum of Socialist Realism Picture Postcards, a Communal 17" (diagonally measured) Television Set and a Young Pioneer Euthanasia Center. Since all the C.I.A. agents we trained in this center have since been captured and shot, we have decided to place it on the disposal list. 400 Acres with 70 buildings for only $85,000!

Anodized Electronic Genital Prods. Developed from the long familiar Cattle Prods used in Wild West Rodeos to excite Brahma bulls to a peak of frenzy before releasing them into the ring, these handy little instruments are excellent for controlling excitable prisoners during mass shower periods in correctional institutions, or for vice squad entrapment officers engaged in clean up sweeps of homosexuals in public comfort stations and park urinals. Only $35.97 each. (Batteries, $3.00 extra)

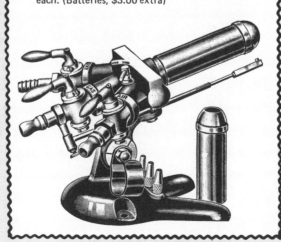

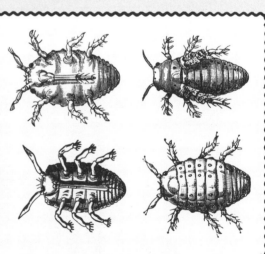

6 Pound "Cooties." We have over seven hundred of these amazing giant mutant vermin, developed through our "Infestation" program which was to be programmed simultaneously with our "Deforestation" program in Viet Nam. These unruly creatures are in perfect health, but are impossible to train and must be kept in maximum security cages. Since they are hybrids and sterile, there will be no danger of their breeding and infesting the countryside. Sold only in pairs; $800.00, including cages and laser whips. NOTE. May not be publicly exhibited without clearance from our Agency.

Splendid Life Size Formal Oil Portraits. These were painted by leading U.S. Portrait Artists, and are framed in beautifully carved and gilded frames with built-in museum type color-corrected lighting devices. These portraits were originally intended to be displayed in the entrance halls of U.S. Embassies and Legations throughout the world. Due to a largely negative local reaction to these paintings, an appreciable number had to be returned to the U.S. in order to avoid Diplomatic Incidents. These handsome paintings are offered "as is." A perfect answer to the problem of suitable decor for Board Room or Corporate Conference Room. Simply hire your local portraitist to paint out Mr. Nixon's face and substitute that of your own Chairman of the Board. A "steal" at only $125.00!

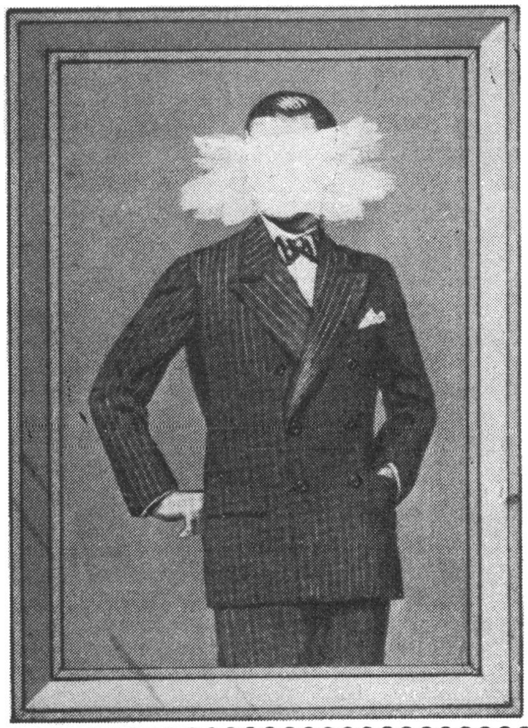

Radioactive Cobalt Vaginal Suppositories. Come packed in special ¼" lead-lined containers, six to a package. As conditions requiring the application of these jazzy little items have changed due to recent political developments, we can now release them to the public (at their own risk). Our loss is your gain: only 75¢ per half dozen. (Postage and handling, including Radiation-Proof Case: $200.00)

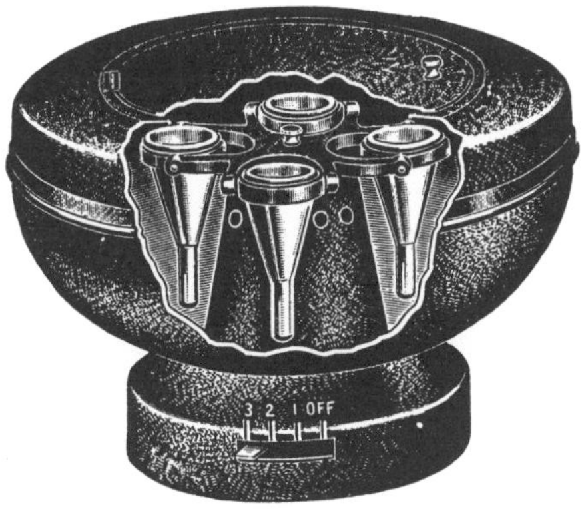
3 2 1 OFF

JOHN FRANCIS PUTNAM AND STEVEN HELLER.
THE REALIST #95, DECEMBER 1972.

Cesar Chavez Targets. Life size octagonal targets bearing a speaking likeness of the notorious Chicano Trouble Maker, Cesar Chavez. Designed for training in use of riot and scatter guns. Targets available in three size-ranges: Close up, closer and point blank. Only $13.75 each F.O.B.

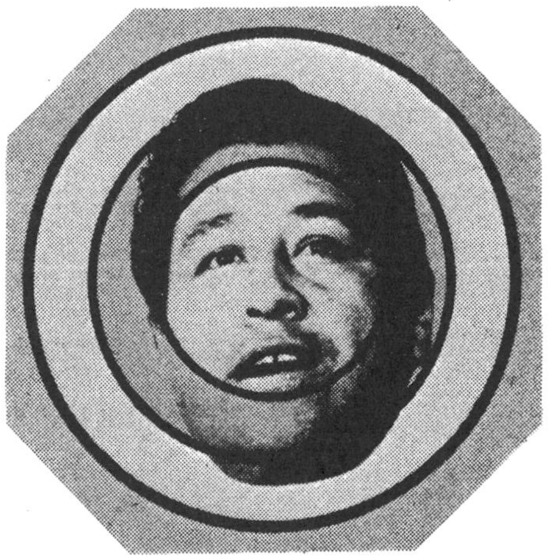

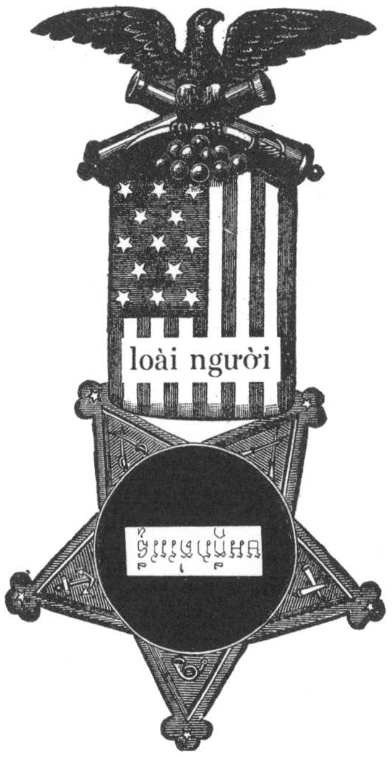
loài người

PEOPLE WILL THINK WE'RE NOT SERIOUS..
SO WHAT ?
The Realist
595 Broadway
New York 10012
Enclosed please find:
$3 for ten extra copies of this issue (number 98)
$6 for a subscription to Mae Brussell's Conspiracy Newsletter
$3 for a six-issue subscription to The Realist
$5 for a 12-issue subscription to The Realist
$7 for a copy of "How a Satirical Editor Became a Yippie Conspirator in Ten Easy Years" by Paul Krassner
$1 for the double-issue (90) of The Realist with the Ken Kesey Interview and details of Scientology's $750,000 lawsuit
$10 for all available back issues including the two with Mae Brussell and the one with Ken Kesey
$3 for a Realist back issues binder
$1 for a red-white-and-blue Fuck Communism poster
$1 for Wally Wood's original Disneyland Memorial Orgy
$1 for The Odd Couple poster (Nixon and Sammy Davis Jr.)
Name .... Apt ....
Address ....
City .... State .... Zip ....
(Note: for Canadian and foreign subscriptions, add $1)

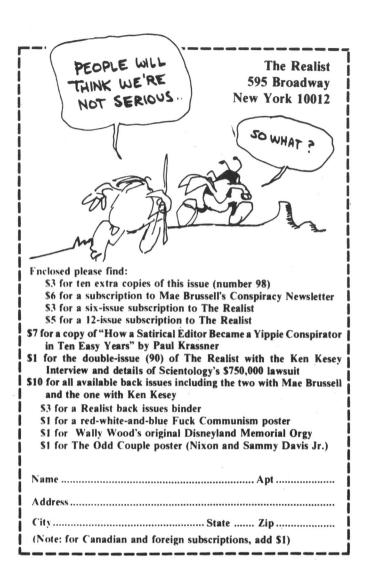

DAN O'NEILL. THE REALIST #98, FEBRUARY 1974.

diet Sperm

KALYNN CAMPBELL. THE REALIST #99, SEPTEMBER-OCTOBER 1985.

KALYNN CAMPBELL. THE REALIST #100, JANUARY-FEBRUARY 1986.

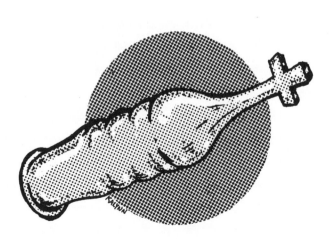

KALYNN CAMPBELL. THE REALIST #99, SEPTEMBER-OCTOBER 1985.

BARBARA HENNIGER. THE REALIST #99, SEPTEMBER-OCTOBER 1985.

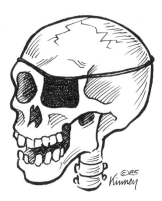

A *Whole Earth Review* correspondent informs us that the pilot of the Air Force's SAC flying command post must wear an eye patch at all times so that he will have sight left in one eye should he happen to gaze at a nuclear bomb going off anywhere above teh United States.

JAY KINNEY. THE REALIST #100, JANUARY-FEBRUARY 1986.

NEWS ITEM: Disneyland has quietly reversed a 28-year-old policy that prohibited partners of the same sex from dancing together in the Magic Kingdom.

KALYNN CAMPBELL. THE REALIST #100, JANUARY-FEBRUARY 1986.

KALYNN CAMPBELL. THE REALIST #101, MAY-JUNE 1986.

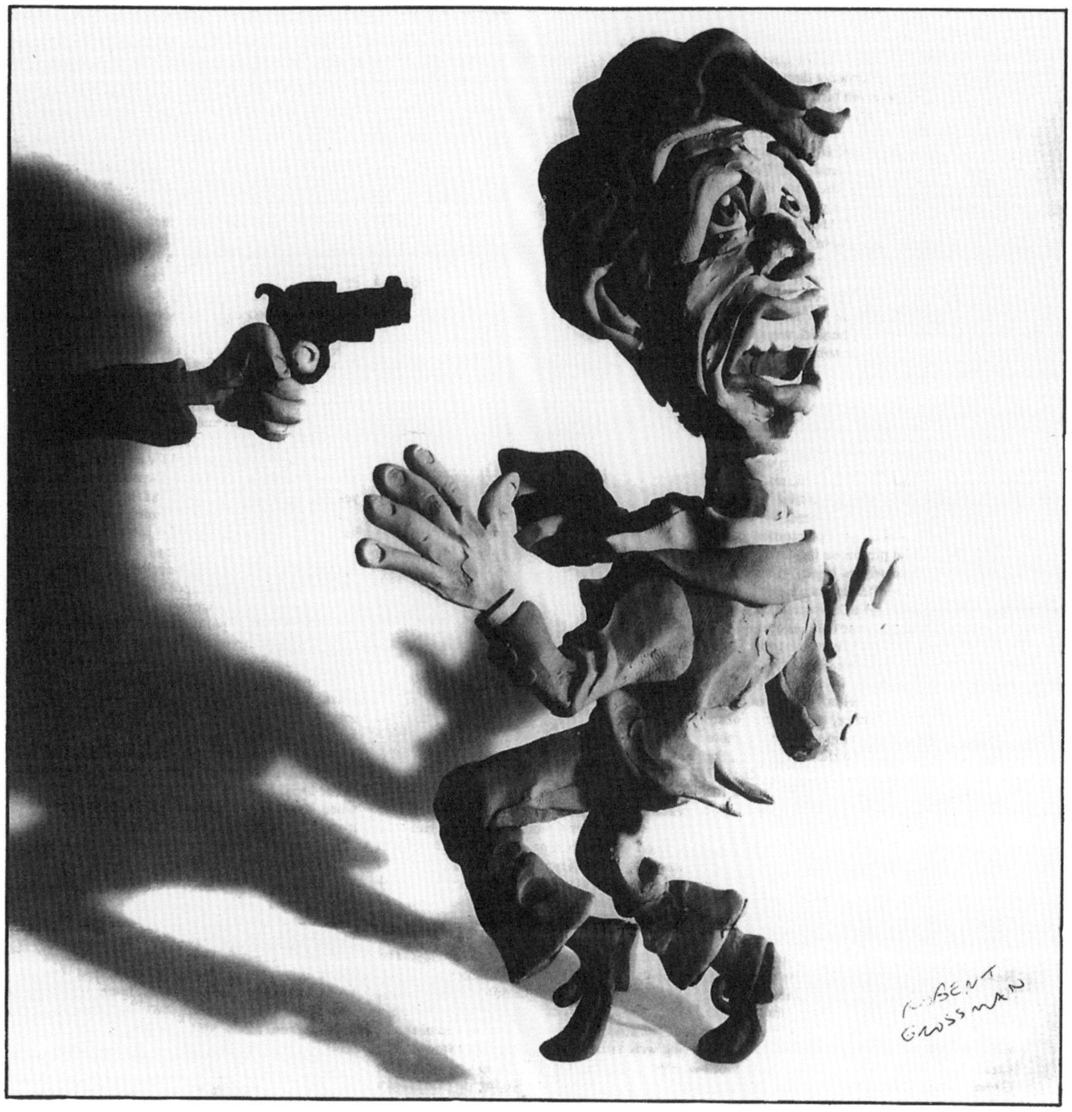
ROBERT GROSSMAN

The Los Angeles Police Commission last month released a 1500-page summary of the investigation into the assassination of Robert F. Kennedy, concluding that: "There was no evidence of a conspiracy." Although one of the bullets was found in the back of Kennedy's neck, the report stated that Sirhan Sirhan acted alone.

The mysterious bullet was explained this way: "Senator Kennedy had been possessed by Satan, and at the precise moment that Sirhan was shooting at him, Kennedy's head turned around 180 degrees, just like Linda Blair in The Exorcist." Thus did the Commission reject the theory of a second gun person.

PAUL KRASSNER AND ROBERT GROSSMAN. THE REALIST #101, MAY-JUNE 1986.

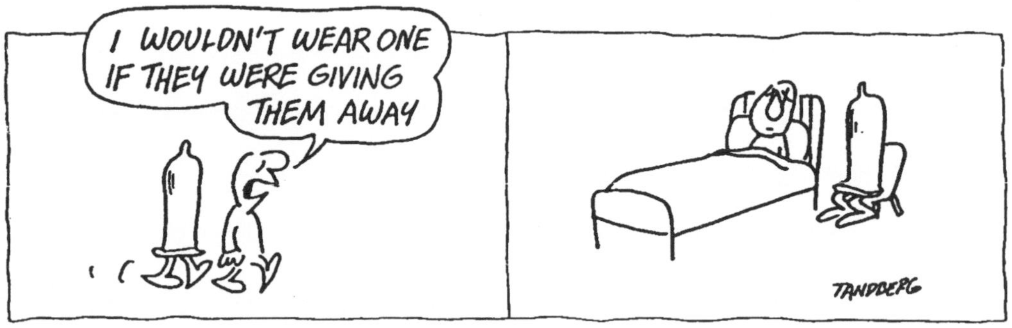
I WOULDN'T WEAR ONE IF THEY WERE GIVING THEM AWAY
TANDBERG

TANDBERG. THE REALIST #101, MAY-JUNE 1986.

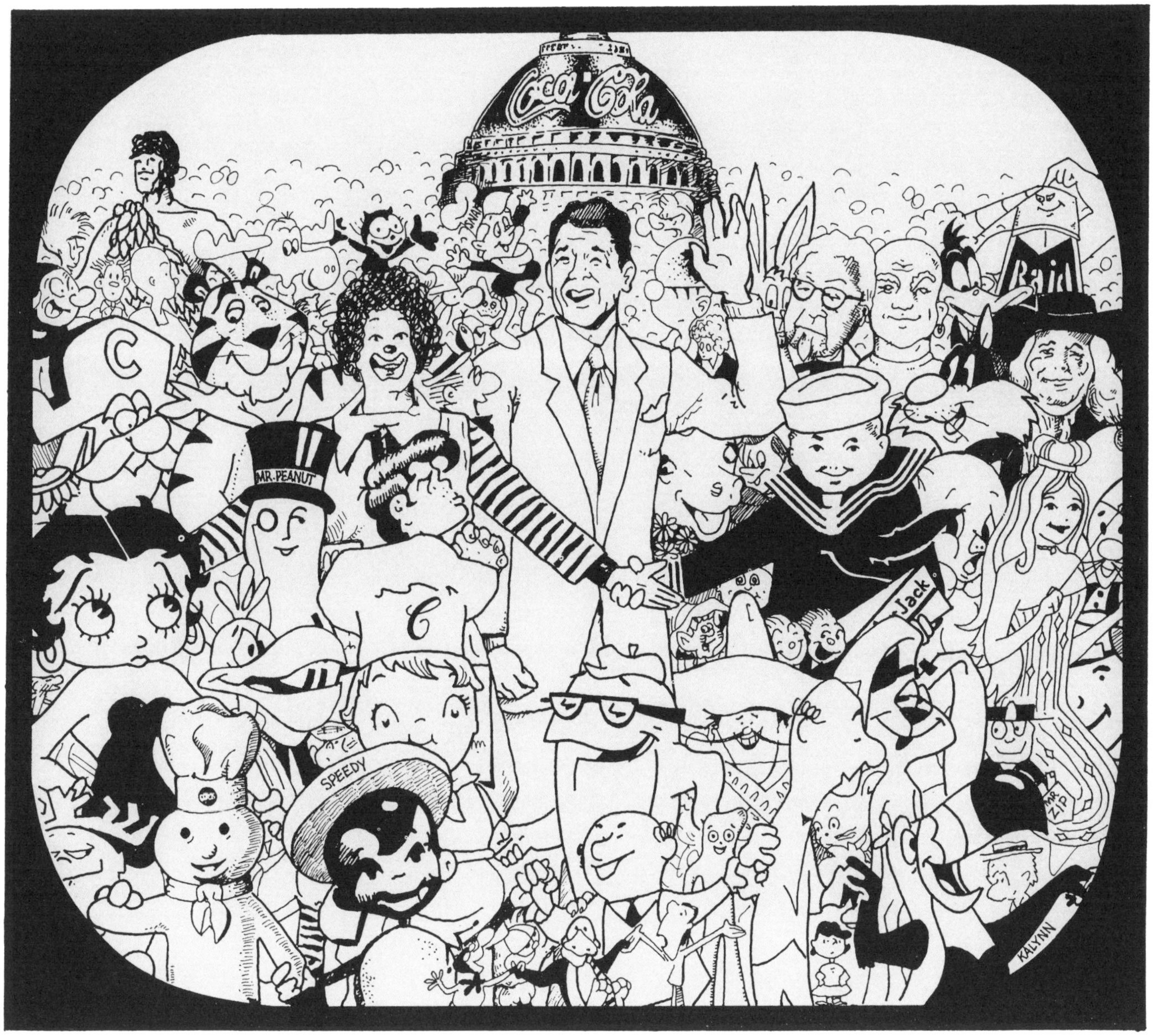
Coca-Cola
MR. PEANUT
SPEEDY
Jack
Raid
KALYNN

KALYNN CAMPBELL. THE REALIST #102, SEPTEMBER-OCTOBER 1986.

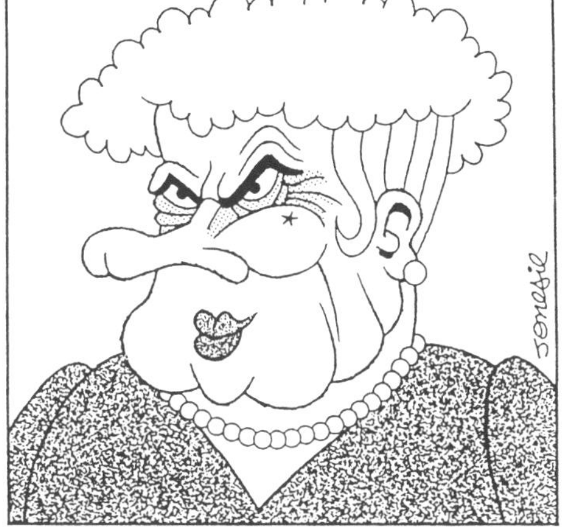
JONESIL

Richard Nixon predicted to the American Newspaper Publishers Association that a woman would be the Republican candidate for Vice President in 1988.

JONESIL. THE REALIST #102, SEPTEMBER-OCTOBER 1986.

Jammed Again!
THESE M-16'S ARE WORTHLESS! FERNANDO! RUN DOWN TO THE ARMS MART AND PICK UP SOME NEW AUTOMATICS!
CLIC CLIC
AW... COLONEL! DO I HAVE TO?
WOULD FRENCH GIATS DO?
NO, NO! TRY PAKISTANI 63A3'S OR MAYBE ISRAELI 5.56'S.
Pay n' Kill
DEATH "R" US
GOOD THING THEY'RE OPEN 'TIL 9:00!
WOW! LOOK AT ALL THE NEAT STUFF!
UH—UH—LEMME SEE THE LASER-SIGHTED ULTIMAX 100...
OH THAT? I'M SURE YOU'D LIKE THE CHINESE D-5 PULSE RIFLE BETTER...OR THE NEW CYBERNETIC SERVICE .45 WITH OPTIONAL A.I. CHIP?!
© 1986 by MAVRIDES & KINNEY
YOU IDIOT! WHERE ARE OUR GUNS?
THEY HAD A GREAT 2 FOR 1 CLOSE OUT SALE ON SHIP-TO-SHIP MISSLES! WHAT SAVINGS!
AY YI YI! THAT WAS OUR CIA FUNDING FOR THE WHOLE WEEK!

ROBERT GROSSMAN. THE REALIST #94, OCTOBER 1972. *89

PAUL MAVRIDES AND JAY KINNEY. THE REALIST #102, SEPTEMBER-OCTOBER 1986.

THE TASTE OF KIEV COMES TO THE WEST!
FROM THE GLOWING WATERS OF THE DNIEPER RIVER–
DIRECT TO YOU!
FIRE-BREWED
MALT DOWN
IT'S THE WATER!
...And remember, E = m-m-m-m-m-mc²!
CIRCLING THE GLOBE SINCE 1986

STEVE MAGNUSON. THE REALIST #102, SEPTEMBER-OCTOBER 1986. *90

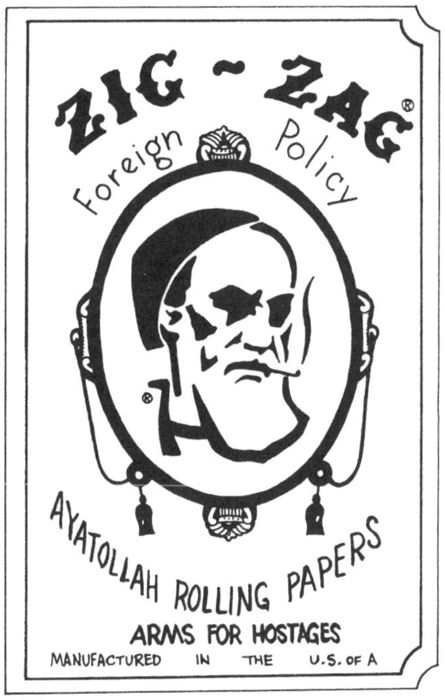
ZIG - ZAG
Foreign Policy
AYATOLLAH ROLLING PAPERS
ARMS FOR HOSTAGES
MANUFACTURED IN THE U.S. OF A

KALYNN CAMPBELL. THE REALIST #103, JANUARY-FEBRUARY 1987.

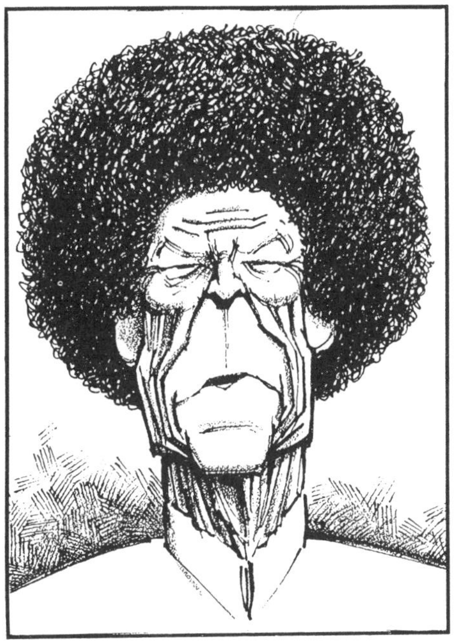

KALYNN CAMPBELL. THE REALIST #102, SEPTEMBER-OCTOBER 1986.

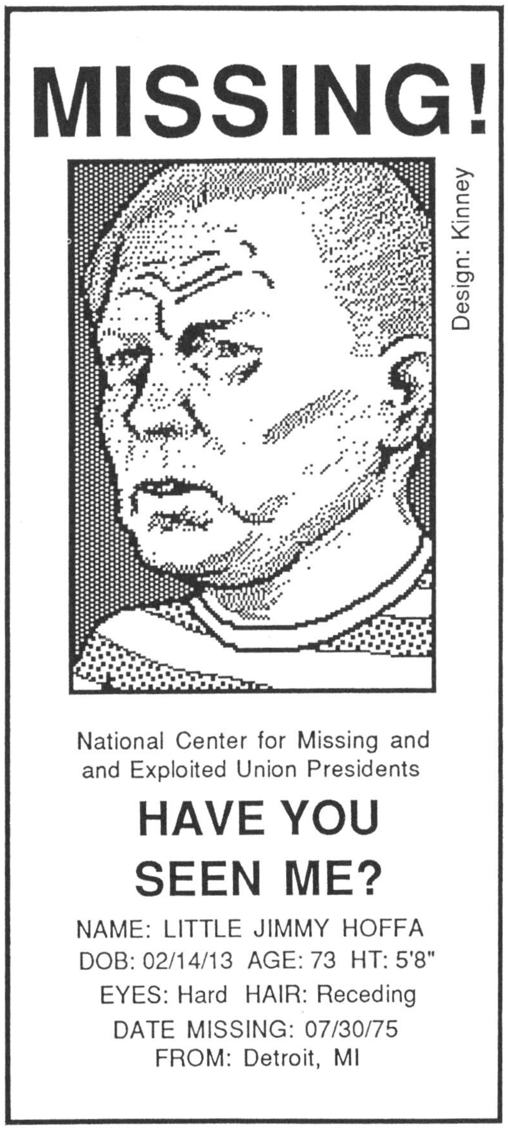
MISSING!
Design: Kinney
National Center for Missing and
and Exploited Union Presidents
HAVE YOU
SEEN ME?
NAME: LITTLE JIMMY HOFFA
DOB: 02/14/13 AGE: 73 HT: 5'8"
EYES: Hard HAIR: Receding
DATE MISSING: 07/30/75
FROM: Detroit, MI

JAY KINNEY. THE REALIST #102, SEPTEMBER-OCTOBER 1986.

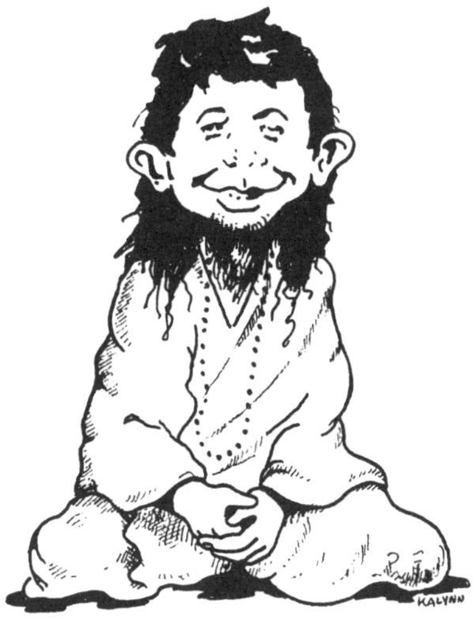

KALYNN CAMPBELL. THE REALIST #103, JANUARY-FEBRUARY 1987.

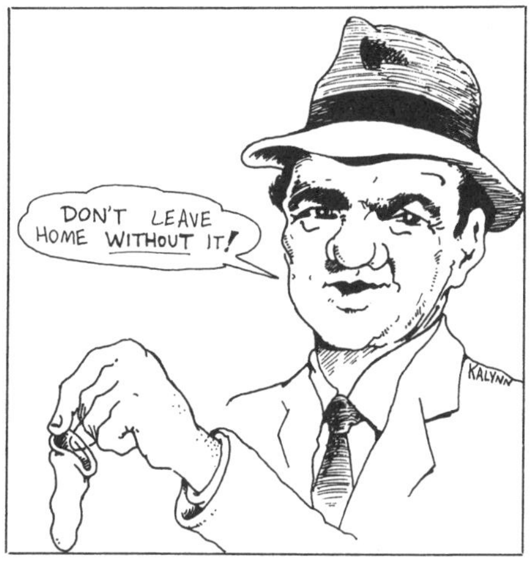
DON'T LEAVE HOME WITHOUT IT!
KALYNN

KALYNN CAMPBELL. THE REALIST #104, JUNE 1987. *91

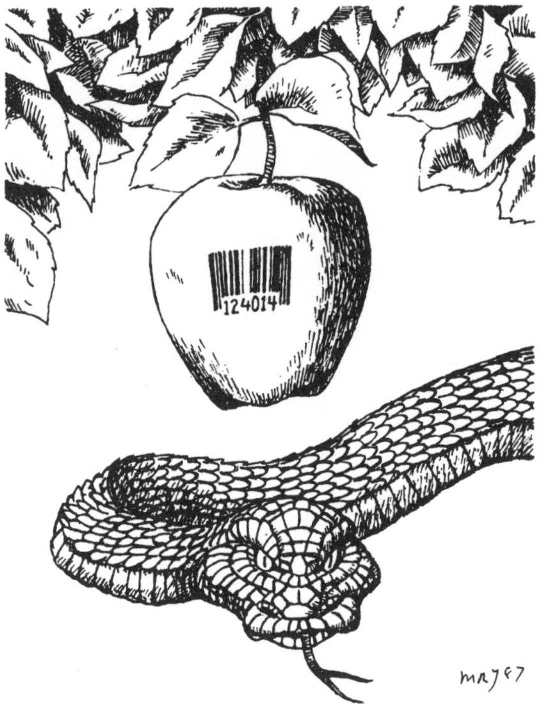
124014

JERRY MAYER. THE REALIST #104, JUNE 1987.

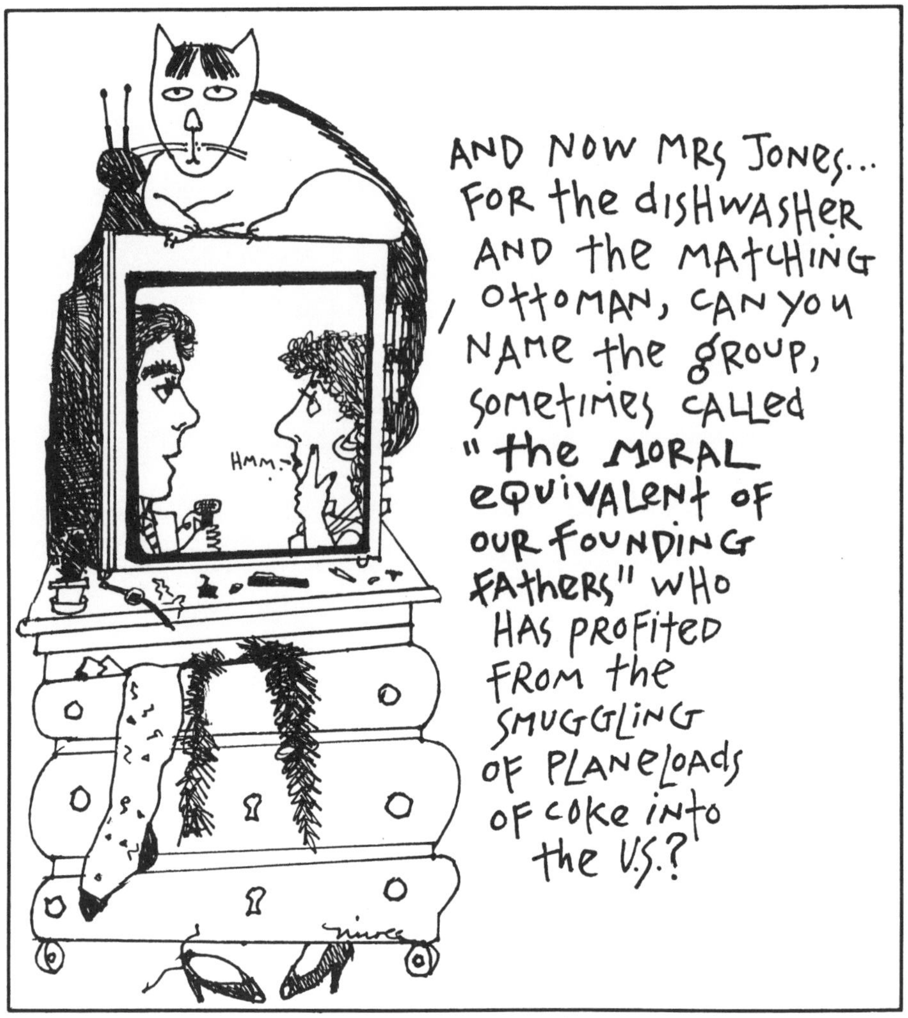
AND NOW MRS JONES... FOR THE DISHWASHER AND THE MATCHING OTTOMAN, CAN YOU NAME THE GROUP, SOMETIMES CALLED "THE MORAL EQUIVALENT OF OUR FOUNDING FATHERS" WHO HAS PROFITED FROM THE SMUGGLING OF PLANELOADS OF COKE INTO THE U.S.?
HMM:-

NICOLE HOLLANDER. THE REALIST #104, JUNE 1987.

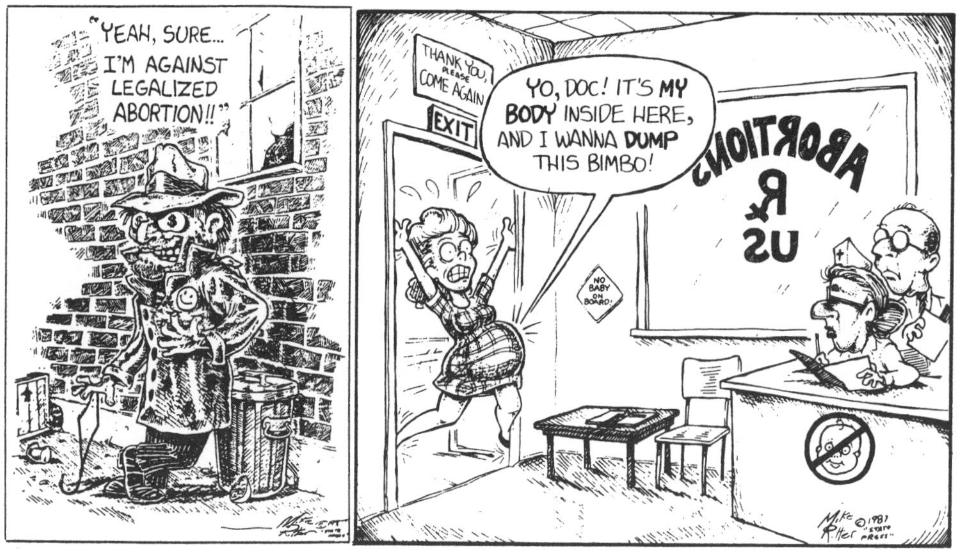
"YEAH, SURE... I'M AGAINST LEGALIZED ABORTION!!"
THANK YOU, PLEASE COME AGAIN
EXIT
YO, DOC! IT'S MY BODY INSIDE HERE, AND I WANNA DUMP THIS BIMBO!
NO BABY ON BOARD

MIKE RITTER. THE REALIST #104, JUNE 1987.

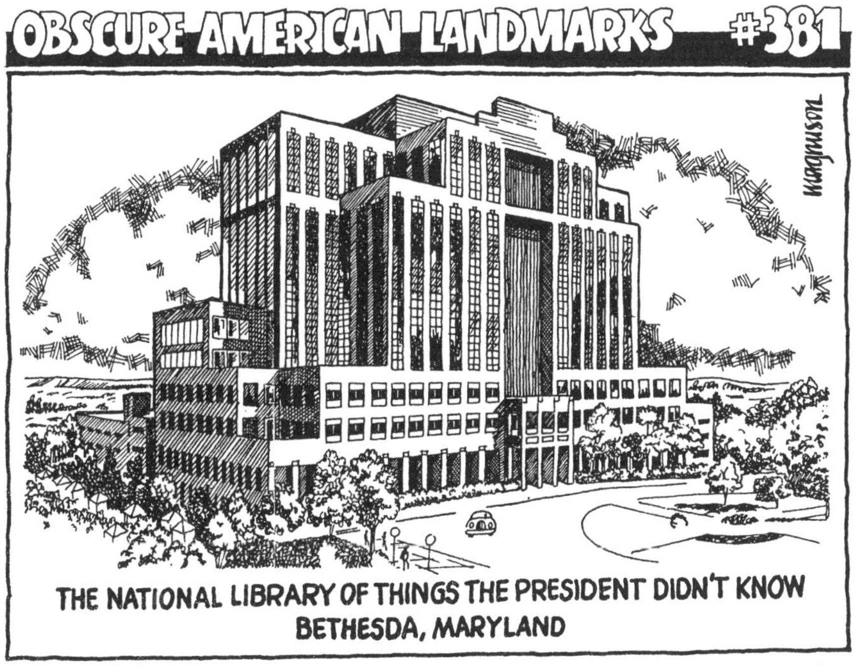
OBSCURE AMERICAN LANDMARKS #381
magnuson
THE NATIONAL LIBRARY OF THINGS THE PRESIDENT DIDN'T KNOW
BETHESDA, MARYLAND

STEVE MAGNUSON. THE REALIST #105, OCTOBER 1987.

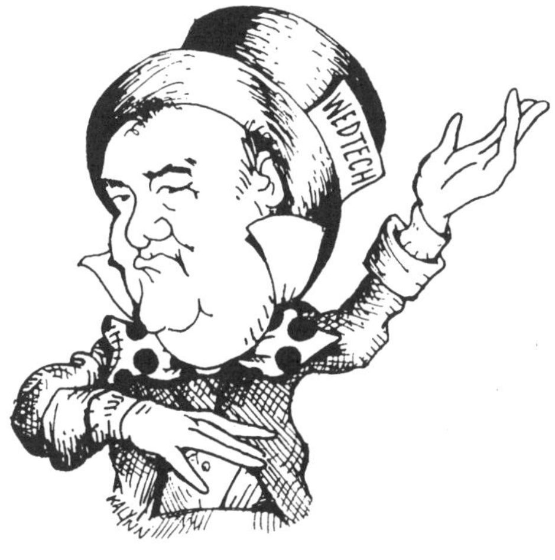
WEDTECH
KALYNN

Testifying before the Senate Judiciary Committee, former deputy attorney Arnold Burns described what it was like working in Ed Meese's Justice Department: "It was a world of Alice in Wonderland, a world of illsion and allusion, a world in which up was down and down was up, in was out and out was in, happy was sad and sad was happy."

KALYNN CAMPBELL. THE REALIST #107, SUMMER 1988.

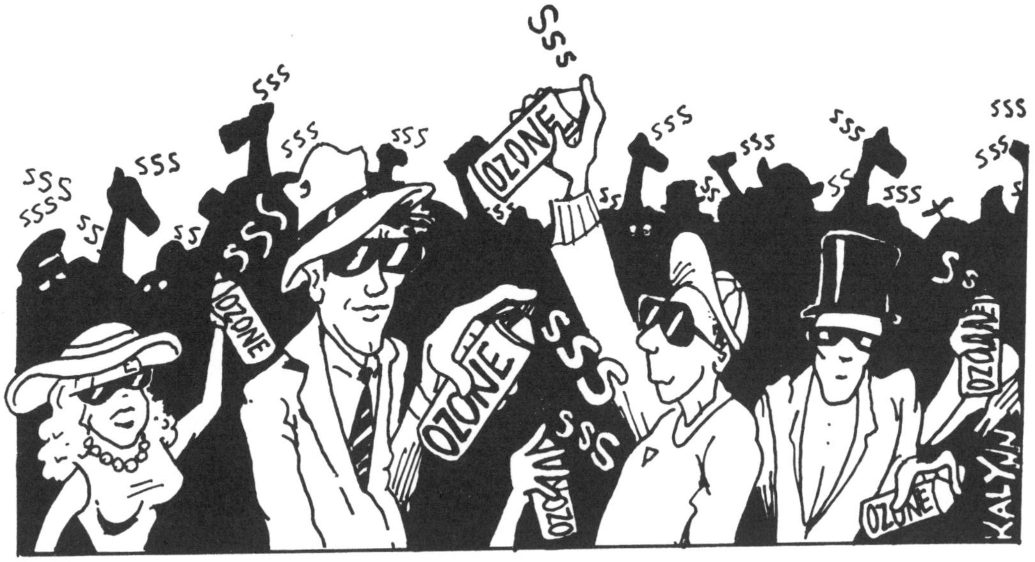
OZONE
OZONE
OZONE
OZONE
OZONE
OZONE
KALYNN

Great Moments in Ecology: According to U.S. News & World Report, "Secretary of the Interior Donald Hodel is only a front man in pushing reversal of Administration policy to counter chloroflourocarbons that erode the earth's protective covering of ozone. The real reason why the White House is switching to a defensive policy of sunglasses, sunbonnets and locations: A heavy attack by the makers of personal-care products, refrigerants and fire extinguishers who complained that a tentative international accord limiting CFC sprays would raise production costs."

KALYNN CAMPBELL. THE REALIST #105, OCTOBER 1987.

WISDOM OF THE AGES #10
"MAN IS THE ONLY ANIMAL THAT LAUGHS AND HAS A STATE LEGISLATURE."
- SAMUEL BUTLER

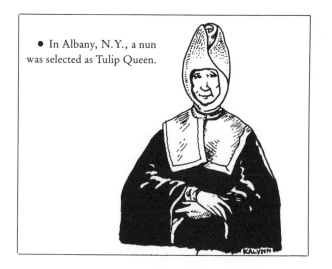

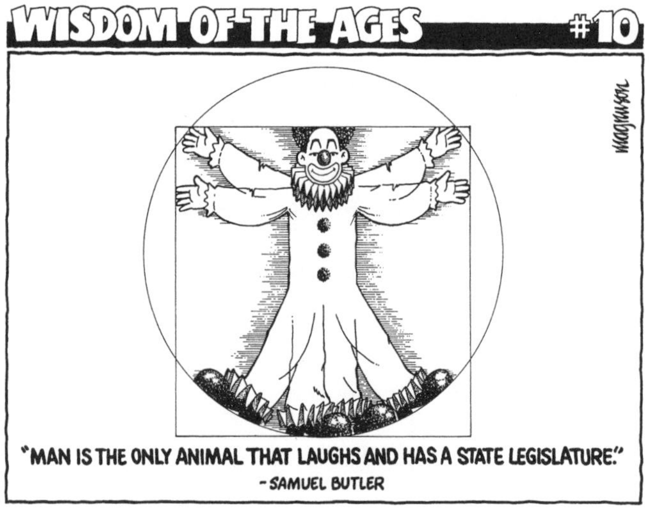

STEVE MAGNUSON. THE REALIST #105, OCTOBER 1987.

• In Albany, N.Y., a nun was selected as Tulip Queen.
KALYNN

KALYNN CAMPBELL. THE REALIST #105, OCTOBER 1987.

HOP DEN
JUST SAY YES
KALYNN FEATURES SYNDICATE

KALYNN CAMPBELL. THE REALIST #107, SUMMER 1988.

IT CAN'T HAPPEN HERE

ROBBIE CONAL. THE REALIST #108, WINTER 1989.

KALYNN

KALYNN CAMPBELL. THE REALIST #107, SUMMER 1988.

Gary Hart, Joan Rivers and Spuds MacKenzie Caught Participating in Kinky Media Orgy

VARIETY
KALYNN

Photo by Jimmy Swaggart

KALYNN CAMPBELL. THE REALIST #106, SPRING 1988.

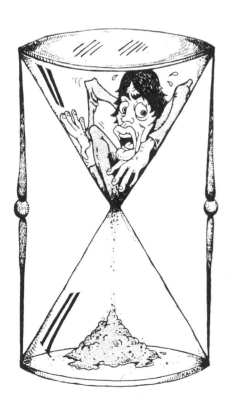

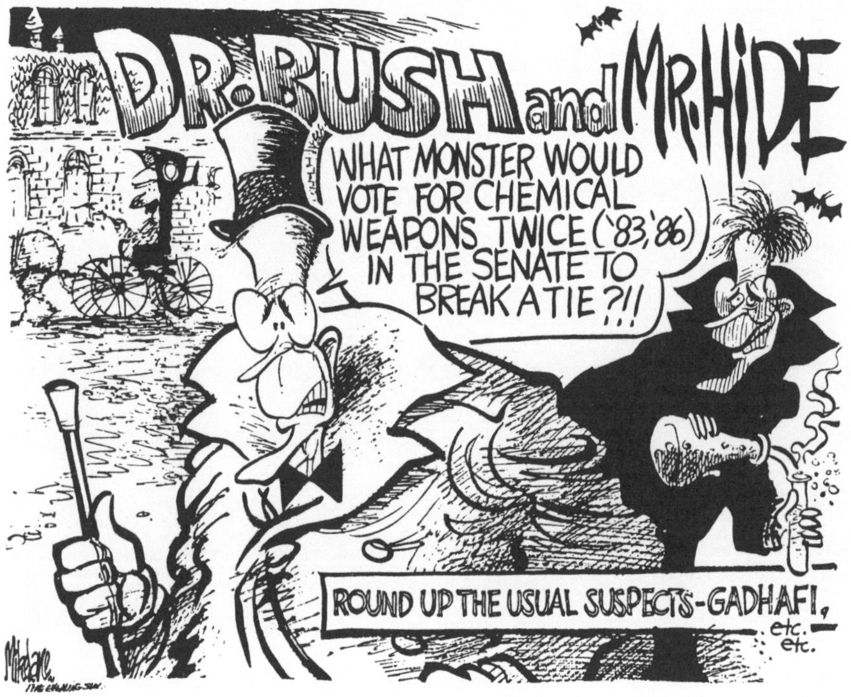
DR. BUSH and MR. HIDE
WHAT MONSTER WOULD VOTE FOR CHEMICAL WEAPONS TWICE ('83, '86) IN THE SENATE TO BREAK A TIE ?!!
ROUND UP THE USUAL SUSPECTS - GADHAFI, etc. etc.

MIKE LANE. THE REALIST #109, SPRING 1989.

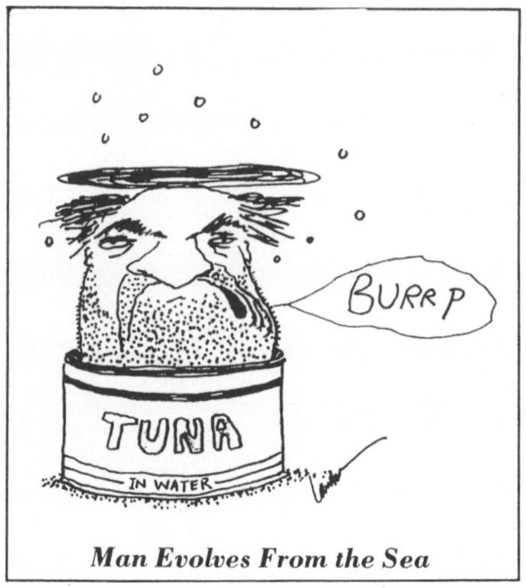
BURRP
TUNA
IN WATER
Man Evolves From the Sea

MARY LAWTON. THE REALIST #108, WINTER 1989.

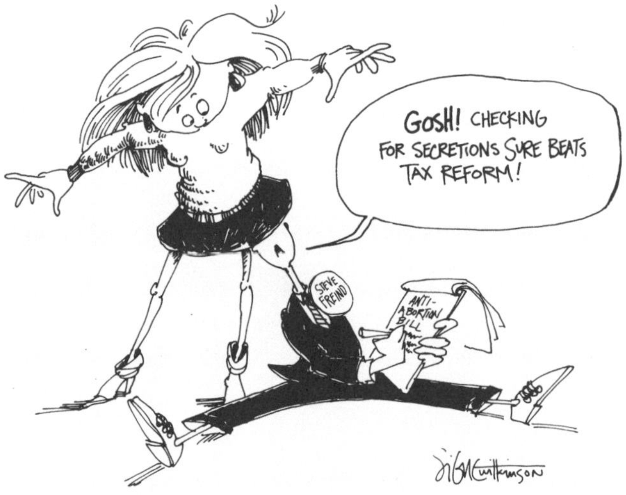
GOSH! CHECKING FOR SECRETIONS SURE BEATS TAX REFORM!
STEVE FREIND
ANTI-ABORTION BILL

SIGNE WILKINSON. THE REALIST #109, SPRING 1989.

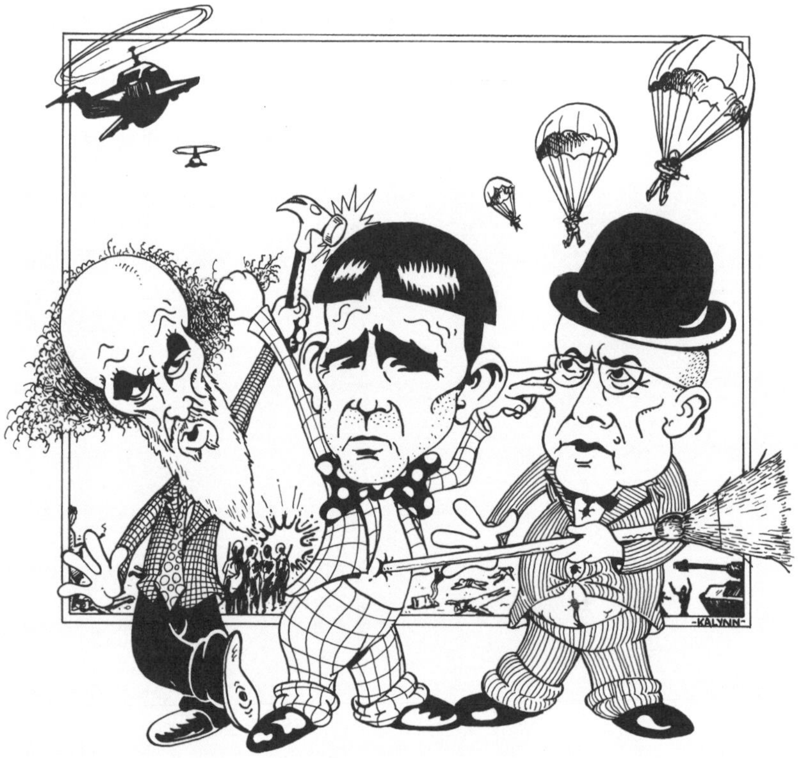
-KALYNN-

The Trial of Oliver North

KALYNN CAMPBELL. THE REALIST #109, SPRING 1989.

CHANNELING DISORDERS
J.Z. KNIGHT GOT RAMTHA, JANE ROBERTS GOT SETH. I GOT HENNY YOUNGMAN.
MIME CHANNELING
Nicole Hollander

NICOLE HOLLANDER. THE REALIST #109, SPRING 1989.

KALYNN

KALYNN CAMPBELL. THE REALIST #109, SPRING 1989. ©92

PRESIDENT
QUAYLE

Georgie We Hardly Knew Ye

There are T-shirts on the market with this sendoff of the famous Edvard Munch painting, "The Scream." And *The Nation* reports that in poster format it's "popping up all over Washington, illustrating the city's bipartisan consensus about the boy Vice President. In the harsher climate of New York, artistic interpreters of the Quayle phenomenon prefer to work in a conceptual style that some critics describe as minimalist, others as felonious. A black-and-white poster spied at the corner of 7th Ave. and 16th St. says, *Murder Dan Quayle in Cold Blood!*"

THE REALIST #109, SPRING 1989.

On the Head Again

The TV program *Incredible Sunday* reported a medical advance in which patients with head injuries are taught to write country music.

PAUL GRUDZINSKI. THE REALIST #109, SPRING 1989.

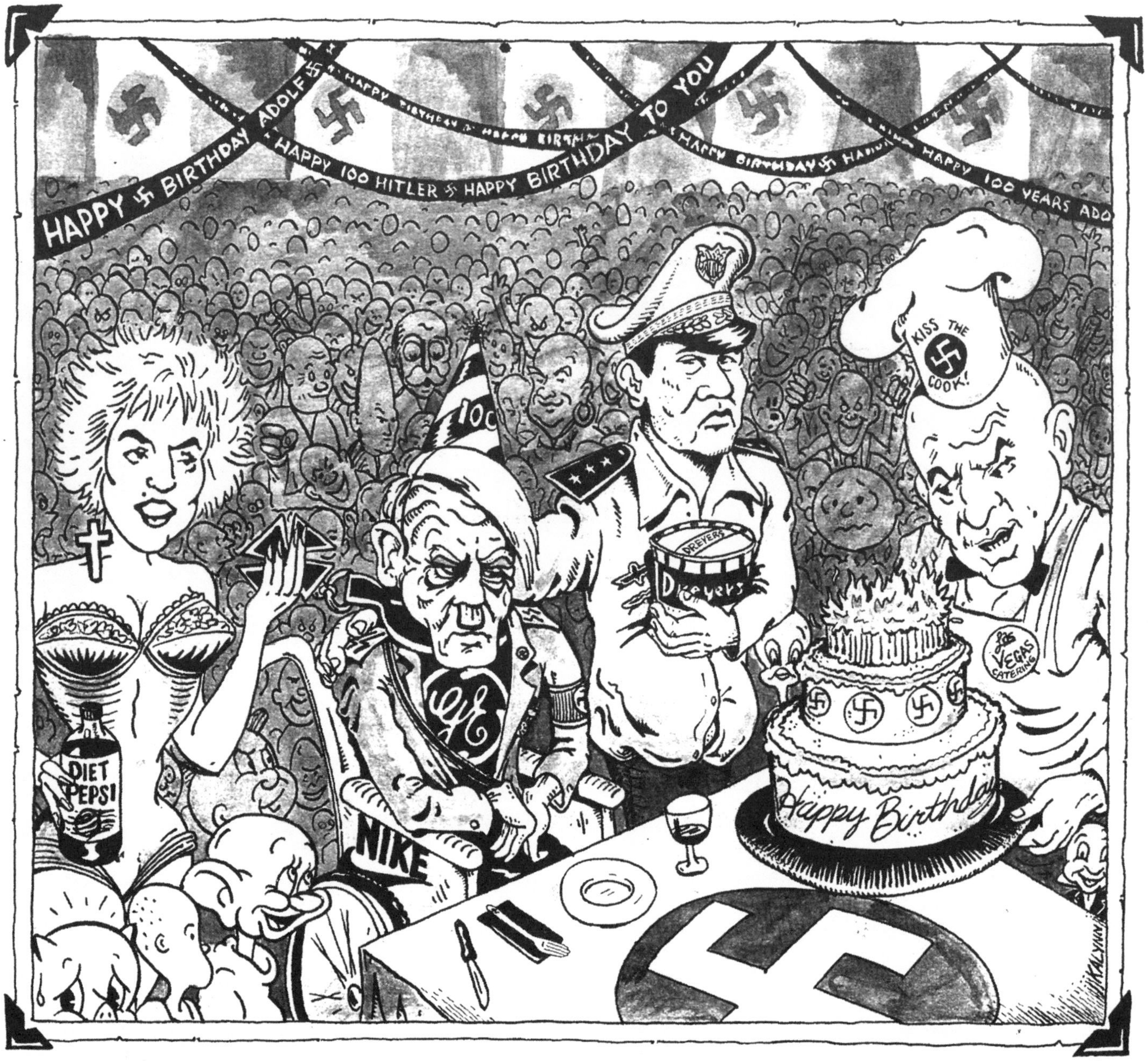
HAPPY BIRTHDAY ADOLF
HAPPY 100 HITLER HAPPY BIRTHDAY TO YOU
HAPPY 100 YEARS
100
KISS THE COOK!
DIET PEPSI
NIKE
LAS VEGAS CATERING
Happy Birthday
KALYNN

KALYNN CAMPBELL. THE REALIST #110, SUMMER 1989.

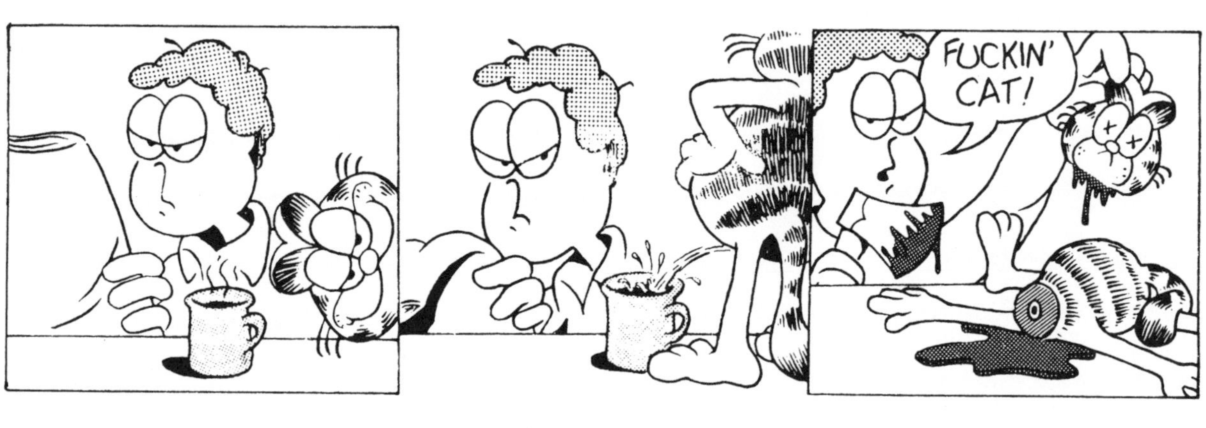
FUCKIN' CAT!

THE REALIST #110, SUMMER 1989.

R
BATMAN
DEAREST
BY ROBIN
KALYNN

KALYNN CAMPBELL. THE REALIST #110, SUMMER 1989. *93

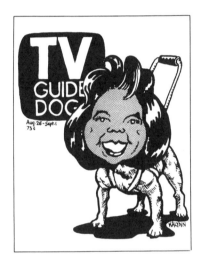

TV
GUIDE
DOG
Aug. 26-Sept. 1
75¢
KALYNN

KALYNN CAMPBELL. THE REALIST #111, WINTER 1990.

MARGE GRUDZINSKI. THE REALIST #111, WINTER 1990.

KALYNN

We're No Angels

KALYNN CAMPBELL. THE REALIST #112, SPRING 1990.

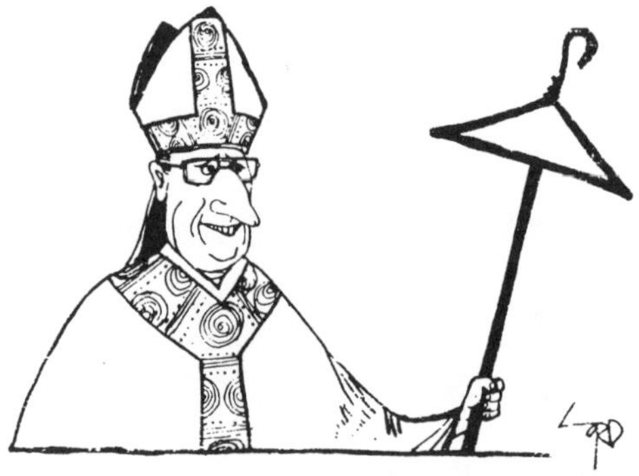

Editorial Cartoon Censored by Newsday

M.G. LORD. THE REALIST #112, SPRING 1990.

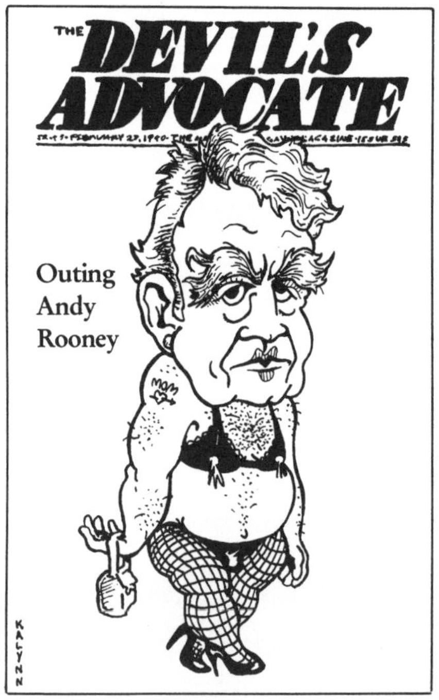
THE
DEVIL'S
ADVOCATE
Outing
Andy
Rooney
KALYNN

KALYNN CAMPBELL. THE REALIST #113, SUMMER 1990.

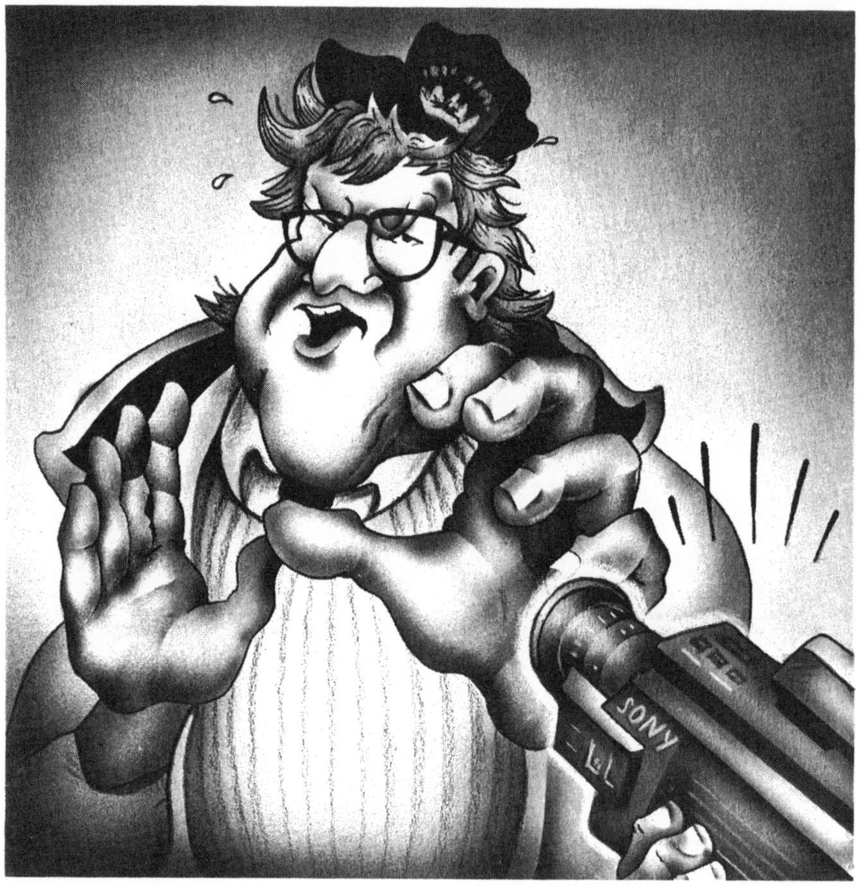
SONY

KALYNN CAMPBELL. THE REALIST #113, SUMMER 1990.

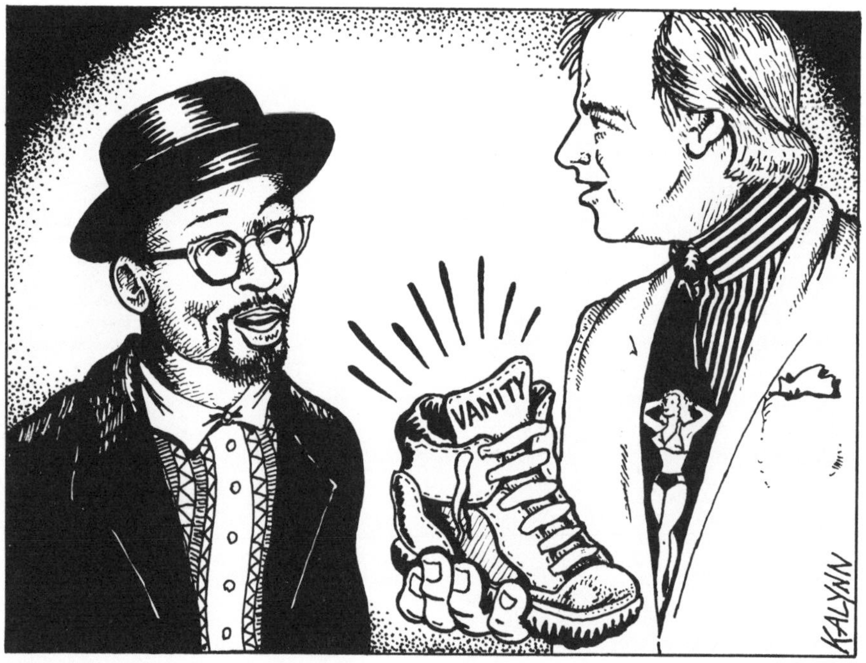
VANITY
KALYNN

KALYNN CAMPBELL. THE REALIST #113, SUMMER 1990.

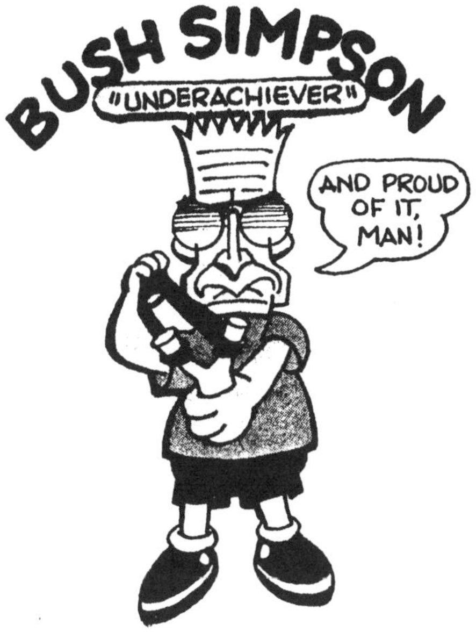
BUSH SIMPSON
"UNDERACHIEVER"
AND PROUD OF IT, MAN!

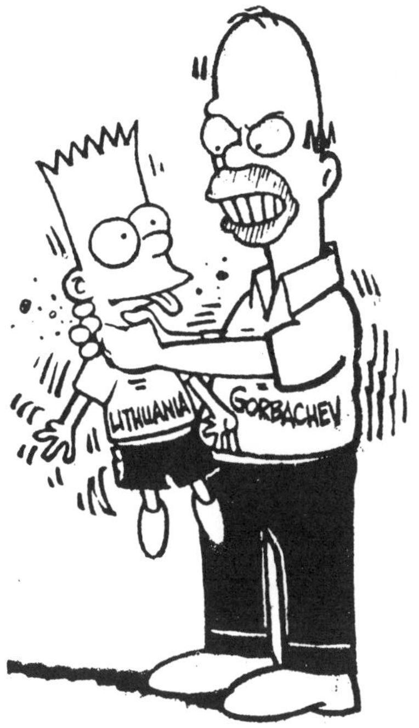
LITHUANIA
GORBACHEV

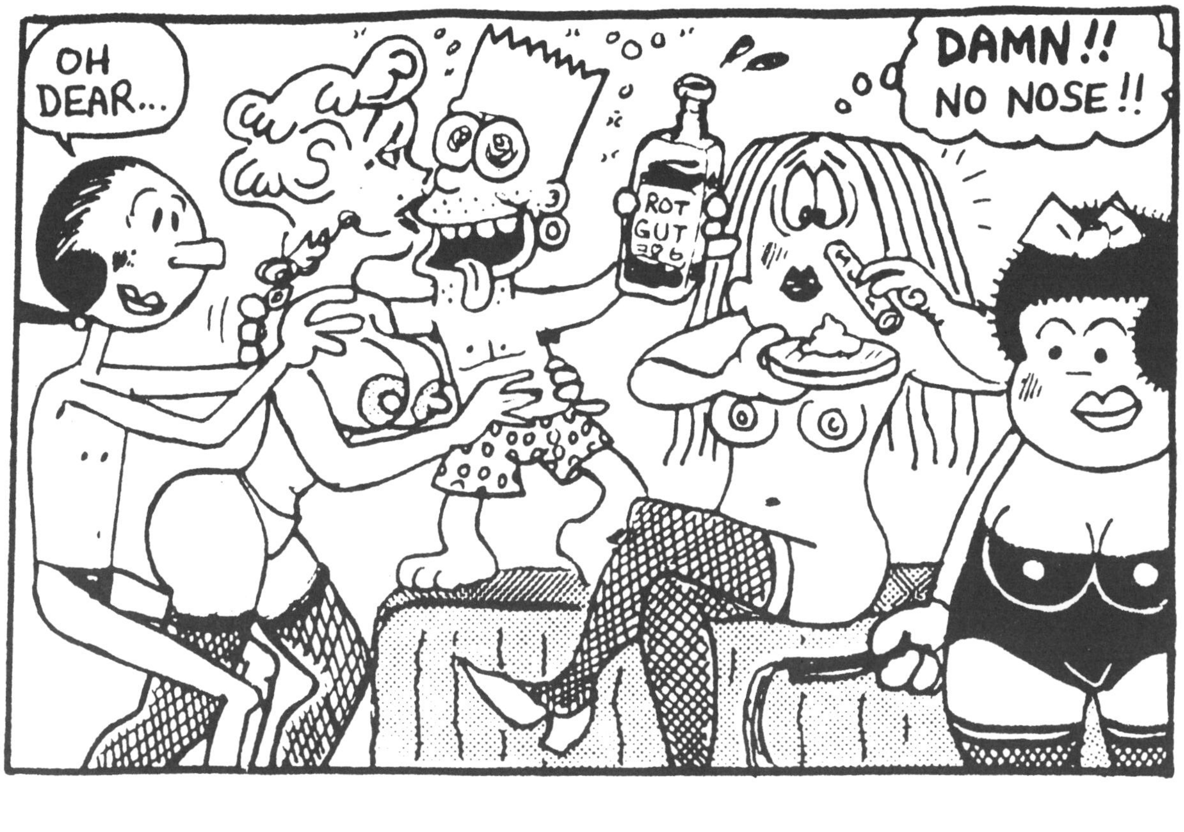
OH DEAR...
ROT GUT
DAMN!! NO NOSE!!

THE REALIST #114, FALL 1990.

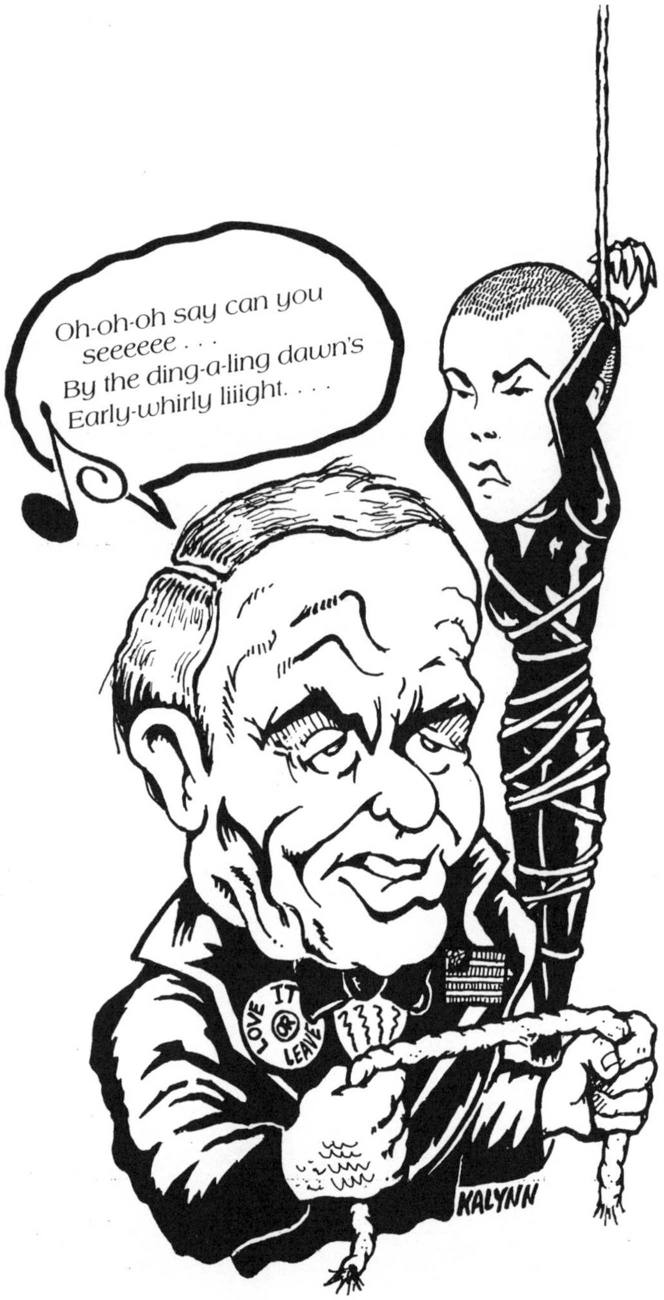
Oh-oh-oh say can you seeeeee . . .
By the ding-a-ling dawn's
Early-whirly liiight. . . .
LOVE IT OR LEAVE
KALYNN

KALYNN CAMPBELL. THE REALIST #115, JANUARY-FEBRUARY 1991. *95

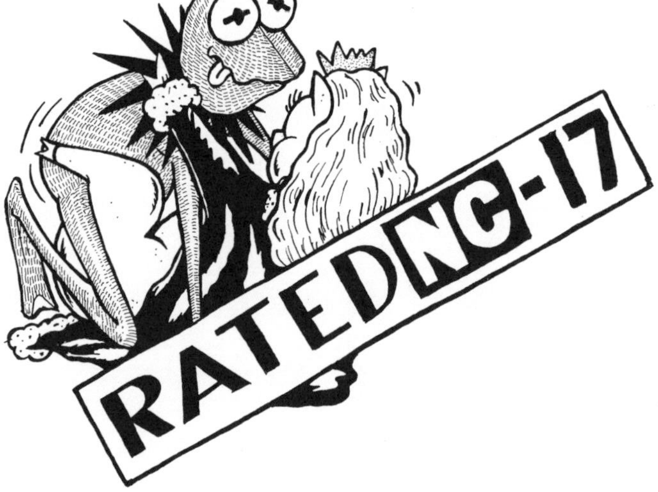
RATED NC-17

KALYNN CAMPBELL. THE REALIST #115, JANUARY-FEBRUARY 1991.

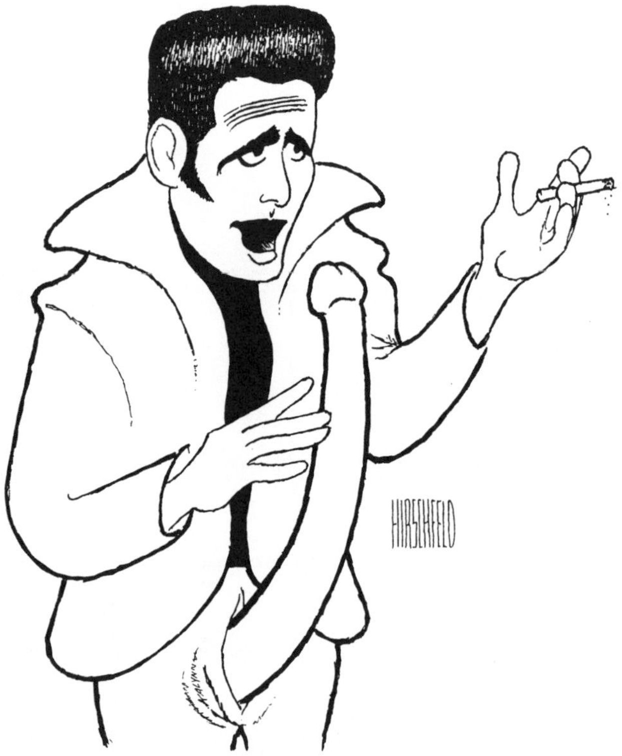
HIRSCHFELD

KALYNN CAMPBELL. THE REALIST #114, FALL 1990.

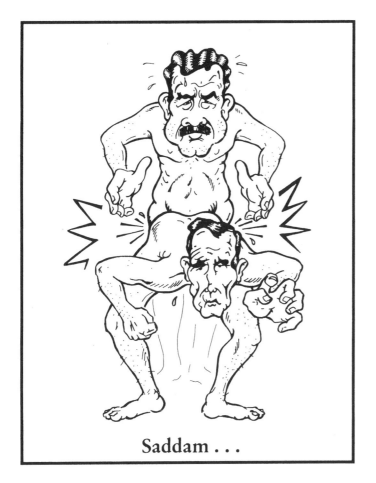

Saddam . . .

. . . and Gomorrah

KALYNN CAMPBELL. THE REALIST #116, MARCH-APRIL 1991.

KALYNN CAMPBELL. THE REALIST #116, MARCH-APRIL 1991.

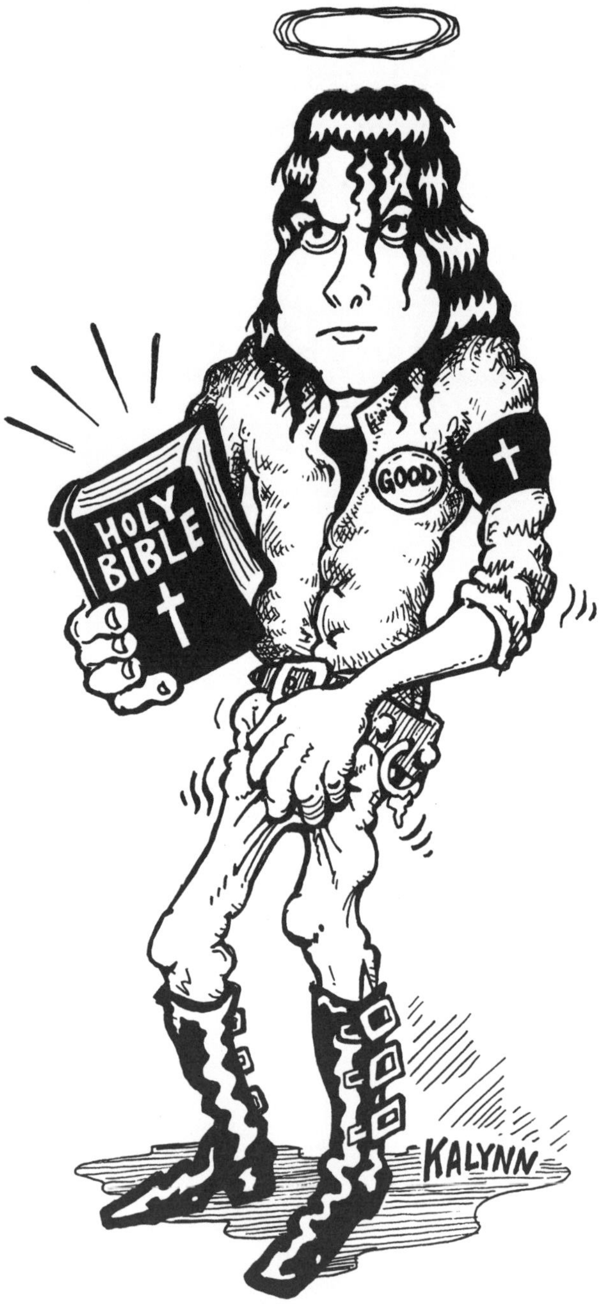
HOLY BIBLE
GOOD
KALYNN

KALYNN CAMPBELL. THE REALIST #120, SUMMER 1992.

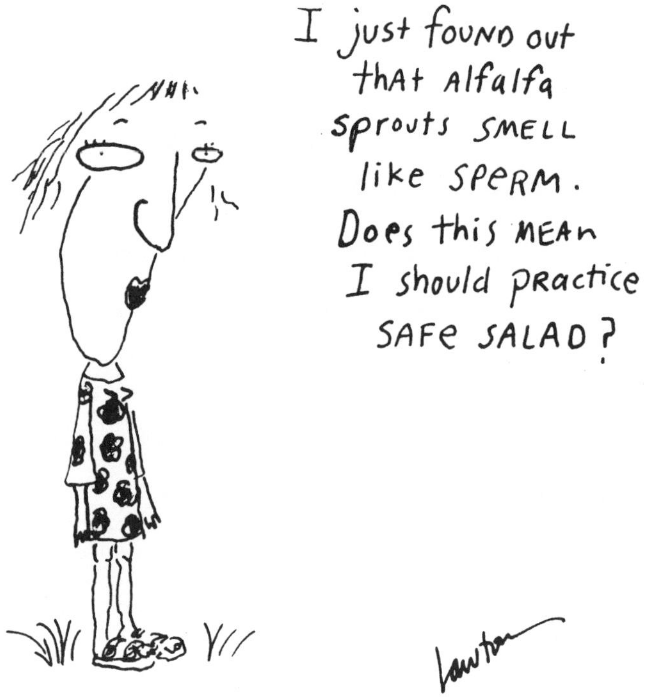
I just found out that alfalfa sprouts smell like sperm. Does this mean I should practice safe salad?
Lawton

MARY LAWTON. THE REALIST #116, MARCH-APRIL 1991.

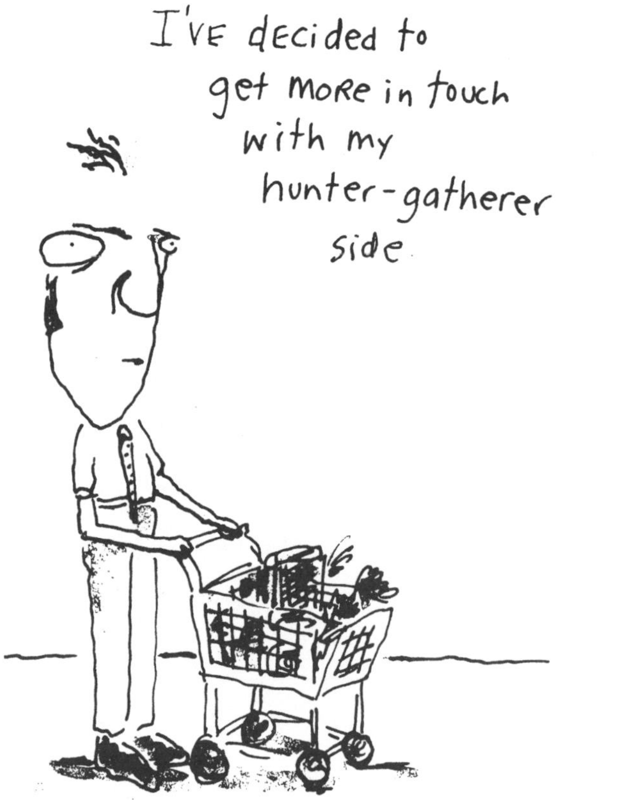
I've decided to get more in touch with my hunter-gatherer side

MARY LAWTON. THE REALIST #117, SUMMER 1991.

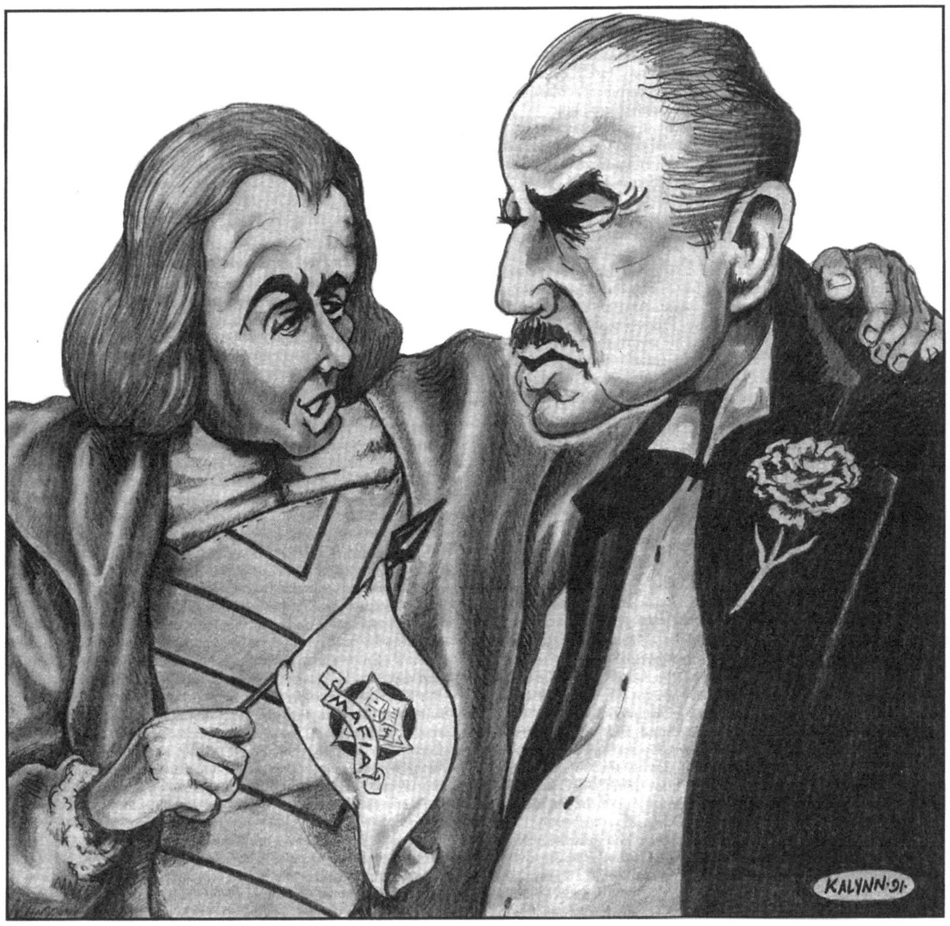
MAFIA
KALYNN·91·

KALYNN CAMPBELL. THE REALIST #118, FALL 1991.

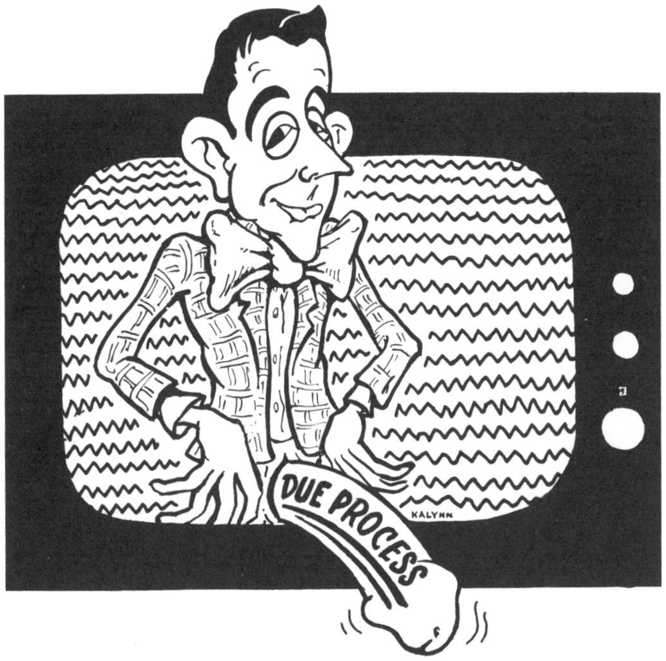
DUE PROCESS
KALYNN

KALYNN CAMPBELL. THE REALIST #118, FALL 1991. *95

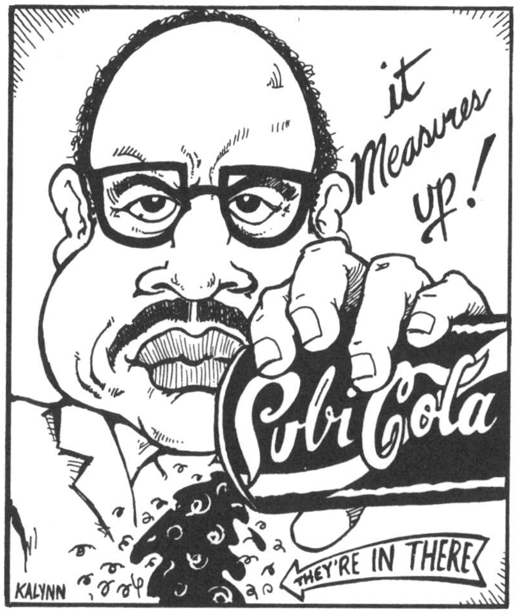
it Measures up!
Pubi Cola
THEY'RE IN THERE
KALYNN

KALYNN CAMPBELL. THE REALIST #119, WINTER 1992. *96

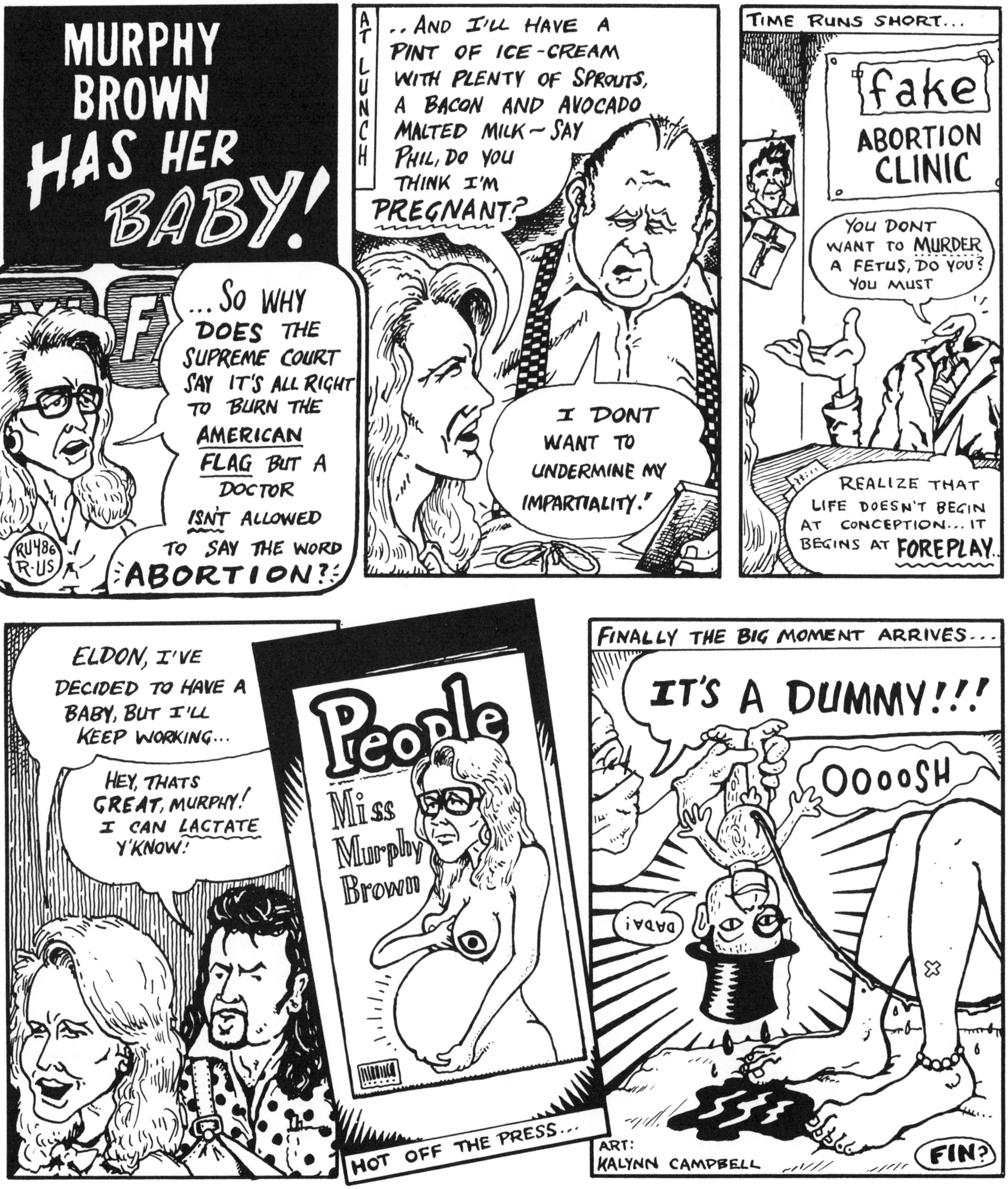

MURPHY BROWN HAS HER BABY!
...SO WHY DOES THE SUPREME COURT SAY IT'S ALL RIGHT TO BURN THE AMERICAN FLAG BUT A DOCTOR ISN'T ALLOWED TO SAY THE WORD ABORTION?
RU486 R-US
AT LUNCH
..AND I'LL HAVE A PINT OF ICE-CREAM WITH PLENTY OF SPROUTS, A BACON AND AVOCADO MALTED MILK ~ SAY PHIL, DO YOU THINK I'M PREGNANT?
I DONT WANT TO UNDERMINE MY IMPARTIALITY!
TIME RUNS SHORT...
fake ABORTION CLINIC
YOU DONT WANT TO MURDER A FETUS, DO YOU? YOU MUST
REALIZE THAT LIFE DOESN'T BEGIN AT CONCEPTION... IT BEGINS AT FOREPLAY..
ELDON, I'VE DECIDED TO HAVE A BABY, BUT I'LL KEEP WORKING...
HEY, THATS GREAT, MURPHY! I CAN LACTATE Y'KNOW!
People
Miss Murphy Brown
HOT OFF THE PRESS...
FINALLY THE BIG MOMENT ARRIVES...
IT'S A DUMMY!!!
OOOOSH
DADA!
ART: KALYNN CAMPBELL
FIN?

PAUL KRASSNER AND KALYNN CAMPBELL. THE REALIST #119, WINTER 1992.

A
B
RIP CORD
WHAT- ME WORRY?
SPY
MAD
FEAR
KALYNN
CAMPBELL

For Bill Gaines So Loved the World He Gave His Only Begotten Icon . . .

KALYNN CAMPBELL. THE REALIST #121, FALL 1992. *97

S. GROSS
THE UNKNOWN TERRORIST
TICK! TICK! TICK!

SAM GROSS. THE REALIST #121, FALL 1992.

With his high-powered telescope, Hank enjoyed examining the nasal hairs of his neighbors.
lawton

MARY LAWTON. THE REALIST #121, FALL 1992.

Young Dr. Jack Kevorkian
Assisting Lemmings with Suicide.
lawton

MARY LAWTON. THE REALIST #120, SUMMER 1992.

PAPER OR PLASTIC
1. DEPLETES THE FORESTS
2. SAW MILLS POLLUTE THE AIR & WATER
3. BURNING PAPER ADDS TO GLOBAL WARMING, ACID RAIN, HALF IN
1. PLASTIC PRODUCTION CREATES TOXIC BY-PRODUCTS
2. NON-BIO-DEGRADABLE
3. DISCARDED PLASTIC PRODUCTS ENDANGER WILD-LIFE, ENVIRON
NICK DOWNES

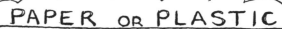

NICK DOWNES. THE REALIST #120, SUMMER 1992.

HONEY, I FUCKED THE KIDS!
WRITTEN AND DIRECTED BY WOO ALLEN
SO WHERE CAN A GUY WHO WORKS ALONE GO TO MEET GIRLS? WHAT AM I SUPPOSED TO DO? GO ON "STUDS"?
CAN I HELP IT IF I FELL IN LOVE WITH SOON-YI?
I WOULD VERY MUCH LIKE TO BE A MODEL AND POSE FOR NATIONAL MAGAZINES
DO YOU REALLY THINK THE 'NEW YORKER' MAGAZINE WILL LIKE THIS?
CLICK
A HARD-ON WANTS WHAT IT WANTS!
ART PIG: KALYNN CAMPBELL
ACTUALLY, MIA IS INSANELY JEALOUS OF MY CAREER...
ACTING IS FUN, BUT THE TRUTH IS, I'VE ALWAYS WANTED TO DIRECT!
AND SO THEN DADDY TOUCHED YOUR PRIVATE PART?
VIDEO CAMERA
IF HE SAYS HE DIDN'T, HE'S LYING
MODERN LIFE IS JUST FULL OF SCHIZOPHRENIC PARADOXES..
WOULD IT BE KOSHER FOR A JEWISH PERSON TO GET A LIVER TRANSPLANT FROM A PIG?
MAYBE IF BIOTECH ENGINEERS COULD DEVELOP A PIG THAT DIDN'T HAVE CLOVEN HOOVES.
A GURU FROM INDIA TOLD BARBARA WALTERS THAT HE DRINKS HIS OWN URINE IN ORDER TO REACH A HIGHER PLATEAU IN HIS SPIRITUAL QUEST.
BUT AFTER THE EARTHQUAKE IN EGYPT, A MAN'S FAMILY DIED BECAUSE THEY REFUSED TO TRANSCEND THAT TABOO AND DRINK THEIR OWN URINE
WHY IS IT WRONG FOR SINEAD O'CONNOR TO TEAR UP A PHOTO OF THE POPE ON 'SATURDAY NIGHT LIVE'?
YET IT'S CONSIDERED AN ARTISTIC STATEMENT WHEN MADONNA SHOVES A CRUCIFIX UP HER VAGINA
OVER THE YEARS, THOUGH, MY PSYCHIATRIST HAS BEEN EXTREMELY HELPFUL.
WOODY ASKS ME PHILOSPHICAL QUESTIONS, LIKE "WHY SHOULD I DENY MYSELF PLEASURE SIMPLY TO AVOID INFLICTING PAIN ON OTHERS?" AND OF COURSE I REPLY, "GO ON." THEN I GIVE HIM AN AUDIOTAPE OF EACH SESSION SO HE CAN GET BUSY WRITING HIS SCREENPLAY
BELIEVE ME, IT HASN'T BEEN SUCH A GREAT THRILL TO BE THE BUTT OF JOKES BY ALL THE TV TALK-SHOW HOSTS...
..HIS NEW MOVIE, 'HUSBANDS AND STEPDAUGHTERS'
RATED D-17, GIRLS UNDER 17 ADMITTED ONLY IF ACCOMPANED BY THE DIRECTOR!
WHY, CHARLIE MANSON HAS BETTER FAMILY VALUES!
WELL, THIS IS MY LAST FILM. I'M GOING TO MARRY SOON-YI AND GO BACK TO MY FIRST LOVE, STANDUP COMEDY
TAKE MY MOTHER-IN-LAW, PLEASE...
END?

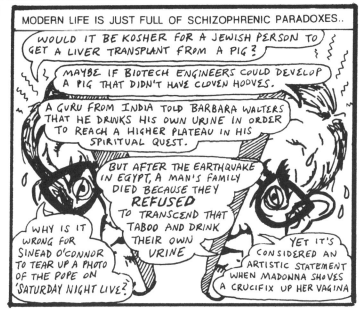

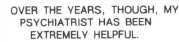

PAUL KRASSNER AND KALYNN CAMPBELL. THE REALIST #122, FALL 1992.

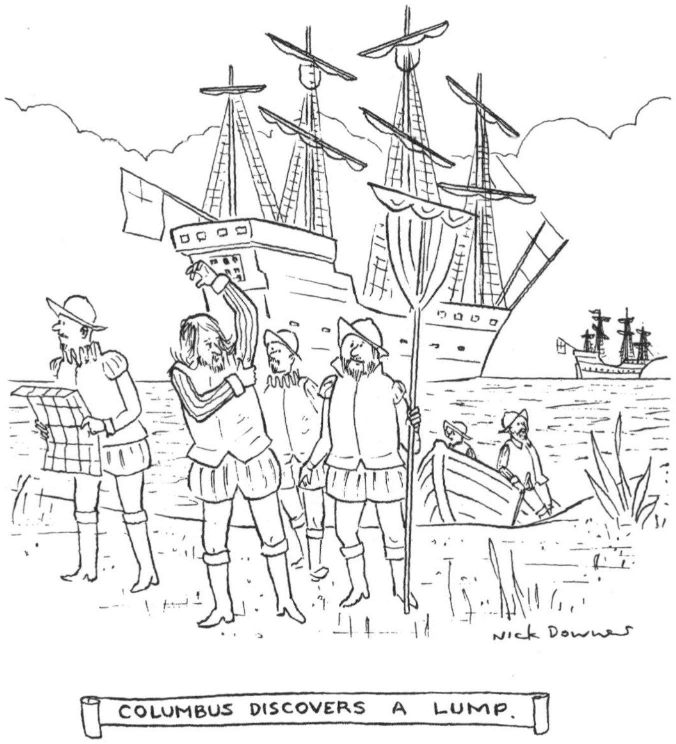
Nick Downes
COLUMBUS DISCOVERS A LUMP.

NICK DOWNES. THE REALIST #121, FALL 1992.

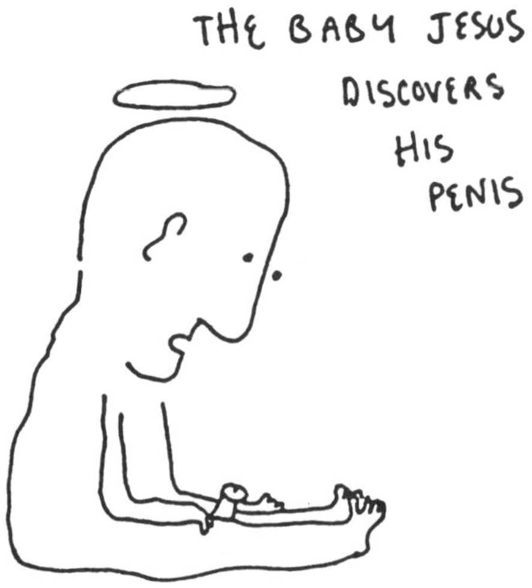
THE BABY JESUS DISCOVERS HIS PENIS

ROZ WARREN. THE REALIST #122, FALL 1992.

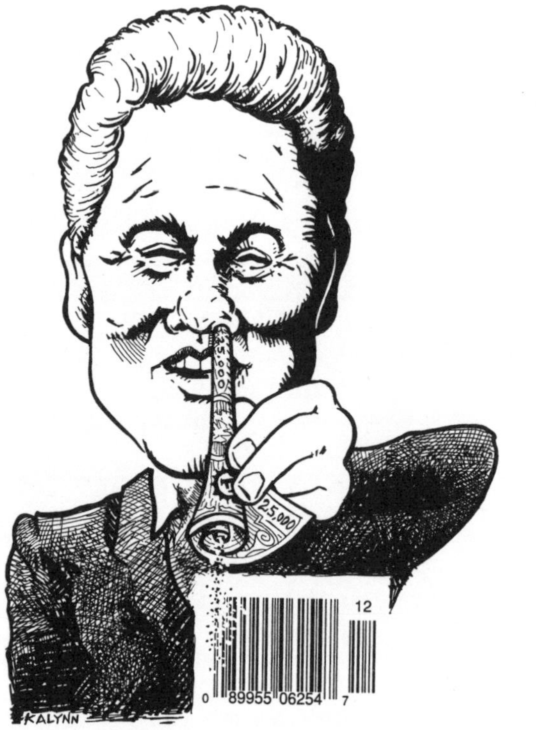
KALYNN

KALYNN CAMPBELL. THE REALIST #122, FALL 1992. *98

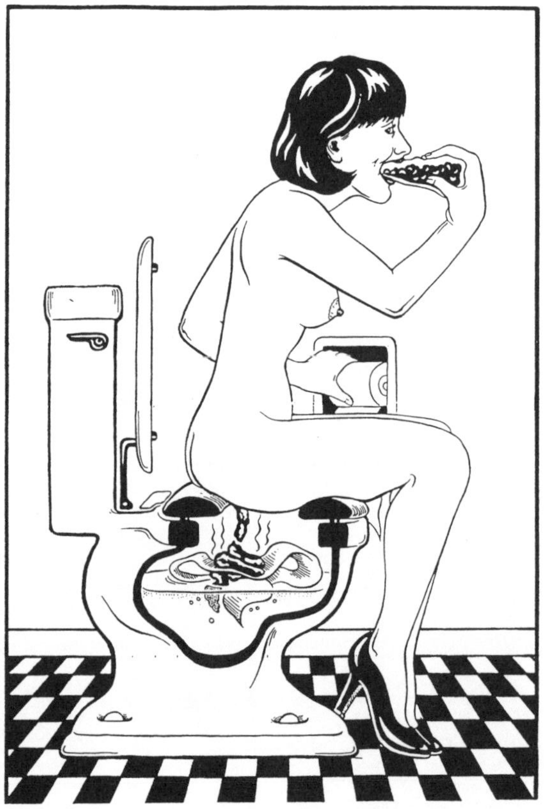

Editor's Note: This was the official centerfold for the special "Holy Shit" issue of *The Religion of the Month Club.*

THE REALIST #122, FALL 1992.

USE
HEIDI-
FLOSS
HEIDI FLOSS
DIPPED IN COCAINE

KALYNN CAMPBELL. THE REALIST #125, FALL 1993. *99

OIL
KALYNN

Let Them Drink Oil

KALYNN CAMPBELL. THE REALIST #123, SPRING 1993.

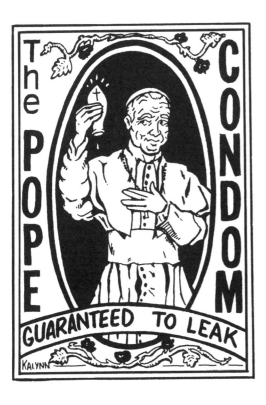

The
POPE
CONDOM
GUARANTEED TO LEAK
KALYNN

KALYNN CAMPBELL. THE REALIST #125, FALL 1993.

ABC's
MAIN ATTRACTION
abc
A LIVING PERSON
A COLLOSSAL ACT
SIAMESE TWINS
SENSATIONAL
HUMAN ODDITY!
KALYNN

KALYNN CAMPBELL. THE REALIST #124, SUMMER 1993.

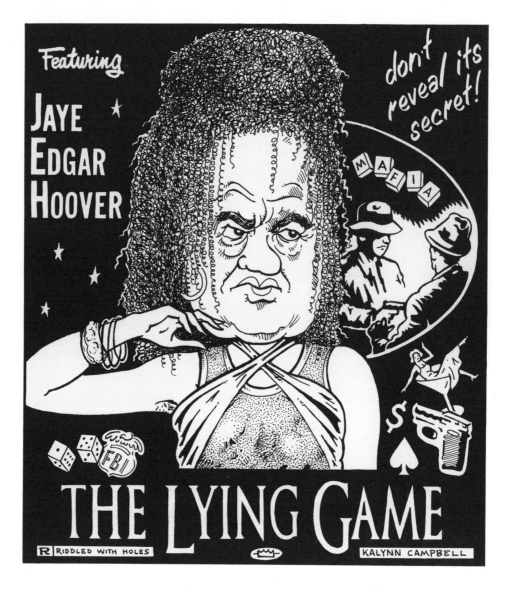

Featuring
JAYE EDGAR HOOVER
don't reveal its secret!
MAFIA
FBI
THE LYING GAME
R RIDDLED WITH HOLES
KALYNN CAMPBELL

KALYNN CAMPBELL. THE REALIST #123, SPRING 1993.

The Romance of Tampons

From the transcript of a taped phone conversation between Prince Charles and Camilla Parker Bowles:

Charles: The trouble is I need you several times a week.

Camilla: Mmm. So do I. I need you all the week, all the time.

Charles: Oh God. I'll just live inside your trousers or something. It would be much easier.

Camilla (laughing): What are you going to turn into—a pair of knickers? *(Laughter from both)* Oh, you're going to come back as a pair of knickers.

KALYNN

Charles: Or, God forbid, a Tampax, just my luck. *(Laughter)*

Camilla: You are a complete idiot! *(She laughs)* Oh, what a wonderful idea.

Charles: My luck to be chucked down the lavatory and go on and on forever swirling around on the top, never going down.

Camilla: *(Laughs)* Oh, darling.

Charles: Until the next one comes through.

Camilla: Or perhaps you could just come back as a box.

Charles: What sort of box?

Camilla: A box of Tampax so you could just keep going . . .

KALYNN CAMPBELL. THE REALIST #123, SPRING 1993.

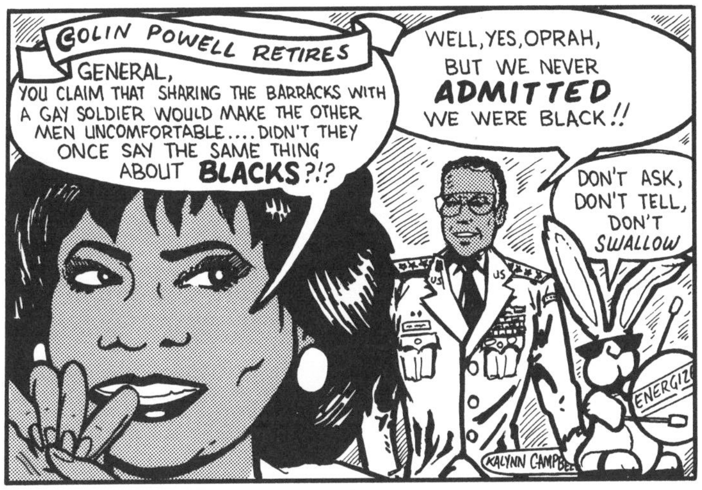
COLIN POWELL RETIRES
GENERAL, YOU CLAIM THAT SHARING THE BARRACKS WITH A GAY SOLDIER WOULD MAKE THE OTHER MEN UNCOMFORTABLE.... DIDN'T THEY ONCE SAY THE SAME THING ABOUT BLACKS?!?
WELL, YES, OPRAH, BUT WE NEVER ADMITTED WE WERE BLACK!!
DON'T ASK, DON'T TELL, DON'T SWALLOW
ENERGIZ
KALYNN CAMPBELL

KALYNN CAMPBELL. THE REALIST #125, FALL 1993.

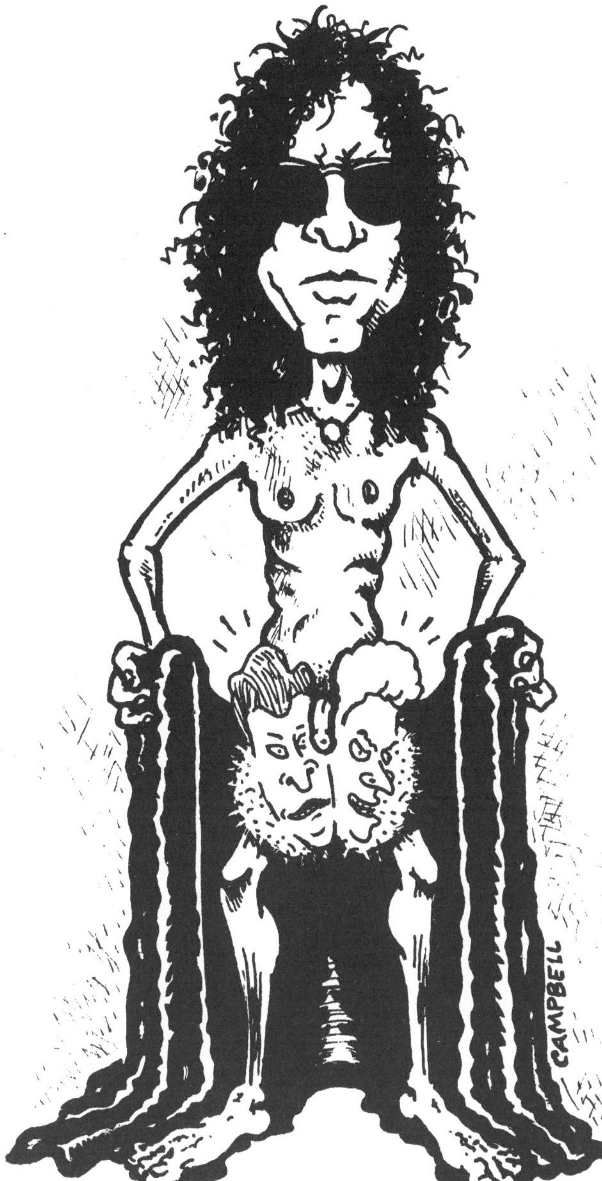
CAMPBELL

KALYNN CAMPBELL. THE REALIST #126, WINTER 1994.

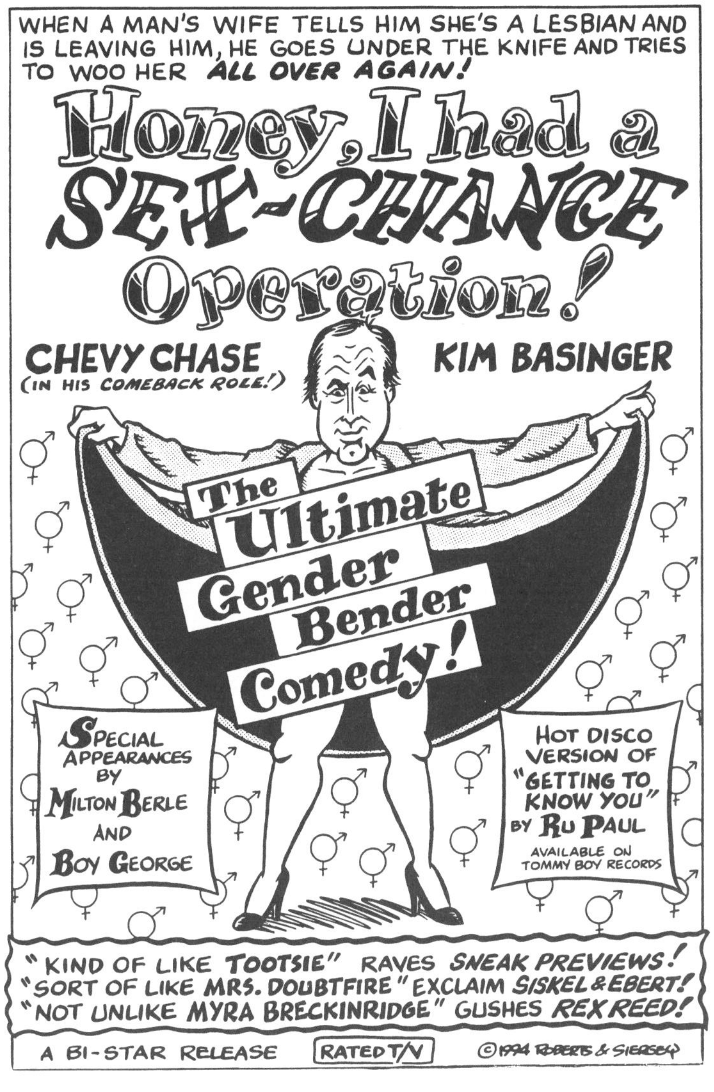
WHEN A MAN'S WIFE TELLS HIM SHE'S A LESBIAN AND IS LEAVING HIM, HE GOES UNDER THE KNIFE AND TRIES TO WOO HER ALL OVER AGAIN!
Honey, I had a SEX-CHANGE Operation!
CHEVY CHASE (IN HIS COMEBACK ROLE!)
KIM BASINGER
The Ultimate Gender Bender Comedy!
SPECIAL APPEARANCES BY MILTON BERLE AND BOY GEORGE
HOT DISCO VERSION OF "GETTING TO KNOW YOU" BY RU PAUL
AVAILABLE ON TOMMY BOY RECORDS
"KIND OF LIKE TOOTSIE" RAVES SNEAK PREVIEWS!
"SORT OF LIKE MRS. DOUBTFIRE" EXCLAIM SISKEL & EBERT!
"NOT UNLIKE MYRA BRECKINRIDGE" GUSHES REX REED!
A BI-STAR RELEASE
RATED T/V
©1994 ROBERTS & SIERSEY

JIM SIERGEY AND TOM ROBERTS. THE REALIST #127, SPRING 1994.

DAN DION AND KNIGHT.
THE REALIST #125, FALL 1993.

A Post-Communism Amusement Park

by Dan Dion

As a result of the increasing activity of the United Nations, we now have the first U.N. boredom relief effort. It is EastEuro Disney, an introduction to both natives and foreigners of the culture, history and limitless possibilities that encompass what used to be the Soviet Union and its satellite countries and Communist neighbors.

Administered and created by the East European governments themselves, but financed by the U.N., it represents a landmark in international cultural cooperation. It is a symbolic pulling back of the Iron Curtain, and a big *willkommen, fzivefen,* and *dobrodošlica* to civilized nations everywhere.

Through globally beloved characters of Walt Disney, the wonders of Eastern Europe are transformed into a magical land of fun and excitement. Like its western counterparts, the park is divided into theme territories, each one a playground in itself. They feature familiar cartoon faces, but with a decidedly EastEuro feel.

The Land of Yesterday

Run by the East Germans, this area showcases the pre-revolution past. Concessions are airlifted in on the hour. Don't miss the *Ich bin ein Berliner* booth with JFK-shaped pastries. Break the head apart to reveal the tasty jelly inside.

ReichVision Super Cinema—Relive the horrors of the blitzkrieg. Take a slow and agonizing journey in a boxcar to Bergen Belsen. Experience the mesmerizing power of a Nazi rally. Be a part of the final solution.

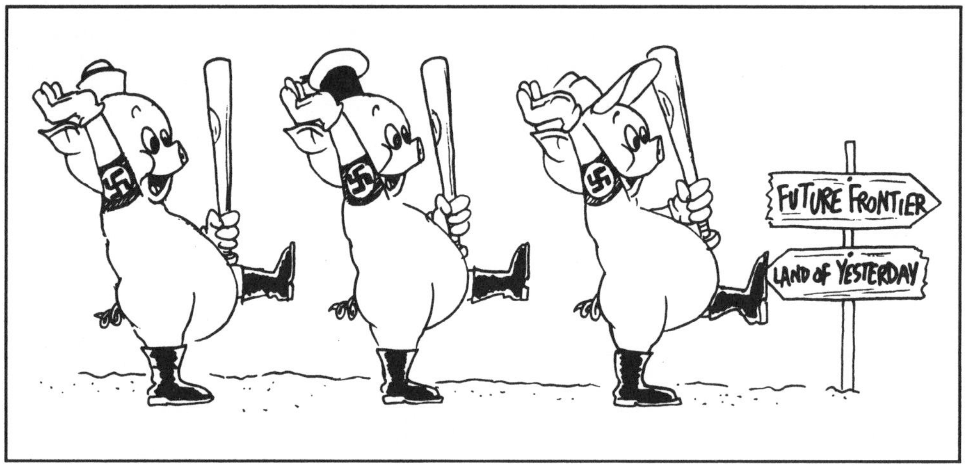
FUTURE FRONTIER
LAND OF YESTERDAY

Animal House: Try to stay dry, and upright, through Beer Bust! Get lucky—or trapped—in the Blind Date tunnel-of-lust! Take wild, felony-filled rides like Road Trip and Parade Gone Mad! Test your wits with Defy The Dean! But be cool. Remember, you can be expelled from the park on any pretext.

Birth of a Nation: Being based on an epic sympathetic to the origins of the KKK, this probably wouldn't get much non-white patronage; but location is everything, and it could become, say, the cash-cow of Moscow (Idaho).

Spartacus: Imagine a Road To Rome rollercoaster, the tracks lined with lifelike crucifixions. Actually, given the success of TV's *American Gladiators,* maybe it's time to bring back the classic Roman approach to popular entertainment for real. It's not all that great a stretch from pro football, boxing, or for that matter, the rodeo. And it's one occupation that youthful gang members wouldn't need costly re-training for, and/or that could be filled by imprisoned lifers without riling the unions.

Six Bonds Over Directed: Rides and attractions patterned after the countless chases, perils, predicaments, traps, and death-defying escapades in the "007" series, with the park divided into sections devoted to the various actors who've played Bond, such as Real Bond Land (Sean Connery), Dumb Bond Land (Roger Moore), Pathetic Bond Land (Woody Allen), and Forgotten Bond Land (George Lazensby).

Poseidon Inferno: Assorted thrills and chills derived from Irwin Allen's "disaster" blockbusters, with daredevil features like Tidal Wave, Highrise Firestorm, Copter Crash, Upside-Down Escape, and a chillingly realistic, holographic "meeting" with the fabled producer himself in Abominable Showman.

French Connection/Blues Brothers/Bullett/ etc.: Every great car chase you ever saw on film, in a computerized, interactive, virtual-reality environment that puts *you* behind the wheel!

The Longest Day: For all those cammo-vested armchair soldiers who lament that they "weren't around for the Big One," here's a chance to see all the combat action of World War II without ever being far from a restroom. Experience the adrenaline rush of utter hopelessness in Hit The Beach; test your nerves in the Minefield obstacle course; charge blazing machineguns in Suicide Bunker Assault; soil your clothing on the Behind Enemy Lines parachute drop. Then enjoy some hearty Shit on a Shingle at one of the K-Rations snack bars, and take in the colorful Andrews Sisters Tribute at the USO pavilion.

Around The World In 80 Days: Ballooning, train rides, storm-tossed schooners, a race against time—it's hard to believe this one hasn't already been built.

The Best Little Whorehouse In Texas: The title pretty much speaks for itself.

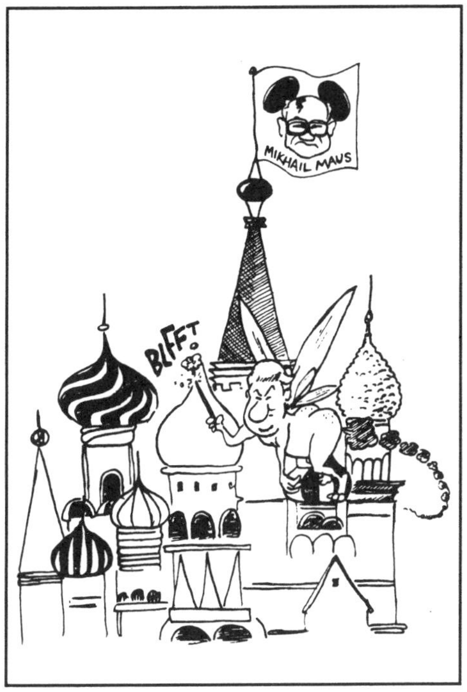
MIKHAIL MAUS
BIFFT

Pinocchio Regimes—Everybody's favorite puppet story is given a new meaning as Gepetto represents the U.S.S.R. in a post-World War II morality tale.

The Hunted House—This chilling and realistic ride is a maelstrom of past Germanic atrocities: elevators that turn into gas chambers; ghosts flying from burning Dresden. Watch Out! You're at the table with Hitler and Chamberlain in 1938!

The Berlin Wall Sprint—Test your luck against Chip and Dale, the Checkpoint Charlie Chipmunks as they do their best to foil your "escape" into Reality World.

Reality World

Presented by the former U.S.S.R., it is designed to give a taste of what Eastern Europe is like to the unknowing traveler. Though not as glamorous or as exciting as the past or future is made up to be, reality has its modest charms. Administrators claim the U.N. has been neglecting its duties and promises, resulting in unsafe and delayed developments.

Others blame stunted growth on the world recession and point to WestEuro Disney's financial failure. True, there are longer lines here, and college students have overrun the Prague Log Adventure, but help is on the way. A large aid package from the United States is expected soon, despite the eroded condition of its own Los Angeles facility.

The Georgian Jug Band Jamboree—Watch the country bears go from frenzied nationalistic music to a drunken stupor as the homemade vodka shows that independence and freedom can be intoxicating.

The Unstable Nuclear Light Parade—Come nightfall it is time to gather in Red Riding Hood Square and marvel at the beautiful hues of iridescent emanations from reactor floats and disarmament waste.

The Rumanian Shooting Gallery—This has only two targets, but fire away at Nicolae Ceausescu and his wife, reenacting the glorious execution of a classic dictator.

Sputnik Mountain—Get trapped as the operator, Mikhail Maus, steps down and nobody accepts responsibility for you. A nice leisure ride for parents.

Reunification Follies—With the cold war having thawed, Beauty and the Beast are skating on thin ice in this re-nuptial celebration. But don't expect a happy ending, as Beauty's family is reluctant to pay the bill, and the Beast just wants to get at the buffet.

The Future Frontier

To get there from the Land of Yesterday, just follow the goose-stepping skinhead pigs. The future is not as far from the past as you might think. This is the only theme area with sponsorship, provided by DuPont. It is the park's commercial center, where free enterprise and consumption meet up with exploitation and poor quality.

101 Corporations—In a virtual maze of 7-11s, Burger Kings, Blockbuster video stores, and *faux*-Levi's vendors, experience the thrill of a market economy. See the cast of *Aladdin* barter for inferior Soviet weapons. Bring your credit cards, but in all fairness, spending limits have been created for Asian visitors.

Pirates of the Mediterranean (under construction)—Watch Macedonian and Grecian forces slaughter each other over a national copyright dispute.

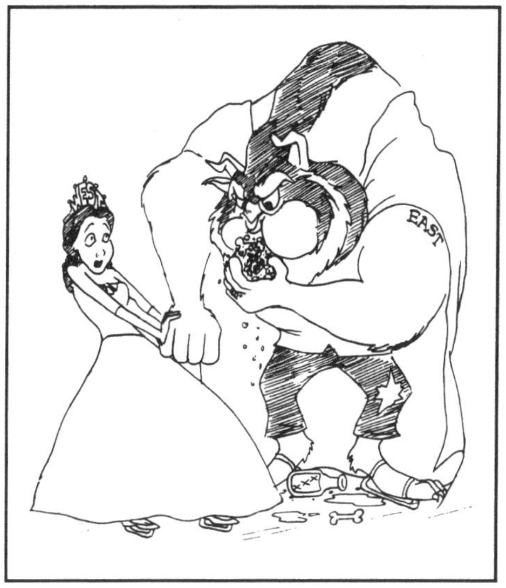
EAST

Helpful Hints

Not blessed with WestEuro Disney's free trade policies, ride tickets are not transferable or interchangeable. The resulting devaluation, inflation and general instability of the many different currencies may prove unsettling. Boundaries between lands may change without notice and perhaps amidst violence. As a guest, you should avert your eyes and leave the civil disputes to the locals. Portions of the Balkan Village are periodically closed for ethnic cleansing. Walt Disney always demanded a pure and immaculate park, so the occasional roundup of heathens is a must.

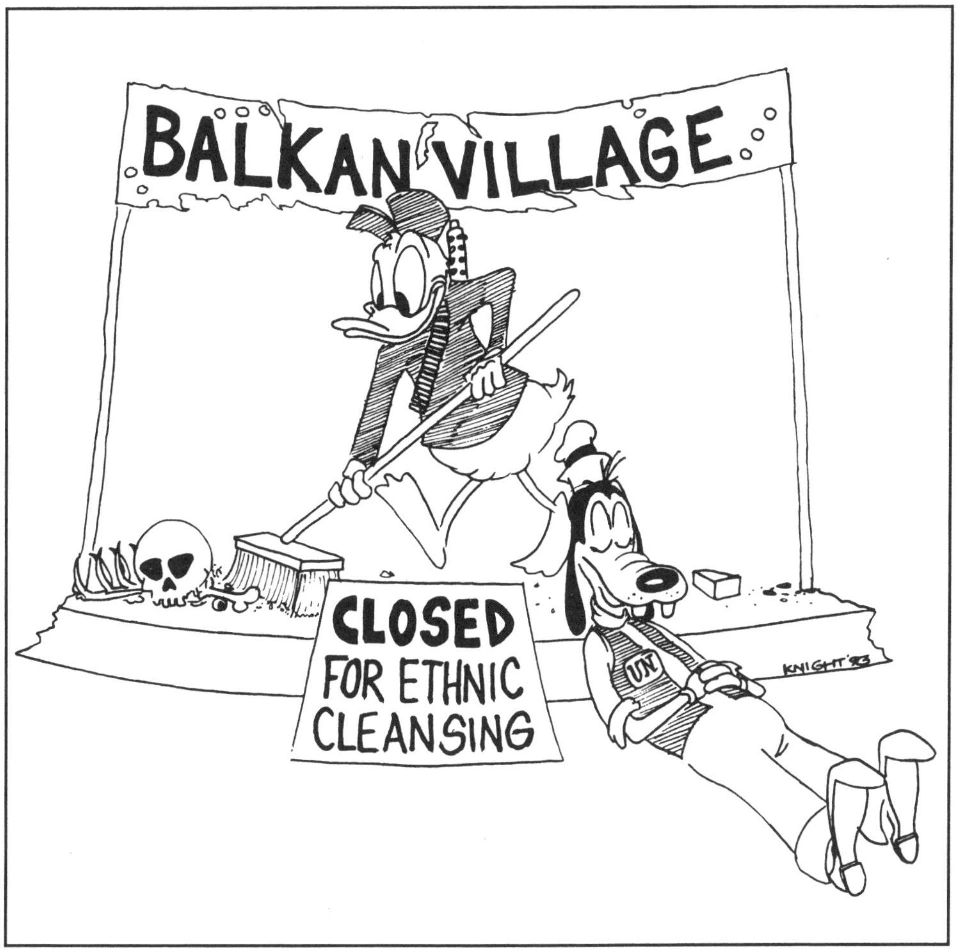
BALKAN VILLAGE
CLOSED
FOR ETHNIC
CLEANSING
UN
KNIGHT '93

The Realist

Spring, 1994
Price: $2

Number 127
Editor: Paul Krassner

- A Home for Problem Priests
- Stewart Brand Was My Roommate
- People Who Drink Their Own Urine

PEANUTS By Charles M. Schulz

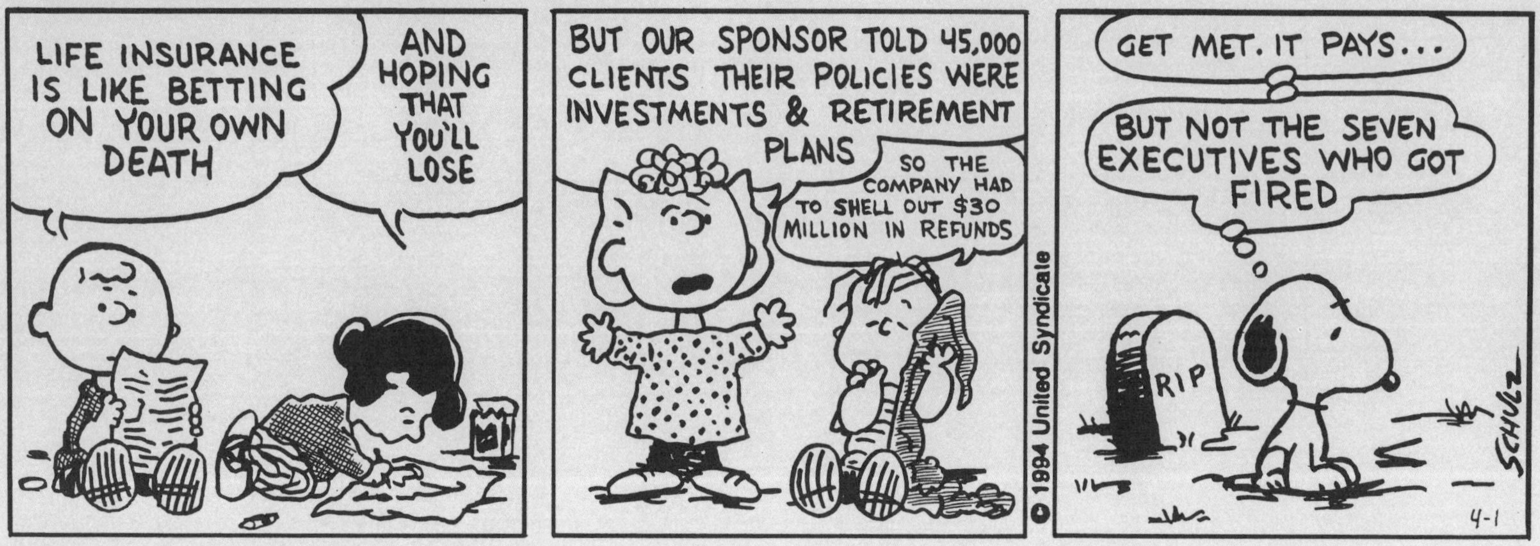

LIFE INSURANCE IS LIKE BETTING ON YOUR OWN DEATH
AND HOPING THAT YOU'LL LOSE
BUT OUR SPONSOR TOLD 45,000 CLIENTS THEIR POLICIES WERE INVESTMENTS & RETIREMENT PLANS
SO THE COMPANY HAD TO SHELL OUT $30 MILLION IN REFUNDS
GET MET. IT PAYS...
BUT NOT THE SEVEN EXECUTIVES WHO GOT FIRED
RIP
SCHULZ
4-1
© 1994 United Syndicate

SYLVIA By Nicole Hollander

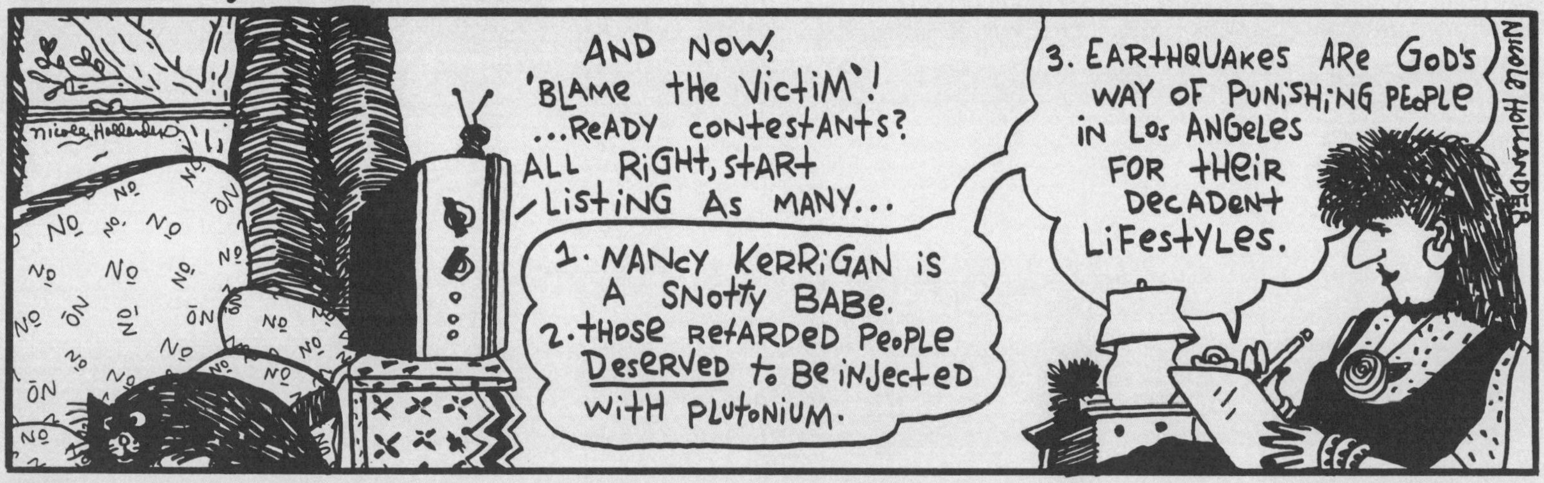

AND NOW, 'BLAME THE VICTIM'! ...READY CONTESTANTS? ALL RIGHT, START LISTING AS MANY...
1. NANCY KERRIGAN IS A SNOTTY BABE.
2. THOSE RETARDED PEOPLE DESERVED TO BE INJECTED WITH PLUTONIUM.
3. EARTHQUAKES ARE GOD'S WAY OF PUNISHING PEOPLE IN LOS ANGELES FOR THEIR DECADENT LIFESTYLES.
NICOLE HOLLANDER

DICK TRACY BY DICK LOCHER & MAX COLLINS

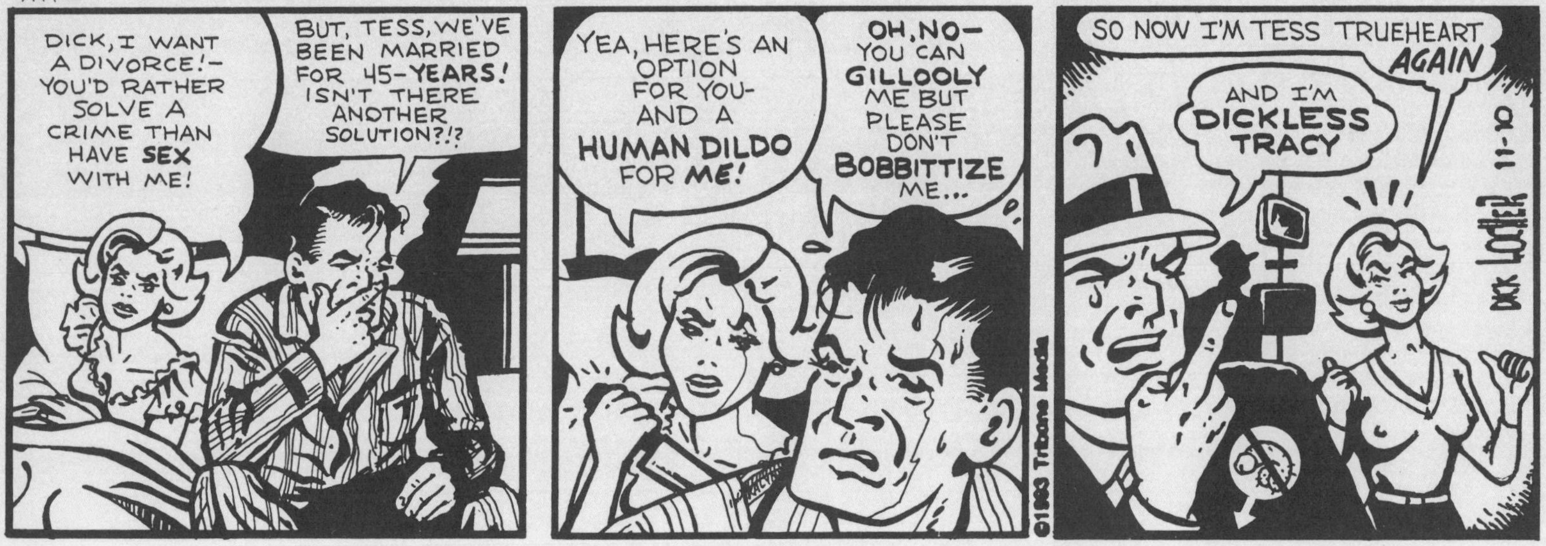

DICK, I WANT A DIVORCE!—YOU'D RATHER SOLVE A CRIME THAN HAVE SEX WITH ME!
BUT, TESS, WE'VE BEEN MARRIED FOR 45-YEARS! ISN'T THERE ANOTHER SOLUTION?!?
YEA, HERE'S AN OPTION FOR YOU—AND A HUMAN DILDO FOR ME!
OH, NO—YOU CAN GILLOOLY ME BUT PLEASE DON'T BOBBITTIZE ME...
SO NOW I'M TESS TRUEHEART AGAIN
AND I'M DICKLESS TRACY
11-10
DICK LOCHER
©1993 Tribune Media

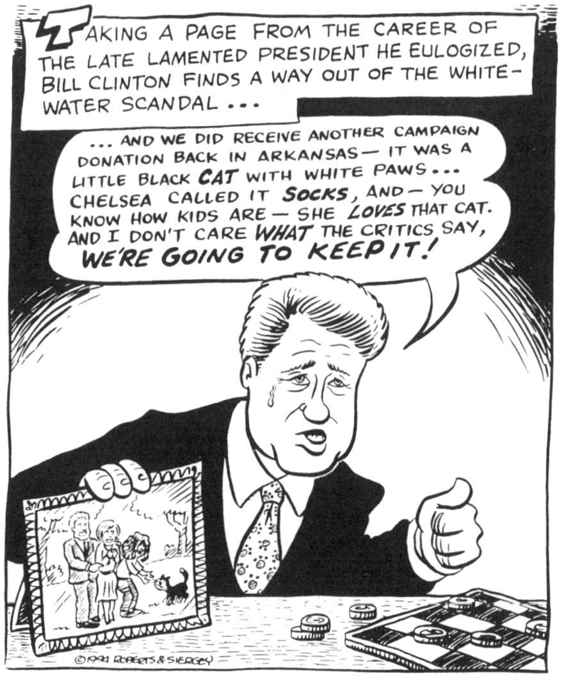
TAKING A PAGE FROM THE CAREER OF THE LATE LAMENTED PRESIDENT HE EULOGIZED, BILL CLINTON FINDS A WAY OUT OF THE WHITE-WATER SCANDAL ...
... AND WE DID RECEIVE ANOTHER CAMPAIGN DONATION BACK IN ARKANSAS— IT WAS A LITTLE BLACK CAT WITH WHITE PAWS... CHELSEA CALLED IT SOCKS, AND— YOU KNOW HOW KIDS ARE— SHE LOVES THAT CAT. AND I DON'T CARE WHAT THE CRITICS SAY, WE'RE GOING TO KEEP IT!
©1994 ROBERTS & SIERGEY

JIM SIERGEY AND TOM ROBERTS. THE REALIST #128, FALL 1994.

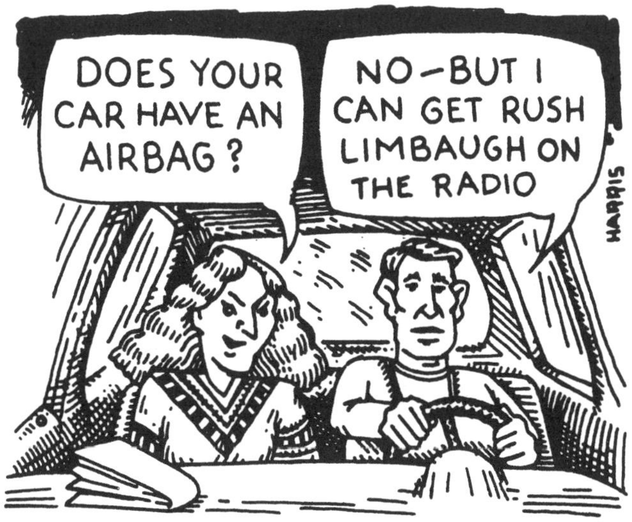
DOES YOUR CAR HAVE AN AIRBAG?
NO—BUT I CAN GET RUSH LIMBAUGH ON THE RADIO
HARRIS

HARRIS. THE REALIST #128, FALL 1994.

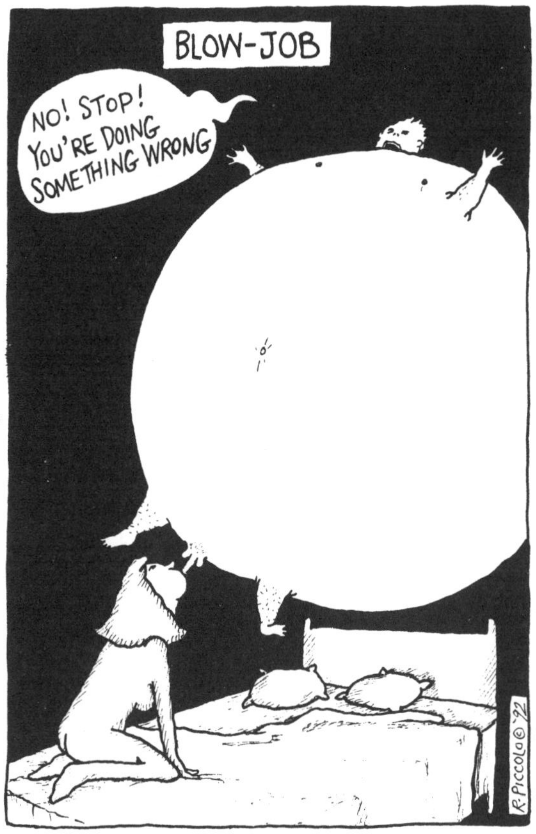
BLOW-JOB
NO! STOP! YOU'RE DOING SOMETHING WRONG
R. PICCOLO © '92

RINA PICCOLO. THE REALIST #128, FALL 1994.

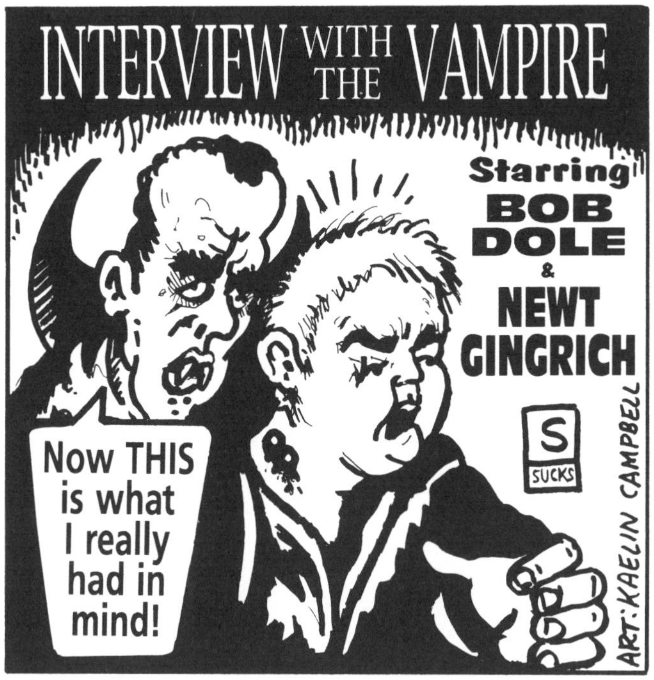
INTERVIEW WITH THE VAMPIRE
Starring BOB DOLE & NEWT GINGRICH
Now THIS is what I really had in mind!
S SUCKS
ART: KAELIN CAMPBELL

KALYNN CAMPBELL. THE REALIST #129, WINTER 1995.

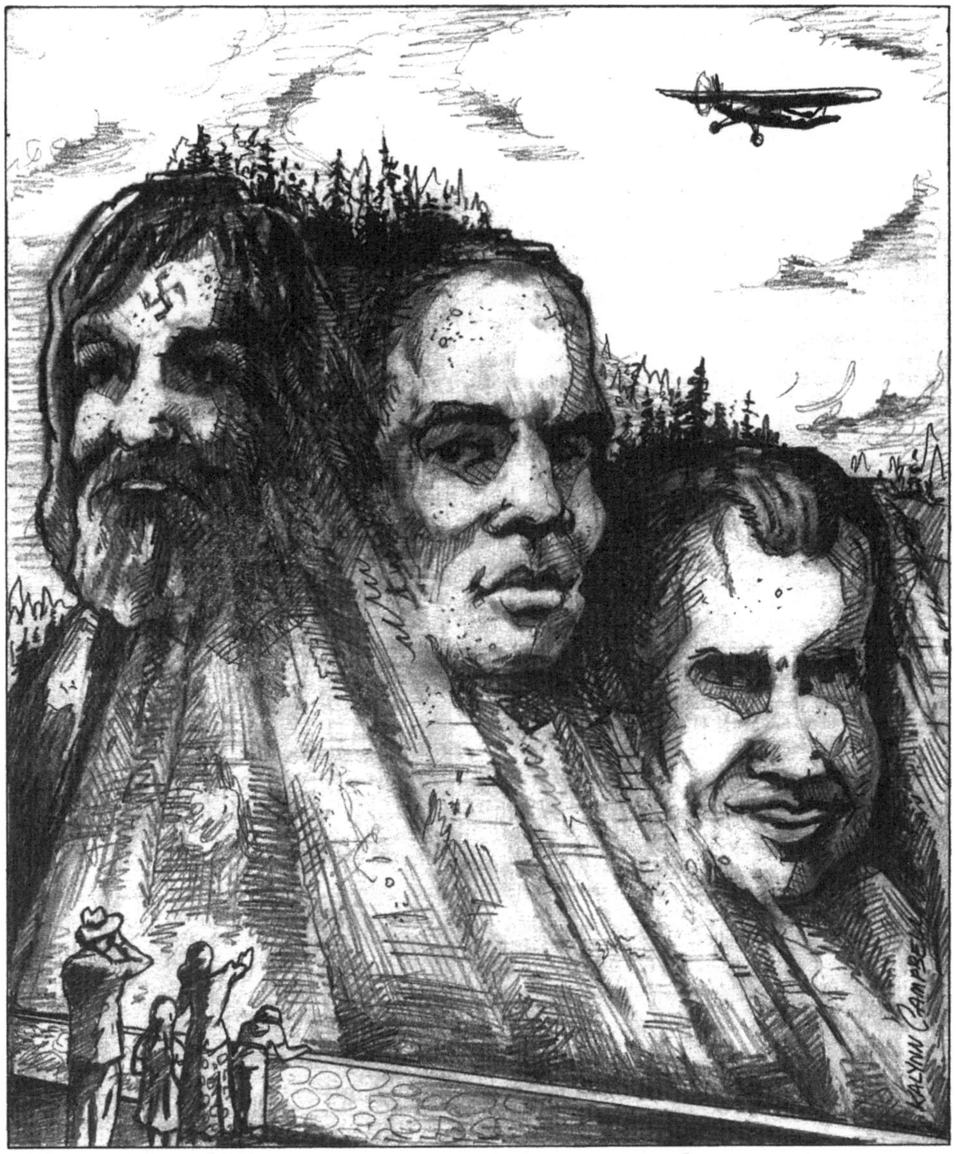
KALYNN CAMPBELL

KALYNN CAMPBELL. THE REALIST #128, FALL 1994. *100

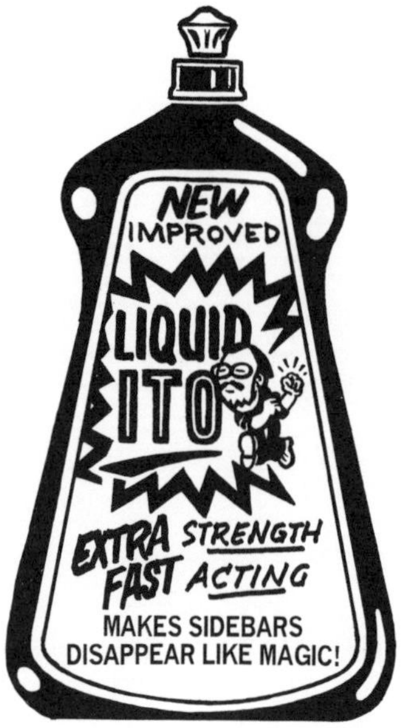
NEW
IMPROVED
LIQUID
ITO
EXTRA STRENGTH
FAST ACTING
MAKES SIDEBARS
DISAPPEAR LIKE MAGIC!

KALYNN CAMPBELL. THE REALIST #130, SUMMER 1995. *101

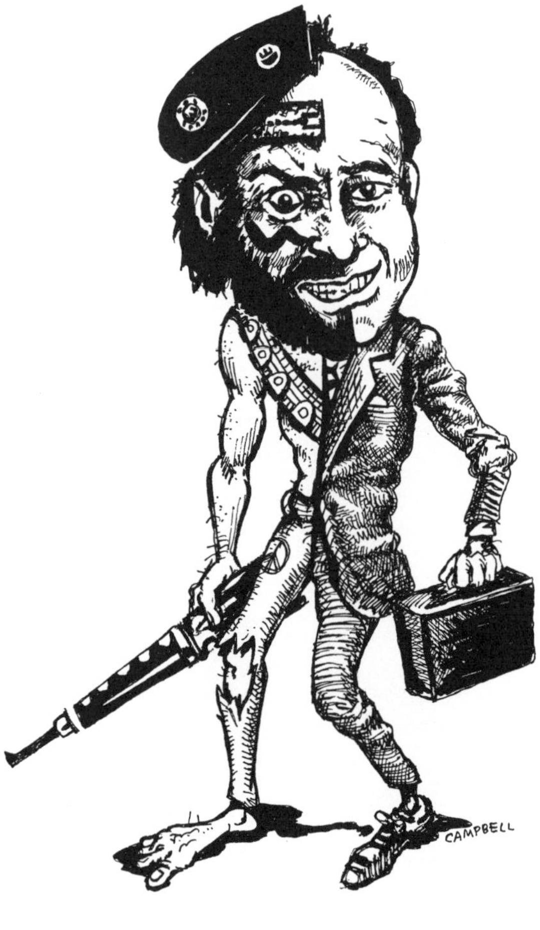
CAMPBELL

KALYNN CAMPBELL. THE REALIST #130, SUMMER 1995. *102

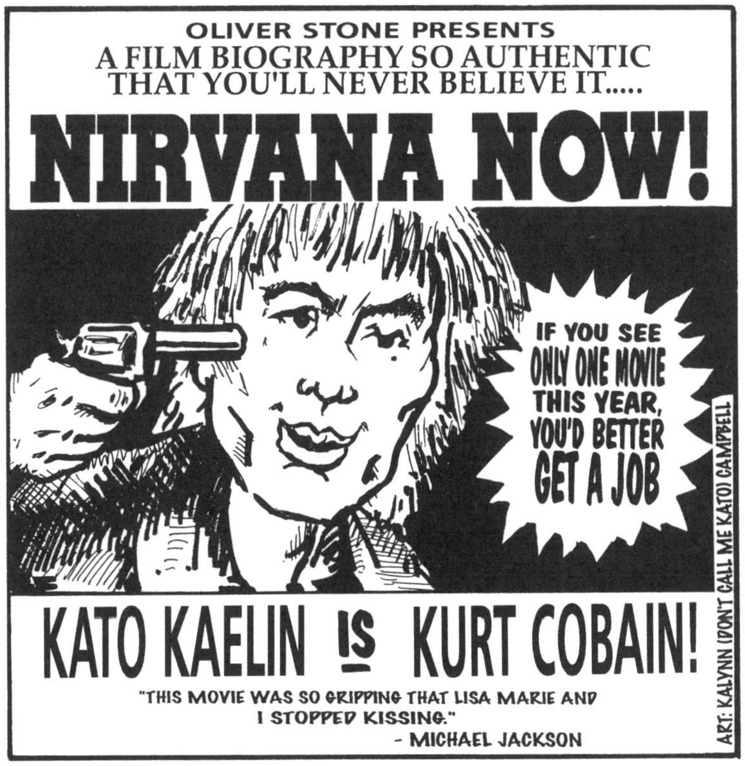
OLIVER STONE PRESENTS
A FILM BIOGRAPHY SO AUTHENTIC THAT YOU'LL NEVER BELIEVE IT.....
NIRVANA NOW!
IF YOU SEE ONLY ONE MOVIE THIS YEAR, YOU'D BETTER GET A JOB
KATO KAELIN IS KURT COBAIN!
"THIS MOVIE WAS SO GRIPPING THAT LISA MARIE AND I STOPPED KISSING."
- MICHAEL JACKSON
ART: KALYNN (DON'T CALL ME KATO) CAMPBELL

KALYNN CAMPBELL. THE REALIST #129, WINTER 1995.

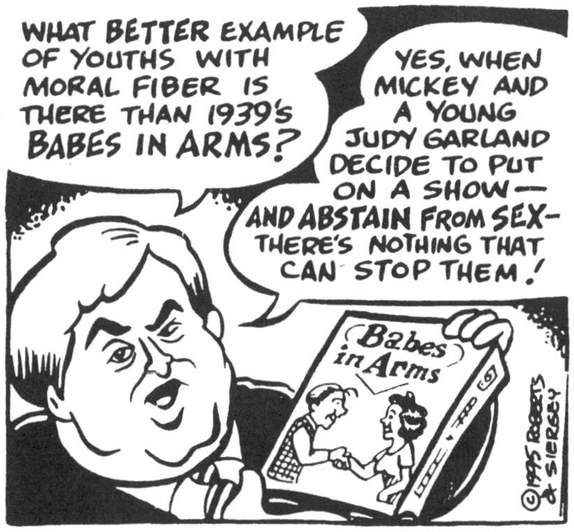
WHAT BETTER EXAMPLE OF YOUTHS WITH MORAL FIBER IS THERE THAN 1939'S BABES IN ARMS?
YES, WHEN MICKEY AND A YOUNG JUDY GARLAND DECIDE TO PUT ON A SHOW— AND ABSTAIN FROM SEX— THERE'S NOTHING THAT CAN STOP THEM!
Babes in Arms
©1995 ROBERTS & SIERGEY

JIM SIERGEY AND TOM ROBERTS. THE REALIST #131, FALL 1995.

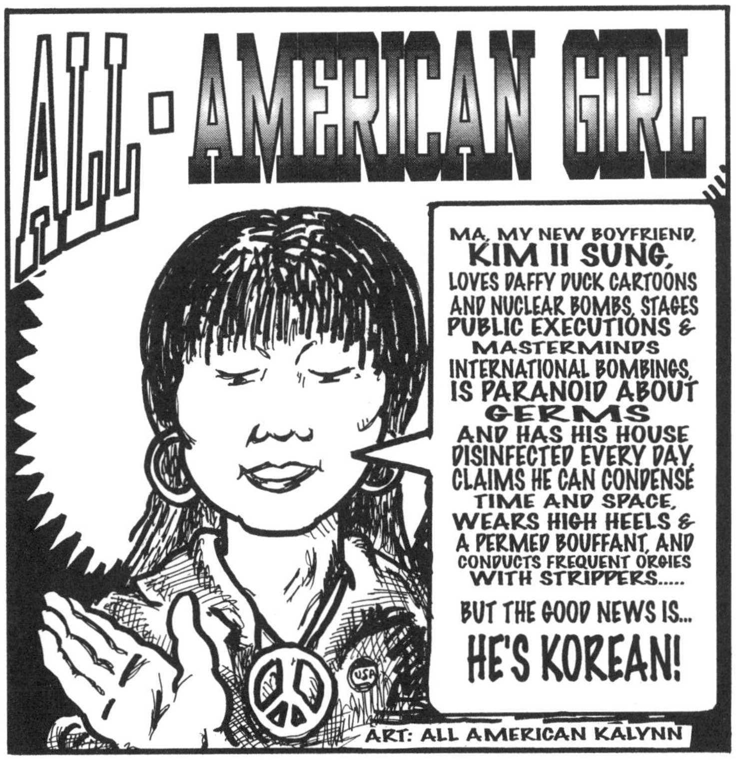
ALL-AMERICAN GIRL
MA, MY NEW BOYFRIEND, KIM Il SUNG, LOVES DAFFY DUCK CARTOONS AND NUCLEAR BOMBS, STAGES PUBLIC EXECUTIONS & MASTERMINDS INTERNATIONAL BOMBINGS, IS PARANOID ABOUT GERMS AND HAS HIS HOUSE DISINFECTED EVERY DAY, CLAIMS HE CAN CONDENSE TIME AND SPACE, WEARS HIGH HEELS & A PERMED BOUFFANT, AND CONDUCTS FREQUENT ORGIES WITH STRIPPERS.....
BUT THE GOOD NEWS IS... HE'S KOREAN!
ART: ALL AMERICAN KALYNN

KALYNN CAMPBELL. THE REALIST #129, WINTER 1995.

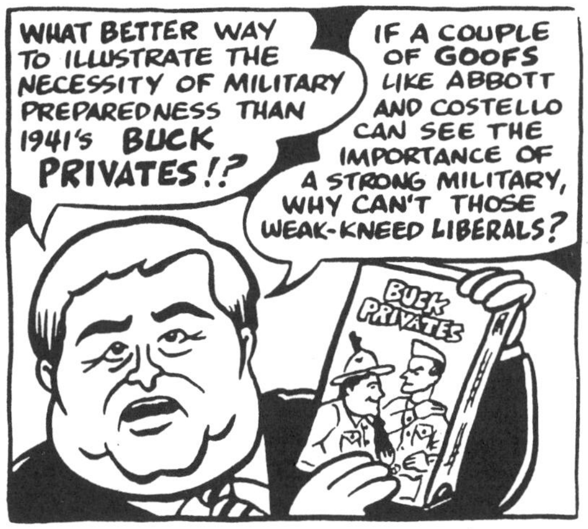
WHAT BETTER WAY TO ILLUSTRATE THE NECESSITY OF MILITARY PREPAREDNESS THAN 1941'S BUCK PRIVATES!?
IF A COUPLE OF GOOFS LIKE ABBOTT AND COSTELLO CAN SEE THE IMPORTANCE OF A STRONG MILITARY, WHY CAN'T THOSE WEAK-KNEED LIBERALS?
BUCK PRIVATES

JIM SIERGEY AND TOM ROBERTS. THE REALIST #131, FALL 1995.

Y-YOU'RE SELLING THE PRISONERS' BODY PARTS?? THEY MUST BE READY TO RIOT!
BEIJING No. 2 PRISON
NO, THEY HAPPIER THAN EVER.
HOW CAN THAT B—
I TOLD YOU! WE NEVER BEAT INMATES IN THIS PRISON!!!
MIGHT DAMAGE HIS KIDNEYS—WORTH 30 GRAND APIECE!
FEIGN

FEIGN. THE REALIST #131, FALL 1995.

Cola
KALYNN

The American Broadcasting Company's New Logo
"The three most graphic images of the 20th century are the Coca-Cola bottle, the Nazi swastika, and Mickey Mouse." –*Life* magazine

KALYNN CAMPBELL. THE REALIST #131, FALL 1995.

SUSAN SMITH WEARS
NO EXCUSE JEANS
NO EXCUSE
NO EXCUSE JEANS
GET CAUGHT IN A PAIR SOON!
KALYNN

KALYNN CAMPBELL. THE REALIST #131, FALL 1995. *103

KALYNN

KALYNN CAMPBELL. THE REALIST #134, FALL 1996.

SOB
KALYNN

From a *Reuters* dispatch: "Former President George Bush nearly drowned earlier this month [July] when he fell into a peat bog during a fishing trip in Canada. Bush was taking a walk through the woods in Newfoundland when he sank up to his armpits in the bog. He was freed by Secret Service and Royal Canadian Mounter Police officers, who struggled for several minutes before they were able to pull him out."

KALYNN CAMPBELL. THE REALIST #131, FALL 1995.

Calvin and Hobbes by WATTERSON
HOW COULD HE DO THIS TO US? WE'RE HELPLESS WITHOUT HIM. JUST THINK ABOUT IT, HOBBES, OUR OWN CREATOR HAS LITERALLY FORCED US OUT OF HAVING OUR DAILY ADVENTURE. I MEAN WHY SHOULD HE HAVE ALL THE POWER? IT'S SIMPLY NOT FAIR! I DON'T UNDERSTAND... I JUST DON'T UNDERSTAND...
...LIFE IS A MYSTERY...
IF IT'S NOT A MYSTERY, WHAT THE FUCK IS IT?!?
COMIC-STRIP CHARACTERS EARLY RETIREMENT HOME
MR. OPUS
KALYNN

PAUL KRASSNER AND KALYNN CAMPBELL. THE REALIST #132, SPRING 1996.

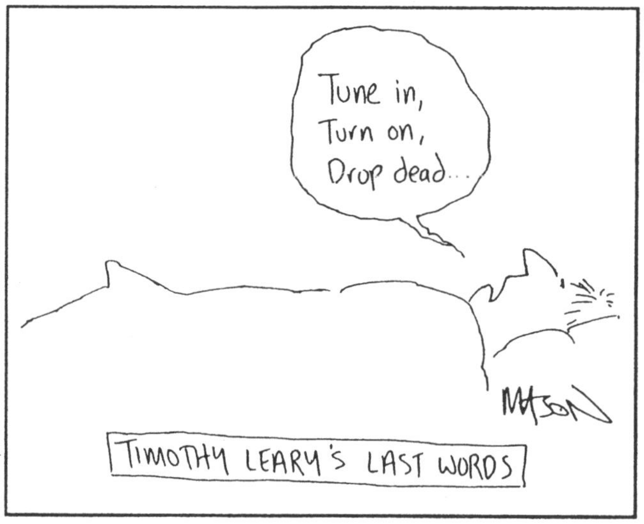
Tune in,
Turn on,
Drop dead...
MASON
TIMOTHY LEARY'S LAST WORDS

MASON. THE REALIST #133, SUMMER 1996.

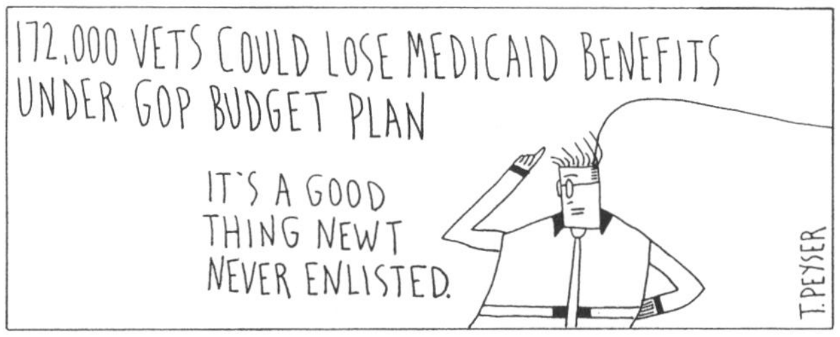
172,000 VETS COULD LOSE MEDICAID BENEFITS UNDER GOP BUDGET PLAN
IT'S A GOOD THING NEWT NEVER ENLISTED.
T. PEYSER

TONY PEYSER. THE REALIST #133, SUMMER 1996.

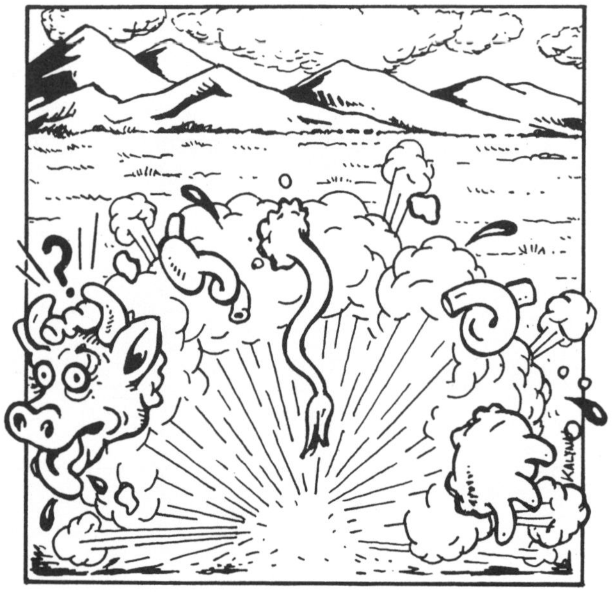

KALYNN CAMPBELL. THE REALIST #133, SUMMER 1996.

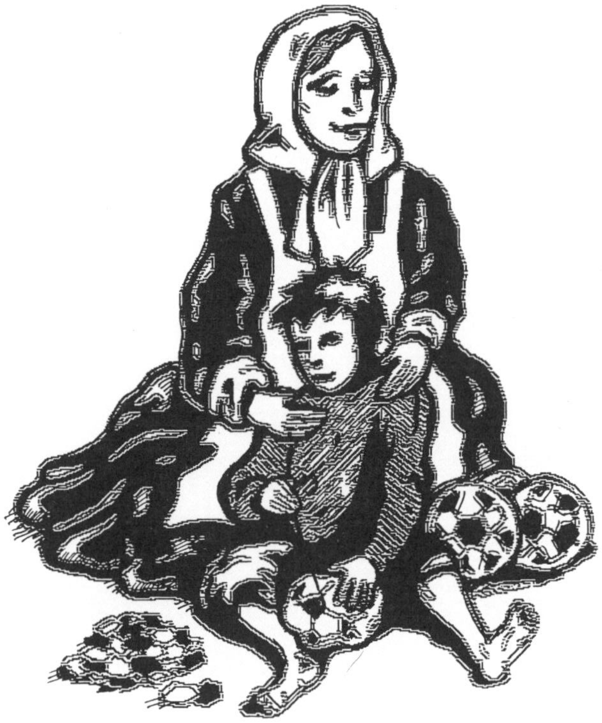

Soccer Mom in Pakistan

THE REALIST #136, SUMMER 1997.

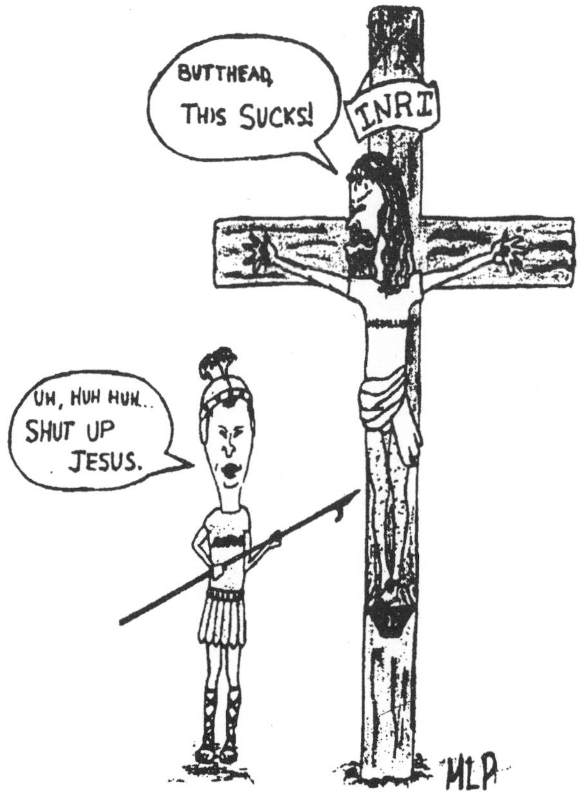
BUTTHEAD, THIS SUCKS!
INRI
UH, HUH HUH.. SHUT UP JESUS.
MLP

Jesus and Butthead

MLP. THE REALIST #135, SPRING 1997.

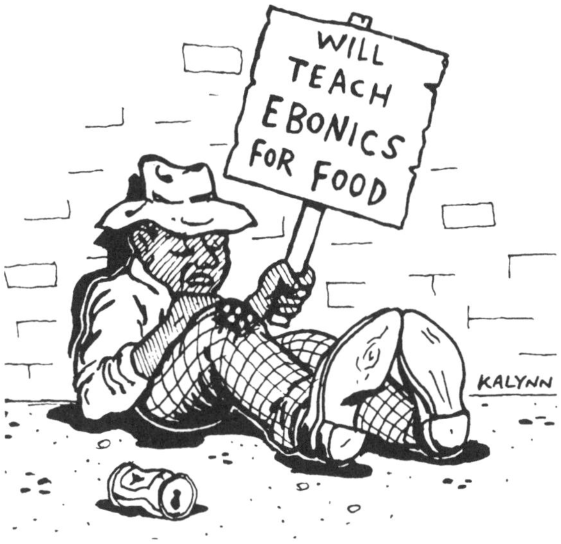
WILL TEACH EBONICS FOR FOOD
KALYNN

KALYNN CAMPBELL. THE REALIST #135, SPRING 1997.

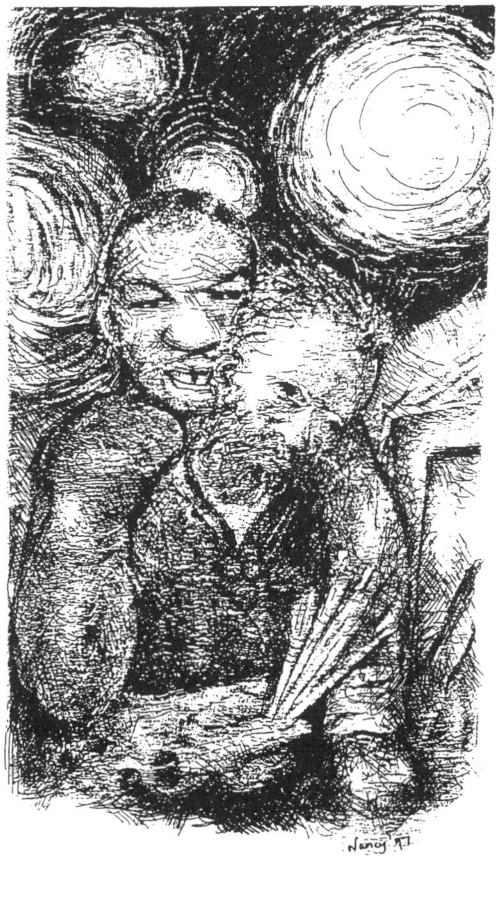

Mike Tyson Meets Vincent van Gogh

NANCY. THE REALIST #137, FALL 1997.

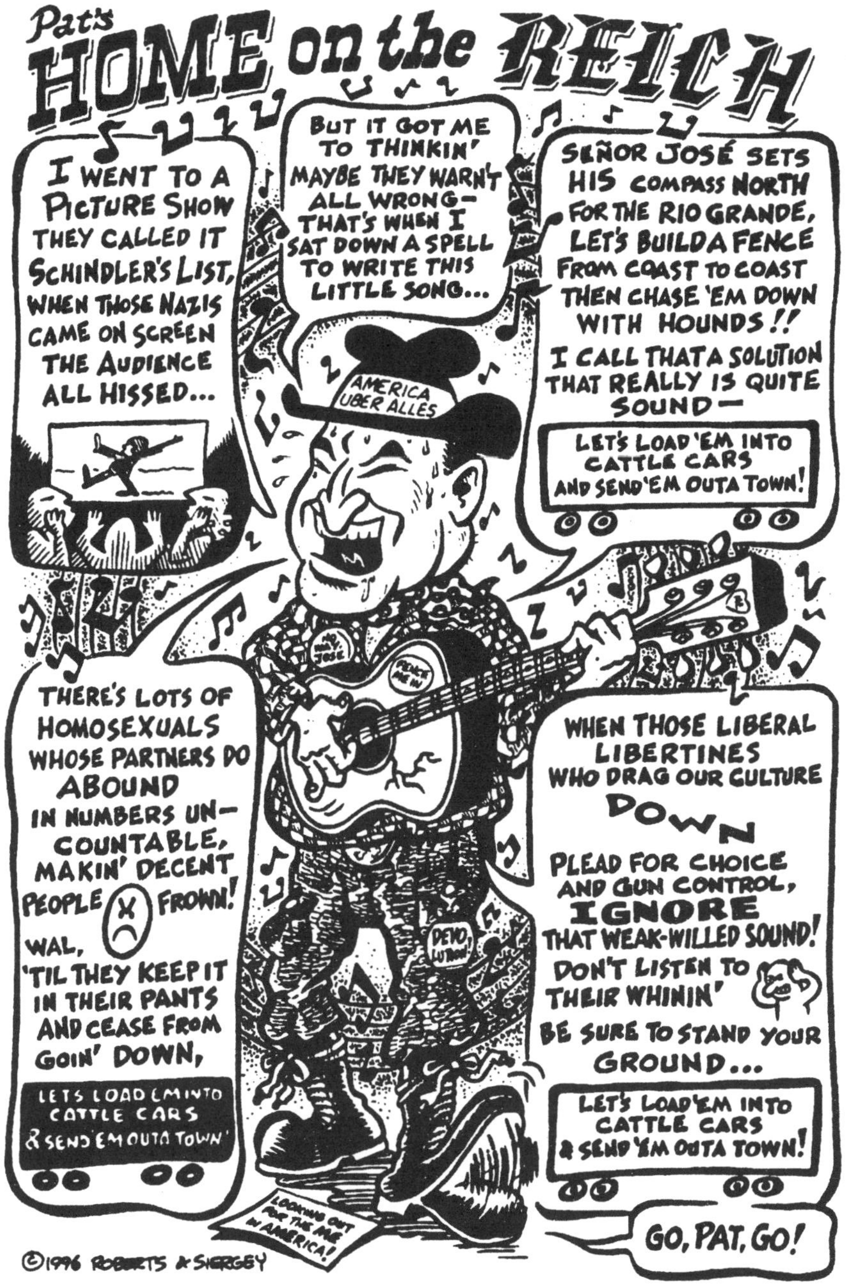
Pat's HOME on the REICH
I WENT TO A PICTURE SHOW THEY CALLED IT SCHINDLER'S LIST, WHEN THOSE NAZIS CAME ON SCREEN THE AUDIENCE ALL HISSED...
BUT IT GOT ME TO THINKIN' MAYBE THEY WARN'T ALL WRONG– THAT'S WHEN I SAT DOWN A SPELL TO WRITE THIS LITTLE SONG...
SEÑOR JOSÉ SETS HIS COMPASS NORTH FOR THE RIO GRANDE, LET'S BUILD A FENCE FROM COAST TO COAST THEN CHASE 'EM DOWN WITH HOUNDS!!
I CALL THAT A SOLUTION THAT REALLY IS QUITE SOUND–
LET'S LOAD 'EM INTO CATTLE CARS AND SEND 'EM OUTA TOWN!
AMERICA UBER ALLES
THERE'S LOTS OF HOMOSEXUALS WHOSE PARTNERS DO ABOUND IN NUMBERS UN-COUNTABLE, MAKIN' DECENT PEOPLE FROWN!
WAL, 'TIL THEY KEEP IT IN THEIR PANTS AND CEASE FROM GOIN' DOWN,
LET'S LOAD 'EM INTO CATTLE CARS & SEND 'EM OUTA TOWN'
WHEN THOSE LIBERAL LIBERTINES WHO DRAG OUR CULTURE DOWN
PLEAD FOR CHOICE AND GUN CONTROL, IGNORE THAT WEAK-WILLED SOUND! DON'T LISTEN TO THEIR WHININ'
BE SURE TO STAND YOUR GROUND...
LET'S LOAD 'EM INTO CATTLE CARS & SEND 'EM OUTA TOWN!
GO, PAT, GO!
©1996 ROBERTS & SIERGEY

JIM SIERGEY AND TOM ROBERTS. THE REALIST #134, FALL 1996.

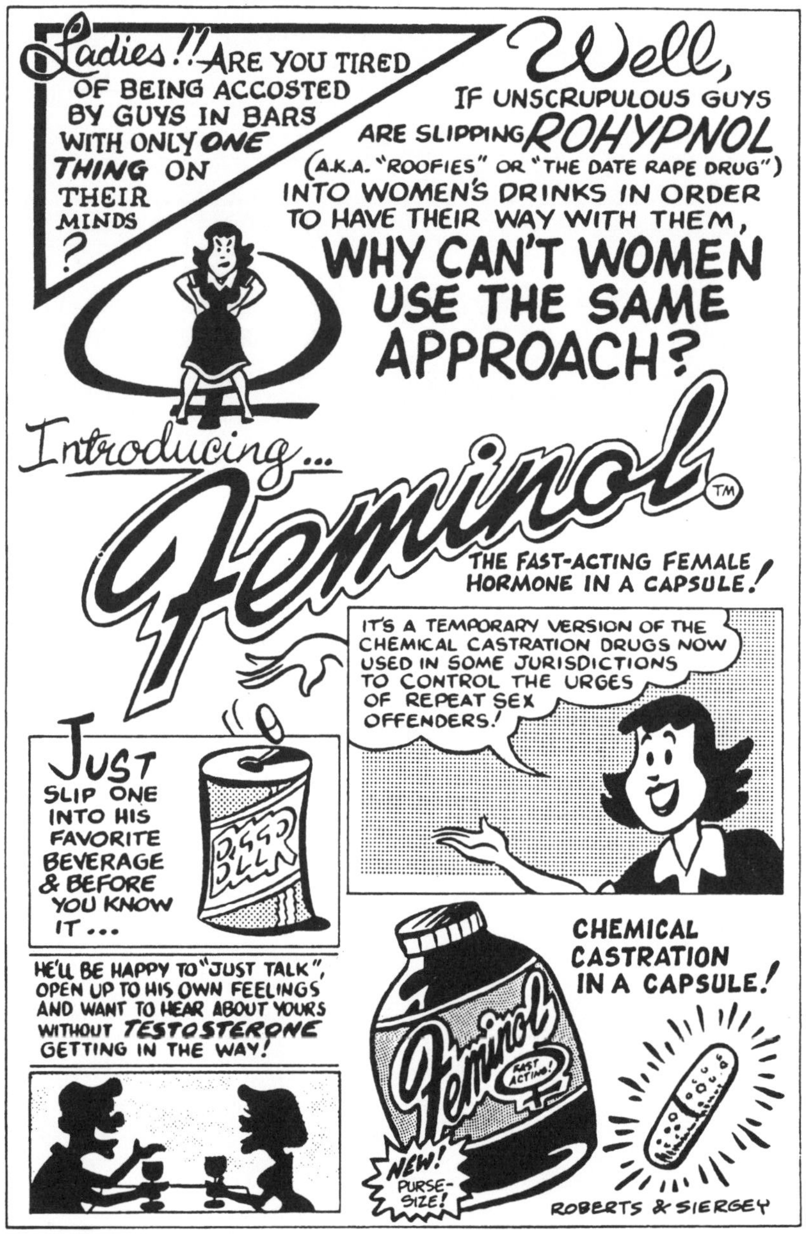

Ladies!! ARE YOU TIRED OF BEING ACCOSTED BY GUYS IN BARS WITH ONLY ONE THING ON THEIR MINDS ?
Well, IF UNSCRUPULOUS GUYS ARE SLIPPING ROHYPNOL (A.K.A. "ROOFIES" OR "THE DATE RAPE DRUG") INTO WOMEN'S DRINKS IN ORDER TO HAVE THEIR WAY WITH THEM,
WHY CAN'T WOMEN USE THE SAME APPROACH?
Introducing...
Feminol TM
THE FAST-ACTING FEMALE HORMONE IN A CAPSULE!
IT'S A TEMPORARY VERSION OF THE CHEMICAL CASTRATION DRUGS NOW USED IN SOME JURISDICTIONS TO CONTROL THE URGES OF REPEAT SEX OFFENDERS!
JUST SLIP ONE INTO HIS FAVORITE BEVERAGE & BEFORE YOU KNOW IT...
HE'LL BE HAPPY TO "JUST TALK", OPEN UP TO HIS OWN FEELINGS AND WANT TO HEAR ABOUT YOURS WITHOUT TESTOSTERONE GETTING IN THE WAY!
CHEMICAL CASTRATION IN A CAPSULE!
Feminol
FAST ACTING!
NEW! PURSE-SIZE!
ROBERTS & SIERGEY

JIM SIERGEY AND TOM ROBERTS. THE REALIST #135, SPRING 1997.

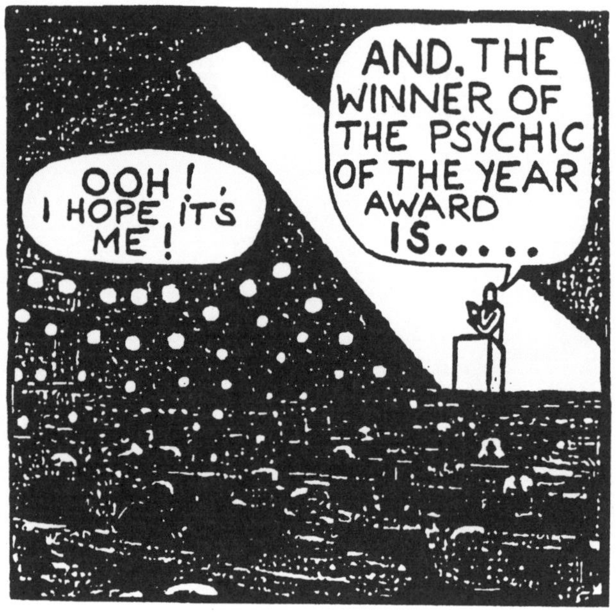

OOH! I HOPE IT'S ME!
AND, THE WINNER OF THE PSYCHIC OF THE YEAR AWARD IS.....

THE REALIST #136, SUMMER 1997.

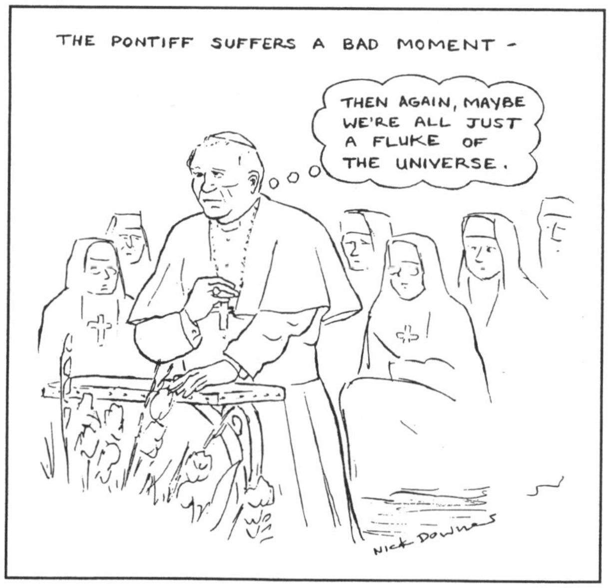

THE PONTIFF SUFFERS A BAD MOMENT -
THEN AGAIN, MAYBE WE'RE ALL JUST A FLUKE OF THE UNIVERSE.
NICK DOWNES

NICK DOWNES. THE REALIST #136, SUMMER 1997.

the Hypno Hotline: For those jobs that can't be accomplished through the usual channels of communication.
Hi, this is Earl, Department of Campaign Finance Reform. Will this be Visa or Master-Card?
Hi—you despair of reforming the system, so you think the best solution is to let the cash flow, but erase the memory of the source from the candidate's mind, so he won't know who he owes... the guys who gave the money have to forget too.
Earl
www.suba.com/~sylvia
Now the candidate has a substantial campaign fund... where does he think it came from? You'd like him to think it came from you... you're the only person you can trust to act re-sponsibly. Sure, no problem.
Earl
10-22
Nicole Hollander

NICOLE HOLLANDER. THE REALIST #138, SPRING 1998.

Blind Item

Stephanie Miller, reacting to the news that organizations for the blind are protesting the reappearance of the nearsighted *Mr. Magoo* animated cartoon character: "Maybe he should be a deaf, gay, Southern Baptist with an irritable bowel problem."

THE REALIST #137, FALL 1997.

Deep Pockets Chopra

From *Newsweek*:

"Spiritual guru Deepak Chopra's enterprises bring in about $15 million a year. He says he enjoys wealth but is not attached to it."

THE REALIST #138, SPRING 1998.

PROMISE KEEPERS DECLARATION
I PROMISE TO KEEP YOU SUBSERVIENT, FOREVER!
Lawton

MARY LAWTON. THE REALIST #138, SPRING 1998.

JANET BODE AND KALYNN CAMPBELL.
THE REALIST #137, FALL 1997.

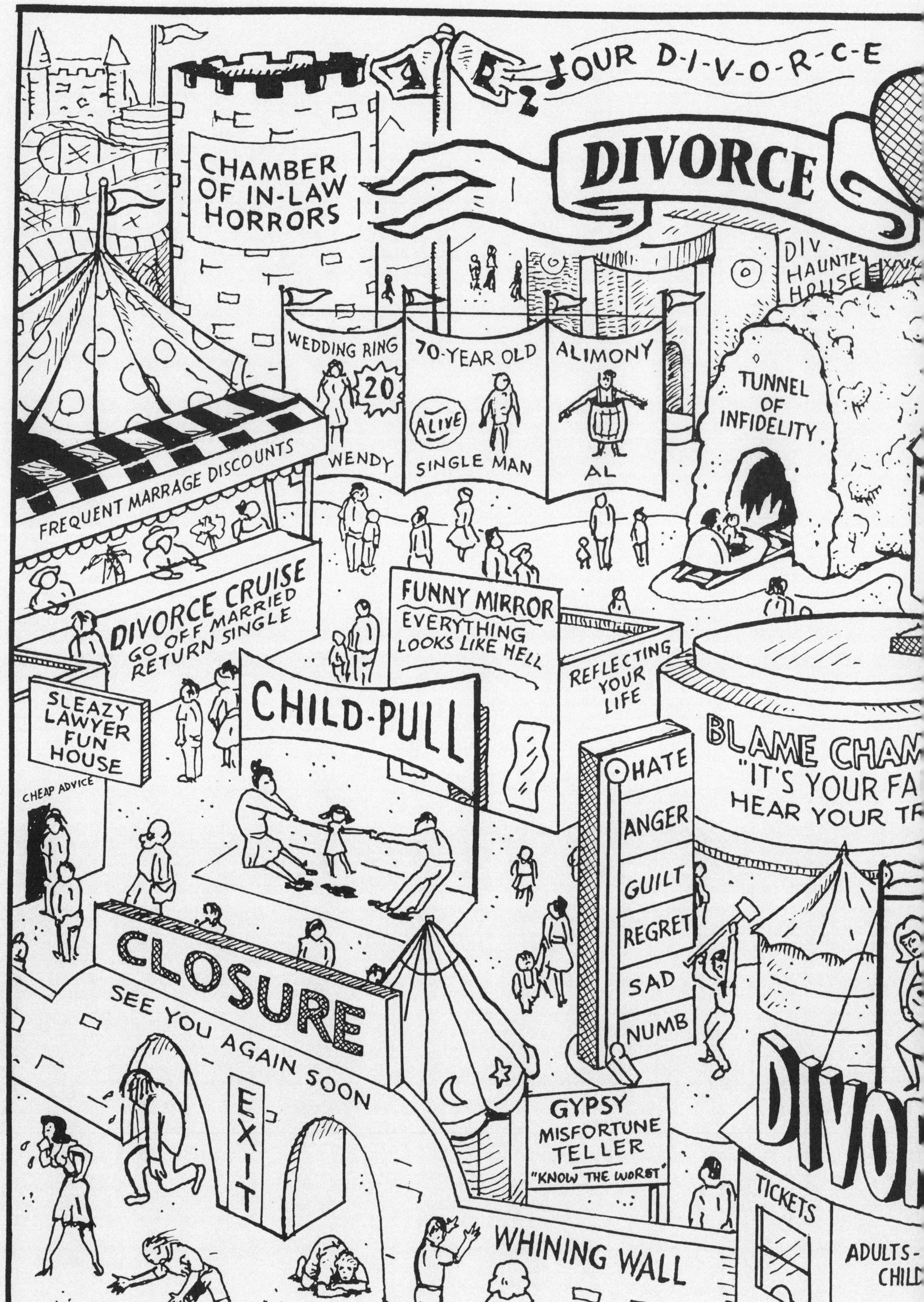
YOUR D-I-V-O-R-C-E
DIVORCE
CHAMBER OF IN-LAW HORRORS
DIV-HAUNTED HOUSE
WEDDING RING 20 WENDY
70-YEAR OLD ALIVE SINGLE MAN
ALIMONY AL
TUNNEL OF INFIDELITY
FREQUENT MARRAGE DISCOUNTS
DIVORCE CRUISE GO OFF MARRIED RETURN SINGLE
FUNNY MIRROR EVERYTHING LOOKS LIKE HELL
REFLECTING YOUR LIFE
SLEAZY LAWYER FUN HOUSE
CHEAP ADVICE
CHILD-PULL
HATE
ANGER
GUILT
REGRET
SAD
NUMB
CLOSURE
SEE YOU AGAIN SOON
EXIT
GYPSY MISFORTUNE TELLER "KNOW THE WORST"
WHINING WALL
TICKETS

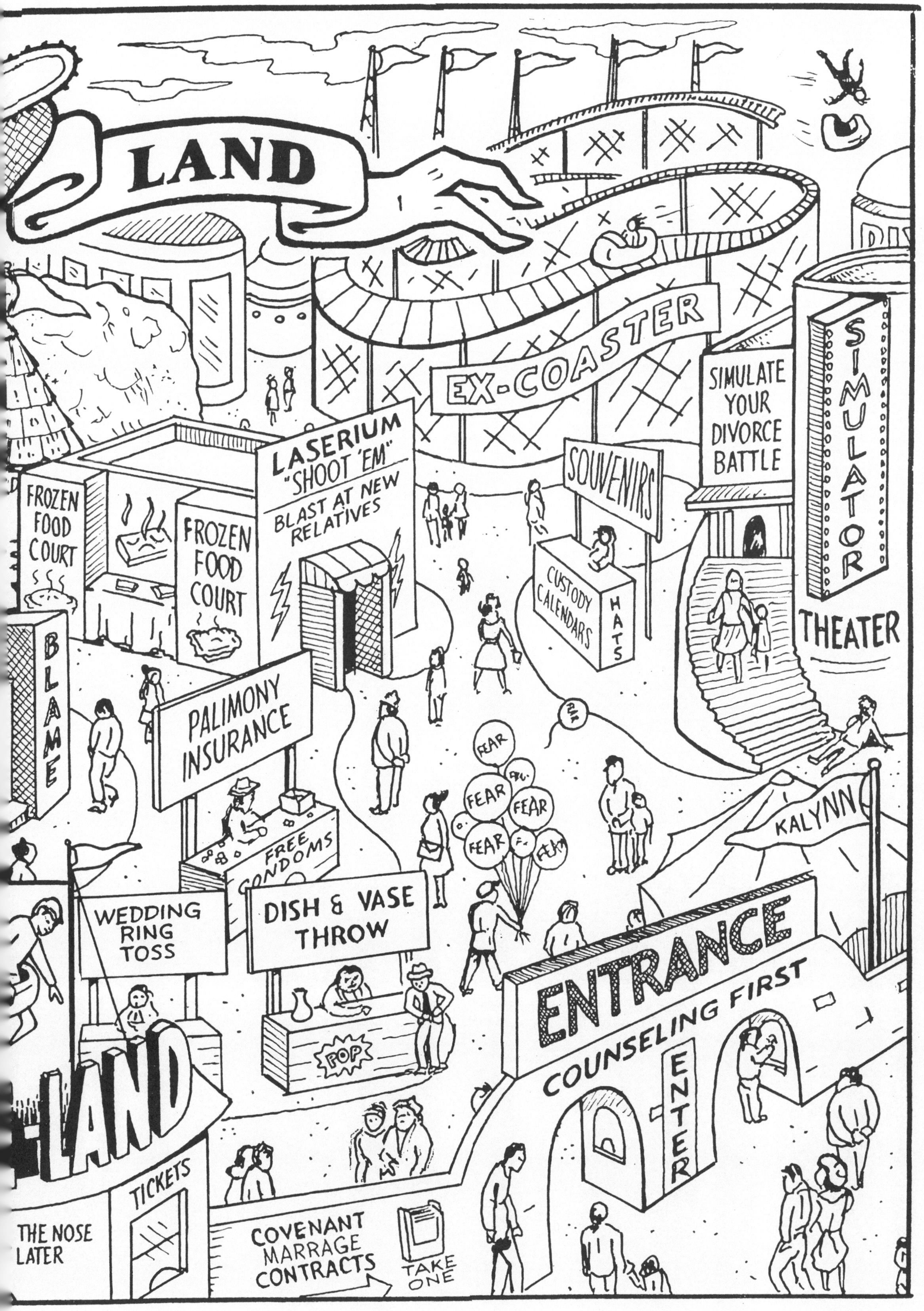
LAND
EX-COASTER
SIMULATE YOUR DIVORCE BATTLE
SIMULATOR
THEATER
LASERIUM "SHOOT 'EM" BLAST AT NEW RELATIVES
SOUVENIRS
CUSTODY CALENDARS
HATS
FROZEN FOOD COURT
FROZEN FOOD COURT
BLAME
PALIMONY INSURANCE
FREE CONDOMS
FEAR
FEAR
FEAR
FEAR
FEAR
FEAR
KALYNN
WEDDING RING TOSS
DISH & VASE THROW
POP
ENTRANCE
COUNSELING FIRST
ENTER
LAND
TICKETS
THE NOSE LATER
COVENANT MARRAGE CONTRACTS
TAKE ONE

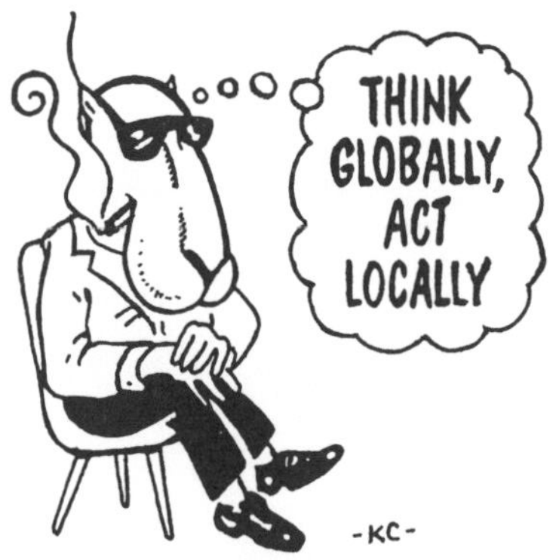
THINK GLOBALLY, ACT LOCALLY
-KC-

KALYNN CAMPBELL. THE REALIST #137, FALL 1997.

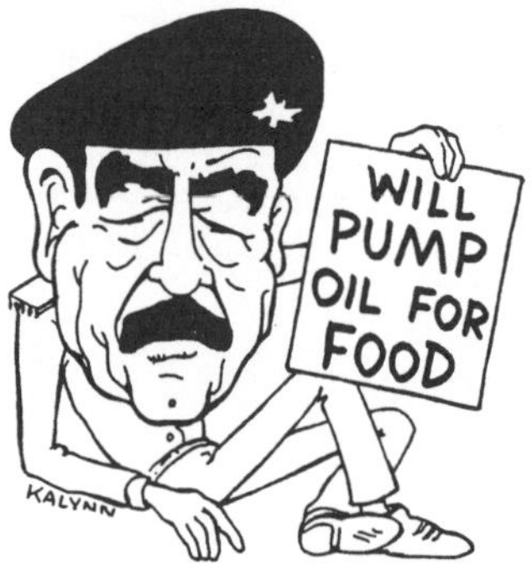
WILL PUMP OIL FOR FOOD
KALYNN

KALYNN CAMPBELL. THE REALIST #138, SPRING 1998.

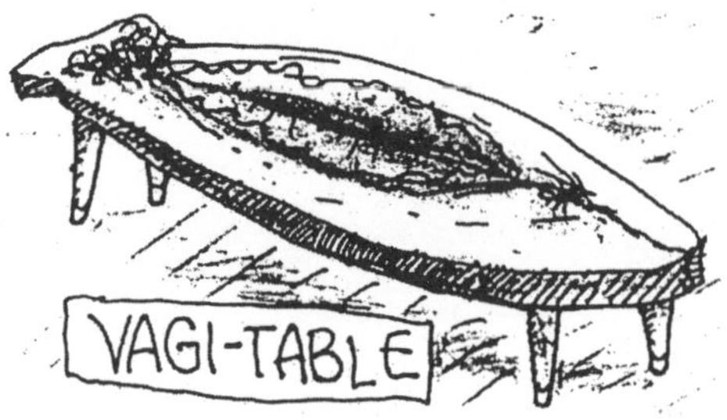
VAGI-TABLE

THE REALIST #140, FALL 1998.

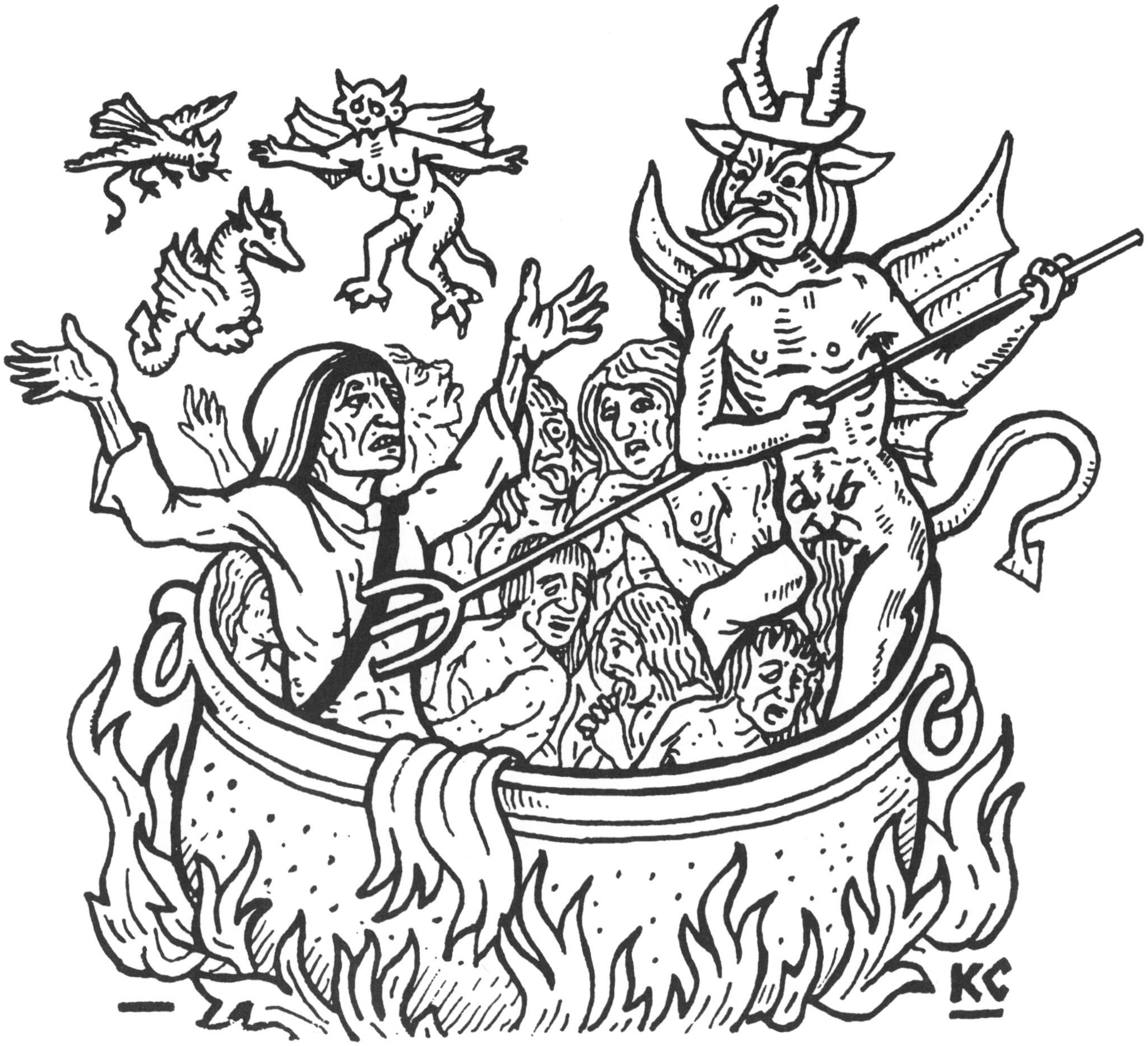
KC

KALYNN CAMPBELL. THE REALIST #138, SPRING 1998.

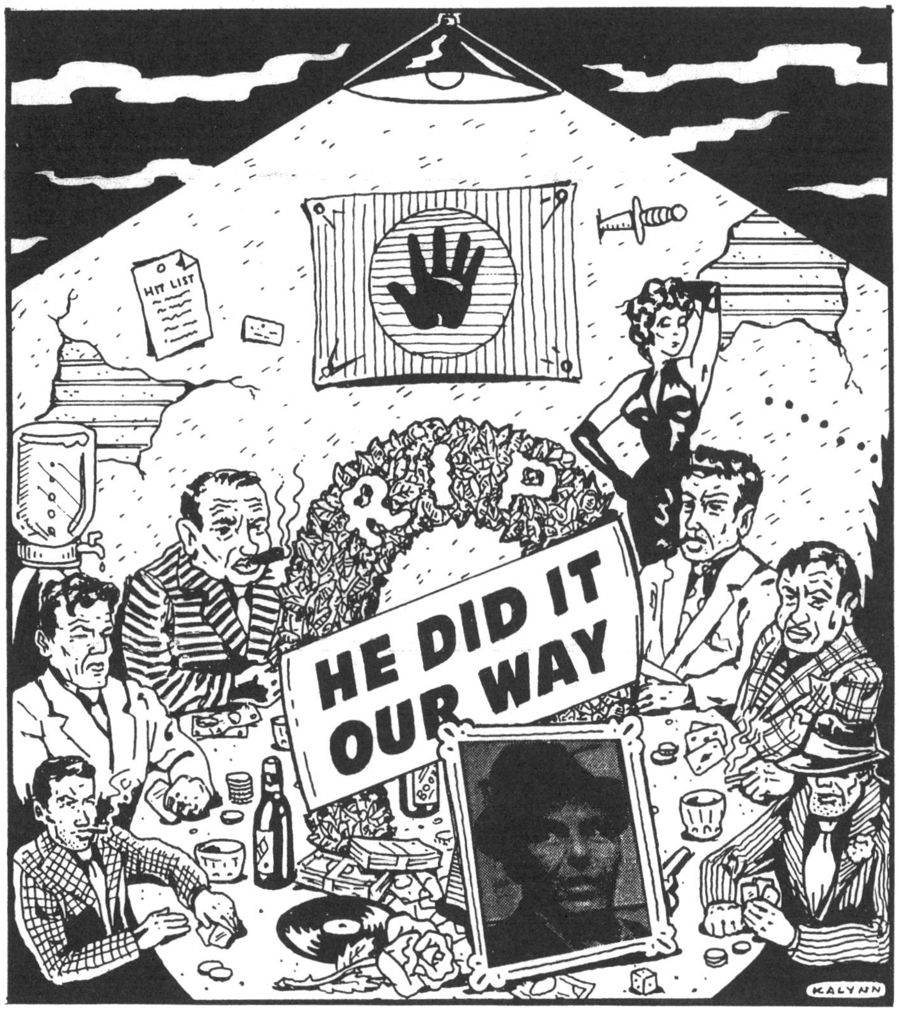
HIT LIST
RIP
HE DID IT OUR WAY
KALYNN

KALYNN CAMPBELL. THE REALIST #140, FALL 1998.

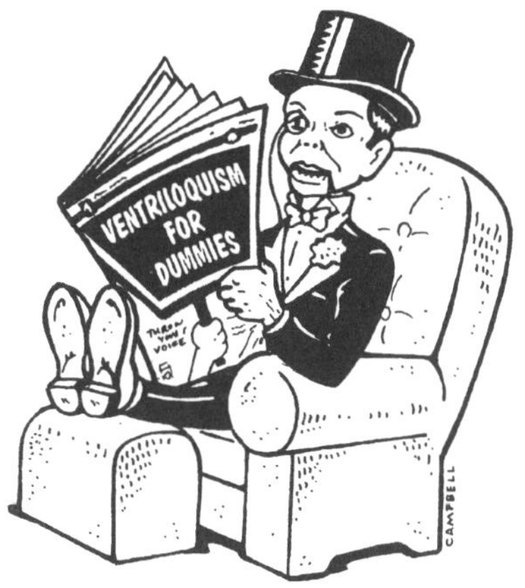
VENTRILOQUISM FOR DUMMIES
CAMPBELL

Sic Transit Mortimer Snerd

Retired ventriloquist Paul Winchell jokes that his dummies Jerry Mahoney and Knucklehead Smiff have taken up a new hobby—collecting dust. "Television and its use of computers can make everything talk," he says, "so there's no need for the art of ventriloquism any more. I don't think young kids today would even understand it."

KALYNN CAMPBELL. THE REALIST #141, SPRING 1999.

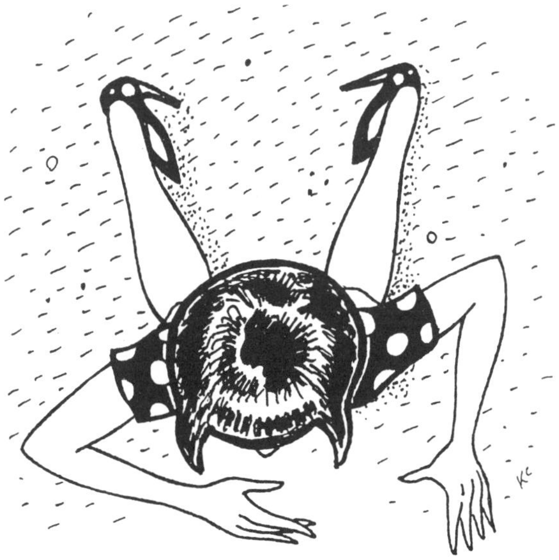
KC

Monica Lewinsky As Seen By the President

KALYNN CAMPBELL. THE REALIST #139, SUMMER 1998.

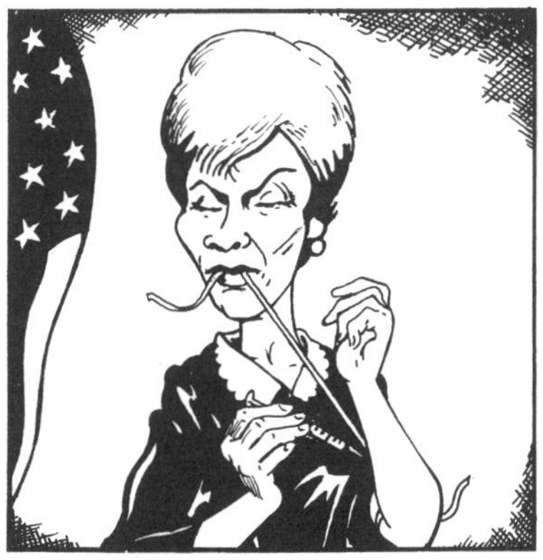

Asshole of the Month

TV's Judge Judy, speaking at a luncheon in Australia, called the debate about needle supply to heroin addicts "an indulgence led by liberal morons." She said, "The solution is simple. Give 'em dirty needles and let 'em die. I don't understand why we think it's important to keep them alive."

THE REALIST #143, SPRING 2000.

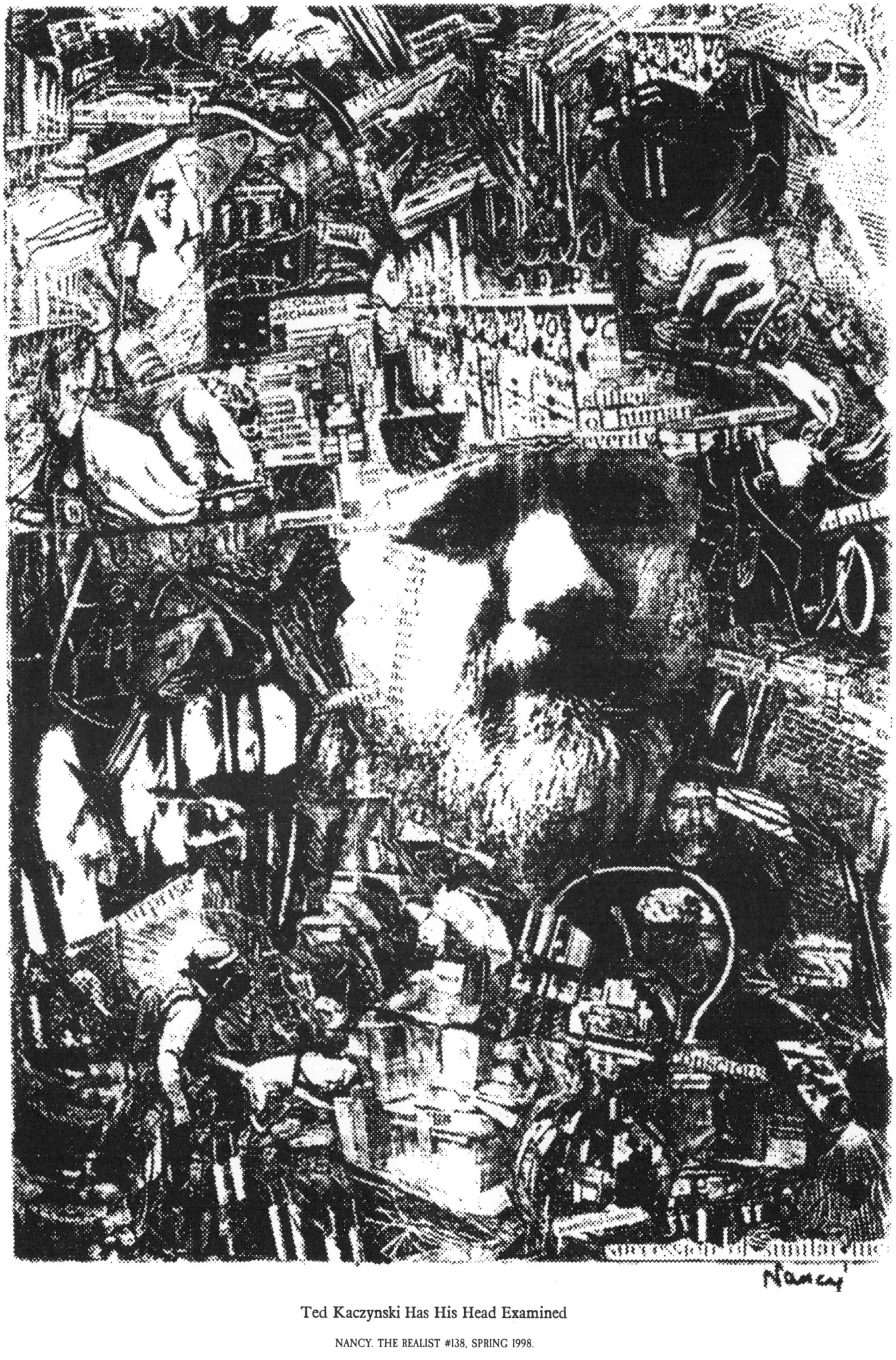

Ted Kaczynski Has His Head Examined

NANCY. THE REALIST #138, SPRING 1998.

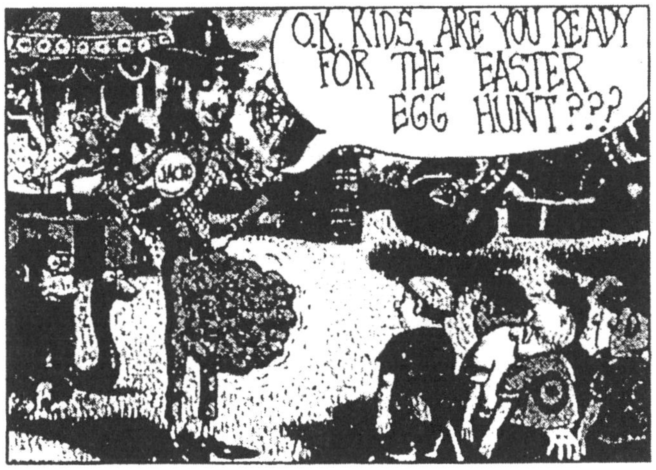
O.K. KIDS, ARE YOU READY FOR THE EASTER EGG HUNT???
JACKO

The *New York Post* refused to publish this cartoon by their regular illustrator, Sean Delonas.

SEAN DELONAS. THE REALIST #140, FALL 1998.

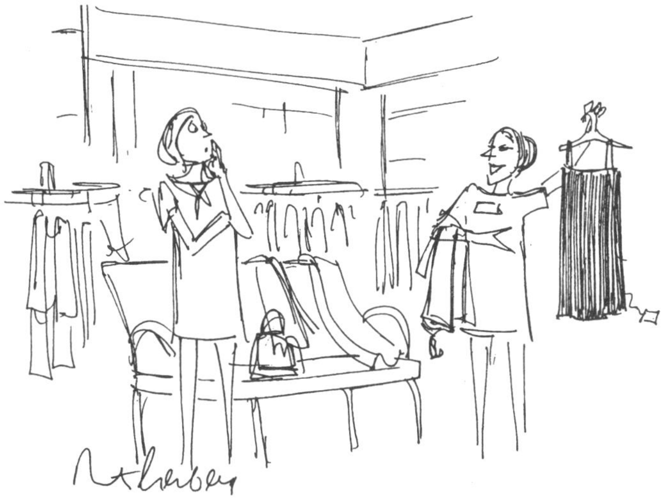

"This one is an exact copy of Monica's — even including a little *faux* stain."

MORT GERBERG. THE REALIST #141, SPRING 1999.

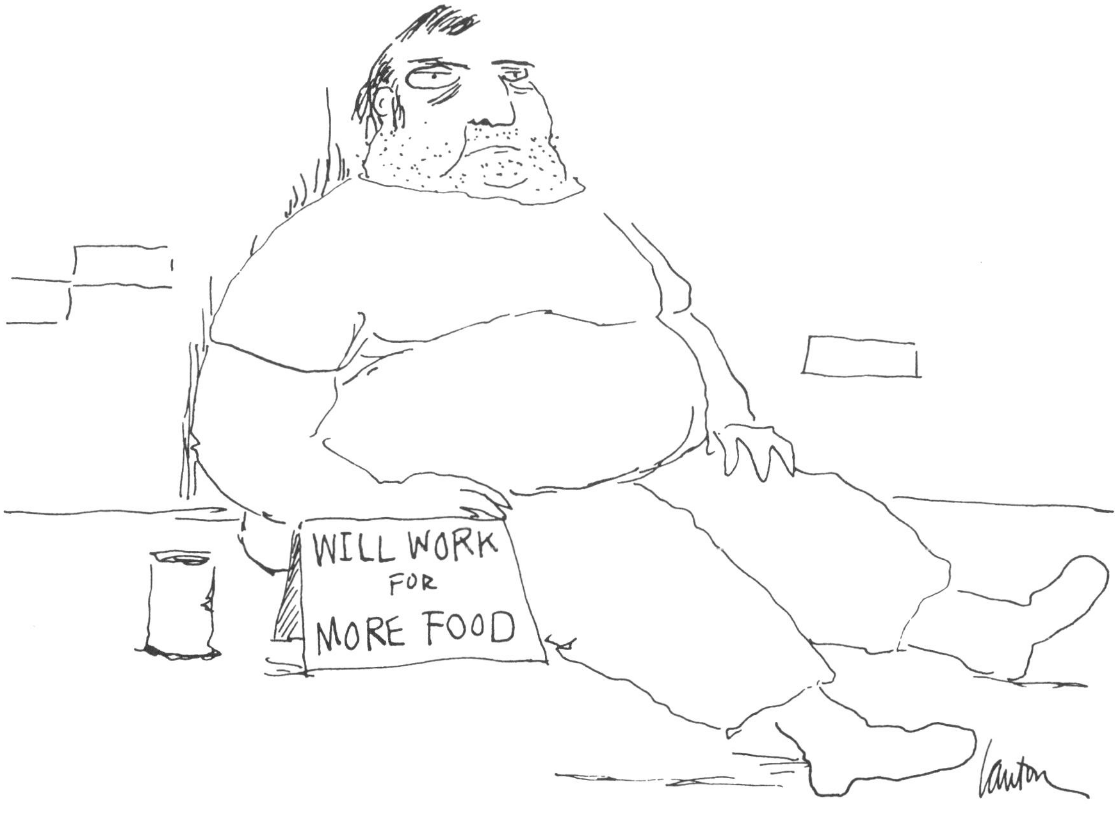
WILL WORK
FOR
MORE FOOD

MARY LAWTON. THE REALIST #144, SUMMER 2000.

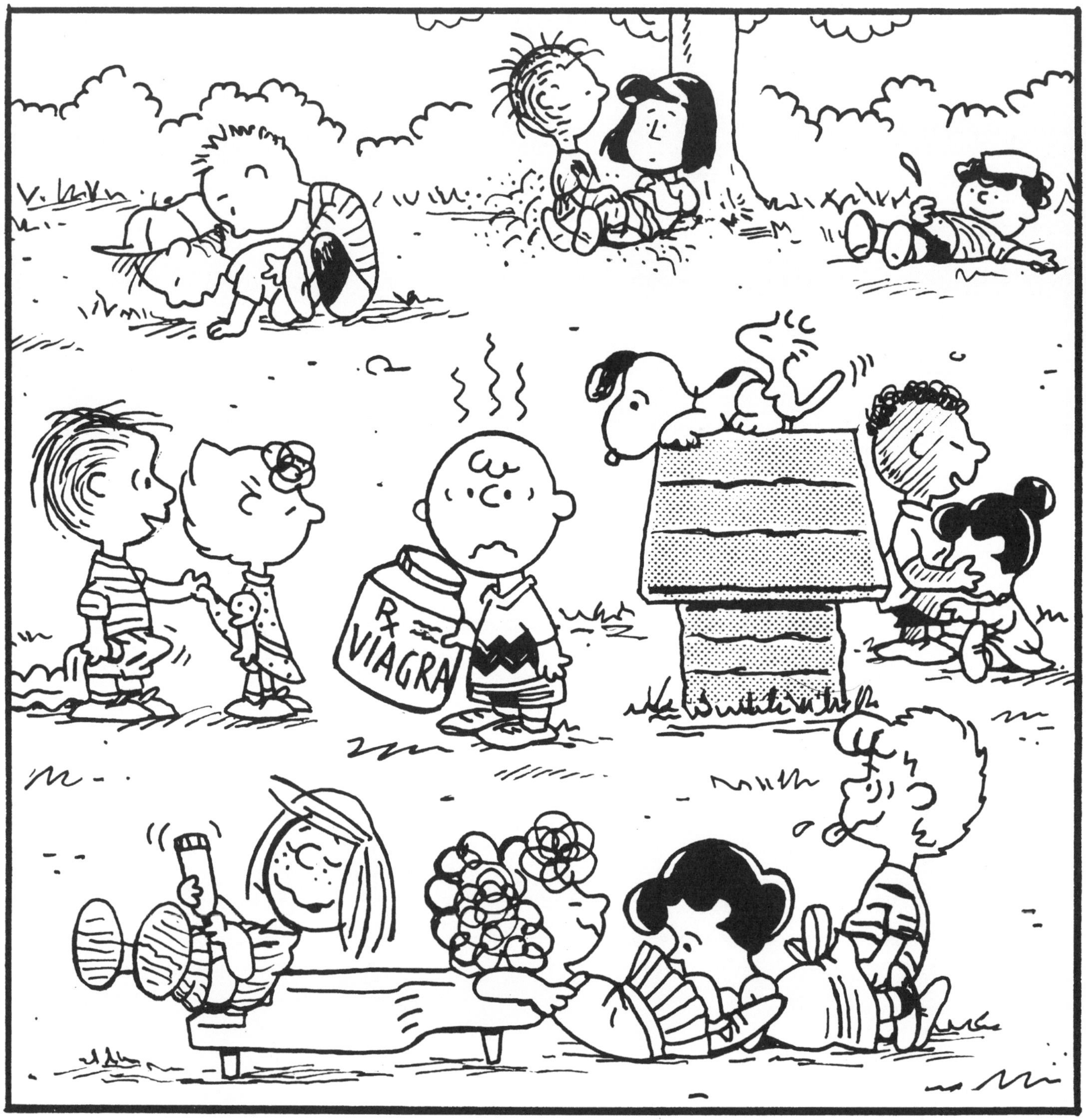
Rx
VIAGRA

The *Peanuts* Memorial Orgy

KALYNN CAMPBELL. THE REALIST #143, SPRING 2000.

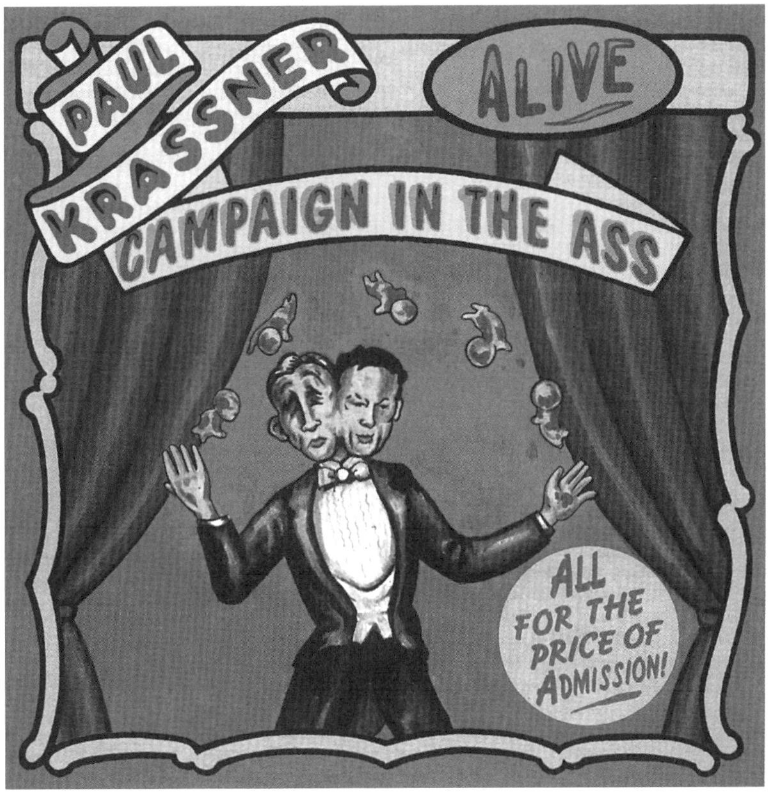
PAUL KRASSNER
ALIVE
CAMPAIGN IN THE ASS
ALL FOR THE PRICE OF ADMISSION!

KALYNN CAMPBELL. THE REALIST #145, FALL 2000.

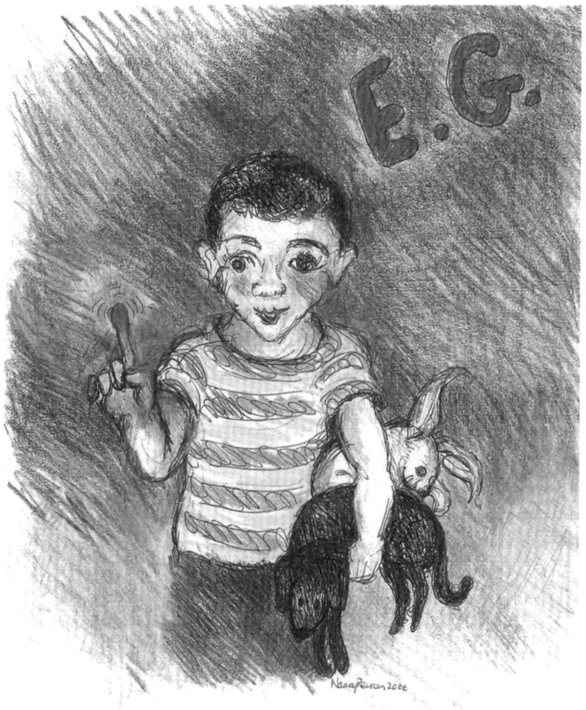
E.G.

Phone Home

NANCY REINER. THE REALIST #145, FALL 2000.

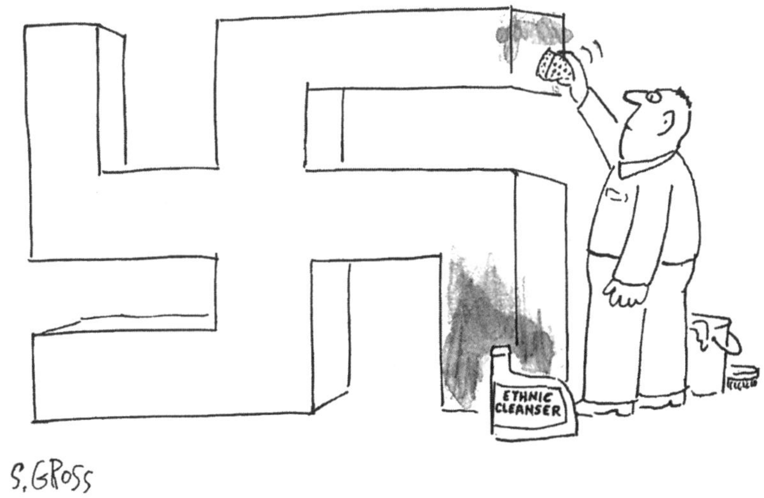
ETHNIC CLEANSER
S. GROSS

SAM GROSS. THE REALIST #144, SUMMER 2000.

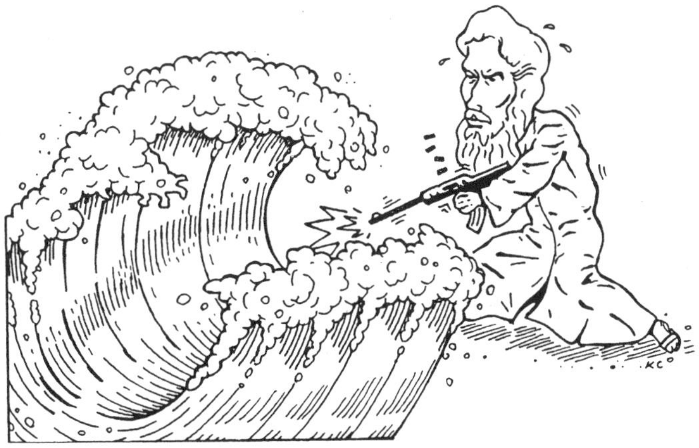

Charlton Heston Parts the Red Sea

KALYNN CAMPBELL. THE REALIST #140, FALL 1998.

KALYNN CAMPBELL. THE REALIST #146, SPRING 2001. *104

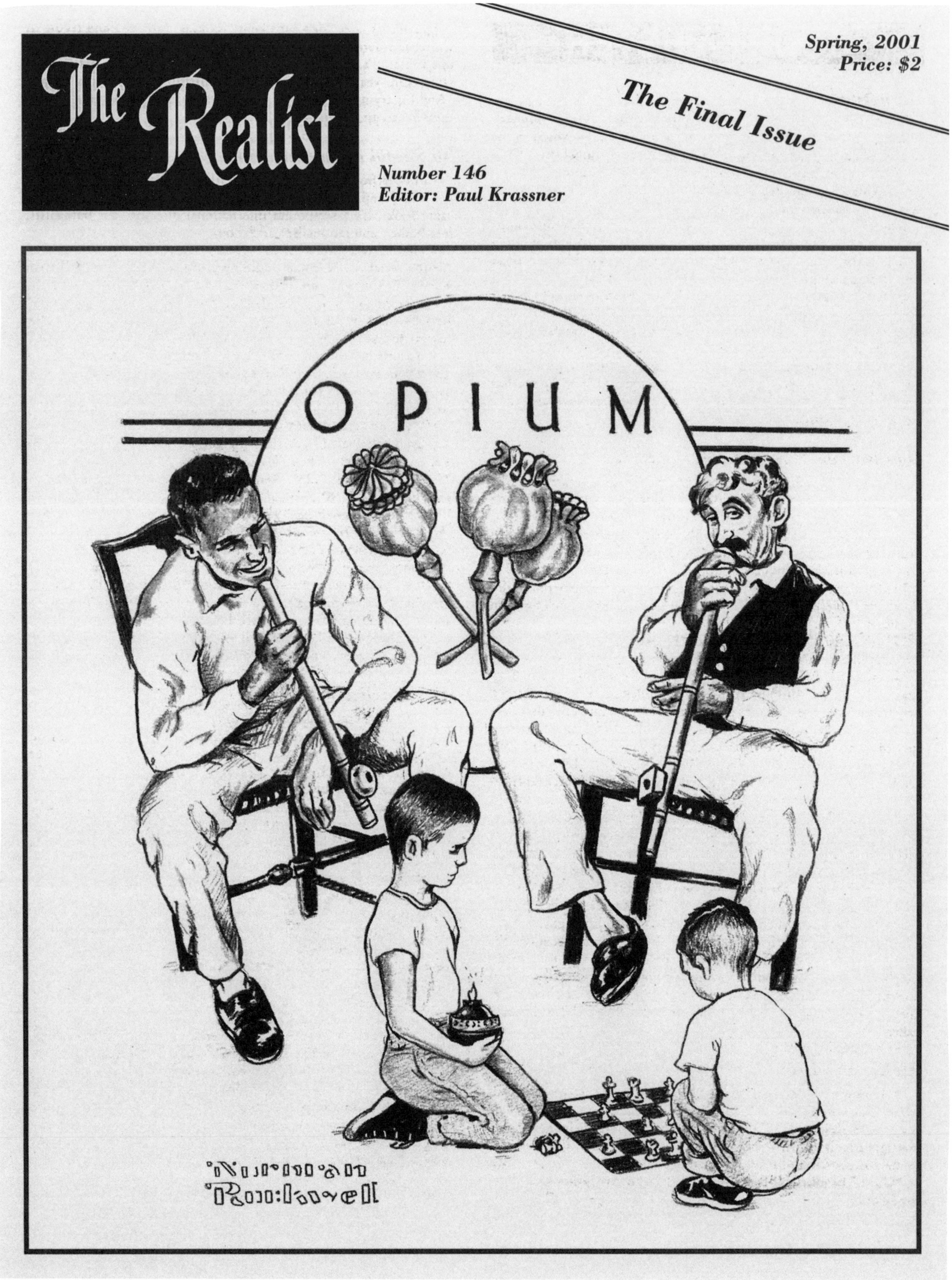
The Realist
Spring, 2001
Price: $2
The Final Issue
Number 146
Editor: Paul Krassner
OPIUM

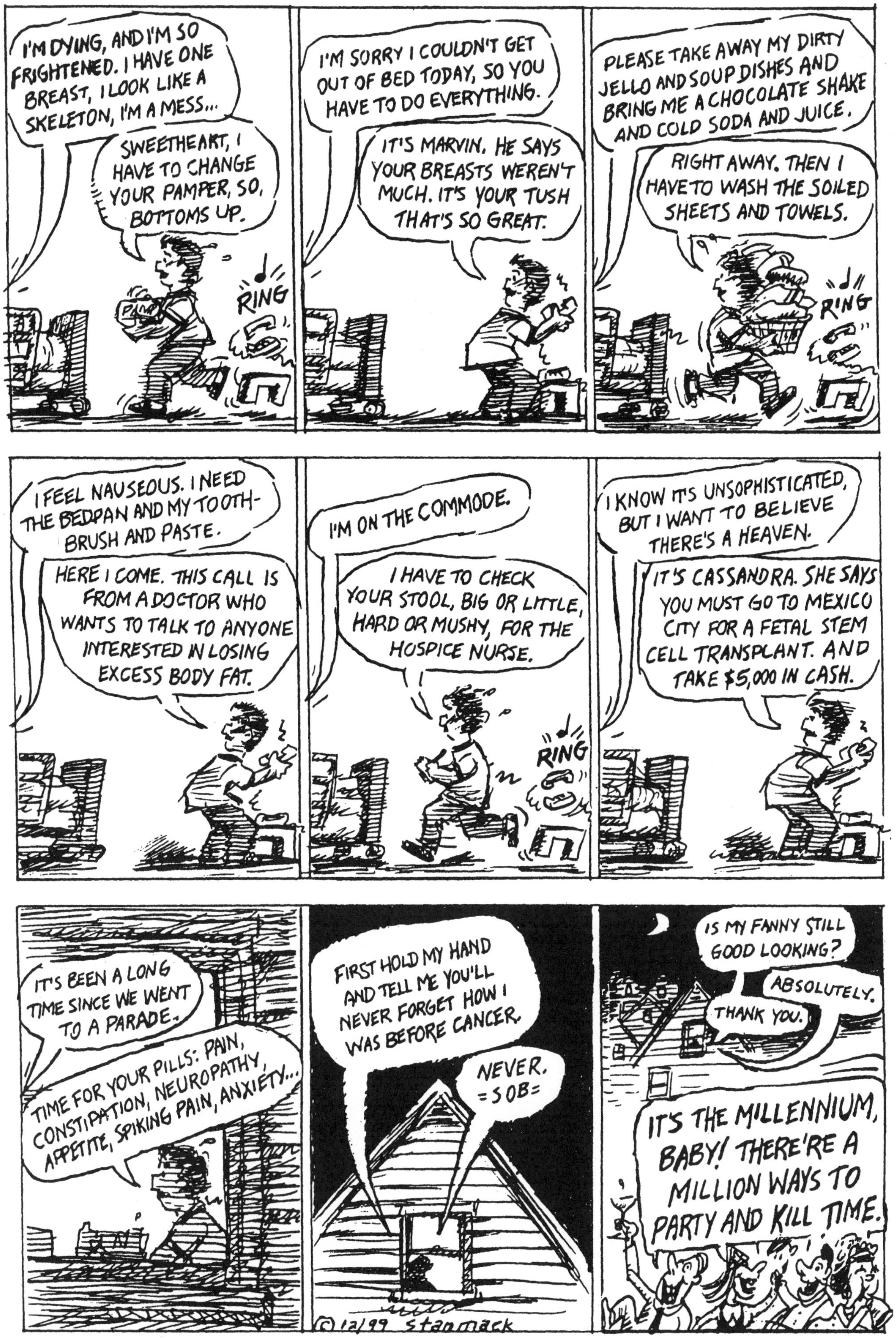
I'M DYING, AND I'M SO FRIGHTENED. I HAVE ONE BREAST, I LOOK LIKE A SKELETON, I'M A MESS...
SWEETHEART, I HAVE TO CHANGE YOUR PAMPER, SO, BOTTOMS UP.
RING
I'M SORRY I COULDN'T GET OUT OF BED TODAY, SO YOU HAVE TO DO EVERYTHING.
IT'S MARVIN. HE SAYS YOUR BREASTS WEREN'T MUCH. IT'S YOUR TUSH THAT'S SO GREAT.
PLEASE TAKE AWAY MY DIRTY JELLO AND SOUP DISHES AND BRING ME A CHOCOLATE SHAKE AND COLD SODA AND JUICE.
RIGHT AWAY. THEN I HAVE TO WASH THE SOILED SHEETS AND TOWELS.
RING
I FEEL NAUSEOUS. I NEED THE BEDPAN AND MY TOOTH-BRUSH AND PASTE.
HERE I COME. THIS CALL IS FROM A DOCTOR WHO WANTS TO TALK TO ANYONE INTERESTED IN LOSING EXCESS BODY FAT.
I'M ON THE COMMODE.
I HAVE TO CHECK YOUR STOOL, BIG OR LITTLE, HARD OR MUSHY, FOR THE HOSPICE NURSE.
RING
I KNOW IT'S UNSOPHISTICATED, BUT I WANT TO BELIEVE THERE'S A HEAVEN.
IT'S CASSANDRA. SHE SAYS YOU MUST GO TO MEXICO CITY FOR A FETAL STEM CELL TRANSPLANT. AND TAKE $5,000 IN CASH.
IT'S BEEN A LONG TIME SINCE WE WENT TO A PARADE.
TIME FOR YOUR PILLS: PAIN, CONSTIPATION, NEUROPATHY, APPETITE, SPIKING PAIN, ANXIETY...
FIRST HOLD MY HAND AND TELL ME YOU'LL NEVER FORGET HOW I WAS BEFORE CANCER.
NEVER. =SOB=
IS MY FANNY STILL GOOD LOOKING?
ABSOLUTELY.
THANK YOU.
IT'S THE MILLENNIUM, BABY! THERE'RE A MILLION WAYS TO PARTY AND KILL TIME.
© 12/99 stanmack

STAN MACK. THE REALIST #146, SPRING 2001. *105

ANNOTATIONS

1. Margaret Mead was a cultural anthropologist famous for her work with indigenous people.

2. *Elmer Gantry* was a 1960 movie starring Burt Lancaster about hucksterism and religion based on the 1926 book by Sinclair Lewis. This was before the movie ratings system was instituted.

3. Dwight D. Eisenhower.

4. "If A Bomb Falls" was one of many awareness campaigns of the 1950s better known for raising anxiety than for inspiring readiness.

5. Barry Goldwater was an iconic conservative senator and 1964 presidential candidate, best known for his tirades against social welfare programs.

6. A riff on school desegregation.

7. Would a Christian cross stave off a Jewish vampire?

8. "Refresh my bowels in The Lord" is an actual line from the King James Bible, Philemon 1:20

9. Pancho Gonzales was a tennis player in the 1950s who kept returning — and winning matches — despite a record of losses.

10. At the time of this cartoon, Germany was divided into two countries, communist East and democratic West, and it was conceivable that soldiers who had served together under Nazi Germany in World War II would be on opposite sides of the East/West divide.

11. "White Negro" was a term of contempt for beatniks in the 1950s for their relationship with the black community.

12. Monroe, North Carolina, was the destination of one of the Freedom Riders campaigns of 1961. The Freedom Riders chartered buses to take them to the segregated South to campaign for civil rights. This joke is particularly ironic, as the Freedom Ride into Monroe was met by an assault on its riders from the KKK.

13. In ancient Rome, the emperor's thumbs-down judgment meant death for a gladiator. The gladiator's middle-finger response here is a modern-day gesture of defiance.

14. This joke riffs off the theme of 1958's *The Ugly American* by Eugene Burdick and William Lederer (made into a 1963 movie starring Marlon Brando) of American arrogance abroad, extending even to the idealistic Peace Corps, which was created to aid developing countries.

15. In 1960, Ruby Bridges, age 6, had to be escorted daily by U.S. marshals through a mob of hateful whites to attend elementary school in New Orleans after a judge's desegregation order.

16. "Taking the red out" meant removing communists from the U.S.

17. The "rhythm method" is an often-unreliable form of birth control endorsed by the Catholic Church (for married couples only).

18. The Phantom and Tarzan are famous fictional jungle heroes. Jane is Tarzan's girlfriend.

19. Most *Realist* readers would have been familiar with the catchphrase "The Shadow knows." The Shadow was a radio and pulp magazine precursor of Batman. His civilian persona was often illustrated casting the shadow of the mysterious crimefighter.

20. In the 1962 New York governor's race, Democrat Robert M. Morgenthau campaigned against incumbent Republican Nelson Rockefeller, who had been granted a divorce from his first wife on the grounds of "extreme mental cruelty" after 31 years of marriage. (Rockefeller won and later became Vice President of the United States under Gerald Ford.)

21. During the Civil Rights Movement, a "sit-in" was a form of demonstration where a group would remain seated in an establishment and refuse to move as a means of passive resistance.

22. Flowers growing in war equipment. Peter, Paul and Mary had a hit with Pete Seeger's "Where Have All the Flowers Gone?" in 1962 and "Flower Power" would become a rallying cry for the hippie movement a few years later.

23. Author J.D. Salinger famously went into seclusion after the massive success of his book, *A Catcher in the Rye*.

24. God finally answers your prayer.

25. Zyklon B was the trade name for the cyanide gas used by the Nazis to kill concentration camp victims during World War II. "That's a gasser" was a famous beatnik phrase meaning "a funny joke."

26. In 1962, The White Citizens Council of New Orleans actually did initiate what some called "Reverse Freedom Rides" — one-way bus tickets out of town for African American residents to cities "up North." Some riders were damn glad to get out of there.

27. "Good grief!" was a frequent catchphrase in *Peanuts*, used here to suggest there was more between Charlie Brown and Lucy than the funny papers suggested.

28. George Lincoln Rockwell was the founder and head of the American Nazi Party; The term "wop" is a slur against Italians, specifically poor Italians who were shunned by their country and not issued passports. The term derives from the phrase "without papers" (or "without passport"); "Spastic" was derogatory slang for an overly nervous (or epileptic) person, so the joke is that they could not color within the lines.

29. How "if I should die before I wake" might be said in Beatnik slang.

30. Dr. Michael Burnhill was the vice president for Internal Affairs for Planned Parenthood and a lifelong advocate for women's health care, family planning, and reproductive health. Abortion was almost completely illegal in 1962.

31. Showing pubic hair was a no-no in *Playboy* and its imitators in the early 1960s. The text here also mocks *Playboy's* profiles of its models.

32. A bit of bohemian word play.

33. A nun counts rosary beads like flower petals to see whether or not God loves her.

34. A traditional hymn reinterpreted in racial terms by a group of "black sunbeams."

35. Mississippi governor Ross Barnett was a staunch segregationist. In 1962, he was appointed registrar of "Ole Miss," the University of Mississippi, to keep out African American students. When James Meredith, a black man, showed up to enroll after a Supreme Court ruling in his favor, a riot ensued and two people were killed. The Kennedy administration sent 30,000 troops to enforce the Court's order and Meredith remained under 24-hour guard by federal troops until he graduated in 1963.

36. World leaders: Soviet Premier Nikita Krushchev, U.S. President John F. Kennedy, and Cuban Prime Minister Fidel Castro comment on the 1962 Cuban Missile Crisis. Pope John XXIII "liberalizes" the Catholic Church's stance on birth control.

37. A joke riffing on *The Defiant Ones,* a famous 1958 movie starring Tony Curtis and Sidney Poitier about two escaped prisoners — one white, one black — who hate each other but are chained together and struggle to survive on the run.

38. Enovid was an early brand of birth control pill. Koromex was a contraceptive vaginal gel. Neither was advertised on TV, but this was a take-off on a high-profile ad campaign promoting Vitalis, a men's hair product, that mocked its competition as "greasy kid stuff."

39. A racial reversal on the advertising slogan for Clairol's hair color product for women.

40. One practical use for an erection.

41. George Lincoln Rockwell was the founder and leader of the American Nazi Party. He was interviewed by Krassner in *The Realist #27* (1961) and contributed a column titled "A Challenge to Consistency" in *The Realist #39* (1962).

42. Pepsi advertisement following a 'nuclear bomb.

43. Statue of Non-Liberty.

44. Don't take candy from strangers — or suspicious vending machines. *Candy* was also a best-selling 1958 novel of sexual hijinks by Terry Southern and Mason Hoffenberg.

45. Disappointment in American symbols

46. A visual joke about evolution.

47. A joke that a Black Muslim would endorse Barry Goldwater, two polar opposites.

48. Tiny showerheads inside the oven. A Holocaust joke.

49. Mother, Father, Child.

50. In the early 1960s, several monks used gasoline to burn themselves to death in protest over the treatment of Buddhists by Vietnamese authorities.

51. Communion crackers with peanut butter.

52. Illustration used to accompany Paul Krassner's announcement about the birth of his daughter, Holly.

53. Judge in kinky stockings and high-heeled boots.

54. Another Nazi showers joke.

55. Rabbi sees Jewish stars when he bumps his head.

56. A joke about "key clubs." Swinging couples would mingle keys in a hat and each wife would retrieve one at random — thereby selecting her partner for the rest of the night's activities.

57. "Ass backward."

58. The Alliance for Progress was an initiative of President Kennedy to establish economic cooperation between the U.S. and Latin America. Here it's represented as a perfume to cover up the smell of imperialism.

59. Barry Goldwater with breasts.

60. During the 1964 Presidential campaign, the Lyndon Johnson campaign famously aired a political ad that equated voting for Barry Goldwater with voting for nuclear war.

61. The Warren Report was the official report of The President's Commission on the Assassination of President Kennedy.

62. Pop fetishism, indeed. When the Beatles toured America, hustlers cut sheets into one-inch squares and sold them to frantic fans by claiming they were the hotel linens the Beatles had slept on.

63. Protest/brothel humor.

64. Among the references in "Superior Man": Patrice Lumumba, the first democratically elected leader of the Congo, who was deposed in a coup some twelve weeks after he took office and later executed; and Carmine DeSapio, the last head of the corrupt New York City Tammany Hall political machine.

65. "Mrs. Brown, You've Got a Lovely Daughter" was a number one U.S. hit for the British band Herman's Hermits in 1965. Eva Braun was Hitler's longtime companion and, for about 40 hours before their mutual suicide, his wife.

66. Even though signed "PK-Bhob" (Paul Krassner-Bhob Stewart), many readers mistook this spoof of a Jules Feiffer cartoon as the genuine article. Feiffer was not amused.

67. Condom reference.

68. When computer punch cards started showing up in consumers' monthly bills to be returned with payment, they carried the instruction "Do Not Fold, Spindle, or Mutilate."

69. *Eros* was a magazine published by Ralph Ginzburg, who was convicted of obscenity in a case that went to the Supreme Court.

70. *Fanny Hill (Memoirs of a Woman of Pleasure),* a 1748 British erotic novel was published in the U.S. in 1963 and the publisher prosecuted for obscenity. In 1966 the Supreme Court ruled the book not obscene.

71. Everett Dirksen was a prominent Republican Senator from 1950 to 1969. Rules permit lengthy statements to be made part of the Congressional Record even though they weren't actually said during floor proceedings.

72. Another joke about a conservative hypocrite and Ralph Ginzburg (*Eros* magazine). *The Realist* ran the entire court transcripts of the *Eros* trial in issues 44, 45, and 46.

73. President Johnson's oldest daughter was known as Lynda Bird. She dated actor George Hamilton for a few months in 1966.

74. A reference to Donald W. Duncan, a green beret who quit the Special Forces and became an anti-war advocate. Duncan later contributed to *Ramparts* magazine.

75. Schwartza: Yiddish or German term for a black person.

76. The "God Is Dead" meme was in the air when Walt Disney died, prompting Paul Krassner to wonder how Mickey Mouse and the other Disney characters might react to the death of their creator. He commissioned this piece by Wallace Wood that became known as "The Disneyland Memorial Orgy."

77. Napalm is a form of jellied petroleum that clings to whatever surface it strikes — including human skin — as it burns. It was manufactured by the Dow Company and used widely against enemy combatants in Vietnam.

78. Adam Clayton Powell represented Harlem in the U.S. Congress from 1945 through 1971. Both he and Senator Thomas Dodd got into financial scandals in the 1960s.

79. The German "Iron Cross" was a military decoration that pre-dated World War II by more than a century but was popularly associated with Nazi Germany. Surfers adopted it as a good luck talisman and called it the "Surfer's Cross" when the surfing fad took off in the 1960s.

80. Israel "above everything else" is a cultural reversal of "Deutschland, Deutschland über alles," the opening line of the "The Song of Germany," and closely identified with the Nazi regime.

81. A Richard Speck joke. Speck was a mass murderer who killed eight student nurses in Chicago.

82. "The Trial of Abbie Hoffman's Shirt." A reference to anti-war activist Abbie Hoffman's shirt, made from an American flag, which Hoffman was arrested for wearing by Washington, D.C. police.

83. LeRoi Jones (Amiri Baraka) was a black militant writer and playwright.

84. Herbert Marcuse was a political theorist known as the "Father of the New Left."

85. A joke on jewish rye bread tasting so good even Hitler would enjoy it. The artist for this strip is John Patler. Patler, who signed his work "Patsalos," was a member of the American Nazi Party. He was the cartoonist for the party's magazine, *Stormtrooper* and is known for the deeply racist comic book *Here Comes Whiteman*. In 1967, Patler was thrown out of the American Nazi Party, and responded by assassinating the Party's leader, George Lincoln Rockwell. Both Patler and Rockwell were also occasional contributors to *The Realist*.

86. Referencing the movie *Midnight Cowboy*, about a male prostitute and a con man, played by Jon Voight (Joe Buck) and Dustin Hoffman (Ratso) using President Richard Nixon and Vice President Spiro Agnew.

87. Referencing the movie *Bob & Carol & Ted & Alice* using Timothy Leary, his wife Rosemary Woodruff, Eldridge Cleaver, and Kathleen Cleaver. The two couples spent an uneasy time together in Algeria on the run from the law.

88. A satirical title based on the Roman Polanski film "Rosemary's Baby," this four-page comic features many cameos of 1970s religious leaders, TV news reporters, and prominent politicians. Spiro Agnew, whose name is demonstrated to be an anagram for "Grow a Penis," was the current Vice President under Richard Nixon.

89. Neil Simon's "The Odd Couple" was a popular play, movie, and TV show. The odd pairing of Richard Nixon and Sammy Davis Jr. came about when Davis, a lifelong Democrat, endorsed Nixon, a Republican, for re-election and gave him a big onstage hug at the Republican convention.

90. A reference to the Chernobyl nuclear reactor meltdown in Kiev.

91. A twist on an American Express commercial starring actor Karl Malden using the company's famous advertising line.

92. Geraldo Rivera, "dickhead."

93. Reference to Joan Crawford's adopted daughter's memoir *Mommie Dearest*.

94. Reference to a feud between Frank Sinatra and Sinead O'Connor after her appearance on *Saturday Night Live* where she ripped up a photo of the Pope.

95. Reference to Pee Wee Herman getting busted for masturbation in an adult theater.

96. Reference to Clarence Thomas's Supreme Court hearing, where it was alleged that his sexual harassment of Anita Hill included inquiring about a pubic hair he said he'd found on his Coca Cola can.

97. Commemorating the death of Bill Gaines, publisher of EC Comics and *Mad* magazine.

98. Reference to Bill Clinton and alleged cocaine use.

99. "Heidi Floss" is a reference to "The Hollywood Madam" Heidi Fleiss.

100. The Mount Rushmore of criminals: Charles Manson, O.J. Simpson, Richard Nixon.

101. Reference to O.J. Simpson criminal trial Judge Lance Ito.

102. Two sides of Jerry Rubin, activist revolutionary and Yippie businessman.

103. Susan Smith was a South Carolina mother who murdered her two children.

104. Paul Krassner writes: Norman Rockwell's paintings on the covers of the *Saturday Evening Post* were always synonymous with saccharine wholesomeness. But his son Peter, speaking at the National Press Club in Washington, mentioned that his father's longstanding ambition was to visit an opium den. Ultimately, he was dissuaded from taking that trip by advertisers in the magazine.

When I saw that on C-Span, I immediately assigned Kalynn Campbell to capture the venerated artist's secret vision. I thought that such an under-the-surface image of the American culture would serve as an appropriate metaphor for the final issue of *The Realist*.

105. Stan Mack based this strip on his real-life experiences with his wife, Janet Bode, in her final days.

Paul Krassner published *The Realist* (1958–2001), but when *People* magazine labeled him "father of the underground press," he immediately demanded a paternity test. And when *Life* magazine published a favorable article about him, the FBI sent a poison-pen letter to the editor calling Krassner "a raving, unconfined nut." George Carlin responded, "The FBI was right. This man is dangerous — and funny; and necessary." While abortion was illegal, Krassner ran an underground referral service, and as an antiwar activist, he became a co-founder of the Yippies (Youth International Party). Krassner's one-person show won an award from the *L.A. Weekly*. He received an ACLU (Upton Sinclair) Award for dedication to freedom of expression. At the Cannabis Cup in Amsterdam, he was inducted into the Counterculture Hall of Fame — "my ambition," he claims, "since I was three years old." He's won awards from *Playboy*, the Feminist Party Media Workshop, and in 2010 the Oakland branch of the writers organization PEN honored him with their Lifetime Achievement Award. "I'm very happy to receive this award," he concluded in his acceptance speech, "and even happier that it wasn't posthumous."

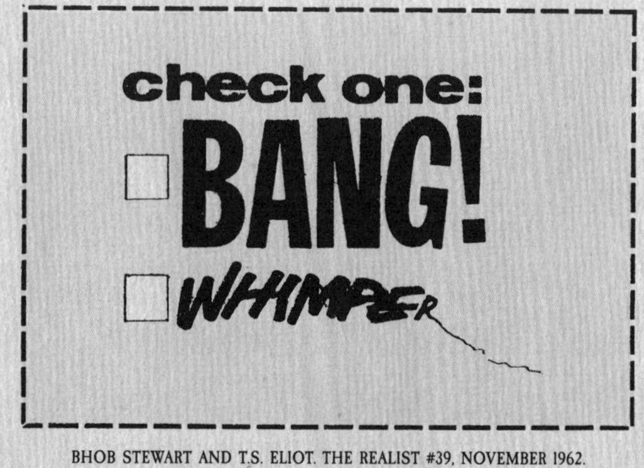
check one:
BANG!
WHIMPER

BHOB STEWART AND T.S. ELIOT. THE REALIST #39, NOVEMBER 1962.